Developing WMI Solutions

Developing WMI Solutions

A Guide to Windows Management Instrumentation

Craig Tunstall and Gwyn Cole

♠Addison-Wesley

Boston • San Francisco • New York • Toronto • Montreal
London • Munich • Paris • Madrid
Capetown • Sydney • Tokyo • Singapore • Mexico City

Many of the designations used by manufacturers and sellers to distinguish their product are claimed as trademarks. Where those designations appear in this book, and Addison-Wesley was aware of a trademark claim, the designations have been printed with initial capital letters or in all capitals.

The authors and publisher have taken care in the preparation of this book, but make no expressed or implied warranty of any kind and assume no responsibility for errors or omissions. No liability is assumed for incidental or consequential damages in connection with or arising out of the use of the information or programs contained herein.

The publisher offers discounts on this book when ordered in quantity for bulk purchases and special sales. For more information, please contact:

U.S. Corporate and Government Sales
(800) 382-3419
corpsales@pearsontechgroup.com

For sales outside of the U.S., please contact:

International Sales
(317) 581-3793
international@pearsontechgroup.com

Visit Addison-Wesley on the Web: www.awprofessional.com

Library of Congress Cataloging-in-Publication Data
Tunstall, Craig.
    Developing WMI solutions : a guide to Windows management instrumentation / Craig
  Tunstall and Gwyn Cole.
      p.   cm.
    ISBN 0-201-61613-0 (pbk : alk. paper)
    1. Microsoft Windows (Computer file)   2. Operating systems (Computers)   I. Cole,
  Gwyn.   II. Title.

  QA76.76.O63 T83   2002
  005.4'469—dc21

                                                        2002026084

ISBN 0-201-61613-0
Text printed on recycled paper
1 2 3 4 5 6 7 8 9 10—CRS—0605040302
First printing, November 2002

Contents

Chapter 2   Existing Management Frameworks   25

Chapter 5   Developing Class Schemas   155

Chapter 6   Method Design and Schema Class Positioning   207

Chapter 11   WMI Scripting and WMIC   545

Preface

Windows Management Instrumentation (WMI) is an impressive technology. For the first time the Windows operating system employs a unified technology to represent software and hardware management. The power of WMI in systems management stretches virtually to every piece of software and hardware. So regardless of whether you're a team leader, software engineer, or system administrator, WMI will probably affect you.

Many applications written for Windows currently do not harness the power of a systems management technology such as WMI: This is why we wrote this book. We want developers to realize that making an application manageable is a key benefit, especially to system administrators. Once system administrators and Information Technology (IT) support departments realize what can be done with WMI, they will demand that applications expose WMI management interfaces. Not only will system administrators be happy, but you'll also be able to harvest the wealth of information available from WMI when building your own management applications. The other side of the coin, apart from making an application manageable, is a "management application." A management application is a program (like an MMC snap-in) or Web interface that can interact with the system to gather, inspect, and manipulate the system's functionality or configuration. We also want system administrators to realize what they can do in a system equipped with a technology such as WMI and how they should go about automating routine tasks.

We are both very excited about WMI and hope to spread the word to help the computing world become a more managed place.

▣ Who Is This Book for and What Is WMI?

This book helps developers and system administrators understand Windows Management Instrumentation (WMI). WMI is a technology built into Windows that enables organizations to manage servers and user PCs connected to their networks. Systems management is becoming much more important as organizational networks become more complex. Systems management is not necessarily a new concept as existing protocols like Simple Network Management Protocol (SNMP) and Desktop Management Interface (DMI) have been around for a while. What is new is that it's been traditionally difficult to envisage a unified picture of the whole system.

Understanding the relationships between hardware and software in an organization's network is equally important. The SNMP world took systems management only as far as the hardware, such as routers. The DMI world took systems management only as far as the desktop. This led to the definition of Web Based Enterprise Management (WBEM), a protocol/schema, by the Distributed Management Task Force (DMTF). Microsoft adopted WBEM and WMI was born. WMI is an implementation of the WBEM standard that is consistent with Microsoft's Total Cost of Ownership (TCO) initiative. WMI brings the power of managing a Windows network to unprecedented levels. For example, through WMI a system administrator can easily write a script that will identify the Windows service packs that have been installed on all the machines in the network.

Administrators can easily develop scripts to perform routine tasks for their network, as well as exploit powerful notification facilities inherent within WMI to identify problems before their users experience them. For this level of system manageability to be made possible, the operating system, devices, and application software need to be instrumented—hardware and software need to expose their management interface through WMI. Hence, for developers, this book is important in learning how to do this; for administrators, it is important in learning how to exploit this technology that helps lower the TCO; and it is important to software team leaders in understanding the impact of this new management model on development.

▣ How to Approach This Book and What You Will Learn

Developers and system administrators, the primary target audience for this book, will benefit from it in several ways. If you know nothing about systems management or WMI, don't worry—this book will help you develop your skills and knowledge of WMI from the beginning. We also intend for this book to be a reference, so if you want to develop a WMI provider in C++ to expose your software management interface, you can go directly to Chapter 12. Likewise, if you want to get system management information in your .NET application, you can go to Chapter 8. Let's have a quick round-up of each chapter.

Chapter 1: Introduction

This chapter introduces the various concepts and terminology used in systems management, in particular, WMI. The chapter highlights the necessity for a unified management standard such as WBEM.

Chapter 2: Existing Management Frameworks

This chapter aims to introduce the goals of WBEM and systems management by examining two existing management frameworks, SNMP and DMI. Still in widespread deployment, both are introduced thoroughly from an architectural perspective and provide an introduction to the basic principles and rationale behind systems management prior to WBEM. The chapter ends by summarizing the characteristics considered desirable in a management framework and how they relate to WBEM.

Chapter 3: Windows Management Instrumentation

This chapter covers a lot of ground to bring you up to speed with WMI. It covers installation and the various components that make up the WMI toolset. It contains some detailed information on the WMI architecture and the various interactions between WMI subsystems. It introduces essential WMI vocabulary so that you can understand the WMI features from a high-level perspective. The latter part of the chapter introduces some of WMI's powerful query language facilities, including queries for data (management information), queries for events (notification of activity), and queries against the class schema (understanding relationships between management information).

Chapter 4: A Guided Tour of the Common Information Model Repository

The chapter continues to help you understand the various class schemas and the WMI tools provided by Microsoft. The class schemas describe virtually every aspect of a network, a computer, and its operating system, as well as the installed software. The chapter includes an in-depth tutorial that provides an extensive introduction to the skills you will need as either an administrator or a developer using the Common Information Model (CIM). The chapter also covers in detail how all the WMI building blocks fit together. It introduces namespaces, classes, properties, qualifiers, flavors, and associations.

Chapter 5: Developing Class Schemas

From a development point of view, a class schema is the most important place to start to use a standard management environment to manage your own software and hardware.

Chapter 5, the first of two chapters in which we discuss this, also is applicable to system administrators who wish to understand more about interpreting a WMI class schema (perhaps for an administration script or simply to obtain information from a user's PC). The chapter introduces schema design by approaching a case study from a project life-cycle perspective that discusses all the stages of the class schema development/design and offers lots of advice and tips along the way, right through to deployment.

Chapter 6: Method Design and Schema Class Positioning

Chapter 6 continues to develop the case study begun in Chapter 5, focusing on interpreting and approaching subtle differences in schema design, such as whether to use a particular method or the WMI standard mechanism to create a management object. It offers advice about looking toward future management requirements in designing classes and their positions within the schema, on localizing schema, and on a number of other topics.

Chapter 7: Developing Management Applications

Accessing the WMI management environment can be achieved in a number of ways. The first of the development-oriented chapters is aimed primarily at developers who need to use C++ and the Component Object Model (COM) to obtain and manipulate information in the management environment. Consider this example, one of the many reasons that you might want to do this: You need access to the management environment so that you can develop a tool, perhaps a user interface administration console, to manage your application's configuration. The chapter contains useful and concise code samples to demonstrate how easy it is to use WMI. It also discusses a number of topics, including event notification, security, and accessing high-performance classes.

Chapter 8: Developing .NET Management Applications

This chapter is on a similar level to Chapter 7, but focuses on how to use the classes in the .NET Framework using C#. The .NET Framework from Microsoft effectively is a new execution environment for applications. C# is a new programming language, ultimately designed to leverage developer productivity. Through the code samples, you'll see how easy the .NET Framework makes management applications development. Virtually every class in the .NET Framework is discussed in detail.

Chapter 9: Developing MMC Snap-ins

The Microsoft Management Console (MMC) is Microsoft's response to the need for a consistent user interface in which administrators can find all their management tools.

The facility to have a similar look and feel across the administrative user interface and the fact that all administration tools can be found in one place mean that MMC helps administrators move toward a lower cost of ownership. This tutorial-style chapter follows the C++ and COM developer through each stage of MMC snap-in development. By the end of the chapter, you will see how to use WMI to access and manipulate Windows Services in a user interface designed for administration. One of MMC's most powerful features is the capability to develop and extend other snap-ins to add your own administration facilities.

Chapter 10: Developing WMI Scripts for Administrators

This chapter is the first of two aimed primarily at the system administrator. It assumes that you have very little, if any, experience in writing scripts and therefore starts at the beginning. It introduces the tools available for system administration and progresses to the VBScript *boot camp*. The boot camp introduces different types of problems you might experience and the techniques used to solve them. It gives detailed instructions for installing the Windows Scripting Host to enable you to use the chapter's sample scripts. By the end of the chapter, you'll learn how to develop your own scripts to use WMI to access and manipulate the management environment.

Chapter 11: WMI Scripting and WMIC

This chapter builds on the lessons learned from Chapter 10. From a systems management perspective (using a case study), you learn how to break down administration problems and solve them using the scripting approach. It discusses remote script execution, because organizational networks contain networked PCs. Windows Management Instrumentation Command-line (WMIC), a new command-line tool that allows administrators to execute tasks and queries against the management environment, exists in Windows XP. The chapter examines WMIC in detail and provides a framework that would be useful for solving problems quickly using WMIC. There's also advice on a number of topics, including how to debug scripts.

Chapter 12: Developing WMI Providers

This crucial chapter describes how software and hardware developers can write their own WMI providers, the gateway for developers to expose their own class schema. The chapter assumes that you have development skills in C++ and COM. It covers virtually all of the many types of providers that can be developed. The chapter implements a very simple fruit basket WMI instance provider in the beginning and progresses to method, event, permanent event consumer, property, and push providers. This chapter provides a solid grounding in developing WMI providers. The source code accompanying the book contains a WMI provider ATL-like framework for accelerating your provider development, although the chapter does not explicitly discuss it.

Chapter 13: High-Performance Instrumentation

Finally, the book covers event tracing, a very little-known subject of the WMI toolset. Event tracing is a powerful and high-performance method of instrumenting applications. It allows applications to expose very detailed information about an operation or task. The operating system uses this technology to expose activity in the Windows kernel, security subsystems, and numerous other subsystems.

Where Can I Find the Sample Source Code and Scripts?

All the source code and scripts can be found at http://www.wbem.co.uk/, the Web site that accompanies the book. This includes the MOF files, Visual C++ 6.0 projects, Visual Studio .NET projects, and the VB Scripts. The projects for the sample code from Chapters 7 and 8 contain many more short functions to demonstrate various aspects of accessing WMI. Check the sample projects if you're not sure how to do something that is not explicitly covered by the chapters.

Glossary

New terms and acronyms are introduced throughout the book. The glossary summarizes these at the end of the book.

■ Acknowledgments

Craig Tunstall

Writing this book has certainly been in equal parts both challenging and rewarding. The book was started in the early days of WMI's deployment when it was available only as an optional add-on for the Windows operating system. Since these early beginnings WMI has become an integral part of the Windows operating system, though sadly not yet an integral part of many companies' enterprise management solution. Both Gwyn and I feel that the world's desktops and networks would be better and more highly managed if WMI received the widespread adoption it deserves. It is my hope that this book goes some way toward encouraging such adoption.

I would first like to thank my parents, Christine and George, for their unfailing support, encouragement, and belief in my abilities. I am indebted to my brother Ryan for without his support, technical feedback, and encouragement this book probably would not have been written.

I would like to thank Gwyn for his enthusiasm, doing such an excellent job on his chapters, working so hard, and providing a great sounding board for ideas. I would also like to thank Mark Priestley and the Cavendish School of Computer Science at Westminster University, London, England, for allowing me to introduce WMI to their students.

I would also like to thank the people who have collectively inspired, motivated, and supported me throughout the production of the book.

Many thanks go to "Doc" Robinson for inspiring me to embrace academia and being a good friend. I would like to thank Kit Ruparel and Gary Clarke for encouraging me in the early days. Thanks also go to all of the reviewers, including Spencer Sturgeon, James Edelen, and Patrick Thompson, for providing such concise feedback. A very big thank you is also owed to the people at Addison Wesley, especially Stephane Thomas for being so supportive and patient throughout this project.

My grateful thanks go to Professor Mark d'Inverno, Professor Steve Winter, and Visiting Professor Mike Luck for their encouragement, support, and enthusiasm.

Finally, I would like to thank Geoff Woods for consistently providing a thought-provoking forum for lively debate; Ian Gallacher for his support, friendship, and sardonic wit; and Muiris, Dewi, and family for their kindness and hospitality.

Gwyn Cole

One day Simon Robinson said to me, "Are you interested in coauthoring a book on WMI?" Overwhelmed by the prospect, I said yes. A few days later I spoke with Craig and we agreed to go ahead with what we hope to be an excellent and comprehensive discussion about developing systems management solutions with WMI. So thanks to Simon for getting Craig and me together and thanks to Craig (who had already completed six chapters) for getting me involved. It's been such an excellent opportunity for me to share my knowledge of WMI with the wider world.

Writing a book like this takes a long time, so I would like to thank all my friends and family for being patient. I haven't been around most of the time and have seen very little of you guys. In particular, thanks to my parents. You have always encouraged me to further my horizons and have provided me with the support I need. Thanks to my brother Steven and his wife, Joanne, for providing me a way to escape every now again. It was very welcome to have a chat, a few beers, and a laugh. Thanks to my friends who haven't seen much of me while I've been writing this book: Mike G., Darryl, Danny, Scott, Beth, Adam, Graham, Nick, Phil, Christophe, Mike M., Mark S., Mark D., and Mark L. In addition, thanks to David and Anna Morley and family who have allowed me to chill out at their place in the south of France every now and again.

A special thanks to the technical reviewers who gave me valuable feedback on my chapters: Patrick Thompson, Andy Cheung, and Paul Westcott.

Thanks to the staff at Addison-Wesley for getting the book through production on a tight schedule, and especially to our editor, Stephane Thomas.

During my college and university years (a while ago now), one lecturer and friend took it upon himself to encourage and guide me in the right direction. Although Brendan Riordan hasn't had any direct input to this book, I would like to thank him for his inspiration.

Finally, a quick thanks to the great software engineers that I work with. Although you may not know it, you've been very helpful to me in bouncing ideas around. Your questions often caused me to go back and research specific aspects of systems management and WMI. Thanks to the Avaya Unified Messenger development team and, in particular, Andy McMullan, Charles Cook, Michael Wilson, Gareth Eley, and Paul Arnold. Also, a little thank you to Mark Coxon for helping me clear my head with a couple of beers on the occasional Thursday night and thanks to Kim and Paula who supplied the beer at Bar Yello.

Chapter 1

Introduction

Welcome to the world of Web-Based Enterprise Management (WBEM) and Windows Management Instrumentation (WMI). The WBEM initiative and Microsoft's implementation of it represent an improved and more complete approach to management of the Information Technology (IT) corporate enterprise. The following chapters will introduce you to enterprise management from the point of view of a software engineer, network administrator, or team leader. In studying this book you will learn not only the rationale behind using WMI for systems management but also, more importantly, how to make use of the tools it provides for the Windows operating system (OS), including Windows XP and the .NET architecture.

The book is structured to provide you with a reference for your future WMI management requirements. It is not a "beginners only" book, but more of a graduated path to enterprise management development. Throughout the book, we explore some existing management frameworks and how they interact with WMI. Obviously, it is not possible within this book to explore every legacy systems management technology and also go into great depth about the WBEM initiative. However, we have selected a number of technologies that you currently will find in the enterprise.

The book is arranged into chapters that cover the following topics:

- Why WBEM represents an evolutionary step for enterprise management
- How this initiative differs from past management frameworks
- How to write code for WMI
- How to write administrative scripts for this environment

We first explore the WBEM initiative and its model for managing enterprise systems. We then take a look at the expertise behind its development and its rationale. We examine Microsoft's WMI. A large percentage of the book discusses WMI's structure and the implementation of code based upon it.

In the book, we use the term "WBEM" to refer to the conceptual enterprise management framework defined by the Distributed Management Task Force (DMTF). We use the term "WMI" to refer to the implementation of WBEM for the Windows operating system.

■ Structure of the Book

One of the most daunting tasks of writing this book was deciding how and in what order to introduce all of the major concepts. The WBEM framework pulls together many different technologies to achieve its goals and integrates with a number of existing management frameworks. Understanding the relationships between these technologies is the key to understanding the WBEM framework fully. In this first chapter we discuss the background of WBEM and introduce many of the relevant technologies. We also introduce the organizations responsible for developing new technologies for management and the World Wide Web, because this will help you develop a fuller picture of the WBEM initiative. The first four chapters describe WBEM and enterprise management in detail, as this is where all implementations, including Microsoft's WMI, draw their inspiration. We also compare the DMTF's WBEM specification and its Microsoft implementation. Chapters 2 and 3 concentrate on defining the relationship between the technologies and their use in the enterprise. Chapter 4 discusses Microsoft's extended schema, Win32. Chapters 5 and 6 examine in depth the issues raised in designing your own extensions for the schema. Chapter 7 provides a detailed introduction and overview for software developers who wish to write management applications. Chapter 8 concentrates on the issues of writing code for .NET management applications, and Chapter 9 covers writing code for the Microsoft Management Console. Chapter 10 is the first of two chapters dedicated to addressing the needs of administrators who wish to use WMI. It introduces the basics of scripting in the form of a VBScript *boot camp* and provides the reader with a series of examples for performing common administrative tasks in WMI. Chapter 11 examines how to write your own script for WMI and also takes a detailed look at the Windows XP tool, WMIC. You don't have to be a programmer to understand this chapter, because basic use of log-in scripts and batch files will be sufficient experience for you to start learning to write WMI scripts. Chapter 12 introduces you to one of the most powerful aspects of Microsoft WMI: the capability for developers to expose their own managed objects through a provider. Chapter 13 looks at high-performance instrumentation and how it can be used to provide detailed trace information and techniques to monitor system usage.

As mentioned previously, the Windows OS, which includes all variants of Windows from version 9x to Windows XP and Windows .NET, is our chosen operating system. Where relevant, we also highlight any issues specific to writing code for each platform, especially those surrounding Windows XP and the .NET architecture.

■ Pedagogical Elements

Our experience of learning new technologies has taught us that one of the main problems developers encounter is making a quick connection between the concepts upon which the technology is based and a practical implementation of code based around it. This book is written with that objective in mind, and we aim to allow you to make the jump from conceptual schema to practical example in as few steps as possible. To make this jump, it is necessary to take the time to learn the WBEM framework. This, however, will pay off when you are required to apply your knowledge of WBEM to real problems in the work environment. From a network administrator's point of view, this approach also makes sense, as it will prove invaluable to know as much as you can about the structure and purpose of WBEM, both to roll out WBEM compliant systems and to support them.

We avoid making abstract references in the text to what is already a conceptual framework, because this slows down learning. Instead, to speed up the cognitive process, we use real-world examples.

■ Target Audience

The book aims to satisfy the needs of the following people wishing to learn more about WBMI and WMI:

- ■ Visual C++ software engineers who wish to develop management applications and expose management objects from their applications
- ■ Visual Studio .NET software engineers who wish to develop .NET management applications using the .NET Framework
- ■ Software team leaders who wish to learn of the impact of the new management model on development
- ■ Systems administrators who wish to gain new skills (WMI Scripting and WMIC) and improve their administrative skills

Some readers may not have written management applications before; the book aims to provide them with some insight into what issues need to be addressed and which technologies are available. The book also caters to the needs of other developers who may be familiar with management frameworks such as Simple Network Management Protocol (SNMP) and Desktop Management Interface (DMI) and builds upon their existing knowledge to introduce them to WMI.

■ Prerequisites

Throughout the book we deal with the object-orientated paradigm. We provide introductions and tutorials for new subjects or concepts as they occur throughout the book so that readers new to this area may grasp the essence of what is written; however, you will obviously be at an advantage if you've encountered this topic before. The same can be said for the diagrams that use the Unified Modeling Language (UML), but we will explain these as they occur.

The chapters that contain C++ code written using the Microsoft WMI Software Development Kit (SDK) require you to be familiar with the Microsoft Developer Studio and Microsoft Visual C++ 6.0 as a minimum. Chapter 8 ("Writing .NET Management Applications") also requires that you have the .NET framework installed. Because the WMI framework uses code that is based upon the Component Object Model (COM), you will also be at an advantage if you are familiar with Distributed Component Object Model (DCOM). If you have never before worked with COM/DCOM, you will find that we explain enough for you to understand the examples and to help you to write your own WMI code. If you wish to delve further into COM, we recommend that you read one of the excellent books available, such as *Essential COM* by Don Box.

Although not essential, it would be advantageous to have a basic knowledge of some existing systems management tools, protocols, and client-server networking. If you are familiar with management frameworks such as DMI and SNMP, you can skip the sections dedicated to explaining them. We introduce these topics as they occur during the course of the book.

■ Terminology

In the first few chapters of the book, you will encounter many new acronyms and concepts that pertain to WMI and systems management in general. We define new terms as they are mentioned and introduce some common terms at the end of this chapter.

■ Software Requirements

The system requirements for developing the samples are much the same as those required for installing and running the Visual C++ Developer Studio environment. All code examples included in the book are written using Visual C++ Developer Studio and/or Visual Studio .NET.

To work with the examples given in the book, you will need the following software installed on your system:

WMI VC++ Developer examples:

Microsoft Visual C++ 6.0 and/or Microsoft Visual Studio .NET

WMI Scripting Administration examples:

Microsoft Windows Scripting Host (WSH), included with Windows 98.

General:

Microsoft Internet Explorer 4.01 and higher

Microsoft WMI SDK [download by going to the Microsoft Web site at http://msdn.
microsoft.com and typing *WMI SDK* in the search facility]

The bulk of the book covers Microsoft's implementation of the WBEM initiative, WMI. We take a look at the Microsoft WMI framework and how it interacts with Windows. The WMI framework is shipped as standard with Microsoft Windows 2000, Microsoft Windows XP, and Microsoft Windows .NET server, but users of Microsoft Windows 95/98 or Microsoft Windows NT4 must install the core or Software Development Kit (SDK) before working with the examples we provide.

■ Operating System Requirements

To develop the examples in the book, you will need a machine with a WMI SDK–supported operating system. Table 1.1 highlights the operating systems that are supported by the WMI SDK.

Microsoft Internet Explorer 4.01 or later is also required and can be downloaded at no cost from the Microsoft Web site at http://www.microsoft.com/ie.

Microsoft's WMI SDK contains a collection of ActiveX components that are an invaluable tool for both developers and administrators who wish to gain a better

Table 1.1   WMI-Supported Operating Systems Required

Operating System	Required
Microsoft® Windows NT® version 4.0	Service Pack 3 or higher
Microsoft Windows 95®	OSR2
Microsoft Windows 98®	
Microsoft Windows Me®	
Microsoft Windows .NET Server®	
Microsoft Windows 2000 Professional and Server®	
Microsoft Windows XP Professional and Server®	

understanding of WMI and the data it provides. The SDK also includes a vast collection of code samples for programmers and administrators. These are installed as part of the WMI SDK under the %/Program files/WMI/Samples directory.

■ Hardware Requirements

The hardware requirements for working with WMI are much the same as those for developing software with Visual C++. The examples given in the book are designed to work with the Visual C++ environment, but they could be altered to work with other C++ compilers with minor modifications. The minimum computer configuration depends largely upon the Microsoft operating system used.

■ Introducing WBEM

Having examined the basic order of the book and the requirements for developing the examples, we introduce the source of WMI's inspiration, the Web-Based Enterprise Management initiative. By understanding the purpose of WBEM, we can begin to understand what part WMI plays in enterprise systems management and how it aims to provide the most comprehensive management architecture currently available for the enterprise.

■ WBEM's Basic Objectives

The aim of the WBEM initiative was to produce an industry-wide standard for managing enterprise systems across heterogeneous networks. Once defined, this standard could enable management of different types of hardware and operating systems across an enterprise network. "Enterprise" refers to the type of networks, computers, and software that support a large business organization. The term typically refers to a large number of systems, connected by multiple Local Area Networks (LANs) and Wide Area Networks (WANs), and, potentially, many sites. Managing these systems has become over the years a complex and costly affair. You will see how the WBEM initiative is designed to reduce administration and management overheads.

■ Core Objectives

The basic premises of Web-Based Enterprise Management can be defined as follows:

- ■ To define a model for representing and classifying enterprise-wide management information

- To provide a way to share that information among various parties across heterogeneous networks

- To remain independent of any proprietary operating system or network architecture

The Central Information Store

At the heart of the WBEM framework is an information model for managing data in a logical and consistent manner. This centralized information model was one of the primary goals of the WBEM initiative; while learning about the initiative, you will learn how WBEM uses the object-oriented paradigm (model) to structure this model. It also adopts XML (eXtensible Markup Language) to communicate this management information in a platform-independent manner. All of these objectives are designed to overcome the shortfalls of existing management frameworks and make WBEM one of the most comprehensive enterprise management solutions. As mentioned earlier, Windows 95/98, Me, NT, 2000, XP, and .NET all utilize these core concepts in WMI and provide access to a single source of detailed system information.

The Common Information Model

The WBEM information model mentioned earlier, the Common Information Model (CIM) is referred to as "common" because it focuses on common aspects found in every enterprise. Specialization of the CIM occurs in the form of extended schemas that are defined by vendors who wish to represent the managed environment of their hardware and software products. Before covering the concept of extended schemas, let's look a little closer at the CIM. The CIM represents a way of storing all enterprise management system information so that it is accessible by all WBEM-compliant systems. The CIM was designed using the object-oriented paradigm.

Object Orientation and CIM

Despite a slow takeoff since its introduction in 1967 in the Simula programming language, the object-oriented paradigm has received a great deal of attention in recent years. Largely, this has been because of the introduction and subsequent widespread popularity of C++, the object-oriented version of C. It was the popularity of C++ that really enabled object orientation to gain a worldwide audience. It quickly became known as the new panacea for analysis, design, and implementation of large or complex systems. Whether this is indeed true may depend upon your personal experiences and objectives, but when initially introduced, object orientation did represent a radical departure from structured methods (in which data and function were separate) and mathematical methods or knowledge-based systems. It is still one of the best approaches to systems development.

The object-oriented paradigm's strengths over traditional approaches included better representation of concepts and a more flexible and complete view of the world. Object orientation could be applied, using objects and classes, to analysis (OOA), design (OOD), and programming (OOP) of complex systems. It also provided an extensible architecture that enabled changes to a system to be implemented more quickly and easily. It is this characteristic of OO that provides the key to the CIM's extensible model. This extensibility allows the CIM to be tailored to represent a particular vendor's hardware or software product.

▪ Building an Information Model

WBEM's core concept, the CIM is founded upon concepts introduced by the object-oriented paradigm. The CIM is WBEM's central information model and is designed so that it can describe all of the hardware, software, and network information found in an enterprise. The information it can represent is useful to management applications administrators and, ultimately, to system administrators. It may help you to imagine the CIM as a blueprint for an information store that contains all the information relevant to a system, but it is not the actual store. The CIM is structured as a series of classes that hold the data (properties), behavior (methods), and inheritance characteristics (parents, or recursive structure and behavior) of the managed objects. In addition, it contains special classes unique to the CIM schema that represent associations between classes. We discuss these in more detail in a later chapter. A *managed object,* referred to as a *management object* in .NET (for the purpose of our discussion we shall use the two terms interchangeably), is a generic term for the software/hardware components on a WBEM-managed network or computer.

▪ Structure of the Centralized Repository

The relationship between the CIM and object orientation means, in plain English, that the CIM arranges management information into many different categories. Each category defines a specific type of managed object in the enterprise, such as a network card, log in account or network protocol, and so forth. Each of these specific categories can inherit a lot of information from parent categories. The category that defines a hard disk, for example, would contain the properties that define the disk, such as its size, make, and model. The class may also inherit more general properties from its parent classes such as its *device id,* which uniquely identifies the device on the system (that is, its hardware base address). The categories would also define the behavior (methods) of the disk. They could define, for example, the type of tasks that the disk is able to perform, such as Reset or PowerSave mode, and so forth. These categories are referred to within the CIM as *classes.* A class, as defined in the CIM, consists of properties and methods that an object supports. Each disk on a WBEM compliant system can create an *instance* of the class *disk,* filling in its own details. An *instance* is an actual data representation of values for each of the properties of the class.

In WMI these *classes* and *instances* could be stored in the CIM repository so that any application wishing to know about which disks are available (instance data) and what their properties are (class information) could access it. (This information could be stored and retrieved in other ways using instance and class providers, but we leave these for later in our discussion.)

In later chapters we refer to *schema.* A *schema* is defined by the DMTF as "a group of classes with a single owner." The CIM schema is not an actual implementation of the structure for storing enterprise management data. It can be imagined instead as more of a template from which the data store can be designed. Implementations of the CIM schema and extended schema are referred to as the CIM *repository.* In most cases, you will find that the CIM repository is a means to store class (and, if necessary, static instance) information. The base classes of CIM define very general characteristics of items found in the enterprise that build in detail with each step further down the hierarchy. The extended schema build upon these generalizations and define an actual (or an aspect of a) managed environment. The Win32 extended schema that defines the Windows operating system is an example. The DMTF defines two models that consist of a number of classes that represent the basic managed elements in the enterprise. These are the *core model* and the *common model* and are collectively referred to as the

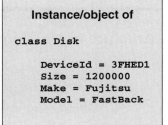

SuperClass	**Derived Class**	**Instance/object of**
```class HardwareDevice { sint32 DeviceId; }```	```class Disk : HardwareDevice { sint32 Size; string Make; string Model; }```	```class Disk DeviceId = 3FHED1 Size = 1200000 Make = Fujitsu Model = FastBack```

Figure 1.1 Inheritance and the difference between class and instance data

CIM schema. The CIM schema is device independent because it does not represent a particular environment and contains elements that are general to all.

Before we look at the implementations of schemas, it is worth looking at the definition of an object as defined by Grady Booch [1994, 83]:

> An object has state, behavior, and identity; the structure and behavior of similar objects are defined in their common class; the terms instance and object are interchangeable.[1]

This definition holds true for objects instantiated in the CIM schema.

Inheritance can be defined as the relationship between classes. Classes inherit information from parent classes, which can pass down their methods and properties. A class that does not have a parent is the root class.

■ The Three-Tiered Model

The DMTF has applied the object-oriented methodology to the information found in a typical managed environment and developed CIM into a multilayered model capable of storing management information. It defines three layers to describe the managed environment (see Figure 1.2).

The core model (2.4 is the latest version at the time of this writing) is very general and contains a small number of classes, associations, and properties that are relevant to all areas of management. It is a starting point from which to extend the common model. The common model is a collection of models that represent five distinct management domains:

- Systems
- Applications
- Networks
- Devices
- Users

We describe the semantics of each domain in later chapters; however, the five distinct areas (*management domains*) are interrelated by associations and subclassing and

---

1. Grady Booch (1994). *Object-Oriented Analysis and Design with Applications,* 2nd ed. Addison Wesley Longman.

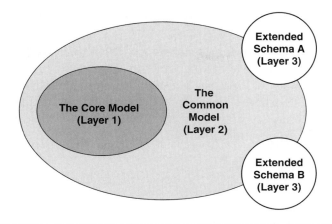

Figure 1.2   The Common Information Model has three tiers

are built on top of the core model. These five domains are broken further into classes that represent specific aspects of each.

The specialization of the common model is created by a series of extended schemas that are submitted by individual vendors. Microsoft has created Win32, a schema that models their Windows operating system environment. We take a closer look at Win32 and the three layers of CIM in later chapters.

Recall that we defined *managed objects* as hardware or software components such as network cards, disk drives, network routers, or gateways. Enterprise management is effectively the discovery, control, and monitoring of these components (such as desktop PCs and their components, network components, and so forth) across LANs and WANs and even the Internet.

Although the preceding points represent a cursory evaluation of the basic aspects of enterprise management, they also represent the basis of the WBEM initiative. Over the course of the next chapters we hope to familiarize you quickly with these core concepts and bring you up to date with the history and rationale behind WBEM. Some of the technologies we discuss in detail in the coming chapters, such as the CIM, were designed specifically for WBEM, and some, such as COM/DCOM, have been designed by other organizations to address implementation-specific issues. We also cover some legacy management frameworks, such as the Simple Network Management Protocol (SNMP), that have been in existence for many years. When we have looked at the history and design, we hope to teach you to write code that will enable you quickly to begin to write professional management applications.

▪ Acronyms and Terminology

Learning some of the more important acronyms and concepts that you will find throughout the rest of the book may speed your understanding of the following chapters. Many of the terms bear a relationship to standards bodies, so before examining them, let's have a look at some standards bodies and the reasons that they exist.

▪ Standards Bodies

Standards bodies exist to govern the development of standards. A standard can be defined as "a documented agreement that contains precise criteria that are used consistently." These criteria include rules, definitions, or guidelines. The members of a standards body ideally must be governmental, industry, or academic leaders within the field that they wish to standardize.

▪ Motivation

Why do we need standards bodies? Java encountered problems because Sun Microsystems and Microsoft, commercially opposed companies, would not adhere to a single standard. Standards bodies are intended to remove commercial interests from the development of standards and act as neutral forums for discussion. They provide an environment in which ideas can be exchanged, developed, and, in the final instance, agreed upon and published as a standard. The result of not developing a standard within an open forum can lead to situations, as with Java, in which inconsistencies occur between different vendors' implementations (for example, HTML).

▪ De Facto and de Jure Standards

Two different types of standards, *de facto* and *de jure,* exist in industry. De facto standards are driven by market forces and exist without formal ratification by a standards body. "Driven by market forces" means that a product or way of doing something has become the *most commonly used and widespread* within a given field. It is called the de facto standard by virtue of its popularity. Obviously, large companies who release a product would all like to define the de facto standard for that product. Problems arise when no clear market leader emerges and multiple standards exist for the same product, leading to product inconsistencies and incompatibilities between rival brands. An example is the use of slightly different mechanisms to achieve similar goals by Microsoft and Netscape in their HTML extensions. The effects of differences in implementation can polarize a market, which normally restricts the users' choices and is not generally good for market growth. Such situations can occur when the market is populated by several large product vendors, like Microsoft and Netscape, each of which holds large market shares.

The second type of standard exists to avoid such complications and open the market to competition based upon value-added products. *De jure* standards are official standards developed by standards bodies. The literal translation of de jure from Latin is "exists in law." Here, this law is defined and upheld by the standards bodies. De jure standards are developed so that they may be adopted and followed by industry as a whole. De jure standards are not open to interpretation by individual vendors: Vendors therefore must adhere to the specifications of the de jure standard. A concept can conform to the standards defined in a de jure standard and also become, by virtue of its popularity, a de facto standard. SNMP is an example of this.

To prevent multiple vendor-dependent implementations of a standard, we turn to a standards body to develop a single universal standard. One of the largest and most internationally renowned standards bodies is the International Organization for Standardization or ISO. (ISO, happily, means "equal" in Greek.) The secret to the success of ISO is its membership. ISO is an umbrella organization for 130 national standards bodies such as the American National Standards Institute (ANSI) and the British Standards Institute (BSI). Each national standards body within ISO represents the interests of its own country. A standard that has been endorsed by ISO has been evaluated and accepted by everyone in the membership, thus giving it global acceptance. To date, ISO has defined thousands of standards covering nearly all areas of technology, including, for example, the software engineering quality standard ISO9001.

ISO is perhaps the most universally well-known organization of its type in the world. Within the Internet also are standards bodies that define technologies specific to the Internet. One such body, the Internet Engineering Task Force (IETF), oversees "the evolution of the Internet architecture and smooth operation of the Internet." It has been responsible for defining hundreds of standards for the protocols that proliferate across the Internet.

Submitting a proposal to ISO or the IETF can ensure widespread acceptance of a given standard and also ensure that everybody develops products that conform to that single standard. The choice of standards body to which to submit a standard depends largely on your chosen audience. Obviously, Internet standards are better ratified by a body specifically set up for Internet-related issues. Part of the CIM specification, the Directory Enabled Networks (DEN) specification, has been submitted to ISO with the aim of gaining worldwide acceptance. We shall discuss the implications of this upon DEN in a later chapter.

The objective of most bodies is to publish standards to which the wider community can adhere. These groups are in place to oversee the development of standards and have no bias toward a particular vendor. They generally organize themselves into working groups to tackle a particular subject and are guided by a board. This structure is used by the Distributed Management Task Force (DMTF), the standards body industry equivalent to the IETF.

■ The Distributed Management Task Force (DMTF)

The difference between the DMTF and the IETF is that the DMTF membership consists exclusively of industry leaders with an interest in developing standards for their product marketplace. The DMTF initially concerned itself with standards pertaining to personal computer desktop management, but since being handed the WBEM initiative, they also encompass the enterprise.

The DMTF consortium was founded in May 1992 by a cooperative of eight companies: Digital Equipment Corporation, Hewlett-Packard, IBM, Intel, Microsoft, Novell, SunSoft, and SynOptics. It now comprises more than 200 commercial technology industry providers whose aim was to work together to develop standards for the maintenance, support, and development of management standards for PC products.

The fees paid by its members support the DMTF. Its vast industry support means that any provisional standards received are viewed internally by a variety of industry-aware sources. After the review process, they are able to suggest revisions to the standard or to endorse it. History has shown that without such an open forum for discussion, industry standards are very hard to secure, leading to different versions of the same standard. This kind of fragmentation is rarely in the interest of the consumer and, in most cases, impedes market progress.

Members of the DMTF include the original team that worked on the initial WBEM initiative before its handover; Microsoft is one of them. Board members of the DMTF include other such giants as IBM/Tivoli Systems, Inc., Novell, and Symantec Corporation. This large volume of contributors gives the DMTF a huge amount of resources and an invaluable amount of expertise.

The DMTF is broken into Technical Development Committees (TDC). Each committee is given a charter—a list of objectives that the team must meet. The CIM TDC's charter is to define a common information model based on object-oriented technologies for use in Web-based management. The TDCs are broken into working groups, each with a charter that explains the objective of the group. For an idea of the diversity of information that CIM holds, examine Figure 1.3, which shows the working groups and their charters in the CIM TDC.

The WBEM initiative was designed to integrate existing management standards such as SNMP and DMI. The time line in Figure 1.4 represents some key stages in the evolution of WBEM and shows the introduction of the DMTF to the WBEM initiative.

Figure 1.3   The DMTF working groups

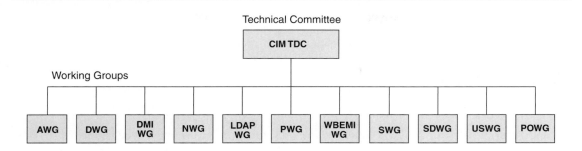

Applications Working Group (AWG)
The objective of this working group is to improve the models that represent application software within the CIM schema.

Database Working Group (DWG)
The objective of this working group is to improve the CIM common models' definition of databases, their requirements, and the relationship between instances of other databases within the enterprise, by identifying the information required to manage databases, the interaction between a database and its environment, and the relationship between database instances throughout the enterprise. The common database model is independent of any particular database implementation.

Desktop Management Interface Working Group (DMI WG)
This working group defines and maintains the DMI specifications. It promotes the DMI technology by creating working groups to address specific management arena issues. It also ensures that the work done by these working groups is in line with the DMTF strategy.

Networks Working Group (NWG)
The objective of this working group is to characterize and control network elements and services. This group also works upon the DEN initiative to enable

seamless integration of CIM with directory services. The networks group anticipates that its schemata will enable applications to learn and navigate a physical or logical network configuration using objects that are independent of the underlying network medium, hardware, or protocols.

Lightweight Directory Access Protocol Working Group (LDAP WG)
The objective of this working group is to develop LDAP schemas from CIM models. The purpose of these LDAP schemas is to support industry standard DEN.

Policy Working Group (PWG)
The objective of this working group is to extend the CIM syntax and metaschema to allow the definition and association of policies, rules, and expressions that enable internal and industry communications with respect to service.

Support Working Group (SWG)
The objective of this working group is to define objects and access methods necessary for support information to be shared between service requesters and providers. This group must define the range of data and means of accessing data that describe the support information exchanged between end users (service requesters) and administrators and support engineers (providers).

Continued

Figure 1.3 *Continued*

System and Devices Working Group (SDWG)
The objective of this working group is to define component and behavioral aspects of the high level system, computer system, operating system, logical device, and physical element classes, and their related and derived objects.

User and Security Working Group (USWG)
The objective of this working group is to define objects and access methods required for principals, where principals include users, groups, consumers, and organizations. This working group further defines the CIM to represent profiles and policies as well as mapping CIM's definitions of principles to existing directory models.

WBEM Interoperability Working Group (WBEMIWG)
The objective of this working group is to define architectures and mechanisms that enable WBEM implementations to interoperate in an open, standard manner, and to address issues that prevent them from doing so.

Pre-OS Working Group (POWG)
The objective of this working group is to define architectures and mechanisms that enable WBEM to monitor and protect environments in the absence of an operating system. For example, the Alert Standard Format Specification (ASFS) is targeted at environments where an OS is absent. POWG defines absent as a networked computer system in the state of inactive or inoperable OS or low power system sleep.

■ The World Wide Web Consortium (W3C)

The World Wide Web Consortium (W3C) was founded in 1994 with the objective of developing common protocols for the World Wide Web. The development of common protocols would enable interoperability in the Internet, an environment that spans the globe. The W3C is an international industry consortium jointly hosted by three academic institutions: the MIT Laboratory for Computer Science in the USA, INRIA[2] in Europe, and Keio University in Japan. Its large membership includes diverse companies such as Lucent Technologies, the British Broadcasting Corporation, America Online, Inc., and American Express.

■ Web-Based Enterprise Management (WBEM)

The WBEM initiative is based upon a set of management and Internet standard technologies developed to unify the management of enterprise computing environments.

2. Institut National de Recherche en Informatique et Automatique

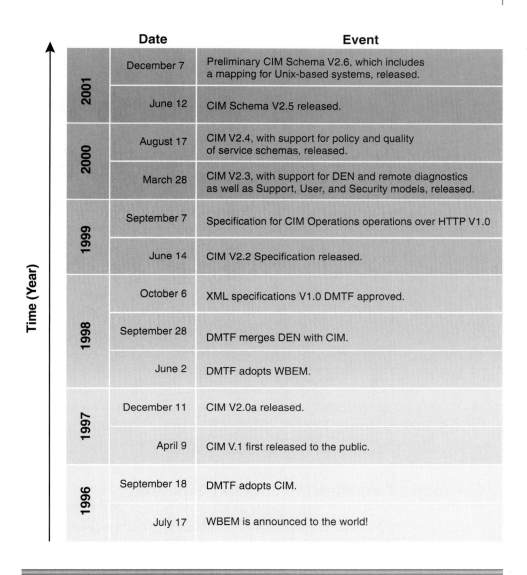

	Date	Event
2001	December 7	Preliminary CIM Schema V2.6, which includes a mapping for Unix-based systems, released.
	June 12	CIM Schema V2.5 released.
2000	August 17	CIM V2.4, with support for policy and quality of service schemas, released.
	March 28	CIM V2.3, with support for DEN and remote diagnostics as well as Support, User, and Security models, released.
1999	September 7	Specification for CIM Operations operations over HTTP V1.0
	June 14	CIM V2.2 Specification released.
1998	October 6	XML specifications V1.0 DMTF approved.
	September 28	DMTF merges DEN with CIM.
	June 2	DMTF adopts WBEM.
1997	December 11	CIM V2.0a released.
	April 9	CIM V.1 first released to the public.
1996	September 18	DMTF adopts CIM.
	July 17	WBEM is announced to the world!

Figure 1.4　Key stages in the evolution of the WBEM

Launched in 1996, its aims were to develop an industry standard to allow administrators to use any Web technologies to manage disparate systems, networks, and applications. WBEM is not a standard in itself: It is an initiative that ties together existing standards with new technologies such as CIM and XML. (XML and HTTP are two standards developed by the W3C that are of particular interest to us with respect to WBEM.)

■ Windows Management Instrumentation (WMI)

The WMI, Microsoft's WBEM-compliant implementation, is a complete management infrastructure for the Windows operating systems. It integrates WBEM's concept of a common information model for management information into the Windows management framework.

WMI provides an application programming interface (API) for developers to access and submit data to this central data store. It provides the capability to write simple scripts that can also perform complex management tasks through the WMI scripting API. WMI also provides administrators with a powerful remote administration tool that is capable of managing objects anywhere on an enterprise network. The WMI framework caters for management applications that need to be notified of events and managed objects that may need to notify a management application of that event. It adds WMI code to the Windows Driver Model (WDM) to enable managed objects to communicate with WMI from the driver level.

WMI offers a powerful set of services, including query-based information retrieval and event notification. We shall explore WMI in detail in coming chapters.

■ Common Information Model (CIM)

The CIM defines a model that represents the manageable elements of the enterprise. It is a core concept of the WBEM initiative and was defined by the DMTF. CIM also defines Managed Object Format (MOF) files, a file format to represent classes and instances of that data.

■ Common Information Model (CIM) Repository

The CIM repository is the store that holds enterprise management information. It uses the CIM as a template for structuring the data held in the repository, and it is implementation specific.

■ Managed Object Format (MOF)

The MOF is used to define the structure and contents of the CIM schema in human- and machine-readable form. A MOF text file describes the class or instances of one or many managed objects. The information held in the MOF can then be imported into the CIM repository. Plain text MOF files can be read using a normal text view, such as

Windows Notepad. We shall examine some examples of MOF files and their structure in later chapters.

Simple Network Management Protocol (SNMP)

The SNMP is an open network management protocol designed to monitor and control network components such as servers, gateways, and routers. SNMP is an Internet standard defined by the IETF and is part of the TCP/IP suite of protocols. It was developed to transmit management information stored in a repository called a *management information base* or MIB. MIBs are managed by SNMP agents and reside on each of the managed objects such as the server or router. Management stations issue queries to these *agents* across the network for system information. SNMP agent software commonly is found integrated into popular brands of dedicated network hardware such as routers.

SNMP is formally specified in a series of requests for comments (RFCs) submitted to the IETF. Requests for comments are documents written about computing or computer communications that usually refer to networking protocols, programs, concepts, or procedures. They can be written by anybody and may be submitted directly to either the IETF or the RFC editor. They are not accepted as a standard until they have been thoroughly reviewed and evaluated by the IETF, which then releases them to the community at large as an RFC.

SNMP was defined formally in RFC 1157 in May 1990 and is used commonly in enterprise networks to manage network components. In Chapter 2 we shall cover the SNMP management framework and how it compares with the Microsoft WMI framework.

Common Management Information Services (CMIS)

The CMIS framework defines a set of messages and their structure and content for use with network management. It also defines intelligent agents that reside upon the managed object. It is similar in concept to SNMP but provides more functionality. This increased functionality has led to its being somewhat more complex, which in turn means that it generates a greater overhead on system resources. This is one of the reasons that it is less commonly found in the enterprise. A second reason for its notable absence as a widespread industry standard is that it is designed to run over the Open Standards Interconnect (OSI) network protocol stack, which also is not found commonly in the enterprise. CMIS uses the Common Management Information Protocol to send information across the network.

■ Common Management Information Protocol (CMIP)

Common Management Information Protocol (CMIP) is part of the OSI body of standards that defines operations and notification services described in the CMIS standard.

CMIS/CMIP are mentioned here for historical reasons rather than for their relevance to our discussion. Their lack of uptake within industry means that they are unlikely to be encountered by a developer or an administrator—we have never worked anywhere they are used or met anyone who has. The focus of this book is on the *typical* aspects of corporate enterprise management and CMIS/CMIP, therefore, will not be mentioned further.

■ Desktop Management Interface (DMI)

The DMI acts as a layer of abstraction between administrators or managers and vendors. It separates those who need to manipulate information from a multitude of products and from the vendors of these products who wish to provide their own unique functionality.

The DMI is developed, maintained, and revised by the DMTF. Whereas the SNMP provided a framework for managing components across a network, the DMI provides a framework based upon managing the components on the desktop.

The DMI is

- Independent of a specific computer or operating system
- Independent of a specific management protocol
- Easy for vendors to adopt
- Useable locally—no network required
- Useable remotely using DCE/RPC, ONC/RPC, or TI/RPC
- Mappable to existing management protocols (for example, CMIP or SNMP)

We shall cover DMI in greater detail in Chapter 2.

■ eXtensible Markup Language (XML)

eXtensible Markup Language (XML) is fast becoming another key industry standard. The XML language is a subset of Standard Generalized Mark-up Language (SGML) and is targeted at data representation. It has been adopted by the DMTF as a means of representing the information stored in CIM across networks. If, for example, we were working in a Windows environment, XML could be imagined as the common language with which a Windows WMI management application would communicate CIM management information to a non-Windows WBEM-compliant management application (such as a Hewlett-Packard UNIX server).

■ Hypertext Transfer Protocol (HTTP)

Hypertext Transfer Protocol (HTTP) is one of the underlying protocols capable of transmitting XML-managed information. You probably know it to be the transport protocol used to send HTML. For now, all you need to know is that it is a very simple protocol that is understood by nearly all networked platforms (especially those that use Web browser technology) and so is potentially of great use in cross-platform communication.

■ Extended Schemas

The DMTF designed the CIM with extensibility in mind: The extended schemas are a specialization of the common and core models of CIM. Vendors who wish to instrument their products have the option to extend the common model to represent their environments. The new extension classes are either derived from or added alongside existing classes. These extensions then are released to the world community with the vendor's product. Microsoft, for example, has released its Win32 extended schema as part of Windows. We shall take a look at the Win32 extended schema and how it models the Windows environment in coming chapters.

■ WMI Scripting

For many years, systems administration has been a reactive (crisis-driven) process in which errors were dealt with only when the customer reported a fault. WMI provides a positive step towards proactive systems administration that enables intelligent decisions to be made before the customer is aware of a fault. WMI scripting is an API for accessing the WMI infrastructure. Developers or administrators can use the Windows Scripting Host (WSH) or Microsoft Internet Explorer (IE) to run their tailor-written scripts. WMI scripting provides a level of control over a network and its components never before known by systems administrators. WMI scripts can be written to monitor any WBEM-compliant hardware or software component and to react to changes in a managed objects state to preempt failure.

Chapter 10 discusses WMI scripting in detail and may also prove valuable reading for developers, as it provides an insight into the role of the system administrator (who most probably will be using the code you write). We shall discuss the merits of using both the WSH and IE in this chapter.

■ Summary

During this chapter we have introduced and discussed the DMTF's initiative Web-Based Enterprise Management (WBEM). The *Web-based* component of the initiative refers to the World Wide Web (or Internet), which is the world's largest and most diverse network. It also refers to Web browser and related technology such as ActiveX and Java. We shall look at their use as administrative tools for the enterprise in future chapters. But why use Web technologies? Mainly, we use them because they are freely available for most operating systems and are platform independent. Thus, the DMTF stays true to its goal of not binding its standards or technology to one particular operating system or vendor. Using this technology also provides a simple and familiar means of controlling and administering across networks.

Chapter 2 examines existing legacy management frameworks SNMP and DMI.

We end the chapter with Ten Fast Facts that sum up the basic points covered in the previous pages to help you to remember the large number of new acronyms and the relationships among the technologies drawn together by WBEM.

Ten Fast Facts: Web-Based Enterprise Management

1. The *WBEM* initiative was originally conceived by five key industry players on July 17th 1996:

BMC Software, Inc.:	*A leader in delivering Application Service Assurance (ASA) solutions.*
Cisco Systems, Inc.:	*A world-wide leader in networking for the Internet.*
Compaq Computer Corporation:	*A PC industry leader.*
Intel Corporation:	*A leader in the development of microchips.*
Microsoft Corporation:	*A leading software vendor.*

2. The WBEM initiative was handed over to the *DMTF* on June 2, 1998, to gain a broader base of industry acceptance.
3. The DMTF comprises more than 200 leading industry players. With the exception of BMC Software, Inc., the board of the DMTF consists only of members of the original initiative.

4. *WMI* is Microsoft's implementation of WBEM for its Windows range of operating systems.

5. *XML* is maintained and developed by the *W3C* not the DMTF. It is the DMTF's proposed means through which WBEM can convey *CIM* management information in a standard format. It is not a communications protocol.

6. Existing popular management frameworks such as *DMI* and SNMP can be integrated into *WBEM/WMI*.

7. The CIM and the *MOF* were designed specifically for the WBEM initiative. Their development is managed by the DMTF.

8. The DMTF does not develop standards biased toward a particular vendor's product. The standards that it defines in WBEM are targeted at the management marketplace as a whole.

9. *XML* is a language designed to communicate structured information in a standard way. One such type of information can be CIM management information. XML is used by WBEM/WMI to convey CIM management information between WBEM-compliant management applications, independent of operating system. For example, a Windows XP Professional client can use XML to convey CIM-compliant management information to a Unix client. For more information on this topic refer to the DMTF website (http://www.dmtf.org/standards/standard_wbem.php).

10. During the definition of WBEM, before handing over to the DMTF, the CIM was referred to as the Hypermedia Management Schema (HMMS). The gap now filled by XML was referred to initially as the Hypermedia Management Protocol (HMMP). The DMTF changed these terms to CIM and XML, respectively.

Chapter 2

Existing Management Frameworks

In Chapter 1 we discussed the core concepts of the WBEM initiative and, briefly, some of the existing enterprise management data gatherers, such as the Simple Network Management Protocol (SNMP) and Desktop Management Interface (DMI). Chapter 2 further develops those definitions and provides a more detailed overview of both SNMP and DMI. Although DMI is not a complete enterprise management solution, it does play an important role in desktop management. Its inclusion in our discussion is justified because of its popularity and because it manages one of the most prominent components in the enterprise, the desktop computer. The same can be said for SNMP, which manages the network-specific domain of the enterprise and has gained widespread popularity among vendors. Consequently, it is safe to assume that you will encounter either or both in some form in many corporate network/desktop managed environments. You can think of DMI and SNMP as managing different parts of the whole enterprise management picture. We illustrate them here to pave the way to introducing the general concepts behind systems management and, subsequently, to lead to our introduction of WMI in Chapter 3. Our discussion outlines the relative strengths and weaknesses of DMI and SNMP and highlights the ultimate need for WBEM. In accordance with their strong market presence, both DMI and SNMP have been integrated into the WBEM initiative to limit the cost implementing WBEM (that is, all existing management software and component instrumentation do not have to be abandoned) and to smooth the integration pathway between old and new technologies.

▪ New and Old Technologies Combined

The universal acceptance of SNMP and DMI by customers and manufacturers has led to their widespread deployment in industry. DMI's broad acceptance by personal computer manufacturers means that management applications written to access DMI have a very good chance of being able to predict and diagnose problems before they occur on a large cross section of hardware. If you somehow could provide interaction between the hardware/software instrumentation provided by DMI and the CIM repository, then you would provide access to yet another rich source of management information. The same is true for the data collected by SNMP. Many existing network devices, such as routers, have embedded SNMP compliance at the lowest level. These devices are not capable of being managed easily by another protocol or framework. Failure to integrate with these existing legacy management frameworks could prevent WBEM's widespread acceptance across industry and lead to a slow uptake by industry.

With this in mind, the DMTF set about defining WBEM, mapping between these existing management frameworks and paradigms. Microsoft also took this objective to heart in designing WMI, which makes ample provision for integration with these existing management frameworks. The focus of this chapter, therefore, is on the operation of both DMI and SNMP in relation to the enterprise. As a software developer writing a management application, you may find much of your effort expended on interconnecting new and old management frameworks.

As mentioned in Chapter 1, the premise of this book is to provide practical advice on WBEM. To do that we use examples of development with Microsoft's WMI. WMI provides integration with SNMP and DMI through a number of built-in *providers*. These providers ensure a layer of abstraction between CIM and SNMP and DMI's legacy data instrumentation. We shall discuss the concept of providers in detail in Chapter 3 and the development of your own providers in Chapter 12. By studying DMI and SNMP frameworks and the differences between them here, you will be able to ascertain both the benefits and the complexities of switching to Microsoft's WMI framework.

We shall examine the information models defined by DMI and SNMP to store management information. As you will find, the WBEM initiative provides a solution that integrates (and in some ways, ultimately replaces) these two management models.

If you are new to enterprise management, this chapter is for you. If you consider yourself an old hand at enterprise management, then you probably can skip to the discussion of WMI in Chapter 3.

▪ The Need for a Universal Management Model

The technological evolution of the modern day office has meant that in the past fifteen years an effective revolution has taken place upon our desks. Although the paperless office is not yet a widespread reality, most offices now are equipped with computers, networks, printers, and servers. An entry-level computer is now capable of being useful for far more than simply typing letters or entering data into a spreadsheet. It is capable of multitasking jobs, playing and recording compact disc–quality sound, displaying digital television–quality images, or rendering high-quality 3D graphics without the need for specialized or expensive hardware.

This revolution means that more and more personnel within a company are required to become at least partly computer literate, which has led to growth in the size and complexity of networks and the computers that populate them. The management complexity of individual machines and networks has grown with their evolution in the workplace. Network administration has become a complex task requiring knowledge of the relationships between various hardware and software products and how they interact.

The complexity of managing these environments partly is because of the speed at which they have grown but also because of the failure of the industry as a whole to agree on a single de facto standard for managing the enterprise. In addition, until now no one has produced a de jure standard to which all companies could adhere. Such a standard would help to reduce the cost of ownership by easing the administrative process. A key objective of such an initiative would be to correlate management data from multiple sources. Figure 2.1 shows a typical network management scenario.

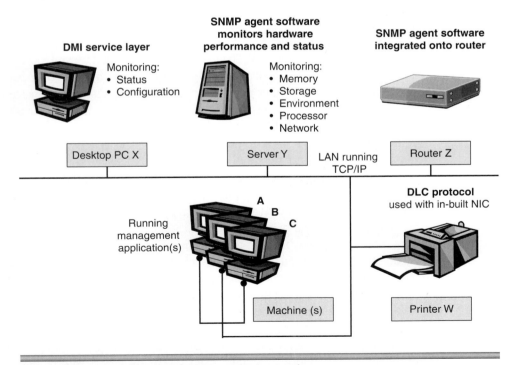

Figure 2.1 A typical network management scenario

Management applications, seen in Figure 2.1 running on machines A, B, and C, can gather information from multiple sources, but the servers, routers, printers, and gateways generally must run tailor-made, "agent" software to communicate with the management application. Multiple management applications may run from single or multiple machines to control and monitor multiple devices on a network, but interchange of information among them is minimal to nonexistent, especially if they monitor information from different vendors. For example, remote administration of printers using the Data Link Control protocol allows status checks on network-aware printers. The management of network-aware printers typically requires a management application different from that needed to manage the routers or servers. Because the printers use a management application and protocol different from the routers on the system, it means as well that neither application can share its information with the other. This also means that no relationship can be established between these managed objects on the system.

> **Note:** The examples cited here are representative of current use in industry. The point of the examples is to demonstrate that these problems are not easily overcome using pre-WBEM technology, NOT that they are impossible to overcome with it.

For example, assume that an application running from Machine A attempts to send a document to Printer W. The print queue is handled by and located on Server Y, which has reached full capacity on its print queue volume (the disk partition on the server that holds the printer queue). Printer W is registered as connected to the network and ready to print, but the Server Y volume sends error messages to users notifying them that it is full. This prevents anyone from printing, but the origin of the fault is not immediately apparent to the administrator. This is because the printer management application is not aware of the relationship between the drive volume and the print queue and, subsequently, cannot remedy the situation. If the system were WBEM compliant, the management application could trigger the relevant defragmentation/purging program to reclaim wasted space when the disk drops below 10 percent of available capacity. The management application could then notify the administrator of the problem and notify users to forward the job to the queue of another printer of equal capability that is not attached to the errant server. WBEM, therefore, enables more intelligent management decisions to be made.

The point of these examples is to show that prior to WBEM it was very difficult to write enterprise management applications that could gather information from every piece of manageable hardware or software in the enterprise. Products from different vendors would report management information in different formats, each potentially using different network protocols. Even the management information produced by printers would vary from vendor to vendor. These problems prompted the DMTF to embark upon producing a management architecture to provide a more complete picture of the enterprise, resulting in the WBEM initiative.

■ The Simple Network Management Protocol

Version 1 of the SNMP was designed in 1987 by the Internet Engineering Task Force (IETF) to send and receive management and status information across networks. Although the name "Simple Network Management Protocol" suggests a network protocol (that is, a means to communicate information), it defines an entire framework for managing internetwork devices. The definition of *internetwork devices* today is flexible in the extreme, but initially meant those components that connect LANs and direct information to and from adjoining networks. This definition has steadily grown with the popularity of SNMP to encompass nearly all network-related components such as servers, routers, printers, bridges, and gateways. An internetwork is a large collection of networks (usually LANs), connected by routers or gateways, that acts as a single network. Large businesses normally have some form of internetwork that supports their enterprise information needs. (This *internetwork* is not to be confused with the 1990s buzzword, the *Internet,* which normally is written with an uppercase "I.") The SNMP framework, as we shall discover, allows administrators of an enterprise internetwork to *remotely* control and monitor network-related components.

SNMP has undergone numerous revisions since its introduction to enable it to manage increasingly complex networks and improve the security model. As you can imagine, networking with every other IT-related field has progressed phenomenally during the past decade, and SNMP's widespread use has meant that the SNMP standards accordingly were revised. The most recent version of SNMP is version 3, which was ratified as a full standard in April 2002. Most current workplace implementations of SNMP, however, are either SNMP version 1 or version 2c, because of the relative newness of the standard. Here we concentrate on the characteristics common to those implementations.

> **Note:** Now that SNMP 3 has gained standardization from the IETF, we expect greater product support for it.

■ A Simple Solution to a Complex Problem

The SNMP framework is called *simple* because its protocol is based upon the two simple functions, *get* and *set* (sometimes called the fetch-store paradigm). The *get* function retrieves a value from a managed device (that is, a network router) and the *set* function alters a value on a managed device. The get and set functions work on a set of data stored on each SNMP agent.

To organize an SNMP-based network, the designers created two logically separate entities. The SNMP topology defines the roles of a network management station and an SNMP agent as follows:

- The network management station manages and initiates management requests on the agent.

- The SNMP agent responds to management stations' requests and can independently issue traps.

■ The SNMP Network Management Station

An SNMP network management station is software that can run on any machine that has a network connection and enough processor power, memory, and hard disk space to perform simple SNMP management tasks. Independent software vendors provide a number of management application products that sit above the network management station to provide a user-friendly front end to the information provided by the network management station (for example, a GUI). A core requirement for running the network management station software is that an SNMP compliant *protocol stack* is installed on the host machine. A *stack* is a commonly-used network term to define a layered collection of protocols bound together to provide a set of functions (for example, transport, error correction and notification, and so forth) to the applications that use them. Perhaps the most well-known stack is TCP/IP, because of its widespread use over the Internet and on corporate LANs and WANs. SNMP also has standards for use with the following protocols:

- The AppleTalk protocol stack (RFC 1419) is commonly used by Apple computers to communicate.

- Novell's IPX/SPX protocol stack (RFC 1420) is commonly found on networks that have Novell Netware servers acting as the central data store.

- The Open Systems Interconnect (OSI) protocol stack is defined by the ISO to represent an international standard for the heterogeneous computer network architecture. This standard is the one upon which most other commonly found protocols is based, but it was never accepted by industry as a protocol stack in its own right. Its lack of popularity in industry mainly is responsible for the failure of the management framework defined by CMIS/CMIP.

RFC means Request for Comments and is the term used by the IETF in defining a standards-related specification. Each RFC starts life as an Internet draft and goes through a six-month period of informal review. A draft that remains unchanged for more than six months without being put forward for publication as a full-blown RFC is removed. A draft that has been considered by the wider community and has met with their approval potentially can be placed on the standards track. The first stage in the standards track is a *proposed* standard, the second stage is a *draft* standard, and the final stage is a full Internet standard (referred to commonly as a *standard*). For more information on this process, see RFC2026 at http://www.ietf.org.

SNMP 1 initially provided only for running SNMP over TCP/IP: You will find that most implementations of the SNMP framework run over this protocol stack.

In Figure 2.2, notice that each SNMP agent comprises a Management Information Base (MIB) component and an SNMP protocol engine. In SNMP 3, the protocol engine may support more than one message processing model, thus creating a multilingual system that provides support for SNMP 1, SNMP 2c, and SNMP 3.

In Figure 2.2, the network management station software is running on a desktop computer using a TCP/IP stack. The SNMP framework has been designed so that the bulk of the processing is done on the network management station and not on the SNMP agent. This enables the hardware that runs the SNMP agent to dedicate most of

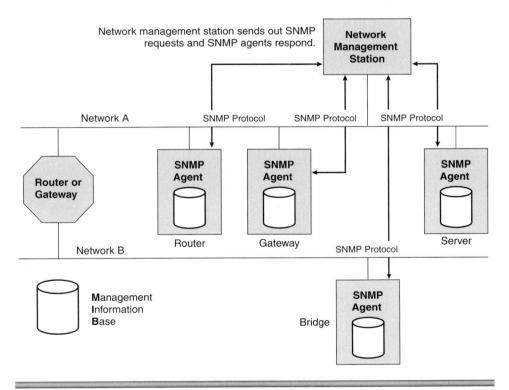

Figure 2.2 An SNMP-managed network

its CPU time to its assigned task, rather than analyzing and managing the SNMP protocol. Remember that when the initial SNMP framework was designed, processors were hardly a fraction as powerful as they now are. A simple network router was not powerful enough to dedicate large percentages of its processing time to interaction with the protocol and still route packets efficiently. Today this is still a design concern, although it is not nearly as big an issue as in the beginning.

The SNMP network management station software commonly is found upon a more powerful machine than the SNMP agent software and, preferably, on one that can display a GUI.

Although the SNMP framework commonly implements a network management station and SNMP agent on different machines, there is no reason that both entities cannot reside on a single machine. The only limiting factor is the resources of the host machines, that is, CPU, memory, disk space, and so forth.

An SNMP agent is software that resides upon the managed device. Typically, you find SNMP agent software integrated into most popular brands of network routers; some vendors even include agent software for use with their servers. The SNMP agent software can field requests issued by the network management station, and when required, it sets/gets information from the Management Information Base (MIB), a local information store.

■ Relevant SNMP Standards

SNMP comprises three basic standards, each defined in RFCs by the IETF:

1. The Structure of Management Information (SMI) defined in RFC 1155. This document specifies how to define managed objects.
2. The Simple Network Management Protocol standard (SNMP 1) defined in RFC 1157. This describes how the SNMP protocol can be used to manage SMI defined objects. An introduction to SNMP 3 can be found in RFC 2570 (the standard RFCs were not available at the time of writing).
3. The Management Information Base (MIB) defined in RFC 1156 and RFC 1213 is a set of standard managed devices for Internet devices.

Figure 2.3 shows how the relationships among the three can be defined.

The SNMP protocol is responsible for packaging the queries and responses to and from agents and network management stations into Protocol Data Units (PDUs). Within these PDUs are Object Identifiers (OIDs) that refer to variables that both a management agent and an SNMP agent can understand. OIDs conform to rules laid down by the SMI document. A collection or scheme of OIDs is a Management Information Base (MIB). We shall discuss the structure of an MIB in a moment, but first let's take a look at the role of PDUs.

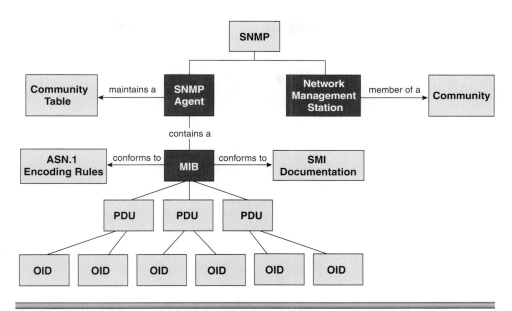

Figure 2.3 The components and relationships between elements of SNMP

In Figure 2.4, you can see that the network management station forms a request and sends it to the SNMP protocol stack. SNMP takes this information from the network management station and creates a PDU, which it passes to the TCP/IP stack. The TCP/IP stack then encapsulates the PDU into a User Datagram Packet (UDP) for connectionless transport. The data is further encapsulated by IP before being passed to the Network Interface Card (NIC). The NIC encapsulates the data with its own specific fields (such as network source and destination address) and passes the information across the network cable.

SNMP was designed initially to use the UDP protocol to send information because of its speed and efficiency. When communicating across multiple networks in which some links are slower than others, network bandwidth and performance become important issues. UDP is more economical in its use of network resources than the Transmission Control Protocol, the connection-based alternative in TCP/IP. UDP provides an unreliable, connectionless delivery service for any information that it sends, which allows it to send and receive information with a very small overhead. The connectionless service provided by UDP is also offered in other protocol stacks such a Novell's IPX protocol in their IPX/SPX stack. "Unreliable" does not mean that the protocol is inherently flawed or is unfit for sending and receiving information. It means that there is a chance that some information may not get through to its destination, although, typically, most does. As well as not guaranteeing arrival at its destination, the UDP protocol does not guarantee the order in which the information will

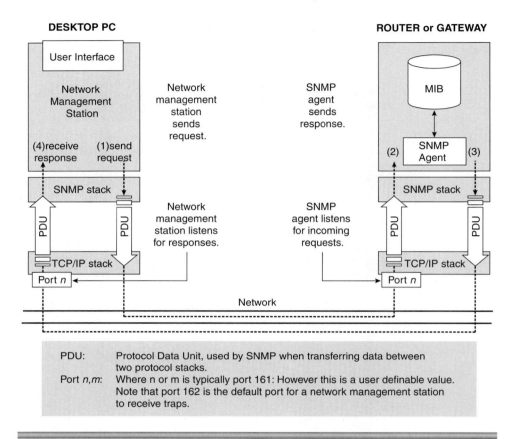

Figure 2.4 An SNMP network management station (NMS) and SNMP agent interacting

arrive. Network protocols work by breaking information down into small, manageable chunks before sending it across the network. Using smaller chunks makes the data easier to transmit and error check and places a more even load upon the network. Once the information has reached its destination, the data segments are reassembled into their original order before being passed up the protocol stack to SNMP and, finally, to the application layer (the network management station or SNMP agent software). The *connectionless* part of the protocol refers to the fact that it does not verify that the destination host is up and running before sending the information, nor does it inform the destination address that it wishes to send information to it. UDP may seem like a bad choice of protocol, considering the importance and urgency of some management information. However, to recap on the points made in the previous paragraphs, the manifest characteristics of UDP do provide the following key advantages:

- Very fast connection times. Unlike a connection-oriented protocol (that is, TCP), it does not have to initiate a connection before sending data.
- Minimal use of network bandwidth. The destination address does not send out requests for packets to be re-sent should a packet be lost en route, nor does it constantly poll the destination address to verify that it is present on the network.

The designers of SNMP who developed the first release believed that the benefits of this type of protocol far outweighed any potential drawbacks. This assumption was proved to be correct if only by the popular acceptance of SNMP over UDP. Had this design feature been a problem, it undoubtedly would have restricted the SNMP acceptance by the networking community as a whole. Today the IETF has released standards that allow SNMP to run over many connection-oriented protocols such as TCP, X.25, and ATM. It is the role of the network administrator to decide which underlying protocol provides the best service to suit the needs of the network. A connection-oriented protocol may be the preferred choice, for example, if the administrator wishes to control an SNMP agent that is located on a particularly unreliable segment of the network.

■ Structure of an SNMP Message

Each SNMP message that is transmitted across the network consists of three components:

- Version number (SNMP 1, SNMP 2c, or SNMP 3)
- If SNMP 3, then a number of authorization and authentication fields as part of the new view-based access control model (VACM) (see RFC 2272 for a complete definition of the SNMP 3 message processing model and VACM.). If SNMP 1 or SNMP 2c, then a community name (0–255 bytes).
- Data (a sequence of PDUs associated with the request)

The data is further encapsulated within the lower layers of the protocol stack before being passed to the NIC, which then sends the data across the network.

Figure 2.5 represents the basic structure of an SNMP message being sent using TCP/IP. You can see from the diagram that the original SNMP message is further encapsulated, first by the UDP header and then by the IP header. If the administrator were using SNMP on a TCP/IP network with a connection-oriented protocol, UDP would be replaced with TCP.

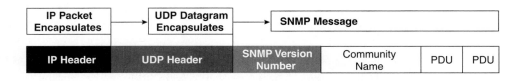

Figure 2.5   The basic structure of an SNMP message over TCP/IP

There can be multiple PDUs in a single message. SNMP 3 introduces a number of new security-related fields that replace the community name at the start of the SNMP message portion of the packet.

■ Communities

To make the framework as flexible as possible, network management stations and SNMP agents are not bound to each other explicitly by a one-to-one relationship. Instead, in SNMP 1 and SNMP 2c the agent maintains a community table. Each community table holds a list of valid communities that the SNMP agent allows to interact with the managed device. Network management stations, therefore, must include a community name to validate their request with each message that they send to an SNMP agent. The word *community* refers to the group of network management stations. Think of community as referring to a collection of network management stations that all pass requests to a single SNMP agent using the same community name. Examples of community names found commonly in SNMP implementation include public, private, and guest. In SNMP 3 this has been updated to achieve better authentication and authorization with View Based Access Control (VACM), which determines whether or not access should be allowed to a managed object in a local MIB by a remote principal. It also uses a MIB to determine the access control for the agent and make it possible for remote configuration to take place. Because of the relative newness of the protocol, we shall concentrate on the more common security features found in SNMP 1 and SNMP 2c.

As mentioned earlier, a community is a group of network management stations that all use the same name. If SNMP had defined a one-to-one relationship between agent and station, then it would have reduced the flexibility and efficiency of the model. Network management stations are grouped into communities by the agent software. Public and private are two of a standard set of groups available to any SNMP implementation. Different communities are granted different levels of access depending on their needs. Access levels determine the tasks that can be carried out on the managed object by a particular community. For example, read-only access could be assigned to the public community, which would prevent all network management stations that were members of that community from writing to any variables. When a network management station sends a request to a particular SNMP agent, the agent immediately checks the community table to verify the network management station's community name. Figure 2.6 provides a simple illustration of the SNMP verification process. Network management stations can be allowed to manage any number of SNMP agent devices across the network, providing there is an entry for the SNMP agent in their community table.

Network management stations can communicate with numerous SNMP agents if the following requirements are met:

1. The network management station has the correct community name to access the data stored on the SNMP agent.

2. The network management station has sent a request that holds the community name and, in some cases, the correct IP address. The SNMP agent checks the details of the community name (and the IP address) in the community table that it holds along with the MIB.

3. The community name specified by the network management station has the appropriate access levels to perform the requested task.

This system, therefore, allows many network management stations to send requests to many SNMP agents, assuming that they satisfy the security requirements. In addition, an SNMP agent can communicate with many network management stations if the stations all specify legal community names. In SNMP 1 the security requirements came in the form of a simple (0–255 octet) community name. If an SNMP agent receives a request from a network management station that provides an invalid community name, it simply drops the packet. In such an instance, it is possible to configure a trap on the agent that sends a message to a predefined, authorized, network management station signalling the attempted access violation (an authentication-failure trap). SNMP can be used to manage network devices on the same network or on multiple networks that support an SNMP-compliant protocol.

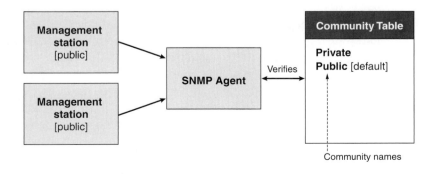

Figure 2.6 Security verification in SNMP 1 and SNMP 2c using communities

■ Event Notification: SNMP Traps and Informs

In SNMP 1, asynchronous notification of events was delegated to "traps." Traps were typically sent by agents to network management stations to signal the occurrence of an asynchronous event and were used to indicate that an event *might* require action, but did not convey the specific action that should take place. They also did not require any form of acknowledgment. It was the responsibility of the network management station, upon receipt of the trap ("event"), to determine the best course of action. An agent might generate any of the following seven predefined types of trap for SNMP 1:

enterpriseSpecific, which implies that an enterprise-specific event has occurred.

coldStart, which implies that the sending agent is reinitializing itself with significant changes in its configuration, for example, after a reboot.

warmStart, which implies that the sending agent is reinitializing itself with no changes in its configuration.

linkUp, which implies that one of the communication links of the sending agent has been restored to normal running status.

linkDown, which implies that a failure has occurred in one of the communication links of the sending agent.

egpNeighborLoss, which implies that an EGP peer relationship of the sending agent's EGP protocol has been lost.

authenticationFailure, which implies that an instance of authentication failure has occurred at the sending agent.

The configuration of agents so that they generated and sent traps to a given network management station was handled by packages supplied by the vendor of the SNMP management environment. Typically, this application came in the form of an agent configuration program that allowed the user to specify destination IP addresses (or network addresses pertinent to the protocol over which SNMP was running) for use in response to one of the above errors. Vendor-defined traps also came with agent software. These traps were designed to monitor events that were specific to particular hardware or software supplied by the vendor. Compaq, which supplies agent software with a wide number of traps that monitor specific conditions that may arise upon their managed devices, is one such vendor. Certain SNMP packages also provide the ability for administrators to define their own traps based upon items in the MIB, although most administrators choose to use vendors' predefined traps. In SNMP 2c, the concept of traps is slightly improved: They were augmented, not replaced, so that when a management station receives an event it must then send an acknowledgment. These improved traps are referred to as *informs*. This meant that the agent sending the event could be programmed to resend the inform until it receives an acknowledgment. This mechanism is again improved upon in the new security features of SNMP 3, which updates informs and traps so that they have to originate from a valid user that is registered in the user database.

The Management Information Base

The IETF standards for SNMP defined a general information store (or *information model*) for holding information pertaining to managed objects on an internetwork that aimed to encompass every possible nonproprietary managed aspect of an internetwork system. Thus, the information defined in the master MIB was very general. The ITEF efforts resulted in a tree with individual data items as leaves, as demonstrated in Figure 2.7. Managed objects or data variables occur at the leaf nodes of the tree. The tree increases in detail as you progress down the hierarchy.

In Figure 2.7 you can see that each node has been assigned a numeric value, for example, ISO has been assigned a value of 1. Each assigned value must be unique within

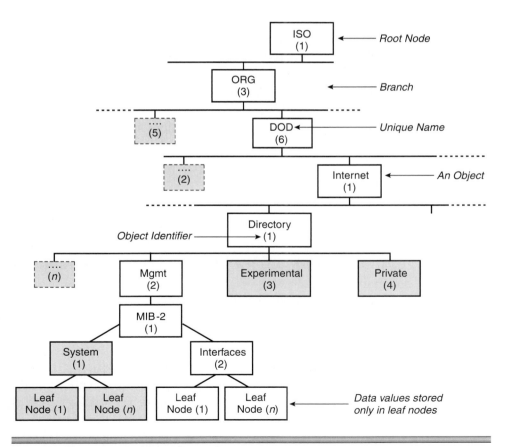

Figure 2.7 A partial MIB tree hierarchy

its branch of the tree. This unique value specifies a component within the MIB. For example, to specify the Interfaces component of the MIB shown in Figure 2.7, the SNMP path would be **1.3.6.1.1.2.1.2.** Each value in the SNMP path represents a specific node in each branch. The last nodes on any branch are leaf nodes. Only leaf nodes can contain objects that possess values accessible to the network management station.

Every managed device in an SNMP controlled network must maintain a set of values that represents the structure of the MIB that it implements. A MIB is the branch of the tree that is relevant to the managed device. The master MIB defined by the IETF is so comprehensive that it is obviously not good use of resources to insist that each managed device on a network carry values for every entry in the master MIB. In the case of a network router, the agent software would maintain the set of values that represent the details of only the router MIB (a generic branch of the master MIB that represents all routers settings). There are MIB branches that define practically all types of internetwork devices.

Each MIB is further broken down into eight subsections that represent object groups, as shown in the following list. The object groups represent the general features of all internetwork devices and, in most cases, are mandatory.

The System Group contains a text definition of the managed device. This definition includes, for example, the version type, operating system, networking software, and so forth. The system group also contains the elapsed time since the network portion of the device was initialized.

The Interfaces Group contains definitions of the available interfaces for receiving and sending SNMP packets.

The Address Translation Group holds a table of mappings of physical-to-network addresses.

The Internet Protocol Group holds all the statistics related to IP.

The Internet Control Message Protocol (ICMP) holds a table of all ICMP-related messages. Among these are error messages relating to the network.

The Transmission Control Protocol (TCP) holds a table of all TCP-related messages.

The User Datagram Protocol holds a table of all UDP-related messages.

The Exterior Gateway Protocol (EGP) stores information pertaining to the EGP protocol.

If the semantics of one of these groups is applicable to an SNMP managed object, then it must implement all items within that group in its MIB definition. For example, an SNMP managed object must implement the EGP group within its MIB if, *and only if,* it uses the EGP protocol.

Central governing bodies are assigned to manage particular branches of the MIB tree by the IETF. The ISO and DOD, who both manage branches in the trees that are related to fields in which they are considered the authority, are examples. Each governing body allocates numbers to the subtrees within their hierarchy. Each subtree further defines a particular type of internetwork device. Additions to these subtrees within the MIB must be registered with the assigned governing body for that branch.

How do vendors specify the features that are particular to their specific products? The MIB definition includes experimental and private enterprise subtrees, which allow vendors to define characteristics of their own products. The experimental branches typically are used by the academic community for research purposes: Industry defines its products under the private/enterprise node of the MIB. The branches developed beneath this node, unlike additions made beneath all other nodes, do not have to be centrally registered, thus creating a more flexible means of defining equipment within the MIB.

SNMP requires that any device to be managed by SNMP must store a set of data values to represent the structure of the MIB that it supports. This allows network management stations to request information from the SNMP agent and guarantees that they will receive a response. For example, the vendor of an SNMP-compliant network card would provide SNMP agent software with the card that stores a list of values that represent the MIB. Certain values within that MIB represent the values specific to the network card. This enables any SNMP network management station to interact predictably with the network card. The information stored on the SNMP agent is implementation-dependent.

The structure of the MIB and the rules for defining MIBs conform to guidelines given in Structured Management Information (SMI) document (see RFC 1155) or MIB-II (see RFC 1213). Managed objects are defined and given places as nodes in the object tree. The master MIB tree places related objects together under a subtree. Each of these subtrees is referred to as a MIB. A managed device, therefore, need only store its particular subtree and not the entire hierarchy from the root down. Each subtree is registered with an administrative authority that assigns a unique OID to the root of the subtree. Any value assigned to objects below the root must be unique for their subtrees. For example, currently MIBs define the TCP/IP protocol, the SNMP protocol, and many others, which are defined in various RFCs. To traverse the tree you specify a series of OIDs, each of which refers to a branch farther down the tree. The standard MIB, to which all SNMP implementations must conform, was designed with the following criteria in mind:

- **Objects must be uniquely named.** There can be no ambiguity when specifying for which object your request is intended.
- **Objects must be essential.** The MIB design is minimalist to reduce the storage overhead of maintaining the structure on each agent.

- **Abstract structure of the MIB must be universal.** The MIB was designed to be of universal use to all vendors and manufacturers.

- **The standard MIB need maintain only a small number of objects.** This is to reduce the hardware requirements for maintaining the MIB.

- **The MIB must allow for private extensions.** These private extensions were for use by independent vendors who wished to customize the MIB to define their products further.

- **Objects must be general and not too device-dependent to allow for extensions.** If an agent is to be SNMP manageable, then it is mandatory to implement the Internet MIB (MIB-II in RFC 1157).

SNMP agents receive requests to get and set (retrieve and change) a particular characteristic of the managed object from network management stations. A managed object could be a particular vendor's network card or a disk controller: We use an Object Identifier to specify a particular object within the MIB hierarchy. An Object Identifier (OID) is a sequence of integer numbers that represent a traversal of the tree hierarchy. It is important to realize that if your managed device requires settings that can be specified only under the private or experimental branch of the MIB, then the additions you have made must be added to every network management stations' central MIB that you wish to communicate with your device. Without this information, the NMS will not have prior knowledge of the properties exposed by your device.

■ SNMP Security

As mentioned previously, each SNMP request contains a community name that is a weak means of authentication. By *weak,* we mean that the authentication can be overcome easily by a malicious user because the community name is not encrypted and IP addresses can be spoofed.

Spoofing or *IP spoofing* is a technique with which an illegal user assumes the identity of a privileged user. In SNMP, the target of spoofing would be a network management station. Imagine that the illegal user is on machine A and the network management station is on machine B. The illegal user changes the IP source address of outgoing packets on machine A to that of the network management station on machine B and captures a community name with a packet sniffer (a piece of software that can intercept or "sniff" the packets transmitted over a network) or uses one of the standard community names. Then machine A can send requests to the SNMP agent that will be processed as if they were from a legitimate network management station.

A *community* is the relationship between an SNMP agent and a collection of network management stations and a *community table* that is maintained by the SNMP agent software. The community table contains a list of communities and their access rights to the SNMP agent's MIB. In some implementations of SNMP, the community table also contains a list of IP addresses (assuming you are using the TCP/IP stack beneath SNMP) that map network management stations' network addresses (that is, 192.142.190.10) to a particular community.

The SNMP agent, upon receiving the request, examines the table to determine whether the SNMP message contains a valid community name. If the message passes the community verification check, the agent examines the table to determine the access levels granted to that station. If the message does not contain a valid community name or the IP address is not recognized, the request is dropped. The SNMP agent can also contain an *authenticationFailure trap* that can notify a predefined network management station of the illegal request. The following list represents the permissions available to a community:

- **No Access.** The SNMP community cannot write to or read SNMP objects on the managed device.
- **Read Only.** The SNMP community can read only readable SNMP objects on the managed device.
- **Clear Statistics.** The SNMP community can write to a limited set of MIB variables on the managed device.
- **Configure.** The SNMP community can read readable SNMP objects on the managed device and can write to writeable SNMP objects on the managed device.

Access privileges can range from *No Access* through administrative level read/write access by setting the configure property to `true`. Read/write access provides the most control, because it allows settings to be changed on the managed device. The agent software can be configured to accept only requests from certain communities, which limits who has control of the device and the level of control with which they are provided. In reality, community names act like passwords, providing certain levels of access for communities.

SNMP 2 introduced a number of improvements to the security model defined in v1. Specifically, in authenticating network management stations that send requests and restricting access to particular variables, it provided a means to prevent intruders from gaining access to information carried along the network and addresses the potential problem of a network management station accidentally crashing an agent by incorrectly setting a variable.

SNMP 3 implements improvements that address the security weaknesses in versions 1 and 2. The User-Security Model (USM), which specifies security and authentication, allows you to encrypt passwords and data at the packet level to help verify the integrity and origin of the packet. The new standard also includes timeliness indicators, data integrity checks, and encryption to protect against threats such as spoofing, message stream modification, and disclosure and modification of information. For more information on these details, refer to RFC 2574.

■ Modus Operandi

SNMP defines a number of operations that get and set data to and from an SNMP agent, as demonstrated in Table 2.1. The Flow column specifies the origin of the call. For example, A -> M means that the agent issues the GetRequest command to the network management station. If the request is completed successfully, the network management station returns the requested value, the GetResponse PDU, containing the original request with the error status field containing no error and the value of the error-index field at zero. The network management station similarly responds with the requested values to the GetNextRequest and SetRequest PDUs.

The GetRequest (see Figure 2.8) is sent by a network management station and received by an SNMP agent. The SNMP agent software then gets the requested item from the Management Information Base (MIB) and returns the corresponding data value.

The SetRequest (see Figure 2.9) is sent by a network management station and received by an SNMP agent. The SNMP agent then accesses the MIB and changes the value specified by set to the value specified by the network management station.

A *trap* (see Figure 2.10) is an asynchronous event that the SNMP agent software is configured to trigger. For example, a trap can be activated to signal a network management station if an SNMP agent is rebooted unexpectedly or if someone has tried illegally to issue a get/set command.

Table 2.1 SNMP Operations

Operation	PDU	Comment	Flow
Get	GetRequest	Contains the values of the requested object instances.	M->A
	GetResponse	Retrieves a variable on an SNMP agent.	A->M
Set	SetRequest	Sets a variable on an SNMP agent.	M->A
	GetResponse	Contains the error status of SetRequest.	A->M
Trap	Trap	Signals the occurrence of an unexpected event.	A->M
Getnext	GetNextRequest	Retrieves object instances.	M->A
	GetResponse	Contains the values of object instances.	M->A

Table Key:

A: SNMP Agent software

M: Network Management Station

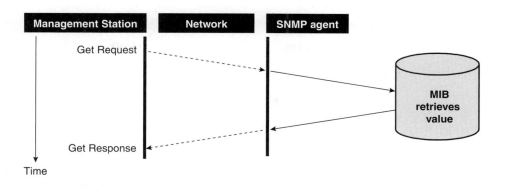

Figure 2.8 The GetRequest operation

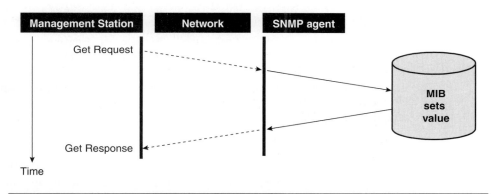

Figure 2.9 The SetRequest operation

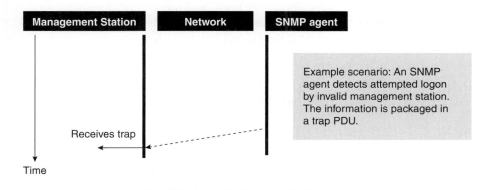

Figure 2.10 The SNMP trap

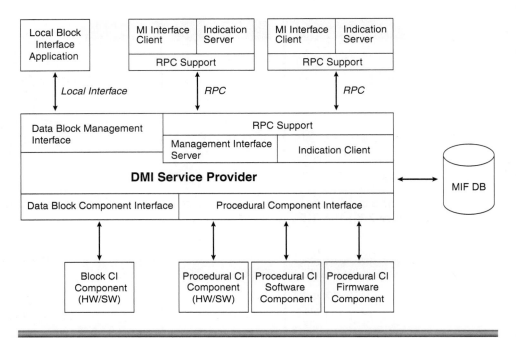

Figure 2.11 A simplified version of the functional block diagram (excluding features unique to DMI 2.0s)

The GetNext operation (see Figure 2.11) is used to retrieve the next lexicographically located object located in the MIB. By lexicographical, we mean that data is sorted according to the hierarchy defined by the MIB and certain data values are next to one another according to this hierarchy. The GetNext operation exploits the fact that related data is stored together in logically related sections of the MIB. Possible uses of this function include retrieving a list of related data, such as a sequence of entries from an IP routing table, from an SNMP agent. GetNext is also useful for network management stations to retrieve extended information from the MIB that is specific to the managed device (for example, custom information defined under the enterprise branch of the MIB).

■ Advantages of the SNMP Protocol

The SNMP protocol has many advantages, including the following:

- It is lightweight use of an enterprise's bandwidth, CPU time, and disk space resources.
- It is simple to set up and use.

- It is relatively simple to implement.

- It is almost an industry-wide solution to systems management—implemented in many hardware products.

- It is extensible. The protocol has been improved upon over time to meet the additional needs of more complex networks (SNMP 2c and SNMP 3).

Disadvantages of the SNMP Protocol

Here are some disadvantages to the SNMP protocol:

- The first SNMP revision's simplistic management information model did not support a modern network's detailed information requirements, but it was updated in SNMP 2c and SNMP 3.

- Information collected by the agents is distributed across the network to many nodes.

- Up-to-date information is not centrally maintained.

- Vendor-specific data cannot be published to the management community without providing an updated MIB file.

- The MIB does not define behavioral characteristics of managed objects.

- The SNMP lacks cohesion with other management paradigms.

- Security flaws exist in many vendors' implementations (see CERT® advisory CA-2002-03 http://www.cert.org).

- New security extensions in SNMP 3 may place an additional processing burden upon managed objects.

With the framework of SNMP for managing devices across a network in mind, we next examine a desktop solution for management.

The Desktop Management Interface

The Desktop Management Interface (DMI) is another specification defined and managed by the DMTF. Representing the DMTF's first initiative to reduce the complexity of desktop management for vendors and administrators, DMI came into existence in 1994. DMI version 1, the initial release, defined a way to manage desktop components and servers while conforming to a consistent and nonproprietary open standard. DMI 2, released in April 1996, encompassed these open standards, defined a means of sending detailed management information across networks to a central site, interacted with agents, and mapped information between SNMP and DMI. Most recently, DMI 2.0s, released in June 1998, subsumes the work of DMI 2 and the errata and adds security extensions: role-based authorization, security indications, logging, and authentication, which secure the interactions between the DMI service provider, management applications, and component instrumentation and protect management information from unauthorized access over the network.

The initial goals specified that DMI was:

■ Independent of any specific operating system, hardware platform, or management protocol

■ Easy for vendors to adopt

■ Scalable, to accommodate a wide range of products from very simple to very complex and extensible, to provide room to grow

■ Mappable to existing management and remoting protocols

But surely this overlaps with the SNMP frameworks objectives? Not really; the facility to remotely access DMI is designed for the remote administration of desktop devices and not network-based devices, as is SNMP.

In the last section we examined how SNMP manages networked devices across one or more networks. The DMI, however, is designed primarily for local desktop and server management.

Why do we need a framework for managing devices on our local machine? As the competition for market share among personal computer component manufacturers has increased, so has the complexity of the devices they produce. Manufacturers constantly "value-add"—revise their products to add new features—with the ultimate hope of capturing a larger market share. This constant movement has led to ever-increasing problems when trying to manage a desktop or server system that consists of numerous software and hardware products built by different vendors. Each product that requires its own set of special management instructions further compounds the management problem. Managing a system with a multitude of different components, each providing different levels of instrumentation, has long been a problem for the system administrator. Simply getting management information from these software and hardware devices is a complex task.

From the manufacturers' perspective, defining proprietary instrumentation for each new product is a costly overhead. The introduction of DMI allows manufacturers to focus on producing a higher quality product and leave the instrumentation and management to DMI.

Instrumentation is the exposure of management data and functions by a managed object. Management data provide management applications with status and configuration information and functions allow management applications to perform actions on the managed object. Instrumentation, therefore, dictates the manageability of a product. Good device instrumentation means good manageability.

DMTF defined a common interface to simplify the management of hardware or software: It provided a layer of abstraction between the managed component and the administrator. The block diagram in Figure 2.11 demonstrates the interface. The common interface, called the *Service layer* in the first release of DMI, in version 2 was renamed the *DMI service provider.* On one side of the DMI service provider is the Component Interface (CI) and on the other is the Management Interface (MI).

The name change in version 2 was partly to reflect changes to the Management Interface that enabled remote access to DMI via DCE/RPC (commonly found on Windows NT), ONC/RPC (implemented mainly on UNIX), and TI/RPC (also known as ONC+ RPC and found on AS/400 and iSeries systems). RPC stands for Remote Procedure Call, a high-level protocol for client-server interaction without concern for the underlying network architecture. In Figure 2.11, observe that the DMI Service Provider and component instrumentation all reside within a single system (that is, a desktop PC). RPC support enables access across a network for DMI management applications to this instrumented data. You can see in Figure 2.11 that DMI provides two choices of component interface: the data block component interface and the procedural component interface. Both perform essentially the same function: passing component instrumentation to the DMI service provider. The Data Block component interface, introduced in DMI 1.0, was superseded by the Procedural Component Interface in DMI 2.0. It is present still in DMI 2.0s to maintain backward compatibility with legacy components.

The procedural interface, in addition to being suitable for remoting via one of the supported RPC mechanisms, is much friendlier to programmers and much less error-prone than the Data Block component interface. A DMI-compliant managed object, such as a network card, may use either component interface to communicate management information.

Management applications use a layer called the Management Interface (MI) to communicate with managed devices on the system. The DMI service provider effectively is sandwiched between the application and the device and marshals requests to and from them. This level of abstraction shields component vendors from decisions about management applications, allowing them to focus on providing competitive management features and functionalities for their products.

For a product to be DMI compliant, it must first go through certification. This process can be performed by the DMTF or by the manufacturer (using the self-certification guidelines provided by the DMTF). Some of the companies that have released DMI-compliant products include:

- 3COM, (DMI-compliant network cards)
- Compaq (DMI-compliant desktop and portable computers)
- Dell Computer Corporation (DMI-compliant desktop and portable computers)
- Fujitsu
- Hewlett-Packard

▪ The DMI Information Model: The Management Store

The DMI model for desktop management defines a localized management repository that must reside on each DMI-managed machine. This repository holds all management information pertaining to the desktop system and is used by the service layer for storage and retrieval of information. This store of information is the Management Information Format (MIF) database. The MIF is a simple text format with a prescribed grammar and syntax and is used to define components and their manageable attributes. Vendors must provide an ASCII text MIF file that details the manageable aspects of that component. These settings are added to the MIF database, usually during installation of the product. Each MIF file is headed by a component (see Figure 2.12). A component can be a manufacturer's product, such as an internal modem. It is important to understand that each MIF file can describe only one component, thus, it is not possible to describe a modem and a hard disk under the same component heading in the same MIF file. Any number of groups can be under each component heading. Groups define a collection of related manageable attributes for the product being described. In the case of an internal modem, you may define a group that defines the attributes for the onboard BIOS, such as whether or not it is Flash upgradeable. A group that defines a single instance of the specified data is scalar; a group that defines multiple instances of data is tabular.

If we were to write a partial MIF file that detailed the Serial Number attribute of **Group:Disk Parameters** from **Component:Harddisk** shown in Figure 2.12, it would appear as in Figure 2.13.

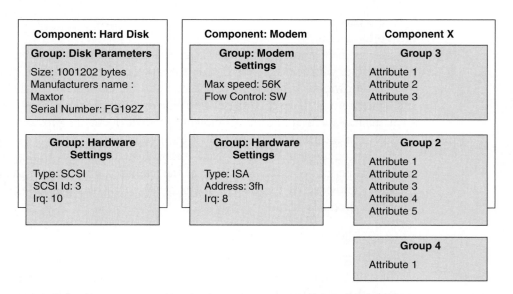

Figure 2.12 Attribute presentation within the DMI Data Model

```
Start Group
  Name = "Hard Disk"
  Class = "DMTF|HardDisk|001"
  ID = 1
  Description = "This group defines the settings of my local harddisk"
  Start Attribute
    Name = "SerialNumber"
    ID = 1
    Description = "Serial number of this disk"
    Type = integer
    Access = Read-Only
    Value = FG192z
  End Attribute
End Group
```

Figure 2.13   An excerpt from a MIF file to describe the attribute Group:Disk

■ Policy

The policy defines which actions can be performed on which objects by which roles. The policy is stored within the MIF database as a table. Each row in the table represents a policy statement, which grants or denies the privilege (role) of a management application to perform a DMI command. The DMI service provider references the policy within the MIF database each time a management application makes a request to perform a command upon an object. The policy statement for that object determines whether the command is carried out or rejected by the service provider.

■ Notification of Events

An *indication* signals a change of state within a DMI-managed system. Indications can be defined to notify a management application of a change of state for either a hardware or a software device. Notification of events is passed up through the DMI provider layer by a DMI-managed object. The DMI provider layer then generates an *indication,* which is then passed to the event consumer. Event consumers must first subscribe to receive a specific *indication.* Indications can also be passed to management applications that are located on remote machines (remote consumers) via RPC, if they have subscribed to that event. To avoid wasteful use of network resources by passing all indications to a remote consumer, the remote consumer must also provide a filter that determines exactly under what circumstances to pass on the indication. The *event severity filter,* for example, can filter out less critical events and prevent them from being sent to a remote management application, thus reserving network resources.

■ DMI Security

The security mechanisms that DMI enforces are based upon those provided by the implementation of RPC that is being used and the features supported by the operating system in use. Windows XP, for example, provides file-level security with its version of NTFS. It is therefore safe to assume that if a malicious user could compromise the security model of RPC or the resident OS, then the security of DMI would also be compromised. DMI 1 and DMI 2 do, however, provide limited security features (such as security indications) to notify management applications of changes in the configuration of DMI or illegal attempts to administer it. With the release of DMI 2.0s, the security model was enhanced and uses authentication to determine whether to perform or reject a DMI command. This decision is reached by considering a variety of factors that include the roles of which the user is a member and policy, which must contain an adequate level of permissions to carry out the command. Having retrieved adequate authorization, the DMI service provider authorizes each subsequent command issued by the management application by referring to the management application role, the current contents of the service provider policy table, and the command parameters.

■ MIF Database Security

The MIF database is located locally on all DMI-managed machines. It is a simple ASCII text file that contains definitions for all the managed objects on a system. The MIF database contains the policy, which you will recall denotes which commands can be performed on which objects, and is therefore a target for malicious attack. The MIF database is protected from unauthorized access from DMI management applications through security mechanisms built into the Management Interface. File level security, however, is very much dependent upon the underlying features provided by the operating system. As mentioned earlier, Windows NT, for example, can provide file-level security to protect important files. If such facilities are available, the DMI service provider will use them to protect the MIF database by allowing access to the file only to privileged processes.

■ Management Interface Security

The MI uses RPC authentication to authenticate the user of a management application, as this is the only entrance for management applications to retrieve DMI management data and instrumentation. Space limitations prevent our going into great detail. Briefly, however, the management application must send the identity of the user invoking the management application (RPC client) to the DMI service provider (RPC server). The RPC server then checks the identity of the user and any associated roles. A role specifies a name and a set of authorization permissions (privileges) that accompany that role (for example, only the role of *network administrator* is allowed to change the speed of the network card from 10Mbps to 100Mbps). DMI 2.0s introduces a number of new features to Management Interface Security. In DMI 2.0s, when a management application registers with the Service Provider, the service provider then authenticates the management application and returns a list of roles associated with the user that invoked it. It also returns a management handle, a unique identifier that allows the service provider to recognize the management application without authenticating the user every time. For every subsequent call, the DMI 2.0s service provider can use the management handle to authenticate the management application and allow tasks to be carried out according to the permissions granted to the associated roles and the policy, which (again) determines which commands can be performed on which objects by which roles.

■ Component Interface Security

The component interface interacts between managed devices and the DMI Service provider. Possible security threats to this interface include software that behaves like component instrumentation but, in fact, is not legitimate instrumentation. DMI, therefore, provides security mechanisms to control registration of components to prevent such actions. DMI provides a group that handles CI security, called *SP Characteristics*. Within that group is the Boolean attribute, *enable local security*. When set to `true`, Component Interface Security is active. This means that any component that tries to register with the DMI service provider through the Component Interface must be a *privileged process*. A privileged process is one that has been executed by a user with special privileges upon the host machine. In Windows NT, for example, a privileged user would be a member of the Windows NT administrators' group. Any process executed by that user is a privileged process. Again, the security mechanism in place varies according to the security features of the host operating system.

■ Security Indications

Security indications can be configured to send notification to authorized management applications if a breach or attempted breach of security is detected. Security indications are fully configurable and are defined in MIF format as special groups and classes with attributes that define what kind of events should trigger an indication.

▪ Advantages of the DMI

DMI has several advantages:

- ▪ It is hardware and platform independent.
- ▪ It is management protocol independent.
- ▪ It works with a variety of authentication and authorization mechanisms.
- ▪ It is usable with or without a network.
- ▪ It maps to existing management protocols such as SNMP.

▪ Disadvantages of the DMI

Here are some disadvantages to the DMI:

- ▪ It is dependent upon underlying operating system for security (for example, Windows version 9x has no file level security—therefore, the DMI MIF file is exposed).
- ▪ It does not provide a cryptographic system to protect data from malicious users.
- ▪ It does not provide fully user-definable event notification (though indications provide notification of certain types of events).
- ▪ It does not illustrate relationship between components outside of the desktop domain through its information model.

▪ Summary

Having examined the DMI and SNMP management frameworks, we have found that certain common features exist in both. We can deem these common characteristics to be necessary attributes for any management framework whether it be DMI, SNMP, or, as we shall discover, WBEM. Furthermore, we can summarize their common features as follows:

Common Elements for Management Frameworks

1. **Security.** Protects from malicious attack or accidental misuse. Management data and instrumentation have always been of potential interest to hackers and subject to malicious attacks. At the most basic level, SNMP provides a basic, community-naming system to authenticate requests. The second version of SNMP adds further security enhancements to prevent illegal access to SNMP agents and to provide a mechanism for assigning access permissions to certain nodes in the MIB. SNMP 3 introduces more features, such as password

and packet-level encryption to help reduce the security threat. In DMI, security is provided by roles, policies, and privileged processes. In DMI, file-level security for the MIF database is largely dependent upon the facilities provided by the host operating system.

2. **Event notification.** Alerts a management application that a certain event has taken place upon a managed object (that is, an external e-mail gateway has been reset). DMI provides indications, a mechanism for event notification. SNMP provides traps.

3. **Dynamic data.** Enables retrieval of management data that is constantly changing.

4. **Structured information store (information model) for static data.** In SNMP, this is the MIB database and in DMI, it is the MIF data store.

5. **Mechanism for device instrumentation.**

6. **Mechanism for control and management across a network.** Examples are RPC, SNMP, or DCOM, and so forth.

7. **Comprehensive integration with legacy management application frameworks.**

8. **Flexibility.** The management framework must be able to work within a broad spectrum of environments.

9. **Efficiency.** It must make efficient use of network resources, such as bandwidth, and still provide effective management.

10. **Extensibility.** Its structure and topology must take into account future advances made in IT enterprise systems.

Another common design feature that we have witnessed in both DMI and SNMP is a two-tiered approach to management data instrumentation. Both include provision for retrieving such information and a mechanism for forwarding it to management applications (or to any other management data consumer). Problems arise, however, when a management application would like to understand and represent both DMI and SNMP data. To do so would require two separate information parsers, one to understand DMI and one to understand SNMP (Figure 2.14).

As we shall discover, WBEM provides a three-tiered approach to data instrumentation (Figure 2.15). The third tier forms a layer of abstraction above the underlying management frameworks data format.

Central to the retrieval of management information in DMI and SNMP is the information model used to logically store management information. Both DMI and SNMP arrange their data in a logically related format for quick storage and retrieval purposes. The structure (or data model) of their respective data stores, however, differs considerably. SNMP's information model was defined by the IETF and managed by various

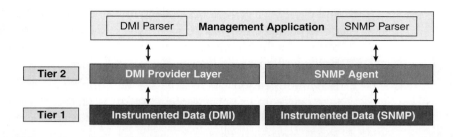

Figure 2.14 A two-tiered approach to data instrumentation

governing bodies. It provides extensibility (as of SNMP 2c and SNMP 3) through vendor-defined extensions that are not published to the community as a whole or governed by the central body. The downside of this mechanism is that a network management station must have the MIB file supplied by the vendor that defines the extended structure to know in detail about these extensions. Typically, this file is compiled to the central network management stations' MIB. There is no way to request this information directly from the managed object, and although you can use GetNext to retrieve the associated data values of these extended attributes, the network management station will have no idea of their relevance to the managed object.

The DMI's data model consists of classifying managed devices as *components,* within which are *groups* that consist of related *attributes.* The definition of DMI-managed objects is contained in vendor-defined MIF files, which are then added to the central MIF database. These MIF file syntax and semantics are flexible enough to allow vendors easily to define any desktop component so that it may be added to DMI's central database. Again, vendors must supply a MIF file to define the manageable aspects of their component.

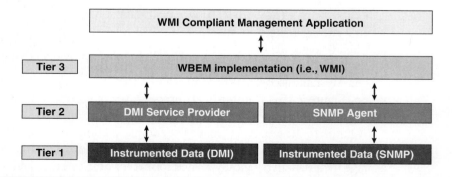

Figure 2.15 A three-tiered approach to data instrumentation

Management information provided by an SNMP network is distributed across the network in the MIBs of the managed devices (SNMP agents). To keep up to date with this data, and to maintain a truly dynamic picture of the values of the data stored in their MIBs, management applications constantly would have to poll all of the SNMP management agents. This is not particularly efficient from the point of view of CPU or network resources. In a DMI-managed machine, all the management information is stored centrally in a MIF database that resides upon the host machine. The MIF database is administered by the DMI service provider. Constantly updated values can be accessed via the DMI service provider, which makes provision for data instrumentation.

The Need for a Unified Management Framework

Both SNMP and DMI are non-vendor-proprietary open standards for management. Each supports managing objects within its specific target environment: the desktop or the network. The weakness of both approaches is in their management information models, which, respectively, hold only information pertinent to network-managed devices or desktops and cannot define relationships with managed objects outside their domain.

Neither information model provides a mechanism with which to represent the sometimes complex relationships that exist between components in the whole enterprise. This makes it very difficult to develop management applications that can track a fault to its source based upon these relationships. In addition, it has not been previously possible to communicate the structure as well as the content of management information across the network.

These limitations have been addressed by the DMTF with the WBEM initiative. The advantages of these additions will be seen mostly in the management applications written to take advantage of its information model, CIM. These applications will be able to make intelligent decisions based upon knowledge supplied by CIM about the objects that it manages. Microsoft implements these standards in its management framework, WMI, which takes the best aspects of proprietary Windows technology, such as COM/DCOM (to allow distributed management), and nonproprietary technology, such as WBEM. As well as being WBEM-compliant and tightly integrated with the Windows Driver Model, Microsoft supplies built-in providers that integrate WMI with both DMI and SNMP.

Ten Fast Facts: SNMP and DMI

1. Prior to WBEM, products from different vendors would report management information in different formats, each potentially using different network protocols. WBEM offers a mapping between DMI and SNMP and provides a solution that integrates (and in some ways, ultimately replaces) them.

2. DMI and SNMP manage different parts of the whole enterprise management picture. DMI manages the desktop-specific aspect whereas SNMP manages the network-specific domain.

3. The SNMP framework is called "simple" because its protocol is based on the two simple functions, get and set (sometimes called the fetch-store paradigm).

4. SNMP 3 addresses the security concerns of version 1 and 2c by introducing authorization and authentication as part of the new view-based access control model (VACM). See RFC 2272 for a complete definition.

5. In SNMP 1, asynchronous notification of events was delegated to "traps." In SNMP 2c, the concept of traps is slightly improved so that when a management station receives an event it must then send an acknowledgment. These improved traps are referred to as "informs." This mechanism is again improved upon in the new security features of SNMP 3, which updates informs and traps so that they have to originate from a valid user that is registered in the user database.

6. The DMI information model is called the Management Store. The SNMP information model is called the Management Information Base (MIB). Events are surfaced in SNMP using traps and informs, and in DMI using indications.

7. WMI provides integration with SNMP through built-in providers. We shall discuss the concept of providers in detail in Chapter 3 and the development of your own providers in Chapter 12.

8. SNMP is lightweight in its use of an enterprise's bandwidth, CPU time, and disk space resources. It is also simple to set up and use, is relatively simple to implement, and is almost an industry-wide solution to systems management. It is also extensible and the protocol has been improved over time to meet the additional needs of more complex networks (SNMP 2c and SNMP 3).

9. SNMP management information can be accessed in WMI using Microsoft's SNMP Provider. The SNMP provider allows users to read and write to SNMP-managed devices as well as surface SNMP traps. WMI providers are discussed in more detail in Chapter 3 and Chapter 12. Microsoft does not currently supply a provider for DMI management information.

10. DMI is hardware- and platform-independent and is management-protocol independent. It works with a variety of authentication and authorization mechanisms and is usable with or without a network. DMI also maps to existing management protocols such as SNMP.

Chapter 3

Windows Management Instrumentation

As we discovered in Chapter 2, both SNMP and DMI provide adequate solutions for their particular management domains. They provide event notification, dynamic and static management information retrieval, and define a logically related store for holding management information. They provide some degree of control over their managed objects and have security mechanisms in place to prevent accidental misuse or abuse.

In any enterprise environment, both DMI and SNMP typically coexist and provide management information for their particular domains. As the coexistence of the two frameworks became more commonplace in the enterprise, the DMTF made provisions for integrating them, and defined a mapping for DMI values into the values understood by SNMP. The aim was to allow systems instrumented by the DMI to be remotely and uniformly managed using the SNMP. Thus, existing SNMP-based management applications could be used to manage DMI-based systems as well as SNMP devices. Unfortunately, a combination of technical incompatibilities between the SNMP and DMI prevented straightforward integration of the two frameworks, causing this attempt to provide interoperability to be time consuming and relatively costly in effort and knowledge.

The biggest problem facing enterprise management in recent years has been the escalating cost associated with the administration of such environments. Despite attempts to instigate some degree of interoperability between de facto management standards, the development of different management frameworks for each domain of the enterprise created a highly complex and error-prone administrative process.

These administrative problems, among other factors, led to a dramatic increase in the cost of owning and maintaining a desktop computer in the enterprise. Indeed, the real cost of maintaining a networked desktop computer in the enterprise goes far beyond its initial purchase. Maintenance, technical support, and hardware and software upgrades and configuration are only some of the ongoing costs associated with a typical desktop computer. Microsoft refers to these ongoing costs as the total cost of ownership (TCO).

Manufacturers of enterprise products have long been aware that corporate customers wished to reduce these running costs. The DMTF was initially formed and a series of initiatives was embarked upon to reduce these overheads. The Web-Based Enterprise Management Initiative (WBEMI) is its most comprehensive and ambitious solution to date.

Microsoft, a member of the DMTF, also launched the Zero Administration for Windows (ZAW) initiative to show its commitment to the problems and costs associated with complex administrative environments. The aim of the ZAW initiative was to reduce the TCO of running and maintaining a Windows desktop computer in the enterprise. It encompassed a variety of technologies, including Windows policy-based management and, more important here, WMI.

When the WBEM initiative was handed over to the DMTF, Microsoft, with many other enterprise software and hardware technology-based companies, maintained an active role in its development. All participants in the development of the WBEM initiative worked toward providing an intuitive, industry-wide solution for centralizing the administration and management of the enterprise that would reduce running costs. Microsoft gained valuable experience from its involvement with the development of WBEM from the drafting phase to its publication, and used it as the core of their management architecture for the Windows range of operating systems. WMI was first shipped as an integral feature in Windows 2000, but it was available long before as an additional feature for Windows 9x and NT4. In addition to conforming to the WBEM standards, Microsoft included a number of Windows-specific instrumentation features (such as those provided by the Windows driver model) to provide tighter cohesion with the Windows operating system, the summation of which we now call Windows Management Instrumentation. Microsoft used the close coupling of WMI with WBEM-compliant technologies to simplify instrumentation and provide consistent, open access to management data. In WMI, we look at a variety of technologies, both proprietary (COM/DCOM) and nonproprietary (XML and CIM), that have been drawn together to manage the enterprise.

▪ The Standard WBEM Components

The primary component of the WBEM initiative is the Common Information Model (CIM), which holds all information pertinent to the enterprise. We briefly defined the CIM, a mandatory component of any WBEM compliant implementation, in Chapter 1.

A distinction must be drawn between the CIM schema as defined by the DMTF and the implementation of the schema by Microsoft. The DMTF CIM schema was a platform-independent blueprint from which people could implement the CIM. The Microsoft implementation, based on the DMTF CIM schema, is the CIM repository and its associated providers. The CIM repository is a physical implementation of the DMTF's CIM.

In addition to CIM, the DMTF specified a number of other basic framework elements for inclusion with any WBEM-compliant implementation.

The DMTF proposed that XML be used to represent CIM objects between management applications across a heterogeneous network. Microsoft adhered to this in implementing WMI. (Chapter 11 introduces WMIC, the administrative tool that provides the ability to output CIM objects in XML format, and offers a practical example.)

MOF files, also a mandatory component, define CIM object definitions in textual format. Any WBEM-compliant implementation must be able to import and export these files to and from the CIM repository.

The DMTF addressed integration with existing legacy management frameworks and documented the process of mapping data from these frameworks into the CIM repository. Microsoft, which supplies both an SNMP and a DMI provider to enable centralized control of both from within WM, completed this work.

In addition to implementing these standard components, implementations of WBEM (a conceptual vendor-neutral framework) must also use some proprietary technologies to bind them. Microsoft, for example, uses the COM/DCOM paradigm to communicate between elements in its architecture.

■ Installing WMI

Installing WMI will make it available for you to use and test the examples provided to help you understand its various components.

> **Note:** Windows2000/Me/XP/.NET users are not required to perform the following steps as WMI will already be installed as part of the operating system.

The WMI core is shipped as an installable option on Windows 98, and is included as part of service pack 4 on Windows NT4. We recommend, however, that you download the latest version of WMI from the Microsoft MSDN Web site, http://msdn.microsoft.com/, and use the search function to locate the latest features in *WMI Core*.

Because WMI requires DCOM to work, WMI does not work on a Windows NT3.51 installation.

Installation Files

Microsoft provides two installation files for download from its Web site. One contains only the core components; the other contains the WMI Software Development Kit (SDK). Many of the examples in this book use components that are shipped as part of the SDK, so downloading the file containing the SDK from Microsoft's site will be worthwhile, whether you are running Windows 9x, NT4, or Windows 2000/XP/.NET. The WMI installable files are as follows:

Core (WMICORE.EXE) (approximately 6.5 Mb)

The core contains the components of WMI that become part of the operating system. System administrators must install the core components on any potentially WMI-managed machine.

WMI SDK (WMISDK.EXE) (approximately 12Mb)

The SDK contains all of the tools, examples, documentation, libraries, and header files required by developers for working with WMI. System administrators may find some of the tools supplied with the SDK interesting, as the SDK contains a number of utilities for navigating the CIM repository, which might be the quickest and most accessible way to learn in detail about WMI.

To start installation, double-click on either of the above and follow the on-screen instructions.

Configuring Windows 98 for WMI

Because Windows 98 does not support the concept of *managed services,* you must configure this operating system to initialize WMI automatically at start-up. The simplest of a number of options is to place a shortcut to `winmgmt.exe` in the Windows startup folder. This solution, although simple, is not ideal, because it leaves the icon on display for inquisitive users. A more secure method of initializing WMI on Windows 98 is to adjust the contents of the system registry, where all but the most determined user fear to tread. You must also configure WMI on Windows 98 to accept remote access by changing certain settings in the DCOM registry.

To enable automatic startup of WMI and remote administration on Windows 98 machines, perform the following steps:

1. Start the registry editor program by clicking on the start menu, selecting Run... and then type `regedit.exe`.

2. You should now be presented with an application window titled Registry Editor. The main window is divided into two panes. The left pane contains a num-

ber of folders that start with the word *HKEY_*. Each folder icon represents a *key* within the registry. Each key at the root of the registry is a *hive* of the registry, hence its abbreviation, `HiveKey`. Select `HKEY_LOCAL_MACHINE` and double-click on it to bring down a selection of subkeys.

3. Double-click the SOFTWARE key.

4. Double-click the Microsoft key.

5. Double-click the OLE key.

6. Two values, *EnableDCOM* and *EnableRemoteConnect,* should be listed in the right pane. Set both of these values to Y by double-clicking each one and entering Y as their data values. EnableDCOM already should be set to Y by default. The default setting for the EnableRemoteConnect? value is N for Windows 98 systems and Y for Windows NT systems. These settings enable remote machines to access the host machine via DCOM.

7. Modify the following entry in the system registry to use `regedit` to activate the automatic start feature supported by WMI. First, go back to the left pane and scroll through it until you locate the key WBEM. Double-click this key and you will be presented several subkeys. Double-click the WMI key and in the right pane locate the *AutostartWin9X* value. Double-click this entry and set its data value to one of the values in Table 3.1.

Optional Setting

While in the HKLM\SOFTWARE\Microsoft\WBEM\WMI key in the registry, you can enable WMI for remote administration. This will allow management applications to administer the machine across the network or phone line using WMI. This setting is disabled by default, as the machine needs to be connected either to a network or to an outside line for this function to work. (Certain security issues are associated with remote administration. WMI security and authentication issues for Windows 98 are discussed later in this chapter.) If you wish to enable this setting, double-click EnableAnonConnections settings and change the data value to 1.

Hint: If you are familiar with the Windows registry, you may prefer to go straight to the keys mentioned by using the Find function under the Edit menu. The keys are

　　　HKEY_Local_Machine\SOFTWARE\Microsoft\OLE

and

　　　HKEY_Local_Machine\SOFTWARE\Microsoft\WBEM

Table 3.1 AutoStartWin9x Registry Value Options

Value	Description
0	Do not automatically start Windows Management Service [default]. This starts Winmgmt.exe only if and when a request is made. The Windows Management Service will unload again after a set period of time. This setting is ideal if you don't anticipate your machine having much interaction with WMI. This setting should not be used if you wish to allow remote administration of WMI on the machines, as this setting does not start the Windows Management Service at the request of remote machines. **Note:** Events will not be forwarded to event consumers while the Windows Management Service is in the unloaded state.
1	Start the Windows Management Service automatically after a system restart *only* if active event consumers were registered with WMI. This option is ideal if you anticipate that the host machine will be providing events for active event consumers. If this is the case, then Windows Management will check for active event consumers before the operating system shuts down. If any are present, then Windows Management Service will start automatically again when the operating system reload is complete, thus enabling it to continue forwarding events to these consumers.
2	Start Windows Management Service automatically every time the system starts up. With this option, the Windows Management Service remains loaded throughout every Windows session, which creates a slightly higher resource overhead but speeds up responses to requests. **Note:** This is the preferred setting for most configurations.

■ Core Components of WMI

When the core components of WMI have been installed, a number of executables, dynamic link libraries (files that end with .dll), MOF, and XSL files will be placed in a directory called WBEM that is located under the Windows system directory. In a Windows XP/.NET/2000/NT4 installation, the path is `%SystemRoot%\system32\wbem`. On a Windows 98/Me installation, the path is `%SystemRoot%\system\wbem`. For Windows 9x/Me/2000 users, it is advisable (although not necessary) to add this installation path to your system environment *path* variable because this will simplify using the command-line driven executables supplied with WMI. The WMI core components are a mixture of command line and GUI-based executables that assist in testing and managing the WMI architecture. This directory also contains the components that make up the management infrastructure.

The WMI SDK is somewhat larger and installs a number of programming samples and applications to allow navigation, interaction, and testing of WMI into a different directory from the core WMI files (by default this directory is \Program Files\WMI).

In the first part of this chapter, we examine the files that are installed as part of the WMI Core. We look at their purpose and use and how they help monitor and control WMI. This is useful for administrators and is helpful for developers in testing code and tracking faults. It also serves as a tangible introduction to WMI, behind which is the conceptual WMI framework. In the second part of the chapter, we explain the WMI framework in detail.

winMgmt.exe: The Windows Management Service

At the very center of the WMI architecture is the executable `winmgmt.exe`. It is capable of functioning both as a standard Windows executable (Windows 9x and Me) and as a service under Windows NT/XP/2000/.NET. The executable was referred to originally as the Common Information Model Object Manager, but the name was changed to Windows Management (or Winmgmt) to reflect its purpose within Windows more clearly. It resides under the `%SystemRoot%\system32\wbem` directory on a Windows NT4.0/XP/2000/.NET installation or `%SystemRoot%\system\wbem` on a Windows 9x/Me installation. When running as a service on Windows NT4/XP/2000/.NET systems, `winmgmt.exe` is started automatically, but this is not the case with either Windows 95 or Windows 98, in which special configuration settings must be made, as detailed at the start of this chapter. On a Windows NT/XP/2000 installation, its state (for example, *started, paused,* or *stopped*) can be monitored under the Services and Applications tab of the computer management snap-in tool, where it is listed as Windows Management Instrumentation.

> **Note:** From here on, we refer to `winmgmt.exe` as the Windows Management Service for the sake of simplicity and readability. This term will refer to `winmgmt.exe` running as a service or as an executable on any of the compatible Windows operating systems.

The Windows Management Service acts as the focal point for all management applications set to retrieve management data from the CIM repository or from instrumented managed objects. (Providers are the mechanism through which we retrieve managed objects and are discussed later in the chapter.) No interactions can take place with the CIM repository, except via the Windows Management Service, which facilitates the gathering and manipulation of information about any type of system information, such as system resources, application performance, and so forth, which are represented as managed objects. When initialized as a service, it starts when the first management application makes a call to connect and runs as long as management applications (or any applications that are making requests) are using its services. When no calls are being made, Windows Management Service eventually shuts down. It can be started from the command line or double-clicked from within Windows Explorer.

`winmgmt.exe` *<optional command line parameters>*

To retrieve a list of the optional command-line parameters type `winmgmt /?` from the command line. Figure 3.1 shows the command line options for the Winmgmt executable.

mofcomp.exe: The Microsoft MOF Compiler

Another technology defined by the DMTF as part of the WBEM initiative is the Managed Object Format or MOF. The MOF language was defined alongside the CIM so that descriptions of classes and instances defined as part of CIM could be created in a

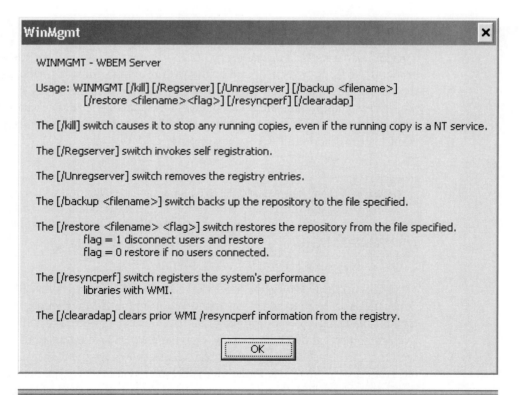

Figure 3.1 The command-line options for the Winmgmt executable

simple ASCII (or Unicode) text format. The MOF file provides a mechanism to import or export these definitions to or from a CIM repository. You may recognize a similarity between MOF and Interface Definition Language (IDL), because MOF's origins lie with IDL.OF, as its origins lay with IDL.

Once you have defined a MOF file (either by hand or by exporting the class and/ or instance definitions from the WMI CIM studio, as demonstrated in Chapter 4) you can use the MOF compiler to add it to the local CIM repository. Microsoft provides a MOF file compiler, `mofcomp.exe` (situated under the WBEM subdirectory), as one of the core components of WMI. It is a command line executable: To compile a MOF file, you must go to a command line prompt and type:

`mofcomp` *<MOF filename>*

Table 3.2 provides the additional command line parameters that are available.

Use the following switches to log into WMI when compiling a MOF file on a local or remote machine and adding it to a CIM repository that could be located upon another machine on the network.

`-U:<UserName>`	User Name
`-P:<Password>`	Login password
`-A:<Authority>`	Example: NTLMDOMAIN:Domain or KERBEROS

Example: `mofcomp -u:Supervisor -p:LetMeIn -A:NT1 <MOF Filename>`

At present, WMI provides basic security features that determine access to the CIM repository as a whole. Windows 9x or NT4 does not allow WMI to define permissions for individual classes, instances, or namespaces. Windows 2000/XP/.NET does, however, introduce namespace-level permissions. The username, password, and authority can all be set using the Security tab in the WMI Microsoft Management Console (MMC) control snap-in, which you can see in Figure 3.2.

The WMI Control

Filename: `Wmimgmt.msc` (Windows 2000/WinXP/.NET)

Wbemcntl (Windows 9x/Me)

Type: GUI-based tool

This Graphical User Interface (GUI)-based tool is released as part of Windows to help configure WMI settings on a local or remote computer. It can be called from the Start/Run menu or command prompt and can provide details on the currently installed version of WMI and its location and status, as well as that of the current OS. The tool makes it possible to perform a manual backup or restore, and can be used to

Table 3.2 mofcomp Command-Line Options

Command-line option	Description
`-check`	This option verifies correctness of the MOF syntax check only. This switch checks the syntax on both binary and text MOF files. When the MOF compiler is used in conjunction with this switch, it does not connect to Windows Management Service nor does it update the CIM repository with any values. It can only be used on its own. Example: `mofcomp -check <MOF filename>`
`-N:<path>`	This option loads a MOF file into the namespace specified. If this switch is not present, then the MOF file is added to the root/default namespace. Alternatively, both these settings can be overridden if the MOF file contains a #pragma namespace ("namespace path"), which specifies another namespace. Example: `mofcomp -n :root\CIMV2 <MOF filename>`
`-class:updateonly`	This option only updates an existing class within the CIM repository. If no such class currently exists within the CIM repository, then this switch tells the compiler to perform no action. Example: `mofcomp -class:updateonly <MOF Filename>`
`-class:createonly`	This option does not change existing classes. This option only creates new classes within the CIM repository. If the class specified with the MOF file already exists, then the compiler will return without making any changes to the CIM repository. Example: `mofcomp -class:createonly <MOF Filename>` Note: Using the two switches, updateonly and createonly, together results in no changes taking place within the CIM repository.
`-class:safeupdate`	Use this switch to update a class that has children when you wish the compiler to avoid possible problems with child classes. If the compiler encounters potential problems, then it will return without making changes to the CIM repository. Note: If an instance of a child class exists then this operation will fail. Example: `mofcomp -class:safeupdate <MOF Filename>`
`-class:forceupdate`	Use this switch to add a new class regardless of any potential conflicts with child classes. If an instance of a child class exists, however, this operation will fail. Example: `mofcomp -class:forceupdate <MOF Filename>`
`-instance:updateonly`	Use this option only to update an existing instance within the CIM repository. If no such instance currently exists within the CIM repository, then this switch tells the MOF compiler to perform no action. Example: `mofcomp -instance:updateonly <MOF Filename>`

Table 3.2 *Continued*

Command-line option	Description
-instance:createonly	This option does not change existing instances. This option will only create new instances within the CIM repository. If the class specified with the MOF file already exists, then the compiler will return without making any changes to the CIM repository. **Example:** mofcomp -instance:createonly <MOF Filename>
-B:<destination filename>	This option creates a binary MOF file but does not add it to the CIM repository. **Example:** mofcomp -b:filename.bin <plain text MOF Filename> Note: Binary MOF files are intended primarily for embedding in WMI for WDM drivers. The use of binary MOF files in other contexts is not encouraged.
-WMI	This switch is for use with binary MOF files. It is intended for use with WMI for WDM and tells the MOF compiler to perform a syntax check without adding the contents to the CIM repository. It requires the -B switch. **Example:** mofcomp -b:filename.bin -WMI <MOF Filename>
-AUTORECOVER	This adds the MOF file to the list of files compiled during DB recovery.
-AMENDMENT	This can be used to split a MOF file into language-specific and language-neutral versions.
-MOF:	This loads a language-neutral MOF file.
-MFL:	This loads a language-specific MOF file.

modify the maximum size of log files, the level of detail entered in them, and the logging directory. It enables an administrator to define authorized users and groups for specific namespaces in WMI, allowing them to be assigned access permissions very similar in appearance and operation to those assigned using the Windows NT user manager. Finally, it allows the changing of the default namespace used for scripting (normally, root\cimv2).

Windows Management Instrumentation Tester

Filename: Wbemtest.exe

Type: GUI-based application

This GUI-based application (see Figure 3.3) enables the user to connect to a namespace and create, delete, and enumerate classes or instances. It also provides an option to enter queries in WMI Query Language (WQL) and execute methods. It can be a useful tool for developing WMI providers.

Figure 3.2 The WMI Control snap-in for Windows 2000/WinXP/.NET

Automatic MOF Registration

Under the WBEM subdirectory, WMI has subdirectories that facilitate automatic registration of MOF files. Any MOF files placed under this directory will be automatically compiled by `winmgmt.exe` if it is running:

```
%SystemRoot%\system32\wbem\mof
```

Or for Windows 9x/Me:

```
%SystemRoot%\system\wbem\mof
```

This directory also contains two subdirectories, *good* and *bad*, in which to store the MOFs after they have been autoregistered. WMI monitors the *wbem/mof* subdirectory and compiles any MOF files placed in it if WMI is running.

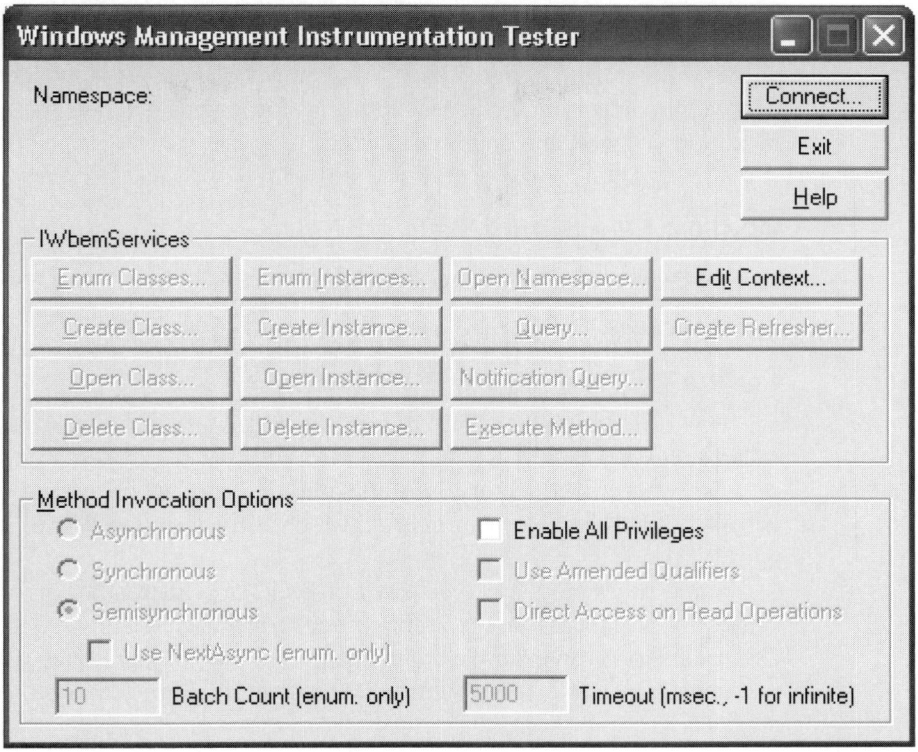

Figure 3.3   The Windows Management Instrumentation Tester

To compile MOF files, WMI uses *mofd.dll,* the dynamic link library that also is held under the WBEM directory.

When the compilation is complete, WMI places the MOF file in either the good or the bad subdirectory, depending on the result of the compilation. To quickly check the outcome of an automatic compilation, it is a good idea to check these directories for the results, because WMI does not generate any visual results (although you can find a detailed account of the results in the log files).

WMI Log Files

```
%SystemRoot%\system32\wbem\logs
```

Or for Windows 9x/Me:

```
%SystemRoot%\system\wbem\logs
```

The components of the WMI framework use the log files to catalog what is happening with WMI over a period of time. They are a good source of information when troubleshooting if you suspect WMI (or one of the components that you have written for WMI!) is malfunctioning. The SystemRoot directory is the default directory in which WMI stores all logs. The WMI Control (`wmimgmt.msc`), which is supplied as a core WMI component, can specify settings for logging, such as the logging directory, maximum log size, and enabled/disabled.

WMI CIM Repository

```
%SystemRoot%\system32\wbem\repository\fs
```

Or for Windows 9x/Me:

```
%SystemRoot%\system\wbem\repository\fs
```

This directory holds the CIM repository (objects.data) as well as an index file called `index.btr`.

The wbem subdirectory also contains the standard providers that are shipped with WMI, for example, *cimwin32.dll,* which is the standard Win32 provider shipped with WMI.

Namespaces are defined as part of the CIM to differentiate among the groups of classes and instances that represent particular management environments. A Windows OS installation is an example of a management environment (`root\CIMV2`), as is all of the management information for the Microsoft Office applications (`root\msapps10`).

■ Windows Management Instrumentation

As mentioned previously, although existing frameworks such as DMI and SNMP provide adequate control and monitoring facilities, they do not represent accurately the data relationships between managed objects from management domains other than their own. For example, most non-WMI management applications are not aware inherently of any physical or logical relationship that may exist between an SNMP-managed object and a DMI-managed object. Using these legacy management frameworks to develop management applications that were aware of these relationships was a complex and costly task. WMI provides a solution to these problems, as well as defining a model of the configuration, status, and operational aspects of a Windows-based enterprise environment. Through its integration with the legacy frameworks, it provides management capability for non-Windows-based managed objects.

Windows Management Instrumentation is an implementation of WBEM based upon the DMTF's guidelines and recommendations. As well as conforming to the DMTF's definitions, DMTF also contains a number of Windows-specific extensions that provide a lower level of integration with the Windows operating system. The extensions to the Windows Driver Model (WDM) that interface directly with WMI, called *WMI for WDM,* are good examples. These extensions form a tight cohesion between the WMI model and instrumented components, providing a very good level of instrumentation.

Microsoft's COM/DCOM is the mechanism that allows communication between the various components in the WMI architecture. The development of software to interact with WMI is in two general areas:

1. Management Application development of software applications that access WMI and read or modify enterprise management data; WMI provides a number of ways of accessing enterprise management information at this level.

2. Device Instrumentation development of software that can provide instrumentation for a hardware or software device; WMI refers to these software components as *providers.*

You must familiarize yourself with WMI's two central components that make up the *management infrastructure:* `winmgmt.exe,` the Windows Management Service, and `object.data`, the CIM central repository for storing enterprise management information. All interactions that take place with the CIM repository must do so via the Windows Management Service (`winmgmt.exe`) in a variety of ways.

The Basic Framework of WMI

The diagram in Figure 3.4 shows the basic structure of WMI. At the top are applications that consume management data. Typically, these are management applications used by system administrators to interact with the managed environment, but they can be applications, such as a database, that collate information. The WMI application programming interface is responsible for interfacing directly with the Windows Management Service (formerly the CIM Object Manager). The Windows Management Service handles all interactions between these *data consumers* and the CIM repository or between data consumers and data providers. *Data providers,* which reside at the bottom of the diagram, provide temporal or dynamic data from managed objects. They encompass instance, event, method, and property providers.

Data providers enable WMI to retrieve dynamic management data, such as the current status of a CD-ROM drive door on a specific machine. Dynamic management data is temporal in nature: A request for such data requires a response within a limited time—otherwise, the data may become invalid. When a management application, for example, makes a request for such data, the Windows Management Service initially looks for the information in the CIM repository. Classes and instances in the CIM repository are registered as either static or dynamic. Dynamic classes and instances are associated with specific providers, which are always called to retrieve the required value(s).

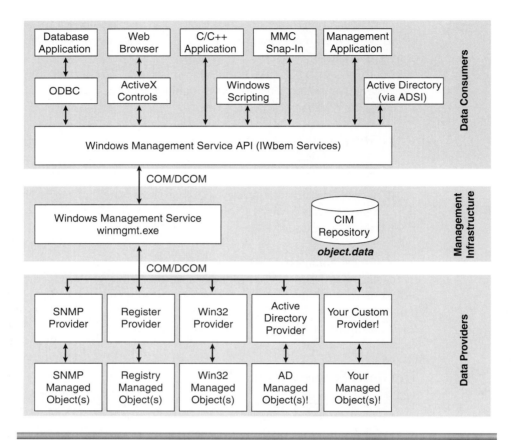

Figure 3.4 An overview of the WMI architecture

The data provider returns the retrieved value to the Windows Management Service. The Windows Management Service forwards this information to the management application. As you can imagine, this kind of operation incurs overhead, but WMI allows for this by calling different kinds of data providers to suit different situations. We discuss these providers later in the chapter.

> **Note:** The only exceptions to this overhead are high-performance providers that use a shared memory interface and are loaded in-proc (short for in-process). This implementation detail, however, is hidden from the user. For more information on high-performance providers see Chapter 13.

The data consumers—management applications—and data providers use Microsoft's COM/DCOM to communicate with Windows Management Service. In general, most data providers and data consumers communicate via Windows Management Services, never directly. An exception is High-Performance (Hi-Perf) providers that communicate between the provider and the consumer.

WMI Management Applications

A management application is an application or Windows service that uses information that originates from one or more managed objects. For WMI to retrieve management information from a managed object, a management application must interact with `winmgmt.exe`, which will retrieve the information.

Management applications attach to the Windows Management Service subject to the usual security password and username verification of the underlying OS. This authentication ensures that users see only what they are authorized to see. Upon meeting the security requirements, a management application has access to a wide range of management information, including a machine's resources, performance, and system inventory. In addition, management applications are able to administer remotely across a network or a telephone line. Windows 98 installations require that WMI be configured correctly. Windows XP is the exception: It enforces a higher level of security when attaching from a remote machine. To attach from a remote machine, remote security access must be enabled for your user account on the target namespace. This can be done with WMI Control. WMI Management applications are also able to register for events.

Access to management information is available through either direct or indirect channels.

Direct Access

Programmers can write applications that access management information directly through the WMI API in C++ or in languages such as Java or Visual Basic that support the automation interface (a COM/DCOM-specific term). Applications written this way do not require the services of an intermediary, such as the WMI ActiveX controls.

Indirect Access

There are three methods for accessing WMI management information indirectly:

1. Use HTML web pages to interact with ISAPI. An indirect channel is available for WMI management information by using HTML pages and a Web browser.

The HTML is parsed by the Internet Server API (ISAPI) layer that interacts with WMI. Microsoft provides a number of ISAPI extensions (*server applications*) that extend a Web server's capability so that it may interact with WMI.

ISAPI is an open standard developed by a number of vendors, including Process Software, in conjunction with Microsoft. ISAPI is available on many popular World Wide Web servers such as Apache for Windows and Microsoft's Internet Information Server (IIS). Netscape Corporation has developed their own ISAPI equivalent for interfacing with the Netscape suite of Web server products. They have named it NSAPI, and as yet no other products have been developed that conform to this standard. As far at the authors are aware no NSAPI extensions have yet been written to interact with the Windows Management Service.

2. Microsoft also provides an ODBC *adapter* that enables ODBC database applications to access the information stored in the CIM. This means that ODBC-based applications such as Microsoft Excel and Microsoft Access can retrieve information from the CIM repository as if it were a database.

3. Use ActiveX controls to access WMI. As part of the WMI SDK, Microsoft provides a number of ActiveX controls that enable access to the CIM Object Manager using calls directly to the native WMI APIs. These controls provide a GUI through which users can view and manipulate management information. Typically, these controls are accessed through a Web browser, although any ActiveX-compliant container application will work.

Providers

The Microsoft WMI architecture relies heavily upon the concept of providers that gather and supply information from managed objects. Providers can be run as stand-alone executables, Windows services, or dynamic link libraries (DLLs). Without providers, the WMI architecture would have no means of gathering dynamic management information or generating "real-world" event notification. Providers are called upon when a management application requests information that is not available in the CIM repository. The CIM repository maintains a number of classes and instances that detail all of the providers that service WMI. Using instance information from these provider classes, the Windows Management Service passes requests to the appropriate provider. Microsoft supplies a suite of standard providers for use with WMI. The standard providers, typically, retrieve management information from a particular subsection of a managed domain such as the registry, DMI, or SNMP.

Table 3.3 lists the built-in providers supplied with WMI. The providers can request information from WMI-managed objects and can send instructions to them.

Table 3.3 Windows Operating System WMI Providers

Provider	Platform(s)	Description	Preinstalled	Namespace
DFS Provider	Windows .NET Server	Allows administrators to logically group shares on multiple servers and seamlessly combine them within a single namespace. The file `dfs_desc.mof` defines the Distributed File System (DFS) provider classes.	Yes	`root\cimv2`
Trustmon Provider	Windows .NET Server	Allows administrators to determine the trust relationships between domains.	Yes	`root\cimv2`
IP Route Provider	Windows .NET Server	Allows administrators to ascertain how IP packets are being routed through a network. The file `route_desc.mof` defines the route provider classes.	Yes	`root\cimv2`
Job Object Provider	Windows .NET Server[0] Windows XP	Allows administrators to retrieve data on named kernel job objects. The file `wmipjobj.mof` defines the job object provider classes.	Yes	`root\cimv2`
Ping Provider	Windows .NET Server[0] Windows XP	Allows administrators to determine if a destination address is responding to requests using the standard ping command. The file `ping_desc.mof` defines the ping provider classes.	Yes	`root\cimv2`
Policy Provider	Windows .NET Server Windows XP	Allows administrators to extend group policy therefore permitting refinements in the application of policy. The file `system.mof` defines the policy provider classes.	Yes	`root\cimv2`
Windows Product Activation Provider	Windows .NET Server[0] Windows XP	Allows administrators to implement Microsoft's anti-piracy technology. This prevents product activation without first establishing a valid association between the hardware ID of the computer and the product ID (PID). This is aimed at reducing casual copying of software.	Yes	`root\cimv2`
Performance Monitoring Provider	Windows .NET Windows XP Windows 2000 Windows NT	Allows administrators to retrieve cooked data. Note Windows XP and .NET users should use the Cooked Counter provider. The file `cimwin32.mof` defines the performance monitoring provider classes.	No	`root\cimv2`

Continued

Table 3.3 *Continued*

Provider	Platform(s)	Description	Preinstalled	Namespace
Performance Counter Provider	Windows .NET Windows XP Windows 2000	Allow administrators to retrieve raw performance counter data. The file `cimwin32.mof` defines the performance counter provider classes.		`root\cimv2`
Power Management Event Provider	Windows .NET Windows XP Windows 2000 Windows NT	Allows administrators to monitor power state changes surfaced through power management events. The file `cimwin32.mof` defines the power management event provider classes.	Yes	`root\cimv2`
Session Provider	Windows .NET Windows XP Windows 2000 Windows NT	Allows administrators to manage network connections and sessions. For example, it is possible to monitor the connections from a remote computer to a shared local resource. The file `session_desc.mof` defines the session provider classes.	Yes	`root\cimv2`
WDM Provider	Windows .NET Windows XP Windows 2000 Windows NT	Provides administrators with access to management data supplied by WDM-compliant hardware drivers.	Yes	`root\wmi`
Active Directory Provider	Windows .NET Windows XP Windows 2000	Allows administrators to retrieve management data from Active Directory.	Yes	`root\cimv2`
Security Provider	Windows .NET Windows XP Windows 2000 Windows NT	Allows administrators to change security settings on NTFS files, shares, or directories. The file `secrcw32_desc.mof` defines the security provider classes.	Yes	`root\cimv2`
SNMP Provider	Windows .NET Windows XP Windows 2000 Windows NT	Allows administrators to access management data generated by SNMP-managed objects. To do this it defines the relationship between objects in the MIB and the WMI CIM classes.	No	`root\cimv2`
System Registry Provider	Windows .NET Windows XP Windows 2000 Windows NT	Allows administrators to read and evoke registry changes to data stored on local or remote machines. It can also notify administrators when changes occur in the target registry.	No	`root\cimv2`
View Provider	Windows .NET Windows XP Windows 2000 Windows NT	Allows administrators to combine existing instances of classes into a single class. This functionality is not restricted by the machine boundary or namespace.	No	Any namespace

Table 3.3 *Continued*

Provider	Platform(s)	Description	Preinstalled	Namespace
Windows Installer Provider	Windows .NET Windows XP Windows 2000 Windows NT	Allows administrators to retrieve information held by the Windows installer and provides access to installer procedures remotely.	Yes	root\cimv2
Win32 Provider	Windows .NET Windows XP Windows 2000 Windows NT	Provides administrators with Windows system data such as the current settings of environment variables or the attributes of a logical disk.	Yes	root\cimv2
Cooked Counter Provider	Windows .NET Windows XP Windows 2000	Allows administrators to retrieve calculated ("cooked") performance data.	Yes	root\cimv2
Disk Quota Provider	Windows XP Windows 2000 Windows NT	Allows administrators to restrict the amount of information a user stores on an NTFS volume. The file `diskquota_desc.mof` defines the disk quota provider classes.	Yes	root\cimv2
Event Log Provider	Windows XP Windows 2000 Windows NT	Allows administrators to retrieve data from the event log service. This includes notification of events. The file `ntevt.mof` contains the classes for the event log provider.	Yes	root\cimv2

■ Types of Providers

Providers are further classified by the actions that they perform. At the most basic level, providers can be classified as either event providers or data providers.

Event Providers

Event providers generate notifications of an event. Once an event has been generated, it is passed to WMI, which attempts to match the event with one or more registered event consumers before passing it on. *Event consumers* are applications that request notification of an event and then perform an action in response to that specific event.

More than one event consumer can be registered to receive the same event, in which case WMI passes notification to all of them. The example in Figure 3.5 has only a single event, a single consumer provider, and a single event provider.

The event provider framework

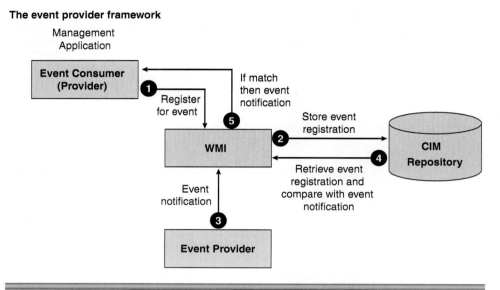

Figure 3.5 The simplified event consumer/event provider model

Data Providers

Data providers deal in management data. They enable a management application to retrieve or modify dynamic instrumented data that must be generated on request. Data providers are further classified as class, instance, method, or property providers. In Chapter 1, we briefly discussed the CIM and how its structure is broken into classes that consist of properties and methods. A class that contains values for its properties and methods is an *instance* of that class. Data from these providers is represented in the CIM repository. Table 3.4 further defines the capabilities of each type of provider.

Table 3.4 Types of WMI Providers

Provider type	Description
Class	Retrieves, modifies, deletes, and/or enumerates a provider-specific class. It can also support query processing.
Instance	Retrieves, modifies, deletes, and/or enumerates the instances of system and/or provider-specific classes. It can also support query processing.
Method	Invokes methods for a provider-specific class.
Property	Retrieves and/or modifies individual property values.

Table 3.5 WMI Provider Classifications

Model	Description
Push	Supplies information directly to CIM repository at startup. Used for data that does not change frequently.
Push-Verify	Supplies information to CIM repository at startup and also periodically as and when it is needed. Used for data that does not change frequently.
Pull	Supplies information directly to WMI and does not use the CIM repository. Used for information that changes frequently.

Data providers also conform to a specific model that determines whether they store information in the CIM repository or pass it directly to WMI. Table 3.5 outlines the three basic types of provider.

■ Event Handling

As we saw in Chapter 2, when we described the operation of the management frameworks DMI and SNMP, event notification plays a key role in managing any environment. Without notification of critical or noncritical situations using events, a management application would not be able to accurately monitor the status of its managed objects. It also would have to poll a managed object repeatedly to determine its status. This would be wasteful of both network resources and processor cycles on the managed object and management application. To avoid this, both DMI and SNMP models support notification of asynchronous events (*traps/informs* in SNMP). The asynchronous event notification mechanism is also part of WMI event-handling architecture. *Asynchronous* in the context of WMI means that it is the responsibility of the management application initially to register for event notification, but then it becomes the responsibility of the event provider to generate notification of that event. The management application, once registered, can carry on its normal administrative duties without having to check the managed object periodically. *Synchronous* event notification would mean it was the responsibility of the management application to check repeatedly to see if the event had occurred. Because of the asynchronous nature of events, WMI provides two models of event subscription. WMI allows developers to subscribe for either asynchronous or semi-synchronous notification of events. Semi-synchronous notification uses the best features of asynchronous and synchronous techniques and avoids the downfalls of each. We discuss the two models in more detail when we develop examples of custom providers in Chapter 12.

WMI's event notification mechanism works for both hardware- and software-instrumented components. The event architecture in WMI centers on *event providers.*

Event providers are supplied as part of the standard providers installed with WMI; for example, they allow you to define events that refer to SNMP or Win32. In addition to the standard event providers, it is also possible to code your own providers to enable event notification for your own managed objects. Any event generated by an event provider is passed to WMI, which in turn passes them to the appropriate management applications for corrective action. Intrinsic, extrinsic, and timer events are the three types of event that can occur within the WMI management framework.

Intrinsic Events

Microsoft defines intrinsic events in WMI as events that occur in response to changes in the standard WMI data model. This refers to the CIM repository and its associated providers. An intrinsic event can be the deletion, creation or modification of a class, an instance, or a namespace. An intrinsic event allows the monitoring of a specific class or property within a class and notification of changes or additions to those values. The event consumer uses a WMI Query Language (WQL) filter to define the conditions that trigger these events. For example, the consumer may wish to be notified about new instances of a process to monitor the processes on a machine.

Extrinsic Events

An extrinsic event in WMI is one that occurs outside the standard WMI data model, that is, any event that is not captured by the CIM repository or providers. Consequently, an extrinsic event must be surfaced using an event provider. Microsoft refers to extrinsic events as "real world" events because they typically take place on actual hardware- or software-managed components. MSDN documentation cites a machine switching to standby mode as an example of an extrinsic event. The conditions that trigger the event are defined by the event consumer (that is, a management application) using a WQL filter.

Timer Events

Timer events are unlike intrinsic or extrinsic events because the event consumer must take explicit action for them to occur. Timer events come in two varieties:

- Absolute timer events are triggered at a certain time.
- Interval timer events are triggered at regular intervals.

In order to receive a timer event, the event consumer must explicitly create within WMI an instance of `_IntervalTimerInstruction`, `_AbsoluteTimerInstruction`, `Win32_LocalTime`, or `Win32_UTCTime`. The event consumer must then define and associate a

WQL event filter and a logical consumer to receive an event. Timer events are merely mechanisms for automating the delivery of events at a given time or time interval. WMI is responsible for forwarding the event at the time specified by the consumer.

■ Event Consumer

An event consumer is an application that registers with WMI to receive notification of certain events. A management application is an example of a typical event consumer. WMI acts as an intermediary between an event consumer and an event provider, receiving and passing on relevant notification to the relevant consumer. WMI matches registered consumers with responsible providers and forwards event notification to them. Event consumers register with WMI to receive notifications using a WBEM Query Language *filter*. We shall take a closer look at filters toward the end of this chapter. Event consumers register without knowing how the provider operates or whether the event type is intrinsic or extrinsic. WMI acts as a layer of abstraction between the two parties, thus shielding the event consumer from the implementation details of the event provider. Event consumers can be either permanent or temporary.

Temporary Consumers

A temporary event consumer is one that receives notification of events only when it is active. It does not receive events when it is no longer active, and it can cancel its registration for an event in WMI. WMI does not store the registration for temporary events in the CIM repository but instead stores the information in memory. Should the CIM repository's host machine be rebooted, all record of the temporary consumer will be lost.

Imagine a Windows-based management application that displays the status and statistics (that is, available space) of all the disks present on a host machine. The application would need to update its statistics should the available disk space on the machine change while it is running. This information, however, would not be important for an application that is not running. The temporary consumer architecture is ideal for such a situation.

Permanent Consumers

The permanent event consumer architecture requires that the consumer explicitly be registered with the CIM repository. WMI describes this registration as the "logical" consumer, and the consumer provider code (that is, the .dll or .exe file) as the "physical" consumer. Registrations of this type are described as "persistent" because they remain in the CIM repository even if the host machine is rebooted. They must be deregistered explicitly (that is, their registration entries must be removed from the CIM repository) to remove them.

Whereas a temporary consumer only receives event notifications while it is active, a permanent consumer, once registered, always receives event notifications, whether its state is active or inactive. If an event takes place and a permanent consumer is not currently active, then WMI uses its registration information to locate the logical consumer and load the physical consumer before forwarding the event.

Permanent consumers are useful when a response to an event always is warranted and is a robust form of event delivery. Events concerning system housekeeping are good examples: Consider a situation in which a disk defragmentation application is registered with WMI as a physical permanent consumer. It registers to receive an event if the amount of fragmentation on the C: drive increases to greater than 10 percent. Once registered, the application terminates. It is not required to remain constantly resident in memory because it needs to perform its task only occasionally, when disk fragmentation exceeds 10 percent. If the disk fragmentation becomes greater than 10 percent, WMI will receive an event and look up the logical consumer in the repository. The logical consumer is associated with an instance of a physical consumer. Having located the logical consumer's entry, WMI will retrieve the details for the physical consumer and attempt to load it. The disk defragmentation program will then execute and perform its task.

Management applications register for notification of events using WMI's subset of the Structured Query Language (SQL, pronounced "Sequel"), which is referred to as WQL (pronounced "Wequal"). Each condition specified by the management application or event provider using WQL is a *filter*. Both management applications (event consumers) and managed objects (event providers) use WQL. We discuss WQL later in this chapter.

■ WMI Security

WMI security is largely reliant upon the facilities provided by the host operating system. For this reason, the local and remote security features of WMI are different on a Windows 98 machine from those on a Windows NT4.0/2000/XP/.NET machine.

Security in WMI is based upon the concept of authentication, which has two stages:

1. Users must have access to Windows systems resources, such as files and directories and the privileges assigned to them. Users gain access by supplying a username, password, and domain name that the host operating system validates. If users do not satisfy these requirements, then they will not proceed to stage 2.

2. Users must have privileges granted at the user or group level to access the CIM repository controlled by WMI. Users gain access by providing a user name, password, and domain.

Access to specific namespaces in WMI is dictated by permissions assigned to user and group accounts with the help of the tool WMI Control. The permissions granted to accounts defined in the Windows computer management snap-in determine access to the underlying Windows system resources. Together they form WMI's security mechanism.

Authentication

User authentication is a username, password, and domain that the user who is attempting to access a particular resource supplies. The authentication process then is handled by marshallers, who verify the account and positively identify the user. Marshallers, based upon DCOM security, have no knowledge of the permissions granted to the user within WMI.

WMI Permission Assignment Using WMI Control

The second part of WMI's security process is based upon the concept of permissions that provide users with specific privileges to access parts of the CIM repository. WMI does not provide a mechanism for assigning permissions to particular classes or instances. Instead, permissions can be assigned only to the entire namespace and thus are called *global permissions*. For example, currently it is not possible to assign read-only permissions to a particular instance of a network card on an installation and to assign write access to all other entries. Microsoft supplies the Winmgmt snap-in to assist in the task of assigning permissions and access level to users or groups. To use this GUI-based application to create users and groups with specific access permissions, first select the Start/Run menu options and then type `winmgmt.msc` at the dialog window. Having started the snap-in, select the Security tab, which, in Figure 3.6, displays a list of namespaces.

Figure 3.7 demonstrates how the namespace security level can be set to allow or deny one or more permissions.

Table 3.6 details the namespace permission types. These settings are relevant only to Windows 9x/Me when accessing the namespace remotely (locally, users have full control).

WMI Security on Windows 9x

On a Windows 98 installation, all local access to WMI is *unauthenticated,* that is, no password or username is required. This is because of the basic security model of the operating system and not because of WMI implementation differences between platforms. Windows 98 requires a password and username only if a remote connection is

Figure 3.6 The WMI Control Security tab displaying the available namespaces

attempted, and only under limited circumstances. To enable authentication for remote access to WMI on this platform, *user level* security must be implemented. User level security requires that a domain that can be used to identify users be specified.

Share level security can provide remote access to WMI's resources; however, it does not enforce any form of authentication and is, therefore, not recommended.

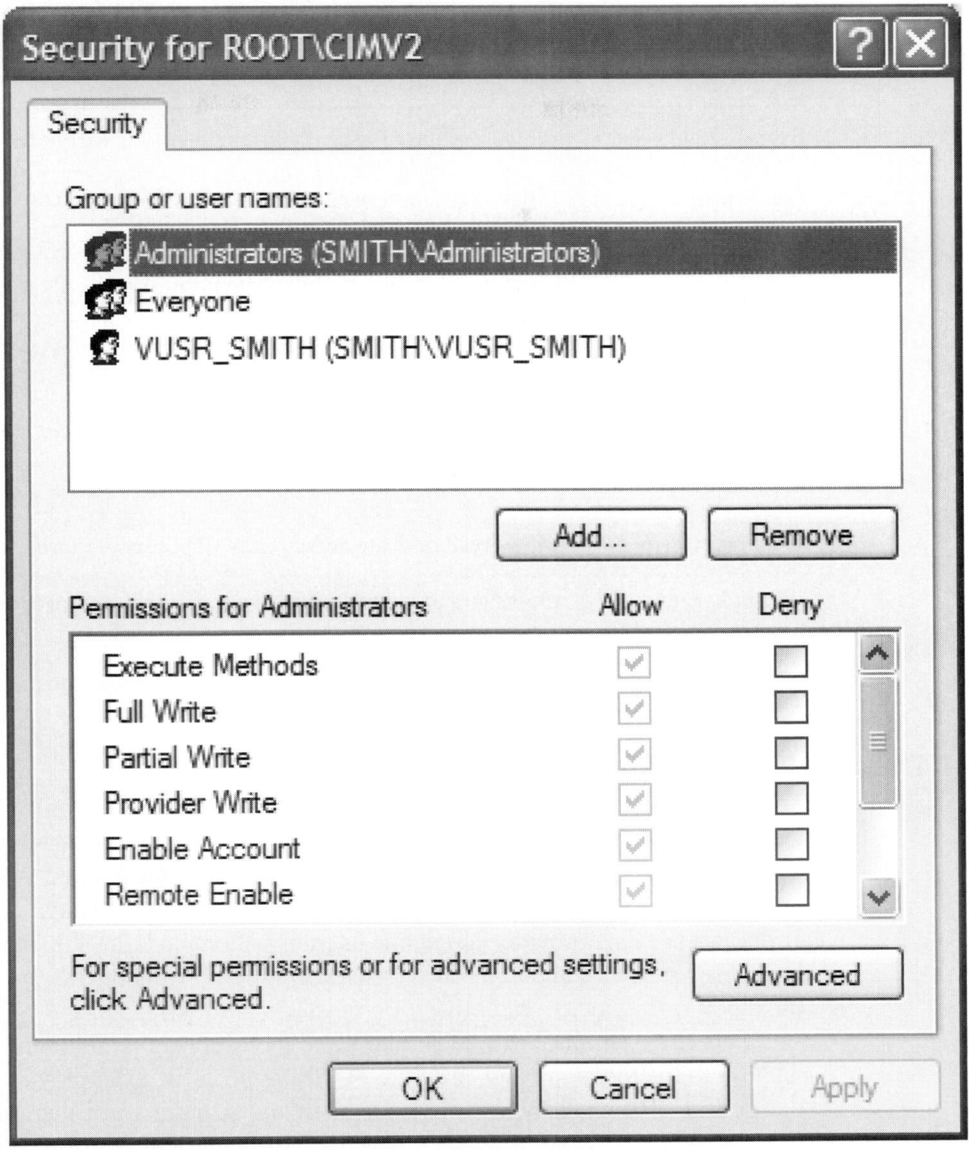

Figure 3.7   Setting the security options for group or user names

Table 3.6   WMI Namespace Permission Types

Model	Description
Execute Methods	Allows a group or user to execute methods within the namespace.
Full Write	Allows a group or user full write/read/delete/execute permissions within the namespace.
Partial Write	Allows a group or user full write permissions only to static objects within the namespace.
Enable Account	Allows group or user read access to WMI objects.
Remote Enable	Allows group or user remote access to namespace.
Read Security	Allows group or user read-only access to WMI security information.
Edit Security	Allows read or write access to WMI security information.
Special Permissions	Allows you to control inheritance on the namespace and/or its sub-namespaces.

■ The WMI Query Language

Central to the concept of receiving and generating event notification or retrieving instances of class data and class definitions, is the Microsoft-defined WMI Query Language. WQL provides a powerful mechanism through which a management application or data provider can define its informational relationship with WMI. WQL is a subset of SQL92 and in its current release, supports only read-only operations, not the modification, deletion, or insertion of values in the CIM repository.

To become familiar with WQL filters and their function and for an informal introduction to the hierarchy and structure of CIM, type in the examples in the definitions that follow. (We shall look in more detail at the structure and hierarchy of CIM in Chapter 4.) The WMI SDK provides the Windows Management Instrumentation Tester (WMI Tester), which is a useful tool for trying out WQL queries (and it has several other useful functions).

The WMI Tester is part of the standard installation of the core components of WMI. If you have successfully installed WMI, the WMI Tester's executable is under the WBEM directory beneath the Windows system directory.

Locate and double-click the file named WBEMtest.exe (in Windows XP, simply go to Start->Run and type WBEMTest.exe) to display the screenshot in Figure 3.8.

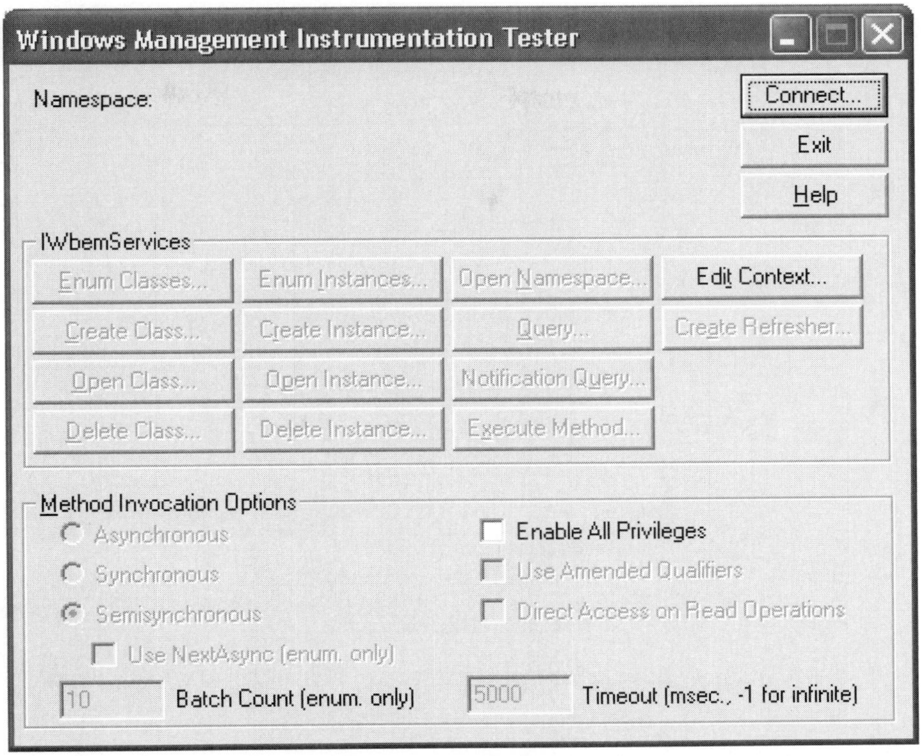

Figure 3.8 The Windows Management Instrumentation Tester main dialog

The dimmed (not enabled) buttons indicate that you are not connected to WMI. To connect, click the Connect… button on the top right. Your screen will display the dialog in Figure 3.9.

Under Namespace, replace the text, `root\default`, with `root\CIMV2` (see Figure 3.9). Leave the Connection settings as they are and leave the User, Password, and Authority fields blank because we will not require them for the following examples.

> **Note:** To connect to WMI on another machine you can specify an explicit path before the namespace as follows:
>
> `\\127.0.0.1\root\CIMV2` or `\\CraigsMachine\root\CIMV2`

As you can see from the example, this can be either a machine name or an IP address. This one, the local loopback address, connects to the host machine.

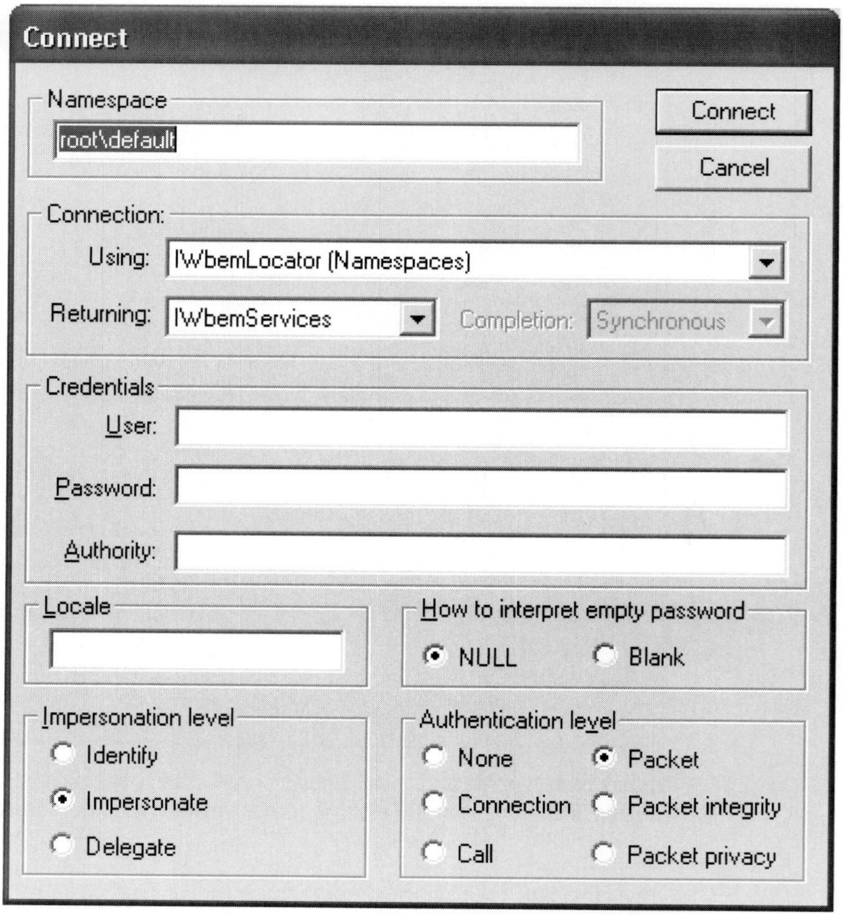

Figure 3.9   The Connect dialog

In Windows 2000/WinXP/.NET, the default is read access to the repository on your own machine. In Windows NT4.0, you should not encounter any restrictions if you are a member of the administrator group. Security restrictions always apply, however, when you access WMI remotely, in which case you must specify a user, a password, and an authority. The authority must be defined with the WMI Control on the target machine.

Click the Connect button to return to the first screen; we have connected to WMI and the Win32 extended schema on our local machine. CIMV2, Microsoft's namespace, contains the Win32 extended schema that defines the manageable components for the Windows OS.

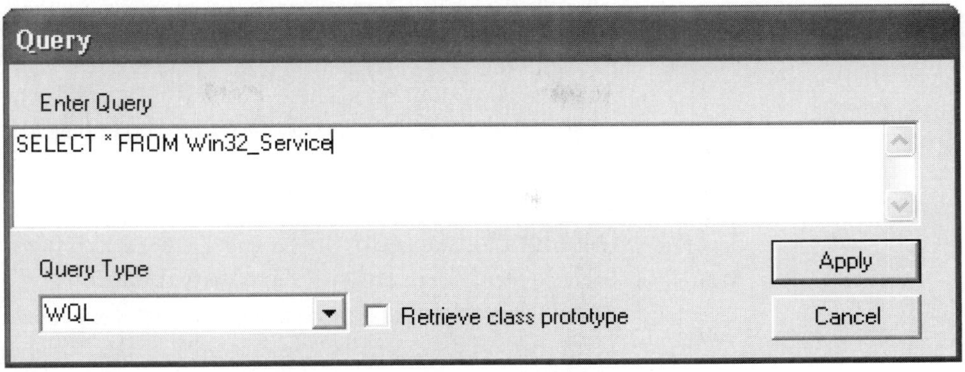

Figure 3.10 The Query dialog

On the right side of the bank of 14 buttons on the main dialog screen, find the button marked Query. (If any of the buttons is not enabled, you have not logged into WMI correctly.) Click this button for the dialog box in Figure 3.10.

You can type WQL queries in the Query dialog box. The Query Type drop-down box specifies the language type of query; at this stage, WQL is the only one available. The *Retrieve class prototype* check box determines whether you would like additional class information returned with your query.

The WQL is able to support three types of query: data, event, and schema. WMI refers to these queries as *filters* because they retrieve only the information specified in the query and filter out all extraneous data.

Data Queries

Data queries allow retrieval of instances of class and data associations through the following three statements:

SELECT retrieves instances of a single class.

Syntax: `SELECT * FROM <CLASSNAME>`

Example: **`SELECT * FROM Win32_LogicalDisk`**

This example retrieves all instances from the CIM repository for class `Win32_LogicalDisk`. This class represents the logical drives associated with a managed environment.

WHERE supports the SELECT statement. It specifies a condition using a property as a value.

Syntax: SELECT * FROM <*CLASSNAME*> WHERE PROPERTY=<*VALUE*>

Examples: **SELECT * FROM Win32_LogicalDisk WHERE FileSystem = "FAT"**

Returns all instances of Win32_LogicalDisk in which the file system is specified as FAT (we could easily have specified the file system as being NTFS).

SELECT * FROM Win32_LogicalDisk WHERE FreeSpace < 102400

Returns all instances of Win32_LogicalDisk in which the amount of free space left on the drive is less than 100 Kilobytes.

SELECT * FROM Win32_LogicalDisk WHERE Compressed = TRUE

Retrieves all instances of Win32_LogicalDisk in which the drive is flagged as compressed. WQL allows the substitution of TRUE and FALSE in place of 1 and 0 for Boolean values.

ASSOCIATORS OF is used alone to retrieve all instances associated with a particular source instance. The source instance is specified in the Object path, which must define a unique instance (that is, class name and key).

Syntax: ASSOCIATORS OF {*Object Path*}

Example: **ASSOCIATORS OF {Win32_Service="WinMgmt"}**

This example will return the classes associated with the WinMgmt instance of class Win32_Service (Windows Management Service—winmgmt.exe.)

The use of curly brackets around the object path is mandatory, and the object path should contain no spaces. Ignoring these rules will result in an error.

The ASSOCIATORS OF statement can include a WHERE clause that can be used in conjunction with one or more of the keywords in Table 3.7.

REFERENCES OF is used alone to retrieve all association instances that refer to a particular source instance.

Syntax: REFERENCES OF {*Object Path*}

Example: **REFERENCES OF {Win32_Service="WinMgmt"}**

This example retrieves all of the associations pertinent to the Windows Management service.

The REFERENCES OF statement can include a WHERE clause that can be used in conjunction with one or more of the keywords in Table 3.8.

Table 3.7 ASSOCIATORS OF Statement Keywords

Keyword	Meaning
AssocClass	Indicates that the returned endpoints must be associated with the source through the specified class or one of its derived classes. Example: `ASSOCIATORS OF {Win32_Service="WinMgmt"} WHERE AssocClass =CIM_Component`
ClassDefsOnly	The **ClassDefsOnly** keyword indicates that a result set of class definition objects is returned, rather than actual instances of the classes. Example: `ASSOCIATORS OF {Win32_Service="WinMgmt"} WHERE ClassDefsOnly`
RequiredAssocQualifier	The **RequiredAssocQualifier** keyword indicates that the returned endpoints must be associated with the source object through an association class that includes the specified qualifier. Example: `ASSOCIATORS OF {Win32_Service="WinMgmt"} WHERE RequiredAssocQualifier = dynamic`
RequiredQualifier	The **RequiredQualifier** keyword indicates that the returned endpoints associated with the source object must include the specified qualifier. Example: `ASSOCIATORS OF {Win32_Service="WinMgmt"} WHERE RequiredQualifier = dynamic`
ResultClass = <class name>	The **ResultClass** keyword indicates that the returned endpoints associated with the source object must belong to or be derived from the specified class. Example: `ASSOCIATORS OF {Win32_Service="WinMgmt"} WHERE ResultClass = Win32_BaseService`
ResultRole	The **ResultRole** keyword indicates that the returned endpoints must play a particular role in their association with the source object. The role is defined by the specified property and must be a reference property of type **ref**. Example: `ASSOCIATORS OF {Win32_Service="WinMgmt"} WHERE ResultRole = Antecedent`
Role	The **Role** keyword indicates that the returned endpoints participate in an association with the source object where the source object plays a particular role. The role is defined by the specified property and must be a reference property of type **ref**. Example: `ASSOCIATORS OF {Win32_Service="WinMgmt"} WHERE Role = PartComponent`

Table 3.8 REFERENCES OF Statement Keywords

Keyword	Meaning
ClassDefsOnly	The **ClassDefsOnly** keyword indicates that a result set of class definition objects, rather than actual instances of the association classes, is returned. **Example:** `REFERENCES OF {Win32_Service="WinMgmt"} WHERE ClassDefsOnly`
RequiredQualifier	The **RequiredQualifier** keyword indicates that the returned association objects must include the specified qualifier. The RequiredQualifier keyword can be used to include particular instances of associations in the result set. **Example:** `REFERENCES OF {Win32_Service="WinMgmt"} WHERE RequiredQualifier = abstract`
ResultClass	The **ResultClass** keyword indicates that the returned association objects must belong to or be derived from the specified class. **Example:** `REFERENCES OF {Win32_Service="WinMgmt"} WHERE ResultClass = Win32_BaseService`
Role	The **Role** keyword indicates that the returned associations are only those in which the source object plays a particular role. **Example:** `REFERENCES OF {Win32_Service="WinMgmt"} WHERE Role = GroupComponent`

Event Queries

Event consumers and event providers, respectively, use event queries to tell WMI of the events in which they are interested and the events that they provide. WMI pairs event consumers and event providers by using their queries for comparison when an event is generated. Both permanent and temporary event consumers use event queries to register their interest in certain events.

Event queries use the SELECT statement (mentioned previously) in conjunction with an optional WHERE clause to specify under what conditions to be notified of an event. The most basic event query filter is

```
SELECT * FROM <EventClass>
```

A basic example of the use of WQL by an event consumer to receive notification of events from class `Win32_LogicalDisk` is

```
SELECT * FROM Win32_LogicalDisk
```

This query registers a consumer to receive notification in the event of a new instance of class `Win32_LogicalDisk`. If, for example, users added a new disk drive to their machine (`Win32_LogicalDisk` would be created as a new instance of class) then the consumer would be notified. The * symbol used after SELECT represents all elements (methods and properties) from within `Win32_LogicalDisk`.WQL does not support consumers that specify individual properties in its place. For example, the following is not a valid event query:

```
SELECT Size,FileSystem FROM Win32_LogicalDisk
```

Although WQL will not reject the query, it will treat it as if it were a * symbol.

Appending the WHERE clause to this invalid query will narrow its scope. The WHERE clause can allow a consumer to specify further conditions under which to be notified of an event:

```
SELECT * FROM Win32_LogicalDisk WHERE FreeSpace < 102400
```

This query will return instances of the `Win32_LogicalDisk` class only when less than 100K free space remains.

The WITHIN clause is appended to a filter so that a time scale within which notification can take place can be specified. The time is specified in seconds. The two types of time interval that can be specified are:

1. a grouping interval
2. a polling interval

When a consumer is interested in the changes to a class and an event provider is not available, the WITHIN clause specifies a polling interval. A polling interval is given when a consumer registers for an intrinsic event.

The WITHIN clause must be used as follows:

```
SELECT * FROM Win32_LogicalDisk WITHIN 600.001 WHERE FreeSpace < 102400
```

The interval is specified in seconds and is a real decimal value. It is not advisable, however, to specify very small values because this creates overhead for CIM. If you specify a minuscule value (such as 0.001) with which CIM is not prepared to work, it can reject the value as being too expensive in terms of overhead. The preceding example generates only one notification instance approximately every 10 minutes (not ignoring the .001 second).

The GROUP clause is used in conjunction with the WITHIN clause:

```
SELECT * FROM Win32_LogicalDisk WHERE FreeSpace < 120000 GROUP
       WITHIN <Interval in seconds>
```

This query registers to receive event notification when the free space on an instance of `Win32_LogicalDisk` falls below 120000 bytes. The time interval specified at the end of the query determines a duration of time (in seconds) before passing the notification of all events of this type to event consumers. GROUP specifies the amount of time spent collecting events before sending an aggregate notification of their occurrence.

The HAVING clause specifies a further condition in conjunction with the GROUP clause. It specifies the minimum or maximum number of events that should take place within the time interval specified by the GROUP command. If the number of events does not satisfy the number specified by the HAVING clause, notification is not passed to the event consumer.

```
SELECT * FROM Win32_LogicalDisk WHERE FreeSpace < 120000 GROUP
       WITHIN 600 HAVING NumberOfEvents > 10
```

In the above example, notification is sent to the consumer only if the number of events is greater than 10 after a period of 10 minutes has elapsed since the first event. Event notification then takes the form of a single aggregate event. *NumberOfEvents* is a member of the `__AggregateEvent` class and represents the number of events combined to produce a single `__AggregateEvent` summary event.

Schema Queries

Schema queries are used to request class information or schema associations and to specify the classes and associations that class providers support. Microsoft normally does not recommend class providers because of the overhead that they place on WMI every time a request is made for them. Schema queries support the following statements:

SELECT retrieves a single class definition. It must be used in conjunction with the keyword meta_class.

```
SELECT * FROM meta_class
```

This query retrieves all of the class definitions found in the current namespace. Like all other uses of the SELECT clause, it can be combined with the WHERE clause to narrow the scope of the query. In this case, however, the WHERE clause must be used in conjunction with two other special keywords, __this and ISA, as follows:

```
SELECT * FROM meta_class WHERE __this "Win32_Service"
```

The __ statement identifies the target class for the query. The preceding query retrieves the class definition for class Win32_Service (not including any of its subclasses). If you wish also to retrieve the subclasses, you must use the following ISA clause:

```
SELECT * FROM meta_class WHERE __this ISA "Win32_Service"
```

ASSOCIATORS OF retrieves associated class definitions. The syntax and semantics of using the ASSOCIATORS OF clause, except for a few minor differences, are the same as those for its use with data queries. The ClassDefsOnly keyword is invalid and every schema query must end with the keywords WHERE and SchemaOnly (in that order, though not necessarily consecutively).

```
ASSOCIATORS OF {Win32_Service} WHERE
        Role = GroupComponent SchemaOnly
```

This query returns a list of associated class definitions for the classes associated with Win32_Service (the Windows NT service class) whose role is that of GroupComponent.

REFERENCES OF retrieves class definitions of classes that are referenced by the source class. The same conditions apply to this clause as to data queries except that each query must contain the two keywords, WHERE and SchemaOnly.

```
REFERENCES OF {Win32_Service} WHERE
        ResultClass = Win32_BaseService SchemaOnly
```

■ Summary

This chapter has explored the basic framework of WMI, including the concepts of events, data consumers, and data providers. We looked at the role that providers play in WMI and examined the use of WQL in defining information requirements. We also examined the files and directories that make WMI and the purposes of these elements.

Consider Chapter 3 a source for reference. You cannot expect to read and remember all of its information in a single sitting. Instead, proceed to Chapter 4, in which we take a practical look at the CIM, which we have already introduced as one of the most important and complex aspects of the WBEM framework.

Ten Fast Facts: Windows Management Instrumentation

1. The primary component and information model of the WBEM initiative is the Common Information Model (CIM), which is designed to hold all information pertinent to the enterprise.

2. The WinMgmt executable is at the heart of the WMI architecture and runs as either a Windows service or executable depending upon the capability of the host operating system.

3. Providers supply management information that can change. They can be run as standalone executables, Windows services, or dynamic link libraries (DLLs). Without providers, the WMI architecture would have no means of gathering dynamic management information or generating "real-world" event notification.

4. Event providers generate notifications of an event. After an event has been generated, it is passed to WMI, which matches the event with registered event consumers before passing it to the event consumers. Event consumers are applications that request notification of an event and then perform an action in response to that specific event.

5. Data providers deal in management data. They enable a management application to retrieve or modify dynamic instrumented data that must be generated on request. Data providers are further classified as class, instance, method, or property providers.

6. Microsoft defines intrinsic events in WMI as events that occur in response to changes in the standard WMI data model. This refers to the CIM repository and its associated providers.

7. An extrinsic event in WMI is one that occurs outside the standard WMI data model, that is, any event that is not captured by the CIM repository or providers. Consequently, an extrinsic event must be surfaced using an event provider. Microsoft refers to extrinsic events as "real world" events because they typically take place on actual hardware- or software-managed components.

8. Timer events can be either absolute or interval based. Absolute timer events are triggered at a certain time. Interval timer events are triggered at regular intervals.

9. Event consumers can be either temporary or permanent. Whereas a temporary consumer receives event notifications only while it is active, a permanent consumer, once registered, always receives event notifications, whether its state is active or inactive. If an event takes place and a permanent consumer is not currently active, then WMI uses its registration information to locate the logical consumer and load the physical consumer before forwarding the event.

10. Central to the concept of receiving and generating event notification, instances of class data, and class definitions is the Microsoft-defined WMI Query Language. Data queries allow retrieval of instances of class and data associations. Event queries tell WMI of the events in which they are interested and the events that they provide. WMI pairs event consumers and event providers by using their queries for comparison when an event is generated. Both permanent and temporary event consumers use event queries to register their interest in certain events. Schema queries are used to request class information or schema associations and to specify the classes and associations that class providers support.

Chapter 4

A Guided Tour of the Common Information Model Repository

Before we take a hands-on look at Microsoft's implementation of the Common Information Model (CIM) repository, let us first examine its structure as defined by the DMTF. In the previous chapters, you have gleaned an idea of the structure and purpose of the CIM. In simple terms, it consists of the following four components:

- Classes that define the structure of the information held in the store
- Associations that define the relationships between elements in the repository
- Methods that define the behavior of the managed objects
- Properties that define individual characteristics of each managed object

Each of these components can have associated instances that hold the management data. They were designed with the basic purpose of providing a platform-independent means of describing the manageable aspects of all types of logical and physical components in the enterprise.

The objective of this chapter is not to describe every class, property, method, and association within the CIM schema and Win32 extended schema. First, this would not make particularly interesting reading, and second, it would prove somewhat overwhelming as an introduction to the CIM. Instead, the focus of this chapter is to examine the classes and associations that hold the elements of most interest to users of WMI. This includes the WMI system classes that define the properties and methods relevant to WMI's security model, the classes that define the WMI provider architecture, and the classes of the CIM schema. By the end of the chapter, you should have a solid enough knowledge of the structure of the repository to move through it with confidence.

We shall use Microsoft's WMI CIM Studio to look at the classes within the CIM repository. During the course of the chapter, we also shall look briefly at the Managed Object Format (MOF) so that you can better understand some of the terminology used in the WMI CIM Studio. For a more complete list of the syntax and semantics used in the MOF, you can refer to the platform SDK documentation available from the MSDN Web site.

Recall from the previous chapter that the CIM is a conceptual model for storing enterprise management information—it is not a physical implementation (that is, the DMTF does not supply a downloadable version of WBEM that you can install as part of your operating system). It is the responsibility of vendors such as Microsoft, Intel, or Hewlett-Packard to adhere to the DMTF's CIM standard and produce their own physical implementations. Microsoft has done this for its range of Windows operating systems. The CIM *repository* supplied as part of WMI is a data store structured in accordance with the DMTF's CIM. It is supplied with any of Microsoft's WMI-compliant operating systems (Windows 9x/2000/NT4.0/WinXp/.NET): It holds management information structured in accordance with the CIM.

The aim of this chapter is to familiarize you with the CIM repository that is shipped with WMI. This will serve two purposes: first, it will give you some idea of the vast array of information that you can retrieve from the repository, and second, it will provide you with an introduction to the structure and relationships of the existing classes. This knowledge will prove useful especially if you are faced with the task of instrumenting your own product within the CIM repository or need to elicit management information from the repository about managed objects. To explore the repository, we shall use the tools supplied with the WMI SDK, so if you did not install the SDK during your study of Chapter 3, you should do so now.

■ Metadata

"Metadata" is a new term to those who are not familiar with data modeling. The Greek word "*meta-*" is a prefix that means "behind" or "hidden." If you are familiar with HTML scripting, you will have encountered the prefix in *meta*tags. Metatags describe the characteristics of information presented on a Web page (for example, to specify text displaying **Bold** or in *Italics*). Metadata is "data that describes data" or, more precisely, *definitional* data.

Admittedly, this is a broad definition, so let us define metadata more fully in terms of the CIM. We know from previous chapters that the information available from CIM is described by a series of classes and associations, and the elements contained therein (methods, properties, and references). These constructs describe the data available to WMI client applications and are classified as metadata, as you can see in Table 4.1.

Table 4.1 Metadata Examples

Property (metadata)	Type (metadata)	Value (instance data)
Model	String	CD99A_EXPRESS
Version	Real32	1.64
BIOSVersion	String	1.23.54.244
Read_errors	Sint32	0

The information in the Property and Type columns is metadata, as it describes the information we can retrieve, which is listed in the Value column. The Property and Type columns represent "data about data." The information in the Value column is instance data—the data that metadata describe. Metadata is a generic term and applies to a broad spectrum of data; for example, class information is metadata. Metadata also includes descriptive information about the context, quality and condition, or characteristics of the data, such as WMI system classes and properties. It is important to make the distinction between metadata and instance data because the CIM repository was envisaged by the DMTF primarily, although not exclusively, as a store for metadata.

■ Dynamic and Static Data

As well as understanding the distinction between metadata and instance data, it is important to understand that the data in WMI is categorized further as either dynamic or static. A simple rule of thumb is that metadata is inherently static and instance data more often is dynamic. As with all generalizations, however, there can always be exceptions to the rule.

Dynamic data is characterized by frequent change. Instance data commonly falls into this category, because the values associated with instance data often change during a managed object's lifetime. For example, the value assigned to a property that represents the amount of free space left on a disk partition is dynamic in nature, because during the day-to-day operation of the disk drive, the value normally will change. Other reasons that the data may change include:

1. The data may persist in other places, such as Active Directory, a database, the Internet, or simply a file on disk.
2. A WMI class can have properties that are retrieved from several sources, thus unifying separate data sources into one logical means of accessing it and its

relationships. For example, the `Win32_Service` might obtain the *Started* property at run time and most of the other properties from the registry.

Static data is slow or nonchanging data, such as class or association definitions or a static property value such as a BIOS version number (although these values can change if the BIOS is stored on flash memory that can be reprogrammed) or a manufacturer's name. WMI class definitions often fall into this category because the classes that define a managed object do not change with great frequency.

Dynamic data (for example, the Read_errors value in the Value column in Table 4.1), is provided externally by WMI providers. Static data and metadata are stored in the CIM repository.

■ Dynamic Data and the CIM Repository

An important concept when retrieving dynamic (volatile) data is *temporal correctness*. For data to be temporally correct, it must be valid in relation to the time of the original query. When a managed object supports dynamic data, it is counterintuitive to import that information into the repository with no means of updating it. Imagine that we are responsible for monitoring the amount of free space on the disk drive partition of a network server. Because the network server is heavily utilized, the space remaining on the disk changes constantly during its day-to-day operation. Without a mechanism for keeping track of these changes, management applications that requested information on the amount of free space could end up retrieving out-of-date information. The solution designed by Microsoft is a WMI provider, a software component that reacts to requests for dynamic data with information that is temporally correct. (Chapter 12 covers WMI providers in detail.) Figure 4.1 shows an example architecture without using WMI providers for dynamic data, and Figure 4.2 demonstrates an architecture that uses WMI providers.

Figure 4.2 shows a management application requesting instance or property data that is supplied dynamically. In this example, class and association information is held statically in the CIM repository. The example does not illustrate the surfacing of events or method invocation.

Figure 4.2 also demonstrates how WMI providers retrieve dynamic data directly from the managed object to respond to the request. The Windows Management service then returns all of the requested information to the client application. Although Figure 4.2 shows a preferred arrangement, it does not preclude storing *instance* information in the CIM repository, which even may be the preferred solution for situations in which the instance information is not expected to change during the lifetime of the managed object (that is, it is static). It is far more likely, however, that some informa-

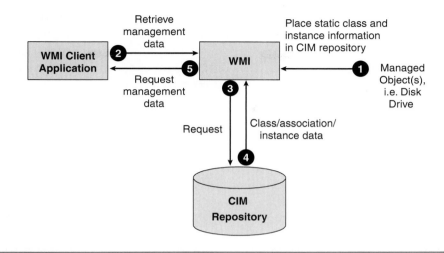

Figure 4.1 Example topology without any mechanism to supply dynamic data

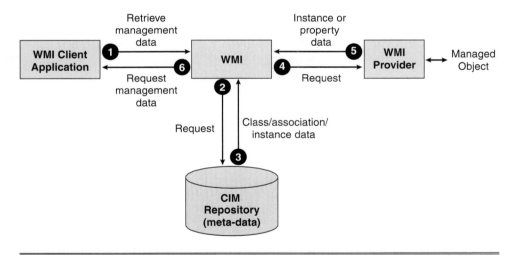

Figure 4.2 Example topology in which product supplies WMI with dynamic data

tion will change over the course of its lifetime. Therefore, WMI providers must keep track of these changes.

In the current release of WMI, the metadata (that is, the classes and associations) in the CIM repository describes local management information pertaining to the host operating system. In future releases, however, WMI technology may concern itself with distributed applications and management information from a variety of sources. Remember that the CIM repository is capable of storing information other than meta-data from any source, local or otherwise, although this is not the preferred arrangement for current products instrumented in WMI.

■ The Common Information Model

As discussed in previous chapters, the CIM has three conceptual layers, each of which builds upon the previous one, providing a greater level of detail. Notice in Figure 4.3 that layer 3 is sometimes referred to as the "layer of extensibility."

The core and common models are referred to collectively as the *CIM Schema*.

The purpose of layering the model is to allow schema designers to view the model as a series of logical progressions from which they can build. The CIM Schema represents the basic classes, properties, methods, and associations of all potentially managed objects within an enterprise.

The Core Model

The core model defines a number of very general classes to describe basic structures and relationships between manageable components in an environment. This information model is independent of any product or implementation.

The Common Model

The common model defines a basic set of classes that represent specific areas of management within the enterprise. The common model consists of a number of models, each of which represents specific management areas. Currently the DMTF defines models that represent the network-, user-, system-, support-, policy-, physical-, metrics-, interoperability-, events-, device-, and application-specific aspects of the enterprise. (A number of submodels extend these models. For more information on the submod-

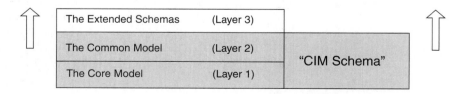

Figure 4.3 The three layers of CIM

els, visit http://www.dmtf.org, the DMTF Web site.) The number of areas represented by classes in the common model are expected to increase over time, the better to represent the variety of advances in technology.

Systems Model

The systems model defines the basic characteristics associated with managed systems. A managed system can be an operating system, a network system, or an application system. It defines the root class `CIM_ManagedSystemElement`, from which all system classes must derive. Included as part of this model are classes that define services, file systems, threads, processes, and software features.

Networks Model

The networks model defines a series of classes, associations, methods, and properties that represent the features of a network environment. Features that are common to a network environment include protocols, services, and the topology of the network. Within the networks model, a number of submodels define the classes, associations, methods, and properties that are specific to their environment.

Devices Model

The devices model defines the physical and logical components that support the system. Examples of classes defined as part of the devices model include `CIM_POTS Modem`, `CIM_Processor`, `CIM_Printer`, and `CIM_DesktopMonitor`.

Physical Model

The physical model is not to be confused with the devices model. Whereas the devices model defines a set of classes that support the managed system, the physical model represents the physical environment. You will find that the physical environment is of surprisingly little concern in the managed environment. Under normal circumstances, you will not often need to come into direct contact with a physical element within an environment but will instead interact with its logical counterpart. Any manipulation of physical elements within the environment normally is a result of manipulation of an associated logical object. For example, imagine an Ethernet network card in an ISA slot of a personal computer running Windows XP. If you were to perform some action that resulted in a series of packets being sent out of the card to the network, it you might trigger the Tx (Transmit) LED on the network card to start blinking. This behavior was the result of the packet being sent out of the card—the Tx LED cannot be addressed directly or polled for its status.

Because the physical model represents the physical aspects of a system, the classes it contains will differ considerably, depending upon the host system (consider the differences in architecture of an HP Mainframe and a desktop computer) and will change to represent the advances in technology.

Applications Model

The applications model describes the details required to manage a set of software applications. The diversity of software applications demands that the model must be flexible enough to describe multiplatform or distributes applications. The applications model borrows heavily from the application software life cycle. The application software life cycle describes the various states of a software application from its initial purchase through its execution.

Event Model

The event model describes CIM Indications and how they are used to communicate occurrences of events in the CIM. It also describes the classes that enable clients to subscribe to CIM Indications, including how to specify a desired mode of delivery. The Specification for CIM Operations over HTTP defines the XML encoding for CIM Indications over HTTP.

Policy Model

The policy model enables application developers, policy administrators, and network administrators to represent and manage policy across a variety of technical domains that include security, networking, and system administration.

Support Model

The support model describes the object and transaction models for the exchange of knowledge related to support activities (Solutions) and the processing of Service Incidents. The object and transaction models are referred to as the Problem Resolution Standard or PRS.

User Model

The user model provides a set of relationships between the various representations of users, their credentials, and the managed system elements that represent the resources and resource managers in system user administration. Thus, the CIM user and security models added to the preexisting set of requirements for the introduction of a "top" object class in the CIM core model.

Metrics Model

The metrics model defines classes to represent a unit of work and its associated metrics. For example, a print job could be a unit of work and the number of pages to be printed could be the metric.

Interop Model

The interop model defines architectures and mechanisms that enable WBEM implementations to interoperate in an open, standard manner, and addresses issues that prevent them from doing so.

In addition to these models is a number of submodels that include:

CIM Network Submodel—IPsec Policy Model. Defines a number of CIM extensions that represent the IP security policy model.

CIM Submodel—Storage Model. Defines the Logical Devices associated with data storage.

CIM Device Submodel—Sensor Model. Defines additional properties and methods for the classes `CIM_Sensor` and `CIM_Numeric Sensor`.

CIM Device Submodel—Printer Model. Describes the management of the functionality and protocols specific to printers.

CIM Submodel—Fault Tolerant Model. Defines a number of fault tolerant extensions to the CIM model.

CIM System Submodel—Diagnostic Model. Describes additional aspects needed for successful diagnostics under multi-tasking operating systems.

The Extended Schemas

Vendors who wish to represent the manageable aspects of their hardware or software product as part of the CIM define the extended schemas. Extended schemas typically derive from classes defined as part of the common model, although it is possible to extend from the core model. An example of an extended schema is the mechanism with which operating system vendors can model the manageable aspects of their operating systems in the CIM. Microsoft uses the Win32 extended schema to represent its Windows platform (Windows 98, NT4.0/2000/WinXP/.NET). The management information you retrieve from WMI about the Windows environment typically will be retrieved from the classes defined as part of the Win32 extended schema, because the majority of CIM schema classes defined within the CIMV2 namespace are declared as abstract.

When designing the CIM, the DMTF envisaged a number of ways to implement it. Among the proposed methods were:

- An application Data Base Management System (DBMS)
- A series of application objects that represent instances of CIM classes
- A structure to pass the instances of CIM between applications

Even from a brief look at the core, common, and extended schemas, it is clear that the DMTF's task in designing the CIM was complex. Because of its complexity, navigating the CIM repository and the query response times on such a large volume of information are design concerns. Too much information to process can be as detrimental to the usability of an information model as not enough information. In addition, a CIM repository might host multiple managed environments, such as local and nonlocal devices. How can we rationalize them?

To overcome these problems, the DMTF developed *namespaces*, a mechanism for partitioning sections of CIM into smaller logical groupings.

■ Namespaces

The purpose of a namespace is to group a set of classes and instances that relate to a particular managed environment logically. The CIMV2 namespace, for example, groups a set of classes and instances that relate to aspects of the local Windows environment. This philosophy would not support defining a network router (its classes, and so forth) within the CIMV2 namespace. It would be logical instead to define a router in the CIM repository by creating a new namespace and populating it with the relevant router classes. To combine instances from both local and nonlocal elements in the same namespace could lead to confusion, because there is no immediate way to distinguish between the two. Placing them in separate namespaces further clarifies the distinction between the nonlocal router's management environment and the local Windows host. If, however, you were defining the manageable aspects of a local internal modem, then it would be most likely that you would place your classes in the CIMV2 namespace. The CIMV2 namespace derives its name from the DMTF's CIM schema that is the basis of its classes.

■ Using the CIMV2 Namespace

Table 4.2 lists an array of hardware- and software-managed objects that you might find in the enterprise. The purpose of the table is to illustrate which devices most likely should appear in the CIMV2 namespace and which should be placed elsewhere. With a technology as complex as WMI, there is always a danger of over-simplifying the issues. For instance, in text we have ignored the fact that a managed object can appear in multiple namespaces in the same CIM repository, but the table shows when it is and is not appropriate to use the CIMV2 namespace. The *Location* field states where the device is located, either on the local host machine, or on another machine on the network.

The DMTF specifies the following points as valid criteria for defining a namespace:

- To define chunks of management information (objects and associations) to limit implementation resource requirements, such as database size
- To define views on the model for applications managing only specific objects, such as hubs
- To pre-structure groups of objects for optimized query speed

Table 4.2 Likely Management Object Locations

Device	Location	Description	Namespace
Network card	Local	Network card residing on host machine.	CIMV2
External modem	Local	56K modem attached to COM1.	CIMV2
Custom designed software application	Local	Simple standalone application that runs on Windows 2000, NT4, and 9x.	CIMV2
Distributed database application	Distributed, Machine A, n	A distributed database with error-recovery and data integrity/fault tolerance built in.	Requires a separate namespace because the CIMV2 namespace does not accommodate distributed applications.
Fax gateway software application	Local	Located on host machine. Runs under Windows. Allows other users on network to send faxes using host machine's fax card.	CIMV2
E-mail gateway	Remote	Located remotely on network. Transmits all external email onto the PSTN.	A separate namespace is required as the CIMV2 namespace merely represents the local managed environment.
Network card	Local	Located on host machine. Instrumented using the DMTF's DMI management architecture.	A separate namespace is required as this object does not use or derive from the CIM schema or object definitions.*
Smart Array SCSI controller card*	Local	Controls a RAID 5 array of hard disk using the SNMP protocol.	A separate namespace is required as this object does not use or derive from the CIM schema or object definitions.*

*Products instrumented with either SNMP or DMI can be represented by classes in the CIM repository. However, they cannot be instrumented as part of the CIMV2 namespace. This is because of architectural differences between the two management paradigms that prevent classes from either SNMP or DMI deriving from those in the CIM schema. In- stead, they must define classes in a separate namespace that does not derive from the CIM schema, but instead illustrates itself using a custom schema. This dynamic or static infor- mation can then be provided to CIM-compliant applications using WMI's built-in SNMP or DMI provider.

test

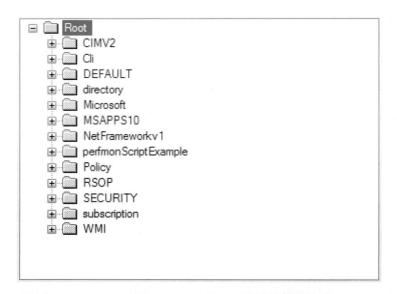

Figure 4.4   Example of namespaces found in a Windows XP installation

WMI Namespaces and the CIM repository

In a typical WMI installation, you will find a number of namespaces defined in the CIM repository. The exact number of namespaces will depend largely upon the version of your operating system and the applications or hardware on your machine. Figure 4.4 shows an example of the namespaces found on an installation of Windows XP.

Table 4.3 provides a quick roundup of the namespaces found in a Windows XP installation.

Defining and Using Your Own Namespace

By using your own namespace, you effectively rid yourself of a number of the constraints of populating a proprietary namespace, such as seeking permission from the owner of the namespace.

You also create potentially more work for yourself because you must define everything from the root up. As we see in Figure 4.5, the CIMV2 namespace contains a collection of classes from the CIM schema as well as from the Win32 extended schema.

If you decide to create a new namespace to define the manageable aspects of your environment, you are not obliged to use or to derive from all (or any) of the classes de-

Table 4.3 Windows XP Namespaces

Namespace	Description
Root	The lowest level in the namespace hierarchy.
CIMV2	Defines the manageable aspects of the host system.
CIMV2\Applications	Defines miscellaneous application-specific data.
Cli	Defines the default WMIC aliases (Windows XP only).
Default	Default namespace (a good place to experiment with your own classes!).
Directory	Groups directory related namespaces.
Directory\LDAP	Defines management information for the Lightweight Directory Access Protocol.
Microsoft	Groups Microsoft technology–specific namespaces, for example, the HomeNet subnamespace on Windows XP, which defines the management information for home networking.
MSAPPS10	Defines class information for the Microsoft Office suite of applications.
NetFrameworkv1	Defines class information for the .NET framework (.NET must be installed on the computer for this to be present).
Perfmonscriptexample	Monitors performance of script-specific information.
Policy	Defines policy-specific management information.
RSOP	Defines resultant set of policy security-related classes for centralized policy-based administration (Windows XP/.NET only).
SECURITY	Defines the WMI system security-related management information.
Subscription	Defines consumer-related classes for triggering scripts in response to an event and sending an e-mail (Windows XP/.NET only).
WMI	Defines management information for the WMI for WDM provider.
<namespace>\MS_XXX	Defines locale-specific information (e.g., MS_409 is the namespace that defines US English locale-specific information).

fined in the CIM Schema or Win32 extended schema. Indeed, as the CIM repository currently stands, a number of namespaces populated by legacy schemas such as the SNMP and DMI exist. Schema designers are required to populate their namespaces only with classes and associations that are pertinent to the managed environment under scrutiny. If, however, you decide not to derive from any of the classes in the CIM schema, then you must question whether the object that you are defining belongs to the enterprise modeled within the CIM. Remember that the CIM schema models the most basic manageable aspects of the enterprise from which you can derive. (If you feel that a vital

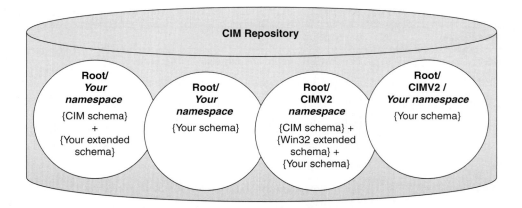

Figure 4.5 Namespaces and the CIM repository

class that will enable you to instrument your product is missing within the CIM schema, then you are encouraged to e-mail the DMTF at cim@dmtf.org with a change request and open a channel of discussion with them. For the Win32 extended schema, e-mail Microsoft at wmgmts@microsoft.com.)

■ Namespaces and Schemas

Imagine a schema as a collection of classes aimed at instrumenting a particular management environment. The scope of a schema can be as diverse or as specialized as the schema designer sees fit, with the understanding that the objects defined within it are related. The DMTF designed the CIM schema to represent the different manageable aspects of the enterprise. Within it are numerous models that target specific aspects of that environment. The Network model, as it defines a group of classes and associations that represent the enterprise network managed environment, is an example. The Win32 extended schema then adds a further level of specialization to this by focusing on the Windows platform. Because schemas are diverse, they contain a large amount of information that may or may not be relevant to a particular managed environment. For example, a schema could contain classes that define every type of microprocessor architecture available. In a real machine, however, only a fraction of those classes may be relevant (perhaps only the x86). A namespace, then, represents the real managed environment by hosting only these relevant classes.

A namespace is a logical abstraction of classes, associations, and instances that limits the visibility and scope to suit a particular managed environment, such as the

Windows OS. By limiting the scope, we can improve response times, reduce the resource overhead for managing the environment, and rationalize the amount of information presented to the end user. A namespace can contain many different classes from many different schemas.

The classes defined within a schema, such as the Win32 extended schema, can be contained in one or many namespaces of the same CIM repository without fear of conflict. The CIM repository can differentiate between these classes by examining the full object path of the class, which can include both the server and the namespace of the CIM repository.

■ Using Existing Schemas

If you use classes defined by the DMTF, Microsoft, or any other schema designer, then you must be careful to adhere to the guidelines and context for their use. Indeed, by using the schemas defined by a third party, you can provide a set of building blocks from which to derive your own classes. If you do not adhere to these rules, there is the risk that the new classes you define may violate the integrity of the schema, thus invalidating the entire class hierarchy. Put simply: your code won't work. The schema designers normally detail the classes that can have subclasses and/or be instantiated in their documentation. Microsoft provides this information in its WMI SDK and in the MSDN platform SDK documentation. If you are still in doubt, e-mail Microsoft at wmgmts@microsoft.com.

■ Subclassing and Instantiating Existing Classes in the CIMV2 Namespace

If your product populates the CIMV2 namespace, you must check with the schema designer for the conditions of its use when subclassing existing classes or creating instances of them. As part of the WMI SDK, Microsoft provides a text file that details which classes may be subclassed or instantiated and which may not. It is vital to check these details before you start designing your classes and deriving them from existing schema.

■ Modifying Existing Classes

If you wish to modify existing classes within the CIM schema or Win32 extended schema, you must obtain permission first from the schema designer. Situations in which you must obtain permission include the addition of a method or property to an existing class or the addition of a completely new class or association. If you decide to populate Microsoft's CIMV2 namespace with your own classes, then you must be careful to obtain permission in case any of your additional classes conflict with the designer's plans for the namespace.

Managed Object Format

Beyond the CIM and extended schemas, we look further at the structure of classes, properties, methods, and associations, initially through examples written in the MOF defined by the DMTF. Later in this chapter, we shall use Microsoft's WMI CIM Studio to explore and modify the CIM repository.

We use the MOF language to define object definitions within the CIM in a textual format. As we shall see in the WMI CIM Studio, MOF is not the only way to modify the CIM repository, but it is beneficial to have some knowledge of the MOF syntax and its semantics. MOF provides a basic understanding of the terminology you will encounter when you use Microsoft's WMI CIM Studio to move through the CIM repository. In addition, it provides you with a concept of the structures that make up the CIM.

MOF files can populate technologies that implement the CIM. In other words, a MOF file exported from a Windows XP/.NET WMI installation theoretically would compile on a UNIX implementation of the CIM. Although this is the DMTF's intention, currently various minor differences exist between Microsoft's and the DMTF's interpretation of the language. In reality, you may have to modify certain elements of the MOF file to remove Microsoft-specific qualifiers to export to non-Microsoft platforms.

To add classes, instances, or associations to the CIM repository, you first must specify the destination namespace of the objects that you wish to add. If you do not specify a destination namespace, WMI will place all entries in the *root/default* namespace in the CIM repository. You have several options for specifying a destination namespace. First, you can specify a namespace as a command-line switch for the MOF comp executable by using the –N switch. This approach is limited, because you can specify only a single destination namespace for the entire MOF file. Second, you can specify the namespace as part of the MOF file. This option will override all others. To do this use, the `#pragma` namespace compiler directive that follows:

```
#pragma namespace (destination namespace)
```

In the next example, any classes, instances, or associations that follow this statement will be destined for the local CIMV2 namespace.

```
#pragma namespace("\\\\.\\Root\\CIMV2")
```

The MOF includes various compiler directives that allow developers to set conditions that affect the compilation process. Compiler directives include `locale`, `source`, `nonlocal`, `include`, and `instancelocale`.

`#pragma locale(language_country)` The locale directive tells the compiler which language and country settings the MOF file will use. Remember that all MOF keywords (such as "class," "instance," and "association") are always listed in English. When not specified, the default value is en_US (language = english and country = United States).

`#pragma source(<namespace type>://<namespace_handle>)` Tells the compiler on which CIM implementation to locate the metadata that follows. You can use this pragma on class instances or association instances. You also can use the source qualifier on individual class and association instances.

`#pragma nonlocal(<namespace type>://<namespace_handle>)` Tells the compiler to reference an object instance in another CIM implementation. This allows the CIM to share management information between machines and to allow enterprise-wide identification of objects. With this compiler directive, we can identify objects located on a machine across the network from the current host machine. For instance, while compiling on host machine A, we could reference an object instance held on a CIM-compliant repository on machine B on a different part of the network (that is, `#pragma nonlocal("namespacetype://namespace_handle")`). `#pragma include("another.mof")` Tells the compiler to insert the contents of the MOF file given as a parameter into the current MOF file from this point onward. `#pragma instancelocale()` Tells the compiler to use the locale that follows the directive for instances declared in the MOF file. This, in effect, means that instances within the MOF file can have a different locale from that declared for classes. We shall cover how to declare instances using MOF later in this chapter.

Terminology checkpoint:

You *compile* class definitions into the CIM repository.

You *import* instance information into the CIM repository.

■ MOF Class Declaration

Declaring a class using MOF syntax is quite simple and not dissimilar from using C++. In Figure 4.6, we declare a fictitious class that represents some of the attributes of a

CD-ROM drive. For the sake of simplicity, we do not derive this class from any classes within the CIM schema or Win32 extended schema.

Figure 4.6 A MOF class declaration

```
[
  abstract,
  Description("This class defines the common characteristics Storage
    devices")
]
class Storage
{
  [read, key: DisableOverride ToSubClass]
  uint64 DeviceId;
  // DeviceId is an unsigned integer 8 bytes
};
class MySchema_CDROM: Storage
{
  string ManufacturerName;
  string Model;
  uint16 ReadSpeed;
  string BIOSVersion;
  // This declares the properties for the CD ROM.
};
```

The class name is the *domain* of the properties or methods that it contains. In Figure 4.6, the property `DeviceId` has a domain of class `Storage` and the property `Model` has the domain of `MySchema_CDROM`. In the case of associations, which we discuss shortly, each reference has a *range*. The range refers to the class to which the reference points.

Note: All keywords in MOF are case INSENSITIVE

In Figure 4.6, we declared the class `CD_ROM` as a subclass of class `Storage`. To compile correctly, we must declare the class `Storage` *before* class `CD_ROM`.

We have declared four properties, `ManufacturerName`, `Model`, `BIOSVersion`, and `ReadSpeed`, as part of the class. Property names must not contain any spaces or underscores; otherwise, the compilation process will fail. Also observe that we used the `//` to place comments in the class declaration. The compilation process ignores these comments.

■ Qualifiers

Qualifiers are the mechanism in MOF through which we can assign characteristics to any of the elements within a schema. These elements include methods, method parameters, properties, classes, and associations. A qualifier has the following components:

- A *name* (that is, description, abstract, read, write,…)
- An *intrinsic data type* (that is, real32, string, uint16,…)
- A *value* of the corresponding type (that is, `Manufacturer_Name` could be assigned the value "Mitsubishi")
- A *scope*, to determine whether the qualifier can be applied to classes, methods, properties, and associations
- A *flavor*, to determine whether the qualifier can be inherited by subclasses or instances, or can be overridden

The DMTF defines a number of *standard* qualifiers for use when working with any schema (which are listed in the DMTF CIM Specification document). It is also possible to define your own qualifiers. Microsoft defines a number of custom qualifiers as part of their implementation of WMI. In Figure 4.7, we add default qualifiers and Microsoft-specific qualifiers to the class.

Figure 4.7 Example qualifiers

```
[
    Description("The CD_Rom class contains characteristics of CDROM drives"):
    ToSubClass,
    Locale(0x409),
    UUID("{BA46D060-7A6D-11d2-BC85-00104B2CF71C}")
]
class MySchema_CDROM:Storage
{
    [ write (true): ToSubClass ]
    string ManufacturerName;
    [ write (true): ToSubClass ]
    string Model;
    [ read,
       Description("This property contains the read speed of the CDROM"
         "Example: 32"): ToSubClass ]
    uint16 ReadSpeed;
    [ read,
    Description("This property defines the BIOS revision of the CDROM"
        "Example: 7.13.1200"): ToSubClass ]
    string BIOSVersion;
};
```

Figure 4.7 shows the qualifiers listed in bold type. Always arrange qualifiers in blocks that immediately *precede* the class, method, or property that they characterize, and always enclose the blocks in square brackets: [ ]. For example:

```
[ Description ("This is a legal qualifier block")]
```

The *Description* qualifier at the start of the class declaration in Figure 4.7 is the qualifier *name* and provides a simple text description of class `MySchema_CDROM`. You must enclose the text itself in curved brackets and straight (nondirectional) quotation marks. Later, applications can use this text to retrieve a description of the class from the CIM repository.

■ Flavors

Qualifiers also are characterized by how they transmit their information from parent to child class or from class to instance. To determine the rules by which a qualifier transmits its information, the MOF language defines special keywords called *flavors*. A colon always must precede qualifier flavors, as in Figure 4.7, and immediately after the description text, a semicolon precedes the qualifier flavor ToSubClass. This flavor indicates that every subclass of `MySchema_CDROM` inherits the qualifiers *Description, Locale,* and *UUID*. Figure 4.8 demonstrates some examples of flavors.

Figure 4.8   Example flavors

```
[ Description("The CDRom class contains characteristics of CDROM drives"):
    ToSubClass, Locale(0x409),
    UUID ("{BA46D060-7A6D-11d2-BC85-00104B2CF71C}")]
```

Other flavors include:

EnableOverride. This indicates that the qualifier can be overridden by child classes. The default value for this parameter is yes.

DisableOverride. This indicates that the qualifier cannot be overridden by child classes. The default value for this is no.

ToSubClass. This indicates that the qualifier is inherited by its child classes.

ToInstance. This indicates that the qualifier is propagated to instances.

NotToInstance. This indicates that the qualifier is not propagated to instances. This is the default.

NotToSubclass. This indicates that the qualifier is not propagated to derived classes. This is the default.

Restricted. This indicates that the qualifier is only valid for the class in which it is declared. Child classes do not inherit this qualifier.

Translatable. This indicates that the value can be specified in multiple locales.

Custom Qualifiers

In designing the WBEM initiative, one of the goals of the DMTF was to provide technologies that were powerful and flexible enough to serve an environment as diverse as the enterprise. The CIM, for example, allows us to design specialized extensions using the extended schema. The MOF language also follows this philosophy to some extent with the creation of user-defined or *custom* qualifiers, whose only constraint is that qualifiers conform to one of the intrinsic data types defined in the MOF language. Schema designers can then use these qualifiers to represent specific characteristics unique to their schema. In Figure 4.8, the Locale qualifier and UUID qualifiers are both custom qualifiers defined by Microsoft and are not part of the default qualifiers defined by the DMTF. Examples of other qualifiers to which you will become accustomed in using WMI are Dynamic and Provider, which specify the use of Microsoft's dynamic providers for a class, instance, or property within the CIM repository.

The Locale qualifier is another Microsoft custom qualifier that provides WMI with a hex value that indicates the language and country of the class information that follows it. In this case, the locale ID 0x409 refers to US English. WMI can use this information to set specific information, such as date and time formats, character-sorting order, and decimal separators, when reading the following class or instance information.

In Figure 4.7, you can also see that the `MySchema_CDROM` class uses another custom qualifier, UUID. The UUID qualifier (which stands for **U**niversally **U**nique **ID**entifier) assigns a unique 128-bit value to each class. UUIDs are randomly generated 8-byte values, which are represented by a string of hex values in the CIM repository. They are so random that no two UUIDs generated on two different machines at the same time ever should be the same. If you are familiar with COM, then you will know UUIDs as the unique means of representing Class Identifiers (CLSIDs) and Interface Identifiers (IIDs). UUIDs also are referred to as GUIDs or **G**lobally **U**nique **Id**entifiers; the two terms can be used interchangeably. The Microsoft Platform SDK supplies two executables, `guidgen.exe` and `Uuidgen.exe`, which can generate these random values on request. WMI uses these values automatically to identify classes and events internally. Then the properties and methods within each class are referred to using a unique index value in conjunction with this UUID. The advantage of using UUIDs/GUIDs is that they are locale independent, that is, they are represented by the same binary value regardless of the locale setting. Microsoft developed a technique called the "Data Block GUID Mapping control" method for WMI that maps these unique UUIDs to a two-character ID within the driver. The driver understands the two-character IDs and therefore can interact with WMI. This mapping between the ID and UUID also enables drivers to support custom events, methods, and properties, which can be instrumented via WMI.

■ User-Defined Qualifiers

New qualifier types are declared at the start of a MOF file: They begin with the *qualifier* keyword. The UUID qualifier, for example, could have been defined using MOF syntax similar to the following:

```
qualifier UUID :string = null, scope (class);
```

This syntax declares the qualifier called UUID, assigns it type string, and gives it a default value of zero. It then declares the qualifier to have a scope that affects only class declarations. Other settings that could have been used here include property, method, and reference, which would have allowed this qualifier to be used on these elements, also.

The *read* qualifier sets the property BIOSVersion to the read-only attribute. It then provides a description for the BIOSVersion property. ToSubClass signifies that any subclasses will inherit the BIOSVersion property.

■ Intrinsic Data Types

In the example class, all of the properties are assigned one of the *intrinsic* data types. Table 4.4 shows the other property data types allowed in MOF format.

■ Instance Creation

Instance creation can take place only after the corresponding class definition within a MOF file, which we declared in the previous section. The only case in which this rule does not apply is if the class definition already exists in the CIM repository within the target namespace. We create instances of classes using the MOF statement

```
instance of <classname>
```

Table 4.4   Intrinsic Data Types

Intrinsic data type	Description
boolean	Boolean value (i.e. TRUE or FALSE, 1 or 0)
char16	Unicode Style 2-byte character
DATETIME	A string that contains the date and time
object	An instance of a class within CIM
real32	4-byte floating point value
real64	8-byte floating point value
<classname>ref	A strongly typed reference
sint64	8-byte signed integer
sint32	4-byte signed integer
sint16	2-byte signed integer
sint8	1-byte signed integer
uint64	8-byte unsigned integer
uint32	4-byte unsigned integer
uint16	2-byte unsigned integer
uint8	1-byte unsigned integer
Array of…	An array of any of the above data types

Remember that MOF keywords are not case sensitive, so the case you use does not matter. To create an instance of the CD_ROM class, we could use the declaration in Figure 4.9.

Figure 4.9   Creating an instance of MOF

```
instance of MySchema_CDROM
{
    DeviceId = 18446744071574384224; //property inherited by class storage
    ManufacturerName = "Sambutsu";
    Model = "CD1F";
    BIOSVersion = "1.34.230";
    ReadSpeed = 64;
};
```

Aliasing

When writing MOF files, it sometimes is expedient to create an *alias* that refers to a specific object instance. This alias can be used later in conjunction with a variable that is a pointer to an object (for example, the *ref:* keyword) to point to that specific object instance. If in the example in Figure 4.9 we declared an association class that referenced the CDROM class, we could use aliasing as in Figure 4.10.

Figure 4.10 Using an alias in MOF

```
instance of MySchema_CDROM as $CDROM
{
    DeviceId = 18446744071574384224; //property inherited by class storage
    ManufacturerName = "Sambutsu";
    Model = "CD1F";
    BIOSVersion = "1.34.230";
    ReadSpeed = 64;
};
[association]
class MYAssociation
{
    MySchema_CDROM REF CDDrive;
    // Note that ordinarily this would not be a legal association as it does
    // not contain the minimum of two REF keywords.
};
instance of MYAssociation
{
    CDDrive = $CDROM;
};
```

▪ A Compileable MOF File

While examining the syntax and semantics of the MOF language by reading examples is an important part of the learning process, it is far more beneficial to gain practical experience through typing and compiling your own examples. Type the following MOF file, which is based upon the previous examples, and follow the instructions to compile it. After you are confident with this process, then experiment and alter sections of the file to see the results.

In the example, we shall create our own namespace, to avoid cluttering any existing system namespaces. Microsoft recommends using the root/default namespace in developing schemas, although we shall create our own in this example.

To write a MOF file, you will need a simple ASCII text editor, such as Microsoft's WordPad or Notepad.

If you have Microsoft Developer Studio, you can configure the settings under Tools/Customize/Tools so the development environment will compile a MOF file for you. For more information, see Microsoft's *Learn WMI* tutorial at http://msdn.microsoft.com/downloads/sample.asp?url=/msdn-files/027/001/574/msdncompositedoc.xml.

First, open your ASCII text editor or Developer Studio. Within the window, type the MOF text in Figure 4.11.

Figure 4.11   A compilable MOF (part 1 of 2)

```
//Beginning of sample MOF file.
#pragma classflags("forceupdate")
#pragma namespace ("\\\\.\\Root")
instance of __Namespace
{
    Name = "Example1";
};
```

The initial `#pragma classflags("forceupdate")` directive tells the compiler to update any existing class definitions in the CIM repository that match those with the class definitions supplied in this MOF file and to resolve conflicts where possible. The update process applies to properties, methods, and qualifiers contained within a class. If the changes within a class are extensive, then it is always better first to delete the existing class from the repository and then to compile the new one. Be aware, however, that doing this deletes all child class definitions!

The CIM repository employs inheritance, which leads to some very real consequences when adding new classes to the repository. For example, replacing an existing class in the hierarchy or changing one of the qualifiers in an existing base class can have direct consequences to the later classes.

Consider a parent class, `Storage`, and a child class, `CDROM`. Imagine that the child class is defined with the class qualifier Write set to true. If we try to add base class, `Storage`, with the class qualifier, Read, set to true, a conflict exists between the child class's qualifier and the base class. In this instance, with the forceupdate flag specified, WMI would remove the qualifier from the child class to make way for the base class. The only situation in which this would not occur is if the child class has instances. If the specified flag were safeupdate, then the update would fail at that point because of the conflict with the child class.

In addition to the forceupdate flag, a number of additional settings exist to resolve conflicts when adding classes. You can combine these options, although you should avoid combining two options that effectively cancel each other out, such as updateonly and createonly. The available options follow.

forceupdate. Upon conflict with existing classes, override this option with new settings. It fails if child classes have instances.

safeupdate. This option allows a safe update of the classes. Do not override existing settings with new settings.

updateonly. This option updates existing classes only. It fails if the classes do not already exist in the target namespace.

createonly. This option adds new classes only. It fails if classes already exist in the repository.

The second `#pragma namespace( )` (see Figure 4.12) tells the compiler to place any classes or instances following the statement into the root namespace on the host machine. The instance declaration of type class `__namespace` tells the compiler to create a new namespace instance. This tells WMI to create a new namespace in the CIM repository with the value assigned to the *name* property. The `__namespace` class in the

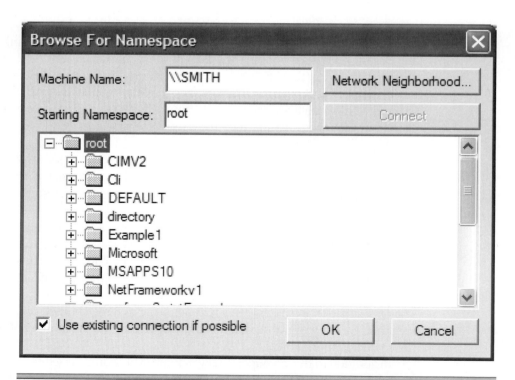

Figure 4.12 The CIM repository with the new namespace, Example1

root namespace is a WMI system class that WMI uses to store all the namespaces held in the CIM repository. We have assigned the key property name a value of **Example1**. The CIM repository now has an additional namespace into which we shall place our example classes.

In Figure 4.13, this section of the MOF file starts by instructing the compiler to place all of the new classes and instances into the newly created Example1 namespace. It does this by specifying `#pragma namespace ("\\\\.\\Root\\Example1")`. In experimenting with new classes and associations within the CIM repository, it is good practice to keep all example classes away from the important systems management classes (such as those stored in the CIMV2 namespace) where they could accidentally cause problems. We do this by placing them in a separate namespace. When you have tested them and are satisfied that they are correct, you can merge them back into your target namespace (for example, the CIMV2 namespace).

Figure 4.13   A compileable MOF (part 2 of 3)

```
#pragma namespace ("\\\\.\\Root\\Example1")
[ abstract,
   Description("This class defines common characteristics of Storage devices")
]
class MySchema_Storage
{
   [ read, key,
      Description("The device ID must be unique for each storage instance"):
         DisableOverride ToSubClass ]
   uint64 DeviceId;
   // Device Id is an unsigned integer 8 bytes
};
[ Description("The CD_Rom class describes characteristics of CDROM drives "):
   ToSubClass
]
class MySchema_CDROM:MySchema_Storage
{
   [write (true): ToSubClass]
   string ManufacturerName;
   [write (true): ToSubClass]
   string Model;
   [read(true), Description("This property contains the read speed of "
      "the CDROM. Example: 32"): ToSubClass ]
   uint16 ReadSpeed;
   [ write, Description("This property defines the BIOS revision of the CDROM."
      "Example: 7.13.1200"): ToSubClass ]
   string BIOSVersion;
};
```

The next statement declares an abstract base class called `MySchema_Storage`. This class has a single property called `DeviceId`, which is declared as both a read-only property and the key property. The read-only qualifier signifies that the value of the property cannot be changed after the instance has been created. From the perspective of a client application, this means that the value of this property cannot be altered. This property also is flagged as a key value because it will uniquely identify instances of the class.

Now type the code in Figure 4.14.

Figure 4.14 A compileable MOF (Part 3 of 3)

```
instance of MySchema_CDROM
{
    DeviceId = 384224; //property inherited by class storage
    ManufacturerName = "Sambutsu";
    Model = "CD1F";
    BIOSVersion = "1.34.230";
    ReadSpeed = 64;
}; // End of sample MOF File
```

The final section of the example declares a single instance of class `MySchema_CDROM`. The instance assigns values to each of the properties and places them in the CIM repository.

Now save the file as `myexample.mof,` go to a command-line prompt, and type the following:

```
C:\ mofcomp  myexample.mof
Microsoft (R) 32-bit MOF Compiler Version 5.1.2600.0
Copyright (c) Microsoft Corp. 1997-2001. All rights reserved.
Parsing MOF file: myexample.mof
MOF file has been successfully parsed
Storing data in the repository...
Done!
C:\
```

Congratulations! You have created your first namespace, added classes to it, and created an instance of a class within the CIM repository.

> **Note:** At this point, you could have used the MOF generator wizard that is part of the WMI Developer Studio to compile your sample MOF file into the CIM repository. We shall look at using the wizards in more detail in Chapter 5.

■ ActiveX Components

You must have Microsoft's WMI SDK installed to participate in the tour of the CIM repository. The WMI SDK contains a collection of ActiveX components to help you administer and access WMI. They install only as part of the WMI SDK: All are in wbemtool.cab file. (CAB, shorthand for CABinet, is Microsoft's mechanism for compressing and packaging files. For more information, go to http://msdn.microsoft.com/workshop/components/activex/packaging.asp.) You can unpack them and use them independently in any compliant ActiveX container. Microsoft supplies the ActiveX controls as freely distributable components with the WMI SDK. You need Internet Explorer 4.01 or later installed to run programs that come with the WMI SDK. Full details of the various ActiveX controls are in the WMI SDK documentation.

You will find short cuts to these tools under the Start/All Programs/WMI SDK folder. This folder contains useful utilities for administering and testing WMI. The ActiveX components all use the WMI API to access WinMgmt.exe.

■ Let the Tour Begin!

To explore the CIM repository, we shall use the Microsoft WMI CIM Studio. This allows us to see all the classes, properties, methods, and associations in the CIM repository in a navigable, graphical format.

To start the WMI CIM Studio, click the `Start/All Programs/WMI SDK/WMI CIM Studio` icon. After your default Web browser (which must support ActiveX controls) loads, it will display the Connect to Namespace dialog box. Click the icon in the right corner that has the ToolTip, "Browse for namespace." First, click the Connect button and click OK to log in as the current user. This should display the Browse for Namespace dialog. Now double-click the root namespace to display the dialog in Figure 4.15.

This dialog displays all of the namespaces available within the target machine's CIM repository. In the present case, the target machine is the local host machine. (Your list of namespaces might differ from the namespaces listed in Figure 4.15.) Namespaces on each machine differ to some extent, depending upon the application suites installed. The namespace list in Figure 4.15 contains the MSAPPS namespace, which was installed with Office 2000. From your list above, you should now select the Example1 namespace and click OK. You created the Example1 namespace when you compiled the earlier MOF file example. Because we are familiar with the classes and instances that we compiled earlier, we shall start our exploration of the repository here. When you click the OK button, the WMI CIM Studio will browse the Example1 namespace in the CIM repository on your local machine. Your display now should show the screen in Figure 4.16.

When browsing among different namespaces in the CIM repository, sometimes you may be asked to reenter your log on credentials. This occurs when the contents of a namespace has altered since you last entered it.

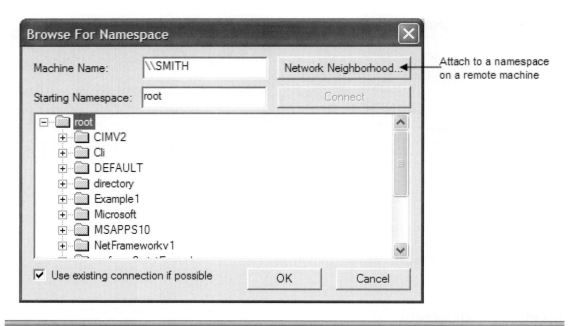

Figure 4.15 Browsing and attaching to a namespace

The viewing area is in two panes: *class explorer*, on the left, displays class information and *class viewer*, on the right, displays property, method, and association information, as well as instance information. The icons in the top of the class explorer pane represent class-related functions provided by the WMI CIM Studio, as described in Figure 4.17.

The class viewer pane in Figure 4.16 displays instance information as well as the properties, methods, and associations in which a class participates. Figure 4.18 describes the icons in this pane.

As is standard with the Windows user interface, any icons that currently are not available are dimmed.

We shall discuss each of the wizard icons and their purposes at the end of the chapter.

■ The Class Explorer Explained

The class explorer contains a list of all the root classes that are part of our Example1 namespace. The presence of a plus sign next to any root class signifies the presence of child classes, and clicking it allows navigation through the class hierarchy tree. The Example1 namespace contains four root classes, three of which are system classes. The __ double underscore prefix denotes WMI system classes. Remember that you cannot derive new classes from WMI system classes. The naming convention for all nonsystem

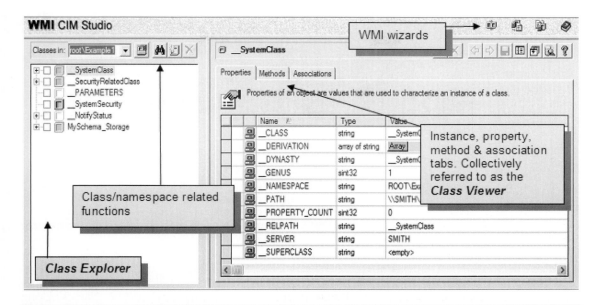

Figure 4.16 The WMI CIM Studio

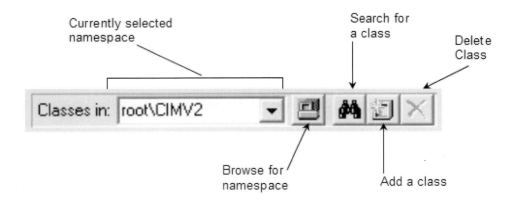

Figure 4.17 Class explorer functions

classes is *schemaname_classname*. In the Example1 namespace, the classes are prefixed with either __ (double underscore) or MySchema_. MySchema_ prefixes the classes we defined in the previous example. It is important to adhere to the naming convention for class visibility, although WMI does not enforce any type of checks in adding new classes to the repository.

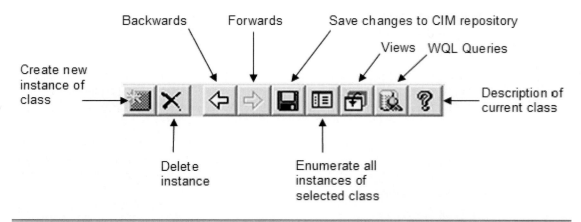

Figure 4.18 Class viewer functions

In the CIMV2 namespace, the majority of classes are prefixed by CIM_, Win32_, or __ (double underscore) to indicate their schemas of origin. All the CIM_ classes belong to the definitions given by the DMTF as part of the CIM schema. All the Win32_ classes belong to the Win32 extended schema defined by Microsoft. All classes prefixed with a double underscore are WMI system classes that define the activities of the CIM Object Manager (WinMgmt).

WMI system *properties* also start with a double underscore, and are present in all classes, system or otherwise. We examine the system classes and properties under the heading "Places of Interest within the CIM Repository" later in this chapter.

> **Note:** Nearly all classes defined as part of the DMTF's CIM schema are declared as abstract classes within Microsoft's CIMV2 namespace. Because they are abstract, you cannot create instances of them.

Two types of icon display next to the class names. The icons discriminate between classes that define regular objects and classes that define association objects. Figure 4.19 shows the icons and their definitions.

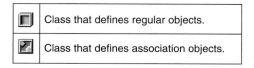

Figure 4.19 CIM Studio icon definitions

Associations

Associations are among the most important aspects of the CIM. They are unique also to any information model defined so far for enterprise management. In Chapter 2, you learned that in fault diagnosis using existing management paradigms, problems occurred because no relationship could be defined easily between managed devices in the information store. That is, it was difficult to define the relationship between a hard disk and the controller card that hosted it, especially if they came from different vendors. Without this kind of information, it was difficult to establish the cause of a particular failure without expert knowledge of the system under scrutiny. Associations provide a powerful mechanism that can define the sometimes complex relationships between managed objects, regardless of whether they are logical (a hard disk partition) or physical entities (a hard disk). MOF signifies an association by placing the Association qualifier before the class definition.

Figure 4.20 shows an example association.

Figure 4.20   An example association

```
[association]
class MySchema_Association
{
    MyClass REF Antecedent;
    YourClass REF Descendent;
};
```

An association is a class that defines a relationship between two or more objects in one or more namespaces. These relationships are vital in tracing faults in a managed environment, because their purpose is to elucidate the connections between components in a system. An association also can include standard properties and methods, although most commonly contain only references.

Association classes are typically the only classes to use the *reference* keyword, which reads in MOF syntax as ref:. The ref: keyword defines the participants in the relationship. The joining of classes in an association does not affect the interface of the class (for example, they are not given any special rights to access to the methods or properties of the associated class, nor do they share nonkey properties or methods). The only exception to this rule is if the association uses key propagation.

Key Propagation

Key propagation occurs in an association when key values from one or more *referenced* classes are propagated to a single *referenced* class defined as *weak*. The weak class must define a property of the same type as those propagated to participate successfully.

But when would we need such a mechanism? Imagine that a class defines the properties of a thread running in a Windows system. The thread is relevant to a management application only in the context of the thread's owning process. Without this information, the management application would be unable to put the thread in context with the operating system. We could define an association that contained a reference to *class thread* and *class process*. We then use key propagation to pass the key property of *class process* (that is, the process handle) to *class thread,* thus, when we declare an instance of our association, we can specify the thread and the process to which the thread belongs. This information then would be available to client applications viewing the association.

As a result, when we retrieve instances of the association, we can identify which thread is running under which process in the operating system. To mark the class in an association as weak, you must use the Weak qualifier. As Figure 4.21 demonstrates, you can declare only one reference per class within an association as weak.

Figure 4.21 Example of key propagation

```
class MySchema_Thread
{
    [key,propagated("MySchema_Process.process_handle")]
    string p_handle;
    string thread_handle;
    // etc.
}
class MySchema_Process
{
    [key]
    string process_handle;
    // etc.
}
[association]
class MySchema_Association
{
    [weak]
    MySchema_Thread REF Thread;
    // The reference to the thread class has now been declared as weak
    MySchema_Process REF Process;
};
```

All other classes in the association then propagate their key properties to the weak class, which must also declare a property using the Propagated qualifier to hold the propagated key values. The key value of the weak class then becomes valid only in the context of the other classes in the association. Figure 4.22 shows how to create an instantiation of the association class MySchema_Association using MOF language.

Figure 4.22   Instance of an association

```
instance of MySchema_Association
{
  Process = "MySchema_Process.process_handle = "1553";
  Thread = "MySchema_Thread.thread_handle = "12",
    MySchema_Process.process_handle = "1553";
}
```

Associations express the relationships between managed objects so that management applications have a means of traversing the CIM hierarchy when searching for related objects. Prior to CIM, existing information models had no way to express the relationships between managed objects at the data model level. Expert knowledge coded into the management application allowed it to understand the relationships when calculating the relationships among managed objects. Associations can now replace expert knowledge to traverse the class hierarchy when tracing a fault to its source. This is one of the major new benefits of writing management applications with WMI.

Namespaces and Associations

It is possible to associate two classes from two different namespaces within the CIM repository; however, WMI will recognize only the association from the side of the namespace that declared the association. For example, if you instrumented a product in your own namespace in the CIM repository and created associations in that namespace that referenced objects in the CIMV2 namespace, management applications that worked with information supplied from within the CIMV2 namespace would be unaware of any associations between the instances in the CIMV2 namespace and your namespace.

In Figure 4.23, two classes, ADevice and BDevice, reside in different namespaces. An association class, MyExample, resides in the *Sample* namespace and has references to both ADevice and BDevice. This is, therefore, a cross-namespace association. A management application in this scenario that works within the CIMV2 namespace and enumerates the associations of class ADevice would not be aware any associations declared in the sample namespace that referenced class ADevice.

The interpretation of each association class depends upon the client application. Microsoft has defined a number of association classes that represent the relationships between Win32 components as part of the Win32 extended schema. Their relationships derive from three basic types of CIM association class:

Component relationship. The component relationship in CIM describes two or more related classes as GroupComponent and PartComponent. The *Group* component can consist of many part components. The relationship can be imagined as a

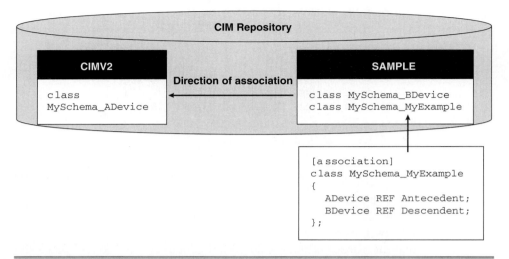

Figure 4.23 The cross namespace associations rule

containment in which the *Group component* object consists of many *Part component* objects. An example within the Win32 schema is the association class `Win32_GroupUser` that associates two classes, the *Group component* (class `Win32_GroupUser`) and the *Part component* (class `Win32_Account`). The association in this case defines the relationship between a Windows NT LAN Manager domain group and individual users who are members of that group.

Dependency relationship. A dependency relationship defines an association where one object, the dependent, is reliant upon another object, the antecedent. An example of this type of association within the Win32 schema is the association class `Win32_DiskDriveToDiskPartition`, which defines a dependency relationship between a disk drive (class `Win32_DiskDrive`) and a partition on that disk drive (class `Win32_DiskPartition`). In this association, the disk drive is the antecedent and the partition is the dependent (that is, the drive partition is dependent upon the drive for its existence).

Element-setting relationship. An element relationship defines the association between a managed element and the settings for that element. An example association class within the Win32 extended schema is `Win32_PrinterSetting`, which references two classes, `Win32_Printer` and `Win32_PrinterConfiguration`. The `Win32_Printer` class defines a printer and is an element. The `Win32_PrinterConfiguration` class defines the settings for a printer and is referenced as a setting.

The nature of each association class is interpreted differently depending upon the context of the reference. These examples represent the associations defined as part of

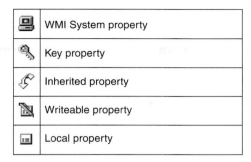

💻	WMI System property
🔑	Key property
🔗	Inherited property
📝	Writeable property
🔲	Local property

Figure 4.24   CIM Studio property types

the Win32 extended schema. You can and should use these associations when you instrument your own product in the Windows environment. You can also define additional forms of association within your own schema to represent the special relationships between components in your own product.

The *class viewer* in the right pane of Figure 4.16 contains three tabs, Properties, Methods, and Associations. Under the Properties tab are the headings Name, Type, and Value, beneath each of which is a series of corresponding properties and their values. As mentioned earlier, property names that start with a double underscore are system properties (that is, __DYNASTY).

An icon next to each property symbolizes certain core attributes of the property. Figure 4.24 shows each icon and the property it represents.

■ System Properties

Earlier, we briefly mentioned WMI system classes. In conjunction with these classes, a number of WMI system properties exist that are present in all classes within the CIM and extended schema. The system properties allow WMI to maintain system information. System properties are not available necessarily to all classes or instances at all times. If they are set to <empty>, they do not apply to a particular object. In the WMI CIM Studio, they can be found in the class viewer pane under the Properties tab. The WMI system property icon represents them. Table 4.5 represents all available system properties and their description.

All the system properties in Table 4.5 are read-only, with the exception of the _Class property, which is read-only for instances but read/write for classes.

We follow our review of the user interface elements that make up the WMI CIM Studio with an examination of the classes and instances within the hierarchy and familiarize ourselves with the functions of the WMI CIM Studio.

Table 4.5 WMI System Properties

Property	Type	Description
__Class	CIM_STRING	Contains the class name.
__Derivation	CIM_STRING array	Contains the class hierarchy of the current class or instance. The first element is the immediate superclass and the last element is the root class.
__Dynasty	CIM_STRING	Name of the top-level class from which this class or instance is derived. When this class or instance is the top-level class, the values of __Dynasty and __Class are the same.
__Genus	CIM_SINT32	Used to distinguish between classes and instances. Set to WBEM_GENUS_CLASS (1) for classes and WBEM_GENUS_INSTANCE (2) for instances.
__NameSpace	CIM_STRING	Name of the namespace from which this class or instance came.
__Path	CIM_STRING	Full path to the class or instance, including server and namespace.
__PropertyCount	CIM_SINT32	Number of nonsystem properties defined for the class or instance.
__RelPath	CIM_STRING	Relative path to the class or instance.
__Server	CIM_STRING	Name of the server supplying this class or instance.
__SuperClass	CIM_STRING	Name of the immediate parent class of the class or instance.

■ Object and Property Qualifiers

First, click the plus sign (+) located next to class MySchema_Storage in the class explorer. This exposes the next branch in the class hierarchy, which contains the subclass MySchema_CDROM. Highlight class MySchema_CDROM with a left mouse click. WMI CIM Studio displays the properties available within that class in the class viewer (right pane). Note the mixture of local, inherited, and system properties. MySchema_CDROM has inherited a single property from its parent class, DeviceId, which is also flagged as a key property. If you now click the value of the __Derivation system property in the right pane (click the array button), the display presents a numerically ordered list of the classes from which MySchema_CDROM derived. The immediate parent class is always the first entry in the array and the last entry in the list is the superclass. Now move the mouse pointer into the class viewer and click the right mouse button. The display presents a menu with two options, Property Qualifiers and Object Qualifiers. Select the Object Qualifiers menu option and the display shows the window in Figure 4.25.

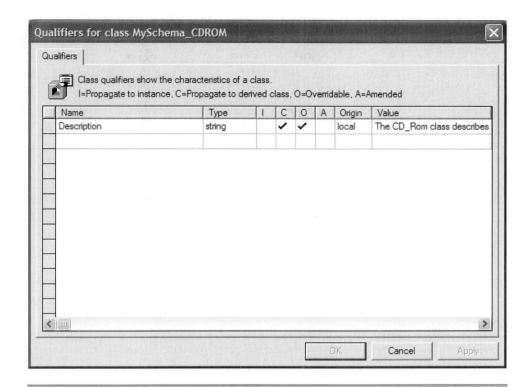

Figure 4.25 The Object qualifiers window for class MySchema_CDROM

The Object Qualifier menu option displays all of the qualifiers that apply to any instance of that particular class. Recall that qualifiers characterize named elements within the schema.

Qualifiers are values that provide additional information about classes, associations, indications, methods, method parameters, triggers, instances, properties, or references.

All qualifiers have a name, type, value, scope, flavor, and default value. Qualifiers cannot be duplicated, and only one qualifier can have any particular name for any given class, instance, or property. The class MySchema_CDROM has one qualifier, Description, assigned to it. The Description qualifier simply provides a human-readable text description of the class.

Remember that we entered this description when we typed the example MOF file. Table 4.6 lists applicable qualifiers.

Now point the mouse to any of the properties listed in the class viewer pane. Double-click the left mouse button on any of these properties and another window will appear that lists the qualifiers for that property.

Table 4.6 Object Qualifiers

Object qualifier	Type	Description
Abstract	Boolean	When set to TRUE this qualifier indicates that instances of the class cannot be created. By default this is set to FALSE.
Association	Boolean	When set to TRUE this qualifier indicates that the class is an association class used to describe a relationship between two or more other classes.
Classcontext	String	This qualifier indicates that the class has instances that are associated with additional information dynamically supplied by a provider.
Dynamic	Boolean	The Dynamic qualifier signals that instances of this class are dynamically created by a provider.
Dynprops	Boolean	When set to TRUE this qualifier indicates that certain properties within this instance are supplied dynamically by a property provider. This is not the same as the *Dynamic* qualifier, which indicates that the instance as a whole is generated by a provider.
InstanceContext	String	This qualifier can be specified on instances that contain values provided by dynamic property providers. The value is passed to the property provider as an argument to `IWbemPropertyProvider::GetProperty`.
Locale	String	This string specifies the locale of the object. This follows the naming convention as defined by Microsoft, for example.
Provider	String	This string contains the name of the dynamic provider that supplies instances of this class. It must be used in conjunction with the Dynamic qualifier.
Singleton	Boolean	When set to TRUE this qualifier indicates that only ONE instance of this class can exist at any one time. This class does not therefore require a KEY property to identify its instance. Only the value TRUE is allowed.

Property qualifiers define characteristics on a per-property basis. The WMI CIM Studio provides a drop-down list of default qualifiers applicable to the properties within CIM. If you wish to define your own qualifier at this point, you can enter a name and a type. Remember that this qualifier will have no meaning to WMI or, more importantly, to your client applications unless you write the code to interpret it.

Notice that between the Type and Value fields in the Property qualifiers box there are the letters "I," "C," and "O." These letters represent the flavors of the qualifier. The "I" determines whether or not this qualifier propagates to instances of the class. For example, it is possible to define a property that is read-only as a class but writeable as an instance. The "C" determines whether this qualifier propagates to a derived class. For example, if a property were assigned the Read qualifier but the "C" flag specified that the qualifier was not propagated to a derived class, then the property could re-

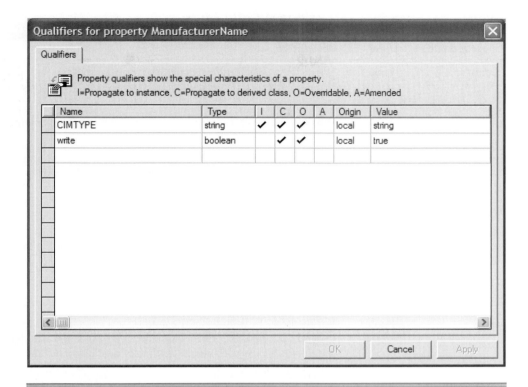

Figure 4.26 The Property qualifiers dialog window

vert to writeable in a child class. The "O" flag indicates whether the qualifier can be overridden in a derived class. Thus, if a property had the read-only flag set, then it could be overridden in the child class. Table 4.7 lists some of the property qualifiers.

■ CIM Studio Functions

? Help for a Class

The help for class icon in the upper right corner of the WMI CIM Studio's class viewer provides a textual description of the class currently selected in the class explorer. By clicking this icon, the WMI CIM Studio retrieves all text entered as part of the description qualifier for the class and all of its properties and methods. In developing the sample MOF file, we used the Description qualifier to describe the usage and purpose of both the class and its key property (see Figure 4.27).

Table 4.7 Property Qualifiers

Property qualifier	Type	Description
Dynamic	Boolean	When set to TRUE indicates that the property value is supplied by a dynamic provider. This qualifier must be used in conjunction with the Provider qualifier.
Implemented	Boolean	When set to TRUE indicates that a method has an implementation supplied by the provider.
Indexed	Boolean	Indicates that the property is indexed. Can be specified on properties of classes to request that those properties be indexed. Only the value TRUE is allowed.
Key	Boolean	When set to TRUE indicates that the property is a KEY property (i.e., used to identify an instance of the class).
Max	sint32	Indicates the maximum number of values a given multivalued reference can have. A value of NULL implies no limit.
Not_Null	Boolean	If set to TRUE indicates that this property must never be set to NULL
Read	Boolean	When set to TRUE indicates that the property is READ only.
Static	Boolean	For methods, indicates that the method is a class method that does not depend on any per-instance data. For properties, indicates that the property is a class variable rather than an instance variable.
Write	Boolean	When set to TRUE indicates that this property can be WRITTEN to.

Figure 4.27 MOF for storage class

```
[ abstract,
  description("This class defines the common characteristics Storage devices")
]
class MySchema_Storage
{
  [ read, key,
     description("The device ID must be unique for each storage class
        instance"): DisableOverride ToSubClass ]
  uint64 DeviceId;
  // Device Id is an unsigned integer 8 bytes
};
```

From the class explorer pane select the MySchema_Storage class. Now click the help for class icon in the class viewer. The display will show the screen in Figure 4.28.

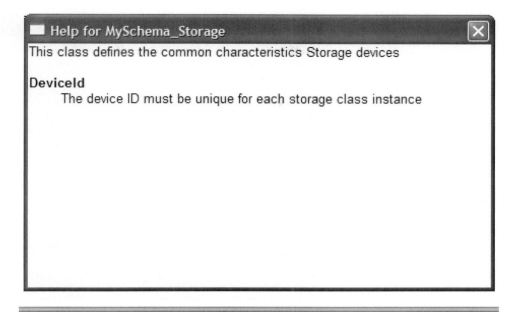

Figure 4.28 The Help dialog for class `MySchema_Storage`

Most of the classes relevant to WMI exist in the CIMV2 namespace. Now that we are familiar with the class explorer and class viewer, we can spend the remainder of the CIM repository tour in this namespace.

Browse for a Namespace

Click the browse for namespace button in the class explorer view. This brings up the Browse for Namespace dialog box that greeted you when you first started the WMI CIM Studio. Double-click the root namespace to reveal all available namespaces and select the CIMV2 namespace before clicking the OK button.

Search for a Class

The search facility within the WMI CIM Studio can be a real time saver when you search for a deeply embedded class in the repositories class hierarchy. Unfortunately, the early release contains no wildcard capability that would enable you to search for possible classes of interest based on a partial name. To search for a class, click the binocular icon in the class explorer pane. Type `Win32_ComputerSystem` (not case sensitive) in the Search for Class dialog box and click the OK button (as in Figure 4.29).

The `Win32_ComputerSystem` class represents a computer system operating in a Win32 environment. For more information, click the help for class button. After the

Search for Class

Enter full or partial class name. If not sure, enter text that may occur in class description or among class properties.

`Win32_ComputerSystem`   [Go!]

Search Options:
- ☑ Search class names
- ☐ Search class descriptions
- ☐ Search property names

Search results:

```
Win32_ComputerSystem
Win32_ComputerSystemEvent
Win32_ComputerSystemProcessor
Win32_ComputerSystemProduct
Win32_ComputerSystemWindowsProductActivationSetting
```

[OK]   [Cancel]

Figure 4.29   The Search for Class dialog

search is completed successfully, the WMI CIM Studio should display the screen in Figure 4.30.

The class explorer pane now highlights class `Win32_ComputerSystem,` and the class viewer pane displays a list of properties associated with that class. If you click the

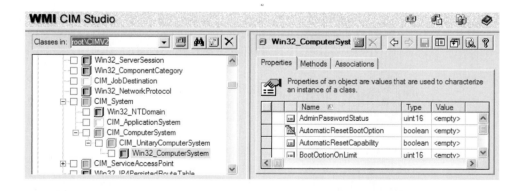

Figure 4.30   Search facility automatically goes to the class you select from the search results

Methods tab in the top of the right pane, all available methods on this object will display. In the case of `Win32_ComputerSystem`, the method `SetPowerState` is available. If necessary, you can call `SetPowerState` to set the power mode (that is, standby, power save, and so forth).

Then click the Associations tab to display a complete list of classes with which the `Win32_ComputerSystem` class is associated (Figure 4.31).

As you can see from Figure 4.31, the Associations tab in the class viewer presents a lot of information. Some of the information is available only by placing the mouse pointer over parts of the display such as the type of relationship (similar to using ToolTips). Double-clicking any of the classes referenced by an association (the classes on the right side of the display) will enumerate all of the associations for that class. Double-clicking the name of the association icon will display the references contained in that association. You can use the forward and back icons to move through these displays.

Next, we examine instances of class `Win32_ComputerSystem`.

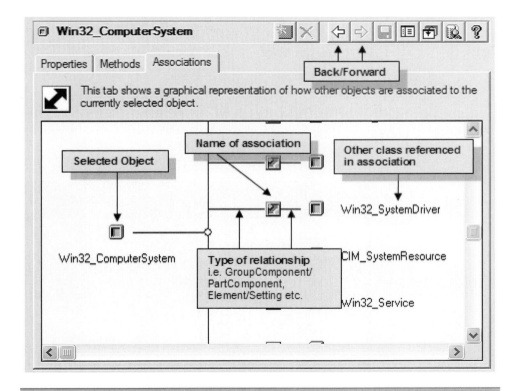

Figure 4.31   The Associations view

Instance Enumeration

Click the instance enumeration icon in the class viewer pane to display all of the instances of Class Win32_ComputerSystem. These instances represent the currently active Win32 computer systems available on the host machine. On a typical installation, there is always only one instance of this class. Select this instance and double-click it to display all of the properties and values for that instance.

Change the View (System Properties and Inherited Properties)

In viewing property information in the class hierarchy, sometimes it is beneficial to filter the view so that system properties or inherited properties are not displayed. This can simplify the number of properties listed on the screen at one time. To filter the on-screen view, click the view icon in the right hand pane and select the Property Filters... option. The display will show the screen in Figure 4.32.

Checking and unchecking these two options allows you to simplify the number of properties shown in the class viewer pane. For example, if you deselect both options, the class viewer pane displays only the local properties for this class.

WQL Queries Tool

The WQL queries tool enables you to create, save, and execute WQL queries in the current namespace. In the example in Figure 4.33, we entered a simple query to retrieve all of the current instances of the class Win32_logicalDisk. This query returns the list of currently available disks on the system that hosts the namespace.

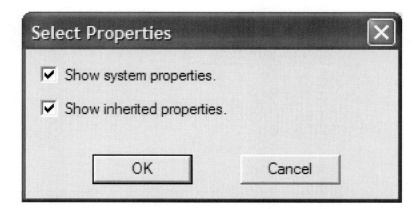

Figure 4.32 The Select Properties dialog

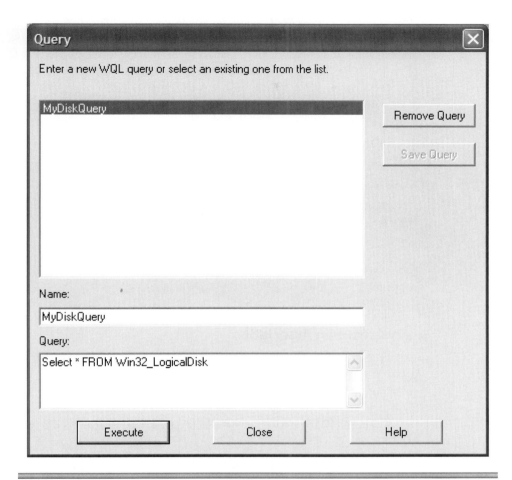

Figure 4.33 The Query dialog box allows you to create, save, and execute WQL queries

Add a Class

With the Win32_ComputerSystem class highlighted in the class explorer pane, click the add class icon in the same pane to display the dialog in Figure 4.34.

Type MySchema_ExtendedComputerSystem as the new class name and click OK. This adds the class ExtendedComputerSystem to the CIM repository. Because Win32_ComputerSystem is listed as the Parent in the edit box, the new class will derive from it. After successfully adding the class to the CIM repository, notice that it inherits a number of system and class properties from its parent classes.

The schema name plus the class name is referred to as the *fully qualified name*. Note that when you create a new class, its name must be unique within its

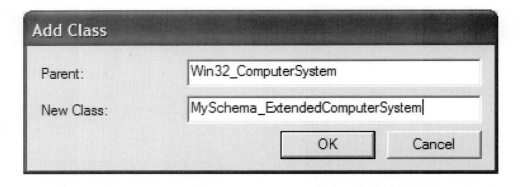

Figure 4.34 The Add Class dialog

schema. If it is not, WMI CIM Studio will report an error when adding it to the CIM repository.

Create an Association

Creating an association class within the CIM repository is not dissimilar to creating a class. The only difference is that the association object qualifier must be set to true and must contain two or more references. To do this, you execute the following steps:

1. Highlight the new class MySchema_ExtendedComputerSystem in the class explorer.
2. Right-click in the class viewer pane and select the Object Qualifiers option from the menu.
3. Left-click under the name field to create a new qualifier. Select Association from the drop-down list and make sure it is set to true (the default).
4. Click the OK button.
5. Use Browse for Namespace to select another namespace, then return to the CIMV2 namespace. The WMI CIM Studio now displays the class Extended ComputerSystem as an association.

Delete a Class or Association

Having created a new association with the fully qualified name, MySchema_Extended-ComputerSystem, we can use the delete icon to delete it. To delete a class within the CIM schema, highlight the target class in the class view with a left mouse click and click the delete icon. If the class contains child classes, WMI CIM Studio will warn you that it will delete them, too, before it carries out the task.

Delete a Property

WMI CIM Studio contains no icon for deleting properties. Instead, simply highlight the desired property and press the delete key. The WMI CIM Studio will verify that you wish to delete the property before it removes it from the class. Note that this function will fail if the class to which the property belongs has children.

Add an Instance

To add an instance of a class to the current namespace, in the right pane, click the icon that looks like the one in the heading of this paragraph. This creates a new blank instance of the currently selected class from the class view. With the mouse, you can select properties within the class and assign values to them. After you finish, click the save button to place the new instance in the CIM repository.

Delete an Instance

To delete an instance from the CIM repository, select the instance to be deleted by clicking the enumerate instances icon. Double-click the instance and then select the delete instance button.

Places of Interest within the CIM repository

First impressions of the CIM repository when viewing via the WMI CIM Studio can be quite overwhelming. This especially is true for the CIMV2 namespace, which contains hundreds of unfamiliar classes with seemingly no relationship to one another or even to elements within the managed environment. To feel more comfortable with the structure of the CIM repository, we start by exploring the classes that glue WMI together. In this exploration, we examine the system classes that represent the core elements of WMI— the security and provider architectures. A series of system classes that begin with the double underscore (__) prefix represent these characteristics.

The Provider Classes

The provider classes define the structure of the WMI provider framework. These classes are present in all namespaces that have properties, methods, or events supplied by WMI providers.

We use the root/CIMV2 namespace to examine the provider classes, so click the browse for namespace button in the class view to select the CIMV2 namespace.

1. Click the search for class button in the class view and type __Provider in the search field. (Remember that it has a leading double underscore.) The system class __Provider is an abstract class that contains the child system class __Win32Provider.

2. Double-left-click class __Provider to display __Win32Provider. The __Win32-Provider class defines a number of local properties that describe, among other things, the name of the Win32 provider (which is a key property) and the CLSID of the provider. (If you are familiar with COM, you know its relevance in calling CoCreateInstance.)

To look at an example instance of class __Win32Provider, click the enumerate instances button in the class viewer pane of WMI CIM Studio. Now double-click the *CIMWin32* instance. This is one of the standard instance and method providers installed with the WMI core. It provides instance information on a wide variety of managed objects within the Win32 environment as well as supporting methods on those objects. In examining its properties, we can see that key property name has the value *CIMWin32* and the CLSID has a value of {d63a5850-8f16-11cf-9f47-00aa00bf345c}.

To gain a better idea of the relationship between the instances of class __Win32-Provider and WMI's architecture, perform the following steps:

1. Use the copy function within WMI Developer Studio to store the CLSID of CIMWin32. (Select the value of CLSID with a single left mouse click and then select Copy from the drop-down menu with a right mouse click).

2. Go to Start/Run and type regedit.exe. This will bring up the system registry editor. Next, in the left pane, highlight HKEY_CLASSES_ROOT. Now select the Edit/Find menu option and paste in the complete CLSID, including its brackets. Click the Find next button to start the search, first making sure that only the Keys checkbox is checked. The registry editor should now bring up the registry key matching the CLSID of the CIMWin32. Beneath this key in the registry is the subkey **InProcServer32**, which contains the path of the dll that hosts CIMWin32. This shows that WMI uses the CLSID stored in the CIM repository to locate the file that hosts the Win32 provider.

At the same branch in the tree as system class __Provider is the system class __ ProviderRegistration. This class serves as an abstract base class for the registration of different types of providers. Table 4.8 summarizes these classes.

Table 4.8 Provider System Classes

Property qualifier	Description
Event provider	__EventProviderRegistration
Method provider	__MethodProviderRegistration
Property provider	__PropertyProviderRegistration
Class provider	__ClassProviderRegistration
Instance provider	__InstanceProviderRegistration
Permanent event consumer registration class	__EventConsumerProviderRegistration

Both the class and instance provider derive from the intermediate abstract class `__ ObjectProviderRegistration`.

The Namespace Classes

Namespaces in the CIM repository are arranged in a hierarchy. At the base of the hierarchy tree is the *root* namespace from which all other namespaces must branch. The hierarchy also allows namespaces to be ordered logically in relation to one another. For example, if *namespace A* were a specialization of *namespace B,* it would be logical to represent this by defining namespace A beneath namespace B in the hierarchy. Remember that we defined a namespace as a logically related set of classes that represents a managed environment. The scope of this relationship is entirely the responsibility of the designer of the namespace. Despite the fact that namespaces are arranged in a hierarchy with root at the bottom, namespaces do not inherit any characteristics, such as classes, from parent namespaces.

Held in the root\ namespace is a series of default system classes that are present in every namespace:

__NotifyStatus	A generic base class for provider-based errors.
__PARAMETERS	The __PARAMETERS system class defines methods and passes input and output arguments to a method provider.
__SystemClass	The __SystemClass system class is the abstract base class from which all system classes derive. Instances of this class cannot be created.

These classes are automatically created with every new namespace. Under the __SystemClass we find the __NAMESPACE class that contains the instances that represent all the namespaces held under the root namespace (for example, CIMV2).

We shall examine the instances of the __NAMESPACE class held in the root namespace, although every namespace will contain this class and, possibly, instances of it.

1. Use the browse for namespace icon to move to the root namespace.
2. Double-click the root class __SystemClass and highlight the __NAMESPACE class.
3. Click the instances button in the class viewer pane. This will display a series of instances, each of which represents a separate namespace within the CIM repository hosted on the machine. Note that the __NAMESPACE class contains a single, nonsystem property name. The name property defines the name of each namespace and is the key for that class. Your screen should now display a view similar to the one in Figure 4.35.

Create a Namespace

To add a new namespace to CIM at this point, click the create instance button in the class viewer pane of WMI CIM Studio. This creates a new instance of class __NAMESPACE. Now click and edit the value of the key property Name. Type a name for your new namespace and click the save button in the class viewer to commit this instance to the CIM repository.

Delete a Namespace

Delete a namespace by enumerating all instances of class __NAMESPACE, selecting the instance you wish to delete, and clicking the delete instance button. This removes the namespace from within the CIM repository *including* all of the classes and instances that it contains. Remember, however, that this action is not easily reversible. (You would have to restore a backup copy of the CIM repository!)

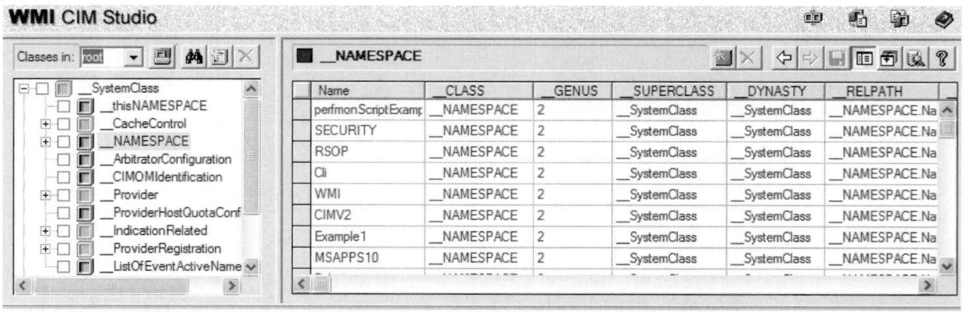

Figure 4.35 Enumerating the __NAMESPACE class

■ Tutorial: Creating a Namespace and Adding Classes, Properties, and an Association

Now that we have examined the concepts of namespaces, classes, properties, and instances, we can become more familiar with some of the tools of the trade. We already have used the WMI CIM Studio to browse the contents of the CIM repository. Now we shall use the CIM repository to create a namespace and experiment by defining some classes, properties, and associations within that namespace.

1. To start the tutorial, make sure that you are connected to the root namespace. Now select the __SystemClass and double-click to reveal its subclasses.

2. Select the __NAMESPACE class in the class explorer and click the create instance button in the class viewer. Left-click the value field of the name property and enter TestNameSpace. Click the save icon to place the instance in the CIM repository.

3. Next we shall populate the namespace with classes and associations, click the browse for namespace icon, and double-click the root namespace to reveal all the available namespaces. Notice that TestNameSpace is now among those listed. Select this namespace and click OK. Notice that the new namespace has already had a number of system classes added to it.

4. For the purpose of the tutorial, we shall add two simple classes and an association class that contains a reference to both of them. First, click the add class icon in the class explorer. Add two root classes, NewClassA and NewClassB, and leave the parent field in the Add Class dialog empty. This will ensure that the classes are created at the root of the namespace.

5. In each class add a string property, *name*. In each case, name a key property as shown in Figure 4.36. Left-click next to the property until you see a key icon appear or use the Property Qualifier dialog box to add the Key qualifier.

6. Click the add class icon again and create a new class, NewAssociation, taking care to leave the parent field blank. Right-click the class viewer and select the Object Qualifiers submenu to display the Object Qualifiers window for the class. Left-click the name field to add a new qualifier and select Association from the drop-down list. This is set to true by default. Click the OK button to return to the class viewer pane. You will not see the association icon next to NewAssociation until you leave the namespace and then return.

7. Now, we shall add two references to the association class, one for each of the new classes. Left-click an empty row in the class viewer (make sure the Properties tab is selected) and name the first reference antecedent. Now left-click the type field and select ref from the drop-down list to make this a reference. A

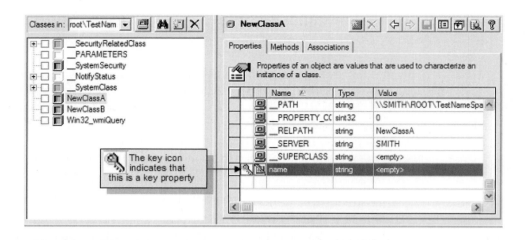

Figure 4.36 Adding a key property

dialog box asking for a reference type will then appear. Type `NewClassA` and click the OK button. Then make sure you click the save button. Repeat this process for the second reference, this time calling it `dependent` and assigning it a reference type of NewClassB. The naming convention for references in an association is purely arbitrary in WMI and the CIM repository, but client applications can use this information to understand the nature of an association and the role a specific managed object plays. The terms *antecedent* and *dependent* simply mean that NewClassB is somehow dependent upon New-ClassA but it is the responsibility of the WMI client to interpret this information fully.

■ The Wizards

The wizards form the final part of any schema modification or design work. They enable you to export the classes and instances that you have added to a namespace using the WMI CIM Studio.

The MOF Generator

The MOF generator can generate MOF files from classes selected within the WMI CIM Studio. This is useful especially when you have used WMI CMI Studio to define classes for your project and wish to export these classes into a MOF file. The MOF generator will also export instance information with the class information.

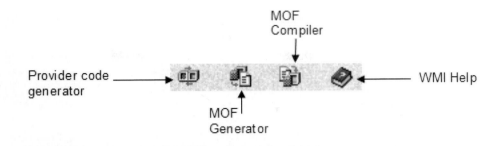

Figure 4.37   The wizards available in the WMI CIM Studio

The MOF Compiler

The MOF compiler can compile a user-selected MOF file into the CIM repository. You can then use the WMI CIM Studio to view the results of the compilation. Experiment by compiling the MOF file you developed in this chapter.

The Provider Code Generator

The provider code generator is a wizard that generates boilerplate code based upon the WMI provider architecture. It allows the selection of classes from the WMI CIM Studio and then generates generic code based upon those classes. In Chapter 12, we use the more flexible ATL-based approach for writing providers and so shall not discuss the provider code generator further.

■ Summary

This chapter was intended to introduce you to the fundamentals of the CIM repository from a practical standpoint. It offers merely an introduction to the CIM repository. Many concepts to understand and tools with which to become familiar remain. Take time to review the chapter, and to modify and expand upon the examples to gain more confidence with the technology. In Chapter 5, we use the wizards that are part of the WMI CIM Studio and develop a set of classes to represent a fictional software product within the CIM repository.

Ten Fast Facts: CIM Repository

1. The correct pronunciation for CIM (according to the folks at Microsoft) is "Sim."

2. The CIM repository is implementation dependent (that is, its implementation differs from platform to platform).

3. Extensions to the schema are expected (although not required) to be made at or below the extensibility layer.

4. The correct nomenclature for classes defined in the CIM is `schemaname_classname`. This also is known as the *full class path* of a given class.

5. A full namespace object path consists of the server and namespace and is formatted using either forward or backward slashes, as shown following:

   \\Server\Namespace

   or

   //Server/Namespace

6. WMI CIM Studio will not allow you to create instances of a new class until you have specified at least one key property. The only exception is if the class is defined as a singleton (using the singleton qualifier).

7. Multiple key properties within a single class are legal and are known as *compound keys.*

8. You cannot derive a new class from a WMI system class.

9. A full object path includes a machine name, a namespace path, and a full class path:

   \\CraigsMachine\Root\CimV2:Win32_Service

   This example points to class `Win32_Service` on machine CraigsMachine in the root\CIMV2 namespace.

10. The Common Information Model is constantly revised and updated. To reflect these changes in the structure of the CIM, the DMTF assigns version numbers to each new release. Minor alterations to classes or other elements within the schema that have little or no impact on existing applications result in updating of the minor version number (that is, after the period: V2.1, V2.2…V2.6, and so forth). Major alterations, such as those that could affect the functioning of existing applications (for example, the removal of a class from the CIM schema) will result in the major version number being incremented (that is, from V2.2 to V3.0, and so forth).

Chapter 5

Developing Class Schemas

In order to manage a product using WMI, we must provide a way of exposing its manageable features to the outside world. To achieve this, the DMTF designed the Common Information Model, which provides a context for the interaction between data consumer and data provider. All discussions so far have assumed that the information a managed object (i.e., a hardware device or software application) wishes to supply is already defined in the CIM schema or Win32 extended schema by existing classes or association. What happens, however, if there are no classes in the CIM schema or Win32 extended schema that represent your product?

In such a case, you are required to design and implement your own classes, methods, and associations. This process is referred to as *schema design* and is the focus of this chapter.

A schema is an abstraction of something that exists in the real world. It is defined by a set of classes/associations that represent the manageable aspects of managed object(s). Each of the classes in a schema contains properties and methods. As you will recall, properties represent the manageable characteristics of a managed object, and methods allow actions to be performed on that managed object. Associations represent the relationships that exist between managed objects.

Both the DMTF and Microsoft provide a great deal of information on the theoretical foundation of schema design; however, the goal of this chapter is to introduce these concepts from a practical standpoint. This chapter does not aim to replace the DMTF and Microsoft documentation but rather to provide an ordered approach to schema design within their constraints. We thoroughly recommend that you keep the DMTF and Microsoft material handy for reference. There is also a wealth of good background material about the CIM to be found on the DMTF website at http://www.dmtf. org (the CIM specification documents are a good place to begin). Both Microsoft and the DMTF provide in-depth coverage on the theory of schema design in their tutorials:

- Search for the WMI tutorial on the MSDN Web site at http://msdn.microsoft.com/
- Search for the CIM tutorial on the DMTF Web site at http://www.dmtf.org/ education/cimtutorial.php

Chapter 5 is for all software engineers who are about to embark upon their first schema design. The main purpose of the chapter is to provide the schema developer with a road map of the steps for schema design using practical examples. The various techniques and structure employed here are by no means definitive (as the proverb goes, "There's more than one way to skin a rabbit") but can provide a starting point from which to base your own approach.

Schema design is a particularly complex process that involves many small steps for successful completion. A detailed discussion easily could fill the remaining chapters of the book; therefore, we do not list every rule and concept explicitly. Instead, the chapter provides an acceptable level of detail in conjunction with other documentation such as that provided by the DMTF and Microsoft.

The example case study is an e-mail package with server and client components. The present chapter and Chapter 6 forward the design, implementation, and testing of a schema and providers for this imaginary product.

■ Schema Design and System Manageability

The foundation of any well-managed product in WBEM and WMI is a well-defined schema that represents the present management needs of that product and is flexible enough to accommodate known enhancements. Defining a schema requires of the designer a mixture of knowledge and experience of the product under scrutiny and the structure, rules, and constraints of the CIM. Although many rules and best practices constrain schema design, often more than one solution to a particular problem becomes clear. As is the case with object-oriented software design, practice and experience are often the only shortcuts to guide you in the direction of the more robust solution.

The present chapter and Chapter 6 present the basic steps required for successful schema design and provide a framework within which to do it. Figure 5.1 offers an overview of the steps in instrumenting a product in WMI.5. We divided this task into two chapters because of the inherent complexity of schema design. Rather than list abstract rules and techniques, we use an imaginary software product to teach by example, providing a real-world context for schema design. In any case study, no matter how general its aims, the example may not demonstrate some specific issues or prob-

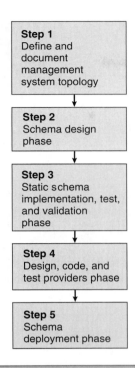

Figure 5.1 WMI product instrumentation life cycle overview

lems. In such instances, we provide additional rules in highlighted boxes to help answer questions that may arise when you approach your own schema design.

In these chapters, we define managed objects from schema design through schema deployment. We practice adding classes, properties, methods, and associations to the CIM repository. Later, in Chapter 12, we examine in detail how to write providers to supply information for these constructs. The next section contains a brief description of a simple case scenario, with which we illustrate the steps of schema design in CIM.

■ Case Study: Client/Server E-mail Package

In the case study, we assume the role of an independent software vendor (ISV) who wishes to instrument a product under development in WMI for the Windows platform. The imaginary product is a basic client-server email system whose target market is small businesses. The software will allow users to send and receive e-mail internally (that is, on machines connected to the same network as the e-mail server or on neighboring visible networks), with or without file attachments. It is basic because it does not communicate

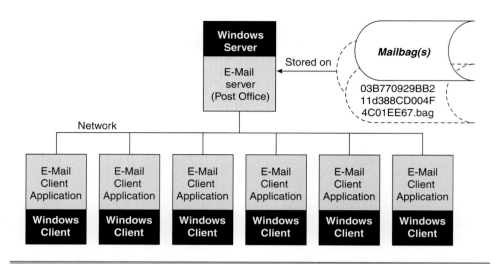

Figure 5.2   Client Server e-mail topology

with other e-mail post offices and does not make provision for mobile users to dial in remotely over the PSTN (Public Switched Telephone Network). The task is to instrument
the server component of the e-mail system—the post office—with WMI. The Post Office
component will reside on a Windows network server and run as a Windows service.

The Post Office should conform to the following requirements:

- The Post Office must verify users when they attempt to log in to the e-mail system. The verification must take the form of a username and a password.

- The Post Office should enable valid users to send and receive mail with or
without attachments between accounts held on the host Post Office.

- The Post Office should return undelivered mail to the sender if it cannot reach
its destination (that is, if the destination address does not exist).

- The Post Office should be manageable under WMI.

Figure 5.2 illustrates the topology of our fictitious e-mail product and shows that
the mailbags associated with each user's e-mail account are centrally located on the
E-Mail Server.

Basic Functionality

Upon creating a user account, the Post Office creates a *mailbag* that resides on a hard
disk partition on the server. A mailbag is a simple sequential file that stores incoming
mail in the order in which it arrives, along with a header of a set length that contains
flags that specify certain characteristics of the e-mail message. Initially, sent e-mail re-

sides in a special directory on the Post Office machine until the user successfully logs into the e-mail client. After the user logs in, the client application requests all new mail from the Post Office. The server application moves all pending mail from one directory and appends it to the destination user's mailbag. Each mailbag has a unique GUID value with the suffix **.bag** to identify its owner. The Post Office server maintains a list of mappings between the GUID and username.

System Requirements for Post Office E-mail

The package has the following software and hardware requirements in order to operate:

- Windows server
- 100 Gigabyte disk space partition for mailbags
- Network card (100mbits or 10mbits Ethernet or token ring)
- 512Mb RAM

Before we can develop the e-mail client/server case study, we must examine some fundamental concepts of schema design. They include using the UML to model a schema and the relevance of the application life cycle on its development.

■ The Unified Modeling Language

In schema design, UML is a tool to create a visual template of schemas to simplify the overall development process. We introduce UML static structure diagrams, first, to help you understand the diagrams supplied by the DMTF and Microsoft, and second, so that you may document your own schema design efficiently and consistently. The DMTF and Microsoft use the UML static structure diagrams (which are about one-tenth of the total set of diagrams available under the UML umbrella) to describe the CIM schema and Win32 extended schema.

The Object Management Group (http://www.omg.org) adopted the UML as a standard in 1997. The UML is language independent and provides notation for inheritance, classes, properties, and methods. We use it in schema design to convey the architecture of a schema and the relationships between the elements that make up the schema. The DMTF and Microsoft, respectively, adopted it as the preferred way to portray their CIM and Win32 extended schema.

Two popular software packages, Rational Rose (http://www.rational.com) and Microsoft Visio (http://www.microsoft.com), allow you to model using the UML rules. With these packages, you can represent the classes in your schema design and provide a permanent record of your schema in UML notation. Another option is to design your schema with a word processing package, such as Microsoft Word, that has basic drawing functionality.

Further Reading in UML

For more detail about UML than this chapter provides, we recommend that you invest in a book dedicated to the subject. Among the numerous good books available that describe UML, two of the best are *Practical Object-Oriented Design with UML,* by Mark Priestley (McGraw-Hill 2000) and *The Unified Modeling Language User Guide* by Grady Booch, James Rumbaugh, and Ivar Jacobson (Addison Wesley Longman 1998), because of their practical, real-world approach to describing UML. Booch, Rumbaugh, and Jacobson, the creators of UML, are chief scientists at Rational Software Corporation. Full publication information is available in our bibliography.

▪ Learning the CIM Schema and Win32 Extended Schemas

The CIM schema and Win32 schema define hundreds of classes. To learn these classes individually would take a great deal of time and not be strictly necessary. The best approach is to familiarize yourself with the basic models defined as part of the common model (applications, services, networks, devices, and physical) and then learn the classes relevant to your product within those models. A basic idea of these models and their purpose should allow you to move through the CIM efficiently. The two steps that follow describe a practical method of achieving this background.

Step 1: Study the Core Model and Common Model UML diagrams provided by the DMTF

For all products, regardless of operating system, that wish to be represented in the CIM, an excellent starting point is to study the CIM schema. These diagrams visually represent the common model (networks, applications, devices, physical, and services) and core model.[1]

Step 2: Study the extended schema provided by your operating system vendor

After you have studied the CIM schema, then study the extended schema UML diagrams provided by the vendor of your target operating system. In our case, this is Microsoft and its Win32 extended schema. Use the Help feature of the WMI CIM Studio while you move through the various namespaces. Microsoft provides WMI CIM Studio as part of the WMI SDK. This approach provides both a visual interpretation of the class hierarchy, inherited properties, and associations as well

---

1. They can be downloaded from the DMTF Web site in Microsoft Visio .vsd format at the following URL: http://www.dmtf.org/standards/. If you do not have Microsoft Visio installed on your computer, you can download the free Web component viewer from http://www.microsoft. com/office/000/viewers.asp

as a description of the purpose of each class. Remember, however that the CIMV2 namespace contains only those classes pertinent to the management of the Windows operating system, which is itself merely a subset of the classes defined by the CIM schema. To obtain a complete picture of the classes available, you must work with the UML diagrams provided by the DMTF on their Web site as well as the material provided by Microsoft (assuming your product runs on the Windows operating system). Use the Help button to display the description of classes and their properties as you view their contents in the class viewer (right pane).

Psychological Requirements

An important mental requirement for anyone wishing to embark upon schema design is a large amount of patience.

Schema designers must learn the many rules associated with schema design and become moderately familiar with the structure and purpose of the CIM schema and extended schemas. This will help you to determine not only which classes and associations are or are not relevant to the design of your product, but also will provide inspiration in designing your own classes and associations. Without doing so, you will not know where to position your own schema (be it in the CIM schema, in the Win32 extended schema, or in a namespace on its own). You should also try to keep up to date with any changes to these schemas by frequenting the Microsoft and DMTF Web sites at the URLs given above.

Schema design is a complex and methodical process and is by no means trivial in relation to the overall instrumentation of the project (which is why Chapters 5 and 6 are dedicated to it). It is vital to the successful instrumentation of your product that your schema adequately defines the manageable aspects of your product in accordance with the rest of the CIM and future developments of your product. So put the coffee on—it is going to be a long night!

Schema Design Timescales

Allocating a timescale for your first attempt at schema design is a tricky job. The amount of time needed to design a schema is very much dependant on the nature of the product being instrumented and the experience of the schema designers. The greater the management bias of the product (that is, the more managing it requires), the more elements the repository must contain, and the longer the schema design process. With experience, however, you will find future releases of your product should have a lower schema design overhead because you can reuse elements of your initial design. The speed at which you progress through the steps of schema design will also increase with repetition and as your knowledge of schema design increases. A good approach is often to try to find an existing schema that looks like what you want and extend it. As Patrick Thompson, Microsoft's schema guru, says, "If you find yourself inventing things from scratch then chances are you haven't understood the existing class structure and are busily wandering off into a vast and trackless desert in which you will probably perish from exposure to the elements!" It is important to appreciate that more or less every possibility is covered at some level of abstraction within the CIM schemas. If it is not at least a subclass of `CIM_ManagedSystemElement` then why are you modeling it?

Software Application Life Cycle

When designing your schema, it is good practice to take into account in which of the four application life cycle states the information in your schema will be available. Figure 5.3 represents a simplified version of the CIM specific software application life cycle, from left to right, in which each box in bold represents one of the *states* available to an application (Deployable, Installable, Executable, Executing). The lines between states represent the available transitions from state to state.

> **Note:** The Executable state displays two similar transitions, *uninstall* and *remove*. The *remove* transition means the application will not be advertised as installable on the system any more. The capability of an application to advertise itself is a function provided by the Windows Installer (see next page).

In the context of the Post Office example, imagine a defined property, `UsersLogged-On`, that represents the number of users currently logged onto our e-mail system. In the context of the application life cycle, this property would contain a value only when the Post Office application was in the *Executing* state. When the e-mail Post Office was not in the Executing state, such information would not be available to a management consumer.

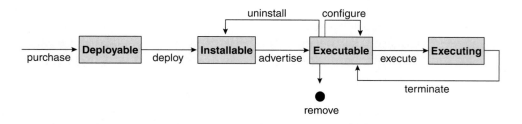

Figure 5.3 The software application life cycle

■ The Windows Installer and WMI

The Windows Installer handles installation and uninstallation of a product as part of the Windows operating system, Microsoft Installer provider, and the Microsoft Installer classes, associations, and so forth (part of the Win32 schema), instrument it in WMI. It maintains a record of all the applications stored on the client machine in the Windows Installer database file. The Windows Installer provider (`%SystemRoot%\system32\wbem\MSIProv.dll`) supplies this information directly from the Windows Installer database. The database stores a variety of information such as the directories and files that belong to the application as well as the registry settings for it. It also stores the features of the product and the elements that make up those features. Despite being introduced with Windows 2000, it is also available as a service pack for the Windows NT4.0 platform and Windows 9x. The Windows 2000 logo certification requirements state that all certified software must install using a Windows Installer-based package (the Windows XP logo requirements are more relaxed and do not specify this requirement). For more information on the Windows Installer, see the Microsoft MSDN Web site under the platform SDK.

The Windows Installer classes expose such information as the version of the components of your product as well as the directory structure for your product, many of which derive from the CIM schema's application model. They also enable methods such as installation, re-installation, and so forth to be carried out. Therefore, when designing your schema, providing your application installs using the Windows installer, you do not have to worry about these aspects.

You can see an example of the Windows Installer in action in the latest version of Microsoft Office. If you select the install on first use option, then the Windows Installer will automatically locate and install any features that are not present (for example, the thesaurus in Word) by first checking the installation state. Features installed on first use are said to be *advertised* (see application life cycle). After a feature is installed, it is available immediately for use without restarting the application or the operating system. Among the other notable changes is that files developed with the Windows Installer install themselves using files with an *.msi suffix instead of the usual setup.exe file.

The CIMV2 namespace contains the classes defined as part of the MSI classes that represent the Windows Installer provider. These classes are derived from the CIM schema's application model as well as the Win32 extended schema. Such classes include `Win32_IniFileSpecification`, which contains the .ini file information that an application needs to set up an .ini file, and `Win32_DirectorySpecification`, which represents the directory layout for a product.[2]

---

2. If you wish to study the Windows Installer classes in more detail, you can find the MOF file under the Windows system directory in `%SystemRoot%\system32\wbem\MSI.MOF`.

Note that existing applications not written with the Windows Installer will not have their information stored in this database.

You can perform any function through WMI using the Windows Installer provider that you can perform with the Windows Installer. For example, you can remotely or locally perform a product reinstallation, upgrade, or uninstallation on any WMI-enabled client machine with WMI.

The Role of WMI with Standard Software Applications and Management Software Applications

Software can be either management-based or not management-based. At this point, it should be clear that WMI is designed for applications from both realms. One of the objectives of WMI is to drive down the Total Cost of Ownership (TCO) for products from both realms through unifying the management architecture. This includes software applications at any state in the software application life cycle.

Our theoretical example program, although not strictly a management product, still will expose management information via WMI to improve its manageability. It is also possible to develop a management application by creating an MMC snap-in. For more details, refer to Chapter 9.

■ Schema Design by Teams vs. by Single Developers

The nature of the product also dictates whether a single person or a team can design the schema. Whether you are part of a team or on your own, be aware of the following potential hazards:

- The CIM repository often offers more than one way to represent a product. Always approach alternative designs with an open mind when they are proffered in team meetings. When you look for the better solution, consider future enhancements to the product that may affect the schema and needs of your customers.

- Too much arguing over minute detail or too much compromise can cause lengthy delays in schema design. Be prepared to take a stand if the situation warrants it! Work in small teams when possible and take design decisions as far as possible within the team before submitting the design to a wider audience.

When Should I Commit My Design to UML?

UML is a good tool to capture your schema design from the very start of development. As your work progresses, so can the level of detail in your diagrams. Schema designers typically use a mixture of UML and MOF files to formalize their ideas.

Can I Design a Schema without UML?

You can design and document a schema without UML but it probably is not advisable. An alternative is to use the WMI CIM Studio to define new classes, properties, and so forth. The advantage of this approach is that it provides a graphical front end for your work that can aid in interpretation. This is not the ideal approach if your schema grows in size or complexity, because the visual breadth and depth of UML is very difficult to recreate. Similarly, if you document your design using flat documents to specify classes and their relationships and so forth, they could quickly become unwieldy and difficult to interpret compared to UML diagrams. UML diagrams also are a permanent visual record for other developers in the team and for developers who may need to continue your work. UML diagrams can represent a very clear and concise portrayal of the intricate relationships between elements in the schema to developers who are familiar with their syntax.

> **Note:** Membership in the DMTF entitles you to a MofEditor tool that allows a MOF to be made into a Visio diagram.

The Unified Modeling Language in Schema Design

The UML is a collection of techniques from its creators, Grady Booch, Ivar Jacobsen, and Jim Rumbaugh (collectively known as "the three amigos"), that can aid in object-oriented analysis and design. Schema design and documentation of the various steps commonly use two UML techniques:

- Use Cases, with which we document the system requirements for schema.
- Object models, which we use in schema design to focus upon class structure, inheritance, and associations, including the relationships between classes in the schema. These models also commonly are called *static structure diagrams*.

> **Note:** UML notation can represent most of the main constructs in a schema (including classes, properties, methods, associations, and aggregate associations) with several exceptions: UML notation does not represent *qualifiers, namespaces, paths,* and *keys.*

A Brief Introduction to UML Object Modeling

Object modeling represents the class structure, inheritance, and associations in schemas. The basic notation associated with object modeling is surprisingly simple. Each class in a UML diagram is represented by a rectangle, which, depending on the level of detail required, can be compartmentalized further (Figure 5.4).

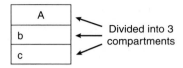

Figure 5.4   Class notation in UML

> **Note:** A fourth compartment to represent events generated by the class may be added.

In the example, the class box is in *compartments.* By default the top compartment, "A" holds the class name (capital letter, center-aligned bold font), the next compartment "b" contains the properties (lowercase, left-aligned), and the final compartment "c" holds the methods or operations (lowercase, left-aligned) for the class (Figure 5.5).

Figure 5.5   Default UML compartment names

Although this format is sufficient for schema design in CIM, the UML neither restricts the number of compartments in a class box nor insists that each compartment have these meanings. UML also is flexible in its level of detail: When drawing classes, for example, you can suppress either the property or the method compartments if they are not required. An example class from our Post Office schema using UML notation would appear as in Figure 5.6.

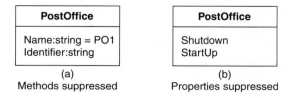

Figure 5.6   Class notation with properties and methods suppressed

In the example in Figure 5.7, we define a single class called PostOffice with two properties (`Name` and `Identifier`) and two methods (`Shutdown` and `StartUp`). Notice that we have also declared the *type* of these properties (that is string) and a default value for `Name`. It would also be possible to specify the signature for the methods `Shutdown` and `StartUp` if required.

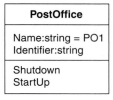

Figure 5.7 Class notation with properties, types, default values, and methods shown

In large or complex UML diagrams such as those provided by the DMTF and Microsoft, the property and method compartments often are suppressed to simplify the notation and improve readability. In addition, it is sometimes not practical to create a diagram that includes this volume of information and still will fit on a single page; that is, readability is as important as the level of detail.

Inheritance Notation

In the example in Figure 5.8, the directional arrow denotes inheritance. DialinAccount and LAN_Account are both subclasses of `EmailAccount`. As subclasses, they can inherit any properties, methods, or associations that belong to class `Email_account` or to its superclasses.

> **Note:** CIM does not support multiple inheritance. The presence of an abstract class implies that a subclass must be present.

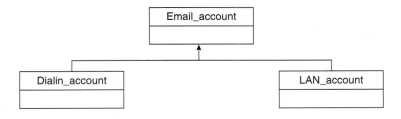

Figure 5.8 Inheritance in UML

Association Notation

Between the two classes, `Mailbag` and `PostOffice`, in the example in Figure 5.9, a connecting line, `Contains`, represents an association class.

Figure 5.9 Associations in UML

The notation tells us that this association contains references to `Mailbag` and `PostOffice`. The asterisk adjacent to `Mailbag` and the numeral 1 adjacent to `PostOffice` tell us that multiple instances of class `Mailbag` can be associated with a single reference to class `PostOffice`. The symbols describe the *cardinality* of the relationship. Table 5.1 lists other options in the notation for cardinality.

It is possible, also, to indicate the role that each class in an association plays. For example, in Figure 5.10, class `Father` is associated with class `Son` in the association class `Related`. In addition to this, class `Father` assumes the role of parent in the association and class `Son` assumes that of the child.

Figure 5.10 Associations in UML

Table 5.1 Relationship Cardinality

Notation	Cardinality
*	Specifies a many-valued optional reference.
1	Specifies a required, single-valued reference.
0…1	Specifies an single-valued optional reference.
0.*n*	Specifies an optional many-valued reference where *n* is the upper limit.
1.*n*	Specifies a required many-valued reference.

Aggregate Associations

An aggregation is a type of association: A diamond symbol at one end of the association indicates that it is an aggregation. The term implies that an aggregation of other entities makes up a given class (*the parent*). We could interpret the diagram in Figure 5.11 in plain English to mean "a Mailbag is made up of many messages" or "many messages are part of a mailbag."

Figure 5.11   Aggregate associations in UML

In logical terms, this means that the CIM repository would host multiple instances of association BelongsTo with each parent object possibly associated with multiple child objects.

Notice in Figure 5.12 that each of the connecting lines between the Mailbag and the Message instances represents a separate instance of the aggregation in the CIM repository.

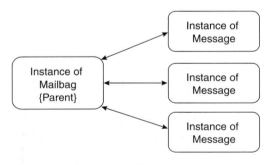

Figure 5.12   Instance association of aggregate relationship

To specify in the MOF language that an association is also an aggregate (Figure 5.13), we use the Aggregation and Aggregate qualifiers as well as the Association qualifier. The Aggregation qualifier specifies that the association is an aggregate and the Reference qualifier, aggregate, identifies the parent reference. For example, the CIM association class CIM_Component specifies that a CIM_ManagedSystemElement (CIM_GroupComponent) can be made up of other CIM_ManagedSystemElements (CIM_PartComponent).

Figure 5.13 Aggregate relationship association class

```
[aggregation, association]
Class PO_BelongsTo
{
  [key, aggregate] PO_Mailbag REF Bag;
  PO_Message REF Letter;
}
```

■ Interpreting the Common Model in UML

Having examined the basic notation for UML object models, let us examine a real-world example, the Common Model from the CIM schema (Figure 5.14). As mentioned earlier, both the DMTF and Microsoft supply their schema diagrams in UML format. It is perfectly acceptable to omit schema names for brevity when you discuss long class names, although in this book we always use the full schema and class name for clarity. From the diagram, we can tell the following about class CIM_ManagedSystemElement:

- The property and method compartments are suppressed for all classes except CIM_ManagedSystemElement.

- The cardinality of associations and the role names for the endpoints have been suppressed.

- CIM_ManagedSystemElement contains five properties: Caption, Description, InstallDate, Name, and Status. The type of each property follows the colon.

- A CIM_ManagedSystemElement can comprise many other CIM_ManagedSystem-Elements. The association class, CIM_Component, whose beginning and endpoint are both on CIM_ManagedSystemElement, illustrates this. Notice the use of the diamond aggregate symbol to represent the aggregation. It is important to understand that the aggregate symbol refers to multiple instances of class CIM_ManagedSystemElement and not necessarily to a single instance (that is, each instance is related to itself). A line that represents an association or aggregate and is attached to itself generally refers to different instances of the same class. The abstract association class CIM_Component is a generic association that establishes part of relationships between managed system elements. For example, the association Win32_SystemProcesses is a child of CIM_Component and represents the fact that processes are part of a computer system.

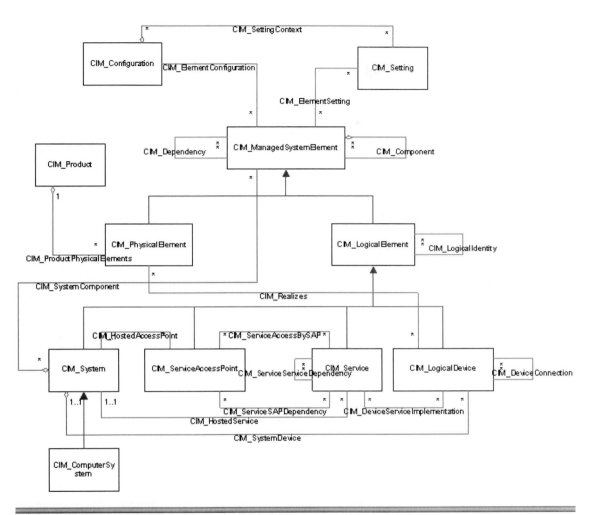

Figure 5.14   The Common Model from the CIM schema

Source: DMTF documentation

- Each CIM_ManagedSystemElement may be dependent on another
  CIM_ManagedSystemElement (see association class CIM_Dependency)
- Each CIM_ManagedSystemElement may be associated with a Setting class (see
  association class CIM_ElementSetting).
- Each CIM_ManagedSystemElement can have a Configuration associated with it
  (see association class CIM_ElementConfiguration).

- `CIM_ManagedSystemElement` has two immediate subclasses, `PhysicalElement` and `LogicalElement`.

- Each `CIM_ManagedSystemElement` may be *part of* a *System*.

Note: The Microsoft and DMTF UML notation uses nonstandard color coding (not seen here because we are in black and white!) to illustrate the differences between connecting lines in their object models. The meanings are as follows:

- Red represents associations
- Blue represents inheritance
- Green represents aggregation

■ The Schema Design Road Map

The schema design road map in Figure 5.15 represents the series of steps in designing a schema. Performing all of the steps depends most on factors such as whether you define your schema from scratch or update an existing schema. The road map shows the inputs each step requires and the outputs each one produces.

Basic Rules for Schema Design

Deciding upon the desired level of detail for the model of the managed object is a subtle challenge that faces any schema designer. We refer to both the nature and the detail of the information you provide in your schema. It is sometimes simpler to understand this concept by examining it from the point of view of the management data consumer than from that of the provider.

First, try to comprehend who, ultimately, will need to interpret the information your schema supplies when your product is finished and shipped. As a simple rule of thumb, do not supply information as part of your schema if you cannot envisage a management consumer requesting it under any circumstances. Schema designers must be very confident that they can imagine all of the possible scenarios in which the product will be managed. If a management data consumer never needs to interpret some (or all) of the information you supply, then that information literally is useless and has no relevance in the schema.

Second, always consider the functionality of a managed object at its most basic level. Consider objects that have multiple roles within a managed system, such as a primary display adapter that is also a three-dimensional accelerator card and MPEG capture board. It would not be in keeping with the ethos of object-oriented design (or

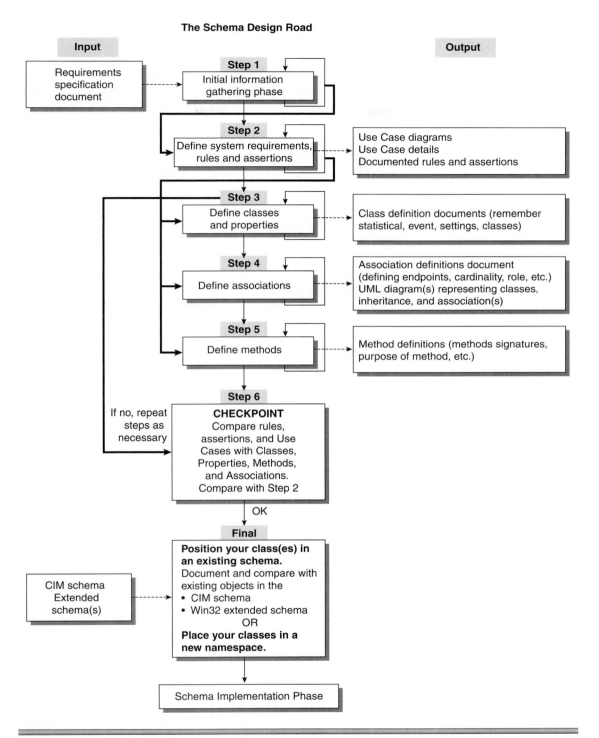

Figure 5.15 The Schema Design Road Map

the CIM) to represent all of these characteristics within a single class. Instead, try to break the object into its constituent roles and use whatever constructs may be necessary to represent each of these roles within the system.

Telephone Operator Example

To illustrate the point, imagine the following telephone operator scenario in which you, the customer (representing a management data consumer), call the telephone operator (representing WMI).

You ask the telephone operator for a specific company's number. The telephone operator returns the details of every employee working for that company before returning the relevant number.

> **Rule 1: Providing too much information in a schema can reduce usability nearly as much as providing too little.**
>
> Although some information may logically belong to a schema, this does not mean that you automatically should include it. Lean is mean!

Determined to get better service, you dial again, but before responding to your query the operator sits on the floor and does 50 sit-ups, followed by 50 push-ups. Breathlessly, the operator returns the telephone number.

> **Rule 2: Avoid expensive computations or use the Expensive and Lazy qualifiers to indicate their presence in a schema when possible.**
>
> Expensive computations are classes, properties, or methods that require excessive CPU time or system resources to compute. The amount of CPU time or system resource is the *cost*. An expensive item, in itself, can render a schema impractical or unreliable to use and, worse still, affect other users of the host CIM repository. Redundancy is permissible in situations where it avoids such overheads.
>
> WMI provides a mechanism for filtering expensive data. If your properties, references, classes, associations, and methods provide such data, you can flag them with the Expensive qualifier. You can use the Lazy qualifier to flag properties individually. Doing so allows management data consumers to specify in a request whether they wish to avoid retrieving any flagged elements. WMI ignores properties marked with this qualifier by default in a WQL query. If classes or properties require a large amount of storage space, they can set the Large qualifier to TRUE.

Several months later, with all previous bad experiences behind you, you call again. This time, the system is down and the telephone operator must plough through 50 volumes of telephone directories, which may take in excess of an hour to complete.

Rule 3: Consider the effect of resource-hungry schema designs.

For example, consider the theoretical maximum number of instances for each class in your schema. If a class generates 10,000 instances, it might not be practical to enumerate all of them at once or to hold that much information in memory. Consider the Post Office example: holding an instance for every message sent in the system (detailing its size, destination, number of attachments, and so forth) could result in the generation of thousands of instances in a relatively short time. This would affect systems resources and performance, especially if a provider were supplying the information dynamically across a low bandwidth connection.

■ WMI Topology Design

A multitude of ways exist to instrument a product in WMI, depending upon the needs of the product and the target environment on which it will run. At this early stage in schema design, consider the management topology of your product. We do this now because decisions made about the topology could ultimately affect the way in which we design the schema. In our fictitious project, the workload is distributed between two teams of developers, one that will design and code the client application and one that will design and code the server application. One of the most powerful aspects of WMI is its architectural flexibility. Normally, many different possible arrangements for a product exist. Here are only two examples of implementations of WMI to instrument our fictitious e-mail package. Notice the different ways in which the management data consumers, WMI, and providers interact.

First Approach

In the first arrangement (Figure 5.16), all of the management schema information is stored together in a single CIM repository located on the Post Office. Therefore, all interactions between WMI and WMI management data consumers are via a single WMI client hosted by the Post Office. The E-mail schema contains classes and associations for the e-mail client as well as the Post Office. When dynamic data is required from the clients, we use providers hosted on the client machines to communicate across the network using the WMI API to the Post Office machine as illustrated in the figure.

All interaction between a management data consumer and WMI is through a single point, the machine that hosts the Post Office. Table 5.2 lists the pros and cons of this approach.

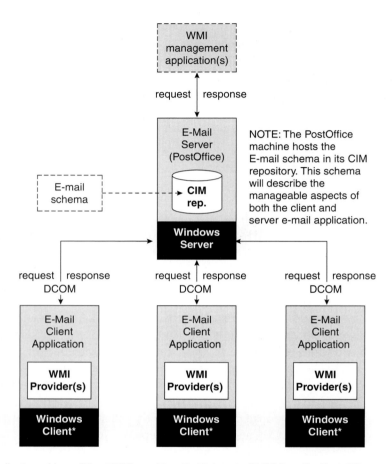

NOTE: The PostOffice machine hosts the E-mail schema in its CIM repository. This schema will describe the manageable aspects of both the client and server e-mail application.

*Each client machine will host WMI providers that interact with WMI on the Post Office machine.

Figure 5.16 A centralized approach to instrumenting the E-mail package

Second Approach

In the decentralized approach (Figure 5.17), the Post Office (server) supplies management information in the CIM repository on its machine. Clients supply management information on their own machines.

Management data consumers must interact with each node in the e-mail architecture to elicit management information. Table 5.3 lists the pros and cons of this approach.

Both approaches are feasible using WMI; however, the decentralized approach has several key advantages over its alternative. From a development viewpoint, the decentralized approach allows schema design in two parts: a Client schema for the client-side application and the Post Office schema for the server side. This means that the

Table 5.2 Pros and Cons of the First Approach

Pros	Cons
Single access point for all management information about the entire e-mail system	This means that there is a single point of failure. If the Post Office machine suffered a network card failure, then no management requests would be channelled to or from client machines.
	Note: If the Post Office service failed this would *not* prevent interaction between WMI and the client machines, because WMI operates as an independent service.
Easy-to-update future releases of the schema as it will be hosted upon a single machine	Potential network latency time when performing nonlocal requests could affect the usability of schema.
	Schema design must be coordinated between the teams—a potential complication when designing by committee.
	Management information (for example, surfacing events) to a single machine could come simultaneously from up to 100 client nodes. This potentially could overload the machine, impeding the performance of the Post Office.
	When fielding management requests on behalf of both the clients and/or server, places an unknown CPU overhead on the Post Office. This is unpredictable and potentially difficult to test.

developers writing the applications can design the schema, therefore separating the management needs of the Post Office from those of the e-mail client applications.

> **Note:** A third approach exists that is a hybrid of the two described. You could use events to forward management information to a central server that then maintains information reflecting the current state of the whole environment. The advantages of this approach are that it can supply the event stream to more than one server, and can recover gracefully after a failure.

This chapter focuses on the design and implementation of the Post Office Schema using the decentralized approach, under which a WMI management information consumer would have to attach to the Post Office machine to retrieve Post Office specific information for the whole system and to each individual e-mail client to retrieve client-specific information. This does not preclude the use of the hybrid approach, which, theoretically, we could add to our design later.

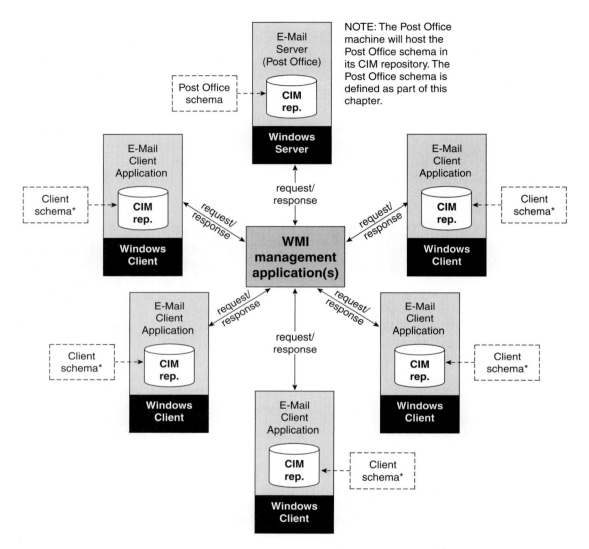

*Each client machine will host the client application schema in its CIM repository. This schema will define the manageable aspects of the e-mail client software. This schema is not defined as part of our example.

Figure 5.17 A decentralized approach to instrumenting the e-mail package in WMI

Table 5.3 Pros and Cons of the Second Approach

Pros	Cons
Schema design can be assigned to the individual teams working on client and server.	Schema updates must take place on each separate machine.
No single point of failure.	Management data consumers must access each client machine individually to retrieve information.
Less potential for system overload.	
Reduced network latency problem (information will travel at most only one hop).	

> **Note:** An input and output box accompanies each of the following schema design steps. The *input* box provides a description of the sources of information needed to complete the step in schema design. The *output* box provides a description of the type of output expected from the step.

■ Schema Design Phase

Schema design includes six phases. In this chapter, we focus on the initial four steps:

Step 1—Gather information

Step 2—Define system requirements, rules, and assertions

Step 3—Define classes and properties

Step 4—Define associations

In Chapter 6, we continue with the final two steps:

Step 5—Define methods

Step 6—Check schema design

Step 1: Gather Information

Input

- Formal and informal questionnaire
- Requirements specification
- Additional documentation when available

Collate Management-Specific Information

The information-gathering phase involves taking information from a variety of sources and sifting out the management-specific details. The requirements specification document, which should provide some guidance on the manageable aspects of the product, is a good starting point for such information. Other sources of information could include formally and informally questioning the target users of the system to gather feedback on their wishes. A formal questionnaire might ask these target users for their requirements for the new system, possible improvements to the management of the existing system, and so on. An informal telephone conversation or e-mail query might elicit responses about the manageable aspects of the product. It is good practice in this step to record clearly and concisely the details of where you gathered your information, from whom, and when. In this step, you should collate any source of information pertaining to the management of your product. You can use this information to help determine the type of information that should be exposed by your managed object and, ultimately, should be made available to management data consumers.

Ascertain Your Management Data Consumers

You must understand who is the target audience of the management data that your product supplies. The IT aspect of many organizations generally is in two key areas:

- **Desktop management,** whose desktop support staff are dedicated to handling all aspects of the desktop. In our example, they would be concerned with the desktop client part of our e-mail package and not directly with the Post Office.
- **Network infrastructure management,** who are dedicated to the handling of all aspects of the network, including network servers and routers. Within this area, a further level of classification, depending upon the size of the organization, exists:

  - **LAN infrastructure,** whose system administrator's aim is to monitor network performance, administer network servers, repair logical faults on a network, and so forth.

  - **WAN/MAN infrastructure,** whose administrator's aim is to manage the overall infrastructure of the corporate network in which the lowest common element is a network router between buildings. Each LAN in the corporate network is a node in the overall network topology. The task of the routers is to enable information to travel between sites to interdepartmental LANs.

Depending on the type of product you develop, you may need to correspond with one or all of these sections within a company to gather a broad enough view of the information you will need to supply in your schema.

Three types of people will interact with our client/server e-mail system:

- Client application users whose goal is to send and receive e-mails (not management biased)

- Desktop managers and support staff whose goal is to help client application users to achieve their goals

- LAN infrastructure system administrators who administer accounts, manage the Post Office housekeeping, and carry out Post Office–based requests from desktop support staff.

Client application users simply use the client application to send and receive e-mail and are not management-focused. They do not interact directly with our Post Office and, therefore, are not target sources of information.

System administrators and/or desktop managers will manage our product, so they are possible sources of information for this step. Establish their management needs and document the key features that we should instrument through WMI.

The Post Office example is based on the assumption that our end user is based in the field and supports the product. Management information consumers might be other independent software vendors (ISV) or independent hardware vendors (IHV), depending upon the nature of the product, in which case they would be the target audience for any questionnaire.

The work in Step 1 will aid us in determining which information we need for Step 2.

Output

The output is a paper-based document containing a description of the management-specific requirements for the system from a variety of sources. The document should contain a record of the sources of the information gathered, the date the information was obtained, and a comprehensive list of who or what will use your management data.

Step 2: Define System Requirements, Rules, and Assertions

Input

- Output from Step 1

Use Case Diagrams and Use Case Details

The first task in this step is to define Use Cases for our Post Office. Use Cases help us to attempt a first draft of system requirements, which in this instance is for the Post Office. To do this, we must consider the type of operations our system must perform based upon the documents produced in Step 1.

The first part of defining our Use Case is to draw a Use Case diagram. To do this, first draw a system boundary (a rectangle) and place within it each required management function as an ellipse. Outside of the system boundary, we place actors (stick people) to represent objects that interact with these management functions.

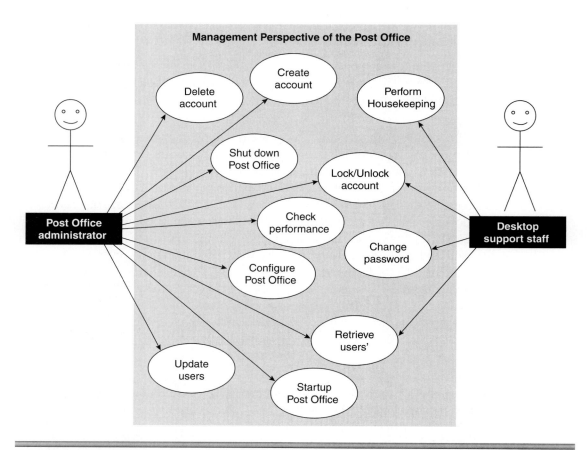

Figure 5.18   Use Case diagram for the Post Office

Note that these can be people (as in our case) or any other kind of management data consumers.

> **Note:** We used nonstandard, "happy" stick people in the diagram to indicate the elation that WMI instrumentation will bring to end users. Sadly, Use Case *actors* normally do not have emotions.

The Use Case diagram shows us that there are two types of system user: Post Office administrators (LAN infrastructure System administrators) and Desktop support staff. Table 5.4 lists the required management functions. For each of the management functions you can provide further detail using a *Use Case detail*. For example, Figure 5.19 describes the management function, Shutdown Post Office.

Table 5.4 Post Office Management Functions

Management function	Description
Shutdown Post Office	Places the Post Office in the executable state.
StartUp Post Office	Places the Post Office in the executing state.
Lock/Unlock account	Locks and unlocks an e-mail account.
Display users' details	Displays contact information for a specific user.
Update users' details	Updates a user's details on the Post Office.
Delete account	Permanently removes an account from the Post Office.
Check performance	Displays information about the number of e-mail messages processed, etc.
Create account	Adds a new account to the Post Office.
Change password	Changes the password on an existing account.
Configure Post Office	Configure settings on the Post Office such as maximum message size, max size of attachment, number of successful login attempts, etc.

[Provide the name of the management function that this Use Case detail describes.]
Use Case Detail: Shutdown Post Office
[Provide the name of the actors who will use this management function]
Used By: **PostOffice administrator**
[Define the constraints or validity checks that must be in place before the Use Case can begin. Refer to the software application life cycle to determine which states are applicable as preconditions.]
Preconditions: **PostOffice must be in the executing state.**
[Provide the details that the PostOffice administrator must supply for this Use Case]
Inputs: **Name of PostOffice to shut down**
[Describe the changes that may occur as a result of this Use Case]
Postconditions: **The PostOffice is in the executable state. The PostOffice no longer responds to client requests or processes email.**
[Provide details of the information that flows from the system to the outside world—in this case, it will be the management data consumer. Do not forget to note the occurrence of events at this stage as well]
Outputs: **Result code that indicates whether or not the task was accomplished successfully.**

Figure 5.19 Use Case details for management function *Shutdown Post Office*

Perform these steps for each of the management functions included in the Use Case diagram.

Rules and Assertions

Next we must look at the rules and assertions that will constrain our system. Remember when specifying these to consider also the occurrence of events and to record them. Events form an integral part of effectively managing a system. We can use the information gathered in Step 1 to help determine our rules and assertions.

Rules   A rule is a principle governing the conduct of our system.

Applying this approach to the Post Office, we can define the rules in Table 5.5.

Note: Rules 1 and 3 generate events if their conditions are met. For example, if the user's mailbag exceeds the 20MB limit, then the administrator should receive notification via an event telling him/her so. It is important at this stage to state any events that may occur as part of your schema because you may need to define event classes for them later if they are extrinsic.

Assertions   An assertion is simply a positive statement (or declaration) of fact about some aspect of the system being modeled.

Table 5.5   Post Office Rules

No.	Rule
1.	If a user attempts to log in to an e-mail account more than n times with an invalid username or password, then the Post Office should lock the account. It should also generate an event to signify that the account has been locked and an attempted security breach has occurred. The account will remain locked until a Post Office administrator unlocks the account.
2.	An e-mail client can only send or receive mail from the Post Office when he/she has supplied a valid user name and password.
3.	If a user's mailbag is > 20 MB, then the Post Office should suspend the user's account and generate an event. This will prevent the user from sending or receiving mail. All pending mail will remain in the intermediate directory and is not added to the mailbag until housekeeping has been performed (that is, the mailbag is <= 20 MB).
4.	If the total number of accounts on the Post Office > 99, then no more accounts may be added to the Post Office.

For example:

"His/her current waist measurement is n"

(where *n* is a waist size in centimeters. Always specify units of measurement where appropriate).

Table 5.6 is the list of assertions for the Post Office system.

Output

Paper-based document that contains the following details:

- Management-specific rules and assertions for the product
- Use Case diagrams to provide details of usage
- Use Case details to provide detailed information on each management function

Table 5.6   Post Office Assertions

No.	Assertions
1.	The Post Office must expose a list of registered accounts.
2.	The Post Office must keep a record of the last time each user successfully logged on the system.
3.	The Post Office must provide a mapping between mailbag GUID IDs and user accounts.
4.	The Post Office must allow only a maximum of 100 e-mail accounts to be logged on the system at once.
5.	There can be only one mailbag per user.
6.	A mailbag cannot exceed 20 MB.
7.	The Post Office must not accept attachments greater than 2 MB.
8.	The Post Office must provide a list of users currently logged on.
9.	The Post Office must monitor the amount of space left on the mailbag disk partition on the Windows2000 server.
10.	The Post Office should provide statistics on the amount of messages being processed. A processed message is one that is sent by the user, processed by the Post Office, and ultimately placed in its destination mailbag.
11.	The Post Office should log the total time in days, hours, and minutes that it has been running since start-up.
12.	Administrators should be able to shut down and restart the Post Office cleanly (that is, without active users losing e-mail messages).
13.	Administrators should be able to add users to and remove users from the Post Office user list while it is running.
14.	Administrators should be able to lock and unlock a user's account from the Post Office.

Step 3: Define Classes and Properties

Input

■ Use Cases and rules and assertions from Step 2

Name Your Schema

Before defining classes and properties, it is good practice to define the name of the schema to which they will belong. Choose a name that will be representative of the real-world object that it characterizes, which in our case is the Post Office. We have chosen to use a short abbreviation to improve readability. Therefore, the fully qualified class name for our PostOffice schema is:

PO_classname *(no whitespaces allowed)*

MOF Qualifiers

We do not address the use of qualifiers until we have documented fully the meaning and purpose of our classes. We look at the addition of object and property qualifiers in the next chapter.

Define Candidate Classes

Next we define candidate classes, but how do we determine which are candidate classes?

To determine which elements are *candidate* classes, look to the Use Cases, rules, and assertions generated in Step 2. We call these elements *candidate* classes because we expect class and property definition to be an iterative process. Indeed, consider it part of the design process to repeat the various stages of Step 3 until satisfied that our classes are an efficient and usable representation of our system. Also, do not be afraid to experiment by adding or removing classes from your schema during this stage.

There are several ways to identify candidate classes. First, look at the Use Cases defined in Step 2. The management functions they describe are a potential source of inspiration. For example, one of the identified management functions is to retrieve the user's details. We could provide a class called UserDetails that contains information such as contact number, surname, first name, title, and so forth.

Second, read the rules and assertions you defined earlier. From the nouns, try to pick out any possible classes and ask:

1. Is there is a definable set of instances for the class?
2. Is the object of relevance to the management data consumers you identified in Step 1?
3. Does it constitute part of the managed system you are modeling?
4. Is there a unique key property or a compound key for the class?
5. Is the class a singleton?
6. How are instances created and deleted?

Although this approach is, perhaps, overly simplistic, it is a good starting point from which to define candidate classes. From the rules and assertions in Step 2, we can identify the candidate classes for the Post Office schema in Table 5.7.

Along with the candidate classes, we include a description of their intended purpose and a discussion on whether or not each class should be part of the Post Office schema. Many factors can affect whether or not a candidate class is required as part of the overall schema.

Always refer back to the information gathered in Step 2 to determine whether a class is required to represent some manageable aspect of your system. In Table 5.7, the classes `Administrator` and `InBox` are irrelevant to the Post Office schema for the reasons listed in the discussion text.

Continue to define candidate classes, looking at the rules and assertions and Use Cases, until you are satisfied that the list of candidate classes is complete.

The next three steps, defining event classes, statistics, and settings, are optional. If your schema does not need to expose these types of information because your management data consumer does not require them, you can skip them.

Define Events

Recall from previous chapters that we defined two types of events in WMI: intrinsic and extrinsic. The next action is defining any intrinsic or extrinsic events that occur as part of your managed environment. Whether you will need to define any classes during this step depends largely on the type of event you wish to supply. In the rules and assertions defined in Step 2, certain conditions specify that a result should be generated.

Intrinsic events occur because of some change of state of which WMI is aware, such as the creation of an instance of a class defined in the CIM repository, regardless of whether that instance is dynamic or static.

Extrinsic events take place outside the scope of the WMI and its managed objects, but in some way, still are relevant to the management of the system. Extrinsic events have nothing to do with namespaces, classes, or instances; instead, they provide notification relevant to the management environment. An example is an event to notify the administrator of a power fluctuation on the Post Office server. Because WMI is not aware of extrinsic events and they have no representation in the CIM repository, extrinsic events rely upon two components to come to the surface successfully. First, an event provider must supply notification of the event (see Chapter 12 for more information) and second, an event class definition (derived from `__ExtrinsicEvent`) must be defined in the CIM repository. This class defines the information supplied in the occurrence of that event.

Note that not all types of event classes provide an enumerable set of instances. As soon as an event occurs, the instance no longer exists.

Microsoft recommends using intrinsic events whenever possible: They are easy to implement because the WMI does the bulk of the work. Our experience, however, suggests that it is more a matter of personal preference that depends upon factors such as the type of product you are instrumenting. Table 5.8 broadly classifies intrinsic events.

Table 5.7 Candidate Classes for the Post Office Schema

Candidate class	Description	Discussion
PostOffice	The `Post Office` class will represent the notion of the e-mail server in our client/server e-mail system. This class will define the manageable aspects of a Post Office and will be central to our schema. The name of the Post Office must be unique; therefore, this could be the key property.	REQUIRED. See Use Case diagram from Step 2.
UserDetails	This class describes the contact details of an account holder in our system (phone number, first name, surname, title, etc.). The username is unique to each person, whereas the surname is not forced to be.	REQUIRED. See Use Case diagram from Step 2.
EmailAccount	The `EmailAccount` class describes the details of an individual account (username, password, date last logged on, etc.). Once again, the username is unique for each instance of this class.	REQUIRED. See Use Case diagram and rules from Step 2.
Mailbag	The `Mailbag` class describes the manageable features and characteristics of each mailbag that belongs to an `EmailAccount`.	REQUIRED. See Use Case diagram from Step 2.
Administrator	The `Administrator` class models the manageable characteristics of an administrator's account on the Post Office.	UNREQUIRED. Upon closer inspection, Class User can subsume this class, because no specific manageable properties belong to an Administrator account that do not apply to a normal account.
Inbox	The `Inbox` class describes the manageable characteristics of each Client applications Inbox that displays all incoming e-mail.	UNREQUIRED. The Post Office schema is concerned only with the manageable aspects of the Post Office. The Inbox is not directly relevant to the Post Office and, therefore, does not need to be modeled in the schema. This class is more likely to appear in the E-mail client application schema (not discussed here).
Message	This class represents each message sent in the e-mail system. It describes characteristics such as the total size of the message including attachments, the destination address, the source address, and the number of attachments.	UNREQUIRED. Although it is theoretically possible to model this component of the e-mail system, is it desirable? First, does a management data consumer need this much information? Secondly, the resource overhead for storing an instance of this class per message sent in the system would be prohibitive (running into the thousands in a short space of time); therefore, we do not need this class.

Table 5.8 Intrinsic Event Classifications

Event	Actions	System class	Description
Instance-related	Creation	__InstanceCreationEvent	Generates events in response to actions taking place on instances.
	Modification	__InstanceModificationEvent	
	Deletion	__InstanceDeletionEvent	
Class-related	Creation	__ClassCreationEvent	Generates events in response to actions taking place on classes.
	Modification	__ClassModificationEvent	
	Deletion	__ClassDeletionEvent	
Namespace-related	Creation	__NamespaceCreationEvent	Generates events in response to actions taking place on namespaces.
	Modification	__NamespaceModificationEvent	
	Deletion	__NamespaceDeletionEvent	

If we examine the list of rules and assertions in Table 5.5, we can see in Rule 1 and Rule 3 that several conditions generate events.

Rule 1: *If a user attempts to log in to an e-mail account more than n times with an invalid username or password, then the Post Office should lock the account. It should also generate an event to signify that the account has been locked and an attempted security breach has occurred.*

Rule 3: *If a user's mailbag is > 20 MB, then the Post Office should suspend the user's account and generate an event.*

To determine whether these events are intrinsic, we can ask the following questions:

"Is the subject of the event represented in either our schema or in another existing schema, such as the Win32 extended schema?"

In Rule 1, the purpose of the event is to notify event consumers if the status of an account changes to *locked*. In the classes we have loosely defined so far, the status of an account would be classified as part of class `EmailAccount.` Therefore, if the status of an e-mail account changed, it would show up as part of this class. This means that the event is part of our schema and, therefore, is intrinsic.

In Rule 2, the subject of the event is the size of the mailbag. Class `MailBag` provides this information and an intrinsic event could again surface.

"Is the event an instance, class, or namespace-related event?"

Both events represent changes to instances that already exist. Therefore, they can be classified as instance modifications, which Table 5.9 explains.

Table 5.9 Intrinsic Event Classifications

Description	Class affected	Type of event
AccountLockedEvent.	PO_UserDetails	Intrinsic instance modification.
An event generated if an account is locked. The property AccountStatus can be used as part of an event filter to indicate that the account is in the locked state.		
LargeMailBagEvent.	PO_Mailbag	Intrinsic instance modification.
An event generated if a mailbag exceeds its disk quota. The property MailbagSize can be used in an event filter to determine whether the mailbag exceeds its quota.		

Intrinsic Event Filter Example

The event queries that follow provide an example of constructing an event filter to subscribe for notification of these events. The bulk of the work is done by WMI when surfacing intrinsic events, because it has to check each instance modification of class PO_UserDetails and PO_MailBag and compare them with every event filter for that instance to determine whether certain conditions are met.

In Figure 5.20, the name property represents the unique identifier WMI uses internally to identify the event filter. You can provide this yourself as part of the event filter; alternatively, WMI will generate one for you. The SELECT statement tells WMI to look in system class InstanceModificationEvent for instances of class PO_UserDetails (always specify the full class name in queries) and notify of an event if property Account-Status has the value of **locked**.

Event providers can notify WMI of both intrinsic and extrinsic events if they report changes to dynamic data (that is, data not held in the CIM repository). Because

```
// AccountLockedEvent intrinsic event query
instance of __EventFilter
{
  Name = "{7ca44681-045f-11d1-ae97-00c04fb68820}";
  Query = "SELECT * FROM __InstanceModificationEvent WHERE
    TargetInstance ISA \"PO_UserDetails\" AND
    TargetInstance.AccountStatus == \"Locked\"";
      QueryLanguage = "WQL";
}
```

Figure 5.20 Event filter for locked accounts

```
// Example of LargeMailBagEvent intrinsic event query
instance of __EventFilter
{
  Name = "{7cb44683-045f-11d1-ae97-00c04fb63821}";
  Query = "SELECT * FROM __InstanceModificationEvent WHERE
    TargetInstance ISA \"PO_MailBag\" AND
    TargetInstance.MailBagSize > 20000";
  QueryLanguage = "WQL";
}
```

Figure 5.21 Event filter for large mailbox accounts

the events are generated in response to extrinsic events, conditions of which the WMI had no knowledge, an event provider must be used to forward the event to WMI. If you consider the relationship between static and dynamic data and CIM repository, then it becomes clear that WMI would not be able to detect changes in dynamic data unless notified by a third party (that is, an instance provider). Because of this step, we identify two intrinsic instance modification events. Figure 5.21 shows the second one. We did not need to define any event classes.

Define Statistical Classes

The CIM provides a CIM_StatisticalInformation class from which to derive classes describing statistical information (Table 5.10). Any classes that define statistical information should derive from this class. We separate statistical information, such as the properties FailMailCount, MailCount, UserLoggedCount, and UserLockCount, so that applications interested in state information do not have to evaluate statistical data and, conversely, applications interested in statistics do not have to access state information.

Finally, CIM does not map statistical information over time. Therefore, only a single instance of each statistical class will exist at any time. Microsoft assumed that if people wanted historical data, they would subscribe for appropriate changes in the statistical classes and write the events to a log. Classes such as the statistics classes, that can have a maximum of a single instance, use the class qualifier, Singleton.

Table 5.10 Candidate Statistical Classes for the Post Office

Candidate class	Description	Base class
PostOfficeStats	Contains the statistics generated by the Post Office since startup	CIM_Statistics

Define Settings Classes

The CIM provides base class `CIM_Setting` (Table 5.11) from which to derive any classes that define the settings for managed objects. In our example, the class `Post Office` defines several properties that fall into this category, such as log in attempt count and maximum size of mailbag (see Table 5.9).

Define Properties

Draw a table listing any properties that all of the classes defined, including statistical and event-based classes, potentially may contain. Use the rules and assertions from Step 2 for guidance but do not worry about creating an exhaustive definition for each class in the first draft. This step will help you think more carefully about the purpose of each class and its role in the schema. You may decide during this stage that certain properties from one class are more suitable in another of the classes. Repeat this process until you are sure that each property in the class is required so that there cannot be any instance for which that property is null. Also, consider which properties might be unique and usable as keys.

After our first pass, we have nine classes and their candidate properties (Table 5.12). Refer once again to the documentation generated in Step 2 to determine which properties are required as part of each class. In addition, ask the following questions for each property:

- What is the type of the property?
- Can you envisage a management consumer ever using the property?
- Does it have a definable range?
- Does the property belong to this class?

The properties define the manageable aspects of the system. After you are satisfied that the list is more or less complete, then create individual tables to represent each class and its properties and scrutinize them in more detail.

Class `PO_PostOffice`

Description: The `PostOffice` class represents the manageable aspects of our Post Office e-mail server (Table 5.13).

Table 5.11 Candidate Settings Classes for the Post Office

Candidate class	Description	Base class
PostOfficeSettings	Contains the settings for the PostOffice	CIM_Setting
MessageSettings	Contains the message specific settings for the PostOffice	CIM_Setting

Table 5.12 Post Office Classes with Candidate Properties

Class	Candidate properties
PostOffice	• List of accounts on system? • Number of user accounts created on Post Office • Post Office name • List of account usernames that are locked out of system • Space remaining on mailbag disk partition on Windows 2000 server • Days, minutes, and hours Post Office has been running
PostOfficeSettings	• Maximum number of log-on attempts allowed
UserDetails	• User name • User's office phone number • User's title (Mr., Miss, Mrs., Dr., etc.) • Forename • Surname • Position in company • Office location • GUID assigned to user's mailbag
Mailbag	• Current size in Megs of mailbag file (including attachments) • Unique GUID assigned to mailbag
MessageSettings	• Max size of message in KiloBytes • Max size of an attachment in KiloBytes • Max number of attachments permitted
EmailAccount	• GUID of mailbag for user • Date user last successfully logged on • User name of account • Current password • The current status of e-mail account (logged in, logged out, locked out, suspended)
PostOfficeStats	• FailedMailCount • TotalMailCount

Table 5.13   Class PO_PostOffice Properties

Property name	Data type	Range	Description
PostOfficeStatus	uint16	Stopped Initializing Running Shutting down Error	The current status of the post office.
PostOfficeName **(key)**	String	Min chars 6 Max chars 100	The PostOfficeName property must be a unique alphanumeric value used for identification purposes. Must be a minimum of 6 alphanumeric octet's length. In future releases more than one Post Office may be visible so the property value must be unique.
StartTime	DATETIME	dd/mm/yy hh:mm:ss Timezone	This property specifies the day, month, year, clock time, and time zone in which the Post Office was started.
TotalMailCount*	uint64	Min 0… Max millions!	Maintaining a count of e-mails successfully delivered since Post Office start-up.
FailedMailcount*	uint64	Min 0 Max millions!	Maintaining a record of how many e-mail messages are currently undelivered.
FreeSpace	uint64	Min 0Kb Max 9,223,372,036,854,775,807!	A property that holds the size in Kb of space remaining on the mailbag partition. Note: Although an object already exists in the CIM repository that represents the space remaining on the mailbag partition, a major goal of schema design is usability. It is also permissible to have two properties within a namespace representing the same thing as long as they do not reside within the same class. The same rule applies to class objects.

Continued

Table 5.13   *Continued*

Property name	Data type	Range	Description
AccountLock	Array of string	Min 0 Max 100	A list of usernames of those who are currently locked out of the system.
AccountLockCount*	uint8	Min 0 Max 100	The current number of users locked out of the system.
RegisteredUsers	Array of string	Min 0 Max 100	A list of usernames of those who are registered with the PostOffice. Note: This is not to be confused with active users. This property merely contains the usernames of all accounts that have been created on the Post Office.
LicenceCount	uint8	Min 1 Max 100	The number of e-mail accounts registered with this Post Office.
UserLoggedCount*	uint8	Min 0 Max 100	A count of the current users logged in the system.

*These properties are statistically based; therefore we move them to a statistics class, see PostOfficeStats.

Discussion

In Table 5.13, we defined a FreeSpace property that already exists as part of Microsoft's Win32 extended schema in the class Win32_LogicalDisk. Should we instrument the same property twice in the repository? In this case, yes, because although we wish generally to eradicate redundant entries in the schema, it is valid to duplicate entries if doing so increases usability. In our case, it is useful for the end users of our schema to have a property that automatically exposes the amount of remaining free disk space on the mailbag volume. This property will eliminate the necessity for the administrator to find out upon which volume and server the mailbag resides and then look up the amount of free space using Win32_LogicalDisk.

> **Note:** Because only a single Post Office exists in our system, only one instance of this class can exist. It, therefore, does not require a key property and can use the class qualifier, Singleton, to specify that no more than one instance of this class will ever exist.

A Brief MOF Interlude

For the `PostOfficeStatus` property, we can use a valuemap and values qualifier. They are similar in function to the enum operator in C++ and similarly map integer values to string literals. In MOF syntax, it would appear as follows:

```
class PO_PostOffice: PO_SoftwareFeature
{
  [ read: ToInstance ToSubClass, description(".."): ToSubClass,
    valuemap {"1", "2", "3", "4", "5"}: ToSubClass ToInstance,
    values {"Stopped", "Initialising", "Running", "Shutting down",
"Error"}:
      ToSubClass ToInstance]
  uint16 PostOfficeStatus;
  ... ..
```

If, for example, the `PostOfficeStatus` property had an instance value of 3, this would denote that the Post Office was in the *Running* state. If a valuemap is not included, CIM assumes that the index value starts at zero by default, in which case, the *Running* state would have a value of 2. We shall cover the assignment of qualifiers to schema constructs in more detail in Chapter 6.

MOF Language Tip

When using the Description qualifier to describe your properties or classes, you can include quotation marks by using the backslash (\).

[input] `description("She said, \"This will print the quotation marks as well\"")`

[output] **She said, "This will print the quotation marks as well"**

Class PO_PostOfficeSettings

Description: The `PostOfficeSettings` class defines the settings for the Post Office (Table 5.14). This class is a singleton.

Class PO_UserDetails

Description: The user class (Table 5.15) will contain the details of an account holder in the Post Office.

Table 5.14 Class PO_PostOfficeSettings Properties

Property name	Data type	Range	Description
MaxFailedLogon	uint8	0 to 255	Determines how many times a user can attempt to log on to the Post Office before the account is locked.

Table 5.15 Class PO_UserDetails Properties

Property name	Data type	Range	Description
Office Location	Array of string	Min 0 chars Max	User's work location (floor, desk number, etc.)
UserName (**key**)	String	Min 6 chars Max 15 chars	Account user's name
Title	String	Mr. Mrs. Sir Dr. Professor Miss Other	Official title of the account holder
ForeName	String	Min 2 chars Max 50 chars	User's first name
Surname	String	Min 2 chars Max 30 chars	User's last name
Job Title	String	Min 2 chars Max 40 chars	Clerk, Director, etc.
ContactNumber	String	Min 0 chars Max 255 chars	User's office phone number

Discussion

Most of the properties in class UserDetails are both read and write (with the exception of the Username, which is read-only because it is a key value). This allows the Post Office administrator to change and update these details in the CIM repository. Class UserDetails provides the details of each user on a per instance basis. If a problem occurs with a particular account, then the Post Office administrator can access instances of this class and contact the user. Note that an instance of this class will exist for each user who has an account with the Post Office, giving a maximum of 100 objects of this class at once.

Class PO_EmailAccount

Description: The e-mail account class (Table 5.16) contains the manageable aspects of an e-mail account on the Post Office. An instance of this class should be created when an account is added to the Post Office.

Table 5.16 Class PO_EmailAccount Properties

Property name	Data type	Range	Description
MailBagIdentifier	String	Max 255 chars	GUID of mailbag for account.
LogonDate	dateTime	dd/mm/yy hh:mm:ss Timezone	Date user last successfully logged on.
Username (**key**)	String	Min 6 chars Max 15 chars	User name of account which serves as our **key**.
Password	String	Min 6 chars Max 200 chars	The current password for the account.
AccountStatus	String	Logged in Logged out Locked Suspended	The current status of the e-mail account. Note that the Post Office administrator can modify this setting, as can the Post Office (automatically) in certain circumstances such as failed log-on attempts.

Discussion

In the Post Office schema design, an object of class EmailAccount will exist for every registered user of the system (maximum 100). It exposes such information as the user's log-on status, the GUID of the mailbag associated with the user, and the date of the user's last successful login. The key property is the Username, which is unique for each instance of the class.

Implementing a password property in the user class brings to light several concerns. First, should we expose such sensitive information in the CIM repository? If so, what precautions can we take to protect it?

WMI imposes several layers of security on accessing data in the CIM repository. First, a user must have a valid Windows user name and password and adequate permission to look at the information in the repository (excluding Windows 9x/Me). Second, WMI requires that users of the CIM repository must possess permission to perform actions such as reading and writing from it. WMI assigns these permissions on a per namespace basis to allow access to specified users or groups of users. Another common technique for storing sensitive information, such as passwords, is to define the password property as write-only (using a property qualifier), ensuring that the existing value of the password cannot be surreptitiously acquired and the e-mail account violated, because WMI administrative users could change it but not view it. You could also put the password in the registry and use standard registry protection techniques to secure it while using the registry provider to get it into WMI.

Finally, Table 5.17 lists the meanings associated with the AccountStatus property.

Table 5.17 AccountStatus Property Values

Status	Meaning
Logged in	The account is currently active and logged in to the system.
Logged out	The account is currently inactive and logged out of the system.
Locked	The account has been locked, which means the user cannot log in and read e-mail, send e-mail, or receive e-mail. This condition is normally imposed when a violation has occurred. Only a Post Office administrator can unlock the account.
Suspended	The account has been suspended, meaning that the user cannot send or receive e-mail but can log in and read existing e-mail. This status is normally enforced when the mailbag exceeds 20 MB.

Class PO_Mailbag

Description: The mailbag class (Table 5.18) represents the manageable aspects of a mailbag (that is the sequential file) on our Post Office. It should be associated with each E-mail account object.

Discussion

Remember that efficiency is a concern when designing a schema. Our mailbag class has an instance for every registered user on the e-mail system (every user must be associated with a mailbag). Therefore, we can assume that, at maximum, WMI will hold 100 mailbag objects.

Class PO_MessageSettings

Description: The message class (Table 5.19) represents the manageable aspects of all messages in our e-mail system. A single instance of this class represents the settings for all messages sent and received within the e-mail system. Because only one instance of this class ever will be created, it does not require a key qualifier. A class that will never have more than one instance is a singleton.

Table 5.18 Class PO_Mailbag Properties

Property name	Data type	Range	Description
MailbagSize	uint16	Min 0 Max 20	Current size of mailbag file (units: megabytes).
MailIdentifier (**key**)	String	None defined	Unique GUID for mailbag.

Table 5.19 Class PO_MessageSettings Properties

Property name	Data type	Range	Description
MaxMessageSize	uint16	Min 0 Max 10,000 (10 Megs)	Max size of message including attachments (units: kilobytes).
MaxAttachSize	uint16	Min 0 Max 10,000	Specifies the maximum size for each attachment (units: kilobytes).
MaxAttachmentCount	unit8	Min 0 Max 10	Max number of attachments permitted per message.

Discussion

The purpose of this class is to allow the Post Office administrator to configure the characteristics of messages and attachments sent within the system. Changes to these values will have a direct impact upon the operation of the Post Office when processing e-mails from client applications.

Class PO_PostOfficeStats

Description: The PostOfficeStats class (Table 5.20) contains statistical information that will be of interest to specialized parties, such as the Post Office administrator. Like all statistical-based classes in CIM, this class is a singleton.

Output

■ UML Object Models of classes

■ Document containing detailed description of schema classes, properties, and associations

Table 5.20 Class PO_PostOfficeStats Properties

Property name	Data type	Range	Description
FailedMailCount	uint64	Min 0 Max millions	The number of messages that the Post Office has failed to deliver.
TotalMailCount	uint64	Min 0 Max millions	The total number of messages successfully delivered.
AccountLockedCount	uint8	Min 0 Max 100	The current number of users locked out of the system.
ActiveAccountCount	uint8	Min 0 Max 100	A count of the current number of accounts logged into the system.

Step 4: Define Associations

Input

- Classes defined in Step 3 considered as endpoints
- Descriptions of the role of the various components in system defined in Step 2

When you are confident that you have defined the classes and properties for your schema, you must consider the associations in which the class objects are expected to participate. You can define associations between classes in existing schemas (such as the Win32 schema) and our Post Office schema or solely between classes defined as part of the Post Office schema. A class can participate in as many or as few associations as required.

Furthermore, associations can define a relationship between two classes, between two instances of classes, or between a class instance and a class. When you define a relationship between two classes, you enable features, such as inheritance, to play a part in the associated objects.

Always remember that the purpose of an association in CIM is to provide management data consumers with a mechanism for tracking the relationships between managed objects in a managed environment. Although, theoretically, it is possible to define an association with more than two *references,* officially it is not supported. It is also possible to define association classes with properties other than type `Ref`. Although DMTF originally discouraged this practice, many of the Win32 schema associations actually do contain properties in addition to references.

The Purpose of Associations

In a scenario in which a managed object ceases to work, associations play an important role in diagnosing the source of the problem. Examples in Chapter 4, such as those of the hard disk and logical partition, illustrate this point.

If you do not adequately define the relationship between your managed object and its environment, you potentially decrease the manageability of the product. Now let us consider the steps in defining associations.

Do any relationships exist between the classes defined in the schema so far and any other classes?

The classes defined in our schema so far are as follows. Note that you need not include every class in an association:

- PO_PostOffice
- PO_UserDetails
- PO_Mailbag
- PO_EmailAccount
- PO_PostOfficeSettings

- PO_MessageSettings
- PO_PostOfficeStats

By examining the purpose of each class listed, we can identify the candidate associations in Table 5.21. Note that we call each of the classes referenced in an association *endpoints*. The endpoints in an association are bidirectional and the association can be traversed from either endpoint, except in special cases.

> **Note:** Cross-namespace associations are allowed, although, for several reasons, they are not recommended.
>
> References to objects outside of the host association's namespace are unaware of the reference because the relationship becomes unidirectional.
>
> If a cross-namespace association refers to a provider-based object, then the relationship will not be included in any query results.

What is the cardinality of each class referenced in the association?

Table 5.22 lists the types of cardinality between two references in an association. Note that associations can contain more than two references, although because Microsoft does not support this, our descriptions use only two classes, A and B.

Table 5.21 Candidate Associations

No.	Endpoint1		Endpoint2	Description
1	PO_EmailAccount	↔	PO_Mailbag	Each e-mail account has an associated mailbag (see topology).
2	PO_UserDetails	↔	PO_EmailAccount	Each EmailAccount object has user details associated with it.
3	PO_PostOffice	↔	PO_EmailAccount	Each Post Office administers many e-mail accounts.
4	PO_PostOfficeStats	↔	PO_PostOffice	The Post Office object generates statistical information.
5	PO_PostOfficeSettings	↔	PO_PostOffice	The Post Office has an associated number of settings.
6	PO_MessageSettings	↔	PO_PostOffice	The Post Office has settings associated with its messages.

Note: The mathematical notation ↔ is used here to represent a relationship between two classes.

Table 5.22 Association Cardinality

Cardinality	Example	Required MOF text
1:1	Each instance of class A is always associated with only one instance of Class B.	Min(1), Max(1)
1:Zero or 1	Each instance of Class A is sometimes associated with only one instance of Class B.	Max(1)
1:Zero or Many	Each instance of Class A can be associated with 1 or more instances of class B.	—
Aggregation	Very strong form of association in which each instance of Class A requires the existence of Class B. This is sometimes referred to as the *part-of relationship*, where Class B is said to be part-of Class A.	—

We can then provide list our association classes, their endpoints, and cardinality from Table 5.23.

> **Note:** Using the PO_PostOfficeAccounts association, it is now possible to determine the current number of users logged in, out, suspended, or locked. By constructing a WQL data query, we can retrieve the list of EmailAccount objects that are currently in any of the four allowed states.
>
> ```
> ASSOCIATORS OF {PO_EmailAccount.AccountStatus ="Logged In"}
>   WHERE AssocClass = PO_PostOfficeAccounts
> ```
>
> The value AccountStatus can be changed to any of the states listed above.

We shall further classify these associations at the end of the schema design phase in Chapter 6 when we position our classes and associations in the CIM repository.

Does the association require any properties other than references?

The purpose of this step is to determine if any properties are required in our associations other than those of type Ref. This is permitted, although not encouraged, in the design of an association because it raises the design issue of whether the association is, in fact, a class that contains references.

In our case, our associations do not require additional properties.

Table 5.23 Association Endpoints

Association class*	Reference Endpoints**	Cardinality	Description
PO_AssociatedMailBag	EmailAccount (*Antecedent*) key Mailbag (*Dependent*) key	1:1	Each e-mail account has only one mailbag.
PO_AccountUserDetails	UserDetails (*Antecedent*) key EmailAccount (*Dependent*) key	1:1	Each e-mail account is associated with a user.
PO_PostOfficeAccounts	PostOffice (*GroupComponent*) key EmailAccount (*PartComponent*) key	1:zero or many	The Post Office has zero or many registered EmailAccounts
PO_StatsForPostOffice	PostOfficeStats (*Stats*) key PostOffice (*Element*) key	1:1	The Post Office generates statistical information.
PO_PostOfficeMsgSettings	PostOffice (*Element*) key MessageSettings (*Settings*) key	1:1	The Post Office processes messages with settings.
PO_PostOfficeHasSettings	PostOffice (*Element*) key PostOfficeSettings (*Settings*) key	1:1	The Post Office has associated settings.

*Each association uses a compound key to uniquely identify it.

**Note that all of the references here are object-based.

■ Representing the PostOffice Schema in UML

Now that we have defined the classes and associations in our schema, the final task in this chapter is to represent this visually using a UML diagram (Figure 5.22).

Output
Paper-based document containing the following:

- Detailed description of schema association classes
- UML Object Models of classes and associations

■ Summary

In this chapter, we have discussed the first four steps involved with schema design, which included:

- Defining the management architecture of a product
- The mechanisms for information gathering

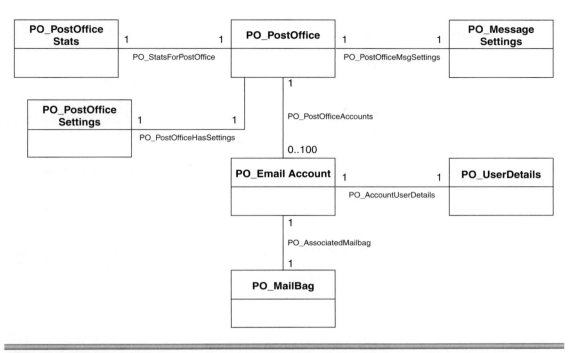

Figure 5.22 A UML object model of the Post Office schema system showing the classes and associations. Note that we position our Post Office schema classes in the next chapter.

- The use of the UML to represent schema constructs
- Interpreting UML diagrams
- Use Cases and Use details
- Defining the rules and assertions pertinent to the management of your system
- Defining classes, properties, associations, and events

In Chapter 6, we conclude the schema design phase by looking at the design of methods to represent the behavior of our system and adding qualifiers to each of our constructs. We also look at positioning our schema in the CIM repository. The final step in schema design is to check that the classes, methods, associations, and properties that we have designed are an efficient and usable representation of the system we are modeling.

Ten Starting Schema Design Tips

1. Learn to interpret UML static structure diagrams.
2. Gather requirements information from as many sources as possible.
3. Generate clear concise documents at every stage of schema design.
4. Learn and understand the CIM metamodel, because it will provide you with a good understanding of the rules of class and association design.
5. Familiarize yourself with the Common model and Win32 extended schema.
6. Use the WMI CIM Studio to browse classes and retrieve descriptions of the purpose of each class (using the Help button).
7. Learn the MOF syntax and semantics.
8. Keep up to date with new revisions of the CIM schema and Win32 extended schema by checking the DMTF and Microsoft Web sites regularly.
9. Repeat each step in schema design until you are satisfied that each is complete. Remember, the further the project progresses, the more time and money it costs to make changes to a schema.
10. Always specify minimum and maximum values for properties where appropriate.

Chapter 6

Method Design and Schema Class Positioning

Now that we have defined the classes, properties, and associations for the Post Office schema, we shall examine the methods required. Superficially, this may appear to be a relatively straightforward task: Decide upon the type of behavior that you would like the managed object to exhibit and then assign this behavior to specific classes within your schema. There are, however, several important considerations before doing this that directly affect the usability of the schema. Always remember that the key strength of an information model like the CIM is that its main source of interaction with the outside world is through flexible WQL queries.

For example, imagine that we define a class, `Person`, that describes somebody's physical characteristics. Instead of using properties to expose the characteristics of height and weight, we use two methods, `GetHeight` and `GetWeight`, to supply these values. Now imagine a scenario in which a data consumer (that is, an administrator of the system) decides to enumerate all of the instances of class `Person` based upon an arbitrary value assigned to weight or height. Theoretically, using WQL the administrator could construct a query as follows:

```
SELECT * FROM MySchema_Person WHERE GetHeight < 210 AND GetWeight >= 200
```

It should be obvious that this won't work! We cannot construct a query to enumerate instances of `MySchema_Person` using height and weight as constraints because we are not exposing them in our class as properties, only as methods. You also eliminate the possibility of detecting or using the properties in an event, because events are entirely query-based. Therefore, use only methods in those conditions in which they will not limit the usability of a schema. The main focus of the first part of this chapter is examining where and when it is appropriate to use methods.

Properties vs. Methods

From the previous example we can see that there are situations in which a property can be a more powerful solution than a method. The advantage of using properties is that they are queryable, which is in keeping with the aims of the CIM and information models in general. Conversely, there are also situations in which a method is preferable to a property.

For example, consider a situation that requires us to change the state of our Post Office from *running* to *stopped*. One possible solution would be to define a property called `State` and allow the management data consumer to change this value from *running* to *stopped*, thus initiating a change of state within the Post Office. The problem with this approach, however, would be in notifying the caller that the operation was or was not successful. If we used a method, we could return a value that signified the outcome of the operation. In some situations, methods are easier to document and understand from a user viewpoint in your schema than a schema construct, such as a property used in conjunction with a query. A good rule of thumb is to use methods for behavior and properties for state. You must use methods if more than one class must be updated at the same time.

> **Note:** We do not suggest that anything is wrong with having properties that indicate the state of a managed object. For example, `Win32_Service` has a read-only property called `State`. Such properties can be used for informational purposes but are not the preferred way to evoke change upon a managed object.

Methods, Operations, and Functions

As well as the stock behavioral definition for methods, we classify them according to the effect they have on the managed objects when run. To further make the distinction between the two types of method, we refer to *operations* and *functions*.

Operations have some type of impact upon their environment, such as causing a change of state, whereas functions, as a general rule, do not cause a change of state and often return a value of some kind. In our example using class `Person`, the methods `GetHeight` and `GetPerson` would be categorized as functions. They have no impact upon the state of the `Person` instance and can be called repeatedly without causing a state change. No special keywords are required to differentiate between the two, and apart from certain syntactic differences in the method signatures, the differences are purely behavioral.

If no keywords or special syntax differentiate between these two types of method, then why mention them?

The methods you define for your schema must conform to one or another of these sets of characteristics. The biggest danger is that your method might exhibit a mixture of characteristics from both. It is best to avoid this type of nonconformance because it can make your methods unpredictable from a user's standpoint and harder to maintain for the developers who work with your schema in the future. Table 6.1 provides a summary of the characteristics of operations and functions.

In Step 5, we define the candidate methods that should belong to our Post Office schema.

■ Step 5: Define Methods

Input

- ■ Requirements Specification that details behavioral characteristics of managed objects
- ■ Assertions and rules defined in Step 2.

Table 6.1 Difference between Operations and Functions

Type of method	Characteristics	Example
Operation	→ Return a status value → Accept input values → Affect the state of the host object or system within which it resides	Our Post Office schema could define two methods that start and stop the Post Office. These would return a status value (i.e., uint32) to indicate whether or not the job was successful or not. These methods would change the state of the Post Office from running to stopped and vice versa.
Function	→ Return a result → Define output parameters → Typically do not have any side effects upon the host object or system within which it resides	For example, in the Post Office schema, we could define a function called GetUserGUID that returned the GUID associated with a specific username. The return type of this function would be a string containing the GUID. Note that this fundamentally differs from an operation because repeated calls to this function would not change the state of the object or have any other side effects; it is used simply to retrieve a value.

Having briefly described the pros and cons of queries and methods, we can state the following about using methods:

> **Note:** Because WQL queries do not operate upon methods, their use, if inappropriate, can constrain the type of queries supported by a schema. This, in turn, can inhibit the usability of the schema.

To maximize the usability of the schema, it is advisable to use methods only when a major change of state needs to be initiated, normally as part of the life cycle of the object.

For example, in the existing CIMV2 schemas, the class `Win32_Service` supports the methods `StartService`, `StopService`, `PauseService`, and `ResumeService`. These state changes are required as part of the life cycle of every `Win32_service` instance.

Methods may be used also to automatically generate a response to a set query, although this would typically be more suited to a view provider. Imagine that users of your schema always will form certain types of queries to retrieve certain data from your schema. You can increase the usability of the schema if you automate the forming of these queries by providing, instead, a method that can be called. Doing this at the present stage requires you to have a very good understanding of how management data consumers will use the schema. You may make several iterations through the design process before you can make any such design decisions.

As with the steps in Chapter 5, we first define a list of *candidate* methods, which represent the behavior of our Post Office.

Candidate Methods

In Table 6.2, we list seven candidate methods for our schema. Among these is the candidate function `GetMailBagIdentifer` that returns the GUID assigned to a user's account (recall that this value forms the prefix of the mailbag's filename ending with .bag). Because users of the schema have no control over this value (it is assigned internally by the Post Office) and management data consumers undoubtedly would want to retrieve this value, it could be a candidate method as defined in the second method rule mentioned in Table 6.2. Admittedly, this is a simple example. Normally, you would want to automate only more complex queries; however, the discussion that follows holds true.

You may recall from our class design that the GUID property, `MailBagIdentifier`, is a member of class `PO_EmailAccount`. Let us look at the advantages and disadvantages of exposing this value as a method (assuming that we removed it from class `PO_EmailAccount` as a property). To do this, we shall look at a couple of possible scenarios in which this information will be retrieved.

Table 6.2 Candidate Post Office Methods

Method	Method category	Description
AddUser()	Operation	This method adds a new user to the Post Office. This method must be passed an object that contains the details of the new user (username, name, contact details, etc.). It must return a status code when completed that denotes the success or failure of the operation.
RemoveUser()	Operation	This method removes an existing user from the Post Office. It takes the username of the user (string) as a parameter and returns a status code upon completion that indicates the success or failure of the operation.
UnlockUser()	Operation	This method changes the status of an existing user's account from locked to unlocked. It returns a status code upon completion that indicates the success or failure of the operation.
LockUser()	Operation	This method locks an existing user's account. It returns a status code upon completion that denotes the success or failure of the operation.
StopPostOffice()	Operation	This method changes the state of the Post Office from running to stopped. It returns a status code upon completion that indicates the success or failure of the operation.
GetMailBagIdentifier()	Function	This method returns the GUID assigned to a user's account. If the value returned is zero then the operation failed. Note: This method is not a suitable candidate and is therefore removed (see discussion below).
StartPostOffice()	Operation	This method changes the state of the Post Office from running to stopped. It returns a status code upon completion that indicates the success or failure of the operation.

Retrieving Information from the Post Office Schema

Scenario 1   In our example, users of the Post Office schema decide that they need to recover the GUID associated with an account by using only the username. Determining the GUID value would make it possible to find the associated mailbag and perhaps delete it, repair it, or restore a previous version from backup. With a Username (Tunstallc), it would be possible to construct a WQL data query that returns the EmailAccount object, if one exists, as follows:

```
SELECT * FROM PO_EmailAccount WHERE UserName="Tunstallc"
```

Assuming that the query returned an object, we could retrieve the GUID associated with the account in the contents of this instance under property `MailBagIdentifier`. If this value were exposed only through a call to function `GetMailBagIdentifier`, then the management data consumer would have to initiate a call to this method to retrieve the value. On this occasion, using a property would require less programming and fewer calls to WMI to read the value held in property `MailBagIdentifier`.

Alternatively, we could construct a query using the Associators Of statement that returned instances of `PO_UserDetails` associated with class `PO_EmailAccount`. We would constrain the query by specifying the `Username` property as the object path; otherwise the query would return every instance associated with `PO_EmailAccount`.

```
ASSOCIATORS OF {PO_EmailAccount.Username="Tunstallc"}
  WHERE AssocClass = PO_AccountUserDetails
```

This query would return the instance of class `UserDetails` (an endpoint in association `PO_AccountUserDetails`) that contains all of the user's personal details (see class definition for more information).

Scenario 2 Imagine a situation in which the only value known is the GUID and we wish to retrieve the user's details. How would we go about doing this with our Post Office schema?

We could construct a data query that searched through the instances of class `EmailAccount` comparing every value of the property `MailBagIdentifier` with our desired GUID, as follows:

```
SELECT FROM * PO_EmailAccount WHERE
  MailBagGUID="1FBA60495EDD41ff82283F3A7FAF06EE"
```

If we exposed only the `MailBagIdentifier` value using the function `GetMailBag-Identifier`, then this query would not be valid and we would have to manually execute every `GetGUID` method on each EmailAccount object and compare the results to find a match! This is hardly in keeping with the usability ethos of CIM and leads us to conclude, in this case, that a method is not the best solution to supply the GUID.

Method Design

As you have with all previous stages in schema design, you should repeat the process until you are satisfied that the methods you have defined are a complete representation of the behavior of your product. After this is the case, you will document the methods in more detail, explaining their roles in the system, their input and output parameters, and any preconditions or postconditions that must exist for their successful initialization and completion.

First, however we must assign our methods to classes within the Post Office schema. We shall do this now, before we describe the method signatures.

Assigning Methods to Host Classes

When positioning methods, it is sometimes judicious to further group methods according to their functionality. Because methods typically are not an element of an information model, their aim is sometimes at odds with your schema design.

In the Post Office schema, we have defined a basic class, `PostOffice`, that represents the general notion of an e-mail server, but we may find it to be insufficient or too general to use as a host class for the numerous methods that we have designed. A best practice, in such a case, is to define one or more abstract classes as an interface for these methods. The Post Office schema does not warrant such action because of the number of methods it supports, but examples of this technique can be found frequently in Microsoft's Win32 extended schema and the CIM Schema. An example is the `Win32_BaseService` class that serves as an abstract superclass for the concrete classes, `Win32_Service` and `Win32_SystemDriver`. Table 6.3 provides a list of methods for the Post Office Schema and their host classes.

> **Note:** The Constructor and Destructor qualifiers can be used to define which methods create and delete instances of their defining class. Both are provided for informational purposes only and are not called automatically by the object manager when the object is created or deleted. Also, the object manager does not have to call any of the constructor or destructor methods defined for any parent class of original class. Both the Constructor and Destructor qualifiers can act upon multiple instances or classes. For example, a Destructor could delete association instances as well as instances of the class that defines the Constructor. Both qualifiers are FALSE by default and cannot be used with the Static qualifier.

Table 6.3   Post Office Methods and Associated Host Class

Method	Host class
AddUser	Post Office
RemoveUser	Post Office
StopPostOffice	Post Office
StartPostOffice	Post Office
UnlockAccount	EmailAccount
LockAccount	EmailAccount

Properties and Parameter Classes After we define the methods for our schema and assign them each to a class, we must consider the signature for each method.

Definition:
A method signature comprises a method name in conjunction with ordered arguments and a return type. If the method is instantiable then the method body is also considered part of that signature.

> **Note:** Although the order of the arguments is considered part of the method signature in CIM, *overloading* is not permitted. Overloading is the circumstance in which methods of the same name, in the same scope, differ only by the order and type of their arguments.

Method Arguments

Several options for defining arguments are open to us at this point. The most common approach is to define them explicitly as part of the method signature (Figure 6.1).

Although defining method arguments as part of the method signature is perfectly adequate when a small number of parameters is required, it can quickly become unwieldy if too many parameters are used. To overcome this problem, we use parameter classes to group sets of parameters, which can then be passed to our methods. Parameter classes offer several key advantages over passing multiple parameters.

Advantages of Parameter Classes

1. They are extensible without affecting existing applications. This means we can extend a parameter class without breaking the method. We do this by deriving from our parameter class and then overriding its properties where needed.

2. They allow specification of default values.

3. They allow us to assign default values, referred to as *initializers*, to parameters when we define our parameter class. This is not possible when we declare the parameters directly.

4. They can be used to simplify the interface of methods that take a large number of parameters.

```
class Person
{
  uint32 ExampleMethod(uint32 myparam1, boolean myparam2,
    uint32 myparam3, uint8 myparam4, string myparam5);
}
```

Figure 6.1 Method arguments specified in method signature

If you are defining your method parameter class within the CIMV2 namespace, it is advisable to make it a subclass of the abstract Microsoft class, `Win32_Method-ParameterClass`. Although this class does not contain any special properties, methods, or associations, placing it here ensures that your schema is consistent with existing schemas and so is easier to maintain. If your schema will occupy its own namespace, it would be judicious to define your own abstract method parameter base class. For our previous example, we could define a class as in Figure 6.2. We omit the qualifiers for readability.

Figure 6.2   Method arguments specified through parameter class

```
[class qualifiers would go here]
class ExampleClassParams : Win32_MethodParameterClass
{
  uint32 myparam1 = 0;        // Here we specify a default value referred to
                              // as an initializer
  boolean myparam2;
  uint32 myparam3;
  uint8 myparam4;
  string myparam5 = 1911;   // Another initializer
}
```

We could then define our method signature as in Figure 6.3.

Figure 6.3   Final method signature

```
class ExampleClass : AllClasses
{
  uint32 AddUser(ExampleClassParams MyObject);
}
```

Notice that the method `AddUser` takes a single argument of type `ExampleClass-Params`. The object passed to the method will be an instantiation of this specifically tailored class defined to hold the parameters required by the method.

Method Overriding and Polymorphism

Caution! These techniques can add substantial complexity to your model, so we advise caution in employing them.

A point to consider during the design of your methods is that the CIM allows both polymorphism and overriding. Commonly, you will not have to consider this until after you derive your classes from classes in existing schemas such as Win32 or CIM.

Polymorphism allows the schema designer to subclass an existing method and then change its implementation, leaving the signature intact. This could be used with the `Win32_Service` class to change the implementation of the `StopService()` method. We could derive from class `Win32_Service` and then use polymorphism to provide an alternate implementation of `StopService` in our new class.

Overriding allows the schema designer to change a property or qualifier while implementing a subclass. In the Post Office schema, we could derive a new class from class `PostOffice` and change the data type of property `LicenseCount` from uint8 to data type uint16. We could also change the Maxvalue qualifier to increase the number of licenses allowed from 100 to 1000. To do this we would specify the MOF qualifier Override in the subclass property.

> **Note:** This is contrary to C++ convention, in which you would specify whether or not a feature of a class could be overridden in the parent class.

Many examples of overriding can be found in CIMV2 namespace, especially in the CIM association classes that have been extended by Win32 classes. It is common practice for many of the Win32 association classes to derive from existing CIM association classes and, in doing so, to override the reference type of the parent association.

Although we have introduced these concepts at this stage in the schema design, we are not able to use them until we have successfully positioned our classes: How can you override a method if you don't know which methods the parent class supports? Therefore, when designing your own schema, you must wait until you have positioned your classes before using these two techniques.

The Post Office Schema Methods

In describing each of our candidate methods in more detail, we include any preconditions and postconditions that may exist.

Why Define Preconditions and Postconditions?

Preconditions and postconditions describe how a method will behave at runtime. It is always good practice to provide as much runtime information as possible at the design stage to aid the implementation. Preconditions and postconditions can be defined as follows:

- A *precondition* describes a set of circumstances that must be true for a method to execute. If the preconditions are not met, then the method will not execute successfully.

- A *postcondition* describes a set of circumstances that must be true before exiting a method. If the postcondition fails, an error code should be returned.

Method `AddUser`

Host Class: `PostOffice`

Description: This method (see Table 6.4) adds a new user to the Post Office. The method takes an object of parameter class `NewUserParam` (defined in Figure 6.4) especially for use with the method. We adopt this approach, as opposed to including each of the parameters explicitly as part of the method signature. Among the reasons we do this is because it makes the method design more flexible should we need to extend it at a later date. Because class `PostOffice` will host the method, we do not need to specify to which Post Office the user must be added. This approach also accounts for any future developments such as the presence of multiple Post Offices on the same machine.

Notice that `NewUserParam` is subclassed under our own abstract parameter base class, `PO_MethodParameterClass`. This class provides a logical grouping for all future method parameter classes.

Table 6.4 AddUser Method Specification

Preconditions	The `AddUser` method can complete its actions only if an identical username does not already exist.
Postconditions	The method can exit successfully only after the user has been added to the Post Office. This indicates the successful creation of the following objects: UserDetails class instance EmailAccount class instance Mailbag class instance AccountUserDetails association object AssociatedMailbag association object PostOfficeAccounts association object If the method does not satisfy these criteria, then the relevant error code must be returned, as detailed below.
Method signature	`uint32 AddUser(NewUserParam object)`
Return codes	0: Operation was completed successfully 1: Unknown error—the method failed to add the user 2: Username already exists 3: Post Office reached maximum number of users 4: Invalid initialization parameters

Figure 6.4 Method parameter class for new users

```
Class NewUserParam : PO_MethodParameterClass
{
  string Title;          // Mr, Mrs, Dr etc..*
  string Forename;       // Users first name*
  string Surname;        // Users last name*
  string Jobtitle;       // Director of finance etc..*
  string Username;       // PostOffice UserName*
  string Password;       // Password at startup
  string Contactnumber;  // User office telephone number*
};
```

*These fields will be used by the Post Office to create a new object of type UserDetails

Method RemoveUser

Host Class: PostOffice

Description: This method (see Table 6.5) removes an existing user from the Post Office. It requires a single parameter, the username of the e-mail account to be

Table 6.5 RemoveUser Method Specification

Preconditions	The method can only complete its actions if the username exists and if the user is not logged in to his or her account.
Postconditions	The method can successfully exit only once after the user has been removed from the Post Office. To do this the following objects must be deleted: EmailAccount object Mailbag Object UserDetails AccountUserDetails association object AssociatedMailbag object PostOfficeAccounts object
Method signature	`uint32 RemoveUser(string UserName)`
Return codes	0: Success: the operation was completed successfully 1: Unknown error—method failed to remove the user 2: Error: Username does not exist 3: Error: UserAccount currently active 4: Error: Invalid initialization parameter

Table 6.6 UnlockAccount Method Specification

Preconditions	The method requires that the username specified is valid and that it is currently in the locked state.
Postconditions	The method can successfully exit only after the user's account has been unlocked.
Method signature	uint32 UnlockAccount()
Return codes	0: Success: the operation was completed successfully
	1: Unknown error—method failed to unlock the user
	2: Error—User account was not locked

removed. The rules and assertions defined in Step 2 state that the Post Office must be capable of carrying out this method while the Post Office is running.

Method UnlockAccount
Host Class: EmailAccount

Description: This method (see Table 6.6) changes a user's account from locked to unlocked. It takes no parameters and returns a status value indicating the success or failure of the operation.

Method LockAccount
Host Class: EmailAccount

Description: This method (see Table 6.7) locks a user account, which prevents the user from accessing mail or sending and receiving mail from that account. It requires no parameters and returns a status value.

Table 6.7 LockAccount Method Specification

Pre-conditions	The method requires that the username specified is valid and that it is currently in the unlocked state.
Post-conditions	The method can successfully exit only after the user's account has been locked.
Method signature	uint32 LockAccount()
Return codes	0: Success—Operation was completed successfully
	1: Unknown error—method failed to lock the user
	2: Error—User's account already locked

Method `StopPostOffice`
Host class: `PostOffice`

Description: This method (see Table 6.8) takes a single parameter and places the Post Office in the stopped state to prevent users from sending or receiving e-mail. Note that this method does not result in the Post Office losing state information and the PostOffice object is not destroyed as a result of the successful completion of this method.

The method takes a single integer value that determines how the Post Office should shut down. The values and their meanings follow:

0—Shut down only if no users are currently logged in

1—Shut down forcibly regardless of whether users are logged in

A similar, more general, method already exists in the Microsoft Win32 schema under the `Win32_Service` class. Because our Post Office, at its most fundamental level, is a service, it can be stopped by executing the `StopService` method on its Win32_Service object. Why reinvent the wheel—or create our own method?

The advantage of creating our own method is that it can take additional parameters should you need them to shut down the Post Office. Although it is true that the

Table 6.8 `StopPostOffice` Method Specification

Preconditions	The method requires that the Post Office is currently in the running state.
Postconditions	The method can successfully exit only after the following are true: 1. The Post Office has been placed in the Stopped state. 2. The Post Office has ensured that no users will lose e-mail messages as a result of shutting down (see rules and assertions in Step 2 for rule) unless the parameter shutdowntype is set to 1.
Method signature	`uint32 StopPostOffice(uint8 shutdowntype)`
Return codes	0: Success—the operation was completed successfully 1: Unknown error—method failed to stop Post Office 2: Error—Post Office was not in running state 3: Error—Users logged in cannot shut down

Post Office will ultimately be coded as a service running as part of the operating system, it is not always useful to view everything at this level of abstraction. For example, we may wish to stop the currently executing Post Office but specify that the Post Office wait until all its users are logged out.

In addition, it is easier, arguably, for schema users to locate and stop a PostOffice object by looking at the `PostOffice` class than by searching through a list of services under Win32_Service.

Method `StartPostOffice`

Host Class: `PostOffice`

Description: This method (see Table 6.9) takes no parameters and places the Post Office in the running state, which allows users to send and receive e-mail. This method call does not reset any values to their default and is not a constructor. The same discussion applies to this method as the `StopPostOffice` method.

Post Office Schema UML Diagram with Methods

Now that we have defined our methods, we can draw up our UML diagram (Figure 6.5) including methods and any parameter classes.

Output

Paper product.

- A document written in plain language describing the methods designed, their signature, purpose, and host class.
- Optional UML diagrams of the schema including the methods.

Table 6.9 `StartPostOffice` Method Specification

Preconditions	The method requires that the Post Office be in the stopped state.
Postconditions	The method can exit successfully only after the Post Office is in the running state.
Method signature	`uint32 StartPostOffice()`
Return codes	0: Success—the operation was completed successfully
	1: Unknown error—method failed to start Post Office
	2: Error—Post Office was not in stopped state

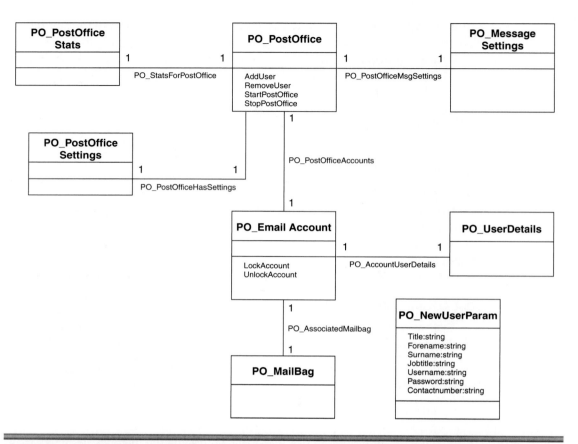

Figure 6.5 The Post Office UML object model (including methods and parameter class)

■ Step 6: Check Schema Design

Input

Requirements Specification document.

- ■ Rules and assertions defined in Step 2.
- ■ UML diagrams from all steps.

At this point in our schema design, we compare our classes, properties, methods, and associations with the rules and assertions we made during Step 2. This purpose is to verify that our schema is able to do exactly what we specified it would do at the start of the design life cycle. Although some of the assertions and rules we defined as part of Step 2, such as the implementation specifics of the Post Office, will undoubtedly fall outside the scope of the design work done so far, we still are able to perform a general check that our design conforms to the requirements.

First, in Table 6.10, we shall compare the rules defined in Step 2 with our schema design. Second, in Table 6.11, we shall compare our assertions with our design.

Rule Generation–Based UML Diagrams

Another final way of checking for conformance to requirements is to translate our UML diagrams back into grammatical rules based upon the relationships between the classes. This involves working with the documentation and diagrams generated in the previous steps to write down the rules that your design enforces. After you have generated these rules, it is then a question of comparing them with your original rules from Step 2.

Table 6.10 Post Office Rules

No.	Rule	Comparison
1.	If a user attempts to log in to an e-mail account more than n times with an invalid username or password, then the Post Office should lock the account. It should also generate an event to signify that the account has been locked and an attempted security breach has occurred. The account will remain locked until a Post Office administrator unlocks the account.	✔ *Our design includes a property under class* `PostOfficeSettings` *that holds the maximum number of login attempts permitted. Users of the schema can define and register an event filter to detect if an account gets locked. The* `EmailAccount` *class contains a status property that holds the current status of an account.*
2.	An e-mail client can send or receive mail from the Post Office only when he/she has supplied a valid username and password.	✘ *This rule falls outside the scope of the design phase and is implementation-specific.*

3.	If a user's mailbag is > 100 megabytes, then the Post Office should suspend the user's account and generate an event. This will prevent the user from sending or receiving mail. All pending mail will remain in the intermediate directory and not be added to the mailbag until housekeeping has been performed (i.e., the mailbag is <= 100 MB).	✔ *Our design defines a property under the* `Mailbag` *class that holds the current size of an account mailbag including attachments. This can be used to construct an event filter that notifies interested parties if the size exceeds a given value.*
		
		i.e. `SELECT * FROM`
		`__InstanceModificationEvent WHERE`
		
		    `TargetInstance ISA PO_MailBag AND`
		    `TargetInstance. MailBagSize > 100000`

4.	If the total number of accounts on the Post Office > 99, then no more accounts may be added to the Post Office.	✔ *Our design stipulates that the maximum number of e-mail account objects per Post Office should never exceed 100. This is stipulated as a precondition in the* `AddUser` *method.*

Table 6.11 Post Office Assertions

No.	Assertions
1.	The Post Office must expose a list of registered accounts.
	✔ *The list of registered accounts can be retrieved from Class PostOffice in property* `RegisteredUsers`.
2.	The Post Office must keep a record of the last time each user successfully logged on the system.
	✔ *See class* `EmailAccount`, *property* `LogonDate`.
3.	The Post Office must provide a mapping between mailbag GUID IDs and user accounts.
	✔ *This information can be retrieved by looking up a user by UserName and then inspecting the value held in property.*
4.	The Post Office must allow a maximum of 100 e-mail accounts to be logged on to the system at once.
	✔ *The number of users allowed on the Post Office is restricted by the method* `AddUser`.
5.	There can be only one mailbag per user.
	✔ *Our design stipulates that there is only one mailbag per user. See UML diagram.*
6.	A mailbag cannot exceed 20 megabytes.
	✔ *Not implemented in the design but will be implemented during the coding of the Post Office.*
7.	The Post Office must not accept attachments greater than 2 megabytes.
	✔ *Class* `MessageSettings/MaxAttachSize` *defines the maximum allowed size of an e-mail attachment on our system.*
8.	The Post Office must provide a list of users currently logged on.
	✔ *Our design allows a list to be supplied using a WQL query. The class* `EmailAccount` *contains an* `AccountStatus` *property that holds the current status of each account. We could retrieve this information using the following query:*
	`SELECT * FROM PO_EmailAccount WHERE AccountStatus = "Logged in"`
	Note: The `AccountStatus` *property also keeps a record of the other states the account might be in, such as locked or suspended.*
9.	The Post Office must monitor the amount of space left on the mailbag disk partition on the Windows 2000 server.
	✔ *Although this is more of an implementation issue, the class* `PostOffice` *contains a* `FreeSpace` *property that holds the amount of free space left on a partition. Using a WQL event filter, it would be possible to monitor the Mailbag partition to see if it dropped below a certain threshold value.*
	i.e. `SELECT * FROM __InstanceModificationEvent WHERE TargetInstance` `        ISA PO_PostOffice AND TargetInstance.FreeSpace < 10000`
	Note: This filter checks to see if space drops below 10 megabytes before triggering an event.

Table 6.11 *Continued*

No.	Assertions
10.	The Post Office should provide statistics on the amount of messages being processed. A processed message is one that is sent by the user, processed by the Post Office, and ultimately placed in its destination mailbag. ✔ *Class* PostOfficeStats *provides this information.*
11.	The Post Office should log the total time in days, hours, and minutes that it has been running since startup. ✔ *Our design incorporates the amount of time that the Post Office has been running since startup. This value is reset when the Post Office is stopped. See* PO_PostOfficeStartTime *for details.*
12.	Administrators should be able to shut down and restart the Post Office cleanly (i.e., without active users losing mail messages). ✔ *We can see at this stage in our design that we have provided for starting and stopping the Post Office. Whether or not we do so cleanly without active users losing messages cannot be determined until we write the associated code for these methods.*
13.	Administrators s--hould be able to add and remove users to and from the Post Office user list while it is running. ✔ *Provision has been made in the design for adding and removing users from the Post Office. Again, run time requirements cannot be verified at this stage in design though they can become -part of the pre or post conditions.njnjn*
14.	Administrators should be able to lock and unlock a user's account on the Post Office. ✔ *The methods* LockUser *and* UnlockUser *enable accounts to be locked and unlocked on the Post Office.*

From interpreting the UML diagrams generated during the design process, we can state the following about our design, which then can again be compared with the rules and assertions from Step 2.

- The Post Office can have a maximum of 100 accounts.
- Each e-mail account has only one mailbag.
- Each e-mail account has associated user details.
- Each Post Office has its own unique message settings.
- Each Post Office generates its own statistics.
- Each e-mail account has its own user details.
- And so forth.

Although this approach is by no means watertight, it does provide a documented way of going through your schema design and verifying its structure and behavior. It also assumes that the rules and assertions that you defined in Step 2 provide a clear specification of how the schema should appear.

Final Considerations—Future Additions

Before signing off your schema design, it is important to consider any developments that will directly or indirectly affect the functioning of your product. Changes in the operation of your product will affect the schema that has been designed to manage it. We include this step to future-proof ourselves against any potential developments that could change aspects of the schema, thus causing incompatibilities between the old and the new. For example, in the Post Office schema we could consider the following:

■ Will a future release of our post office system be able to send and receive e-mail outside of our single Post Office? What impact would this have upon our schema design?

■ What type of advances in hardware or software design will take place that would change the boundaries within which the product must operate? For example, not long ago machines had only 30 megabyte hard disks and 2 megabytes of RAM. If your design is built around such limitations (that is, if you are using an uint8 property to expose how much free RAM your product has available), you could find in the near future that your design is inadequate. The Y2K problem was an outstanding example!

■ Will the Post Office be able to send and receive mail using e-mail protocols other than SMTP (Simple Mail Transfer Protocol)? What are the ramifications of this on our schema design?

■ Will the next release of the Post Office be able to handle more than 100 licensed users? What effect will this have on our schema design? In our example, this could mean that the *usercount* and any properties concerning the user count should be adjusted to take numbers greater than 100. Currently, we use an uint8, but we could increase this to uint16 to support greater numbers of accounts.

■ Will the mailbag size restriction increase in future releases of the Post Office? Have we accounted for such changes in our design?

■ Will future releases of the e-mail product allow a single machine to host multiple Post Offices? If so, what are the ramifications for our Post Office schema if multiple Post Offices were hosted on a single repository?

What would be the impact upon our schema should the answer to any of these questions be true? Use this phase to bring to light any possible design frailties that may exist in your design, and then make the necessary alterations.

■ Final Step: Positioning Classes

Having designed our classes, associations, properties, and methods, we position the classes in the final step. The last stage of design is possibly one of the most complex in class and namespace positioning, because of the available array of choices.

The Win32 extended schema contains some well-instrument products that do not require the number of classes we defined for the Post Office schema. Your schema, at this point in the design, might require merely that you add some properties to an existing class in the CIM or Win32 schemas. You can derive them from the relevant class, or, in special cases, might add them to the existing class. To add to an existing class, you must obtain approval from the owner of the schema before shipping your product. If your product runs on the Windows operating system and uses the CIMV2 namespace and classes in the Win32 schema, request approval from Microsoft's schema validation team (wmgmts@microsoft.com). If the DTMF owns the class you wish to modify, request its approval (CIM@dmtf.org).

The schema positioning process outlined here is in stages for the benefit of first-time schema designers. With practice and increased familiarity with the CIM schema and Win32 extended schema, you can omit many of the initial stages.

The four categories in Table 6.12 represent choices you may make in positioning classes.

If this is your first attempt at schema positioning, your lack of familiarity with the CIM schema or Win32 Schema classes will limit your understanding of the positioning stages. We will remedy this by starting with the most general classes and progressing down the hierarchy to the more specific ones.

■ Step-by-Step CIMV2 Namespace Class Positioning

The following steps take you through the process of class positioning. Your goal in positioning any class is to place it as close as possible to a leaf node (a class with no descendants).

1. Select a class from your schema.
2. Identify a general start point under which to classify the class and ask yourself fundamental questions about the class:
   - Does your product fall under the core of any of the common models (Networking, Applications, Systems, Physical, and so forth)?
   - Then, does your class represent the manageable characteristics of a logical element (`CIM_LogicalElement`), that is, software, or of a physical element (`CIM_Physical` Element), that is, a network cable?

Table 6.12 Schema Positioning Stages

No.	Description
1.	**Your classes derive from an extended schema such as the Win32 schema.** The Win32 extended schema is likely to be relevant to your product because it represents extensions to the Common model that are OS specific. In most cases, you must derive from a class that belongs to an extended schema. You do not need Microsoft's permission to add classes to the CIMV2 namespace, but you do need permission if you intend to modify one of the Win32 schema classes. In either case, you should check with Microsoft before shipping an extension or modifying one of their classes.
2.	**Your classes derive from existing CIM schema classes.**
3.	**Your classes do not derive from any schema class.**
4.	**An identical class already exists; therefore, you need not augment the schema.** This situation is ideal, although unlikely if your product is at all complex.

> **Hint:** Look first at the classes that belong to the core model, then to the Common model, and then to the extended schemas for inspiration.

> **Note:** If no class is relevant to the management application you are building, you probably have not understood the CIM schema. Its abstract layers are so generic that they should cover practically anything. If you are not dealing with a managed object, why is the element part of a management application? If the element is neither logical nor physical, then you are operating under very strange epistemic assumptions!

Next, create a new namespace (possibly under root/CIMV2/Applications) and place the class there. **End of Process.**

or

Apply to the DMTF (cim@dmtf.org) for the inclusion of the class in the CIM schema and obtain an implementation from Microsoft. Then, normalize your class and repeat Step 2.

Else **proceed to the next step.**

3. Progress down the hierarchy and ask more specific questions until one of the following occurs:

   a. There are multiple potential superclasses at the same level: Normalize your class and **return to Step 2.**

   b. There exists a single superclass at this level: **Repeat Step 3.**

   c. No suitable superclass exists: **Proceed to the next step.**

4. If the last relevant class belongs to the CIM schema, then apply for an implementation from Microsoft (winmgmts@microsoft.com), normalize, and start the process again with that implementation in place. **Return to Step 2.**

Else **proceed to the next step.**

5. If the class belongs to the Win32 extended schema, then normalize your class and extend the Win32 class (check Microsoft documentation to determine which classes in the CIMV2 namespace may or may not be extended). **End of Process.**

Extending the CIMV2 Namespace

Microsoft limits the CIM classes and associations within the CIMV2 namespace that it allows schema extension designers to derive from or instantiate to gain Microsoft Windows BackOffice logo certification. Table 6.13 lists the classes that can be subclassed. Table 6.14 lists associations that can be subclassed.

A number of classes do not allow direct instantiation and subclassing. These are high-level classes or classes that contain instances that are not local to the machine.

Classes

- `CIM_ManagedSystemElement` and `CIM_LogicalElement` (subclasses addressed separately)
- `CIM_System` and `CIM_ComputerSystem` (subclasses addressed separately)
- `CIM_LogicalDevice` (subclasses addressed separately)
- `CIM_VirtualComputerSystem`
- `CIM_Cluster`
- `CIM_ClusteringService`

Associations

- `CIM_ApplicationSystemSoftwareFeature`
- `CIM_ComponentCS`

Table 6.13 Classes That Can Be Subclassed

Class	Description
CIM_FRU	The CIM_FRU class is a vendor-defined collection of products and/or physical elements that is associated with a product for the purpose of supporting, maintaining, or upgrading that product at the customer's location. FRU is an acronym for 'field replaceable unit'.
CIM_SupportAccess	The CIM_SupportAccess class defines how to obtain assistance for a product.
CIM_MonitorResolution	CIM_MonitorResolution describes the relationship between horizontal and vertical resolutions, refresh rate, and scan mode for a desktop monitor.
CIM_RedundancyGroup and its subclasses	A collection of managed system elements that together indicate that the aggregated components together provide redundancy.
CIM_ManagementController	Capabilities and management of a management controller. An I2C microcontroller is a type of management controller.
CIM_Statistics and its subclasses	Defines any statistical information about our managed objects.
CIM_StorageError	CIM_StorageError defines blocks of media or memory space that are mapped 'out of use' due to errors. The key of the class is the StartingAddress property of the bytes in error.

- CIM_HostedClusterService
- CIM_ClusterServiceAccessBySAP
- CIM_HostingCS
- CIM_ParticipatingCS
- CIM_DeviceAccessedByFile (n/a for Win32 environment)

> **IMPORTANT:** For more detailed information about which CIM and Win32 classes can and cannot be subclassed see schema.txt, which is installed as part of the WMI SDK and resides in ./Program files/WMI/License/schema.txt.

Normalization

The purpose of normalization is to avoid problems, such as duplicate data, multiple in-heritance, selective inheritance, and incorrect property placement. Any of these can re-

Table 6.14 Associations That Can Be Subclassed

Associations
All CIM_Product associations with the exception of the CIM_ProductSoftwareFeatures association
All CIM_FRU and CIM_SupportAccess associations
All CIM_Configuration associations
All CIM_Statistics associations
CIM_Realizes and most associations of the Physical Model (exception is the CIM_Container association).
CIM_DeviceSoftware
CIM_AssociatedSensor and its subclasses
CIM_BIOSLoadedInNV
CIM_StorageDefect
CIM_RedundancyComponent and its subclasses
CIM_ActsAsSpare
CIM_CollectionOfSensors
CIM_DeviceServiceImplementation
CIM_DeviceSAPImplementation

duce the efficiency and usability of the schema extension. They also can make it difficult to correctly position your class in an existing class hierarchy such as the CIM schema.

Normalization is particularly relevant during class positioning because you will inherit new properties, methods, associations, and qualifiers from the parent classes after you place your class in the hierarchy. You already may have defined some of these characteristics in your class and will have to normalize them before you position it in the hierarchy. Additionally, you may find that your class inherits irrelevant characteristics from its parent.[1]

CIMV2 Class Placement Objectives

■ Your aim in most cases is to extend a Win32 class not a CIM schema class directly.

---

1. More information can be found on data modeling topics in J. P. Thompson's *Data with Semantics: Data Models and Data Management* (Van Nostrand Reinhold, 1989). Another good reference is William Kent's guide to normalization, "A simple guide to five normal forms in relational database theory" from *Communications of the AMC,* 26:2, pp. 120–125, 1983.

■ If a Win32 class is not available then extend a CIM schema class.

■ You should be as close towards a leaf node as possible when placing your class.

Remember: If your class does not appear to derive from a class in the CIM schema or Win32 schema you can
- Apply for an extension to the CIM schema and then get an implementation in the Win32 schema. Then you must derive from the Win32 class.
- Create your own namespace in which to place your class.

■ Putting Class Placement Theory into Practice

Use the `PO_PostOffice` class from our Post Office schema to practice the class placement steps.

To determine the start point, we shall examine the core model and CIM schema. You will recall that the core model and the Common model make up the CIM schema. In most cases, the core model will be too general a start point for class positioning, so we can progress immediately to the Common model. When you position schema classes, they must start somewhere, most commonly as a subclass of an existing class. The purpose of starting at the schema level is to locate a model within which our class fits. Note that in most cases you will not need to define a new root class because the CIM schema encompasses the most general aspects of the enterprise. (If the CIM schema does not support your product at this level, then you should contact the DMTF about adding a new class.)

First, we must consider under which of major areas within the Common model in CIM we can place our class (Table 6.15).

Following the earlier steps, we have an entry point in the applications model, CIM_LogicalElement. We must now work through its subclasses, identifying possible parent classes. Use the WMI CIM Studio to inspect the descriptions of the applications model classes, their properties, methods, and associations, and its help facility (Figure 6.6) to retrieve descriptions of classes, methods, and properties.

The help facility in CIM Studio can provide useful information about individual classes in the CIM schema and Win32 Schema. In this example, we have the description of the `CIM_ManagedSystemElement` class.

In the DMTF UML Application Model diagram (http://www.dmtf.org/standards/cim_schema_v26.php), we can see are a number of direct CIM schema descendants of CIM_LogicalElement (Table 6.16).

Table 6.15 CIM Models

Model	Discussion
Networks	The networks model represents the manageable features of a network environment. Our PostOffice class, however, does not add any features to this environment and generates no management information that could be viewed as network specific. Therefore, we shall not be working with any of the classes from this model.
✔ Applications	The applications model represents the set of details required to manage a software product, which may be any of a range of products, from a simple stand-alone desktop application to a complex distributed application. Our PostOffice class fits within this category because it defines a set of features for the Post Office software product. This is the logical entry point for our PostOffice class: The base class is CIM_LogicalElement. For a detailed description of each class, use the WMI CIM Studio help facility and DMTF documentation that includes UML diagrams in Visio format.
Systems	The systems model defines the basic characteristics associated with managed systems. Recall that a system is an entity, such as a router, server, or workstation, that stands alone in an environment. Our PostOffice class does not fit this model because it can only be managed only in the context of the host operating system upon which it runs.
Physical	The physical model represents the actual physical environment. In the CIMV2 namespace, the CIM_PhysicalElement class holds much of the information gathered as part of this model. Because our product is purely software-based, this model is not relevant to our schema design.
Devices	The devices model defines the physical and logical components that support the system. Our software application is not a device and so does not fall under this category.

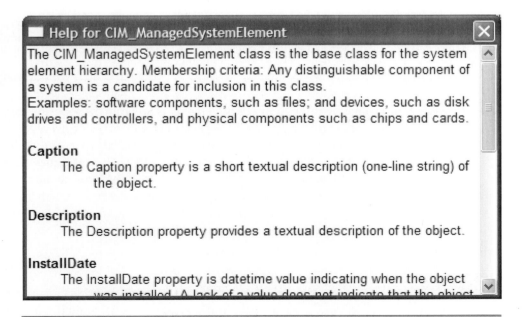

Figure 6.6 The help facility in WMI CIM Studio

Table 6.16 Post Office Class Positioning in the CIM Namespace

Class	Description
CIM_Service	A CIM_Service is a logical element that contains the information necessary to represent and manage the functionality provided by a device and/or SoftwareFeature. A service is a general-purpose object to configure and manage the implementation of functionality. It is not the functionality itself. ✗ Our class does not represent this characteristic.
CIM_SoftwareFeature	The CIM_SoftwareFeature class defines a particular function or capability of a product or application system…. It does so though only in the context of a product and propagates properties from the CIM_Product class. ✗ Our PostOffice class does not participate in this tightly bound association with the CIM_Product class and therefore cannot derive from here.
CIM_SoftwareElement	The CIM_SoftwareElement class is used to decompose a CIM_SoftwareFeature object into a set of individually manageable or deployable parts for a particular platform. ✗ This class is not directly relevant to the PostOffice class.
CIM_System	A CIM_System is a logical element that aggregates an enumerable set of managed system elements. The aggregation operates as a functional whole. Within any particular subclass of system, there is a well-defined list of managed system element classes whose instances must be aggregated. ✗ This class is not directly relevant to the PostOffice class.
CIM_ServiceAccessPoint	CIM_ServiceAccessPoint represents the ability to utilize or invoke a service. Access points represent that a service is made available to other entities for use. ✗ This class is not directly relevant to the PostOffice class.

Our aim in iterating through the class hierarchy is to locate the subclass nearest a leaf node. When we can no longer classify our PostOffice class under any of the available subclasses, we look to the most suitable superclass and derive from that. In our example, the PostOffice class does not fit under the CIM_SoftwareFeature class, so we take CIM_LogicalElement as our superclass. Because we shall not extend a Win32 class and the class CIM_Software feature is not one of the classes to which Microsoft allows extensions in the CIMV2 namespace, the most salient solution is to place the class in its own namespace.

▪ Namespace and Schema Placement

In Chapter 4, we discussed namespaces and their relevance to holding information about managed environments. When positioning our schema on a Windows platform, we face three choices, placing our classes within the existing CIMV2 namespace, creating our own custom namespace, or a mixture of the two. The choice we make depends wholly on the type of information we wish to add to the CIMV2 namespace and whether or not we can derive from any of the existing classes without conflicting with Microsoft's plans for the namespace.

> **Note:** The Windows 2000 logo requirements state that all products written for Windows 2000 must use the Windows Installer to install and uninstall themselves. This means that regardless of your end choice of namespace, ultimately you must instrument the application to some extent within the CIMV2 namespace. Microsoft relaxed this rule for Windows XP, although it still appears under the list of future requirements (F1.5). For detailed information on the logo requirements see:
>
> http://msdn.microsoft.com/certification/default.asp (Windows 2000 and WinXP)
>
> http://www.microsoft.com/PRODUCTS/servers/designed (BackOffice)

Where does the management-specific information defined for our Post Office reside? Microsoft provides strict rules about class placement within the CIMV2 namespace for logo certification: All of your schema classes might not meet Microsoft's requirements. In the Post Office example, because the information we are going to supply in our schema is unique to our application, it does not apply generally to all other Win32 applications. The solution is to create a new namespace under the CIMV2\Applications namespace. This does not preclude using the CIMV2 namespace to host certain classes from your schema and placing the remaining classes in your own namespace; we shall consider the implications of this later. You can use the view provider to include classes from the CIMV2 namespace in your namespace if you want to integrate your management data with data available in the CIMV2 or any other namespace.

■ The Applications Namespace

The Applications namespace accommodates application management information that does not follow Microsoft's guidelines for the CIMV2 namespace. Microsoft anticipates that more and more products will use the CIMV2 namespace, creating their own sub-namespaces to store product-specific management information. Microsoft's Internet Explorer places management information in its own namespace defined in the CIMV2 namespace. Table 6.17 represents a few of the advantages and disadvantages of using the Microsoft CIMV2 namespace and creating your own namespace.

Table 6.17 Advantages and Disadvantages of Namespace Positioning

Using the CIMV2 namespace	Using an Applications/proprietary namespace
Easy for applications to access.	Requires more thought about how you will deploy your schema.
Must adhere to strict rules defined by Microsoft for use of the CIMV2 schema.	Allows unrestricted usage (you are the owner) and is easier to extend.
Many features implemented already using the Windows Installer and other providers.	Requires you to use the view provider to include classes/instances from other namespaces. Note: You can import the DMTF definition of abstract CIM classes into your namespace as and when needed.
	All cross-namespace associations are unidirectional.*

*This is relevant if you compromise, positioning part of your classes in the CIMV2 namespace and positioning specific management elements that are unique to your product in a proprietary namespace. Cross-namespace associations are allowed, but remember that they are unidirectional from the direction of the association's host namespace.

Limitations of Multinamespace Class Positioning

Figure 6.7 is an arrangement of classes from the Post Office schema that demonstrates the limitations of cross-namespace associations.

In the three examples that follow, we positioned some Post Office application-specific classes in the PostOffice namespace and the associations in the CIMV2 namespace

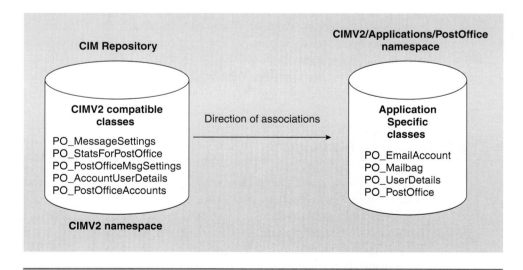

Figure 6.7 An arrangement of classes from the Post Office schema

(ignoring the suitability of these classes to be positioned in the CIMV2 namespace). As a result of this positioning, some of the association classes make cross-namespace associations to the classes based in the PostOffice namespace. Although this approach is perfectly valid, it brings about certain considerations when constructing WMI queries. We use the *Associators of* or *References of* statement to illustrate this point.

Example 1. Executed in the CIMV2 Namespace

```
ASSOCIATORS OF
  {\\MyMachine\root\CIMV2\applications\PostOffice:PO_UserDetails.
Username="Tunstallc"}
  WHERE AssocClass=PO_AccountUserDetails
```

Example 2. Executed in the PostOffice Namespace

```
Associators of (PO_UserDetails.Username="Tunstallc")
  WHERE AssocClass=PO_AccountUserDetails
```

The query in Example 1 would attempt to find all the endpoint objects bound to association `PO_AccountUserDetails` with a PO_userdetails object that had a username of Tunstallc. The query will work if you give the full class object path of the User Details object and run the query from the namespace that hosts the association class `PO_AccountUserDetails` (in this example CIMV2).

The query in Example 2 would fail to return any instances because the association class `PO_AccountUserDetails` does not exist in the PostOffice namespace.

Example 3. Executed in the PostOffice Namespace

```
REFERENCES OF {PO_UserDetails="Tunstallc"}
```

The query in Example 3 would return no references because the CIMV2 namespace within their respective association classes hosts them. This highlights the unidirectional problem of association classes in which only the host namespace is aware of the association. In our example, class `PO_UserDetails` is unaware of any of the associations in which it may be involved if they fall outside the scope of the PostOffice namespace.

Post Office Schema Namespace Positioning

The Post Office schema will reside in a new namespace called PostOffice, placed beneath the root/CIMV2/applications namespace. This is because not all of the classes belonging to the Post Office schema can be positioned in the CIMV2 namespace and because of the problems highlighted previously about cross-namespace associations.

The Post Office Schema Class Positions

By repeating this class-positioning process for each of the classes in the Post Office schema, we position the classes as in Figures 6.8, 6.9, 6.10, 6.11, 6.12, and 6.13.

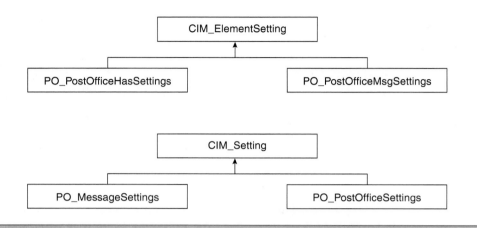

Figure 6.8   Post Office schema settings classes

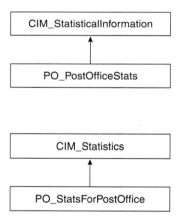

Figure 6.9   Post Office schema statistical classes

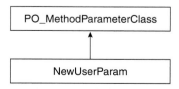

Figure 6.10   Post Office schema method parameter classes

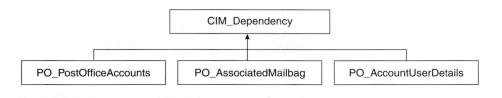

Figure 6.11   Post Office schema dependency classes

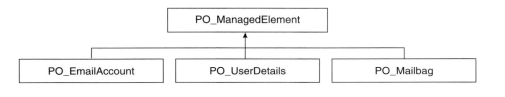

Figure 6.12   Post Office schema managed element classes

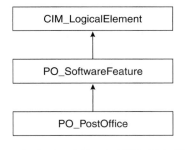

Figure 6.13   Post Office schema element classes

PO_MethodParameterClass in Figure 6.10 is a new abstract base class that hosts the parameter classes specific to our Post Office schema. Had we placed our schema classes in the CIMV2 namespace, we could have used the Win32_MethodParameter class.

PO_ManagedElement in Figure 6.12 is an abstract base class for the classes Mailbag, UserDetails, and EmailAccount. It groups them together as manageable aspects of our Post Office application that are unique to it. We cannot classify these classes under CIM_ManagedSystemElement, because they represent objects outside the managed system domain and are, instead, a logical representation of the managed elements in our Post Office.

PO_SoftwareFeature in Figure 6.13 is a new abstract superclass for class Post-Office. Derived from class CIM_LogicalElement, it represents the manageable features of our software application. It contains several inherited properties and defines a single key name property that replaces our `PostOffice` name property.

Managed Object Format (MOF) Qualifiers and Flavors

Before you add your schema to the CIM repository, you must use qualifiers and flavors to characterize your properties, classes, associations, and methods.

We have already assigned a type to the elements in our schema, but we must complete some additional tasks before creating the code.

- ✔ Decide which properties should be read-only and which should be read/write.
- ✔ Decide which elements are key properties.
- ✔ Decide which elements to flag as *required* properties
- ✔ Decide which methods are constructors and destructors.
- ✔ *Always* explicitly state Max and Min values for properties.
- ✔ Explicitly state the upper length and minimum length of strings using Max-Len(n) and Minvalue(n) where *n* is a natural number.
- ✔ Decide which qualifiers to pass to ToInstance's and ToSubclasses.
- ✔ Decide which classes are concrete/abstract.
- ✔ Decide which classes are singletons.
- ✔ Always specify a locale. If you do not, the MOF compiler will default to the locale of the installation that hosts the CIM repository.
- ✔ Provide clear descriptions for each class, property, method, and association using the Description qualifier.

■ MOF Creation and Testing

Before we can begin to write the first lines of Post Office schema MOF code, we must consider an additional problem. Although at this early stage in development we have designed the elements of our schema, we have not considered how to supply them to management data consumers. Will the objects, classes, or properties in our schema be provided dynamically by a provider, will they be stored within the CIM repository, or will a mixture of both apply? The means of supplying the elements affects the contents of the MOF file (the inclusion of the dynamic qualifier, among others), but more important is the necessity for testing our schema properly, regardless of having made this decision. If we write our schema as static, meaning that all elements (objects, classes, properties, and associations) are held within the CIM repository at this stage, we can test them before writing provider code. As you will see after we code our MOF file, it is not difficult to add the dynamic qualifier after the provider code.

■ Implementing the Schema: WMI API Calls vs. MOF Code

In the Post Office example, we provide the source code in the form of a MOF file. It is listed in its entirety to provide you with the full source for the Post Office schema and to help you understand how the MOF language represents the schema. The comments in shaded boxes are given to assist your interpretation of the code and to help you understand why we use certain techniques.

By using the WMI API, you can add schema constructs programmatically and avoid using MOF files altogether. Exclusively adopting this approach, however, assumes that your product will work only on the Windows platform and that you don't require the multiplatform compatibility of the MOF language. Experience also suggests that unless you are familiar with the MOF language, writing directly via the WMI API could be overwhelming for a first-time WMI developer. From a testing perspective, it is far less labor intensive to write a MOF file and import it into the CIM repository than to write a program that makes a series of calls to the WMI API. Maintenance of the schema becomes overwhelming in the WMI API. In comparison, a MOF file is simple to update, is understood by other developers, and is version-control friendly. Considering the recovery aspect, if you mark your MOF appropriately, WMI will remember it and recompile it if the repository becomes corrupted.

> **Tip:** For WMI recompiling, mark your MOF file with the `#pragma autorecover` command. This adds the MOF file to the list of files that WMI will compile during recovery of the repository. The registry holds the list of MOF files registered for recovery under `HKEY_LOCAL_MACHINE\SOFTWARE\Microsoft\WBEM\CIMOM`.

You can manually trigger a restore of the CIM repository with the wmimgmt.msc snap-in by moving to the Backup/restore tab.

With the WMI CIM Studio, you can add your schema to the CIM repository easily. The Studio permits you to add classes, properties, and associations to a namespace and then export them to a MOF text file for editing and documentation. We do not use the WMI CIM Studio because of limited space, because we reviewed the fundamentals of performing these tasks in earlier chapters, and because the quickest way to learn the syntax of MOF is to read and type an example.

■ Multilanguage Support

Support for multiple languages is a key issue in developing any software application, and schemas in the CIM repository are no exception. This section describes how MOF files accommodate multilanguage support.

Begin by marking any locale-specific data using the Amendment qualifier at the class level and the Amended qualifier flavor at the qualifier level. Items that may be locale specific include the descriptions that are part of classes, properties, methods, or associations. The Amendment qualifier indicates that a class contains locale-specific information. If you use the Amendment qualifier, you must also use the Locale qualifier to tell the compiler for which locale the class has information. In Figure 6.14, the MOF excerpt declares that class `PO_PostOffice` contains locale-specific information in US English (0x409).

Figure 6.14 Example of the amendment qualifier

```
[ description("The PostOffice class exposes management information pertinent
to our PostOffice. It supplies all the main properties for monitoring the
PostOffice, its performance and the accounts on it. This class is a singleton
in this release"): amended ToInstance, amendment, locale(0x409)]
class PO_PostOffice: PO_SoftwareFeature
{
  .. ...
  ...
```

Notice that the Description qualifier for the class has the Amended qualifier flavor to signify that its contents are locale specific.

In the MOF excerpt in Figure 6.15, we declare that the description for property `StartTime` within class `PO_PostOffice` is locale specific. Notice that the locale value assigned to the class is global for all properties and methods within it unless it is overridden with another locale qualifier.

Figure 6.15 Example of the amended qualifier

```
[ read: ToSubClass ToInstance, required: ToSubClass ToInstance, description
("The StartTime property contains the start date and time of the current
PostOffice session.") : amended ToSubClass]
DATETIME StartTime;
```

WMI uses this information in responding to requests from management information consumers. It determines the locale of the consumer and returns the information marked with that locale value, if it is available, from the repository. To determine the locale, WMI divides the information from a schema into language-neutral and language-specific namespaces. When returning information to the consumer, it constructs a composite of data from both namespaces. This is an extremely powerful feature, especially considering that Windows can now support multiple languages on a single installation. This feature makes it feasible for an American and a Japanese office to access the CIM repository simultaneously, each retrieving management information in its respective language.

If you want your schema to be readable in a specific locale, use the DisplayName qualifier to specify the name of the property, method, class, or association in a locale-specific format. For example, we could append all of our manageable classnames, properties, methods, and association names using the MOF excerpt in Figure 6.16.

Figure 6.16   Example of the DisplayName qualifier

```
[ displayname("PostOffice (PO)") : amended,
description("The PostOffice class exposes management information pertinent
to our PostOffice. It supplies all the main properties for monitoring the
PostOffice, its performance and the accounts on it. This class is a
singleton in this release"): amended ToInstance, amendment, locale(0x409)]
class PO_PostOffice: PO_SoftwareFeature
{
  .. ...
  ...
```

Having defined which classes, properties, methods, and associations contain locale-specific information, we can compile this information into the CIM repository.

Use the *amendment* pragma at the top of the MOF file, following the namespace pragma, to notify the compiler that the file includes locale-specific information (see Figure 6.17).

Figure 6.17   Example of the amendment MOF compiler directive

```
#pragma namespace ("\\\\.\\Root\\CIMV2\\Applications\\PostOffice")
#pragma amendment("MS_409") // Specifies U.S. English
// The naming convention for these namespaces is ms_xxx where xxx equals
// the LCID hex digits after 0x...
```

This directive tells the compiler to create a language-specific schema that will reside immediately beneath the namespace specified by the namespace directive. In our example, this would create the localized namespace root\CIMV2\Applications\PostOffice\ms_409.

> **Important:** WMI treats all of the amended classes placed in the locale-specific namespace (for example, MS_409) as abstract, regardless of their initial definition. This means that it is not possible to instantiate them in the localized namespace.

Instead of declaring the #pragma amendment ("ms_XXX") in your MOF file, you can use the amendment directive to notify the MOF compiler that your MOF contains locale-specific information. You still must mark locale-specific classes and data using the AMENDMENT and Amended qualifiers. Use the mofcomp -*amendment* directive from the command prompt as follows:

```
C:\mofcomp -MOF:PostOfficeLN.mof MFL:PostOfficeLS.mfl amendment:MS_409
PostOffice.mof
```

This command places the output not in the CIM repository but in two files: a localized MOF file (which ends with mfl) and a language-neutral one (which ends with mof). You must then use mofcomp without any special switches to compile these two files individually to place them in the CIM repository.

▪ The Post Office Schema in MOF

Having completed the steps of schema design, we can create our Post Office schema in MOF format. The code is annotated throughout at points of interest, although, because of its length and the syntactical unfriendliness of the MOF language, you will want to download the example from the Web site and use the text for reference only.

Brief MOF Syntax Reminder

Remember that commas delimit qualifiers and spaces delimit qualifier flavors. Colons separate flavors from their qualifiers. Square brackets enclose qualifiers and flavors before the property, class, association, or method to which they apply.

```
e.g. [Qualifier : flavor1 flavor2 , Qualifier 2: flavor1 ]
     [Read: ToSubClass ToInstance, Description("Textual description"):
     ToSubclass]


     #pragma autorecover
     #pragma classflags("forceupdate")
     //    Create namespace for PostOffice under CIMV2/Applications
```

```
#pragma namespace ("\\\\.\\Root\\CIMV2\\Applications")

instance of __Namespace
{
  Name = "PostOffice";
};


//    Change focus to PostOffice namespace

#pragma namespace ("\\\\.\\Root\\CIMV2\\Applications\\PostOffice")
#pragma amendment("MS_409")
```

The amendment pragma tells the MOF compiler to create separate MOF files: a locale-neutral version and a locale-specific version. This means that compilation becomes a two-step process.

Step 1. Compile the MOF file and generate two output files: a locale-neutral version and one or more locale-specific versions.

Step 2. Compile each of these files to add their contents to the CIM repository.

We offer more detail about this process at the end of the chapter.

We used the WMI CIM Studio's MOF Generator to export the class definitions that follow directly from the CIMV2 namespace and place them here. Because we derive some of the PostOffice classes from these classes, we need their definitions before we declare our own classes. These classes do not exist in the PostOffice namespace, so if we did not export them, we would generate a compilation error.

```
//**************************************************************************
//* Class: CIM_ManagedSystemElement
//* Derived from:
//**************************************************************************
[ Abstract, Locale(1033): ToInstance, UUID("{8502C517-5FBB-11D2-AAC1-
   006008C78BC7}"): ToInstance]
class CIM_ManagedSystemElement
{
    [MaxLen(64): ToSubClass, read: ToSubClass] string Caption;
    [read: ToSubClass] string Description;
    [MappingStrings{"MIF.DMTF|ComponentID|001.5"}: ToSubClass, read:
    ToSubClass] datetime InstallDate;
    [read: ToSubClass] string Name;
    [read: ToSubClass, MaxLen(10): ToSubClass, ValueMap{"OK", "Error",
      "Degraded", "Unknown", "Pred Fail", "Starting", "Stopping",
      "Service"}: ToSubClass]
    string Status;
};
```

```
//***********************************************************************
//* Class: PO_ManagedElement
//* Derived from:
//***********************************************************************
[ Abstract, Locale(1033): ToInstance, UUID("{6131164E-FDF5-4085-8064-
  0A84BF8957FB}"): ToInstance]
class PO_ManagedElement
{
   [MaxLen(64): ToSubClass, read: ToSubClass] string Caption;
   [read: ToSubClass] string Description;
};


//***********************************************************************
//* Class: CIM_LogicalElement
//* Derived from: CIM_ManagedSystemElement
//***********************************************************************
[ Abstract, Locale(1033): ToInstance, UUID("{8502C518-5FBB-11D2-AAC1-
  006008C78BC7}"): ToInstance]
class CIM_LogicalElement : CIM_ManagedSystemElement
{
};


//***********************************************************************
//* Class: PO_SoftwareFeature
//* Derived from: CIM_LogicalElement
//***********************************************************************
[ Locale(1033): ToInstance, UUID("{E527D7F2-E3D4-11d2-8601-
  0000F8102E5F}"): ToInstance, abstract]
class PO_SoftwareFeature : CIM_LogicalElement
{
   [read: ToSubClass, key, override("Name"), Maxlen(256): ToSubClass]
   string Name = NULL;
};


//***********************************************************************
//* Class: CIM_Dependency
//* Derived from:
//***********************************************************************
[ Association: DisableOverride ToInstance ToSubClass, Abstract,
  LOCALE(0x409): ToInstance, UUID("{8502C53A-5FBB-11D2-AAC1-
  006008C78BC7}"): ToInstance]
class CIM_Dependency
{
   [read: ToSubClass] CIM_ManagedSystemElement ref Antecedent;
   [read: ToSubClass] CIM_ManagedSystemElement ref Dependent;
};
```

```
//*******************************************************************
//* Class: CIM_ElementSetting
//* Derived from:
//*******************************************************************
[ Abstract, Association: DisableOverride ToInstance ToSubClass,
   LOCALE(0x409): ToInstance, UUID("{8502C577-5FBB-11D2-AAC1-
   006008C78BC7}"): ToInstance]
class CIM_ElementSetting
{
   [read: ToSubClass] CIM_ManagedSystemElement ref Element;
   [read: ToSubClass] CIM_Setting ref Setting;
};


//*******************************************************************
//* Class: CIM_Setting
//* Derived from:
//*******************************************************************
[ Abstract, LOCALE(0x409): ToInstance, UUID("{8502C572-5FBB-11D2-AAC1-
   006008C78BC7}"): ToInstance]
class CIM_Setting
{
   [read: ToSubClass, MaxLen(256): ToSubClass] string SettingID;
   [read: ToSubClass, MaxLen(64): ToSubClass] string Caption;
   [read: ToSubClass] string Description;
};


//*******************************************************************
//* Class: CIM_StatisticalInformation
//* Derived from:
//*******************************************************************
[ Abstract, LOCALE(0x409): ToInstance, UUID("{956597A1-7D80-11D2-AAD3-
   006008C78BC7}"): ToInstance]
class CIM_StatisticalInformation
{
   [read: ToSubClass, MaxLen(256): ToSubClass] string Name;
   [read: ToSubClass] string Description;
   [read: ToSubClass, MaxLen(64): ToSubClass] string Caption;
};


//*******************************************************************
//* Class: CIM_Statistics
//* Derived from:
//*******************************************************************
[ Abstract, Association: DisableOverride ToInstance ToSubClass,
   LOCALE(0x409): ToInstance, UUID("{956597A3-7D80-11D2-AAD3-
   006008C78BC7}"): ToInstance]
class CIM_Statistics
```

```
{
    [read: ToSubClass] CIM_StatisticalInformation ref Stats;
    [read: ToSubClass] CIM_ManagedSystemElement ref Element;
};


//************************************************************************
//* Class: PO_MethodParameterClass
//* Derived from:
//************************************************************************
[ Abstract, LOCALE(0x409): ToInstance, UUID("{6AF1A338-5671-4d3d-8A12-
  0532E9D0C97F}"): ToInstance]
class PO_MethodParameterClass
{
};


//************************************************************************
// THE FOLLOWING CLASSES ARE ALL PART OF THE POSTOFFICE SCHEMA
//************************************************************************


//************************************************************************
//* Class: PO_PostOffice
//* Derived from: PO_SoftwareFeature
//************************************************************************
```

> The UUID qualifier has been included in the class definitions for completeness.
> WMI does not require that you supply this value in your class definitions and will
> generate one automatically on your behalf if you do not. The value must be
> unique. It is used by WMI to identify classes.

```
[ Description("The PostOffice class exposes management information
  pertinent to our PostOffice. It supplies all the main properties
  for monitoring the PostOffice, its performance and the accounts on
  it. This class is a singleton in this release"): amended,
  UUID("{6F0DD128-6546-4636-9DDC-C1F86692616B}") : ToInstance,
  AMENDMENT, LOCALE(0x409)]
```

The AMENDMENT class qualifier specifies that locale-specific information is held in
this class. The Locale qualifier specifies the class has been localized for US English
(0x409).

```
class PO_PostOffice:PO_SoftwareFeature
{
```

You will notice that class PO_PostOffice does not contain a key property. This is
because it inherits the key property name from its parent class PO_SoftwareFeature.

```
[ Read: ToInstance ToSubClass, Description("The PostOfficeStatus
  property contains the current status of the PostOffice.") :
  ToSubClass amended,
  valuemap {"1","2","3","4","5"}: ToSubClass ToInstance,
  values {"Stopped","Initialising","Running","Shutting down","Error"}:
  ToSubClass ToInstance Amended]
uint16 PostOfficeStatus;


[ Read: ToSubClass ToInstance, Required: ToSubClass ToInstance,
  Description("The PostOfficeVersion property contains the version
  of the PostOffice."): ToSubClass amended, Minvalue(6): ToSubClass
  ToInstance ,
  Maxlen(100): ToSubclass ToInstance]
string PostOfficeVersion;


[ Read: ToSubClass ToInstance, Required: ToSubClass ToInstance,
  Description("The PostOfficeName property contains the version of the
  PostOffice."):
  ToSubClass amended, Minvalue(6): ToSubClass ToInstance,
  Maxlen(100): ToSubclass ToInstance]
string PostOfficeName;


[ Read: ToSubClass ToInstance, Required: ToSubClass ToInstance,
  Description("The StartTime property contains the start date and time
  of the current PostOffice session."): ToSubclass amended]
datetime StartTime;


[ Write: ToSubClass ToInstance, Required: ToSubClass ToInstance,
  Description("The MaxFailLogon property stipulates the maximum logon
  attempts."):ToSubClass amended, Maxvalue(100) : ToSubclass]
uint8 MaxFailLogon;


[ Read: ToSubClass ToInstance, Description("The FreeSpace property
  stipulates the amount of freespace left on the mailbag partition."):
  ToSubClass amended, Units("Kilobytes"): ToSubclass ToInstance]
uint64 FreeSpace;
```

Notice the Units qualifier that describes the property values units of measurement. In this case, it is measured in KB.

```
[ Read: ToSubClass ToInstance, Description("The UserCount property
  indicates the number of registered users on the PostOffice."):
  ToSubClass amended, MinValue(1): ToSubClass ToInstance, Maxlen(100):
  ToSubclass ToInstance]
uint8 UserCount;
```

```
[ Read: ToSubClass ToInstance, Description("The UserLogged array
  property holds the usernames of those currently logged in to the
  PostOffice."): ToSubClass amended, MinValue(1): ToSubClass
  ToInstance, Maxlen(100): ToSubclass ToInstance]
string UserLogged[];

[ Read: ToSubClass ToInstance, Description("The UserLoggedCount
  property counts the number of users logged on the PostOffice."):
  ToSubClass amended, MinValue(1) : ToSubClass ToInstance, Maxlen(100):
  ToSubclass ToInstance]
uint8 UserLoggedCount[];
```

Now we define the methods that belong to class `PostOffice`. The method descriptions that follow are reformatted to make them more readable. Note that the MOF compiler will flag an error if you attempt to compile text strings that contain a carriage return.

```
[ Description("The AddUser method adds a user to the PostOffice. It
  returns the following status values:\n0 : Operation was completed
  successfully\n1 : Unknown error - the method failed to add the user\n2
  : Error: Username already exists\n3 : Error: PostOffice reached
  maximum number of users\n4 : Error: Invalid initialisation
  parameters"): ToSubClass amended, Values {"Success", "Unknown error",
  "Error: Username exists",
  "Error : Max number of users exceeded",
  "Error: Invalid initialisation parameters"}: Amended ToSubclass]
uint32 AddUser([in, Id(0)] NewUserParam object);
```

The In qualifier specifies this parameter as an input parameter. The Id(0) qualifier uniquely tags each parameter in a method. WMI automatically assigns an Id value if one is not given.

```
[ Description("The RemoveUser method removes a user from the
  PostOffice. It returns the following status values:\n0 : Operation
  was completed successfully\n1 : Error: Unknown error - the method
  failed to remove the user\n2 : Error: Username does not exist\n3 :
  Error: UserAccount Current Active\n4 : Error: Invalid initialisation
  parameters "): ToSubClass amended, Values{"Success", "Unknown error",
  "Error: Account does not exist", "Error: Account Active",
  "Error: Invalid initialisation parameters"}: Amended ToSubclass]
uint32 RemoveUser([in,id(0)] string Username);
```

> **Note:** When the Post Office is installed, a single PostOffice object will be created. This `StartPostOffice` method places it in the running state, allowing users to use it to send and receive e-mail.

```
[ Description("The StartPostOffice method places the PostOffice in the
  running state. It returns the following status values:\n0 : Success -
  the operation was completed successfully\n1 : Unknown error - the
  PostOffice failed to start\n2 : Error: PostOffice was not in stopped
  state" ): ToSubClass amended, Values{"Success", "Unknown error",
  "Error: PostOffice not in stopped state"}:
  Amended ToSubclass]
uint32 StartPostOffice();
```

The Amended qualifier flavor indicates that the qualifier contains localized information. In this case the description is written in English and belongs to locale 0x409 (see locale qualifier declared with the class). This information is placed in a language-specific child namespace and merged with the language-neutral version when requested. On an American installation, typically /MS_409 would hold this locale-specific information.

```
[ Description("The StopPostOffice method places the PostOffice in the
  stopped state. It takes a single parameter, Shutdowntype, that
  specifies how the PostOffice shuts down. It returns the following
  status values:\n0 :
  Success - the operation was completed successfully\n1 :
  Unknown error - the PostOffice failed to shutdown\n2 : Error: PostOffice
  was not running" ): ToSubClass, Values{"Success", "Unknown error",
  "Error: PostOffice not in running state"}: Amended ToSubclass]
uint32 StopPostOffice([in, id(0), Description("Shutdowntype can be
  assigned a value of 0 or 1.\n A value of zero means shut down only
  if no users are currently logged in\n A value of one means shut
  down forcibly regardless of whether users are logged in")] uint8
  shutdowntype);
};


//********************************************************************
//* Class: PO_EmailAccount
//* Derived from:
//********************************************************************

[ Description("The EmailAccount class exposes management information
  about each user of our system. It supplies all the main properties
  about each including the accounts status, user name and password."):
  amended,
  UUID("{E8415E1E-5E11-4f5e-8F2F-FBE3E0A25857}") : ToInstance,
  AMENDMENT, LOCALE(0x409)]
class PO_EmailAccount: PO_ManagedElement
{

  [ Read: ToSubClass ToInstance, Description("The MailBagIdentifier
    property contains the unique value assigned to this accounts
    mailbag."): ToSubClass amended]
  string MailBagIdentifier;
```

```
[ Read: ToSubClass ToInstance, Description("The LogonDate property
  contains the date and time this account was successfully
  accessed."): ToSubClass amended]
datetime LogonDate;


[ Key: ToSubClass ToInstance DisableOverride, Read: ToSubClass
  ToInstance, Description("The UserName property contains the date and
  time this account was successfully accessed."): ToSubClass amended]
string UserName;
```

By specifying the password property `Read(false)`, we ensure that nobody can read the password for the user's account. The password property is writeable, however, which allows administrators to change the password when required.

```
[ Read(False): ToSubClass ToInstance,Write: ToSubClass ToInstance,
  Description("The UserName property contains the date and time this
  account was successfully accessed."): ToSubClass amended]
string Password;


[ Read: ToSubClass ToInstance, Description("The AccountStatus string
  property contains the current status of the account.\n Acceptable
  values are: \n Logged In\n Logged Out\n Locked\n Suspended"):
  ToSubClass amended]
string AccountStatus;


// Now we define the methods for class PO_EmailAccount


[ Description("The LockAccount method locks a users account on the
  PostOffice. It returns the following status values: \n0 : Operation
  was completed successfully\n1 : Error: Unknown error - the method
  failed to lock the user \n2 : Error: Users account already locked "):
  ToSubClass amended, Values{"Success", "Unknown error",
  "Error: Account already locked"}: Amended ToSubclass]
uint32 LockAccount();


[ Description("The UnLockAccount method unlocks a users account on the
  PostOffice. It returns the following status values:\n0 : Operation
  was completed successfully\n1 : Error: Unknown error - the method
  failed to unlock user \n2 : Error: Users account not locked"):
  ToSubClass amended, Values{"Success", "Unknown error", "Error:
  Account not locked"}:
  Amended ToSubclass]
uint32 UnLockAccount();
};
```

```
//************************************************************************
//* Class: PO_PostOfficeStats
//* Derived from: CIM_StatisticalInformation
//************************************************************************

[ Abstract(false),Description("The PostOfficeStats class is a singleton
  and exposes statistical management information about the PostOffice.
  It is of special interest to management data consumers that wish to
  monitor performance of the Post Office in terms of message processing
  ability and delivery failures."): amended ToSubClass, AMENDMENT,
  LOCALE(0x409),
  UUID("{C83E84AE-318F-4dae-B91C-19EB12E143DC}"): ToInstance,
  Singleton : ToInstance ToSubclass]
```

We must declare that this class is a singleton bcause it does not contain a key value.
Without specifying this, WMI CIM Studio will not allow us to instantiate it.

```
Class PO_PostOfficeStats:CIM_StatisticalInformation
{

  [ Read: ToSubClass ToInstance, Description("The FailedMailCount
    property contains the total number of emails that have failed to
    reach their destination address since startup. "): amended
    ToSubClass]
  uint64 FailedMailCount;


  [ Read: ToSubClass ToInstance, Description("The TotalMailCount
    property contains the total number of emails successfully delivered
    since startup."): amended ToSubClass]
  uint64 TotalMailCount;


  [ Read: ToSubClass ToInstance, Description("The AccountLockedCount
    property maintains a count of the total number of accounts locked at
    the present time."): amended ToSubClass]
  uint8 AccountLockedCount;


  [ Read: ToSubClass ToInstance, Description("The ActiveAccountCount
    property maintains a count of the total number of users currently
    logged in"): amended ToSubClass]
  uint8 ActiveAccountCount;
};
```

```
//*******************************************************************
//* Class: PO_MessageSettings
//* Derived from: CIM_MessageSetting
//*******************************************************************


[ Singleton: ToInstance ToSubclass, Description("The MessageSettings
   class is a singleton and contains the settings for messages sent on
   our PostOffice. It is here that management data consumers can
   configure the message settings for our PostOffice. "): amended
   ToSubClass,AMENDMENT, LOCALE(0x409),
   UUID("{340B7585-BD27-48d7-9A0F-4BD6E20A8951}") : ToInstance]
Class PO_MessageSettings:CIM_Setting
{

   [ Write: ToSubClass ToInstance, Description("The MaxMessageSize
      property contains the maximum permitted size of a message sent on
      the PostOffice. The value includes attachments and is measured in
      kilobytes"): amended ToSubClass, Units("Kilobytes"):ToSubClass
      ToInstance]
   uint16    MaxMessageSize;


   [ Write: ToSubClass ToInstance, Description("The MaxAttachSize
      property contains the maximum permitted size of an individual
      attachment on the PostOffice. The value is measured in kilobytes"):
      Amended ToSubClass, Units("Kilobytes"): ToSubClass ToInstance]
   uint16    MaxAttachSize;


   [ Write: ToSubClass ToInstance, Description("The MaxAttachmentCount
      property contains the maximum number of attachments permitted per
      email on the PostOffice. "): amended ToSubClass]
   uint8    MaxAttachmentCount;
};


//*******************************************************************
//* Class: PO_Mailbag
//* Derived from: PO_ManagedElement
//*******************************************************************


[ Description("The Mailbag class exposes management information about
   the mailbag files on the PostOffice. It is of special interest to
   management data consumers that wish to ascertain the size of a users
   mailbag and the GUID associated with their mailbag."): amended
   ToSubClass, AMENDMENT, LOCALE(0x409),UUID("{F9828C0E-AEC6-40ec-877C-
   E75849FF0560}") : ToInstance]
Class PO_Mailbag: PO_ManagedElement
{
```

```
[ Read: ToInstance ToSubClass, Description("The MailbagSize property
  states the current size of the mailbag for a particular user on the
  PostOffice. The unit of measurement is megabytes"): amended
  ToSubClass, Units("Megabytes"): ToSubClass ToInstance]
uint16 MailbagSize;

[ Key: ToSubClass ToInstance DisableOverride, Read:ToSubClass
  ToInstance, Description("The MailIdentifier property contains the
  GUID assigned to a mailbag on the PostOffice. "): amended ToSubClass]
string MailBagIdentifier;
};


//*******************************************************************
//* Class: PO_PostOfficeSettings
//* Derived from: CIM_Setting
//*******************************************************************

[ Singleton: ToInstance ToSubClass, Description("The PostOfficeSettings
  class is a singleton and exposes management information pertinent to
  the PostOffice. It contains a single value that dictates the maximum
  number of logon attempts allowed"): amended ToSubClass, AMENDMENT,
  LOCALE(0x409), UUID("{8571C9CA-1E6E-4f9a-8ACE-60C574F25CFE}") :
  ToInstance]
Class PO_PostOfficeSettings: CIM_Setting
{
```

The Write qualifier declares the MaxFailLogon property value as read/write.

```
[ Write: ToSubClass ToInstance, Description("The MaxFailedLogon
  property specifies the maximum number of logon attempts permitted to
  users of the PostOffice. The range is between 0 and 255."): amended
  ToSubClass]
uint8    MaxFailedLogon;
};


//*******************************************************************
//* Class: PO_UserDetails
//* Derived from: PO_ManagedElement
//*******************************************************************

[ Description("The UserDetails class exposes management information
  pertinent account holders on the PostOffice. It contains a values
  that describe contact details such as phone number, location, title
  etc.."): amended ToSubClass, AMENDMENT, LOCALE(0x409),
  UUID("{78687D99-6758-49c5-A090-6ADC8CB9D181}") : ToInstance]
class PO_UserDetails:PO_ManagedElement
{
```

```
[ Write: ToSubClass ToInstance, Description("The title property
  contains the title"): amended ToSubClass, Maxlen(32):ToInstance
  ToSubClass]
string Title;// Mr, Mrs, Dr etc..


[ Write:ToSubClass ToInstance, Description("The forename contains the
  users first name"): amended ToSubClass,Maxlen(32): ToInstance
  ToSubClass]
string ForeName;// Users first name


[ Write:ToSubClass ToInstance, Description("The surname contains the
  users last name"): amended ToSubClass,Maxlen(32): ToInstance
  ToSubClass]
string SurName;// Users last name


[ Write: ToInstance ToSubClass, Description("The jobtitle contains
  the users job title"): amended ToSubClass,Maxlen(64): ToInstance
  ToSubClass]
string JobTitle;// Director of finance etc..


[ key: ToInstance ToSubClass DisableOverride, Write: ToInstance
  ToSubClass, Description("The Username contains the users name"):
  amended ToSubClass, Maxlen(16): ToInstance ToSubClass]
string UserName; //PostOffice UserName


[ Write: ToInstance ToSubClass, Description("The password contains
  the users password"): amended ToSubClass,Maxlen(16): ToInstance
  ToSubClass]
  string Password; // Password at startup


[ Write: ToInstance ToSubClass, Description("The ContactNumber
  contains the users contact number"): amended ToSubClass,Maxlen(32):
  ToInstance ToSubClass]
  string ContactNumber;//User office telephone number*
};


//***************************************************************************
//* Class: PO_NewUserParam
//* Derived from: PO_MethodParameterClass
//***************************************************************************


[ Abstract(false),Description("The NewUserParam class is a parameter
  class used in calls to PostOffice method adduser ."): amended
  ToSubClass, AMENDMENT, LOCALE(0x409): ToInstance,
```

```
  UUID("{BE56E4DD-8BEA-4016-9B97-A09D17DE71A1}") : ToInstance]
Class PO_NewUserParam: PO_MethodParameterClass
{

  [ Write: ToSubClass ToInstance, Description("The title property
    contains the title"): ToSubClass, Maxlen(32):ToInstance ToSubClass]
  string Title;// Mr, Mrs, Dr etc..


  [ Write:ToSubClass ToInstance, Description("The forename contains the
    users first name"): amended ToSubClass,Maxlen(32): ToInstance
    ToSubClass]
  string ForeName;// Users first name


  [ Write:ToSubClass ToInstance, Description("The surname contains the
    users last name"): amended ToSubClass, Maxlen(32): ToInstance
    ToSubClass]
  string SurName;// Users last name


  [ Write: ToInstance ToSubClass, Description("The jobtitle contains
    the users job title"): amended ToSubClass,Maxlen(64): ToInstance
    ToSubClass]
  string JobTitle;// Director of finance etc..


  [ Write: ToInstance ToSubClass, Description("The Username contains
    the users name"): amended ToSubClass,Maxlen(16): ToInstance
    ToSubClass]
  string UserName; //PostOffice UserName


  [ Write: ToInstance ToSubClass, Description("The password contains
    the users password"): amended ToSubClass,Maxlen(16): ToInstance
    ToSubClass]
  string Password; // Password at startup


  [ Write: ToInstance ToSubClass, Description("The ContactNumber
    contains the users contact number"): amended ToSubClass,Maxlen(32):
    ToInstance ToSubClass]
  string ContactNumber;//User office telephone number*
};


//************************************************************
//
// Now we define the associations for the PostOffice schema
//
//************************************************************
```

```
//************************************************************************
//* Class: PO_AssociatedMailbag
//* Derived from: CIM_Dependency
//************************************************************************

[ Description ("The AssociatedMailbag relationship defines the
  dependency relationship between class EmailAccount and Mailbag"):
  amended ToSubClass, LOCALE(0x409): ToInstance ,UUID("{37186F00-4D97-
  474c-882A-C816378D949E}") : ToInstance]
class PO_AssociatedMailbag: CIM_Dependency
{

   [ read : ToSubclass, key : ToInstance ToSubclass DisableOverride,
     Override("Antecedent") : ToSubclass]
   PO_EmailAccount Ref Antecedent = NULL;

   [ read : ToSubclass,key : ToInstance ToSubclass DisableOverride,
     Override("Dependent") : ToSubclass]
   PO_Mailbag Ref Dependent = NULL;
};


//************************************************************************
//* Class: PO_AccountUserDetails
//* Derived from: CIM_Dependency
//************************************************************************

[ Description ("The AccountUserDetails relationship defines the
  dependency relationship between class UserDetails and EmailAccount"):
  amended TosubClass,LOCALE(0x409): ToInstance,
  UUID("{04428CAD-30D3-4841-B94B-435890C708B3}") : ToInstance]
class PO_AccountUserDetails: CIM_Dependency
{

  [ read : ToSubclass,key : ToInstance ToSubclass DisableOverride,
    Override("Dependent") : ToSubclass]
  PO_UserDetails Ref Dependent;

  [ read : ToSubclass,key : ToInstance ToSubclass DisableOverride,
    Override("Antecedent") : ToSubclass]
  PO_EmailAccount Ref Antecedent;
};


//************************************************************************
//* Class: PO_PostOfficeMsgSettings
//* Derived from: CIM_ElementSetting
//************************************************************************

[ Description ("The PO_PostOfficeMsgSettings relationship defines the
  relationship between class PostOffice and MessageSettings"): amended
  ToSubClass, LOCALE(0x409): ToInstance ,
```

```
       UUID("{358B159A-D3E1-4aa7-80CC-16750727C281}") : ToInstance]
class PO_PostOfficeMsgSettings: CIM_ElementSetting
{

  [ read : ToSubclass,key : ToInstance ToSubclass DisableOverride,
    Override("Element") : ToSubclass]
  PO_PostOffice Ref Element;

  [ read : ToSubclass,key : ToInstance ToSubclass DisableOverride,
    Override("Setting") : ToSubclass]
  PO_MessageSettings Ref Setting;
};


//*********************************************************************
//* Class: PO_StatsForPostOffice
//* Derived from: CIM_Statistics
//*********************************************************************

[ Abstract(false),Description ("The StatsForPostOffice relationship
   defines the statistical relationship between class PostOfficeStats and
   PostOffice"): amended ToSubClass,Locale(0x409) : ToInstance,
   UUID("{3918547B-4A68-4817-9B7D-6EB319BC4F7F}") : ToInstance]
class PO_StatsForPostOffice: CIM_Statistics
{

  [ read : ToSubclass,key : ToInstance ToSubclass DisableOverride,
    Override("Stats") : ToSubclass]
  PO_PostOfficeStats Ref Stats;

  [ read : ToSubclass,key : ToInstance ToSubclass DisableOverride,
    Override("Element") : ToSubclass]
  PO_PostOffice Ref Element;
};


//*********************************************************************
//* Class: PO_PostOfficeHasSettings
//* Derived from: CIM_ElementSetting
//*********************************************************************

[ Description ("The PostOfficeHasSettings relationship specifies the
   element-setting relationship between classes of type PostOffice and
   PostOfficeSetting"): amended ToSubClass, Locale(0x409) : ToInstance,
   UUID("{B669107D-6B17-453a-B097-9CA844A57990}") : ToInstance]
class PO_PostOfficeHasSettings: CIM_ElementSetting
{

  [ read : ToSubclass,key : ToInstance ToSubclass DisableOverride,
    Override("Element") : ToSubclass]
  PO_PostOffice Ref Element;
```

```
  [ read : ToSubclass,key : ToInstance ToSubclass DisableOverride,
    Override("Setting") : ToSubclass]
  PO_PostOfficeSettings Ref Setting;
};


//************************************************************************
//* Class: PO_PostOfficeAccounts
//* Derived from: CIM_Dependency
//************************************************************************

[ Description ("The PostOfficeAccounts relationship specifies the
  antecedent-depejndent relationship between classes of type PostOffice
  and EmailAccount"): amended ToSubClass, Locale(0x409) : ToInstance,
  UUID("{3A9BB2B4-8790-444f-8AFA-C5109A3D14A7}") : ToInstance]
class PO_PostOfficeAccounts:CIM_Dependency
{

  [ read : ToSubclass,key : ToInstance ToSubclass DisableOverride,
    Override("Antecedent") : ToSubclass]
  PO_PostOffice Ref Antecedent;

  [ read : ToSubclass,key : ToInstance ToSubclass DisableOverride,
    Override("Dependent") : ToSubclass]
  PO_EmailAccount Ref Dependent;
};


//*** END OF POSTOFFICE SCHEMA MOF FILE
```

■ Compiling a Multilanguage MOF File

Before we can test our schema, we must import it into the CIM repository. In this instance, we shall use the mofcomp command line executable to compile it. Because we have used the Amendment qualifier to specify locale-specific information, we need to perform two steps to successfully import our schema.

Step 1.

In the first step, we generate two separate MOF files, a language-neutral file (*.mof) and a language-specific version (*.mfl).

Syntax:

```
Mofcomp –MOF: <language neutral mof file> –MFL: <language specific
mof file>
  <Master MOF>
```

In the case of the Post Office, we would specify our two output files by typing the following at the command prompt and pressing return.

```
C:\MOFS\Mofcomp -MOF:PostOfficeLN.mof -MFL:PostOfficeLS.mfl
PostOffice.mof
```

Note that it is important to specify the file names for both the MOF and MFL. Failure to do so will result in the mof compiler not generating any files.

> **Note:** The MOFcompiler button that is part of the WMI CIM Studio does not support compilation of MOF files with the amendment pragma. In this case, you must use the command-line executable version of mofcomp to create locale-neutral and locale-specific MOF/MFL files.

After the compiler has completed a successful run, the source directory should contain three files: the original MOF file, a language-neutral version of the MOF file (PostOfficeLN.mof), and the language-specific version (PostOffice.mfl). Nothing has been placed in the CIM repository, and we must complete the second step to import our Post Office schema.

Step 2.

The second step simply is to compile the two MOF files into the CIM repository. Note that if this is your first time to compile files, you must compile the language-neutral MOF file (*.mof) before compiling the language-specific file (*.mfl) to avoid compilation errors. In our example, go to the command line and type the following:

```
C:\Mofcomp PostOfficeLN.mof
```

Then type:

```
C:\Mofcomp PostOfficeLS.mfl
```

This action should have successfully placed the Post Office schema in the CIM repository. If you are anxious to see the fruits of your labor, start up the WMI CIM Studio and move to the root\CIMV2\Applications\PostOffice namespace, where you should see the screen in Figure 6.18.

The compilation process has also created a subnamespace, ms_409, that contains all of the language-specific qualifiers, such as our class and property descriptions.

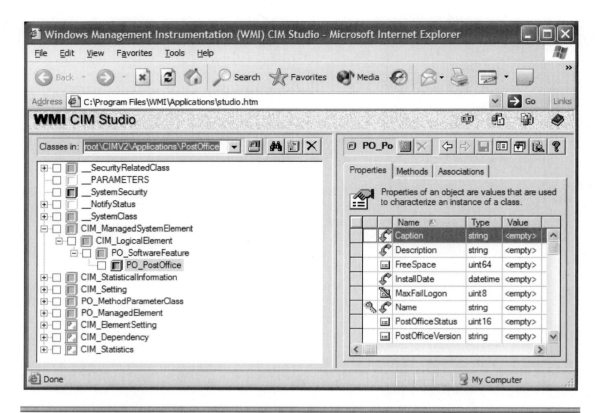

Figure 6.18 The root/CIMV2/Applications/PostOffice namespace

Also, note that if you highlight any of the classes in the class view (left pane) and then click the help button, you will see a description of the class and its members. These details came from the description qualifiers included in the MOF file.

You also can examine the associations and methods in which each class participates by clicking the Associations tab and the Methods tab in the right pane.

■ Testing

Testing at this stage in schema development typically revolves around the creation of static class instances of your schema, populated with dummy realistic data. Then it is possible to test your schema by constructing a series of WQL queries or dummy method invocations using either the WMI CIM Studio or the WMI Tester (`%systemroot%/system32/wbem/wbemtest.exe`). The WMI CIM Studio is slightly better for this task because it allows you to save your queries for each namespace. This approach is beneficial because it can assist concurrent development of your WMI projects. For example, the client team can code against the dummy data while the provider team writes the provider until it is ready to replace the static data. In that way, client development is not delayed and the provider should slot into place.

The feedback provided by the users of the schema during the requirements phase should also provide you with guidance about the type of tests you should perform upon your schema. As you construct the WQL queries, imagining yourself in the position of the person using the schema sometimes can be useful. In the Post Office schema, our requirements suggest that we should test the following aspects of our design:

- Are we able to start the Post Office and shut it down using the schema?
- Can we retrieve user's details from the schema by providing a MailbagIdentifier?
- Can we add users and delete users?
- Can we determine how many accounts have been created?
- Can we determine which e-mail users are currently logged on?
- Can we determine the size of a user's mailbag?

This is a quick and easy way to assess whether or not the schema meets your requirements, as defined in Step 1 of the life cycle, and can be carried out independent of those developing other parts of the project. It is far less costly and time-consuming to test your schema using static instances with dummy data than to commit to an early schema design and then have to alter your code.

■ Schema Deployment

Schema deployment in WMI consists of two main options. The first option is to add your schema to the target namespace programmatically using the WMI API. This is not the ideal solution, however, because potentially it can become very complex to maintain if your schema evolves. The second, more commonly adopted, option is to add your schema by using MOF files, which have the advantage of being relatively simple to interpret, maintain, and deploy as part of the installation of your managed product.

■ Summary

That concludes our introduction to schema design. In Chapters 5 and 6, we have looked at many techniques and best practices to guide you through your first attempts at schema design. With practice, you will gain your own set of best practices and no doubt will establish a good idea of some of the potential pitfalls. Mainly, schema design is complex because of the multitude of intermediate steps in performing it and the potential to omit one or more of them. We hope that the basic framework presented here will reduce the chances of this and will give you a reasoned, methodical approach to designing your schema. The MOF file in this chapter is by no means complete: To supply any of our Post Office's management information dynamically requires a provider. So that the components of the schema can be supplied dynamically, we examine the writing of providers in depth in Chapter 12. In Chapter 7 we concentrate on the other side of the management equation, developing management applications.

Schema Design and Positioning Q & A

Doesn't the Win32 extended schema provided by Microsoft supply all of the classes I need to instrument my product? Surely I can merely populate these classes with instances and find my product represented in the CIM repository!

In most cases, the Win32 extended schema certainly provides a starting point from which to derive your own classes. It is designed to represent the general aspects of the Windows 32-bit environment. In many cases, though, it most probably will not fully encompass the specific manageable aspects of your product. For example, Microsoft has defined a class called Win32_POTSModem that represents a "Plain Old Telephone Service Modem" on a Win32 system. If, however, you had designed your own modem and were instrumenting it in the CIM repository, you could derive from this existing class, adding the unique manageable elements of your product to the new class (after all, it's these added features that differentiate your product from the competition).

One of the abstract CIM classes in the CIMV2 namespace perfectly represents the management needs of my product. Can I instrument that class?

No, this is not permitted within the CIMV2 namespace.

My product encompasses the concepts of an e-mail account user, an application running as a service, and an e-mail delivery system. How can I derive from a class that encompasses all of these?

The simple answer is that you should break the management of your product into its constituent roles and define these varying elements under separate classes. These classes then can be positioned within the hierarchy under the relevant superclass.

My product seems to fit equally well under two superclasses at the same level in the hierarchy. How should I decide which one to pick?

In a situation like this, you should normalize your class further and attempt to position it again.

The PostOffice class in our example could be viewed as a Win32 service because it will run as a service on Windows NT platforms (see last chapter) and also as an application in its own right. Which is the correct interpretation when trying to place it in an existing schema?

With the vast array of classes available in CIM and the extended schema, one potential problem when positioning classes is viewing them at the correct layer of abstraction. For example, in our case, the PostOffice class could be viewed as either a specialization of the class Win32_service that has the manageable characteristics of a service (that is, it is controlled by the service control manager and can start, stop, pause, and so forth) or as a separate software feature.

The first school of thought would lead us to classify Post Office as derived from class `Win32_Service`. At the operating system level, the Post Office would be a service running on the local machine. However, we are instrumenting the product from the point of view of management data consumers, that is, system administrators. The consumers' view of the Post Office will be at a different layer of abstraction, not merely as a service but as an application that exhibits manageable qualities with which they can interact. If we did not write the Post Office as a service, would it still perform the same function from the point of view of system administrators? The answer is yes, despite that the system views it differently. Therefore, the correct approach would be to classify it not as a service, but as a software application, specifying the features that can be managed.

Chapter 7

Developing Management Applications

With schema design and provider development complete, the next step is to learn to write applications to administer the managed objects. Typically, client-side applications will provide a presentation layer for the managed objects. The presentation layer usually includes creating and deleting management objects, getting and setting properties, and calling methods.

For example, let's assume that you have created a class for managing the debug-logging configuration of your Windows 2000 service. A client-side application will allow you set the properties that will enable debug logging, and your Windows 2000 service will typically retrieve this configuration to decide whether it should perform debug logging.

This chapter focuses on the COM APIs that allow you to interact with WMI so that you can manage your objects. Later, in Chapter 9, we will focus on how you can write an MMC snap-in to provide a presentation layer for your managed objects.

This chapter assumes your familiarity with C++ programming, COM, and the Active Template Library (ATL). It also assumes that you are aware that managed objects can be created, updated, deleted, enumerated, and queried. You can manipulate the properties on objects, execute methods, and subscribe to receive WMI events. In this chapter, we discuss in detail how you can write applications to manage management objects. We discuss issues such as flag parameters to give you a complete guide to making WMI calls in your applications. By the end of this chapter, you should be knowledgeable about virtually every key aspect of writing a managed application. The first half of this chapter covers the basics, probably enough for most people; the second half covers more advanced topics.

In this chapter we use the terms "management object," "managed object," "object," and "instance" interchangeably.

■ Getting Started

The first thing you must do is connect to the WMI service. The WMI architecture is based on manipulating objects in a single namespace. In the debug logging example, to enable debug logging on machine A and machine B, you must connect to machine A, set the appropriate properties, and then connect to machine B and do the same for that machine. Let us look at some code that connects to WMI.

```
HRESULT hr = S_OK;

CComPtr<IWbemLocator> spLoc;
hr = spLoc.CoCreateInstance(CLSID_WbemLocator);

CComBSTR bstrNamespace("\\\\.\\root\\CIMV2");
CComPtr<IWbemServices> spServices;

// Connect to CIM
hr = spLoc->ConnectServer(bstrNamespace, NULL, NULL, 0,
  NULL, 0, 0, &spServices);

// Switch the security level to IMPERSONATE so that the provider
// will grant access to system-level objects.
hr = CoSetProxyBlanket(spServices, RPC_C_AUTHN_DEFAULT,
  RPC_C_AUTHZ_NONE, NULL, RPC_C_AUTHN_LEVEL_CALL,
  RPC_C_IMP_LEVEL_IMPERSONATE, NULL, EOAC_NONE);
```

The first call we make is to get a WMI locator interface from the Windows 2000/XP WMI service. This is always the first operation you will do. The `IWbemLocator` interface is our gateway to connect to any namespace on any machine. This, of course, assumes that the namespace exists and that the machine has the WMI service. Under Windows 2000, the WMI service runs in a process called WinMgmt.exe under the local system account. Under Windows XP, WMI is a service process within SVCHOST.

The WMI locator interface looks like this:

```
interface IWbemLocator
{
HRESULT ConnectServer(
  const BSTR strNetworkResource,
  const BSTR strUser,
  const BSTR strPassword,
```

```
   const BSTR strLocale,           // MS_409 for example
   LONG lSecurityFlags,            // must be zero
   const BSTR strAuthority,        // Security authority
   IWbemContext *pCtx,             // Used in calls within provider
   IWbemServices **ppNamespace);   // Your link to the WMI world
};
```

The first parameter, *strNetworkResource*, specifies both the machine and the namespace to which to connect. Format the string in the following way:

```
\\<machine name>\<namespace>
```

In the previous code sample, "\\." specifies the current machine, although we could have specified "\\MACHINE_A" to connect to a specific machine. The "root\CIMV2" specifies the namespace. The connect string to connect to the CIMV2 namespace on MACHINE_A would look like:

```
\\MACHINE_A\root\CIMV2
```

The *strLocale* parameter allows you to specify the locale for retrieving localized class information, such as class or property descriptions. The format of this parameter starts with "MS_" and you append the Win32 LCID locale identifier in hex. "MS_409" is U.S. English and "MS_407" is German. Inclusion of this parameter makes sense only when you have a localized namespace. If a namespace is localized in U.S. English and German, you will see subnamespaces "ms_409" and "ms_407", respectively. Localized namespaces use amended qualifiers, which we discuss later in the chapter. If the namespace is not localized, then you should pass NULL.

Use the *pCtx* parameter only to make WMI calls within dynamic providers. We discuss this in Chapter 12.

The final parameter, *ppNamespace*, is virtually everything you will need when you access management objects. You will need the IWbemServices interface for:

- Getting, deleting, and updating WMI instances
- Enumerating all instances of a specific WMI class
- Performing WQL queries
- Subscribing to events

Before you can use the IWbemServices interface, you must set up the proxy's security context by calling CoSetProxyBlanket, which allows you to specify the authentication and impersonation details of the user's security context. If you do not call CoSetProxyBlanket, then you may experience access-denied errors from the WMI provider. This is the case when accessing management objects from the Win32 providers supplied with Windows 2000/XP. Providers may make calls to system-level APIs and/or make security checks against an ACL, and, therefore, you must ensure that you use the correct security context. In this chapter, we assume that you will not be able to call `CoInitializeSecurity`; this is why we call `CoSetProxyBlanket` instead. We will discuss security in greater detail later in the chapter.

All the code samples in this chapter demonstrate how to use the `IWbemServices` interface. First, let's examine the three ways that you can make method calls.

1. **Synchronous.** This performs an operation, and the thread stays blocked until the call completes. Depending on the operation, a synchronous method call can turn out to be lengthy, especially when performing queries and enumerating large sets of instances. Most of the code samples in this chapter use the synchronous approach to describe the steps necessary to code your own applications. It is a good starting point.

2. **Asynchronous.** This starts an operation and immediately returns. You must implement `IWbemObjectSink`, which WMI will use to send all instances and other progress information back to you. For example, `IWbemObjectSink`'s `Indicate` method passes an instance found during a query back to you. This mechanism may be a little harder to use and involves the development of more code. Asynchronous development usually involves writing applications with multiple threads and determining program flow may be a little unpredictable. We cover this in more detail later in the chapter.

3. **Semisynchronous.** This combines parts of the synchronous and asynchronous approaches. It allows you to make a call and return immediately without having to provide an implementation of `IWbemObjectSink`. Instead, the call returns an `IWbemCallResult` interface for you to poll and gather the results of the operation, such as a query. This solves the problem of thread blockage and the use of multiple threads with no additional code. We cover this in more detail later in the chapter.

■ Object Paths Explained

Throughout the rest of this chapter, you will see the terms "object paths" or "object reference" mentioned regularly. Understanding object paths is important because it is your way to ask WMI for a management object that you want, and it is also WMI's way of providing you a reference about a particular object.

An object path is a string that can reference either a class or object instance specifically. This can be easily explained with an example from file systems. The following string represents a path to a particular file:

```
C:\MyDocuments\MyLetter.doc
```

If you provide this path to the file system (using the appropriate APIs), the file system can provide you with a file handle that you can later use either to read or to write to. This concept is the same for object paths.

An object path can be either a fully *qualified path* or a *relative path*. The format for a fully qualified path is:

```
\\machine\namespace:classname.keyproperty1=value,keyproperty2=value
```

In the following two examples, the first references a user account and the second references a shared directory.

```
\\GWCOLE\root\CIMV2:Win32_UserAccount.Domain="GWCOLE",Name=
  "Administrator"
\\GWCOLE\root\CIMV2:Win32_Share.Name="C$"
```

Notice that a *dot* separates the class name from the first key property and that a *comma* separates all subsequent key properties. We collectively refer to a class with multiple key properties as a *compound key*.

Relative object paths omit the machine and namespace names. The format for a relative object path is:

```
classname.keyproperty1=value,keyproperty2=value
```

The same object path examples above would look like this as relative object paths:

```
Win32_UserAccount.Domain="GWCOLE",Name="Administrator"
Win32_Share.Name="C$"
```

Using relative object paths is easiest in most cases because you specified the machine and namespace during the initial connection to WMI (using the `ConnectServer` call).

All key properties that use a string data type need to be enclosed in quotation marks (as in the above examples). The following data types use strings: strings, dates and times, and object references. Key properties that are numbers follow the equals operator, as in this example:

```
Win32_DMAChannel.DMAChannel=2
```

All the examples so far have been references to actual management objects. Let us look at how you can refer to classes, which is useful when you want to gather information about a class (such as enumerating the defined properties). As you will see later, static method calls require class references, rather than an object reference. You will find more on method calls later. The format for a fully qualified path to a class is:

```
\\machine\namespace:classname
```

Here is an example referencing the `Win32_VideoController` class on a particular machine:

```
\\GWCOLE\ROOT\CIMV2:Win32_VideoController
```

As before, relative class paths are a bit friendlier than fully qualified paths. The format for a relative path to a class is:

```
classname
```

Finally, this is an example of a relative reference to the `Win32_VideoController` class:

```
Win32_VideoController
```

Object paths are not case sensitive, and they must not contain spaces except inside string literals.

■ Getting an Object

Getting an object is one of the most basic operations to perform. This kind of operation is especially useful when you know which management object you're after. For example, if you decide to gain access to some properties of a shared directory on a machine, `GetObject` is the operation you should perform. Before you can gain access to a management object, you need a valid object path. Here is an example: If you look at the `Win32_Share` class in the CIMV2 namespace, you will see that it has one key property, "Name". If you expect the C$ shared directory on a machine to exist, you can get a management object that represents the shared directory. You need to generate an object path that includes the one and only key value, `Win32_Share.Name="C$"`, and call `GetObject.`

You may also get an object path from a property. WMI includes a data type that can reference other objects; this is an *object reference*. Association classes include properties that are object references to make an association. You may read one of these properties and pass the object reference (which is a string) straight into the `GetObject` call. Either way, as long as you have a valid object path, you will be able to access the management object.

The following code illustrates how to get the path of a shared directory:

```
CComBSTR bstrPath("Win32_Share.Name=\"C$\"");

// Get the shared directory object
CComPtr<IWbemClassObject> spInstance;
```

```
hr = spServices->GetObject(bstrPath, WBEM_FLAG_RETURN_WBEM_COMPLETE,
  NULL, &spInstance, NULL);

// Get a property from the object
CComVariant var;
hr = spInstance->Get(CComBSTR("Path"), 0, &var, 0, 0);

_tprintf(_T("Win32_Share.Name=\"C$\" path is %ls\n"), V_BSTR(&var));
```

The above example merely retrieves the path of the shared directory and outputs it to the screen. `WBEM_FLAG_RETURN_WBEM_COMPLETE` means complete the entire call before returning (implied by default because it has a value of zero). Manipulating object properties will be covered later in the chapter, as will other flags that can be used.

A portion of the `IWbemServices` interface looks like this:

```
interface IWbemServices
{
HRESULT GetObject(
  const BSTR strObjectPath,          // The object path
  LONG lFlags,                       // How to obtain the object
  IWbemContext *pCtx,                // Used in provider
  IWbemClassObject **ppObject,       // The managed object
  IWbemCallResult **ppCallResult);   // Don't use this for now
};
```

The *strObjectPath* parameter lets you pass the object path of the management object to which you'd like to gain access.

The *lFlags* parameter specifies how the `GetObject` call should be made. More advanced flags that can be passed, such as `WBEM_FLAG_RETURN_IMMEDIATELY`, which allows you to perform semisynchronous calls, will be covered later in the chapter.

The *ppObject* out-parameter returns the management object specified in the *strObjectPath* parameter. All management objects are represented through an *IWbemClassObject* interface, which provides access to all the properties as defined in the management class.

■ Enumerating Objects

In some cases, you will want a complete list of all management objects of a given class. Suppose you have a user interface that allows the user to select a shared directory to complete some task; you would want to display a list of all the available shared directories. You can achieve this by enumerating all the instances of the `Win32_Share` class. You could perform the following query to achieve the same result:

```
SELECT * FROM Win32_Share
```

However, performing a query involves processing the query, obtaining a list of objects, and comparing the query against each object. In this case, it is more efficient to enumerate the objects in a class. To perform an enumeration, all you need to know is the name of the class you would like to enumerate.

Enumerating objects for a given class is one of the easiest ways to discover what management objects are available. When you move through classes in CIM Studio (which comes as a developer tool in the Platform SDK), one of the first things you do is to look at a list of instances to see what can be managed. Review Chapter 4's quick introduction to CIM Studio. You may also want to check out wbemtest, another WMI SDK tool that very closely mimics the IWbemServices interface. It can be useful in developing your management applications.

The following code sample illustrates how to obtain a list of shared directories:

```
// Get list of objects for the Win32_Share class
CComPtr<IEnumWbemClassObject> spEnumInst;
hr = spServices->CreateInstanceEnum(CComBSTR("Win32_Share"),
  WBEM_FLAG_SHALLOW, NULL, &spEnumInst);

bool bFinished = false;
while (!bFinished)
{
  // Get the Win32_Share instance
  ULONG uNumOfInstances = 0;
  CComPtr<IWbemClassObject> spInstance;
  HRESULT hrNext = spEnumInst->Next(10000, 1, &spInstance,
    &uNumOfInstances);

  if (hrNext == WBEM_S_FALSE)
    bFinished = true;
  else if (hrNext == WBEM_S_NO_ERROR)
  {
    // Get properties from the Win32_Share instance
    CComVariant varRelPath;
    hr = spInstance->Get(CComBSTR("__RELPATH"), 0,
      &varRelPath, 0, 0);

    CComVariant varPath;
    hr = spInstance->Get(CComBSTR("Path"), 0, &varPath, 0, 0);

    _tprintf(_T(" %ls path is %ls\n"), V_BSTR(&varRelPath),
      V_BSTR(&varPath));
  }
}
```

The CreateInstanceEnum call creates an enumerator that can be used to gain access to every instance of that class. The enumerator is returned in an IEnumWbemClassObject interface and the `Next` method call provides access to an `IWbemClassObject` interface (that is, an instance). The code sample specified `WBEM_FLAG_SHALLOW`, which instructed `CreateInstanceEnum` to return only an enumerator that has the instances of the `Win32_Share` class. A quick check is done to determine whether there are more instances to retrieve and if there are, some output is made. Notice that `__RELPATH` was specified as a property name: `_RELPATH` is the relative path of the object. WMI has many system-provided properties for classes and instances; we discuss these in more detail later in the chapter. The output of this on our machine produces the following:

```
Win32_Share.Name="C$" path is C:\
Win32_Share.Name="IPC$" path is
Win32_Share.Name="ADMIN$" path is C:\WINNT
```

A portion of the `IWbemServices` interface looks like this:

```
interface IWbemServices
{
HRESULT CreateInstanceEnum(
  const BSTR strClass,            // Class name to enumerate
  LONG lFlags,                    // WBEM_FLAG_SHALLOW
  IWbemContext *pCtx,             // Used in providers
  IEnumWbemClassObject **ppEnum );  // Your Enumerator
};
```

The *strClass* parameter specifies the name of the class you want to enumerate and is returned in the *ppEnum* out-parameter. You can specify how the enumerator should be built based on the *lFlags* parameter. For instance, if the class you want to enumerate is a base (or abstract) class (introduced in Chapter 5), then you might want to use `WBEM_FLAG_DEEP` instead of `WBEM_FLAG_SHALLOW` to build your enumerator. This will cause WMI to provide instances not only of the base class but also of all its derived classes in the enumerator. Let us have a look at an example. Suppose you want to see all security accounts on your system. If you use CIM Studio (see Figure 7.1) to look at the CIMV2 schema, you will see that the `Win32_Account` is a base class for `Win32_SystemAccount`, `Win32_Group`, and `Win32_UserAccount` classes. If you call `CreateInstanceEnum` for the `Win32_Account` class and specify `WBEM_FLAG_DEEP`, you will get an enumerator that will contain all instances of `Win32_SystemAccount`, `Win32_Group`, and `Win32_UserAccount`.

Figure 7.1 Win32_Account class hierarchy

To recap, the following call will provide only an enumerator of all the instances of the `Win32_SystemAccount` class.

```
CComPtr<IEnumWbemClassObject> spEnumInst;
hr = spServices->CreateInstanceEnum(CComBSTR("Win32_SystemAccount"),
  WBEM_FLAG_SHALLOW, NULL, &spEnumInst);
```

This call will provide an enumerator of all the instances of the `Win32_System-Account`, `Win32_Group`, and `Win32_UserAccount` classes. Note that `WBEM_FLAG_DEEP` typically is used when all instances of classes derived from a base class are required.

```
CComPtr<IEnumWbemClassObject> spEnumInst;
hr = spServices->CreateInstanceEnum(CComBSTR("Win32_Account"),
  WBEM_FLAG_DEEP, NULL, &spEnumInst);
```

Other flags can be specified in the *lFlags* parameter. `WBEM_FLAG_FORWARD_ONLY` is one of them; its use produces a forward-only enumerator. This type of enumerator generally is faster and requires less memory; however, you won't be able to call the `Clone` or `Reset` methods. If you do not need to use `Clone` or `Reset`, we recommend that you specify this flag on all your calls.

The `WBEM_FLAG_BIDIRECTIONAL` is implied by default (because it has the value zero). This flag means that WMI will retain pointers to instances until the enumerator is released. In practice, the instances are not released immediately. If the class you are enumerating has a very large collection of instances, you may experience `WBEM_E_OUT_OF_MEMORY` being returned by `CreateInstanceEnum`. In this case, you should use the asynchronous version, `CreateInstanceEnumAsync`. (A forward-only enumerator can save some memory, but it typically won't be enough of a saving if you expect a very large collection of instances.) Other flags will be discussed later in the chapter.

▪ Creating an Object

When writing applications to create management objects, you need to take into account how, if at all, those objects can be created. This applies equally to how you foresee the creation of your own management objects when designing your schema. Creating a shared directory on a machine is an example of creating an object. There are three ways to look at the creation of objects.

1. Use the standard mechanism provided by WMI through `IWbemServices`.
2. Use a method such as `Create`. The `Win32_Share` class does this.
3. You cannot create instances at all, as in the case of the `Win32_ComputerSystem` class.

First Point

When creating instances in the standard mechanism, you need to spawn an uncommitted instance based on the class definition, set your properties, and call `PutInstance` on the `IWbemServices` interface. (The code sample later in this section illustrates this process.)

Generally, you are required to set all the key properties on the newly spawned instance before passing it to `PutInstance`. Key properties identify an object explicitly and are required to access it in the future. In some cases, the provider may assign a value to a key property if it discovers that one does not exist, but this is not common. It is considered *best practice* that the key properties be set when you create your management objects. To see what this means, let us look at the following class:

```
class Sample_Book
{
  [key] string BookTitle;
  [key] string AuthorName;
  string Summary;
  DATETIME DatePublished;
  uint8 NumberOfChapters;
};
```

The only properties that have to be set are `BookTitle` and `AuthorName`. This means that the other properties need not be set to create a valid instance. This can pose some danger, especially if you decide that you also require `Summary` and `NumberOfChapters` properties. However, this danger is not so bad if you control the source code in the provider. You simply ensure that the remaining two required properties are set; otherwise `PutInstance` could return something like `WBEM_E_INVALID_OBJECT`. Of course, this isn't guaranteed with other providers.

WMI classes that support the standard mechanism of creating management objects have the `supportsCreate` qualifier.

Second Point

To clearly state what information is required to create an instance, some classes use a method to create an instance. This is the case with the `Win32_Share` class, which has a method called `Create`. You first would need to set up a method call and then execute it. The next time you enumerate the `Win32_Share` class, the new instance will be listed as part of the collection. Let us look again at the `Sample_Book` class, this time with a method to create an instance:

```
class Sample_Book
{
  [key] string BookTitle;
  [key] string AuthorName;
```

```
    string Summary;
    DATETIME DatePublished;
    uint8 NumberOfChapters;

    [static, implemented] boolean Create([in] string BookTitle,
      [in] string AuthorName, [in] string Summary,
      [in] uint8 NumberOfChapters);
};
```

As it is clear to see, the `Create` method requires both `Summary` and `NumberOf-Chapters` values, as well as the key values. Also, notice that the method returns a `boolean` value to indicate whether the method succeeded. (You could instead return a `uint32` if you want to return a HRESULT. However, remember that the method can be called from scripting environments where HRESULTs may not be the most suitable return value.) Here are other reasons that you might want a method for the creation of instances:

1. The key values are not known in advance and are generated by the provider.
2. You may want to have specific flags passed into the method for more context information when creating the instance.
3. You may want to receive one or more out-parameters (other than the return value).

If you find that a method exists for the creation of instances, it may contain the `Constructor` qualifier to signify that the method creates instances.

Third Point

Instances cannot be created for some classes, as in the case of the `Win32_ComputerSystem` class. If you think about it, it does not make sense to have more than one instance of this class. You may find with your own schema that you cannot create instances and the only supported operations allowed are to update, enumerate, and perform queries.

Example

Let's examine how you might create an object with the standard mechanism. We discuss calling methods on classes later in the chapter.

```
// Get class so we can spawn an instance of it
CComPtr<IWbemClassObject> spClass;
hr = spServices->GetObject(CComBSTR("Sample_Book"), 0,
  NULL, &spClass, NULL);
```

```
// Make new object
CComPtr<IWbemClassObject> spInstance;
hr = spClass->SpawnInstance(0, &spInstance);

// Set some properties on the object
CComVariant varBookTitle("Developing WMI Solutions");
hr = spInstance->Put(CComBSTR("BookTitle"), 0, &varBookTitle, 0);

CComVariant varAuthor("Gwyn Cole");
hr = spInstance->Put(CComBSTR("AuthorName"), 0, &varAuthor, 0);

CComVariant varSummary("A cool book on Windows Management
  Instrumentation");
hr = spInstance->Put(CComBSTR("Summary"), 0, &varSummary, 0);

CComVariant varNumOfChapters(int(11));
hr = spInstance->Put(CComBSTR("NumberOfChapters"), 0,
  &varNumOfChapters, 0);

// Commit to create instance in WMI
hr = spServices->PutInstance(spInstance, WBEM_FLAG_CREATE_ONLY,
  NULL, NULL);
```

The first task is to spawn an uncommitted instance based on the class definition. Calling `SpawnInstance` does this for the `Sample_Book` class in this case. We call this an *uncommitted instance* because it has not yet been passed to WMI and normal operations such as setting and getting properties can be performed. Next, we do exactly that, setting all the properties (as long as we include the key properties) of the new instance. After all the properties have been set, use the `IWbemServices` interface to pass the instance to WMI by calling `PutInstance`. The provider will extract all the properties from the instance and physically do whatever the provider needs to do to create the instance.

This is what the `SpawnInstance` method looks like:

```
interface IWbemClassObject
{
HRESULT SpawnInstance(
  LONG lFlags,                          // must be zero
  IWbemClassObject **ppNewInstance);    // New instance
};
```

When `SpawnInstance` returns, the *ppNewInstance* out-parameter will contain the new instance, ready for properties to be set. The *lFlags* parameter is documented as having to be 0.

The `PutInstance` method looks like this:

```
interface IWbemServices
{
HRESULT PutInstance(
  IWbemClassObject *pInst,              // Instance to create/update
  LONG lFlags,                          // Create/update flags
  IWbemContext *pCtx,                   // Used in providers
  IWbemCallResult **ppCallResult);      // Don't use this for now
};
```

The uncommitted instance is passed in the *pInst* parameter. The *lFlags* parameter specifies the kind of put-operation that must be performed. In the code sample, we used `WBEM_FLAG_CREATE_ONLY`, which tells WMI that this operation can create only instances. If you already had an instance with identical key properties, the `PutInstance` call would fail with `WBEM_E_ALREADY_EXISTS`. If we had used `WBEM_FLAG_CREATE_OR_UPDATE` instead, the `PutInstance` call would not have failed and an update would have been attempted. Use `WBEM_FLAG_CREATE_ONLY` when you do not intend for the instance to be updated accidentally. We cover updating instances such as `WBEM_FLAG_UPDATE_ONLY` in the next section.

If the *lFlags* parameter has `WBEM_FLAG_RETURN_IMMEDIATELY` set, then you will receive an `IWbemCallResult` interface pointer from the *ppCallResult* out-parameter. This allows you to perform semisynchronous calls. We discuss this later in the chapter.

An example of creating an object with a method will be demonstrated later in the chapter when we discuss WMI method calls.

■ Updating Objects

Updating existing management objects with new property values is a common requirement when writing applications. As with creating instances, there are three options: to use the standard mechanism to update, to use a method to update, and to be unable to update at all. The standard mechanism for updating instance property values is very similar to creating a new instance because you still make a call to `Put-Instance`. The general process is to get your instance, change the properties, and call the PutInstance method. The following code sample changes a property value on the book instance we created earlier:

```
// Generate the object path
CComBSTR bstrPath = _T("Sample_Book.BookTitle=\" Developing WMI
  Solutions\", AuthorName=\"Gwyn Cole\"");
```

```
// Get the Sample_Book object we want
CComPtr<IWbemClassObject> spInstance;
hr = spServices->GetObject(bstrPath, 0, NULL, & spInstance, NULL));

// Change the number of chapters
CComVariant varNumOfChapters(int(12));
hr = spInstance->Put(CComBSTR("NumberOfChapters"), 0, &
  varNumOfChapters, 0);

// Commit to update instance in WMI
hr = spServices->PutInstance(spInstance, WBEM_FLAG_UPDATE_ONLY,
  NULL, NULL);
```

As you can see, updating an instance is straightforward. We changed only the number of chapters property for this book; all the other property values remained unaffected. However, notice the flags parameter in the `PutInstance` call: This time `WBEM_FLAG_UPDATE_ONLY` was specified. The `WBEM_FLAG_UPDATE_ONLY` will allow only for an update to an already existing instance. If the `Sample_Book` instance did not exist, the `PutInstance` method would return `WBEM_E_NOT_FOUND`. Using `WBEM_FLAG_CREATE_OR_UPDATE` instead would have allowed the provider to do whatever is necessary to update the instance, even if it had to create it. Use `WBEM_FLAG_UPDATE_ONLY` in situations where you do not want accidental creation of instances.

Some classes use methods to update instances with very similar reasons to those described in the previous section. For example, the `Win32_Share` class has a method called `SetShareInfo` in which the description of the shared directory, together with some other properties, can be changed. The `Win32_Service` class is another example: It has two methods to update an instance, `Change` and `ChangeStartMode`.

WMI classes that support the standard mechanism of updating management objects have the `supportsUpdate` qualifier.

▪ Deleting an Object

When writing applications, you will occasionally want to delete management objects. For instance, you might want to remove access to an already existing shared directory, which would involve deleting the instance of the shared directory management object. As with creating and updating instances, you have three options: to use the standard mechanism to delete, to use a method to delete, and to be unable to delete at all.

For some classes, such as the `Win32_VideoController` class, it makes no sense to delete instances. This is a hardware device, and to remove the instance would involve physically removing the video controller from your computer.

The easiest method of removing instances is to use the standard mechanism to delete an object. All you need is a valid object path and to make a call to `Delete-Instance`. WMI classes that support the standard mechanism of deleting management objects have the `supportsDelete` qualifier.

In some classes, you may find that a deletion method is available. Here are some reasons that you might want a method for the deletion of instances:

1. You may want to have specific flags passed into the method for more context information when deleting the instance.

2. You may want to receive one or more out-parameters other than the return value.

If you find that a method exists for the deletion of instances, then you can expect the standard mechanism to fail. This depends on the provider.

Let us look again at the `Sample_Book` class, this time with a method to delete an instance:

```
class Sample_Book
{
  [key] string BookTitle;
  [key] string AuthorName;
  string Summary;
  DATETIME DatePublished;
  uint8 NumberOfChapters;

  [static, implemented] boolean Create([in] string BookTitle,
    [in] string AuthorName, [in] string Summary,
    [in] uint8 NumberOfChapters);
  [implemented] boolean Delete();
};
```

Did you observe that the `Delete` method does not include the key properties of the class? How will the `Delete` method know which book to delete? The key reason is that the `Delete` method is an object method and is relative to the management object. The `Create` method was defined with the `static` qualifier, which defines it as a class method. This effectively means the method can be called without reference to any instances of the class. The `static` qualifier is the same concept as in object-oriented programming. The `Delete` method can be called only relative to the management object.

Deleting an instance is a very easy operation with the standard mechanism. You need only to pass an object path to `DeleteInstance` and the provider will attempt to remove the instance. Let us remove the `Sample_Book` instance that we created earlier:

```
// Generate the object path
CComBSTR bstrPath = _T("Sample_Book.BookTitle=\" Developing WMI
  Solutions\", AuthorName=\"Gwyn Cole\"");
```

```
// Delete Sample_Book
hr = spServices->DeleteInstance(bstrPath, 0, NULL, NULL));
```

The `DeleteInstance` method looks like this:

```
interface IWbemServices
{
HRESULT DeleteInstance(
  const BSTR strObjectPath,          // Object path to DELETE
  LONG lFlags,                       // Usually zero
  IWbemContext *pCtx,                // Used in providers
  IWbemCallResult **ppCallResult);   // Not needed for now
};
```

The *strObjectPath* parameter specifies the object path of the management object to delete. When `DeleteInstance` is called, the provider will verify that the object path does reference a valid instance and then it will attempt to remove it permanently. When writing your applications, be careful not to hold onto an object (an *IWbemClass-Object* pointer) and later delete the object while still holding a reference to the instance. This will result in unpredictable behavior.

The *lFlags* parameter allows just one flag, `WBEM_FLAG_RETURN_IMMEDIATELY`, which is used when executing semisynchronous calls.

■ Performing Queries

Performing queries is one of the most popular mechanisms of gaining access to managed objects. The reason is that it allows great flexibility in specifying exactly what you want. When writing your own applications, you will inevitably find that you must perform queries that fall into one of two categories:

1. You need context-relative information.
2. You need to improve performance.

For an example of context-relative information, suppose that a task requires a security principle (that is, a user) from a particular domain. A user interface application could formulate the following WQL query:

```
SELECT * FROM Win32_UserAccount WHERE Domain="DOMAIN_A"
```

This query would provide you with a full list of all the users in DOMAIN_A. You can also use a query to improve performance by specifying the properties you require. The above example asked for all properties from the `Win32_UserAccount` class (that is, the SELECT *). You do not need all the properties if you simply want to display a list of users and use the SID (security identifier) to perform some task. You can revise the query to ask specifically for the display name and SID.

```
SELECT FullName, SID FROM Win32_UserAccount WHERE Domain="DOMAIN_A"
```

This query would return only the FullName and SID property values for each instance that matches the query (WHERE Domain="DOMAIN_A"). However, the performance improvement can vary from provider to provider. WMI providers do not have to support query optimization, in which case WMI calls CreateInstanceEnumAsync for a complete list of all the instances together with all the property values set. WMI then processes each instance and if the instance matches the query, WMI copies the instance and the required properties to the query enumerator that is output to the caller. The bottom line is that the speed of queries is dependent on whether providers support query optimization in their implementation.

Performing queries is in some ways similar to enumeration. When we dealt with enumeration earlier in the chapter, you learned that you could get all of the instances of a specific class and access the instances through an enumerator (IEnumWbemClass-Object). When performing queries, you still end up with an enumerator that allows you to enumerate all of the instances that match your query.

For more information on all the different types of queries that can be performed, review Chapter 3 and the Platform SDK documentation.

The following code sample illustrates how to obtain a list of Windows Services that have been started:

```
CComBSTR bstrQuery("SELECT * FROM Win32_Service WHERE Started=true");

// Execute query
CComPtr<IEnumWbemClassObject> spEnumInst;
hr = spServices->ExecQuery(CComBSTR(_T("WQL")), bstrQuery,
  WBEM_FLAG_FORWARD_ONLY | WBEM_FLAG_RETURN_IMMEDIATELY, NULL,
  &spEnumInst);

bool bFinished = false;
while (!bFinished)
{
  // Get the instance
  ULONG uNumOfInstances = 0;
  CComPtr<IWbemClassObject> spInstance;
  HRESULT hrNext = spEnumInst->Next(10000, 1, &spInstance,
    &uNumOfInstances);

  if (hrNext == WBEM_S_FALSE)
    bFinished = true;
```

```
    else if (hrNext == WBEM_S_NO_ERROR)
    {
      // Get properties from the object
      CComVariant varName;
      hr = spInstance->Get(CComBSTR(_T("DisplayName")), 0, &varName, 0, 0);

      _tprintf(_T(" %ls\n"), V_BSTR(&varName));
    }
  }
}
```

In this code sample, the `ExecQuery` call performs the query (if it is valid) and creates an enumerator that can be used to gain access to every instance that matches the query. The enumerator is returned in an `IEnumWbemClassObject` interface. It does a quick check to ensure that there are more instances to retrieve, and if there are, some output (the display name of the service) is made.

The `ExecQuery` method looks like this:

```
interface IWbemServices
{
HRESULT ExecQuery(
  const BSTR strQueryLanguage,        // Must be 'WQL'
  const BSTR strQuery,                //The WQL query to perform
  LONG lFlags,                        // How to perform the query
  IWbemContex *pCtx,                  // Used in providers
  IEnumWbemClassObject **ppEnum);     // Results from query
};
```

The *strQueryLanguage* parameter specifies the type of query to perform. The current implementation of WMI supports only "WQL".

The *strQuery* parameter is the query that you wish to perform. If the query is successful, you will get an enumerator in the *ppEnum* out-parameter that you can use to gain access to each management object. If the query is invalid or the class specified is not found, `ExecQuery` will return `WBEM_E_INVALID_QUERY` or `WBEM_E_NOT_FOUND`, respectively.

Several flags can be specified in the *lFlags* parameter. `WBEM_FLAG_FORWARD_ONLY`, which produces a forward-only enumerator, is one of them.

If the query you are processing has a very large collection of instances, `WBEM_E_OUT_OF_MEMORY` may be returned by `ExecQuery`. In this case, you must use the asynchronous version, `ExecQueryAsync`.

As mentioned earlier, WMI has some system-provided properties that are automatically included in every object. These properties are __SUPERCLASS, __DYNASTY, __RELPATH, __DERIVATION, __SERVER, __NAMESPACE, and __PATH. The meaning and purpose of these properties are discussed in Chapter 3. We mention these now because, depending on the type of query you perform, these system-provided properties may or may not be set.

If you perform any query that starts with SELECT *, you can be assured that all the system-provided properties will be available for you, as in the following case:

```
SELECT * FROM Win32_UserAccount WHERE Domain="DOMAIN_A"
```

If you perform any query that specifies specific properties in the SELECT statement, then the system-provided properties will not be available, as in the following case:

```
SELECT FullName, SID FROM Win32_UserAccount WHERE Domain="DOMAIN_A"
```

All is not lost; you can instruct WMI to include the system-provided properties that can identify the location of a management object. To do this, you need to specify WBEM_FLAG_ENSURE_LOCATABLE when calling ExecQuery. The resulting instances in the returned enumerator will include __RELPATH, __SERVER, __NAMESPACE, and __PATH.[1]

There are occasions when you depend on the system-provided properties being available. The MMC snap-in in Chapter 9 will demonstrate the use of system-provided properties when creating and updating management objects in the user interface.

Microsoft Systems Management Server implements an extended version of WQL called Extended WQL. Extended WQL offers additional SELECT clauses such as DISTINCT, JOIN, and DATEPART. The WBEM_FLAG_PROTOTYPE allows you to obtain a class definition in the result set that uses the JOIN clause.

■ Making Method Calls

So far in this chapter, you have seen a few occasions in which you might want or need to make method calls. For instance, you saw that we could have called methods for the creation and deletion of our Sample_Book class. Other examples include changing the configuration of shared directories and Windows Services (as well as starting and stopping them). You may discover in your own schema designs that you need to add behavior to your classes, and in this case methods are the answer. Although we see methods for creating, changing, and deleting instances, we urge you to use the standard mechanisms provided by WMI for these types of operations where possible. However, exceptions are appropriate when you find yourself in one or more of the following situations:

1. You may want to have specific flags passed into the method for more context information when creating and deleting instances.

---

1. Note that you can achieve the same result by specifying the system properties in the SELECT statement, although it is much easier simply to use the WBEM_FLAG_ENSURE_LOCATABLE flag.

2. You may want to receive one or more out-parameters other than the return value.

3. None of the WMI HRESULTs accommodate the types of errors you'd like to return. You can define the method return value so that you can return an appropriate data type for the errors you would like to pass back to the caller.

4. You may want to create multiple instances at the same time.

Calling methods fall into two categories:

1. Calling static methods on classes

2. Calling methods on objects

To illustrate making method calls in detail, we shall use a fictitious class with a method called `foo` and decorate the method with different parameters so that you can gain a clear understanding. Let us look at this declaration:

```
class Sample_Class
{
  [key] string Name;
  [static, implemented] void foo();
};
```

The class has a static method that takes no parameters and returns `void` (effectively meaning no return value). So let us see what code is needed to make this method call:

```
hr = spServices->ExecMethod(CComBSTR("Sample_Class"), CComBSTR("foo"),
  0, NULL, NULL, NULL, NULL);
```

That's it! The first parameter provides a class or object context of the method you would like to call. In the above case, we passed a class reference, `Sample_Class`. The second parameter is the name of the method you want to call—in this case, `foo`. Let us revise our method declaration:

```
class Sample_Class
{
  [key] string Name;
  [implemented] void foo();
};
```

Not much difference. The only change we made was the removal of the `static` qualifier. The `static` qualifier meant that the method could be called without reference to any instances of the class. This is exactly what happened in the code sample:

We passed a class reference. With the above change to `foo`, we must now use an object reference. Let us look at the following code:

```
hr = spServices->ExecMethod(CComBSTR("Sample_Class.Name=\"Gwyn\""),
  CComBSTR("foo"), 0, NULL, NULL, NULL, NULL);
```

Simple. As you can see, an object reference was passed instead. Unfortunately, methods that take no parameters and have no return value are not practical for most purposes. So let's extend `foo` to return a value:

```
class Sample_Class
{
  [key] string Name;
  [implemented] string foo();
};
```

From a code perspective, things start getting more involved. We now need to obtain the return value from the `ExecMethod` call. This is the purpose of the sixth parameter, which returns an `IWbemClassObject` interface. But, you're probably asking yourself, isn't the `IWbemClassObject` interface used for representing object instances? The best way to visualize the `IWbemClassObject` interface is as a container for useful information. All method calls use this interface to pass back the method out-parameters as well as the return value. The return value exists in a property called `ReturnValue`, hence none of your method out-parameters can use this name. Let's see some code that retrieves our string return value on `foo`:

```
CComBSTR bstrMethod("foo");
CComBSTR bstrObject("Sample_Class.Name=\"Gwyn\"");

CComPtr<IWbemClassObject> spOutParams;
hr = spServices->ExecMethod(bstrObject, bstrMethod, 0, NULL, NULL,
  &spOutParams, NULL);

// Inspect out-parameters for return value
CComVariant varReturnValue;
hr = spOutParams->Get(L"ReturnValue", 0, &varReturnValue, 0, 0);

_tprintf(_T("\n %ls::%ls returned %ls\n"), bstrObject, bstrMethod,
  V_BSTR(&varReturnValue));
```

The above code now has all the information you will need to make the `Delete` method call on the `Win32_Share` class. Finally, let's make our `foo` method take an in- and out-parameter.

```
class Sample_Class
{
  [key] string Name;
  [implemented] string foo([ in] uint32 inparam, [out] boolean outparam);
};
```

Developing code to pass method in-parameters is significantly more involved. To prepare the method's in-parameters requires access to the method declaration (made from the class definition). You will need to spawn a brand new instance of the method in-parameter definition so that parameter values can be set. Finally, the in-parameters are passed to the `ExecMethod` call and the provider will extract the parameters for the operation. Let's see some code:

```
CComBSTR bstrMethod("foo");
CComBSTR bstrObject("Sample_Class.Name=\"Gwyn\"");
CComBSTR bstrClass("Sample_Class");

// Get the class definition so we can get access to the method in-parameters
CComPtr<IWbemClassObject> spClass;
hr = spServices->GetObject(bstrClass, 0, NULL, &spClass, NULL);

// Get the methods in-parameters
CComPtr<IWbemClassObject> spInParamsDefinition;
hr = spClass->GetMethod(bstrMethod, 0, & spInParamsDefinition, NULL);

// Spawn an instance of the in-parameters for our use
CComPtr<IWbemClassObject> spInParams;
hr = spInParamsDefinition ->SpawnInstance(0, &spInParams);

// Setup required in-parameters for method
CComVariant varInParam(int(12345));
hr = spInParams->Put(L"inparam", 0, & varInParam, 0);

// Execute method
CComPtr<IWbemClassObject> spOutParams;
hr = spServices->ExecMethod(bstrClass, bstrMethod, 0, NULL, spInParams,
  &spOutParams, NULL);

// Inspect out-parameters for return value
CComVariant varReturnValue;
hr = spOutParams->Get(L"ReturnValue", 0, &varReturnValue, 0, 0);

// ReturnValue contained in V_BSTR(&varReturnValue)
```

```
// Inspect the methods out-parameters (other than the method return value)
CComVariant varOutParam;
hr = spOutParams->Get(L"outparam", 0, & varOutParam, 0, 0);

// outparam value contained in V_BOOL(&varOutParam)
```

As with out-parameters, all in-parameters are contained within an instance of the `IWbemClassObject` interface. Each property corresponds to a method parameter, so if the method you plan to call has six parameters, then you will have to set six properties (assuming that all the parameters are required and are not optional).

To provide a more serious code sample and introduce some other issues that you most likely will have to deal with, we shall create a shared directory with the `Win32_Share` class. Here is an almost complete declaration of the `Win32_Share` class:

```
class Win32_Share: CIM_LogicalElement
{
  [read] string Name;
  [read] boolean AllowMaximum;
  [read] uint32 MaximumAllowed;
  [read] string Path;
  ...

  [static, implemented] uint32 Create([in] string Path, [in] string Name,
    [in, ValueMap {"0",...}, Values {"Disk Drive",...}] uint32 Type,
    [in] uint32 MaximumAllowed,
    [in, optional] string Description,
    [in, optional] string Password,
    [in, optional] Win32_SecurityDescriptor Access);

  [implemented] uint32 SetShareInfo([in, optional] uint32 MaximumAllowed,
    [in, Optional] string Description,
    [in, optional] Win32_SecurityDescriptor Access);

  [implemented] uint32 Delete();
};
```

Let's focus on the `Create` method. It has seven in-parameters, `Path`, `Name`, `Type`, `MaximumAllowed`, `Description`, `Password`, and `Access`. Each of these parameters should be straightforward to understand; if you look at the sharing property page for a directory, you will see the user interface that map to these parameters. Let's discuss the `Create` method's parameter types and declarations in detail.

First, you will see that most parameters take standard types that you already recognize, such as `string` and `uint32`. The `Access` parameter is an exception: It passes a `Win32_SecurityDescriptor` object. Classes intended for use in method parameters usually are inherited from `Win32_MethodParameterClass`.

All parameter declarations use qualifiers to provide more context information. The [in] qualifier specifies that the parameter is an in-parameter and [optional] means that it is not required. The ValueMap qualifier specifies the values that are valid for the property or parameter. The full ValueMap declaration that follows shows various integers' values that are valid for the Type parameter.

```
ValueMap
{
  "0", "1", "2", "3",
  "2147483648", "2147483649", "2147483650", "2147483651"
}
```

What do these values mean or represent? That is the role of the Values qualifier, which provides a textual description of the values in the ValueMap. Here is the full Values declaration:

```
Values
{
  "Disk Drive", "Print Queue", "Device", "IPC",
  "Disk Drive Admin", "Print Queue Admin", "Device Admin", "IPC Admin"
}
```

Using the Values and ValueMap qualifiers, it is possible to work out what the Type parameter means or should be. The parameter is 0 (in integer form), specifies "Disk Drive" and 1 specifies "Print Queue" and so on. You should use these types of qualifiers in your own schema to aid the understanding of your method parameters and class properties.

The code that follows calls a static method to create a shared directory:

```
CComBSTR bstrMethod("Create");      // Method to call
CComBSTR bstrClass("Win32_Share");  // The class the method belongs to

// Get the class definition so we can get access to the method from the class
CComPtr<IWbemClassObject> spClass;
hr = spServices->GetObject(bstrClass, 0, NULL, &spClass, NULL);

// Get the methods in-parameters
CComPtr<IWbemClassObject> spInParamsDefinition;
hr = spClass->GetMethod(bstrMethod, 0, & spInParamsDefinition, NULL);

// Spawn an instance of the in-parameters for our use
CComPtr<IWbemClassObject> spInParams;
hr = spInParamsDefinition ->SpawnInstance(0, &spInParams);
```

```
// Setup required in-parameters for method
CComVariant varName("Temp");
hr = spInParams->Put(L"Name", 0, &varName, 0);


CComVariant varPath("C:\\Temp");
hr = spInParams->Put(L"Path", 0, &varPath, 0);


CComVariant varType(int(0));
hr = spInParams->Put(L"Type", 0, &varType, 0);


// Execute method
CComPtr<IWbemClassObject> spOutParams;
hr = spServices->ExecMethod(bstrClass, bstrMethod, 0, NULL,
  spInParams, &spOutParams, NULL);


// Inspect out-parameters for return value
CComVariant varReturnValue;
hr = spOutParams->Get(L"ReturnValue", 0, &varReturnValue, 0, 0);


_tprintf(_T("\n %ls::%ls returned %d\n"), bstrClass, bstrMethod,
  V_I4(&varReturnValue));
```

Most of the details were discussed in earlier code, so we will focus on the new information. We completed only the required parameters (that is, parameters that don't have the `optional` attribute set) for two reasons: first, to keep the code sample small and second, we needed to fill in only the required parameters to create a shared directory. The `Type` parameter has a value of 0 (integer), if you recall, and this, according to the `Values` qualifier, will specify "Disk Drive". We finally pass the in-parameters to the ExecMethod call and we get the out-parameters through `spOutParams`. If a method being called returns a value other than `void`, then you will always get an out-parameter named "ReturnValue".

Let's look at the `GetMethod` method call:

```
interface IWbemClassObject
{
HRESULT GetMethod(
  LPCWSTR wszName,                      // Name of the method
  LONG lFlags,                          // Must be zero
  IWbemClassObject **ppInSignature,     // In-params definition
  IWbemClassObject **ppOutSignature);   // Out-params definition
};
```

A key point to notice is that `GetMethod` can be called only if the `IWbemClassObject` instance represents the definition of a class. If this were an object, `GetMethod` would return a `WBEM_E_ILLEGAL_OPERATION` error. Ultimately, `GetMethod` allows you to obtain a definition of both the in-parameters and the out-parameters of a method. The `wszName` parameter specifies the name of the method. Both the `ppInSignature` and `ppOutSignature` out-parameters contain the parameter definitions. If you are not interested in either `ppInSignature` or `ppOutSignature` then you can simply pass NULL to ignore the parameter. In the code sample above, we ignored `ppOutSignature`. The `lFlags` parameter is documented as having to be 0.

Next, the `ExecMethod` method looks like this:

```
interface IWbemServices
{
HRESULT ExecMethod(
  const BSTR strObjectPath,          // The class or object ref
  const BSTR MethodName,             // The name of the method
  long lFlags,                       // How to make the call
  IWbemContext *pCtx,                // Used in providers
  IWbemClassObject *pInParams,       // The in-parameters
  IWbemClassObject **ppOutParams,    // The out-parameters
  IWbemCallResult **ppCallResult);   // Not used for now...
};
```

As mentioned already, the *strObjectPath* parameter is either a class reference for static methods or an object reference for object methods.

The *lFlags* parameter allows only one flag, `WBEM_FLAG_RETURN_IMMEDIATELY`, which you use when you want to execute a semisynchronous call. We discuss semisynchronous calls later in the chapter.

If a method has in-parameters, you must supply your in-parameters (as already discussed) in the *pInParams* parameter. If the method does not have any in-parameters, then you can simply pass NULL.

If a method has out-parameters, you will receive them through `ppOutParams` when `ExecMethod` returns. If you wish to ignore the out-parameters, you can simply pass NULL.

■ Manipulating Object Properties

As you already have seen, setting and getting property values is one of the most common operations performed when writing management applications. Throughout nearly all of the code samples so far in this chapter, you've seen properties being set and property values being retrieved. We have been careful, however, to use strings or integers to aid understanding. In the next couple of sections, we will cover in more detail how to get and set properties of different data types. Let's quickly recap the calls made earlier that involve getting and setting property values. The following call was made in the section in which you saw how to create a management object. Notice that it uses the `Put` method call.

```
CComVariant varNumOfChapters(int(11));
hr = spInstance->Put(CComBSTR("NumberOfChapters"), 0, &
  varNumOfChapters, 0);
```

The next call was made in the section where you saw how to obtain a management object. Notice that it uses the `Get` method call.

```
CComVariant var;
hr = spInstance->Get(CComBSTR(_T("Path")), 0, &var, 0, 0);
```

Both of these code samples either are getting a value or setting a value. Note that calling `Put` will change the property of the instance in memory, but will not persist the change to the real object in WMI. To persist the change requires a call to `PutInstance`. To move this discussion forward, let's examine the `Put` and `Get` methods in the `IWbemClassObject` interface.

```
interface IWbemClassObject
{
HRESULT Put(
  LPCWSTR wszName,          // Name of the property
  LONG lFlags,              // Must be zero
  VARIANT *pVal,            // Value of property to set
  CIMTYPE vtType);          // The CIM type, info in variant anyway

HRESULT Get(
  LPCWSTR wszName,          // Name of the property
  LONG lFlags,              // Must be zero
  VARIANT *pVal,            // Value of property obtained
  CIMTYPE *pvtType,         // The CIM type, info in variant anyway
  LONG *plFlavor);          // Info about the origin of the property
};
```

If the `IWbemClassObject` interface pointer represents a management object, then the *wszName* parameter specifies the name of a property in the class. If, however, the `IWbemClassObject` interface pointer represents method parameters, then the `wszName` parameter specifies the name of the parameter.

The *lFlags* parameter is documented as having to be 0.

In the case of `Put`, the *pVal* parameter is the property value to set, and for `Get`, the *pVal* parameter is the property value obtained from the object. The variant contains the type and value of the property. In addition, there are also separate integer declarations that describe the CIM data types; the *vtType* and *pvtType* parameters refer to them. The data type definitions all start with CIM_*xxxx*, where *xxxx* is the name of the data type. The *vtType* parameter is used when creating properties in a class. You can use the WMI API to create classes in the WMI repository, but this topic is beyond the scope of this book. The *pvtType* out-parameter specifies the type contained within pVal. Generally, you will probably end up ignoring the *pvtType* parameter because all the information you need is contained within the variant. Table 7.1 describes all the CIM data types and the variant mapping used.

Table 7.1 CIM Data Type to Variant Mappings

Data type	VT type	CIM type	Comment
sint8	VT_I2	CIM_SINT8	Signed 8-bit integer.
sint16	VT_I2	CIM_SINT16	Signed 16-bit integer.
sint32	VT_I4	CIM_SINT32	Signed 32-bit integer.
sint64	VT_BSTR	CIM_SINT64	Signed 64-bit integer in string form. The string follows the hexadecimal or decimal format according to the American National Standards Institute (ANSI) C rules.
real32	VT_R4	CIM_REAL32	32-bit floating point number.
real64	VT_R8	CIM_REAL64	64-bit floating point number.
uint8	VT_UI1	CIM_UINT8	Unsigned 8-bit integer.
uint16	VT_I4	CIM_UINT16	Unsigned 16-bit integer.
uint32	VT_I4	CIM_UINT32	Unsigned 32-bit integer.
uint64	VT_BSTR	CIM_UINT64	Unsigned 64-bit integer in string form. The string follows the hexadecimal or decimal format according to the ANSI C rules.
boolean	VT_BOOL	CIM_BOOLEAN	Boolean value.
DATETIME	VT_BSTR	CIM_DATETIME	All dates and times in WMI use the format designed by the Distributed Management Task Force (DMTF).
object	VT_UNKNOWN	CIM_OBJECT	Represents an object. Query for the IWbemClassObject interface to gain access to the object properties.
object ref	VT_BSTR	CIM_REFERENCE	An object path string. See the discussion earlier in the chapter about object paths.
char16	VT_I2	CIM_CHAR16	16-bit Unicode character.
string	VT_BSTR	CIM_STRING	Unicode character string.
[array]	VT_ARRAY | *	CIM_FLAG_ARRAY	An array of any of the above data types. Arrays are accessed using SAFEARRAYs.

The *plFlavor* parameter can be used to determine where the property originated. If you do not care where the property originated, then you simply pass NULL. The flavor of the property can be local, inherited, or system-provided.

For all system-provided properties, the *plFlavor* parameter will contain WBEM_FLAVOR_ORIGIN_SYSTEM. This applies to __SUPERCLASS, __DYNASTY, __RELPATH, __DERIVATION, __SERVER, __NAMESPACE, and __PATH properties.

The *plFlavor* parameter will contain WBEM_FLAVOR_ORIGIN_LOCAL if the property is at a local level. For classes, a local property is the most derived property in the class; for example, the Win32_Share class has AccessMask, AllowMaximum, MaximumAllowed, Path, and Type, all of which are declared within the class.

The *plFlavor* parameter will contain WBEM_FLAVOR_ORIGIN_PROPAGATED if the property is inherited from a parent (or super) class. The following code sample enumerates all the property definitions for the Win32_Share class:

```
// Get the class definition
CComPtr<IWbemClassObject> spClass;
hr = spServices->GetObject(CComBSTR("Win32_Share"),
  WBEM_FLAG_RETURN_WBEM_COMPLETE, NULL, & spClass, NULL);


// Start enumerating the properties in the class
hr = spClass->BeginEnumeration(WBEM_FLAG_NONSYSTEM_ONLY);

CComBSTR bstrName;
CComVariant varValue;
LONG lFlavor = 0;
while (spClass->Next(0, &bstrName, &varValue, 0, &lFlavor) ==
  WBEM_S_NO_ERROR)
{
  CComBSTR bstrFlavor;

  switch (lFlavor)
  {
    case WBEM_FLAVOR_ORIGIN_SYSTEM: bstrFlavor = _T("system-provided");
      break;
    case WBEM_FLAVOR_ORIGIN_PROPAGATED: bstrFlavor = _T("inherited");
      break;
    case WBEM_FLAVOR_ORIGIN_LOCAL: bstrFlavor = _T("local"); break;
  }

  _tprintf(_T("  %ls is %ls\n"), bstrName, bstrFlavor);

  // Free these before we get the next property details
  bstrName.Empty();
  varValue.Clear();
}
hr = spClass->EndEnumeration();
```

This code conveniently introduced you to the enumeration of properties. As you can see, it is straightforward; all you need to do is start the enumeration and call `Next` until it returns `WBEM_S_NO_MORE_DATA` (this signifies that you reached the end of the enumeration). You should always call EndEnumeration when you have finished with an enumeration operation. In the code sample, we used `WBEM_FLAG_NONSYSTEM_ONLY`, but other flags can be passed into `BeginEnumeration`. See the Platform SDK documentation for more information.

Let's get back to property flavors. The preceding code produces the following output:

```
AccessMask is local
AllowMaximum is local
Caption is inherited
Description is inherited
InstallDate is inherited
MaximumAllowed is local
Name is inherited
Path is local
Status is inherited
Type is local
```

You can now see proof that `AccessMask`, `AllowMaximum`, `MaximumAllowed`, `Path`, and `Type` are declared locally within the `Win32_Share` class. `Caption`, `Description`, `Install-Date`, `Name`, and `Status` are inherited from `CIM_ManagedSystemElement`.

For instance, local properties are those set by the provider for the class. Code similar to the previous enumeration, except for an instance of a `Win32_Share` class instead of class definition, produces the following output:

```
AccessMask is inherited
AllowMaximum is local
Caption is local
Description is local
InstallDate is inherited
MaximumAllowed is inherited
Name is local
Path is local
Status is local
Type is local
```

You can now see that the provider for the `Win32_Share` class has set the inherited class properties `Caption`, `Description`, `Name`, and `Status` (as well as most of its local properties). The properties `AccessMask`, `InstallDate`, and `MaximumAllowed` were inherited from the class declaration, because the provider did not set their values.

Now let's turn our focus to some of the more unusual property data types. We assume that you are comfortable with such data types as a string (VT_BSTR) and sint32 (VT_I4). The types we think need more explanation are arrays, object, and DATETIME.

Table 7.2 DATETIME Field Descriptions for Absolute Date/Time

Field	Comment
yyyy	Four-digit year (0000 through 9999). Providers can restrict the supported range.
mm	Two-digit month (01 through 12).
dd	Two-digit day of the month (01 through 31).
HH	Two-digit hour of the day using the 24-hour clock (00 through 23).
MM	Two-digit minute in the hour (00 through 59).
SS	Two-digit number of seconds in the minute (00 through 59).
mmmmmm	Six-digit number of microseconds in the second (000000 through 999999).
s	Plus sign (+) or minus sign (−) to indicate a positive or negative offset from Universal Time Coordinates (UTC).
UUU	Three-digit offset indicating the number of minutes that the originating time zone deviates from UTC.

The array and object data types will be covered later in the chapter, so let's discuss DATETIME.

The DATETIME data type can represent either a date and time or an interval. Both types are strings that use formats designed by the DMTF. Each format is a fixed-length string that contains fields for each type of time specification. The string format for the date and time specification is:

```
yyyymmddHHMMSS.mmmmmmsUUU
```

Table 7.2 describes each field.

Each of the nine fields either must be completed or ignored and replaced with asterisks. Here are some examples:

```
20050704******.********* // date only: 4 July 2005
********1230**.********* // hours & minutes only: 12:30 pm
200507********.********* // year & month only: July 2005
20050704123029.********* // date & time: 4 July 2005-12:30 pm 29 seconds
200507041230**.***** +060 // date & time: 4 July 2005-12:30 pm,
                          //              1 hour ahead of universal time
```

The string format for the interval time specification is:

```
ddddddddHHMMSS.mmmmmm:000
```

Table 7.3 describes each field.

Table 7.3   DATETIME Field Descriptions for Interval Times

Field	Comment
dddddddd	Eight digits representing a number of days (00000000 through 99999999).
HH	Two-digit hour of the day using the 24-hour clock (00 through 23).
MM	Two-digit minute in the hour (00 through 59).
SS	Two-digit number of seconds in the minute (00 through 59).
mmmmmm	Six-digit number of microseconds in the second (000000 through 999999).
:000	Interval times always have a trailing :000 as the last four characters.

All five fields must be completed. Here are some examples of interval times:

```
00000002030756.000000:000  // interval: 2 days, 3 hours, 7 minutes & 56 sec
00000000000100.000000:000  // interval: every minute
00000000000015.000000:000  // interval: every 15 seconds
00000000000000.500000:000  // interval: 500 milliseconds (half a second)
```

■ Manipulating Array Object Properties

When writing your applications, you more than likely will have to use arrays to obtain the property values you are after. You might need to use arrays to get your own array-based property values in your own schema design. As mentioned in the last section, you can have an array of any CIM data type. You can represent binary data as an array of uint8.

Let's examine some code that accesses an array-based property. The purpose of the code sample is to list the derivation hierarchy for a class, in this case Win32_Physical-Memory. The __DERIVATION system-provided property is declared as an array of strings (that is, VT_ARRAY | VT_BSTR).

```
// Get the class definition
CComPtr<IWbemClassObject> spClass;
hr = spServices->GetObject(CComBSTR("Win32_PhysicalMemory"),
  WBEM_FLAG_RETURN_WBEM_COMPLETE, NULL, & spClass, NULL);

// Get a property from class definition
VARIANT var; VariantInit(&var);
hr = spClass->Get(CComBSTR(_T("__DERIVATION")), 0, &var, 0, 0);

// var.vt is VT_ARRAY | VT_BSTR
```

```
// Calculate the number of elements
long lUpper = 0;
long lLower = 0;
hr = SafeArrayGetUBound(V_ARRAY(&var), 1, &lUpper);
hr = SafeArrayGetLBound(V_ARRAY(&var), 1, &lLower);

long lNumOfElems = lUpper-lLower + 1;

// Gain access to the SAFEARRAY
BSTR HUGEP *pbstrArray;
hr = SafeArrayAccessData(V_ARRAY(&var), (void**)&pbstrArray);

_tprintf(_T(" Derivation:\n"));
for (int nIndex = 0; nIndex < lNumOfElems; nIndex++)
{
  _tprintf(_T(" %ls\n"), pbstrArray[nIndex]);
}

hr = SafeArrayUnaccessData(V_ARRAY(&var));
VariantClear(&var);
```

You should be reasonably familiar with the above code. We have obtained the class definition and requested the system-provided property __DERIVATION. The variant of the property contains the SAFEARRAY and so we use the appropriate API calls to access the array directly. The output of the above example produces the inheritance hierarchy for the Win32_PhysicalMemory class. Win32_PhysicalMemory first inherits from CIM_PhysicalMemory, and that inherits from CIM_Chip, and so forth.

```
Derivation:
  CIM_PhysicalMemory
  CIM_Chip
  CIM_PhysicalComponent
  CIM_PhysicalElement
  CIM_ManagedSystemElement
```

Saving array-based properties is also straightforward. Create your SAFEARRAY and bind it to a VARIANT. Ensure that the VARIANT's vt (variant type) member is set correctly when passing it to Put.

■ Accessing Objects from Object Properties

When writing your applications, you will occasionally have to access properties or method parameters that are not strings, integers, or arrays, but in fact are complete objects. You have already seen an example of this earlier in the chapter. The `Access` in-parameter for the `Win32_Share Create` method took a `Win32_SecurityDescriptor` object. To explain the concept of embedding objects within properties (or method parameters) more fully, we extend the `Sample_Book` class that was introduced earlier in the chapter.

Here is the `Sample_Book` class with a small change. The `Summary` property no longer is defined as a string data type. Instead, we encapsulate the summary string within a new class called `Sample_BookSummary`.

```
class Sample_Book
{
  [key] string BookTitle;
  [key] string AuthorName;
  Sample_BookSummary Summary;
  DATETIME DatePublished;
  uint8 NumberOfChapters;
};
```

As you can see, the `Summary` property is defined now as an object of type `Sample_BookSummary` (effectively a new data type). Let's see what the `Sample_BookSummary` class looks like:

```
class Sample_BookSummary
{
  string BookSummary;
};
```

All we have done is move the string describing the summary of the book into another class (through the `BookSummary` property). To visualize the sample code better, let's create an instance of the `Sample_Book`. Here is the MOF code that does this (also, notice that the `Summary` property is a new instance):

```
instance of Sample_Book
{
  BookTitle = "Developing WMI Solutions";
  AuthorName = "Craig Tunstall & Gwyn Cole";
  NumberOfChapters = 12;
  Summary = instance of Sample_BookSummary
  {
    BookSummary = "A cool book on Windows Management Instrumentation";
  };
};
```

Now let's view some sample code that obtains this object (`Sample_Book`) and accesses a property that is an also an object (`Sample_BookSummary`). When designing your own schemas you might want to employ this technique. However, be careful: The disadvantage of this approach is that it limits your capability to query and form associations. The capability of querying and forming associations on your managed objects is a key benefit, and you should try to keep your options open for future schema revisions.

This sample code obtains the instance we created:

```
CComBSTR bstrPath =
  "Sample_Book.BookTitle=\"Developing WMI Solutions\","\
  "AuthorName=\"Craig Tunstall & Gwyn Cole\"";

// Get the Sample_Book object
CComPtr<IWbemClassObject> spInstance;
hr = spServices->GetObject(bstrPath, WBEM_FLAG_RETURN_WBEM_COMPLETE,
  NULL, &spInstance, NULL);

// Get the property which is an object
CComVariant varObject;
hr = spInstance->Get(CComBSTR(_T("Summary")), 0, &varObject, 0, 0);

// QueryInterface for the property's object interface
CComQIPtr<IWbemClassObject> spSummaryObject = V_UNKNOWN(&varObject);

// Get property from embedded object
CComVariant varSummary;
hr = spSummaryObject->Get(CComBSTR(_T("BookSummary")), 0, &varSummary,
  0, 0);

_tprintf(_T(" BookSummary is'%ls'\n"), V_BSTR(&varSummary));
```

Most of this code sample should be straightforward by now. We get the object we want and obtain the Summary property value. We highlighted the code that actually extracts the embedded object in bold font. The Summary property variant is of type VT_UNKNOWN. This means we have a valid IUnknown interface pointer with which you can call QueryInterface to ask for an interface that can provide access to the properties of the object. This is what the ATL class CComQIPtr does. Use the IWbemClassObject interface to get and set property values by calling the Get and Put methods, as we do next: We call Get to retrieve the BookSummary property from the embedded object. The code outputs:

```
BookSummary is 'A cool book on Windows Management Instrumentation'
```

Creating objects that have properties with embedded objects is a little more involved. You may need to create objects like this in your own applications because your schema uses embedded property objects. The process of creating embedded property objects is not dissimilar to creating instances, which was covered earlier in the chapter. The general process is to get the class definition and (this is the crucial part) spawn an instance of it. The spawned instance represents the object that you will use when you set the property value. You set all your properties on the spawned instance before calling Put.

Let's extend the code sample from the earlier section that covers the creation of objects. In that section, we created a Sample_Book instance in which we declared the Summary property as using a string data type. Now with the revised Sample_Book class definition, let's recreate the Sample_Book instance. The following code will do the same task as the MOF complier did earlier with the MOF code. We have highlighted the code we shall discuss in bold font:

```cpp
// Get class so we can spawn an instance of it
CComPtr<IWbemClassObject> spClass;
hr = spServices->GetObject(CComBSTR("Sample_Book"), 0,NULL,
  &spClass, NULL);

// Make new object
CComPtr<IWbemClassObject> spInstance;
hr = spClass->SpawnInstance(0, &spInstance);

// Set some properties on the object
CComVariant varBookTitle("Developing WMI Solutions");
hr = spInstance->Put(CComBSTR("BookTitle"), 0, &varBookTitle, 0);

CComVariant varAuthor("Craig Tunstall & Gwyn Cole");
hr = spInstance->Put(CComBSTR("AuthorName"), 0, &varAuthor, 0);

CComVariant varNumOfChapters(int(11));
hr = spInstance->Put(CComBSTR("NumberOfChapters"), 0,
&varNumOfChapters,0);

// We're going to create the object for the Summary property
// First get the definition of the Sample_BookSummary class
CComPtr<IWbemClassObject> spBookSummaryClass;
hr = spServices->GetObject(CComBSTR("Sample_BookSummary"), 0, NULL,
  &spBookSummaryClass, NULL);

// Make new Sample_BookSummary object
CComPtr<IWbemClassObject> spSummaryObject;
hr = spBookSummaryClass->SpawnInstance(0, &spSummaryObject);

// Set property on embedded object
CComVariant varSummary("A cool book on Windows Management
  Instrumentation");
hr = spSummaryObject->Put(CComBSTR(_T("BookSummary")), 0, &varSummary, 0);
```

```
// Finally, encapsulate object in variant and set the Summary property
CComVariant varSummaryObject(spSummaryObject);
hr = spInstance->Put(CComBSTR(_T("Summary")), 0, &varSummaryObject, 0);

// Commit to create instance in WMI
hr = spServices->PutInstance(spInstance, WBEM_FLAG_CREATE_ONLY,
  NULL, NULL);
```

Creating an instance and creating an instance for a property is virtually the same sort of code: You get the class definition, spawn an instance of the class, and set your properties. The only difference between saving object instances and saving property objects is:

1. When you create a management object, you save (commit) it by calling `PutInstance`.

2. When you create a property object, you save (commit) it by calling `Put` on the management object.

When you call methods that use parameter objects in either the in-parameters or the out-parameters, then you will need to write similar code to that demonstrated earlier.

■ Making Semisynchronous Calls

All the examples in this chapter so far have been making synchronous calls to WMI. The main problem with making synchronous calls is that the thread blocks for the duration of the method call. This can decrease the responsiveness of your application, especially if the call you are making is lengthy. A solution to this problem is to make asynchronous calls instead, but this is a little harder to implement. You have to handle multiple threads and provide an additional implementation of the `IWbemObjectSink` interface. We shall cover asynchronous calls in the next section.

Semisynchronous calls aim to solve both of these problems. They reduce code complexity by not having to deal with multiple threads and without having to implement an `IWbemObjectSink` interface.

You can make two types of semisynchronous calls:

1. Some of the methods on the `IWbemServices` interface return an `IWbemCallResult` interface. This interface can be polled when you are ready to deal with the result of the operation. The `IWbemCallResult` interface is implemented by WMI.

2. Other methods return an `IEnumWbemClassObject` enumerator. This enumerator also can be polled for the results of the operation by using the `Next` method call when it times out.

Let's look at the methods that return an `IWbemCallResult` interface first. They include `GetObject`, `PutInstance`, `DeleteInstance`, and `ExecMethod`. To make a semisynchronous call, follow this process:

1. Make your `IWbemServices` method call passing `WBEM_FLAG_RETURN_IMMEDIATELY` into the *lFlags* parameter. This specifies that you wish to make a semisynchronous call.

2. You have to pass the address of an `IWbemCallResult` pointer into the *ppCallResult* out-parameter. This will communicate the call progress when you poll it.

3. Make `GetCallStatus` calls on the *ppCallResult* interface pointer until it returns `WBEM_S_NO_ERROR`. When `WBEM_S_NO_ERROR` is returned, it means that there is a valid result for you to grab in the `GetResultObject`, `GetResultServices`, or `GetResultString` methods.

4. You can now make a call to `GetResultObject`, `GetResultServices`, or `GetResultString`, depending on the `IWbemServices` call made.

Let's see how you might make a semisynchronous call to `GetObject`. In this example, we get an instance that represents the Windows 2000 Fax service:

```
CComBSTR bstrPath;
bstrPath = (_T("Win32_Service.Name=\"Fax\""));

// Get object
_tprintf(_T(" Making call to GetObject()\n"));
CComPtr<IWbemCallResult> spCallResult;
hr = spServices->GetObject(bstrPath, WBEM_FLAG_RETURN_IMMEDIATELY,
  NULL, NULL, &spCallResult);

HRESULT hrStatus = S_OK;
do
{

  // Has the call finished yet? My poll timeout is 100 ms
  HRESULT hrCallResult = S_OK;
  hrStatus = spCallResult->GetCallStatus(100, &hrCallResult);

  _tprintf(_T(" IWbemCallResult::GetCallStatus(timeout=100ms, 0x%X)")\
    _T(" returned 0x%X\n"), hrCallResult, hrStatus);

  if (hrStatus == WBEM_S_NO_ERROR && hrCallResult == WBEM_S_NO_ERROR)
  {
    _tprintf(_T(" GetObject() call complete\n"));
```

```
      // Get object instance from call as there should be one now...
      CComPtr<IWbemClassObject> spInstance;
      hr = spCallResult->GetResultObject(WBEM_INFINITE, &spInstance);

      // Get a property from the object
      CComVariant var;
      hr = spInstance->Get(CComBSTR(_T("PathName")), 0, &var, 0, 0);

      _tprintf(_T("  Win32_Service.Name=\"Fax\" path is %ls\n"),
        V_BSTR(&var));
    }
  } while (hrStatus != WBEM_S_NO_ERROR);
```

We've highlighted in bold each of the four steps we outlined earlier. The code produces the following output:

```
Making call to GetObject()
IWbemCallResult::GetCallStatus(timeout=100ms, 0x8004100A) returned 0x40004
IWbemCallResult::GetCallStatus(timeout=100ms, 0x8004100A) returned 0x40004
IWbemCallResult::GetCallStatus(timeout=100ms, 0x8004100A) returned 0x40004
IWbemCallResult::GetCallStatus(timeout=100ms, 0x0) returned 0x0
GetObject() call complete
Win32_Service.Name="Fax" path is C:\WINNT\system32\faxsvc.exe
```

As you can see, the call to GetCallStatus timed out and we went back to try again and again until the call reported that it had completed. The HRESULT reported from GetCallStatus is WBEM_S_TIMEDOUT. When a time-out occurs, the HRESULT reported from GetCallStatus's out-parameter is WBEM_E_CRITICAL_ERROR under Windows 2000. Windows XP returns WBEM_S_NO_ERROR, which is what you would expect, because the semisynchronous call has not completed.

Let's look at the interfaces we have seen and discuss them in more detail. Here is the IWbemCallResult interface:

```
      interface IWbemCallResult
      {
      HRESULT GetCallStatus(
        LONG lTimeout,                      // timeout in milliseconds
        LONG *plStatus);                    // returned HRESULT from call

      HRESULT GetResultObject(
        LONG lTimeout,                      // timeout in milliseconds
        IWbemClassObject **ppResultObject); // returned instance

      HRESULT GetResultServices(
        LONG lTimeout,                      // timeout in milliseconds
        IWbemServices **ppServices);        // returned namespace
```

```
HRESULT GetResultString(
  LONG lTimeout,                        // timeout in milliseconds
  BSTR *pstrResultString);              // object path of new object
};
```

The `GetCallStatus` method would be used in all cases, because it is the primary source to discover whether the call has completed and to obtain the returned HRESULT from the initial call. You can make the time-out as short or as long as you like; you probably will need to experiment to find a happy medium for keeping your application responsive.

If you are making calls with either `GetObject` or `ExecMethod`, then you must call `GetResultObject` to gain access to the `IWbemClassObject` for the completed operation. When the `GetObject` call completes, the returned `IWbemClassObject` will be the desired object instance. When the `ExecMethod` call completes the returned `IWbemClassObject` will be the out-parameters of the method call that also includes the `ReturnValue` property.

If you are making calls to `OpenNamespace`, then you will need to call `GetResultServices` to gain access to the `IWbemServices` interface for the newly opened namespace. We have not discussed `OpenNamespace` because it is similar to `IWbemLocator::ConnectServer`. The real difference between `OpenNamespace` and `ConnectServer` is that you can open namespaces relative to the current namespace by passing a relative namespace reference.

If you are making calls to `PutInstance`, then you might want to call `GetResultString`. `GetResultString` is a way for the provider to return an object path of a newly created instance. This is especially useful if the provider assigns or generates a unique value for a key property.

Having reviewed the `IWbemCallResult` interface, let's focus on the other semisynchronous methods that return an `IEnumWbemClassObject` enumerator. They include `CreateInstanceEnum` and `ExecQuery`. To make a semisynchronous call with either of these functions, you have to follow this process:

1. Make your `IWbemServices` method call passing `WBEM_FLAG_RETURN_IMMEDIATELY` into the `lFlags` parameter. This specifies that you wish to make a semisynchronous call.

2. You can now call `Next` on your returned enumerator. If the time-out expires, you will receive `WBEM_S_TIMEDOUT`. If it is successful, you will receive `WBEM_S_NO_ERROR` and, finally, `WBEM_S_FALSE` when you get to the end of the enumerator.

In fact, there is barely any difference between synchronous and semisynchronous calls. The only differences in making them are to add `WBEM_FLAG_RETURN_IMMEDIATELY` to the `lFlags` parameter and to add additional logic to check for `WBEM_S_TIMEDOUT`. The following code displays a list of running Windows 2000/XP Services:

```
// Get list of running services
CComPtr<IEnumWbemClassObject> spEnumInst;
CComBSTR bstrQuery("SELECT * FROM Win32_Service WHERE Started=true");
```

```
// Perform query
hr = spServices->ExecQuery(CComBSTR(_T("WQL")), bstrQuery,
  WBEM_FLAG_BIDIRECTIONAL | WBEM_FLAG_RETURN_IMMEDIATELY, NULL,
  &spEnumInst);

bool bFinished = false;
while (!bFinished)
{

  // Get the object instance
  ULONG uNumOfInstances = 0;
  CComPtr<IWbemClassObject> spInstance;
  HRESULT hrNext = spEnumInst->Next(100, 1, &spInstance,
    &uNumOfInstances);

  if (hrNext == WBEM_S_FALSE)
    bFinished = true;
  else if (hrNext == WBEM_S_TIMEDOUT)
  {
    _tprintf(_T("  IEnumWbemClassObject::Next(timeout=100ms) ")\
      _T("returned 0x%X\n"), hrNext);
  }
  else
  {

    // Get properties from the object
    CComVariant varName;
    hr = spInstance->Get(CComBSTR(_T("DisplayName")), 0, &varName, 0, 0);

    _tprintf(_T("  %ls\n"), V_BSTR(&varName));
  }
}
```

We have highlighted in bold the two steps we outlined earlier. The code produces a portion of the following output:

```
...
...
Print Spooler
Telephony
Distributed Link Tracking Client
Windows Time
World Wide Web Publishing Service
  IEnumWbemClassObject::Next(timeout=100ms) returned 0x40004
  IEnumWbemClassObject::Next(timeout=100ms) returned 0x40004
Windows Management Instrumentation
Windows Management Instrumentation Driver Extensions
```

From this output, you can deduce that we had to poll twice before we successfully got an object instance of the WMI service. The 0x40004 HRESULT is WBEM_S_TIMEDOUT.

Making Asynchronous Calls

The main benefit of accessing management objects asynchronously is that an operation can be started and, if necessary, be cancelled later. This enables an application to be optimized for performance more easily and solves the problem of thread blockage while the operation is in progress.

Developing asynchronous access to management objects requires the development of a sink. The sink's whole purpose is to monitor the delivery of management objects and handle call status notifications. Applications that access management objects asynchronously typically are multithreaded and therefore require that the sink be thread safe. The drawbacks of writing asynchronous applications are that it is more difficult to determine the sequence of operations between threads and you must develop a sink for each type of operation.[2]

Calling an asynchronous method starts the desired operation and returns immediately. It reports the results of the operation to the sink until the asynchronous operation completes. To demonstrate this, we shall reimplement the earlier code sample in which we obtained a list of Windows Services that had already started.

Let's see what the sink interface looks like:

```
interface IWbemObjectSink
{
HRESULT Indicate(
  LONG lObjectCount,                  // Number of objects returned
  IWbemClassObject **ppObjArray);     // Array of objects

HRESULT SetStatus(
  LONG lFlags,                        // Call status
  HRESULT hResult,                    // Call result or progress
  BSTR strParam,                      // For PutInstanceAsync only
  IWbemClassObject *pObjParam);       // For complex error/status
};
```

The Indicate method is called when WMI has management objects that satisfy the asynchronous operation. To draw a parallel to what you've seen already, let's review what was involved with a semisynchronous query. When an ExecQuery call completes, an

2. We do not recommend reusing an existing instance of a sink for multiple asynchronous operations. Use one sink instance for one asynchronous operation.

enumerator is returned that contains the result set for the query. Each instance can be obtained by iterating through the enumerator. An asynchronous call is a little different. It has no enumerator, because each instance is obtained when WMI delivers it to your sink through the `Indicate` method. The query will continue until it completes or it is cancelled.

The `lObjectCount` parameter is the number of objects contained within the `ppObj-Array` parameter. The `ppObjArray` parameter contains the instances returned by WMI.

The `SetStatus` method allows WMI to notify you with call status information. This is critical in determining when the call completes. The `lFlags` parameter can be either `WBEM_STATUS_COMPLETE` or `WBEM_STATUS_PROGRESS`. The `WBEM_STATUS_COMPLETE` is obvious; this flag is set when the asynchronous operation is complete. When `WBEM_STATUS_COMPLETE` is set, the `hResult` parameter contains the result of the completed call. The `WBEM_STATUS_PROGRESS` flag may or may not be set, depending on whether the asynchronous method call had specified `WBEM_FLAG_SEND_STATUS`. When `WBEM_STATUS_PROGRESS` is set, the `hResult` parameter contains both the progress and total. The progress value is contained in `LOWORD(hResult)` and usually represents a percentage, although this depends on the provider. The total value is contained in `HI-WORD(hResult)` and usually represents the total number of instances, but again, this depends on the provider.

All WMI providers do not necessarily support the delivery of progress information and so the `WBEM_FLAG_SEND_STATUS` may be ignored. If the `WBEM_FLAG_SEND_STATUS` is not set when making an asynchronous method call, it is guaranteed that `SetStatus` will be called only once.

If you are making calls to `PutInstanceAsync`, then you might want to inspect the `strParam` parameter. This parameter allows the provider to return an object path of a newly created instance. This is especially useful if the provider assigns or generates a unique value for a key property. The equivalent of this functionality for a semisynchronous call is the `GetResultString` method on the `IWbemCallResult` interface.

The `pObjParam` parameter allows the provider to return very rich information about the error or status of an operation. This is useful especially where the error and/or status simply cannot be encapsulated in an HRESULT. When writing your own providers, keep this in mind if you want to provide richer information to the client. The `pObjParam` parameter works like any other `IWbemClassObject` instance. Properties on the instance can be inspected for the desired information. Making asynchronous calls is the only means of getting at this rich information.

Let's look at a code sample. It does nothing very interesting except output some information to the console window:

```
class CQuerySink : public IWbemObjectSink
{
private:
  CRITICAL_SECTION m_csLock;      // We need to be thread safe
  bool m_bIsComplete;             // An internal flag for call completion
```

```
public:
  CQuerySink(): m_lRefCount(0), m_bIsComplete(false)
  {
    InitializeCriticalSection(&m_csLock);
  }
  ~CQuerySink()
  {
    DeleteCriticalSection(&m_csLock);
  }

  // Helper function to determine if the query is complete
  bool IsComplete()
  {
    bool bRetVal = false;

    EnterCriticalSection(&m_csLock);
    bRetVal = m_bIsComplete;
    LeaveCriticalSection(&m_csLock);

    return bRetVal;
  }

  // IUnknown method implementations skipped for brevity
  //... ...
  //...

  // IWbemObjectSink methods
  STDMETHOD(Indicate)(long lObjectCount, IWbemClassObject** apObjArray)
  {
    HRESULT hr = S_OK;

    for (int nIndex = 0; nIndex < lObjectCount; nIndex++)
    {
      // Get properties from a Win32_Service object
      CComVariant varName;
      hr = apObjArray[nIndex]->Get(CComBSTR(_T("DisplayName")), 0,
        &varName, 0, 0);

      _tprintf(_T("  %ls\n"), V_BSTR(&varName));
    }
      return WBEM_S_NO_ERROR;
  }

  STDMETHOD(SetStatus)(long lFlags, HRESULT hResult, BSTR strParam,
    IWbemClassObject* pObjParam)
  {
    if (lFlags == WBEM_STATUS_COMPLETE)
```

```
        {
          _tprintf(_T(" Call complete, returned HRESULT 0x%X\n"), hResult);

          EnterCriticalSection(&m_csLock);
          m_bIsComplete = true;
          LeaveCriticalSection(&m_csLock);
        }
        else if (lFlags == WBEM_STATUS_PROGRESS)
        {
            // You could also check LOWORD(hResult) for progress info
            // and check HIWORD(hResult) for the total.
            _tprintf(_T(" Call still in-progress\n"));
        }

        return WBEM_S_NO_ERROR;
     }
  };
```

In your own applications, you would perform something more interesting for both the `Indicate` and `SetStatus` methods. An example would be to set a progress bar position in a user interface application with the `LOWORD(hResult)` during an `WBEM_STATUS_PROGRESS` notification. However, this is possible only if the provider publishes the progress in the `LOWORD(hResult)` and the total in the `HIWORD(hResult)`. Most providers do not know how many management objects there will be in advance, so setting a progress bar may not be possible.

Asynchronous calls typically will be made in a multithreaded environment, so let's examine how you might execute a task by using another thread to perform a query. The following code sample is not very interesting; it merely spawns a new thread for a new task.

```
HANDLE hThread = HANDLE(_beginthread(ThreadGetWin32Sevices, 0, 0));
```

Next, let's look at the `ThreadGetWin32Sevices` function that is used for the thread execution:

```
void ThreadGetWin32Sevices(void *param)
{

  CoInitializeEx(NULL, COINIT_MULTITHREADED);
  HRESULT hr = S_OK;

  // Connecting to WMI skipped for brevity
  //... ...
  //...

  CComBSTR bstrQuery("SELECT * FROM Win32_Service WHERE Started=true");
```

```
    CQuerySink *pSink = new CQuerySink;
    hr = spServices->ExecQueryAsync(CComBSTR(_T("WQL")), bstrQuery,
      WBEM_FLAG_BIDIRECTIONAL, NULL, pSink);

  while(!pSink->IsComplete())
    Sleep(50);

  CoUninitialize();
}
```

The first task we performed was to create a multithreaded apartment. A single-threaded apartment is not very useful if we don't have a message pump in our thread. A message pump is necessary for proxy calls to make it back on the sink. The lack of a message pump would cause the thread to hang. The next step was to connect to WMI and start an asynchronous query by calling `ExecQueryAsync`.

The method parameters for `ExecQueryAsync` are quite similar to `ExecQuery`. The only difference is that instead of receiving an `IEnumWbemClassObject` enumerator, an `IWbemObjectSink` implementation is passed. All asynchronous method calls require an `IWbemObjectSink` implementation.

■ WMI Error Messages

On occasion, it is useful to provide more meaningful error information for HRESULTs and, in particular, for WMI HRESULTs. There is a COM interface provided by WMI that can be used to get both the facility and the error strings. This typically would be used when displaying errors to a user.

It consists of one interface, `IWbemStatusCodeText`, that has two methods, `GetError-CodeText` and `GetFacilityCodeText`. Both methods take a HRESULT and return a string.

Here is sample code that retrieves the strings:

```
void DisplayError(HRESULT hrDesc)
{
  HRESULT hr = S_OK;

  CComPtr<IWbemStatusCodeText> spError;
  hr = spError.CoCreateInstance(CLSID_WbemStatusCodeText);

  CComBSTR bstrError;
  hr = spError->GetErrorCodeText(hrDesc, 0, 0, &bstrError);

  CComBSTR bstrFacility;
  hr = spError->GetFacilityCodeText(hrDesc, 0, 0, &bstrFacility);

  _tprintf(_T("\n%ls HRESULT 0x%X is: %ls"), bstrFacility, hrDesc, bstrError);
}
```

The following calls:

```
DisplayError(WBEM_E_ACCESS_DENIED);
DisplayError(WBEM_E_INVALID_OBJECT_PATH);
DisplayError(WBEM_E_INVALID_QUERY);
DisplayError(WBEM_E_PROVIDER_NOT_CAPABLE);
DisplayError(STG_E_WRITEFAULT);
DisplayError(HRESULT_FROM_WIN32(ERROR_FILE_NOT_FOUND));
```

Produce the following output:

```
Wbem HRESULT 0x80041003 is: Access denied
Wbem HRESULT 0x8004103A is: Invalid object path
Wbem HRESULT 0x80041017 is: Invalid query
Wbem HRESULT 0x80041024 is: Provider is not capable of the attempted
   operation
Storage HRESULT 0x8003001D is: A disk error occurred during a write
   operation.
Win32 HRESULT 0x80070002 is: The system cannot find the file specified.
```

■ Overview of Events

One of the most powerful features in WMI is that it has the capability to deliver events when something interesting happens. "Something interesting" might include notification when disk space runs low on a machine. The event mechanism employed by WMI is based on a publish and subscribe approach. An event is published when either a client or an event provider delivers it to WMI. Figure 7.2 shows the events being published to WMI and applications subscribing for event notification. Event notification opens the possibility for one or more applications to react to events in which they are interested. For example, a management application may want to capture System Event Log activity so that it can analyze specific events and raise potential problems immediately.

An application can subscribe to receive one or more events. Events are delivered to the application if the published event satisfies the subscribed event query.

There are three types of events: intrinsic, extrinsic, and timer.

1. *Intrinsic events* occur in response to changes to namespaces, classes, and instances. Changes to instances are the most useful event notifications.
2. *Extrinsic events* are custom-defined events. These types of events allow you great flexibility in your own applications to deliver specialized events.
3. *Timer events* are events that WMI delivers using preconfigured information.

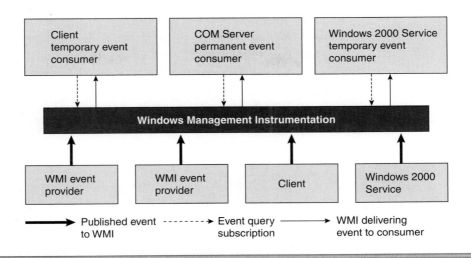

Figure 7.2 WMI event interaction

No events are delivered unless an application asks WMI for event notifications. An application that requests events from WMI is an *event consumer.* There are two types of event consumers: temporary event consumers and permanent event consumers. The following sections cover temporary event consumers in detail.

Temporary event consumers are applications (clients or Windows services) that subscribe to WMI for event notification. All event subscriptions use a WQL event query, which enables an event consumer to specify precisely what events to deliver.

Permanent event consumers offer a more robust event delivery and are implemented as COM servers (local or in-proc). When an event is delivered to a permanent event consumer, WMI calls `CoCreateInstance` (if it has not already been created from a previous event delivery) followed by passing the event to the consumer. These types of consumers are very powerful if you think about the possibilities! Permanent event consumers are discussed in detail in Chapter 12.

> **Note:** Key properties are meaningless in an event class. You cannot use normal enumeration techniques to address instances of an event class; you can access them only through an event consumer.

The WMI SDK comes with a few tools that you can use to test and develop event queries for your applications. The WMI Event Registration facility (which comes as a developer tool in the Platform SDK) can create event registrations, including timer instructions. These event registrations will be used by the Event Viewer consumer application (when loaded) to make the event subscriptions. The Event Viewer allows you to visualize the events as and when they occur. If you need quick raw access to test your event query, use `wbemtest`, which is installed with Windows XP and very closely mimics the `IWbemServices` interface.

Let's examine the different kinds of events.

▪ Intrinsic Events

As already mentioned, *intrinsic events* occur in response to specific types of changes to data. In the CIM, there are three types of data: namespaces, classes, and instances. All intrinsic events follow a common pattern: an event for creation, another for deletion, and finally an event for modification (Table 7.4).

Given that most applications either commit changes to management objects or respond to management object changes, you will find that the `__InstanceModification-Event` will become one of your best friends. Every time an instance changes, you will get one of these events (if you subscribe for it, of course). The `__InstanceCreation-Event` also is very useful, as you will see later when we subscribe for new Windows event log events.

All event classes ultimately inherit from the CIM class `__Event`, as you can see in Figure 7.3.

The `__InstanceModificationEvent` class is derived from the `__Instance-OperationEvent` class. The `__InstanceOperationEvent` class has only one property,

Table 7.4 Intrinsic Event Classes

Intrinsic class	Comment
__ClassCreationEvent	Notifies a consumer when a class is created.
__ClassDeletionEvent	Notifies a consumer when a class is deleted.
__ClassModificationEvent	Notifies a consumer when a class is modified.
__InstanceCreationEvent	Notifies a consumer when a class instance is created.
__InstanceDeletionEvent	Notifies a consumer when an instance is deleted.
__InstanceModificationEvent	Notifies a consumer when an instance is modified.
__NamespaceCreationEvent	Notifies a consumer when a namespace is created.
__NamespaceDeletionEvent	Notifies a consumer when a namespace is deleted.
__NamespaceModificationEvent	Notifies a consumer when a namespace is modified.

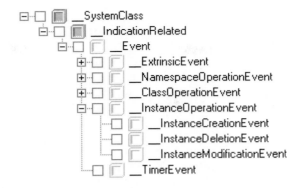

Figure 7.3 WMI event classes

Source: CIM Studio

`TargetInstance`. The `TargetInstance` property represents a copy of the managed object[3] that was created, deleted, or changed.

```
class __InstanceOperationEvent: __Event
{
  object TargetInstance;
};
```

The `__InstanceModificationEvent` class adds another property, `PreviousIn-stance`. This is a copy of the managed object before it was changed.

```
class __InstanceModificationEvent: __InstanceOperationEvent
{
  object PreviousInstance;
};
```

■ Extrinsic Events

Events that have nothing to do with namespaces, classes, or instances are called *extrinsic events*. WMI providers can publish both intrinsic and extrinsic events that offer a customized environment for new types of events. All extrinsic events are derived from `__ExtrinsicEvent`. To obtain more information about the extrinsic event classes in

3. `TargetInstance` is of type *object*, which means that any WMI object can be represented.

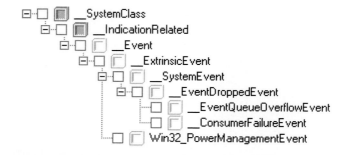

Figure 7.4 WMI extrinsic event classes

your namespace, use a tool like CIM Studio and iterate through the __ExtrinsicEvent derived classes. You will see something like Figure 7.4 under Windows 2000.

As you can see, there are three extrinsic event classes: __EventQueueOverflow-Event, __ConsumerFailureEvent, and Win32_PowerManagementEvent. The first two event classes are system-defined classes,[4] so there is really only one custom event class, Win32_PowerManagementEvent. Windows XP, on the other hand, publishes around 100 extrinsic events that include events for provider activity, the Service Control Manager, and some event traces from the Operating Systems event tracer (as covered in Chapter 13).

Let's look at the Win32_PowerManagementEvent extrinsic event:

```
class Win32_PowerManagementEvent: __ExtrinsicEvent
{
  [read,
   ValueMap
   {
     "4", "7", "10", "11", "18"
   },
   Values
   {
     "Entering Suspend", "Resume from Suspend",
     "Power Status Change", "OEM Event","Resume Automatic"
   }
  ] uint16 EventType;

  [read] uint16 OEMEventCode;
};
```

4. The reasons that the system event classes are not intrinsic are (1) they have nothing to do with namespaces, classes, or instances, and (2) the classes are used by the WMI event generator, which can be viewed as a specialized event provider. This is why they ultimately derive from __ExtrinsicEvent.

The `Win32_PowerManagementEvent` class description is:

The `Win32_PowerManagementEvent` class represents power management events resulting from power state changes. These state changes are associated with either the Advanced Power Management (APM) or the Advanced Configuration and Power Interface (ACPI) system management protocols.
Source: CIMV2 namespace in Windows XP

The `EventType` property contains one of the values specified in the `ValueMap`, which can be interpreted into a human-readable form with the strings in the `Values` qualifier. We introduced `Values` and `ValueMaps` earlier in the chapter. If the `Event-Type` property has the value `11` ("`OEM Event`"), then the `OEMEventCode` property will contain the specific power management code provided by the original equipment manufacturer.

This is an excellent example of an extrinsic event. It has nothing to do with namespaces, classes, and instances (that is, intrinsic events), but it completely defines a new event within the managed environment.

■ Timer Events

Timer events are a specialized kind of intrinsic event. WMI uses preconfigured event timers within the repository to generate timer events. There are two types of timers, absolute and interval. Absolute timers specify a specific time in the future. Interval timers are continuously generated and are specified in milliseconds. Configuring when timer events get generated is called a *timer instruction*.

As can be seen from the class hierarchy in Figure 7.5, there are two timer instruction classes. Creating instances of `__AbsoluteTimerInstruction` and `__IntervalTimer-Instruction` set up absolute and interval timer instructions, respectively.

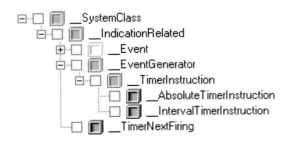

Figure 7.5 WMI timer instruction classes

To examine the timer classes, let's first look at the `__TimerInstruction` base class:

```
[abstract] class __TimerInstruction: __EventGenerator
{
  [key] string TimerId;
  boolean SkipIfPassed = FALSE;
};
```

The `TimerId` property specifies the name of the timer instruction (this must be unique), and the `SkipIfPassed` property indicates whether WMI should skip the delivery of the event if it is unable to deliver it at the appropriate time. The default setting for this is *false,* which instructs WMI that it must deliver the event, even if delivery time has passed. If this property is set to *true,* the event will not occur if WMI was unable to generate the event at the appropriate time. The `__AbsoluteTimerInstruction` class looks like this:

```
class __AbsoluteTimerInstruction: __TimerInstruction
{
  [not_null] DATETIME EventDateTime;
};
```

The `EventDateTime` property specifies an exact time for the delivery of the event. The `DATETIME` property must be a fully qualified date-time value. WMI will not generate an absolute timer event based on a partially completed `DATETIME`. `DATETIME` properties are covered earlier in the chapter. The `__IntervalTimerInstruction` class looks like this:

```
class __IntervalTimerInstruction: __TimerInstruction
{
  [not_null, units("milliseconds")] uint32 IntervalBetweenEvents;
};
```

The `IntervalBetweenEvents` property represents the interval between events.

To set up timer instructions requires new instances of either `__AbsoluteTimer-Instruction` or `__IntervalTimerInstruction`, depending on the type of timer you want to set up. For example, let's instruct WMI to generate an absolute timer event. The following MOF code will cause WMI to fire an absolute timer event at 7:57 P.M. on January 31, 2005 (GMT):

```
instance of __AbsoluteTimerInstruction
{
  TimerId = "MyAbsoluteTimer";
  SkipIfPassed = FALSE;
  EventDateTime = "20050131195700.000000+000";
};
```

An absolute timer event may be useful if your application is supposed to perform a task at a specific time. Once the time has passed and the event delivered, the application could alter the `EventDateTime` property to fire at another predetermined time for the same task.

Next, let's instruct WMI to generate interval timer events. The following MOF code will cause WMI to fire an interval timer event every two seconds:

```
instance of __IntervalTimerInstruction
{
  TimerId = "MyIntervalTimer";
  SkipIfPassed = FALSE;
  IntervalBetweenEvents = 2000;
};
```

Interval timer events may be useful if your application is supposed to perform a task at regular intervals. Suppose you have a distributed application that manages its own replication of data to other servers (perhaps every 10 minutes). Such a regular activity would benefit from an interval timer.

■ How to Subscribe to Events

As mentioned earlier, no events will be delivered unless an event consumer subscribes for them. All event subscriptions use a WQL event query. To demonstrate what an event query looks like, let's subscribe to be notified when a CD-ROM drive management object changes:

```
SELECT * FROM __InstanceModificationEvent WITHIN 5 WHERE TargetInstance
  ISA "Win32_CDROMDrive"
```

The query asks to be notified for any changes to any `Win32_CDROMDrive` management object (there may be more than one CD-ROM drive). If the CD-ROM drive door opens and closes, two events will fire as each operation caused a change to the managed object. All event queries should start with `SELECT *`, because WMI does not support event queries that specify properties in the SELECT statement. If properties are specified, WMI ignores them and treats the query as `SELECT *`.

The next piece of information the event query requires is the type of event to which the event consumer is subscribing. The query asked to be notified for the intrinsic event, `__InstanceModificationEvent`. Most intrinsic event queries must specify how often WMI should poll the provider to determine if there are any changes to the management objects. This is the reason for the `WITHIN` clause. The query instructs WMI to poll all the CD-ROM drives every 5 seconds for modification changes. Next, the event query needs to know what object class it should monitor: This is the purpose of the ISA operator. The ISA operator requests notification of events for any class deriving from the specified class. The TargetInstance is a property on the event class.

Let's review the query: It requests notification every 5 seconds for any instance modification events for all instances that are members of any class deriving from the Win32_CDROMDrive class.

To make queries more specific, the query can include other WQL operators (like AND, OR, and so forth) to narrow the events that will be delivered to event consumers. Consider the following event query:

```
SELECT * FROM __InstanceModificationEvent WITHIN 30 WHERE
  TargetInstance ISA "Win32_CDROMDrive" AND
  TargetInstance.MediaLoaded = true
```

This query instructs WMI to poll all the CR-ROM drives every 30 seconds and requests an event notification if the CD-ROM drive has changed and has media loaded.

All WMI event providers register the events they can publish. This information is especially useful when determining what event queries can be subscribed for. To view the event registrations, use a tool such as CIM Studio to enumerate the instances of the __EventProviderRegistration class and inspect the EventQueryList property. The power management event provider has only one event query registered, which is:

```
SELECT * FROM Win32_PowerManagementEvent
```

Notice that this event provider publishes an extrinsic event, Win32_PowerManagement-Event. The Windows event log event provider also has only one event query registered:

```
SELECT * FROM __InstanceCreationEvent WHERE
  TargetInstance ISA "Win32_NTLogEvent"
```

This event query will cause WMI to fire creation events to event consumers for every new event added to the Windows event log service. Notice that this event provider publishes an intrinsic event, __InstanceCreationEvent.

Subscribing to timer events is similar to subscribing for intrinsic and extrinsic events. Delivery of all timer events uses the __TimerEvent class. The class looks like this:

```
class __TimerEvent: __Event
{
  string TimerId;
  uint32 NumFirings;
};
```

The TimerId property specifies the name of the timer instruction that generated this event. The NumFirings property is the number of times the event occurred before a notification was delivered to the consumer. The following event query subscribes for event notification from one of the timers we created earlier in the chapter.

```
SELECT * FROM __TimerEvent WHERE TimerId = "MyIntervalTimer"
```

Virtually all timer event queries will look like this one. To subscribe to other timers involves specifying a different timer instruction name for the `TimerId` value.

To try out the various types of event subscriptions, go to Appendix A for a short tutorial on the WMI SDK event tools. If you are using Microsoft Visual Studio.NET, then Appendix B covers a short tutorial on using the WMI server explorer, which includes support for making event subscriptions.

■ Writing Applications to Receive Semisynchronous Events

There are two choices for event notification: polling for the event deliveries yourself or having them delivered to you asynchronously. Synchronous event notification is not possible because of the nature of events. Events get delivered to the consumer at any time after the event query is registered. Both semisynchronous and asynchronous calls are discussed earlier in the chapter.

Let's see some sample code that uses one of the queries discussed earlier to subscribe for event notification. We want to discuss only the highlighted sample code; the rest of the code is standard semisynchronous polling on an enumerator, which is included for completeness.

```
// Register event query for the events we want
CComBSTR bstrEventQuery("SELECT * FROM __InstanceModificationEvent "\
  "WITHIN 5 WHERE TargetInstance ISA \"Win32_CDROMDrive\"");

CComPtr<IEnumWbemClassObject> spEnumInst;
hr = spServices->ExecNotificationQuery(CComBSTR("WQL"), bstrEventQuery,
  WBEM_FLAG_RETURN_IMMEDIATELY | WBEM_FLAG_FORWARD_ONLY,
  NULL, &spEnumInst);

bool bFinished = false;
while (!bFinished)
{
  ULONG uNumOfInstances = 0;
  CComPtr<IWbemClassObject> spInstance;
  HRESULT hrNext = spEnumInst->Next(1000, 1, &spInstance,
    &uNumOfInstances);

  // As this is a test console application, this allows the user to
  // terminate the event subscription (when the spEnumInst is released)
```

```
    if (_kbhit())
    {
      _getch();
      bFinished = true;
    }
    if (hrNext == WBEM_S_TIMEDOUT)
    {
      _tprintf(_T("  IEnumWbemClassObject::Next(timeout=1000ms)\n"));
    }
    else
    {
      // What type of event do we have?
      CComVariant varClass;
      hr = spInstance->Get(CComBSTR(_T("__CLASS")), 0, &varClass, 0,0);

      // Get the object (created, changed or deleted) of the
      // intrinsic event
      CComVariant varType;
      hr = spInstance->Get(CComBSTR(_T("TargetInstance")), 0,
        &varType, 0, 0);

      CComQIPtr<IWbemClassObject> spObject = V_UNKNOWN(&varType);

      // What type of object was changed?
      CComVariant varTypeClass;
      hr = spObject->Get(CComBSTR(_T("__CLASS")), 0, &varTypeClass, 0, 0);

      _tprintf(_T("Received a %ls event of type %ls\n"),
        V_BSTR(&varClass), V_BSTR(&varTypeClass)
    }
  }
```

The event query in the preceding sample code instructs WMI to poll all the CD-ROM drives every 5 seconds, and to send an event notification if there are any changes to any of the CD-ROM drives.

To subscribe for semisynchronous event notification requires a call to `ExecNotificationQuery`. This method instructs WMI to send event notifications through the returned `IEnumWbemClassObject` enumerator. If there are no events to deliver, the `Next` call will time out, requiring you to make another call to `Next`; this is done until an event is delivered (if at all). The code outputs the following result; notice the event polling in action.

```
IEnumWbemClassObject::Next(timeout=1000ms)
Recieved a __InstanceModificationEvent event of type Win32_CDROMDrive
IEnumWbemClassObject::Next(timeout=1000ms)
IEnumWbemClassObject::Next(timeout=1000ms)
```

When an event is received, the preceding code determines what kind of event was delivered (we're expecting only `__InstanceModificationEvent`) and then obtains the class name of the instance that was modified. In a real application, you would extract one or more properties from the changed object in `TargetInstance` and formulate an appropriate response to the event.

Let's see what the `ExecNotificationQuery` method looks like:

```
interface IWbemServices
{
HRESULT ExecNotificationQuery(
  const BSTR strQueryLanguage,      // Only WQL is supported
  const BSTR strQuery,              // Your event query
  long lFlags,                      // Semisynchronous flags
  IWbemContext *pCtx,               // Used in providers
  IEnumWbemClassObject **ppEnum);   // Your access to the events
};
```

The *strQueryLanguage* parameter specifies the type of event query subscription. The current implementation of WMI supports only WQL.

The *strQuery* parameter specifies the event query for the events for which you want to receive notifications. If the event query subscription is successful, you will get an enumerator in the *ppEnum* out-parameter that you poll to access the events when they are delivered. To cancel the event subscription, release the returned enumerator in the *ppEnum* out-parameter.

The *lFlags* parameter must specify both `WBEM_FLAG_RETURN_IMMEDIATELY` and `WBEM_FLAG_FORWARD_ONLY`. If you don't, the call to `ExecNotificationQuery` will fail. These flags specify that you want to make a semisynchronous call and return only a forward-only enumerator. Remember that you will not be able to call the `Clone` or `Reset` methods on the forward-only enumerator.

■ Writing Applications to Receive Asynchronous Events

As with all the other asynchronous calls you've seen, you must supply a custom implementation of `IWbemObjectSink`. Whenever WMI delivers an event, your sink will be called. Asynchronous method calls are discussed earlier in the chapter.

Use asynchronous event subscription if you want event notifications delivered in the background using another thread. The thread that performs the event query subscription is immediately available to perform other tasks.

The following asynchronous sink is a reimplementation of the semisynchronous example given in the previous section.

```
class CEventSink : public IWbemObjectSink
{
```

```cpp
public:
  CEventSink() {}
  ~CEventSink() {}

  // IUnknown methods skipped for brevity...

  STDMETHOD(Indicate)(long lObjectCount, IWbemClassObject** apObjArray)
  {
    HRESULT hr = S_OK;

    for (int nIndex = 0; nIndex < lObjectCount; nIndex++)
    {
      // Get properties from the object
      CComVariant varClass;
      hr = apObjArray[nIndex]->Get(CComBSTR(_T("__CLASS")), 0,
        &varClass, 0, 0);

      CComVariant varType;
      hr = apObjArray[nIndex]->Get(CComBSTR(_T("TargetInstance")),
        0, &varType, 0, 0);

      CComQIPtr<IWbemClassObject> spObject = V_UNKNOWN(&varType);

      CComVariant varTypeClass;
      hr = spObject->Get(CComBSTR(_T("__CLASS")), 0,
        &varTypeClass, 0, 0);

      _tprintf(_T(" Received a %ls event of type %ls\n"),
        V_BSTR(&varClass), V_BSTR(&varTypeClass));
    }

    return WBEM_S_NO_ERROR;
  }

  STDMETHOD(SetStatus)(long lFlags, HRESULT hResult, BSTR strParam,
    IWbemClassObject* pObjParam)
  {
    if (lFlags == WBEM_STATUS_COMPLETE)
    {
      _tprintf(_T(" Call complete, returned HRESULT 0x%X\n"),
        hResult);
    }

    return WBEM_S_NO_ERROR;
  }
};
```

You probably will have noticed the similarities of this sink to the one provided earlier in the chapter. This demonstrates the flexibility of the IWbemObjectSink interface: It can be applied to different operations that deliver objects or events. When an asynchronous event query is cancelled, WMI will call the SetStatus method passing WBEM_STATUS_COMPLETE for the *lFlags* parameter and WBEM_E_CALL_CANCELLED in the *hResult* parameter.

To make an asynchronous event subscription requires the following steps:

1. Create an instance of the sink.
2. Call ExecNotificationQueryAsync with the event query and a pointer to the sink.

Unfortunately, this is not the whole story. We must also consider DCOM security. When you call ExecNotificationQueryAsync, WMI keeps a record of the event registration together with the sink that WMI will use to deliver the events. When it is time for WMI to deliver an event, it makes a call to the sink's Indicate method. If DCOM security has not been set up on the client to accept calls from another COM server, such as WMI, then the call will never reach the client and will be rejected by the COM runtime with access denied. In a production system, it is not practical to reconfigure all the client DCOM security settings on every machine. Figure 7.6 summarizes what happens.

To overcome this problem, the event sink must be placed in an *unsecured apartment*. An unsecured apartment is a separate process (a local COM server) that turns off DCOM security when it is loaded. You provide the unsecured apartment with your local sink and you get back a new unsecured sink. The unsecured sink is then passed to WMI for event notification. When WMI delivers an event, it is delivered through the

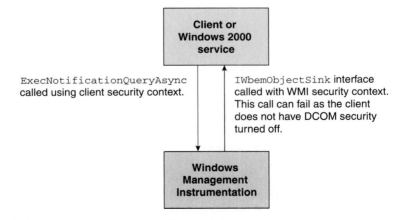

Figure 7.6 DCOM client callback problem

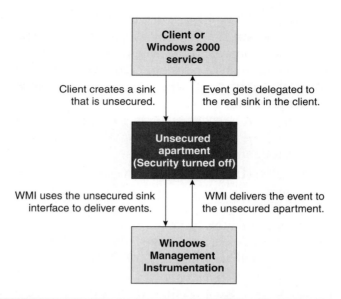

Figure 7.7 DCOM client callback solution

unsecured apartment, which allows any incoming method calls. The unsecured apartment delegates the calls to the client's local sink (Figure 7.7).

You might have come across this DCOM problem in which client callbacks cannot be made from the server in your own software solutions. Unfortunately, the unsecured apartment only works with WMI interfaces, more specifically, IWbemObjectSink.

The following code sample demonstrates how to subscribe asynchronously for event notifications. The highlighted portions represent the code necessary to create and use an unsecured apartment:

```
// Create sink for events
CEventSink* pSink = new CEventSink;

// Create DCOM middle-man
CComPtr<IUnsecuredApartment> spSink;
hr = spSink.CoCreateInstance(CLSID_UnsecuredApartment, NULL,
  CLSCTX_LOCAL_SERVER);

// Make the sink accessible to DCOM
CComPtr<IUnknown> spStubUnk;
hr = spSink->CreateObjectStub(pSink, &spStubUnk);

CComQIPtr<IWbemObjectSink> spStubSink = spStubUnk;
// The event query
```

```
CComBSTR bstrEventQuery("SELECT * FROM __InstanceModificationEvent "\
  "WITHIN 5 WHERE TargetInstance ISA \"Win32_CDROMDrive\"");

// Register the event query for the event notification we want
hr = spServices->ExecNotificationQueryAsync(CComBSTR("WQL"),
  bstrEventQuery, WBEM_FLAG_SEND_STATUS, NULL, spStubSink);

.. ... ..
... .
..

// Cancel registered event query
hr = spServices->CancelAsyncCall(spStubSink);
```

After you create the sink, you need to place it into an unsecured apartment. Load the unsecured apartment local COM server and call `CreateObjectStub`. You supply the local sink and `CreateObjectStub` returns a new unsecured sink. You will need to call `QueryInterface` for the unsecured `IWbemObjectSink` so that `ExecNotification-QueryAsync` and `CancelAsyncCall` can be called correctly. To cancel the event subscription, you will have to call `CancelAsyncCall`, passing in the unsecured sink used in making the event subscription.

Let's look at the `IUnsecuredApartment` interface:

```
interface IUnsecuredApartment
{
HRESULT CreateObjectStub(
  IUnknown *pObject,          // Your local sink
  IUnknown **ppStub);         // Your new unsecured sink
};
```

The *pObject* parameter is your local sink that you wish to place into an unsecured apartment. If the call is successful, you will receive a new unsecured sink in the *ppStub* out-parameter.

■ More on Security

All the code samples in this chapter have assumed that `CoInitializeSecurity` cannot be called. We did this on purpose, because it is not possible to call `CoInitializeSecurity` when developing MMC snap-ins: An interface has been marshalled by the time the snap-in is called. That is why we called `CoSetProxyBlanket` in the early part of the chapter; this sets the correct client security context on the proxy. The `IWbemServices` is the only interface that requires the proxy security context to be set.

If you are the sole owner of a process, you may find it easier to call `CoInitialize-Security` (which can be called only once per process). Calling `CoInitializeSecurity` sets the client security context for all DCOM calls to WMI and other DCOM services you may use. If you are developing a DLL, however, it is safer to call `CoSetProxyBlanket`, because you will have no idea whether the process that you are joining has already marshalled an interface.[5]

In particular, we want to discuss the authentication level and impersonation level parameters that can be passed into both `CoInitializeSecurity` and `CoSetProxyBlanket.` The parameters you pass here also depend on what the providers require to do their work.

Authentication is the process by which one principle (your client) proves its identity to another principle (ultimately the WMI provider). To specify what type of authentication you want requires one of the `RPC_C_AUTHN_LEVEL_xxx` values. In most cases, all you will need is `RPC_C_AUTHN_LEVEL_CONNECT`. This value requires the client to prove its identity on the first connection with WMI, which is usually adequate for most interactions. Supplying `RPC_C_AUTHN_LEVEL_CALL` causes the client to prove its identity on every WMI call it makes. Alternatively, you can use `RPC_C_AUTHN_LEVEL_DEFAULT`, which allows DCOM to use its normal security blanket negotiation algorithm (under Windows 2000/XP) to choose the authentication level. Under Windows NT 4.0, this value defaults to `RPC_C_AUTHN_CONNECT`. Check the MSDN documentation for more information on the other `RPC_C_AUTHN_LEVEL_xxx` values.

In addition to the authentication level, you also supply the authentication capabilities. The capabilities we discuss specify what security context to use when making calls to WMI. A security token is attached to each process. A security token is like a handle to a principle's security context. You can alter a security token to represent another principle. By default, threads do not have security tokens and any calls on a thread in the end use the process security token. You can override this behavior and assign the desired security token within a thread. The `EOLE_AUTHENTICATION_CAPABILITIES` values can specify how the thread security token is assigned to DCOM proxies. The `EOAC_NONE` flag ignores the thread token and always uses the process security token. When you use the `EOAC_STATIC_CLOAKING` flag, the thread security token that is assigned when calling `CoInitializeSecurity` or `CoSetProxyBlanket` will be used for the proxy's security context.

Cloaking is a means to track principle identities when making DCOM calls. The most flexible capabilities flag is `EOAC_DYNAMIC_CLOAKING`. This flag uses whatever thread security token is set when it makes DCOM calls within the thread. If you use this flag, then you should specify the `RPC_C_AUTHN_LEVEL_CALL` flag to authenticate the user's identity on every call to WMI.

Impersonation specifies the limitations on a principle on another machine within your security context. To specify the type of impersonation you will allow requires one

---

5. Our aim for this section is to provide you with enough information for practical use. For a more detailed discussion on security, we recommend reading *Programming Windows Security* by Keith Brown (ISBN 0-201-604426).

of the `RPC_C_IMP_LEVEL_xxx` values. `RPC_C_IMP_LEVEL_IMPERSONATE` allows WMI and the providers to perform tasks on your behalf. Ultimately, this means that you can access any local executive objects for which you have access permission. Any calls made by a WMI provider to another machine will result in an access denied error. This level of impersonation does not allow your security context to be passed to anybody else. As we mentioned earlier, providers can dictate the minimum impersonation level. Consider the following: If a provider performs a task that results in another WMI call to another machine on the network, then your security context needs to be passed. This is called *delegation,* and it requires the `RPC_C_IMP_LEVEL_DELEGATE` flag. Delegation is a form of impersonation that allows WMI to pass your security context to another machine, which can make calls on your behalf. However, there is a down side to delegation. Your security credentials can be passed to an unlimited number of other machines that then can perform tasks on your behalf (and can be audited). This level of impersonation is dangerous if the provider is not trustworthy.

Let's also consider the connection options that affect security. Earlier in the chapter, we introduced you to the `IWbemLocator::ConnectServer` method call. Let's recapitulate the method:

```
interface IWbemLocator
{
HRESULT ConnectServer(
  const BSTR strNetworkResource,
  const BSTR strUser,
  const BSTR strPassword,
  const BSTR strLocale,            // MS_409 for example
  LONG lSecurityFlags,             // must be zero
  const BSTR strAuthority,         // Security authority
  IWbemContext *pCtx,              // Used in calls within provider
  IWbemServices **ppNamespace);    // Your link to WMI
};
```

When making a connection to a different machine, you can include the `strUser` and `strPassword` parameters to specify the user credentials with which to connect. For local connections, you must pass NULL, which effectively uses the currently logged-on user credentials. You may need to complete these parameters if you do not want to use the currently logged-on user for a connection to another machine. The `strUser` parameter can also include the domain of the user/principle, for example, `DOMAIN_A\User_A`.

If you need to use Kerberos security authentication or if you need to use a different NTLM domain to authenticate the user credentials, then you must complete the `strAuthority` parameter. In most cases, you simply may pass NULL to use the default domain security authority of the currently logged-on user. To use Kerberos authentication, you must pass a string formatted like this: "`Kerberos:<principle name>`", in which

`<principle name>` is the principle of the machine to authenticate against. To use NTLM authentication for a specific domain, you will need to pass a string formatted like this: `"NTLMDOMAIN:<domain name>"`, where `<domain name>` is the domain to authenticate against. If you specify this parameter, do not include domain information in the *strUser* parameter.

■ Classes that Require Specific Security Privileges

All the classes so far have not required any special security privileges to access instance data. However, you will more than likely come across classes that fall into this category in your own applications. A good example is the Windows event log WMI class, `Win32_NTLogEvent`, which requires that the `SeSecurityPrivilege` be set when accessing instance data. Let's have a look at the class:

```
[
  dynamic,
  provider("MS_NT_EVENTLOG_PROVIDER"),
  EnumPrivileges {"SeSecurityPrivilege"}
]
class Win32_NTLogEvent
{
  [key] uint32 RecordNumber;
  [key] string Logfile;
  uint32 EventIdentifier;
  uint16 EventCode;
  string SourceName;
  .... ..
  ...
};
```

The `EnumPrivileges` qualifier contains an array of strings that represent the privilege names of the privileges that must be set on the thread that wants to access the event log instance data.

Here's some pseudocode of the steps required to correctly set up the security token on the current thread.

```
Get a security token for the thread and create one if necessary

Get the WMI class definition and inspect the EnumPrivileges qualifier

While (not end of qualifier list)
{
  Create a valid token privilege using the privilege name in list
  Adjust the token privilege
}

Set-up the IWbemServices proxy blanket with the thread security token
```

To ease the process of setting up the correct privileges, here are two helper functions to do just the job: `WMIImpersonateClassPrivilege` and `WMIRevertToSelf`. The following gives an outline of how to use these helper functions:

```
// Connect to WMI

WMIImpersonateClassPrivilege(spServices, _T("Win32_NTLogEvent"));

// Do something interesting with spServices that requires privileges

WMIRevertToSelf();        // Revert to process security context
```

This should clearly outline that you set up your thread security token with the correct privileges, and when the privileged operation is complete, to revert back to the process security token. The following code is necessary if you plan to subscribe to Windows event log events from WMI.

```
HRESULT WMIImpersonateClassPrivilege(IWbemServices* pServices,
                                     LPCTSTR lpszClass)
{
  USES_CONVERSION;
  HRESULT hr = S_OK;

  // Do we have a token on this thread?
  HANDLE hToken = NULL;
  BOOL bRes = OpenThreadToken(GetCurrentThread(),
    TOKEN_QUERY | TOKEN_ADJUST_PRIVILEGES, TRUE, &hToken);

  if (!bRes && !hToken)
  {
    // Create a copy of the process token
    ImpersonateSelf(SecurityImpersonation);

    // Get the token just created
    bRes = OpenThreadToken(GetCurrentThread(),
      TOKEN_QUERY | TOKEN_ADJUST_PRIVILEGES, TRUE, &hToken);
  }

  // Get the class so that we can inspect the class qualifiers
  CComPtr<IWbemClassObject> spClass;
  hr = pServices->GetObject(CComBSTR(lpszClass),
    WBEM_FLAG_RETURN_WBEM_COMPLETE, NULL, &spClass, NULL);

  // Get qualifier set
  CComPtr<IWbemQualifierSet> spQualifiers;
  hr = spClass->GetQualifierSet(&spQualifiers);
```

```
// Get the EnumPrivileges array
VARIANT var; VariantInit(&var);
hr = spQualifiers->Get(L"EnumPrivileges", 0, &var, NULL);


// Calculate the number of elements
long lUpper = 0;
long lLower = 0;
hr = SafeArrayGetUBound(V_ARRAY(&var), 1, &lUpper);
hr = SafeArrayGetLBound(V_ARRAY(&var), 1, &lLower);


long lNumOfElems = lUpper-lLower + 1;


// Gain access to the SAFEARRAY
BSTR HUGEP *pbstrArray;
hr = SafeArrayAccessData(V_ARRAY(&var), (void**)&pbstrArray);


for (int nIndex = 0; nIndex < lNumOfElems; nIndex++)
{

  // Construct the desired privilege
  TOKEN_PRIVILEGES tpEnable = {0};
  tpEnable.PrivilegeCount = 1;
  tpEnable.Privileges[0].Attributes = SE_PRIVILEGE_ENABLED;

  LookupPrivilegeValue(NULL, OLE2T(pbstrArray[nIndex]),
    &tpEnable.Privileges[0].Luid);
  // Set new privileges
  bRes = AdjustTokenPrivileges(hToken, FALSE, &tpEnable, 0,
    NULL, NULL);
}

hr = SafeArrayUnaccessData(V_ARRAY(&var));
VariantClear(&var);
CloseHandle(hToken);


// Set the proxy blanket to use the new security settings
hr = CoSetProxyBlanket(pServices, RPC_C_AUTHN_WINNT, RPC_C_AUTHZ_NONE,
  NULL, RPC_C_AUTHN_LEVEL_CALL, RPC_C_IMP_LEVEL_IMPERSONATE, NULL,
  EOAC_STATIC_CLOAKING);

  return hr;
}


HRESULT WMIRevertToSelf()
{
  HRESULT hr = S_OK;
```

```
    if (RevertToSelf() == FALSE)
      hr = HRESULT_FROM_WIN32(GetLastError());

    return hr;
}
```

This code assumes that you will use static cloaking for the `IWbemServices` DCOM proxy. You might want to make this a parameter if you plan to use different types of authentication identity tracking (that is, static or dynamic cloaking, and so forth).

■ Localized Namespaces

All the MOF examples you've seen throughout this chapter have provided very little information about what the classes, methods, and properties actually are. Apart from the names of the classes and properties, only a few qualifiers have provided a little more meaning. At most, properties have been qualified as a key property. In the previous section, we introduced the `EnumPrivileges` qualifier for classes. Classes, methods, and properties can provide helpful text descriptions through a *description* qualifier. If you are creating and implementing a new class, then you should consider supplying description qualifiers. They will help others understand and use your new class. You also could use them in your own applications as help items. Let's see an example MOF file that uses description qualifiers in a class definition.

```
#pragma namespace("\\\\.\\root")

instance of __namespace { name = "WMIBook";};

#pragma namespace("\\\\.\\root\\WMIBook")

[
  description("This manages user accounts for the voicemail system"):amended
]
class Sample_VoicemailAccount
{

  [key, description("The Directory common name of the user"):amended]
  string UserID;

  [description("Telephone extension number of the user"):amended]
  string TelephoneExtension;

  string DisplayName;

  [description("Binary WAVE stream of the user's name"):amended]
  uint8 SpokenName[];
};
```

In this example, the class and most of the properties have a `description` qualifier. The `amended` flavor means that the qualifier (`description` in this case) will be retrieved from the localized namespace. Recall that the initial connection to the namespace through `IWbemLocator::ConnectServer` specifies the locale.

The process of making a localized namespace was covered briefly in Chapter 6. In this section, we shall use the previous example to expand on localized namespaces and shall provide sample code to show the localization support in action.

The previous MOF example demonstrates exactly what you need before you consider making a localized version of the file. Everything that requires localization has been marked with the `amended` flavor. When the MOF compiler processes this file, it outputs two files: a language-neutral version and a localized version.

The language-neutral MOF file contains all the class definitions. The localized file will contain only those classes, methods, and properties that used the `amended` flavor. When the MOF compiler processes the localized file, it creates a new localized namespace for the amended classes.

Let's make a localized namespace (assume the above example is in a file called `WMIVoicemail.mof`):

```
mofcomp -MOF:WMIVoicemailLN.mof -MFL:WMIVoicemailLS.mfl -Amendment:MS_409
  WMIVoicemail.mof
```

The `-MOF:` switch instructs the MOF compiler to place the language-neutral version into a file called `WMIVoicemailLN.mof`. The `-MFL:` switch specifies that the classes, methods, and properties that use the `amended` flavor be output to a file called `WMIVoicemailLS.mfl`. The `-Amendment:MS_409` switch determines what language the localized output file will represent. The `MS_409` portion of the switch specifies the U.S. English locale.

Here is the output of the language-neutral MOF file:

```
#pragma namespace("\\\\.\\root")

instance of __namespace { name = "WMIBook";};

#pragma namespace("\\\\.\\root\\WMIBook")

class Sample_VoicemailAccount
{
  [key] string UserID;
  string TelephoneExtension;
  string DisplayName;
  uint8 SpokenName[];
};
```

Notice that there are no *description* qualifiers. These are contained in the localized MOF file:

```
#pragma namespace("\\\\.\\root\\WMIBook")

instance of __namespace { name="ms_409";};

#pragma namespace("\\\\.\\root\\WMIBook\\ms_409")

[
  description("This manages user accounts for the voicemail system"):
    Amended, AMENDMENT, LOCALE(0x409)
]
class Sample_VoicemailAccount
{

  [key, description("The Directory common name of the user"):Amended]
  string UserID;

  [description("Telephone extension number of the user"):Amended]
  string TelephoneExtension;

  [description("Binary WAVE stream of the user's name"):Amended]
  uint8 SpokenName[];
};
```

You will notice that the DisplayName property does not exist in this MOF code, which demonstrates that a localized namespace contains only classes, methods, and properties that have the amended flavor.

When the language-neutral files and all the localized MOF files are compiled, namespaces take the structure in Figure 7.8. The WMIBook namespace contains localized content for U.S. English and German.

Connecting to the WMIBook namespace for the German locale requires the following call:

```
hr = spLoc->ConnectServer(CComBSTR("root\\WMIBook"), NULL, NULL,
  CComBSTR("MS_407"), NULL, 0, 0, &spServices);
```

Figure 7.8 Example WMI namespace structure

Refer to the `ConnectServer` discussion earlier in the chapter for more information about the locale parameter.

Whenever you wish to access localized content in your applications, you must use `WBEM_FLAG_USE_AMENDED_QUALIFIERS` on calls to the `IWbemServices` interface. This includes all variants of `GetObject`, `ExecQuery`, and `CreateInstanceEnum`. This flag instructs WMI to obtain the localized content for the locale specified in the `ConnectServer` call. The following code sample retrieves the U.S. English descriptions for the class and UserID property that we created earlier:

```
CComBSTR bstrClass("Sample_VoicemailAccount");

// Get class definition using amended qualifiers
CComPtr<IWbemClassObject> spClass;
hr = spServices->GetObject(bstrClass, WBEM_FLAG_USE_AMENDED_QUALIFIERS,
  NULL, &spClass, NULL);

// Get class qualifiers
CComPtr<IWbemQualifierSet> spClassQualifiers;
hr = spClass->GetQualifierSet(&spClassQualifiers);

// Get description for class
CComVariant varClassDesc;
hr = spClassQualifiers->Get(L"Description", 0, &varClassDesc, NULL);

_tprintf(_T(" Class is'%ls'\n"), V_BSTR(&varClassDesc));

// Get property qualifiers
CComPtr<IWbemQualifierSet> spPropQualifiers;
hr = spClass->GetPropertyQualifierSet(L"UserID", &spPropQualifiers);

// Get description for property
CComVariant varUserIDDesc;
hr = spPropQualifiers->Get(L"Description", 0, &varUserIDDesc, NULL);

_tprintf(_T(" User ID is'%ls'\n"), V_BSTR(&varUserIDDesc));
```

The above code outputs the following:

```
Class is 'This manages user accounts for the voicemail system'
User ID is 'The Directory common name of the user'
```

■ Overview of High Performance Classes

No software instrumentation interface would be complete without a mechanism for accessing high performance data. All Windows NT-based Operating Systems from the outset have included monitoring tools (such as the System Monitor in Windows 2000/XP) that use performance counters to capture and analyze system performance. This is useful especially in determining system bottlenecks and fine-tuning system and application performance. High performance software instrumentation allows services and drivers to provide real-time information about current activity.

Fortunately, all applications can benefit from performance monitoring without exposing any customized performance objects. Windows 2000/XP instruments standard objects such as a process, thread, network interface, and processor, to name a few. Every performance object has one or more counters. A process, for example, includes process ID, private bytes, handle count, and thread count counters. The Windows 2000/XP System Monitor can determine whether an application is leaking memory by inspecting the Private Bytes counter.

Adding your own customized performance counters to the system was not easy and programmatically reading them was not much better until the Performance Data Helper (PDH) library emerged. PDH provided a much simpler API that made it considerably easier to access instrumented data from the Operating System, a Windows service, or a device driver.

One of the original performance-monitoring design goals was to monitor other machines on the network, not just the local machine. This requirement turned into a solution that uses special registry keys that provide fast access to the data. However, there is little optimization of this data when it is transmitted over the network.

One of the truly great benefits of WMI is that it is a unified API for accessing management information in an enterprise environment. It describes all management information through classes. High-performance data is no exception. WMI can access all the performance counters that exist in Windows 2000/XP through the generic performance counter provider. For example, the `Win32_PerfRawData_PerfProc_Process` class exposes all the counters of the process object. WMI terms these types of classes Hi-Perf (high-performance). Applications wishing to expose high-performance information don't necessarily need to go through the anguish of exposing performance counters any more. WMI supports a special type instance provider that exposes high-performance information.

One of the benefits of accessing high-performance classes is that you don't need to use any special API to access them; you can use the standard `IWbemServices` interface and call either `GetObject` or `CreataInstanceEnum`. However, using this approach makes calls across process boundaries, which is a relatively slow process. To take maximum advantage of a high-performance class, you need to use a special WMI API called a *refresher*. The refresher loads the high-performance provider in-process and copies data directly from provider to the client, using a shared memory interface. If the refresher is accessing objects on another machine, then the refresher on the remote machine caches the objects and transmits only a minimal data set over the network.

■ Writing Applications to Access High-Performance Data

All Windows 2000/XP performance counters are exposed in classes that are derived from `Win32_PerfRawData`. If you need to access any performance counters, use a tool like CIM Studio to identify the class and its properties. Let's examine ways in which the `Win32_PerfRawData_PerfProc_Process` class can be accessed. This is a portion of the class definition:

```
class Win32_PerfRawData_PerfProc_Process: Win32_PerfRawData
{
  [key] string Name;
  uint64 PercentProcessorTime;
  uint64 PercentUserTime;
  uint64 PercentPrivilegedTime;
  uint32 WorkingSet;
  uint64 PrivateBytes;
  uint32 ThreadCount;
  uint64 ElapsedTime;
  uint32 IDProcess;
  .. ... ..
  ...
};
```

The `Name` property identifies the name of the process and the `PrivateBytes` property identifies how much memory the process is using. (We mention these properties specifically because we shall use them in sample code later.) As already mentioned, you can access high-performance classes in two ways: either by using the standard `IWbemServices` interface or by using a refresher. Although it is not desirable for high-performance, you could make the following calls to obtain the memory usage of a process.

```
CComBSTR
bstrPath("Win32_PerfRawData_PerfProc_Process.Name=\"MyProcess\"");

CComPtr<IWbemClassObject> spInstance;
hr = spServices->GetObject(bstrPath, 0, NULL, &spInstance, NULL);

CComVariant var;
hr = spInstance->Get(CComBSTR("PrivateBytes "), 0, &var, 0, 0);
```

A refresher is required to achieve high-performance. A refresher is a mechanism that can update a number of refreshable objects speedily. A refresher updates only the objects that were added prior to calling `Refresh`. The following sample code leaks some memory and then monitors the private bytes property to inspect the amount of memory that is allocated for the process:

```
// Create a refresher, this accesses the Hi Perf data
CComPtr<IWbemRefresher> spRefresher;
hr = spRefresher.CoCreateInstance(CLSID_WbemRefresher);

// We need to add objects to the refresher
CComQIPtr<IWbemConfigureRefresher> spConfig = spRefresher;

CComBSTR bstrPath("Win32_PerfRawData_PerfProc_Process.Name=\"WMIHiPerf\"");
```

```
// Add the instance we want refreshed
CComPtr<IWbemClassObject> spRefreshableObject;
hr = spConfig->AddObjectByPath(spServices, bstrPath, 0L, NULL,
  &spRefreshableObject, NULL);

// Using IWbemObjectAccess for fast property retrieval.
CComQIPtr<IWbemObjectAccess> spObjectAccess = spRefreshableObject;

// Obtain the property handles, this is used in reading properties.
long lPrivateBytesHandle = 0;
hr = spObjectAccess->GetPropertyHandle(L"PrivateBytes", NULL,
  &lPrivateBytesHandle);

// Small loop to show that there is a memory leak!
for(int x = 0; x < 5; x++)
{

  // Update all the objects added to the refresher
  hr = spRefresher->Refresh(WBEM_FLAG_REFRESH_AUTO_RECONNECT);

  hr = spObjectAccess->Lock(0);

  // Read the processes PrivateBytes memory usage
  DWORD dwPrivateBytes = 0;
  spObjectAccess->ReadDWORD(lPrivateBytesHandle, &dwPrivateBytes);

  hr = spObjectAccess->Unlock(0);

  _tprintf(_T("Process is using %lu bytes\n"), dwPrivateBytes);

  // Leak some more memory
  char* pLeakMemory = new char[20000];
}
```

After creating a refresher (in-process), the next task is to configure the refresher with the objects that require monitoring. Call AddObjectByPath for as many objects as you want to monitor. AddObjectByPath requires an object path of the high-performance object referred to by the namespace to which the IWbemServices parameter points. The IWbemConfigureRefresher interface has a number of other methods that can add objects to the refresher, including AddEnum, AddObjectByTemplate, and AddRefresher. We find AddRefresher interesting because all the objects added to another refresher (also called a *child refresher*) result in all objects being updated with a single call to Refresh. Objects also can be removed by calling Remove.

The IWbemClassObject returned by AddObjectByPath allows you to inspect the properties of the high-performance object by calling Get for the property value. However, you should consider using another interface called IWbemObjectAccess. This interface is optimized for very fast property access, but the downside is that property names cannot be used to access properties. Instead, you need to obtain property access handles by calling GetPropertyHandle. Property handles represent the named properties and allow direct access to the property in the refresher. Another downside is that the interface is not thread-safe, so depending on your circumstances, you should consider using the `Lock` and `Unlock` methods. Surround calls to `ReadDWORD`, `ReadQWORD`, and `ReadPropertyValue` with calls to `Lock` and `Unlock`.

Part of the reason that `IWbemClassObject::Get` is slower is that it has to translate the property name into a property handle that is then used to access the property directly.

Calling `Refresh` regularly is critical to monitoring changes to objects and objects in child refreshers. The `WBEM_FLAG_REFRESH_AUTO_RECONNECT` specifies that even if the connection is broken, the refresher will attempt to reconnect to the high-performance provider automatically. If you do not want to do this, use `WBEM_FLAG_REFRESH_NO_AUTO_RECONNECT`.

The previous sample code outputs the following. Notice that memory is being leaked:

```
Process is using 1294336 bytes
Process is using 1314816 bytes
Process is using 1335296 bytes
Process is using 1359872 bytes
Process is using 1380352 bytes
```

▪ Access High-Performance Enumerated Data

In the last section, we explained how a single object could be added, refreshed, and retrieved from a refresher. Another way of adding objects to a refresher is to add an *enumerator*. An enumerator adds all the objects of the class that you can later retrieve by iterating through the conformant array of `IWbemObjectAccess` objects. To add an enumerator, you need to call `IWbemConfigureRefresher::AddEnum`. This returns an `IWbemHiPerfEnum` interface that you later use to obtain the list of all the objects in the enumerator, after a refresh. The following code includes an enumerator that will add all the process instances to the refresher for monitoring:

```
// Create a refresher, this accesses the Hi Perf data
CComPtr<IWbemRefresher> spRefresher;
hr = spRefresher.CoCreateInstance(CLSID_WbemRefresher);

// We need to add objects to the refresher
CComQIPtr<IWbemConfigureRefresher> spConfig = spRefresher;

// Add an enumerator to the refresher.
CComPtr<IWbemHiPerfEnum> spEnumObjects;
hr = spConfig->AddEnum(spServices,
    L"Win32_PerfRawData_PerfProc_Process", 0, NULL,
    &spEnumObjects, NULL);

// Update all the objects added to the refresher.
hr = spRefresher->Refresh(WBEM_FLAG_REFRESH_AUTO_RECONNECT);
```

```
DWORD dwNumReturned = 0;
IWbemObjectAccess** apEnumAccess = NULL;

// Find out how many objects there are in the refresher.
hr = spEnumObjects->GetObjects(OL, 0, apEnumAccess,
  &dwNumReturned);

// We expect this, best to check anyway.
if (hr == WBEM_E_BUFFER_TOO_SMALL)
{
  apEnumAccess = new IWbemObjectAccess*[dwNumReturned];

  // Get all the objects that are now updated
  hr = spEnumObjects->GetObjects(OL, dwNumReturned, apEnumAccess,
    &dwNumReturned);
}

// Obtain the property handles. Used when reading properties.
long lPrivateBytesHandle = 0;
hr = apEnumAccess[0]->GetPropertyHandle(L"PrivateBytes", NULL,
  &lPrivateBytesHandle);
long lNameHandle = 0;
hr = apEnumAccess[0]->GetPropertyHandle(L"Name", NULL, &lNameHandle);

// Examine all the properties
for(DWORD dwIndex = 0; dwIndex < dwNumReturned; dwIndex++)
{
  hr = apEnumAccess[dwIndex]->Lock(0);

  // Read PrivateBytes
  DWORD dwPrivateBytes = 0;
  hr = apEnumAccess[dwIndex]->ReadDWORD(lPrivateBytesHandle,
    &dwPrivateBytes);

  // Read Name
  long nNameSizeInBytes = 0;
  LPWSTR szName[64];
  hr = apEnumAccess[dwIndex]->ReadPropertyValue(lNameHandle,
    sizeof(WCHAR) * 64, &nNameSizeInBytes, (LPBYTE)szName);

  hr = apEnumAccess[dwIndex]->Unlock(0);

  _tprintf(_T("Process '%ls' is using %lu bytes\n"), szName,
    dwPrivateBytes);
}
```

To obtain the objects within the IWbemHiPerfEnum enumerator, you must call GetObjects twice. The first call determines how big the conformant array should be, and the second call retrieves the enumerated objects. It is now possible to iterate through all the currently active processes. Note that the number of instances in the enumerator can change with every call to `Refresh`.

The previous code sample conveniently introduced the `ReadPropertyValue` call. You can use this call to retrieve data that is neither a `DWORD` nor `QWORD`. In this case, we wanted the name of the process (all strings are more than likely in Unicode, hence the `WCHAR`).

The following is small portion of the output from the above code:

```
Process 'Idle' is using 0 bytes
Process 'System' is using 90112 bytes
Process 'SMSS' is using 1126400 bytes
Process 'csrss' is using 1777664 bytes
Process 'LSASS' is using 2916352 bytes
.. ... ..
...
```

■ Summary

This chapter has introduced you to virtually every aspect of managing objects in WMI. The first half of the chapter introduced you to the most fundamental and basic operations. You learned how objects could be accessed, created, deleted, updated, enumerated, and queried. Methods provided you with a powerful mechanism for adding behavior to classes and objects. Some detailed discussion outlined how you could manipulate properties, especially objects or arrays.

Leading into the sections covering WMI events, we introduced semisynchronous and asynchronous calls and how you could use them to good effect. We covered all three types of events and the distinctions among them. Intrinsic events involve changes to classes, namespaces, and object instances. Extrinsic events allow providers to add new types of events to the management environment. Finally, timer events allow you to set up configurable timers to remind you to perform some task at a specific time or interval.

The last few sections covered advanced topics that include more information about security and dealing with localized namespaces (using amended qualifiers). The WMI high-performance refreshers were discussed in detail to make it easier for you to access this sort of monitoring information.

Ten Fast Facts: Developing C++/COM Management Applications:

1. You always have to connect to WMI using the `ConnectServer` method on the `IWbem-Locator` interface. The resulting `IWbemServices` out-parameter will provide you with all the facilities you are mostly likely to require.

2. Use `CreateInstanceEnum` to easily identify the currently available management objects for a class. For example, you could call `CreateInstanceEnum` to determine quickly what shared directories there are by supplying the class name, "Win32_Share".

3. Use `GetObject` if you know the specific management object to which you require access. This involves creating a valid *object path*.

4. Be aware that properties may supply `Values` and `ValueMap` qualifiers to describe how to interpret property data.

5. WMI offers a powerful means to extract information from the management environment by using data queries. Data queries are specified using WQL and are passed to `ExecQuery`.

6. Many WMI classes use methods to add behavior. Always check whether the class you want to use has any methods in which you may be interested. In particular, many classes in the CIMV2 namespace use methods to create and update management objects. Call `ExecMethod` to execute a management class or management object method.

7. Interpreting WMI class properties involves dealing with VARIANTs. If you are unsure what VARIANT types you need to use, consult Table 7.1.

8. Always consider using semisynchronous or asynchronous techniques in your management applications. Either of these approaches will make your applications more responsive.

9. Event notification is one of WMI's most powerful features. WMI has the capability to deliver events when something interesting happens. "Something interesting" might include being notified when disk space runs low on a machine, for example. Call `ExecNotificationQuery` to make an event subscription.

10. If you need to obtain values from performance counters, remember WMI provides a means to access them using high-performance classes that are optimized for communication across a network.

Chapter 8

Developing .NET
Management Applications

Microsoft has introduced the .NET Framework, a whole new paradigm in the way that developers write and run software. This new platform contains many new technological features that make it a great way to write, deploy, and run software. The .NET Framework is an execution platform that is not tied to a specific processor architecture.

The key in achieving this is based on the Common Language Run-time (CLR). When a .NET application is compiled, the object code that is generated is in an Intermediate Language (IL). Upon installation or the first execution of the application, the .NET run time will compile the IL code into processor-specific instructions (native code).

All applications that use the .NET Framework can use the large library of built-in classes. This means that .NET applications can be developed faster, making the developer more productive. Applications will be able to use the same classes as another application, such as the Thread class in the `System.Threading` namespace. All .NET classes exist in a namespace. The WMI classes, for instance, exist in the `System.Management` namespace. Another major advantage of the .NET Framework is that it offers programming language independence. This makes the programming language you use irrelevant. For instance, you could develop a component using the new C# programming language, and extend it (using inheritance) with Visual Basic. After that, you may decide to use the component in your favorite COBOL application! This type of platform and programming language independence is a great technological breakthrough. In addition, because all .NET applications use the same libraries, applications usually have a much smaller footprint.

In Chapter 7, we covered the WMI COM APIs that allow you to interact with WMI. This chapter takes a similar form but covers the .NET classes. It assumes that you are familiar with the C# programming language and are familiar with the .NET platform. It also assumes that you are aware by now that management objects can be created, updated, deleted, enumerated, and queried. You can manipulate properties on management objects, execute methods, and subscribe to receive WMI events. This chapter details how you can write applications to manage management objects. Some specific topics are discussed in detail to give you a complete guide to how you might want to make WMI calls in your own applications. By the end of this chapter, you will know about virtually every key aspect of writing a .NET management application.[1]

During this chapter we use the terms "management object" and "instance" interchangeably.

■ Getting Started

This chapter focuses on the classes within the `System.Management` namespace. All the samples and classes in this chapter are based on the .NET Framework and Visual Studio .NET.

When creating .NET management applications with Visual Studio .NET, do not forget to include a reference to the `System.Management` namespace in your projects.

Figure 8.1 highlights some of the major classes in the `System.Management` namespace with which you will become familiar by the end of the chapter.

■ Getting a Management Object

Getting a management object is one of the most basic operations to perform. This kind of operation is useful especially when you know what management object you want. For example, you can gain access to properties for a shared directory (which may be on another machine) by executing an operation that retrieves the management object from WMI.

Before you can gain access to a management object, you must have a valid object path. An object path is a string that can specifically reference either a management class or a management object. For example, if you look at the `Win32_Share` class in the `CIMV2` namespace, you'll see that it has one key property, "Name". If you expect the C$ shared directory on a machine to exist, you therefore can attempt to get a management object that represents the shared directory. You must generate an object path that includes the one and only key value, `Win32_Share.Name="C$"`. We explained object paths in more detail in Chapter 7.

1. If you are not familiar with the .NET initiative, we suggest you read one of the many books available on programming within the .NET environment and, in particular, C#.

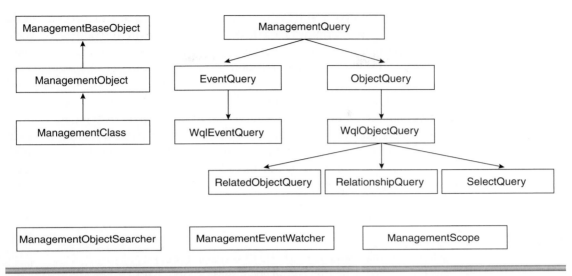

Figure 8.1 Major .NET Framework management classes

You may also get an object path from a property. WMI includes an object reference, which is a data type that can reference other management objects. Association classes include properties that are object references in order to make an association. You may read one of these properties and merely pass the object reference (which is a string) straight into the `ManagementObject` class's constructor. Either way, as long as you have a valid object path, you'll be able to gain access to a management object.

The following code illustrates how to get the path of a shared directory:

```
ManagementObject mo = new ManagementObject("Win32_Share.Name=\"C$\"");

Console.WriteLine("Win32_Share.Name=\"C$\" path is {0}", mo["Path"]);
```

The above example retrieves the path of the shared directory and outputs it to the screen. This probably will be the most common way to retrieve properties from a management object. However, the above code sample employs a lazy object retrieval technique. The properties for the management object are retrieved when the `mo["Path"]` property is required, not when the `ManagementObject` is created. To specify explicitly when an object is retrieved from WMI requires a call to `Get` on the `ManagementObject` class. Let's look at an example:

```
ManagementObject mo = new ManagementObject("Win32_Share.Name=\"C$\"");

mo.Get(); // Explicit. Object retrieved here!

Console.WriteLine("Win32_Share.Name=\"C$\" path is {0}", mo["Path"]);
```

The management object in this example now is retrieved at specific point in the code. This offers you a deterministic method to specify where in the code the overhead of retrieving the object is made. If there are any problems in retrieving the management object, you are in a better position to place exception error handling code appropriately.

Let's look at the `ManagementObject` class in more detail. To do this, let's take a step back and examine the base class, `ManagementBaseObject`, which is the base class for both management objects and management classes. We've just now seen how we can get a management object, so we will focus on some of the other available operations that can be performed for both classes and objects. Here is a portion of the `ManagementBaseObject` class declaration:

```
public class ManagementBaseObject
{
  // Properties
  public virtual ManagementPath ClassPath {get;}
  public object this[string propertyName] {get; set;}
  public virtual PropertyDataCollection Properties {get;}
  public virtual QualifierDataCollection Qualifiers {get;}
  public virtual PropertyDataCollection SystemProperties {get;}
  . ... .
  .. .. ...


  // Methods
  public bool CompareTo(ManagementBaseObject otherObject,
    ComparisonSettings settings);

  public object GetPropertyQualifierValue(string propertyName,
    string qualifierName);

  public object GetPropertyValue(string propertyName);

  public object GetQualifierValue(string qualifierName);

  public void SetPropertyQualifierValue(string propertyName,
    string qualifierName, object qualifierValue);

  public void SetPropertyValue(string propertyName, object
    propertyValue);

  public void SetQualifierValue(string qualifierName,
    object qualifierValue);
  ... ... .
  ..
};
```

The `ClassPath` property provides information about the class of the object referenced by the management object. This sometimes is useful when you want to construct a new object path for other objects of the same class or to generate a WQL query. The `ManagementPath` class will be discussed in more detail shortly.

The `[]` index operator is a very useful shorthand for `GetPropertyValue` and `SetPropertyValue`. The index operator allows easy access to set and get property values. The code samples shown earlier use this technique to retrieve the path of a shared directory (`mo["Path"]`). We discuss getting and setting properties in more detail later in the chapter.

The `Properties` property represents all the properties of a management class or management object. This is useful when you must process the values for all of the properties. You will see an example of this later in the chapter. The system-provided properties can be found in the `SystemProperties` property collection.

Like the `Properties` property, the `Qualifiers` property represents all the qualifiers for a management class or management object. For similar reasons, you also may want to process all of the qualifier values. Qualifiers are a way to provide context information for the classes, objects, properties, and methods. If you want to set or get a specific qualifier for a class or object, use `SetQualifierValue` or `GetQualifierValue`, respectively. You'll see an example shortly that retrieves a class qualifier. If you want to set or get a specific qualifier for a property, use `SetPropertyQualifierValue` and `GetPropertyQualifierValue`, respectively. If you were writing the CIM Studio application (which ships with the Platform SDK) using the .NET Framework, then you would need to use `Properties`, `SystemProperties`, and `Qualifiers` properties to display the enumerations.

If you want to compare two management objects derived from `ManagementBaseObject`, then you may consider the `CompareTo` method. This makes the job of comparing management objects an easy task. In the .NET management library, you will find many such useful methods that make life easier. We include more examples later.

Let's examine a portion of the `ManagementObject` class:

```
public class ManagementObject: ManagementBaseObject
{
  // Constructors
  public ManagementObject();
  public ManagementObject(ManagementPath path);
  public ManagementObject(string path);
  public ManagementObject(ManagementPath path, ObjectGetOptions
    options);
  public ManagementObject(string path, ObjectGetOptions options);
  ... ...
  .
};
```

Earlier you saw some code samples that referenced a management object by specifying an object path as a string, such as:

```
ManagementObject mo = new ManagementObject("Win32_Share.Name=\"C$\"");
```

This code uses a relative object path. Retrieving an object (or a class) from a specific namespace on a specific machine requires a fully qualified object path. A fully qualified object path includes the machine name, the namespace, and an object reference. On the reverse side, if you obtain an object reference from WMI (either through an object reference or through the __PATH property), you may end up parsing the object path string into its separate elements. In the .NET environment, another way to specify an object path is to use the ManagementPath class. Two of the ManagementObject constructors (in the preceding declaration) use the ManagementPath class instead of an object path string. Let's look at how this class is used. The following code sample obtains the shared directory information from another machine:

```
ManagementPath path = new ManagementPath();
path.Path = "Win32_Share.Name=\"C$\"";
path.Server = "BOB";
path.NamespacePath = "root\\CIMV2";

ManagementObject mo = new ManagementObject(path);

Console.WriteLine("Win32_Share.Name=\"C$\" path is {0}", mo["Path"]);
```

This code sample specifies all the elements of a fully qualified object path, that is, the machine name (BOB), the namespace (root\CIMV2), and the object reference (Win32_Share.Name="C$"). Let's look at what else the ManagementPath class offers:

```
public class ManagementPath
{
  // Constructors
  public ManagementPath();
   public ManagementPath(string path);

  // Properties
  public string ClassName {get; set;}
  public static ManagementPath DefaultPath {get; set;}
  public bool IsClass {get;}
  public bool IsInstance {get;}
  public bool IsSingleton {get;}
  public string NamespacePath {get; set;}
  public string Path {get; set;}
  public string RelativePath {get; set;}
  public string Server {get; set;}
```

```
    // Methods
    public void SetAsClass();
    public void SetAsSingleton();
};
```

The `ClassName` property exposes the management class specified within the `Path` property. You can determine if the `Path` property references a class by inspecting the `IsClass` property. Likewise, if you want to determine whether the `Path` property has an object reference, you can inspect the `IsInstance` property. In addition, if the `Path` property references a singleton object, you can inspect the `IsSingleton` property.

To determine the machine on which the class or object resides, examine the `Server` property. If you are specifying a specific machine for an object (or a class) request, do something similar to the code sample and set the `Server` property.

To determine the namespace in which the class or object resides, examine the `NamespacePath` property. To specify a namespace, do something similar to the recent code sample and set the `NamespacePath` property.

The `DefaultPath` property specifies the default machine and namespace (as a string) that will be used when no machine (`Server`) and/or namespace (`NamespacePath`) is specified. This is currently "\\.\root\CIMV2".

The `SetAsClass` method will convert the path (whatever it is) into a class reference. This can be useful when you want to create another management object of the same class as another currently existing object. The following demonstrates what happens to the `Path` property:

```
ManagementPath path = new ManagementPath();
path.Path = "Win32_Share.Name=\"C$\"";

path.SetAsClass();

Console.WriteLine("Path is {0}", path.ToString());
```

The `WriteLine` statement outputs: "Path is Win32_Share".

The `SetAsSingleton` method will convert the path into a singleton reference. Sometimes this is useful when you need a quick way of converting a class reference to a singleton reference. For instance, the `__SystemSecurity` class has a singleton reference and the class reference can be converted easily, as the following code sample demonstrates:

```
ManagementPath path = new ManagementPath("__SystemSecurity");

path.SetAsSingleton();

Console.WriteLine("Path is {0}", path.ToString());
```

The `WriteLine` statement outputs: `"Path is __SystemSecurity=@"`. Notice that the class reference was specified through the `ManagementPath`'s constructor.

Here is another portion of the `ManagementObject` class declaration:

```
public class ManagementObject: ManagementBaseObject
{
  // Properties
  public ObjectGetOptions Options {get; set;}
  public virtual ManagementPath Path {get; set;}
  .. ... .
  ...
};
```

Microsoft has rationalized all the various options for different WMI operations into single encapsulated classes. The WMI COM API specified the various options either through flags or through calling specific methods. For example, if you wanted to access amended qualifier values, you had to specify `WBEM_FLAG_USE_AMENDED_QUALIFIERS` in the flags parameter in methods on the `IWbemServices` interface. If you wanted to specify the WMI call context, you had to specify that through another parameter. If you wanted to specify the time-out for a semisynchronous call, you had to specify that through another method call on another interface. In the .NET environment, all of this is unified into option classes derived from `ManagementOptions`. The `Options` property in the previous class declaration allows you to inspect and modify the various options when retrieving objects and classes. The `ManagementClass` class also has an `Options` property.

Let's look at an example for retrieving an object using the `ObjectGetOptions` class:

```
ObjectGetOptions options = new ObjectGetOptions();
options.UseAmendedQualifiers = true;

ManagementClass mc = new ManagementClass("Win32_Share", options);
Console.WriteLine("Win32_Share description is '{0}'",
  (string)mc.GetQualifierValue("Description"));
```

This code sample enables the amended qualifiers so that the localized description of the `Win32_Share` class can be obtained. All the options for retrieving objects or classes are provided through the `ObjectGetOptions` class. The output of this code sample produces the following:

Win32_Share description is 'The Win32_Share class represents a shared resource on a Win32 system. This may be a disk drive, printer, inter-process communication, or other shareable device. Example: C:\PUBLIC.'

Let's look at the `ObjectGetOptions` class in more detail. To do this, let's go back to the base class, `ManagementOptions`. `ManagementOptions` is the base class for all management operation options.

```
public abstract class ManagementOptions
{
  // Properties
  public ManagementNamedValueCollection Context {get; set;}
  public TimeSpan Timeout {get; set;}
};
```

The `Context` property is usually used from within WMI providers that make WMI calls. This helps to avoid infinite loops from occurring within the provider. However, in some cases providers use the mechanism so that clients can set additional context information that the provider may extract for a specific operation.

The `Timeout` property is required only for semisynchronous calls. In general, we do not cover semisynchronous calls in this chapter because it is so easy to use the .NET classes to do true asynchronous operations. We discuss semisynchronous event subscription, the only exception, later in the chapter.

Now let's look at the `ObjectGetOptions` class:

```
public class ObjectGetOptions: ManagementOptions
{

  // Constructors
  public ObjectGetOptions();
  public ObjectGetOptions(ManagementNamedValueCollection context);
  public ObjectGetOptions(ManagementNamedValueCollection context,
    TimeSpan timeout, bool useAmendedQualifiers);

  // Properties
  public bool UseAmendedQualifiers {get; set;}
};
```

The `ObjectGetOptions` class is one of the simpler options classes because it has only one property, `UseAmendedQualifiers`. The earlier code sample created an `Object-GetOptions` object and separately set the `UseAmendedQualifiers` property. Alternatively, we could have specified this by using the correct `ObjectGetOptions` constructor.

Let's continue examining the `ManagementObject` class:

```
public class ManagementObject: ManagementBaseObject
{
  // Methods
  public void Get();
  public void Get(ManagementOperationObserver watcher);
  . ... .. ..
  ... ...
        .
};
```

Earlier in this section we described the lazy management object retrieval employed within the `ManagementObject` and `ManagementClass` classes. We also described how you could use the `Get` method to specify explicitly when the object was retrieved. This class declaration shows the prototype for the `Get` method as well as another `Get` method that takes a `ManagementOperationObserver` parameter. Use this for asynchronous retrieval operations as discussed in more detail later in the chapter.

■ Enumerating Management Objects

In some cases, you will want a complete list of all the management objects of a given class. Suppose you have a user interface that allows the user to select a shared directory to complete a task. In this case, you would want to display a list of all the available shared directories. You can achieve this by enumerating all the instances of the `Win32_Share` class. You also could perform the following query to achieve the same result:

```
SELECT * FROM Win32_Share
```

However, performing a query involves processing the query, obtaining a list of objects, and comparing the query against each object. In this case, it is more efficient to enumerate the objects in the class. To perform an enumeration, all you must know is the name of the class you want to enumerate.

Enumerating objects for a given class is also one of the easiest ways to discover which management objects are available. When you move through classes using CIM Studio (which comes as a developer tool in the Platform SDK), one of the first things you do is look at a list of instances to see which objects can be managed.

The following code sample illustrates how to obtain a list of shared directories:

```
ManagementClass mc = new ManagementClass("Win32_Share");

ManagementObjectCollection mcCollection = mc.GetInstances();

foreach( ManagementObject mo in mcCollection )
{
  Console.WriteLine("'{0}' path is '{1}'", mo["__RELPATH"], mo["Path"]);
}
```

The `GetInstances` call creates a collection (`ManagementObjectCollection`) that you can later enumerate to gain access to every instance of that class. You may see the terms *collection* and *enumeration* used interchangeably, but there is an important difference. A collection is a container of values or objects. You can enumerate a collection, providing access to every value, element, or object, but you cannot navigate it (that is, move back and forth through the collection). To move through a collection requires an enumerator. Call the `ManagementObjectCollection` class's method `GetEnumerator` to obtain an enumerator for the collection. `GetEnumerator` returns an enumerator object of class `ManagementObjectCollection.ManagementObjectEnumerator`. All collection classes in the `System.Management` namespace also have an enumerator class.

Notice that `__RELPATH` was specified as a property name. `__RELPATH` is the relative path of the object. WMI has many system-provided properties for classes and instances that we will discuss in more detail later in the chapter. The output of the preceding code on our machine produces the following:

```
Win32_Share.Name='C$' path is 'C:\'
Win32_Share.Name='IPC$' path is '
Win32_Share.Name='ADMIN$' path is 'C:\WINNT'
```

Retrieving collections of management objects also uses an options class derived from `ManagementOptions`. The `EnumerationOptions` class has many more options than `ObjectGetOptions` (described earlier).

Let's consider a simple example of how we might want to use the `Enumeration-Options` class. By default, the enumeration collection enumerates only the instances of objects of a specific management class. This is called a *shallow enumeration,* and you saw it in the preceding code sample. Here is another example, one that will provide only an enumeration of all the instances of the `Win32_SystemAccount` class.

```
ManagementClass mc = new ManagementClass("Win32_SystemAccount");
ManagementObjectCollection mcCollection = mc.GetInstances();
```

If the class you want to enumerate is a base class, then you might want to build your enumeration collection so that it includes all classes derived from the base class. This is called a *deep enumeration.* To specify a deep enumeration, you must create and complete an `EnumerationOptions` object. Let's look at an example. Suppose you want to see all security accounts on your system. If you look at the CIMV2 schema using CIM Studio, you will see that the `Win32_Account` is a base class for `Win32_SystemAccount`, `Win32_Group`, and `Win32_UserAccount` classes. By specifying a deep enumeration for the `Win32_Account` class, you'll get a collection that will contain all instances of `Win32_SystemAccount`, `Win32_Group`, and `Win32_UserAccount`. Here is an example:

```
ManagementClass mc = new ManagementClass("Win32_Account");

EnumerationOptions options = new EnumerationOptions();
options.EnumerateDeep = true;

ManagementObjectCollection mcCollection = mc.GetInstances(options);
```

```
foreach( ManagementObject mo in mcCollection)
{
  Console.WriteLine("Account '{0}' is '{1}'", mo["__RELPATH"],
    mo["Status"]);
}
```

Let's look at the `EnumerationOptions` class in more detail.

```
public class EnumerationOptions: ManagementOptions
{
  // Constructors
  public EnumerationOptions();
  public EnumerationOptions(ManagementNamedValueCollection context,
    TimeSpan timeout, int blockSize, bool rewindable,
    bool returnImmediately, bool useAmendedQualifiers,
    bool ensureLocatable, bool prototypeOnly, bool directRead,
    bool enumerateDeep);

  // Properties
  public int BlockSize {get; set;}
  public bool DirectRead {get; set;}
  public bool EnsureLocatable {get; set;}
  public bool EnumerateDeep {get; set;}
  public bool PrototypeOnly {get; set;}
  public bool ReturnImmediately {get; set;}
  public bool Rewindable {get; set;}
  public bool UseAmendedQualifiers {get; set;}
};
```

The `BlockSize` option allows you to specify how many management objects will be obtained and placed into the collection before they pass to the caller. This can improve performance when you expect large collection sets of objects in which the caller can process a group of objects at a time. The default value for this option is 1.

The `DirectRead` option allows the caller direct access to the WMI provider.

As you have seen, the `EnumerateDeep` option allows you to enumerate an entire class hierarchy if it is set to true.

The `ReturnImmediately` option is required only for semisynchronous calls. This chapter does not cover semisynchronous calls.

The `Rewindable` option instructs WMI whether to build an enumerator that can be rewound (that is, allow the caller to move back and forth through the collection). If this option is set to false, WMI builds a forward-only enumeration. This type of enumeration generally is faster and requires less memory. If you do not need to navigate your collection, then we recommend that you set `Rewindable` to false. If the class you are enumerating has a very large collection of instances, you may experience out-of-memory exceptions. In this case, you must obtain the collection asynchronously.

The `UseAmendedQualifiers` option allows access to localized content. This was demonstrated earlier.

The `EnumerationOptions` class also is used in performing queries, so the `Ensure-Locatable` and `PrototypeOnly` options will be discussed later.

■ Creating a Management Object

When writing applications to create objects, you must take into account how those objects can be created, if at all. This consideration applies equally to how you foresee the creation of your own objects when you design your schema. Creating a shared directory on a machine is an example of creating an object. There are three ways to look at the creation of objects.

1. Using the standard mechanism provided by WMI.
2. Using a method such as `Create`. The `Win32_Share` class does this.
3. You cannot create instances at all, as in the case of the `Win32_ComputerSystem` class.

First Point

When creating instances using the standard mechanism, you must spawn an uncommitted instance based on the class definition, set your properties, and commit the instance to WMI. (The code sample later in this section illustrates this process.)

As a general rule, you must set all the key properties on the newly spawned instance before committing it. Key properties identify an object explicitly and are required to access it in the future. In some cases, the provider may assign a value to a key property if it discovers that one does not exist, but this is not common. *Best practice* is that you set the key properties when you create your objects. To see what this means, let's look at the following class:

```
class Sample_Book
{
  [key] string BookTitle;
  [key] string AuthorName;
  string Summary;
  DATETIME DatePublished;
  uint8 NumberOfChapters;
};
```

The only properties that must be set are `BookTitle` and `AuthorName`. This means that the other properties do not need to be set to create a valid instance, which can pose some danger, especially if Summary and NumberOfChapters properties also are required. However, this danger is not so bad if you control the source code in the provider, because you simply could ensure that the remaining two required properties are set; otherwise, you could return something like WBEM_E_INVALID_OBJECT from the provider. Of course, this is not guaranteed when using other providers.

WMI classes that support the standard mechanism of creating management objects have the supportsCreate qualifier.

Second Point

To state clearly the information that is required to create an instance, some classes use a method to create an instance. This is the case with the Win32_Share class, which has a method called Create. You would first set up a method call and then execute it. The next time you enumerate the Win32_Share class, the new instance is listed as part of the collection. Let's have another look at the Sample_Book class, this time with a method to create an instance:

```
class Sample_Book
{
  [key] string BookTitle;
  [key] string AuthorName;
  string Summary;
  DATETIME DatePublished;
  uint8 NumberOfChapters;

  [static, implemented] boolean Create([in] string BookTitle,
    [in] string AuthorName, [in] string Summary,
    [in] uint8 NumberOfChapters);
};
```

Now it is clear that the Create method requires both the Summary and NumberOfChapters values, as well as the key values. Also notice that the method returns a Boolean value to indicate whether the method succeeded. (You could instead return a uint32 if you want to return a HRESULT. However, remember that you can call the method from scripting environments where HRESULTs might not be the most suitable return value.) Here are some other reasons that you might want a method for the creation of instances:

1. The key values are not known in advance and are generated by the provider.
2. You may want to have specific flags passed to the method for more context information when creating the instance.
3. You may want to receive one or more out-parameters (other than the return value).

If you find that a method exists for the creation of instances for a class, then you can expect the standard mechanism to fail. However, this depends on the provider. Methods that create management objects may contain the `Constructor` qualifier. The `Constructor` qualifier signifies that the method can create one or more management objects.

Third Point

For some classes, instances cannot be created, as in the `Win32_ComputerSystem` class. If you think about it, it does not make sense to have more than one instance of this class. You may find in your own schema that you cannot create instances and the only supported operations allowed are to update, enumerate, and perform queries.

Example

Let's look how you might create an object using the standard mechanism. We discuss calling methods on classes later in the chapter.

```
// Get class so we can spawn an instance of it
ManagementPath path = new ManagementPath();
path.ClassName = "Sample_Book";
path.NamespacePath = "root\\WMIBook";

ManagementClass mc = new ManagementClass(path);

// Make new object
ManagementObject mo = mc.CreateInstance();

// Set some properties on the object
mo["BookTitle"] = "Developing WMI Solutions";
mo["AuthorName"] = "Gwyn Cole";
mo["Summary"] = "A cool book on Windows Management Instrumentation";
mo["NumberOfChapters"] = 11;
// Commit to create instance in WMI
mo.Put();
```

The first task is to spawn an uncommitted instance that is based on the class definition. Calling `CreateInstance` does this for the `Sample_Book` class. We call this an uncommitted instance because it has not yet been passed to WMI and we can perform normal operations like setting and getting properties. That is exactly what we do next—set all the properties (as long as we include the key properties) of the new instance. After all the properties have been set, we pass the instance to WMI by calling `Put` on the management object. The provider will extract all the properties from the instance and physically do whatever it needs to do to create the instance.

Let's see the `Put` methods the `ManagementObject` class:

```
public class ManagementObject : ManagementBaseObject
{
  // Properties
  public ManagementPath Put();
  public ManagementPath Put(PutOptions options);
  ......
  ...
};
```

Committing management objects also has an options class, `PutOptions`, derived from `ManagementOptions`. Let's look at the `PutOptions` class:

```
public class PutOptions: ManagementOptions
{
  // Constructors
  public PutOptions();

  // Properties
  public PutType Type {get; set;}
  public bool UseAmendedQualifiers {get; set;}
};
```

The `Type` option can be `UpdateOrCreate`, `UpdateOnly`, or `CreateOnly` and specifies the kind of put-operation that must be performed. The code sample specified no `Put-Options` : `Put()` defaults to `UpdateOrCreate`. By specifying the `UpdateOrCreate`, `Put-Options` allows the provider to commit the desired change in any way it sees fit, regardless of whether the management object existed or not. If `CreateOnly` were specified, WMI would allow only the creation of the instance. If you already had an instance with identical key properties, the `Put` call would fail by throwing an "object already exists" exception. Use `CreateOnly` option when you do not intend the instance to be updated accidentally. There is a `PutOptions` example in the Updating Management Objects section that follows.

■ Updating Management Objects

When writing applications, updating existing instances with new property values is one of the operations you most often end up doing. As in creating instances, you have three options: using the standard mechanism to update, using a method to update, and not being allowed to update at all. The standard mechanism of updating instance property values is very similar to creating a new instance, because you still make a call to `Put`. The general process is to get your instance, change the properties, and then call `Put`. The following code sample changes a property value on the book instance we created earlier:

```
// Generate the object path
ManagementPath path = new ManagementPath();
path.Path = "Sample_Book.BookTitle=\" Developing WMI Solutions\",
  AuthorName=\"Gwyn Cole\"";
path.NamespacePath = "root\\WMIBook";

// Get the Sample_Book object we want
ManagementObject mo = new ManagementObject(path);

// Change the number of chapters
mo["NumberOfChapters"] = 12;

PutOptions options = new PutOptions();
options.Type = PutType.UpdateOnly;

// Commit to update instance in WMI
mo.Put(options);
```

As you can see, updating an instance is straightforward. We only changed the number of chapters property and all the other property values remained unaffected. However, notice the use of the `PutOptions` class, which specifies the type of put operation that WMI should allow, in this case `UpdateOnly`. The `UpdateOnly` option will allow an update only to an already existing instance. If the `Sample_Book` instance did not exist, the `Put` method would throw an "object not found" exception. If we had specified the `UpdateOrCreate` option (which is the default type) instead, `Put` may not have failed, because the provider would have attempted to create the instance. Use `UpdateOnly` in situations in which you do not want accidental creation of instances.

Some classes use methods to update instances for very similar reasons to those described in the previous section. For example, the `Win32_Share` class has a method called `SetShareInfo` in which the description of the shared directory, together with some other properties, can be changed. The `Win32_Service` class is another example; it has two methods, `Change` and `ChangeStartMode`, to update an instance.

WMI classes that support the standard mechanism of updating management objects have the `supportsUpdate` qualifier.

Deleting a Management Object

When writing applications, you occasionally will want to delete management objects. For instance, you might want to remove access to an already existing shared directory, which would involve deleting the shared directory management object. As with creating and updating instances, you have three options: using the standard mechanism to delete, using a method to delete, and not being allowed to delete at all.

For some classes such as the `Win32_VideoController` class, it makes no sense to delete instances. The `Win32_VideoController` class is a hardware device and to remove the instance would involve physically removing the video controller from your computer. Using the standard mechanism to delete an object is the easiest method of removing instances. In some classes you may find that a deletion method is available. Here are some reasons that you might want a method for the deletion of instances:

1. To have specific flags passed to the method for more context information when deleting the instance
2. To receive one or more out-parameters (other than the return value)

If you find that a method exists for the deletion of instances, then you can expect the standard mechanism to fail, but this depends on the provider. WMI classes that support the standard mechanism of deleting management objects have the **supportsDelete** qualifier.

Let's have another look at the above `Sample_Book` class, this time with a method to delete an instance:

```
class Sample_Book
{
  [key] string BookTitle;
  [key] string AuthorName;
  string Summary;
  DATETIME DatePublished;
  uint8 NumberOfChapters;

  [static, implemented] boolean Create([in] string BookTitle,
    [in] string AuthorName, [in] string Summary,
    [in] uint8 NumberOfChapters);

  [implemented] boolean Delete();
};
```

Did you observe that the `Delete` method does not include the key properties of the class? How will the `Delete` method know which book to delete? The key is that the `Delete` method is not static and is relative to the management object. The `Create` method was defined with the **static** qualifier, which effectively means the method can be called without reference to any instances of the class. This is the same concept as in object-oriented programming. The `Delete` method can be called only relative to the management object. Using the standard mechanism, deleting an instance is an easy operation. All you need do is obtain a `ManagementObject` and call `Delete` and the provider will attempt to remove the instance. Let's remove the `Sample_Book` instance that we created earlier:

```
// Generate the object path
ManagementPath path = new ManagementPath();
path.Path = "Sample_Book.BookTitle=\" Developing WMI Solutions\",
AuthorName=\"Gwyn Cole\"";
path.NamespacePath = "root\\WMIBook";

ManagementObject mo = new ManagementObject(path);

// Delete Sample_Book
mo.Delete();
```

Let's look at the `Delete` method in the `ManagementObject` class:

```
public class ManagementObject: ManagementBaseObject
{
  // Properties
  public void Delete();
  public void Delete(DeleteOptions options);
  .. .... .
  ...
};
```

Deleting management objects also has an options class derived from `Management-Options`. However, there is not much interesting in it because delete is a relatively simple operation. Let's look at the `DeleteOptions` class:

```
public class DeleteOptions : ManagementOptions
{
  // Constructors
  public DeleteOptions ();
  public DeleteOptions(ManagementNamedValueCollection context,
    TimeSpan timeout);
};
```

As you can see, there are no properties to speak of, which just leaves the constructor to discuss. The only reason you would want to create and specify a `DeleteOptions` object is if you have specific context information to pass to the provider. Although not explicitly mentioned, all options classes have a constructor that takes a `Management-NamedValueCollection`. This is a reasonably low-level mechanism for supplying additional information to the provider. Of course the provider will query the context information only if it is expecting any specific named context values.

■ Performing Queries

Performing queries is one of the most popular mechanisms for gaining access to management objects, because it allows great flexibility in specifying exactly what you want. When writing your own applications, you will inevitably find that you must perform queries that fall into one of two categories:

1. You need context-relative information.

2. You need to improve performance.

For an example of context-relative information, suppose that a task requires a security principle (that is, a user) from a particular domain. A user interface application could formulate the following WQL query:

```
SELECT * FROM Win32_UserAccount WHERE Domain="DOMAIN_A"
```

This query would provide you with a full list of all the users in DOMAIN_A. You can also use a query to improve performance by specifying what properties you require. The previous example asked for all properties from the `Win32_UserAccount` class (that is, the `SELECT *`). You do not need all the properties if you simply want to display a list of users and use the SID (security identifier) to perform some task. The query can be revised to specifically ask for the display name and SID.

```
SELECT FullName, SID FROM Win32_UserAccount WHERE Domain="DOMAIN_A"
```

The above query would return the `FullName` and `SID` property values only for each instance that matches the query (`WHERE Domain="DOMAIN_A"`). However, the performance improvement can vary from provider to provider. WMI providers do not have to support query optimization, in which case WMI obtains the complete list of all the instances together with all their property values. WMI then processes each instance and if the instance matches the query, WMI copies the instance and the required properties to the query collection that is passed to the caller. The bottom line is that the speed of queries depends on whether providers support query optimization in their implementation.

Performing queries is, in some ways, similar to enumeration. When we dealt with enumeration earlier in the chapter, you learned that you could get all of the instances of a specific class and you could access the instances through an enumeration collection (`ManagementObjectCollection`). When performing queries, you still end up with a collection that allows you to enumerate all of the instances that satisfy your query. For more information on all the different types of queries that can be performed, review Chapter 3 and the Platform SDK documentation.

The following code sample illustrates how to obtain a list of Windows Services that have already been started:

```
ManagementObjectSearcher query = new ManagementObjectSearcher(
  "SELECT * FROM Win32_Service WHERE Started=true");
ManagementObjectCollection queryCollection = query.Get();
foreach(ManagementObject mo in queryCollection)
{
  Console.WriteLine("Service:'{0}'", mo["DisplayName"]);
}
```

In the code sample, the `Get` call (on the `ManagementObjectSearcher` class) performs the query (if it is valid). The `Get` operation creates and returns a collection that can be used to gain access to every management object that matches the query. The display name for every running Windows service is output to the console.

Let's see what the `ManagementObjectSearcher` class looks like:

```
public class ManagementObjectSearcher: Component
{
  // Constructors
  public ManagementObjectSearcher();
  public ManagementObjectSearcher(string queryString);
  public ManagementObjectSearcher(ObjectQuery query);
  public ManagementObjectSearcher(ManagementScope scope, ObjectQuery
    query, EnumerationOptions options);

  // Properties
  public EnumerationOptions Options {get; set;}
  public ObjectQuery Query {get; set;}
  public ManagementScope Scope {get; set;}

  // Methods
  public ManagementObjectCollection Get();
  public void Get(ManagementOperationObserver watcher);
};
```

Notice that the only methods available allow the execution of a query by calling either of the `Get` methods. The first `Get` method executes the query synchronously and the second version executes the query asynchronously. Asynchronous WMI operations will be discussed later in the chapter. The query executed is specified in the `Query` property. The WMI connection used to execute the query is supplied through the `Scope` property. The `ManagementScope` class will also be discussed later in the chapter. When executing the query, if it is found to be invalid or the class specified is not found, be prepared to handle a `ManagementException`.

We mentioned earlier that querying for objects is similar to returning all instances of a class. Earlier you saw a detailed discussion involving the `EnumerationOptions` class. We will reveal more detail about some of the enumeration options shortly.

Let's examine the different ways that a query can be specified. In the previous code sample, the `ManagementObjectSearcher` object was created by using the second constructor in the above class declaration. That is, a complete WQL plain text query was specified.

```
ManagementObjectSearcher query = new ManagementObjectSearcher(
  "SELECT * FROM Win32_Service WHERE Started=true");
```

Another way to specify the WQL query is through an `ObjectQuery` object. `ObjectQuery` has a few derived classes that allow you to use alternative methods of assembling your queries. You can code the preceding query alternatively as follows:

```
ObjectQuery myquery =
  new ObjectQuery("SELECT * FROM Win32_Service WHERE Started=true");

ManagementObjectSearcher query = new ManagementObjectSearcher(myquery);
```

The above case specifies the plain text `SELECT` query into an `ObjectQuery` object rather than it being specified through the `ManagementObjectSearcher` constructor. Let's take a quick look at the `ObjectQuery` class:

```
public class ObjectQuery: ManagementQuery
{
  public ObjectQuery();
  public ObjectQuery(string query);
  public ObjectQuery(string language, string query);
};
```

The second constructor specifies the query that WMI should execute. The third constructor also specifies the query language used by the query. The current implementation of WMI supports only WQL. When using the second constructor, the WQL query language is assumed.

Notice that the `ObjectQuery` class inherits from `ManagementQuery`. All WMI query classes in the .NET Framework inherit from this class, which is an abstract class that forces query classes to support both the query language and the query. Here is what the class looks like:

```
public abstract class ManagementQuery: ICloneable
{
  public virtual string QueryLanguage {get; set;}
  public virtual string QueryString {get; set;}
};
```

So far, the `ObjectQuery` class hasn't offered many advantages over using a plain text string. So let's look at one of the derived classes, `WqlObjectQuery`:

```
public class WqlObjectQuery: ObjectQuery
{
  public WqlObjectQuery();
  public WqlObjectQuery(string query);

  public override string QueryLanguage {get;}
};
```

The main purpose of this class is that all queries are WQL object queries, hence, the `QueryLanguage` property will always return WQL. A similarly named class, `Wql-EventQuery`, specifies WQL event queries. Although it, too, offers little benefit, this is how the query could have been specified:

```
WqlObjectQuery myquery =
  new WqlObjectQuery("SELECT * FROM Win32_Service WHERE Started=true");

ManagementObjectSearcher query = new ManagementObjectSearcher(myquery);
```

Again, we do not achieve much benefit, so let's look at the next derived class, `SelectQuery`. This class's purpose is to encompass all WQL SELECT queries for either management classes or management objects. From the following class declaration, you can see that there are many more useful constructors and properties.

```
public class SelectQuery: WqlObjectQuery
{
  // Constructors
  public SelectQuery();
  public SelectQuery(string queryOrClassName);
  public SelectQuery(string className, string condition);
  public SelectQuery(string className, string condition,
    string[] selectedProperties);

  // Properties
  public string ClassName {get; set;}
  public string Condition {get; set;}
  public bool IsSchemaQuery {get; set;}
  public override string QueryString {get; set;}
  public StringCollection SelectedProperties {get; set;}
};
```

If you really wanted to, you could still pass an entire WQL plain text query into one of the constructors, but let's see how this class differs. Consider the following alternative method of specifying the query:

```
SelectQuery myquery = new SelectQuery("Win32_Service", "Started=true");

ManagementObjectSearcher query = new ManagementObjectSearcher(myquery);
```

This query shows that the class and condition statements are supplied through two separate parameters. This has the added benefit that if you must generate complex queries, you do not have to assemble all the query strings yourself. Most of this can be managed easily through the `SelectQuery` class.

There are also `RelatedObjectQuery` and `RelationshipQuery` classes. The `Related-ObjectQuery` class represents a WQL `ASSOCIATORS OF` query and `RelationshipQuery` represents a WQL `REFERENCES OF` query. Review Chapter 3 and the Platform SDK documentation for more information.

As mentioned earlier, WMI has some system-provided properties that are included automatically in every object. These properties are `__SUPERCLASS`, `__DYNASTY`, `__RELPATH`, `__DERIVATION`, `__SERVER`, `__NAMESPACE`, and `__PATH`. The meaning and purpose of these properties are discussed in Chapter 3. The reason we mention these now is that depending on the type of query you perform, these system-provided properties may or may not be set.

If you perform any query that starts with `SELECT`, you can be assured that all the system-provided properties will be available for you, as in the following case:

```
SELECT * FROM Win32_UserAccount WHERE Domain="DOMAIN_A"
```

If you perform any query that specifies specific properties in the `SELECT` statement, then the system-provided properties will not be available, as in the following case:

```
SELECT FullName, SID FROM Win32_UserAccount WHERE Domain="DOMAIN_A"
```

All is not lost! You can instruct WMI to include the system-provided properties that can identify the location of a management object. To do this, you must set the `EnsureLocatable` option to true in the `EnumerationOptions` class. The resulting instances in the returned management object collection will include `__RELPATH`, `__SERVER`, `__NAMESPACE`, and `__PATH` properties.

Microsoft Systems Management Server implements an extended version of WQL, called Extended WQL. As part of Extended WQL, there are additional SELECT clauses such as DISTINCT, JOIN, and DATEPART. The `PrototypeOnly` option in the `Enumera-tionOptions` class allows you to obtain a class definition in the result set that uses the JOIN clause.

■ Making Method Calls

So far, you saw a few occasions in which you might want or must make method calls. For instance, you've seen that we could have called methods for the creation and deletion of our `Sample_Book` class. Other examples include changing the configuration of shared directories and Windows Services (as well as starting and stopping them). You may discover in your own schema designs that you must add behavior to your classes, in which case methods are the answer. Although we see methods for creating, changing, and deleting instances, we urge you to use the standard approaches for these types of operations where possible. However, exceptions are made when you find yourself in one or more of the following situations:

1. You may want to have specific flags passed to the method for more context information when creating and deleting instances.
2. You may want to receive one or more out-parameters (other than the return value).
3. None of the WMI HRESULTs supports the types of errors you would like to return. You can define the method return value so that you can return an appropriate data type for the errors you would like to pass back to the caller.
4. You may want to create multiple instances at the same time.

Calling methods fall into two categories:

1. Calling static methods on classes
2. Calling methods on objects

To illustrate making method calls in detail, we shall use a fictitious class with a method called foo, and decorate the method with different parameters so that you can gain a clear understanding. Let's look at this declaration:

```
class Sample_Class
{
  [key] string Name;
  [static, implemented] void foo();
};
```

The class has a static method that takes no parameters and returns void (effectively meaning no return value). So let's see what code we need to make this method call:

```
ManagementClass mc = new ManagementClass("Sample_Class");

mc.InvokeMethod("foo", null);
```

Invoking static methods in a class requires that you first retrieve the class from WMI. We do this through the ManagementClass class. The previous code sample gets access to the Sample _Class class followed by invoking the method with InvokeMethod. Let's revise our method declaration:

```
class Sample_Class
{
  [key] string Name;
  [implemented] void foo();
};
```

We do not see much difference. The only change we made was the removal of the `static` qualifier. The `static` qualifier meant that the method could be called without reference to any instances of the class. With the change to `foo`, we must now use an object reference. Let's look at the following code:

```
ManagementObject mo = new
ManagementObject("Sample_Class.Name=\"Gwyn\"");

mo.InvokeMethod("foo", null);
```

An object reference is now used instead of a class reference. To access a management object requires the `ManagementObject` class, which also has an `InvokeMethod` method. Unfortunately, methods that take no parameters and have no return value are not practical for most purposes. So let's extend `foo` to return a value:

```
class Sample_Class
{
  [key] string Name;
  [implemented] string foo();
};
```

Here is how you can easily retrieve the string return value from `foo`:

```
ManagementObject mo = new
ManagementObject("Sample_Class.Name=\"Gwyn\"");

string myString = (string)mo.InvokeMethod("foo", null);
```

The code now has all the information you'll need to make the `Delete` method call on the `Win32_Share` class. Finally, let's make our `foo` method take an in- and out-parameter.

```
class Sample_Class
{
  [key] string Name;
  [implemented] string foo([in] uint32 inparam, [out] boolean outparam);
};
```

From a code perspective, things start getting more involved. All in-parameters and out-parameters are encapsulated into a kind of management object. `Management-Object`s make it very easy to get and set properties. Preparing and accessing parameters is also like getting and setting properties, except the terminology is slightly different where they are not properties but are in- or out-parameters. `Management-`

`BaseObject` objects are used as a container of parameters. Each property corresponds to a method parameter, so if the method you're planning to call has six parameters, then you'll have to set six properties (assuming all the parameters are required and are not optional).

A method's return value exists in a property called `ReturnValue`, hence, none of your method out-parameters can use this name. If the method also has one or more out-parameters, then the `ManagementBaseObject` passed back to the caller will contain the `ReturnValue` as well as the other out-parameters. Let's see some code:

```
ManagementObject mo = new ManagementObject("Sample_Class.Name=
  \"Gwyn\"");

// Get the method parameters
ManagementBaseObject inParams = mo.GetMethodParameters("foo");

// Complete method in-parameters
inParams["inparam"] = 12345;

// Call method on management object
ManagementBaseObject outParams =
  mo.InvokeMethod("foo", inParams, null);

// Get return value and out-parameters
string retVal = (string)outParams["ReturnValue"];
bool mybool = (bool)outParams["outparam"];
```

Writing code to pass in-parameters to a WMI method is significantly more involved. The preparation of the method's in-parameters is achieved most suitably by calling `GetMethodParameters`. This is followed by setting each parameter in the `ManagementBaseObject` instance, `inParams`. You must complete the associated value for each in-parameter. Finally, the in-parameters are passed to the `InvokeMethod` call and the provider extracts the parameters for the operation. After the provider has done its work, it will populate a `ManagementBaseObject` instance that will contain the method's out-parameters and return value.

To provide a more serious code sample and introduce some other issues that you most likely will have to deal with, we shall create a shared directory with the `Win32_Share` class. Here is an almost complete declaration of the `Win32_Share` class:

```
class Win32_Share: CIM_LogicalElement
{
  [read] string Name;
  [read] boolean AllowMaximum;
  [read] uint32 MaximumAllowed;
  [read] string Path;
  ...
```

```
[static, implemented]
uint32 Create([in] string Path, [in] string Name,
  [in, ValueMap {"0",...}, Values {"Disk Drive",...}] uint32 Type,
  [in] uint32 MaximumAllowed,
  [in, optional] string Description,
  [in, optional] string Password,
  [in, optional] Win32_SecurityDescriptor Access);

[implemented] uint32 SetShareInfo([in, optional] uint32
    MaximumAllowed,
  [in, Optional] string Description,
  [in, optional] Win32_SecurityDescriptor Access);
[implemented] uint32 Delete();
};
```

Let's examine the `Create` method. It has seven in-parameters, `Path`, `Name`, `Type`, `MaximumAllowed`, `Description`, `Password` and `Access`. Each of these parameters should be straightforward to understand; if you look at the sharing property page for a directory, you'll see the user interface that maps to these parameters. Let's discuss the `Create` method's parameter types and declarations in detail.

First, you'll see that most parameters take standard types that you already recognize, like `string` and `uint32`. The `Access` parameter is an exception: It passes a `Win32_SecurityDescriptor` object. Classes intended for use in method parameters are usually inherited from `Win32_MethodParameterClass`. All parameter declarations use qualifiers to provide more context information. The `[in]` qualifier specifies that the parameter is an in-parameter and `[optional]` means that it is not required to be set. The `ValueMap` qualifier specifies the values that are valid for the property or parameter. The full `ValueMap` declaration that follows shows various integers values that are valid for the `Type` parameter:

```
ValueMap
{
  "0", "1", "2", "3",
  "2147483648", "2147483649", "2147483650", "2147483651"
}
```

But what do these values mean or represent? Describing them is the role of the `Values` qualifier. This qualifier provides a textual description of the values in the `ValueMap`. Here is the full `Values` declaration below:

```
Values
{
  "Disk Drive", "Print Queue", "Device", "IPC",
  "Disk Drive Admin", "Print Queue Admin", "Device Admin", "IPC Admin"
}
```

Using the `Values` and `ValueMap` attributes, it is now possible to work out what the `Type` parameter means or should be. The parameter 0 (in integer form) specifies "Disk Drive", 1 specifies "Print Queue", and so on. You should use these types of attributes in your own schema to aid the understanding of your method parameters and class properties.

Let's look at some code that calls a static method to create a shared directory:

```
// Get the class definition so we can get access to the method from the
  class
ManagementClass mc = new ManagementClass("Win32_Share");

// Get the methods in parameters
ManagementBaseObject inParams = mc.GetMethodParameters("Create");

// Setup required in parameters for method
inParams["Name"] = "temp";
inParams["Path"] = "C:\\temp";
inParams["Type"] = 0;

// Execute method
ManagementBaseObject outParams =
  mc.InvokeMethod("Create", inParams, null);

// Inspect out parameters for return value
uint retVal = (uint)outParams["ReturnValue"];
```

Most of the details of the preceding code sample have been discussed, so we'll examine only the new ones. Did you notice that we completed only the required parameters (that is, parameters that do not have the `optional` attribute set)? We did this for two reasons: first, to keep the code sample small, and second, we needed to fill in only the required parameters to create a shared directory. The `Type` parameter has a value of zero (integer), which, if you recall, according to the `Values` attribute will specify "Disk Drive." We finally pass the in-parameters to the `InvokeMethod` call and we shall get the out-parameters through `outParams`. If a method being called returns a value other than `void`, then you'll always get an out-parameter named "ReturnValue."

Let's have a look at the WMI method-related methods in the `ManagementObject` class:

```
public class ManagementObject : ManagementBaseObject
{
  // InvokeMethod declarations
  public object InvokeMethod(string methodName, object[] args);
  public ManagementBaseObject InvokeMethod(string methodName,
    ManagementBaseObject inParameters, InvokeMethodOptions options);
  public void InvokeMethod(ManagementOperationObserver watcher,
    string methodName, object[] args);
```

```
public void InvokeMethod(ManagementOperationObserver watcher,
  string methodName, ManagementBaseObject inParameters,
  InvokeMethodOptions options);

// GetMethodParameters declaration
public ManagementBaseObject GetMethodParameters(string methodName);
};
```

There are four variants of the InvokeMethod method. The first declaration is the one we used earlier when we called foo—the version that had no method parameters. From its declaration, you can now see that a method with in-parameters can use the same version of InvokeMethod (by passing an array that represents the method's in-parameters). Did you also notice InvokeMethod 's return type, object? This version of InvokeMethod automatically extracts the ReturnValue out-parameter and returns it, using the base data type, object.

The second InvokeMethod method declaration is the one we used in the code samples involving in-parameters. The third parameter options specifies how the WMI method should be called, which includes additional context information. The InvokeMethodOptions class is derived from ManagementOptions. Let's have a look:

```
public class InvokeMethodOptions: ManagementOptions
{
  public InvokeMethodOptions();
  public InvokeMethodOptions(ManagementNamedValueCollection context,
    TimeSpan timeout);
};
```

This class has no additional properties other than those inherited from the ManagementOptions class. This is why we did not include the use of the class in the earlier code samples. One possible use would be to pass additional context information through the Context property (ManagementNamedValueCollection).

The third and fourth InvokeMethod declarations are asynchronous versions of the first and second declarations.

▪ Manipulating Management Object Properties

As you've already seen, setting and getting property values is one of the most common operations when writing management applications. Throughout nearly all the code samples in this chapter so far, you've seen properties' get, set, and property values retrieved. We have, however, been careful to use strings or integers to aid understanding. In the next couple of sections, we shall cover in more detail how to get and set properties of different data types. Let's quickly recapitulate the calls we made earlier that involve getting and setting property values. The following call was made in the section in which you saw how to create a management object. Notice how the value is assigned:

```
mo["NumberOfChapters"] = 11;
```

The next call was made in the section where you saw how to obtain a management object. Notice how the value is obtained:

```
Console.WriteLine("Win32_Share.Name=\"C$\" path is {0}", mo["Path"]);
```

Both of these code samples are either getting a value or setting a value using the indexing [] operator. The code sample also could have been written to use the Get-PropertyValue and SetPropertyValue methods. The following example demonstrates incrementing the number of chapters (notice that the value uses a byte cast because the property CIM type is uint 8):

```
byte NumOfChapters = (byte)mo.GetPropertyValue("NumberOfChapters");
NumOfChapters++;
mo.SetPropertyValue("NumberOfChapters", NumOfChapters);
```

Note that calling SetPropertyValue will change the property of the instance in memory, but will not persist the change to the real management object in WMI. To persist the change, a call to Put is required on the management object. Here are the prototypes for accessing the properties:

```
public class ManagementObject : ManagementBaseObject
{
  public object GetPropertyValue(string propertyName);
  public void SetPropertyValue(string propertyName, object
  propertyValue);

  public object this[string propertyName] {get; set;}
  .. ... .
  ...
};
```

You may find that you must cast the object return value to the desired C# data type, like the preceding case in which GetPropertyValue returned a uint 8 that maps to the C# data type, byte. Table 8.1 describes all the CIM data types and the C# data type mappings. The CimType enumeration is defined in the System.Management namespace.

In addition to the values of properties, determining where the property originated also can be obtained from WMI. This is called the property flavor and can be local, inherited, or system-provided.

Table 8.1   CIM Data Type to C# Mappings

MOF data type	C# data type	CimType enumeration	Comment
sint8	sbyte	SInt8	Signed 8-bit integer.
sint16	short	SInt16	Signed 16-bit integer.
sint32	int	SInt32	Signed 32-bit integer.
sint64	long	SInt64	Signed 64-bit integer.
real32	float	Real32	32-bit floating point number.
real64	double	Real64	64-bit floating point number.
uint8	byte	UInt8	Unsigned 8-bit integer.
uint16	ushort	UInt16	Unsigned 16-bit integer.
uint32	uint	UInt32	Unsigned 32-bit integer.
uint64	ulong	UInt64	Unsigned 64-bit integer.
boolean	bool	Boolean	Boolean value.
DATETIME	string	DateTime	All dates and times in WMI use the format designed by the Distributed Management Task Force (DMTF).
object	object	Object	Represents an object. Cast to ManagementBaseObject to gain access to the object properties.
object ref	string	Reference	An object path string. See the discussion earlier in the chapter about object paths.
char16	short	Char16	16-bit Unicode character.
string	string	String	Unicode character string.
[array]	[] index operator		An array of any of the above data types. Arrays are accessed using the array [] index operator. For example, an array of strings is string[].

System-provided properties can be separately accessed via the ManagementBase-Object property, SystemProperties. The SystemProperties property will contain a collection that will include __SUPERCLASS, __DYNASTY, __RELPATH, __DERIVATION, __SERVER, __NAMESPACE, and __PATH properties.

In classes, a local property is the most derived property, for example, the Win32_Share class has AccessMask, AllowMaximum, MaximumAllowed, Path, and Type, all declared within the management class. Inherited properties are declared in a parent (or super) class. To see this in action, the following code sample enumerates all the property definitions for the Win32_Share class:

```
ManagementClass mc = new ManagementClass("Win32_Share");

PropertyDataCollection props = mc.Properties;

foreach (PropertyData pd in props)
{
  if (pd.IsLocal)
    Console.WriteLine("{0} is Local", pd.Name);
  else if (!pd.IsLocal)
    Console.WriteLine("{0} is Inherited", pd.Name);
}
```

This code conveniently introduced you to the enumeration of properties. As you can see, it is straightforward: All you must do is obtain the property collection (`Property-DataCollection`) and enumerate through each item. Each property is identified through the `PropertyData` class, and whether it is local or not can be determined by inspecting the `IsLocal` property.

The previous code produces the following output:

```
AccessMask is local
AllowMaximum is local
Caption is inherited
Description is inherited
InstallDate is inherited
MaximumAllowed is local
Name is inherited
Path is local
Status is inherited
Type is local
```

You can now see proof that `AccessMask`, `AllowMaximum`, `MaximumAllowed`, `Path`, and `Type` all are declared locally within the `Win32_Share` class. The `Caption`, `Description`, `InstallDate`, `Name`, and `Status` all are inherited from `CIM_ManagedSystem-Element`.

For management objects, local properties are those that are set by the provider for the class. Code similar to the previous enumeration, except for an instance of a `Win32_Share` class instead of a class definition, produces the following output:

```
AccessMask is inherited
AllowMaximum is local
Caption is local
Description is local
InstallDate is inherited
MaximumAllowed is inherited
Name is local
Path is local
Status is local
Type is local
```

You can now see that the provider for the `Win32_Share` class has set the inherited class properties `Caption`, `Description`, `Name`, and `Status` (as well as most of its local properties). The properties `AccessMask`, `InstallDate`, and `MaximumAllowed` were inherited from the class declaration because the provider did not set them.

Now let's examine some of the more unusual property data types. We assume that you're comfortable with most of the data types such as string and sint32. The types we think need more explanation are arrays, object, and DATETIME. The array and object data types will be covered later in the chapter, so let's talk about DATETIME.

The DATETIME data type can represent either a date and time or an interval. Both types are represented as strings using formats designed by the Distributed Management Task Force (DMTF). Each format is a fixed-length string that contains fields for each type of time specification. The string format for the date and time specification is:

```
yyyymmddHHMMSS.mmmmmmsUUU
```

Table 8.2 describes each field.

Each of the nine fields must either be completed or ignored and replaced with asterisks. Here are some examples:

```
20050704******.********** // date only: 4 July 2005
********1230**.********** // hours & minutes only: 12:30 pm
200507********.********** // year & month only: July 2005
```

Table 8.2 DATETIME Field Descriptions for Absolute Date/Time

Field	Comment
yyyy	Four-digit year (0000 through 9999). Providers can restrict the supported range.
mm	Two-digit month (01 through 12).
dd	Two-digit day of the month (01 through 31).
HH	Two-digit hour of the day using the 24-hour clock (00 through 23).
MM	Two-digit minute in the hour (00 through 59).
SS	Two-digit number of seconds in the minute (00 through 59).
mmmmmm	Six-digit number of microseconds in the second (000000 through 999999).
s	Plus sign (+) or minus sign (–) to indicate a positive or negative offset from Universal Time Coordinates (UTC).
UUU	Three-digit offset indicating the number of minutes that the originating time zone deviates from UTC.

```
20050704123029.********** // date & time: 4 July 2005 - 12:30 pm
                          29 seconds
200507041230**.******+060 // date & time: 4 July 2005 - 12:30 pm,
                          // 1 hour ahead of universal time
```

The string format for the interval time specification is:

ddddddddHHMMSS.mmmmmm:000

Table 8.3 describes what each field is.

Table 8.3 DATETIME Field Descriptions for Interval Times

Field	Comment
dddddddd	Eight digits representing a number of days (00000000 through 99999999).
HH	Two-digit hour of the day using the 24-hour clock (00 through 23).
MM	Two-digit minute in the hour (00 through 59).
SS	Two-digit number of seconds in the minute (00 through 59).
mmmmmm	Six-digit number of microseconds in the second (000000 through 999999).
:000	Interval times always have a trailing :000 as the last four characters.

All five fields must be completed. Here are some examples of interval times:

```
00000002030756.000000:000 // interval: 2 days, 3 hours, 7 minutes
                          & 56 sec
00000000000100.000000:000 // interval: every minute
00000000000015.000000:000 // interval: every 15 seconds
00000000000000.500000:000 // interval: 500 milliseconds (half a second)
```

Manipulating Array Object Properties

When writing your applications, you more than likely will have to use arrays to obtain the property values you want. You might even need to use arrays to get your own array-based property values in your schema design. As mentioned in the last section, you can have an array of any CIM data type. Binary data can be represented as an array of uint8.

Let's examine some code that accesses an array-based property. The purpose of the following code sample is to list the derivation hierarchy for a class, in this case Win32_PhysicalMemory. The __DERIVATION system-provided property is declared as an array of strings.

```
ManagementClass mc = new ManagementClass("Win32_PhysicalMemory");

string[] classes = (string[])mc.GetPropertyValue("__DERIVATION");

foreach (string classname in classes)
{
  Console.WriteLine("{0}", classname);
}
```

You should be reasonably familiar with this code, as we have obtained the class definition and requested the system-provided property __DERIVATION. The array of strings can be accessed easily by enumerating the array. The output of this example produces the inheritance hierarchy for the Win32_PhysicalMemory class. Win32_PhysicalMemory first inherits from CIM_PhysicalMemory and that inherits from CIM_Chip and so on.

```
CIM_PhysicalMemory
CIM_Chip
CIM_PhysicalComponent
CIM_PhysicalElement
CIM_ManagedSystemElement
```

Saving array-based properties is also straightforward. Create your array and pass it to SetPropertyValue (or perform an assignment using the index operator).

The previous code sample demonstrates how to access a property and cast it to the desired array data type. However, accessing the class derivation (in this specific case) also could have been achieved using the ManagementClass's Derivation property:

```
ManagementClass mc = new ManagementClass("Win32_PhysicalMemory");

foreach (string classname in mc.Derivation)
{
  Console.WriteLine("{0}", classname);
}
```

■ Accessing Objects from Object Properties

When writing your applications you will occasionally have to access properties or method parameters that are not strings, integers, or arrays, but, in fact, are complete objects. You've already seen an example of this earlier in the chapter. The Access in-parameter for the Win32_Share Create method took a Win32_SecurityDescriptor object. To explain the concept of embedding objects within properties (or method parameters) more fully, we shall extend the Sample_Book class that was introduced earlier in the chapter.

Here is the `Sample_Book` class with a small change. The `Summary` property no longer is defined as a string data type. Instead, we encapsulated the summary string within a new class called `Sample_BookSummary`.

```
class Sample_Book
{
  [key] string BookTitle;
  [key] string AuthorName;
  Sample_BookSummary Summary;
  DATETIME DatePublished;
  uint8 NumberOfChapters;
};
```

As you can see, the `Summary` property now is defined as an object of type `Sample_Book-Summary` (effectively a new data type). Let's see what the `Sample_BookSummary` class looks like:

```
class Sample_BookSummary
{
  string BookSummary;
};
```

All we have done is move the string describing the summary of the book into another class (through the `BookSummary` property). To visualise the sample code better, let's create an instance of the `Sample_Book` using the MOF code below. Notice that the Summary property is a new instance:

```
instance of Sample_Book
{
  BookTitle = "Developing WMI Solutions";
  AuthorName = "Craig Tunstall & Gwyn Cole";
  NumberOfChapters = 11;
  Summary = instance of Sample_BookSummary
  {
    BookSummary = "A cool book on Windows Management Instrumentation";
  };
};
```

The next sample code obtains this object (`Sample_Book`) and accesses a property that is an also an object (`Sample_BookSummary`). When designing your own schemas, you might want to employ this technique. However, be careful, because the disadvantage of this approach is that it limits your capability to query and form associations. The ability to query and form associations on your management objects is a key benefit. Keep your options open for future schema revisions.

This sample code obtains the instance we created:

```
ManagementPath path = new ManagementPath();
path.Path = "Sample_Book.BookTitle=\" Developing WMI Solutions\",
  AuthorName=\"Craig Tunstall & Gwyn Cole\"";
path.NamespacePath = "root\\WMIBook";

ManagementObject mo = new ManagementObject(path);

ManagementBaseObject mp =
  (ManagementBaseObject)mo.GetPropertyValue ("Summary");

Console.WriteLine("BookSummary is '{0}'", mp["BookSummary"]);
```

Most of the previous code sample should be straightforward by now. We get the object we want and obtain the `Summary` property value. We have highlighted in bold text the code that actually extracts the embedded object. After the object is extracted from the property it becomes easy to get and set property values. We do that next, retrieving the `BookSummary` property from the embedded object. The previous code outputs:

```
BookSummary is 'A cool book on Windows Management Instrumentation'
```

Creating objects that have properties with embedded objects is a little more involved. You may need to create objects like this in your own applications because your schema uses embedded property objects. The process of creating embedded property objects is not dissimilar to creating instances, covered earlier in the chapter. The general process is to get the class definition and (this is the crucial part) spawn an instance of it. The spawned instance represents the object that you will use when you set the property values. You set all your properties on the spawned instance before calling `SetPropertyValue` (or an assignment using the index operator).

Let's extend the code sample from the earlier section covering the creation of objects. In that section, we created a `Sample_Book` instance when the `Summary` property was declared as using a string data type. Now with the revised `Sample_Book` class definition, let's recreate the `Sample_Book` instance. The following code will do the same task as the MOF compiler did earlier with the MOF code. We have highlighted in bold text the code that we discuss:

```
// Get class so we can spawn an instance of it
ManagementPath path = new ManagementPath();
path.ClassName = "Sample_Book";
path.NamespacePath = "root\\WMIBook";

ManagementClass mc = new ManagementClass(path);

// Make new object
ManagementObject mo = mc.CreateInstance();
```

```
// Set some properties on the object
mo["BookTitle"] = "Developing WMI Solutions";
mo["AuthorName"] = "Gwyn Cole";
mo["NumberOfChapters"] = 11;

// We're going to create the object for the Summary property
// First get the definition of the Sample_BookSummary class
ManagementPath proppath = new ManagementPath();
proppath.ClassName = "Sample_BookSummary";
proppath.NamespacePath = "root\\WMIBook";

ManagementClass propmc = new ManagementClass(proppath);

// Make new Sample_BookSummary object
ManagementObject propmo = propmc.CreateInstance();

// Set property on embedded object
propmo["BookSummary"] =
  "A cool book on Windows Management Instrumentation";

// Finally, set the Summary property
mo["Summary"] = propmo;

// Commit to create instance in WMI
mo.Put();
```

Creating an instance and creating an instance for a property are virtually the same sort of code. You get the class definition, spawn an instance of the class, and set your properties. The only differences between saving management objects and saving property objects are:

1. When you create a management object, you save (commit) it by calling `Put`.
2. When you create a property object, you save (commit) it by calling `SetProperty-Value` (or perform an assignment using the index operator) on the management object.

When you call methods that use parameter objects in either the in- or the out-parameters, then you must write similar code to that demonstrated earlier.

■ Making Asynchronous Calls

The main benefit of accessing management objects asynchronously is that an operation can be started and, if necessary, be cancelled later. This enables an application to be optimized more easily for performance and solves the problem of thread blockage while the operation is in progress.

Developing asynchronous access to management objects requires the development of one or more delegate methods. A delegate method's purpose depends on the type of event that occurs. For instance, when a management object is ready to be passed to the caller from WMI, the .NET management classes call an `ObjectReady` delegate method with the object details supplied through the method's arguments.

Calling an asynchronous method starts the desired operation and returns immediately. The results of the operation are reported to the delegate methods (as events) until the asynchronous operation completes. All asynchronous operations use the `ManagementOperationObserver` class. This class contains the delegate methods (these are like function pointers in C++) for the four different types of events: Progress, ObjectReady, ObjectPut, and Completed. Let's take a look at the `ManagementOperationObserver` class:

```
public class ManagementOperationObserver
{
  // Constructors
  public ManagementOperationObserver();

  // Properties
  public event ProgressEventHandler Progress;
  public event ObjectReadyEventHandler ObjectReady;
  public event ObjectPutEventHandler ObjectPut;
  public event CompletedEventHandler Completed;

  // Methods
  public void Cancel();
};
```

To start an asynchronous operation a `ManagementOperationObserver` object must be created and then the delegate handlers for the types of events that are required must be set. The `Cancel` method allows a caller to cancel a currently executing asynchronous operation. We shall focus on the four event delegate handler properties later.

Let's reimplement the earlier code sample in which a list of running Windows Services was obtained:

```
// Create WQL query
ManagementObjectSearcher query = new ManagementObjectSearcher(
  "SELECT * FROM Win32_Service WHERE Started=true");

// Create class with event handlers
MyQueryObjectAsyncHandler handler = new MyQueryObjectAsyncHandler();

// Create an asynchronous control and handler object
ManagementOperationObserver moo = new ManagementOperationObserver();
```

```
// Set event delegate methods
moo.ObjectReady += new ObjectReadyEventHandler(handler.WMIObject);
moo.Completed += new CompletedEventHandler(handler.Done);

// Start the asynchronous operation
query.Get(moo);

// Wait until the asynchronous operation has completed
while (!handler.Completed)
{
  Console.WriteLine(" Waiting 100ms...");
  System.Threading.Thread.Sleep(100);
}
```

The first step in coding your own asynchronous operations is to develop a handler class. In the sample code this is `MyQueryObjectAsyncHandler`. (We shall discuss this shortly.) The next step is to create the asynchronous operation observer that provides control and event delivery to your handlers. This is followed by passing the `ManagementOperationObserver` object to the asynchronous version of the desired WMI operation. All WMI operations have some way of specifying a `ManagementOperationObserver` object.

Although it may not be obvious, the code sample in fact does receive all the objects that match the WQL query. The delivery of the objects is made through the event handlers on the `MyQueryObjectAsyncHandler` object, `handler`. Two handlers are set up, one for `ObjectReady` events and other for asynchronous operation `Completed` events. Let's take a look at the `MyQueryObjectAsyncHandler` class:

```
public class MyQueryObjectAsyncHandler
{

  // A helper member to assess whether the operation has completed
  private bool completed = false;

  // The CompletedEventHandler delegate
  public void Done(object sender, CompletedEventArgs e)
  {
    completed = true;

    Console.WriteLine("Query has completed!");
    Console.WriteLine("CompletedEventArgs.Status is {0}", e.Status);
  }

  // The ObjectReadyEventHandler delegate
  public void WMIObject(object sender, ObjectReadyEventArgs e)
  {
    Console.WriteLine("Service: '{0}'", e.NewObject["DisplayName"]);
  }
```

```
    // A property to determine if the operation has completed
    public bool Completed
    {
      get
      {
        return completed;
      }
    }
};
```

The `MyQueryObjectAsyncHandler` class has two of the event delegate methods implemented, `WMIObject` and `Done`. The `WMIObject` method conforms to the `Object-ReadyEventHandler` prototype and `Done` conforms to the `CompletedEventHandler` prototype. The `WMIObject` method just outputs the `DisplayName` of the Windows service and the `Done` method outputs the result of the asynchronous operation.

Let's discuss the event delegate methods in detail. The `Progress` delegate handler property (in the `ManagementOperationObserver` class) has the following declaration:

```
public delegate void ProgressEventHandler(object sender,
  ProgressEventArgs e);
```

A method conforming to this prototype (without specifying `delegate`) will be able to receive progress information from the provider. The handler will not be called unless the delegate is specified through the `Progress` property. The `sender` parameter usually points to the `ManagementOperationObserver` object that sent the event. You will find that in most cases, you'll ignore this parameter. This applies to all `ManagementOperationObserver` event handlers. The progress information is supplied through a `ProgressEventArgs` object. The handler should inspect this object to obtain the progress details. Here is the declaration of the `ProgressEventArgs` class:

```
public class ProgressEventArgs: ManagementEventArgs
{
  // Properties
  public int Current {get;}
  public string Message {get;}
  public int UpperBound {get;}
};
```

The progress value is contained in the `Current` property and usually represents a percentage, although this depends on the provider. The total value is contained in the `UpperBound` property and usually represents the total number of instances, but again, this depends on the provider. The `Message` property represents optional additional information regarding the operation's progress. WMI providers do not necessarily support the delivery of progress information.

The `ObjectReady` delegate handler property has the following declaration:

```
public delegate void ObjectReadyEventHandler(object sender,
  ObjectReadyEventArgs e);
```

A method conforming to this prototype (without specifying `delegate`) will be able to receive the management objects from the provider as and when WMI has been able to satisfy the desired operation. The handler will not be called unless the delegate is specified through the `ObjectReady` property. The management object is passed through an `ObjectReadyEventArgs` object. The handler should inspect this object to access the management object. Here is the declaration of the `ObjectReadyEventArgs` class:

```
public class ObjectReadyEventArgs: ManagementEventArgs
{

  // Properties
  public ManagementBaseObject NewObject {get;}
};
```

Inspect the `NewObject` property to gain access to the management object. When performing a query or enumerating all the instances of a class, the assigned `Object-Ready` delegate handler will be called each time a management object satisfies the query. The `ObjectPut` delegate handler property has the following declaration:

```
public delegate void ObjectPutEventHandler(object sender,
  ObjectPutEventArgs e);
```

A method conforming to this prototype (without specifying `delegate`) will be able to receive the details of the `Put` (or commit) operation. The handler will not be called unless the delegate is specified through the `ObjectPut` property. The details are passed through an `ObjectPutEventArgs` object. Here is the declaration of the `ObjectPutEvent-Args` class:

```
public class ObjectPutEventArgs: ManagementEventArgs
{
  // Properties
  public ManagementPath Path {get;}
};
```

When making asynchronous `Put` calls, you might want to inspect the `Path` property. This property is set by the provider to return an object path of a newly created instance.

This is especially useful if the provider assigns or generates a unique value for a key property. The `Completed` delegate handler property has the following declaration:

```
public delegate void CompletedEventHandler(object sender,
  CompletedEventArgs e);
```

A method conforming to this prototype (without specifying `delegate`) will be able to determine the outcome of an asynchronous operation by inspecting the `Completed-EventArgs` object. The handler will not be called unless the delegate is specified through the `Completed` property. Here is the declaration of the `CompletedEventArgs` class:

```
public class CompletedEventArgs : ManagementEventArgs
{
  // Properties
  public ManagementStatus Status {get;}
  public ManagementBaseObject StatusObject {get;}
};
```

The outcome of the operation is supplied through the `Status` property. Check the Platform SDK for all the management status enumeration values.

The `StatusObject` property allows the provider to return very rich information about the error or status of an operation. This is especially useful where the error and/or status simply cannot be encapsulated in the `ManagementStatus` enumeration. When writing your own providers, keep this in mind if you want richer information provided to the client. The `StatusObject` property works like any other management object in which inspecting the properties of the object provides the detailed information. Making asynchronous calls is the only means of getting at this rich information.

▪ Overview of Events

One of the most powerful features in WMI is that it has the capability to deliver events when something interesting happens. "Something interesting" might include being notified when disk space runs low on a machine. The event mechanism employed by WMI is based on a publishing and subscription approach. An event is considered published when either a client or an event provider delivers it to WMI. For a fully detailed explanation of WMI events, refer to Chapter 7.

As mentioned in Chapter 7, no events will be delivered unless an event consumer subscribes for them. All event subscriptions are made using a WQL event query. To demonstrate what an event query looks like, let's make a subscription to be notified when the CD-ROM drive management object changes:

```
SELECT * FROM __InstanceModificationEvent WITHIN 5 WHERE
   TargetInstance ISA "Win32_CDROMDrive"
```

The above query asks to be notified for any changes to any `Win32_CDROMDrive` management object (perhaps they have more than one CD-ROM drive). If the CD-ROM drive door opens and closes, two events will get fired as each operation causes a change to the management object. All event queries should start with `SELECT *`; WMI does not support event queries that specify properties in the SELECT statement. If properties are specified, WMI ignores them and treats the query as `SELECT *`.

The next piece of information the event query requires is the type of event to which the consumer is subscribing. The earlier query asked to be notified for the intrinsic event, `__InstanceModificationEvent`. Most intrinsic event queries must specify how often WMI should poll the provider to determine if there are any changes to the management objects. This is the reason for the `WITHIN` clause. The query instructs WMI to poll all the CD-ROM drives every 5 seconds for modification changes. Next, the event query needs to know what object class it should monitor; this is the purpose of the `ISA` operator. The `ISA` operator requests notification of events for any class deriving from the *specified* class. The `TargetInstance` is a property on the event class.

Let's review the query: It requests notification every 5 seconds for any instance modification events for all instances that are members of any class deriving from `Win32_CDROMDrive`. To try out the various types of event subscriptions, go to Appendix A for a short tutorial on using the WMI SDK event tools. Appendix B covers a short tutorial on using the WMI server explorer in Microsoft Visual Studio .NET, which includes support for making event subscriptions.

■ Writing Applications to Receive Asynchronous Events

There are two choices for event notification: polling for the event deliveries yourself or having them delivered to you asynchronously. Synchronous event notification is not possible because of the nature of events. Events get delivered to the consumer at any time after the event query is registered.

As with the other asynchronous calls you have seen, you must supply one or more delegate methods to handle the events fired from the .NET Framework. Whenever WMI delivers an event, the .NET Framework calls your delegated method with the event details supplied through method arguments. We discussed asynchronous method calls earlier in the chapter.

WMI asynchronous event operations use the `ManagementEventWatcher` class. This class contains the delegate methods (these are like function pointers in C++) for the two different types of .NET Framework events, `EventArrived` and `Stopped`. The event watcher manages all the event interactions between WMI and caller (that is, the application). Let's take a look at the ManagementEventWatcher class:

```
public class ManagementEventWatcher
{
  // Constructors
  public ManagementEventWatcher();
  public ManagementEventWatcher(EventQuery query);
  public ManagementEventWatcher(string query);
  public ManagementEventWatcher(ManagementScope scope, EventQuery
    query,  EventWatcherOptions options);

  // Properties
  public EventWatcherOptions Options {get; set;}
  public EventQuery Query {get; set;}

  // Event delegates
  public event EventArrivedEventHandler EventArrived;
  public event StoppedEventHandler Stopped;

  // Methods
  public void Start();
  public void Stop();
  public ManagementBaseObject WaitForNextEvent();
};
```

To start an asynchronous operation, a ManagementEventWatcher object must be created and then the delegate handlers for the types of events that are required must be set. The Start method actually registers the event watcher with WMI as an event consumer. This is when the delegate event handlers can expect to receive WMI events as and when they occur. The Stop method unregisters the event watcher as an event consumer. The WaitForNextEvent method is used only when the event watcher is configured as a semisynchronous event consumer. We discuss this in the next section and discuss the two event delegate handler properties later.

The event query can be specified in one of two ways. The event query can be either specified as a string or as an EventQuery based object when a ManagementEventWatcher object is created. The resulting event query can be accessed through the Query property. If the ManagementEventWatcher was created using the default constructor, you can supply the query afterward by setting the Query property (as long as it is before Start is called). The next code sample will supply the event query as a string.

You should use asynchronous event subscription when you want event notifications to be delivered in the background using another thread. The thread that performs the event query subscription is available immediately to perform other tasks. The .NET Framework neatly manages the background thread.

The following code sample demonstrates how to asynchronously subscribe for event notifications:

```
string eventquery = "SELECT * FROM __InstanceModificationEvent
  WITHIN 5 WHERE TargetInstance ISA \"Win32_CDROMDrive\"";

// Create class with event handlers
MyEventAsyncHandler handler = new MyEventAsyncHandler();

// Create an asynchronous event watcher
ManagementEventWatcher watcher =
  new ManagementEventWatcher(eventquery);

// Set event delegate methods
watcher.EventArrived +=
  new EventArrivedEventHandler(handler.EventArrived);
watcher.Stopped += new StoppedEventHandler(handler.StoppedEvent);

// Register the watcher as an event consumer
watcher.Start();

// Thread is available to do other stuff. In this case, waits//
for 30 seconds
System.Threading.Thread.Sleep(30000);

// Stop and the watcher is no longer a registered event consumer
watcher.Stop();
```

The event query in the sample code instructs WMI to poll all the CR-ROM drives every 5 seconds, and if there are any changes to any of the CD-ROM drives, to send an event notification. Each time a WMI event gets delivered to a .NET event watcher (an event consumer), the `EventArrived` delegate method will be called. In the code sample, after the event watcher has registered with WMI (through `Start`), the calling thread just hangs around for 30 seconds before unregistering itself as an event consumer. This means that WMI events are captured only for a 30-second window (if any events are fired at all). Your applications will probably do something more useful than just sitting around for 30 seconds.

The WMI events are delivered through the delegate handlers in the `MyEventAsync-Handler` class (in this case). The event handlers determine how the WMI event should be processed, so let's have a look at what the handlers do:

```
public class MyEventAsyncHandler
{
  public void EventArrived(object sender, EventArrivedEventArgs e)
  {
    // Extract the TargetInstance from the __InstanceModificationEvent
```

```
    ManagementBaseObject TargetInstance =
      (ManagementBaseObject)e.NewEvent["TargetInstance"];

    Console.WriteLine("Received a {0} event of type {1}",
      e.NewEvent["__CLASS"], TargetInstance["__CLASS"]);
  }

  public void StoppedEvent(object sender, StoppedEventArgs e)
  {
    Console.WriteLine("StoppedEventArgs.Status is {0}", e.Status);
  }
}
```

The `EventArrived` handler simply outputs to the console what type of event occurred (we're expecting `__InstanceModificationEvent`) and the class of the management object that had changed (in `TargetInstance`). The `StoppedEvent` handler simply outputs to the console how the event watcher was stopped.

The `EventArrived` delegate handler property has the following declaration:

```
public delegate void EventArrivedEventHandler(object sender,
  EventArrivedEventArgs e);
```

A method conforming to this prototype (without specifying `delegate`) will be able to receive the event objects from WMI as and when an event matches the event query. The handler will not be called unless the delegate is specified through the `Event-Arrived` property. The `sender` parameter points to the `ManagementEventWatcher` event consumer that registered for the event. You will find that in most cases, you'll ignore this parameter. This applies to all `ManagementEventWatcher` event handlers. The event object is passed through an `EventArrivedEventArgs` object. The handler should inspect this object to access the details about the WMI event. Here is the declaration of the `EventArrivedEventArgs` class:

```
public class EventArrivedEventArgs: ManagementEventArgs
{
  // Properties
  public ManagementBaseObject NewEvent {get;}
};
```

Inspect the `NewEvent` property to gain access to the WMI event. The assigned `Event-Arrived` delegate handler will be called each time WMI is able to match an event with the event query.

The `Stopped` delegate handler property has the following declaration:

```
public delegate void StoppedEventHandler(object sender,
  StoppedEventArgs e);
```

A method conforming to this prototype (without specifying `delegate`) will be able to identify when the event consumer stopped being registered to receive events from WMI. The handler will not be called unless the delegate is specified through the `Stopped` property. The event object is passed through an `StoppedEventArgs` object. The handler should inspect the `Status` property to understand why the event watcher is no longer an event consumer. Here is the declaration of the `StoppedEventArgs` class:

```
public class StoppedEventArgs: ManagementEventArgs
{
    // Properties
    public ManagementStatus Status {get;}
};
```

▪ Writing Applications to Receive Semisynchronous Events

Capturing WMI events semisynchronously offers a solution through which an application thread can start and receive WMI events using a polling technique. No other threads are required and the executing thread blocks for a predefined time-out. The time-out can be as short or as long as is required. Developing applications to receive semisynchronous events reduces code complexity by not having to develop event handlers. Instead, the events are usually processed inline.

Developing code to receive semisynchronous WMI events is quite similar to setting up an asynchronous event watcher. In an asynchronous event watcher, you have to create the delegate event methods and assign them to the event watcher. A semisynchronous event watcher leaves the `EventArrived` event handler property with a null value and the `Timeout` property is set to a predefined time-out.

Let's examine some sample code that subscribes for event notification using the query discussed earlier. The sample code that follows demonstrates how to receive just one semisynchronous WMI event. To receive multiple events typically would require a `while` loop. Let's have a look:

```
// Create the event query
WqlEventQuery query = new WqlEventQuery("__InstanceModificationEvent",
  new TimeSpan(0, 0, 5), "TargetInstance ISA \"Win32_CDROMDrive\"");

// Specify a timeout of 15 seconds
EventWatcherOptions options = new EventWatcherOptions();
options.Timeout = new TimeSpan(0, 0, 15);

// Make ourselves an event watcher
ManagementEventWatcher watcher =
  new ManagementEventWatcher(null, query, options);
```

```
try
{
  // Wait for an event to occur
  ManagementBaseObject NewEvent = watcher.WaitForNextEvent();

  // Extract the TargetInstance from the __InstanceModificationEvent
  ManagementBaseObject TargetInstance =
    (ManagementBaseObject)NewEvent["TargetInstance"];

  Console.WriteLine("Received a {0} event of type {1}",
    NewEvent["__CLASS"], TargetInstance["__CLASS"]);
}
catch(System.Management.ManagementException e)
{
  // Maybe the event timed-out after 15 seconds?
  Console.WriteLine("Caught ManagementException ->'{0}'", e.Message);
}

// Stop receiving events
watcher.Stop();
```

Notice how the query is specified? This demonstrates the other .NET Framework alternatives in setting up an event query. The `WqlEventQuery` class ensures that the query is a WQL event query. (WQL is the only currently supported WMI query language.) The `EventQuery` class could have also been used.

The next task is to setup the time-out that will be used when waiting for an event to occur. To specify the time-out requires the `EventWatcherOptions` class. Like the other options classes, it is derived from `ManagementOptions`. Setting the `Timeout` property, which is inherited from `ManagementOptions`, provides the event watcher with a predefined time-out when waiting for an event. Both the query and the event watcher options are passed when the `ManagementEventWatcher` object is created. Notice that a semisynchronous event consumer does not require `Start` to be called. The `Start` method is used by an asynchronous event consumer to register the event watcher (review the previous section for more information). The difference between asynchronous and semisynchronous event handling is that the `WaitForNextEvent` method replaces the functionality provided by the asynchronous `EventArrived` event handler. The `WaitForNextEvent` method blocks until a WMI event occurs. If no event matches the event query within the specified time-out (15 seconds in our case), `WaitForNextEvent` throws a time-out `ManagementException`. You will notice that the code to extract the details of the WMI event is similar to the asynchronous `EventArrived` delegated handler. It merely outputs what type of event occurred and the class of the object that had changed. Finally, the semisynchronous event watcher is unregistered from WMI as an event consumer, using `Stop`.

Let's look at the `EventWatcherOptions` class:

```
public class EventWatcherOptions: ManagementOptions
{
  // Constructors
  public EventWatcherOptions();
  public EventWatcherOptions(ManagementNamedValueCollection context,
    TimeSpan timeout, int blockSize);

  // Properties
  public int BlockSize {get; set;}
};
```

Apart from the inherited properties `Context` and `Timeout`, the options class defines `BlockSize`. The `BlockSize` property specifies how many events to wait for before returning from a block operation.

■ Managing Connections to WMI

At this point in the chapter, you've seen code samples in which the connections to WMI have been automatically managed by the .NET management classes. This probably is good enough for most cases you are likely to encounter. The .NET management classes give you the opportunity to fine-tune your connections to WMI namespaces, which could possibly be on different machines. You may also discover that the providers for the classes you want to access require higher security privileges, or that you must provide specific security credentials for another authorized user to gain access to a particular management namespace. There are many other reasons why you might want to fine-tune access to WMI in .NET applications.

Before diving into the details of managing connections to WMI, let's take a quick tour of the following code sample that encompasses all the main points we want to bring to your attention:

```
ConnectionOptions options = new ConnectionOptions();

options.Authentication = AuthenticationLevel.Call;
options.Impersonation = ImpersonationLevel.Impersonate;
options.EnablePrivileges = true;
options.Locale = "MS_409";
options.Username = "DOMAIN_A\\gcole";
options.Password = "mypassword";

ManagementScope ms = new ManagementScope("\\\\OSAKA\\root\\CIMV2",
  options);

// Explicit connection to WMI namespace
ms.Connect();
```

```
ManagementObject mo = new ManagementObject("Win32_Share.Name=\"C$\"");

// Reuse existing connection for this ManagementObject retrieval
mo.Scope = ms;

// Connection scope used when object is retrieved here
mo.Get();

Console.WriteLine("Win32_Share.Name=\"C$\" path is {0}", mo["Path"]);
```

First, notice that there is another options class, ConnectionOptions. This also derives from ManagementOptions and contains many important properties which we shall discuss.

All connections to WMI are managed through the ManagementScope class. This class allows you to set up a connection to a machine and namespace that is retained for the lifetime of a management scope object. The connection is physically set up after the Connect method is called. If there are any problems in making the connection, then you can expect to catch a ManagementException that will detail the nature of the problem—an access-denied error, for instance.

After you have a connected ManagementScope object, you can use it in the .NET management classes ManagementObject, ManagementClass, ManagementObjectSearcher, and ManagementEventWatcher, which all have a property called Scope. Assigning a management scope object to Scope allows an already configured WMI connection session to be supplied for an operation. The preceding code sample does this. The management object mo uses the connection set up by ms. When the shared directory object is retrieved from WMI, it is done so with the connection set up through ms.

Let's take a look at the ManagementScope class:

```
public class ManagementScope: ICloneable
{
  // Constructors
  public ManagementScope();
  public ManagementScope(ManagementPath path);
  public ManagementScope(string path);
  public ManagementScope(ManagementPath path, ConnectionOptions
    options);
  public ManagementScope(string path, ConnectionOptions options);

  // Properties
  public bool IsConnected {get;}
  public ConnectionOptions Options {get; set;}
  public ManagementPath Path {get; set;}

  // Methods
  public void Connect();
};
```

The `IsConnected` property can be used to evaluate whether a connection to WMI exists. The management path of the WMI connection can be set and retrieved from the `Path` property. However, the `Path` property is usually set up with one of the `ManagementScope` constructors.

Let's move our attention to the all-important `ConnectionOptions` class:

```
public class ConnectionOptions: ManagementOptions
{
  // Constructors
  public ConnectionOptions();
  public ConnectionOptions(string locale, string username,
    string password, string authority,
    ImpersonationLevel impersonation,
    AuthenticationLevel authentication,
    bool enablePrivileges, ManagementNamedValueCollection context,
    TimeSpan timeout);

  // Properties
  public AuthenticationLevel Authentication {get; set;}
  public ImpersonationLevel Impersonation {get; set;}
  public string Locale {get; set;}
  public string Username {get; set;}
  public string Password {set;}
  public string Authority {get; set;}
  public bool EnablePrivileges {get; set;}
};
```

This class is tremendously important because it is your gateway to set up a connection that has the specific security settings required to access the management objects you want to query or manipulate.[2] Let's look at each property in detail.

Our aim for the rest of this section is to provide you with enough information that can be of some practical use. In particular, we want to discuss the authentication level and impersonation level options that can be specified. The enumeration values you pass for these properties also depend on what the providers require to do their work.

Authentication is the circumstance in which one principle (your client) proves its identity to another principle (ultimately the WMI provider). To specify the type of authentication you want requires that the `Authentication` property be set to one of the `AuthenticationLevel` enumeration values. In most cases, all you will need is `Connect`. This value requires the client to prove its identity on the first connection with WMI, which is usually adequate for most interactions. Supplying `Call` causes the client to prove its identity on every WMI call it makes. Alternatively, you can use `Default`,

---

2. For a more detailed discussion on security, we recommend reading *Programming Windows Security* by Keith Brown (ISBN 0-201-60442-6).

which allows DCOM layer to choose the authentication level using its normal security blanket negotiation algorithm (under Windows 2000). Under Windows NT 4.0, this value defaults to `Connect`. Check the MSDN documentation for more information on the other `AuthenticationLevel` enumeration values.

Impersonation specifies what a principle on another machine is allowed to do with your security context. To specify what type of impersonation you want requires that the `Impersonation` property be set to one of the `ImpersonationLevel` enumeration values. `Impersonate` allows WMI and the providers to perform tasks on your behalf. This ultimately means that you can access any local executive objects that you have permission to access. Any calls made by a WMI provider to another machine will result in an access-denied error. This level of impersonation does not allow your security context to be passed to anybody else. As we mentioned earlier, providers can dictate the minimum impersonation level. Consider the following—if a provider performs some task that results in another WMI call to some other machine on the network, then your security context needs to be passed. This is called *delegation* and you must use `Delegate`. Delegation is a form of impersonation that allows WMI to pass your security context to another machine so that machine can make calls on your behalf. However, the downside to delegation is that your security credentials can be passed to an unlimited number of other machines and those machines can perform tasks on your behalf (and can be audited). Needless to say, this level of impersonation is dangerous if you do not completely trust the provider.

The `Locale` property allows you to specify the locale that will be used to retrieve localized class information, such as class or property descriptions. The format of this property starts with "MS_" and you append the Win32 LCID locale identifier in hex. U.S. English is `"MS_409"` and German is `"MS_407"`. Specifying this property makes sense only when you have a localized namespace. If a namespace is localized in U.S. English and German, you will see sub- (or child) namespaces called `"ms_409"` and `"ms_407"` respectively. Localized namespaces use amended qualifiers, which were covered briefly earlier in the chapter. For a more detailed discussion of localized namespaces, refer to Chapter 7.

When making a connection to a different machine, you can optionally include the `Username` and `Password` properties to specify the user credentials with which to connect. Local connections do not require these properties to be specified and the currently logged-on user credentials are used. You may need to complete these properties if you do not want to use the currently logged-on user for a connection to another machine. The `Username` property can also include the domain of the user/principle, for example, `DOMAIN_A\User_A`.

If you need to use Kerberos security authentication or to use a different NTLM domain to authenticate the user credentials, then you specify the authority in the `Authority` property. In most cases, you will just leave the `Authority` property empty, which will cause the default domain security authority of the currently logged-in user to be used. To use Kerberos authentication, you must pass a string formatted like this: "Kerberos:<principle name>", where <principle name> is the principle of the machine against which to authenticate. To use NTLM authentication for a specific domain, you must pass a string formatted like this: "NTLMDOMAIN:<domain name>", where <domain name> is the domain against which to authenticate. If you specify this property, do not include domain information in the Username property.

All the classes we have discussed so far have not required any special security privileges to access instance data. However, you will more than likely come across classes that fall into this category. An example is the Windows event log WMI class, Win32_NTLogEvent, which requires that the SeSecurityPrivilege be set when accessing instance data. Let's have a look at the class:

```
[
  dynamic,
  provider("MS_NT_EVENTLOG_PROVIDER"),
  EnumPrivileges {"SeSecurityPrivilege"}
]
class Win32_NTLogEvent
{
  [key] uint32 RecordNumber;
  [key] string Logfile;
  uint32 EventIdentifier;
  uint16 EventCode;
  string SourceName;
  .... ..
  ...
};
```

The EnumPrivileges qualifier contains an array of strings that represent the privilege names of the security privileges. The security privileges must be set on the thread that wants to access any information from the management class or a management object.

The .NET Framework makes it very easy to enable the security privileges of a management class. All that is required is to set up a connection in which the connection options have the EnablePrivileges property set to true. To get an idea of what happens out of sight, review Chapter 7. You will realize quickly how useful it is to set one property that automatically applies the correct security privileges on the calling thread.

■ Summary

This chapter has introduced you to virtually every aspect of managing objects in WMI using the .NET Framework management classes. We explained some of the most fundamental and basic operations through which objects could be accessed, created, deleted, updated, enumerated, and queried. Our coverage of methods provided you with a powerful mechanism for adding behavior to classes and objects. Detailed discussion outlined how properties could be manipulated, especially those that are either objects or arrays.

We provided details about how to make asynchronous calls within your own applications. (Asynchronous calls make your applications much more responsive and allow for operations to be easily cancelled.) Our very quick introduction to WMI events discussed both semisynchronous and asynchronous event subscriptions in detail.

Throughout the chapter, some off-topic discussions brought your attention to some of the more obscure functionality provided by the .NET management classes, such as determining whether or not a property is locally defined. In addition, we pointed out some programming shortcuts (such as the management class's `Derivation` property) to highlight that it is worth taking some time to explore fully what is available to you in the .NET management classes.

Finally, we discussed in detail how you can manage your connections to WMI. This chiefly covered how you can set up a connection with very specific options, including advanced security configuration.

Ten Fast Facts: Developing .NET Management Applications

1. Connections to WMI are automatically managed by the .NET Framework. However, you can manage and set up your own connections using the `ManagementScope` class.

2. The `ManagementObject` class makes it easy to gain access to a WMI management object. Simply supply your own object path or use the `ManagementObjectCollection` to gain access to each management object.

3. The .NET Framework management classes have an "options" class that unifies all the options for a particular operation. The option classes are inherited from `ManagementOptions`.

4. Be aware that properties may supply `Values` and `ValueMap` qualifiers to describe how to interpret property data.

5. WMI offers a powerful means to extract information from the management environment by using data queries. Data queries are specified using WQL and can be assembled through one of the many query classes, starting with `ObjectQuery`.

6. Many WMI classes use methods to add behavior. Always determine if the class you want to use has any methods in which you may be interested. In particular, many classes in the CIMV2 namespace use methods to create and update management objects. Call `InvokeMethod` on either the `ManagementObject` or the `ManagementClass` to execute a method.

7. Interpreting WMI class properties involves dealing with C# data types. If you are unsure what data types you need to use, consult Table 8.1.

8. Always consider using asynchronous techniques in your management applications. This will make your applications more responsive.

9. Event notification is one of WMI's most powerful features. WMI has the capability to deliver events when something interesting happens. "Something interesting" might include being notified when disk space runs low on a machine, for example. Use the `ManagementEventWatcher` class to make an event subscription. Also, explore which of the event query classes is the most appropriate for your situation, starting with `EventQuery`.

10. The .NET Framework has many useful helper functions, more than those covered in this chapter. It is worth taking some time to explore fully what is available to you in the .NET management classes.

Chapter 9

Developing MMC Snap-ins

Chapter 12 covers in detail how applications can expose management objects with Windows Management Instrumentation (WMI). This chapter explores how you can develop management user interfaces to manage your own management objects. The Microsoft Management Console is Microsoft's answer to providing a consistent user interface in which administrators can find all their management tools. Let's review where management tools were a few years ago to see why the Microsoft Management Console was developed.

In recent years, networked computer systems have become more complex and as a result have become harder to administer. Administrators in the past had relatively simple tasks compared to today. Their tasks included correctly setting security permissions for users and configuring print servers. Now, computer systems are used for many more business functions within the enterprise, and system administration has become a complex task. The administrator's tasks now include the setting up of the Active Directory, IP telephony solutions, e-mail servers, unified messaging solutions, complex databases, and many more. System administration became fragmented as software and hardware vendors developed their own administration tools with different and usually nonstandard user interfaces. The administrator was overwhelmed with the array of administration tools. An administrator who wanted to administer some aspect of the system had to find the correct program before changes could be made. In addition, every time the system expanded with new services, the administrator had another learning curve in using the new administration tools. This resulted in another program to add to the already vast collection of administration software. Administration tools and the knowledge of and the ability to find the correct ones were fragmented across the system. This ultimately increased the total cost of ownership. To address this problem, Microsoft developed the

Microsoft Management Console (MMC). MMC is an administration environment that integrates all machine, network, and systems management in one place. There are no more fragmented administration tools across the system: MMC is the center point for any administration facility. An administrator who can't find the appropriate tool simply looks for it in the list of installed administration tools. All MMC administration software has a similar look and feel, which helps reduce the learning curve required by the administrator. This moves toward a lower total cost of ownership. In addition, administrators, especially in large production sites, also rely on the ability to script their administration tasks. Making administration possible through WMI, which is scriptable, moves further toward a lower total cost of ownership. We cover scripting WMI from an administrator's perspective in Chapter 10.

MMC by itself does not do anything useful for the administrator. Instead, it relies on snap-ins that form the administration tool-set. Snap-ins hook into the MMC user interface and extend it with the administration tasks of the hardware or software. The Explorer-like user interface is extended by snap-ins that add menus, toolbars, property sheets, wizards, and new items within both the scope and result panes. Microsoft provides some guidelines that vendors writing MMC snap-ins should follow in an effort to make all administration tools coexist and be consistent with each other.

Administrators can personalize their administration environments by selecting one or more snap-ins to the console and saving it to a file. This enables them to make different console files for all their common administration tools.

Figure 9.1 shows a screen shot of the management console from the Computer Management snap-in. This snap-in can administer the most common administration tasks for a single machine. The scope pane allows snap-ins to partition their administration tasks into different namespaces, such as the Shared Folders item. The result pane usually contains a collection of items that relate to the namespace. The Shares namespace lists all the machine's shared folders and has a toolbar button for creating new, shared folders. The toolbar is a convenient host for common tasks. Every snap-in item has a common set of verbs in either the scope or the result panes. These verbs include rename, delete, refresh, and properties. Verbs help in maintaining a consistent user interface and a set of operations across all snap-ins. The E$ shared folder in Figure 9.1 displays two enabled verbs: properties and refresh. All items can individually enable the supported verbs that are communicated through the context menu and toolbar.

■ Snap-in Architecture

MMC categorizes two types of snap-ins: primary and extension. Primary (or standalone) snap-ins provide the entry point for any administration tool. This type of snap-in is added to the root of the console tree in the scope pane and has full control over all

Standard verbs (e.g., refresh, delete, and properties) provided by the MMC user interface

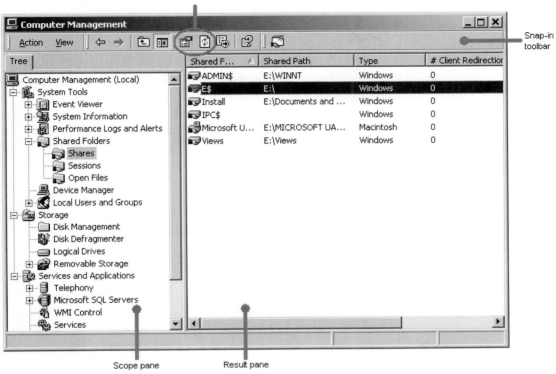

Figure 9.1 The Microsoft Management Console

aspects of the user interface. Extension snap-ins can extend any other snap-in (both primary and extension) by extending its namespace, menus, toolbars, taskpads, and property pages. The extension snap-in architecture provides a good solution in separating related but different administration tasks into smaller and more maintainable code bases.

Do you develop a primary snap-in or do you develop an extension snap-in? The basic rule to follow is:

1. If your administration requirements are distinct from any other existing administration snap-in, then develop a primary snap-in.

2. If your administration requirements are related but different from an existing administration snap-in (primary or extension), develop an extension snap-in. For instance, if you want to provide system information for your software, then

you should consider an extension snap-in to extend the System Information snap-in.

How does any snap-in know how to extend another snap-in? Every type of item within the console must have a unique identifier called a GUID (globally unique identifier). This is fundamental to the snap-in extension architecture. Figure 9.2 illustrates the GUIDs that identify two types of items within the Shared Folders snap-in. If you need to extend the Shared Folders item, you do so using its GUID identifier to bind it to the item.

Note that not every item in the console must have a unique GUID. Every *type of item* must have a unique GUID. Consider the Shares item in the Shared Folders snap-in. All the *shares* listed in the result pane have the same GUID because they are all of the same *item type*. Extending this item affects all the Share items in the result pane.

Registration brings the snap-in architecture to life. All snap-ins make registrations in the registry, and MMC uses this information to determine what snap-ins to load and what notifications to deliver to them.

When administrators want to construct their own personalized administration environments, they can use the Add/Remove Snap-ins menu item. From the list of installed snap-ins, administrators can add one or more primary snap-ins to the console. The screen shot in Figure 9.3 displays a list of installed primary snap-ins.

One of the useful features in MMC is that you can create configuration files that store references to a number of snap-ins. The console loads the snap-ins when the file opens. Software vendors use this mechanism for their own administration environments. For instance, Windows 2000 Computer Management uses a configuration file called compmgmt.msc.

■ Getting Started

The rest of this chapter focuses on the COM APIs that allow you to integrate with the Microsoft Management Console (version 1.2). We assume that you are familiar with C++ programming, COM (Component Object Model), and ATL (Active Template Library). The first half of this chapter covers the basics, probably enough for most peo-

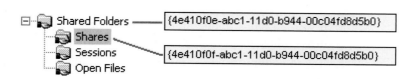

Figure 9.2 MMC item unique identifiers

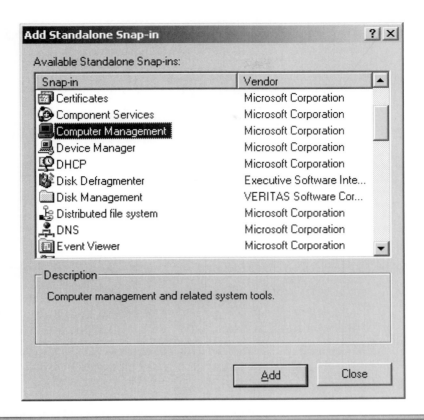

Figure 9.3 MMC's installed snap-ins list

ple, and the second half covers more advanced topics. You may consider this chapter an introduction to snap-in development. Therefore, you will not find any deep analysis of every interface and method call, but after completing it, you should know enough to find what you need. The key to understanding snap-in development is knowing which interfaces need to be provided by the snap-in and which interfaces are provided by the console. Let's examine the diagram in Figure 9.4.

The diagram clearly shows that a snap-in typically implements two COM coclasses: the snap-in and its about information. Don't be alarmed at the number of interfaces that need to be implemented by the snap-in. You need to implement only the interfaces for the features that you plan to support. If you do not want to add any buttons to the toolbar, you do not need to implement the IExtendControlbar interface. ATI's snap-in support has implementations for the most common interfaces. The snap-in's about information is provided through the ISnapinAbout interface and is used when displaying the Add/Remove Snap-in's dialog. The console interfaces provide a set of services that snap-ins use to interact and customize the administration user interface.

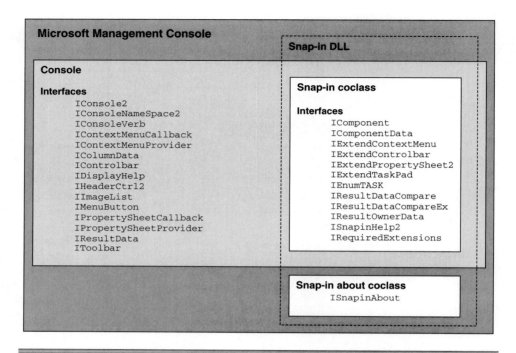

Figure 9.4 MMC interfaces and snap-in components

For example, the `IConsoleNameSpace2::InsertItem` call will add an item into the console's tree in the scope pane. Table 9.1 briefly describes what each of the console interfaces means to the snap-in.

The snap-in implements a number of interfaces to deliver its user interface. For instance, if a snap-in wants to add some menu items, it must implement the `IExtendContextMenu` interface. The menu items are added when the console calls the snap-in's implementation of `AddMenuItems`. The interfaces that determine the snap-in's capabilities are briefly discussed in Table 9.2.

We hope you now have a rough idea of the services provided by the console and the snap-in interfaces that you can implement. Assuming that most snap-ins will extend menus, toolbars, and property sheets, we shall focus specifically on these through the first half of this chapter.

Let's have a quick look at a snap-in in Figure 9.5. The entry point for any snap-in is the scope pane object. The console creates this object and calls `Initialize` on the `IComponentData` interface. The `Initialize` method supplies the snap-in with an `IConsole` interface—this later becomes the lifeline for the snap-in so that it can socialize with the console. All future interactions with the `IComponentData` interface allow the snap-in to extend the scope pane user interface. The `IComponentData::CreateComponent` method is an exception—the console calls this to instantiate a result pane object

Table 9.1 MMC Console Interfaces

Console Interface	Comment
IConsole2	Provides core console services, like setting up image lists, obtaining the console's window handle, expanding and selecting items in the namespace, and updating all views of the snap-in. MMC passes a pointer to this interface when the snap-in is being initialized.
IConsoleNameSpace2	Allows the snap-in to add new items to the scope pane with support for updating the items, navigating the child/parent relationships, and deleting items.
IConsoleVerb	Allows the snap-in to manage the state of the verbs available for an item. It is the snap-in's responsibility to correctly set up the verbs when an item is selected.
IContextMenuCallback	Allows the snap-in to add menu items to a context menu. You'll rarely need to use this interface when using ATL's snap-in support.
IContextMenuProvider	Allows the snap-in to provide its own context menu. You'll rarely need to use this interface unless you are using a customized result view.
ColumnData	MMC automatically retains column configuration by the user and persists the data into the configuration file (.msc). This interface allows snap-ins to gain access to the user-defined column configuration. For example, a snap-in may not want to fetch data for columns that are hidden in order to improve performance.
IControlbar	Allows the snap-in to add menus and toolbars in the console. You'll rarely need to use this interface when using ATL's snap-in support.
IDisplayHelp	Allows the snap-in to display help for an item.
IHeaderCtrl2	Allows the snap-in to insert, remove, and change column configuration.
IImageList	Allows the snap-in to set up image lists that will be used for its user interface— the scope and result pane items, for instance.
IMenuButton	Allows the snap-in to add menu items to the console's menu bar. There is only one menu bar per console view. Depending on the function of the snap-in, this generally does not get used.
IPropertySheetCallback	Allows the snap-in to add property pages to a property sheet.
IPropertySheetProvider	Allows the snap-in to provide its own property sheet or wizard without responding to the properties verb. You'll rarely need to use this interface unless you're planning on providing customized property sheets and wizards.
IResultData	Allows the snap-in to add new items to the result pane with support for updating the items, enumerating the result list, and deleting items.
IToolbar	Allows the snap-in to add buttons to the console's toolbar. You'll rarely need to use this interface when using ATL's snap-in support.

Table 9.2 MMC Snap-in Interfaces

Snap-in Interface	Comment
IComponent	This implements the snap-in's interactions with items in the result pane. All snap-ins should implement this interface.
IComponentData	This implements the snap-in's interactions with items in the scope pane. All snap-ins should implement this interface.
IExtendContextMenu	Implement this interface only if the snap-in will add context menu items.
IExtendControlbar	Implement this interface only if the snap-in will add toolbars or menu items to the console's control bar.
IExtendPropertySheet2	Implement this interface only if the snap-in will add property pages.
IExtendTaskpad	Implement this interface only if the snap-in will support taskpads. The IEnumTASK also must be implemented.
IEnumTASK	Implement this interface only if the snap-in will add one or more tasks to a taskpad. The IExtendTaskpad also must be implemented.
IResultDataCompare	Implement this interface only if you want the snap-in to compare result items so that the items can be sorted in the result pane.
IResultDataCompareEx	Similar to IResultDataCompare except that scope items can also be compared.
IResultOwnerData	Implement this interface only if the snap-in plans to use virtual lists for the list view control in the result pane.
ISnapinHelp2	Implement this interface only if the snap-in provides help for items in the scope and/or result panes.
IRequiredExtensions	Implement this interface only if the snap-in requires that the console load other extension snap-ins. This is irrespective of the extension snap-ins specified in the Add/Remove Snap-ins console menu item.
ISnapinAbout	This implements the snap-in's about information. This includes the snap-in description, vendor details, and an icon.

that extends the result pane's user interface. The console initializes the result pane object (that is, the IComponent interface) in a similar way to the scope pane object by calling Initialize. Both the scope and result pane objects (Figure 9.5) support a number of interfaces that extend specific console user interface elements. All items in the scope and result panes are represented as objects that support the IDataObject interface. The IDataObject interface is used through many Windows APIs and was originally used for OLE drag-and-drop operations. The concept behind this interface is that objects can expose a number of data formats (or structures) that anybody else can read. This provides a perfect solution for snap-ins because both primary and extension

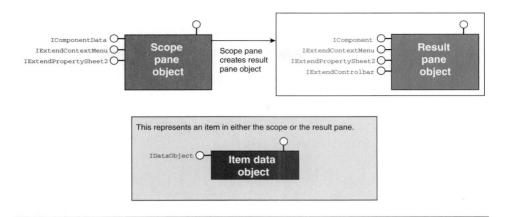

Figure 9.5   MMC snap-in objects

snap-ins can exchange information about an item. Snap-in items expose the following information using the **IDataObject** interface.

- The item's GUID (both in binary and string form)
- The item's display name
- The snap-in's class identifier (CLSID)
- The item's object data (provided through ATL)

There are more data structures and formats exposed by items, but we discuss them later in the chapter. The Figure 9.5 diagram can be expressed simply as:

A snap-in provides the console with three types of objects. The *scope* and *result* pane objects extend the console's user interface. The *item* object allows communication with other snap-in items and the console.

Another important aspect of snap-in development is controlling the delivery of an item's user interface. This depends, in part, on how an item responds to MMC notifications. Item notifications are another important communication medium for a snap-in. For instance, when a user selects or expands an item in the user interface, a notification gets delivered to the appropriate item. All notifications are delivered through the **Notify** method on either the **IComponentData** or **IComponent** interface. Here are a few examples:

MMCN_SELECT—received when an item is selected.

MMCN_EXPAND—received when an item is expanded.

`MMCN_PROPERTY_CHANGE`—received when a property sheet changes values in an item.

`MMCN_REFRESH`—received in response to the refresh verb.

`MMCN_RENAME`—received in response to the rename verb.

`MMCN_DELETE`—received in response to the delete verb.

`MMCN_COLUMN_CLICK`—received when a user clicks a column header.

■ Snap-in Implementation Basics

Typical snap-in development largely relies on the COM infrastructure provided by ATL.[1] All snap-ins are COM components that implement **IComponentData** and friends. When you embark on a snap-in development project, we highly recommend that you use the Microsoft Visual C++ Developer Studio MMC snap-in wizard. This generates boilerplate code that starts you in the right direction. All the ATL snap-in support is encapsulated in the atlsnap.h header file. Perform the following steps to create an MMC snap-in project with Visual C++ Developer Studio 6.0:

1. Load Visual C++ Developer Studio 6.0.
2. Select the File menu and then the New option.
3. On the Project tab, ensure that the ATL COM AppWizard item is selected. Enter a name for the project in the Project name field. Press OK. On the next wizard page, go with the default selections and press Finish. The final dialog confirms the wizard options; press OK.
4. Select the Insert menu and then the New ATL Object... option.
5. On the ATL Object Wizard dialog, select the MMC SnapIn item under the Objects category. Press Next. This enters you into the MMC Snap-in wizard. The next page requests some information about the project setup. Enter a name for the snap-in in the Short name field (the other fields automatically get populated). Switch to the MMC Snapin tab on the same wizard page. To go with the simplest options, select all the interfaces in the Interfaces group box and deselect the Supports Persistence check box (most projects won't require this). Press OK.
6. You now have a MMC snap-in project.

Earlier in the chapter, we discussed what a snap-in looks like in terms of COM objects and interfaces. Let's take a quick tour (Figure 9.6) and see what the three objects look like using ATL.

1. For more information about ATL, we recommend reading *ATL Internals* by Brent Rector and Chris Sells, ISBN-0-201-69589-8.

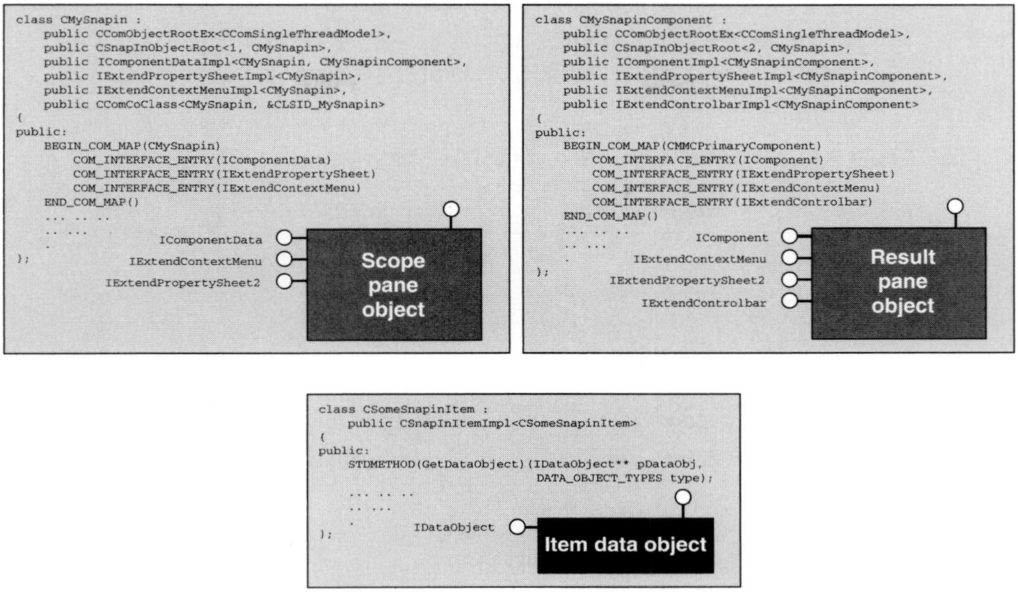

```
class CMySnapin :
    public CComObjectRootEx<CComSingleThreadModel>,
    public CSnapInObjectRoot<1, CMySnapin>,
    public IComponentDataImpl<CMySnapin, CMySnapinComponent>,
    public IExtendPropertySheetImpl<CMySnapin>,
    public IExtendContextMenuImpl<CMySnapin>,
    public CComCoClass<CMySnapin, &CLSID_MySnapin>
{
public:
    BEGIN_COM_MAP(CMySnapin)
        COM_INTERFACE_ENTRY(IComponentData)
        COM_INTERFACE_ENTRY(IExtendPropertySheet)
        COM_INTERFACE_ENTRY(IExtendContextMenu)
    END_COM_MAP()
    ... ... ..
    .. ...
    .
};              IComponentData
                IExtendContextMenu
                IExtendPropertySheet2
```

Scope pane object

```
class CMySnapinComponent :
    public CComObjectRootEx<CComSingleThreadModel>,
    public CSnapInObjectRoot<2, CMySnapin>,
    public IComponentImpl<CMySnapinComponent>,
    public IExtendPropertySheetImpl<CMySnapinComponent>,
    public IExtendContextMenuImpl<CMySnapinComponent>,
    public IExtendControlbarImpl<CMySnapinComponent>
{
public:
    BEGIN_COM_MAP(CMMCPrimaryComponent)
        COM_INTERFACE_ENTRY(IComponent)
        COM_INTERFACE_ENTRY(IExtendPropertySheet)
        COM_INTERFACE_ENTRY(IExtendContextMenu)
        COM_INTERFACE_ENTRY(IExtendControlbar)
    END_COM_MAP()
    ... ... ..
    .. ...
    .
};              IComponent
                IExtendContextMenu
                IExtendPropertySheet2
                IExtendControlbar
```

Result pane object

```
class CSomeSnapinItem :
    public CSnapInItemImpl<CSomeSnapinItem>
{
public:
    STDMETHOD(GetDataObject)(IDataObject** pDataObj,
                             DATA_OBJECT_TYPES type);
    ... .. ..
    .. ...
    .
};              IDataObject
```

Item data object

Figure 9.6   MMC snap-in ATL objects

The diagram shows the scope and result pane classes with the user interface elements that the snap-in extends (by looking at the supported interfaces). For instance, the `IExtendContextMenu` interface allows the snap-in to add and respond to context menu commands.

The key to understanding snap-in development is that the *item* is the heart of an application. Let's briefly look at the folder example presented earlier (Figure 9.1). The Shares item provided a menu, a toolbar, and a list of shares in the result pane. If this were your snap-in, you could encapsulate the functionality for this item into one class. In ATL, this class would be derived from `CSnapInItemImpl`. The `CSnapInItemImpl` template class effectively wraps up the `IDataObject` interface to the extent that you probably never will need to get near it. When approaching your own snap-in development, focus on what each *item type* needs to do. Ask yourself the following questions for every item type:

- What menu actions will I have (that are not verb-related)?
- What verbs do I need to enable (refresh, delete, properties, etc.)?
- What property pages do I need to add?
- What toolbar buttons should I display?

Asking these questions should focus your attention on the requirements for each type of item you have. This exercise will provide the answer to what interfaces your scope and result objects must support. The items in the Figure 9.6. diagram can display context menus, property pages, and toolbars.

Table 9.3 is a list of the ATL snap-in classes that you can use to extend your snap-in.

Table 9.3 MMC ATL Snap-in Component C++ Templates

ATL Snap-in C++ Template Class	Snap-in COM Interface
IComponentImpl	IComponentData
IComponentDataImpl	IComponent
IExtendContextMenuImpl	IExtendContextMenu
IExtendPropertySheetImpl	IExtendPropertySheet
IExtendControlbarImpl	IExtendControlbar

The `IResultDataCompareImpl` template class also is provided by ATL, but it does not implement anything. Table 9.4 shows the other classes provided by ATL.

Table 9.4 MMC ATL Snap-in Framework C++ Templates

ATL Snap-in Class	Comment
CSnapInItemImpl	All *items* derive from this class. The ATL implementations of the snap-in interfaces forward all method calls for an item to an object derived from this class.
CSnapInPropertyPageImpl	This offers a basic implementation of a property-page base class. You can choose other ATL-based application frameworks for their property-sheet base classes (such as the Windows Template Library in the Platform SDK). All that a snap-in requires is a HPROPERTYPAGE handle.

The `CSnapInItemImpl` class is the cornerstone of snap-in development. Later in the chapter, we shall expand on how notifications and interface methods calls get routed to this class. But for now, just note this class will be the basis for all your snap-in development.

■ Let's Make a Snap-in

Before we dive into the details of ATL and other aspects of snap-in development, let's first discuss the design of a snap-in and then add features to it as we move through the chapter. Designing a snap-in is an exercise that will help you determine the functionality of each item type and what interfaces you must support. Let's develop something similar to the Windows 2000 Services snap-in (shown in the screen shot in Figure 9.7).

The item labeled Console Root is always present and is added by MMC. All other items are added by snap-ins. There are two types of items that we will have to design: the *Services item* in the scope pane and all the *service items* in the result pane. The *Services item* is a container for all the Windows service items in the result pane. Each Windows *service item* in the result pane is of the same type. Let's focus on the functionality we want for each of the two item types.

The Services item (in the scope pane):

1. Must create and add all the Windows service items in the result pane when expanded.

2. Must support the refresh verb so that the list of all the services in the result pane can be updated. The console will display the enabled verbs through the context menu and toolbar.

3. Must set up the columns in the result pane so that the service items can populate them.

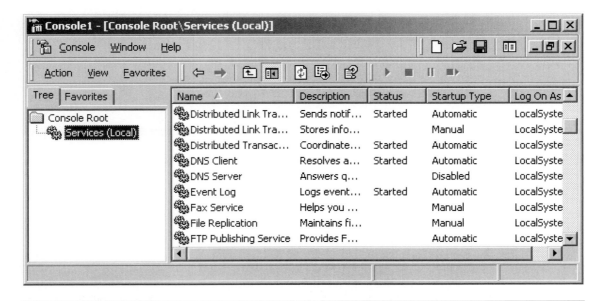

Figure 9.7 Windows 2000 Services snap-in

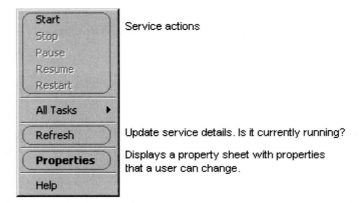

Figure 9.8   Service item's menu

The Windows service item (in the result pane):

1. Must display some service details in the provided columns, such as name, status, startup type, and so forth.

2. Must add some context menu actions, like start and stop. Figure 9.8 shows what the Windows 2000 Services snap-in context menu looks like.

3. Must add a toolbar so that the service easily can be started and stopped. Figure 9.9 shows what the Windows 2000 Services snap-in toolbar looks like.

Figure 9.9   Service item's toolbar

4. Must support the properties verb so that service details can be edited through property sheets.

Here is a summary of the interfaces that must be supported:

1. Verbs and columns do not require additional interfaces. The snap-in uses the console interfaces to set up the user interface.

2. The snap-in will require `IExtendContextMenu`, `IExtendControlbar`, and `IExtendPropertySheet` because service items (in the result pane) will have a context menu, toolbar, and property sheet.

In fact, in our snap-in, we will have a third item type because we want to use the same snap-in to expand other snap-in features later. The Services item will hang off the root item.

■ Implementing `IComponentData`

You should have gathered by now that a snap-in delivers its user interface by supporting many COM interfaces. One of the most important interfaces is `IComponentData`. The two main purposes of this interface are (1) to customize the scope pane's user interface, and (2) to create a COM object that extends the result pane's user interface. Fortunately, ATL provides an implementation of this interface. In addition, an important feature of ATL is that it delegates console interactions to the appropriate item. A snap-in can have many items within its user interface and so all interactions need some way of being routed to the correct item. This delegation mechanism is important because it makes it easier to develop items that can be added to either the scope or the result pane. The `CSnapInObjectRoot` base class provides this mechanism, which is why you see it in the following declaration:

```
class CMMCPrimary:
  public CComObjectRootEx<CComSingleThreadModel>,
  public CSnapInObjectRoot<1, CMMCPrimary>,
  public IComponentDataImpl<CMMCPrimary, CMMCPrimaryComponent>,
  public CComCoClass<CMMCPrimary, &CLSID_MMCPrimary>
{
protected:
  // I added this to make it easier to call base class methods
typedef IComponentDataImpl<CMMCPrimary, CMMCPrimaryComponent>
  _CompDataBase;

public:
  CMMCPrimary();
  ~CMMCPrimary() {}

  BEGIN_COM_MAP(CMMCPrimary)
    COM_INTERFACE_ENTRY(IComponentData)
  END_COM_MAP()
  DECLARE_REGISTRY_RESOURCEID(IDR_MMCPRIMARY)
  DECLARE_NOT_AGGREGATABLE(CMMCPrimary)

  STDMETHOD(Initialize)(LPUNKNOWN pUnknown);

  static void WINAPI ObjectMain(bool bStarting)
  {
```

```
      if (bStarting)
        CSnapInItem::Init();
    }
};
```

The CMMCPrimary class in this declaration is the minimum you have to implement for a snap-in. After the console calls CoCreateInstance to load the snap-in, it queries for IComponentData and calls Initialize. This is where you should perform your own initialization tasks. The wizard-provided initialization includes obtaining an IConsole interface (by calling the ATL base class implementation) and setting up the images used by the items.

All the icons that a snap-in intends to use are embedded in a bitmap that is called an *image list*. All snap-ins have two image lists: one for small icons (16×16 pixels) and one for large icons (32×32 pixels). The Visual Studio snap-in wizard creates both of these image lists ready for you to extend with new icons. Setting an image list requires the use of the IConsole::QueryScopeImageList method. This method returns an IImageList interface that is used subsequently to add the image list to the console through ImageListSetStrip. The image mask [RGB(255, 0, 255) in this case] specifies the transparency color mask used by the image list. As we shall see throughout the chapter, the IConsole interface is used frequently to harness the services provided by the console.

```
HRESULT CMMCPrimary::Initialize(LPUNKNOWN pUnknown)
{
  HRESULT hr = _CompDataBase::Initialize(pUnknown);

  if (FAILED(hr))
    return hr;

  CComPtr<IImageList> spImageList;
    return E_UNEXPECTED;

  // Load bitmaps associated with the scope pane
  HBITMAP hBitmap16 = LoadBitmap(_Module.GetResourceInstance(),
    MAKEINTRESOURCE(IDB_MMCPRIMARY_16));

  HBITMAP hBitmap32 = LoadBitmap(_Module.GetResourceInstance(),
    MAKEINTRESOURCE(IDB_MMCPRIMARY_32));

  hr = spImageList->ImageListSetStrip((long*)hBitmap16,
    (long*)hBitmap32, 0, RGB(255, 0, 255)) != S_OK)

  return hr;
}
```

Before a snap-in can add any user interface, it must have a root item. This should not to be confused with the Console Root item provided by MMC. The root item is the starting point for adding other scope and result pane items to the console. Depending on your application, the root item may end up doing very little, perhaps just adding one or more scope pane items. The following snap-in constructor creates a new root item that is held by m_pNode.

```
CMMCPrimary::CMMCPrimary()
{
  m_pNode = new CMMCPrimaryRootItem;

  m_pComponentData = this;
}
```

The m_pComponentData in this code fragment is used by most of the ATL snap-in base classes. The snap-in wizard also adds the following destructor code that cleans up the root item.

```
CMMCPrimary::~CMMCPrimary()
{
  delete m_pNode;
  m_pNode = NULL;
}
```

The ObjectMain method is an ATL facility that allows a COM component to perform initialization when the DLL is loaded. As briefly mentioned earlier, snap-in items are represented through an IDataObject. The CSnapInItem::Init() call registers the clipboard formats that are used to communicate the item information. We shall cover this later.

■ Implementing IComponent

The IComponent interface allows the snap-in to connect to the console's result pane. All item activity in the result pane is controlled through this object. When an item sends a notification or when a property sheet is displayed, this object handles those interactions. Like the scope pane object, all notifications and interface method calls get routed to the appropriate item. Hence the inclusion of the CSnapInObjectRoot template base class. The code sample below is the snap-in's result pane class declaration.

```
class CMMCPrimaryComponent:
  public CComObjectRootEx<CComSingleThreadModel>,
  public CSnapInObjectRoot<2, CMMCPrimary >,
```

```
public IComponentImpl<CMMCPrimaryComponent>
{
public:
  CMMCPrimaryComponent() {}

  BEGIN_COM_MAP(CMMCPrimaryComponent)
    COM_INTERFACE_ENTRY(IComponent)
  END_COM_MAP()
};
```

The `CMMCPrimaryComponent` class is the minimum you have to implement. As mentioned earlier, the console creates the result pane object by calling `CreateComponent` on the `IComponentData` interface. This is what the `IComponentDataImpl::CreateComponent` implementation looks like (roughly):

```
STDMETHOD(CreateComponent)(LPCOMPONENT *ppComponent)
{
  HRESULT hr = E_POINTER;

  // Create result pane object
  CComObject<Component>* pComponent;
  hr = CComObject<Component>::CreateInstance(&pComponent);

  // Component may need this to communicate with the scope pane object

  // Return the IComponent interface to the console
  hr = pComponent->QueryInterface(IID_IComponent,
    (void**)ppComponent);
  return hr;
}
```

■ The Root Item and General Item Basics

The heart of an MMC snap-in is the items contained within it. All items have some common (boilerplate) tasks that they must implement. Fortunately, the Visual Studio snap-in wizard creates a generic item that is derived from the `CSnapInItemImpl` base class. Unfortunately, it does not do anything very useful, but it does contain code that all snap-in items must have. You can use the generic item code as the basis for your own snap-in items.[2] Let's determine what code you need to put in place before we look at some of the more interesting snap-in features.

---

2. You may wish to make an item template–based class in your own snap-ins.

The `CSnapInItemImpl` class is designed to support both the scope and the result panes, which is why you can see `GetScopePaneInfo` and `GetResultPaneInfo` in the class declaration below. These functions provide a means to get data structures that describe an item and are used when adding (or updating) items in either the scope or the result pane.

```
class CMMCPrimaryRootItem: public CSnapInItemImpl<CMMCPrimaryRootItem>
{
public:
  static const GUID* m_NODETYPE;
  static const OLECHAR* m_SZNODETYPE;
  static const OLECHAR* m_SZDISPLAY_NAME;
  static const CLSID* m_SNAPIN_CLASSID;

public:
  CMMCPrimaryRootItem();
  ~CMMCPrimaryRootItem() {}

  STDMETHOD(GetScopePaneInfo)(SCOPEDATAITEM *pScopeDataItem);

  STDMETHOD(GetResultPaneInfo)(RESULTDATAITEM *pResultDataItem);

  STDMETHOD(Notify)( MMC_NOTIFY_TYPE event, long arg, long param,
    IComponentData* pComponentData, IComponent* pComponent,
    DATA_OBJECT_TYPES type);

  LPOLESTR GetResultPaneColInfo(int nCol);
};
```

To be able to add or update a scope item (using either `IConsoleNameSpace2::Insert-Item` or `IConsoleNameSpace2::SetItem`) requires a structure called `SCOPEDATAITEM`. This structure contains information such as the item's icon and display name. The `lParam` member of this structure is a cookie (set by the snap-in) that uniquely identifies an item. ATL requires the cookie value to be the item's object address (that is, `m_pNode = new CMMCPrimaryRootItem` where `m_pNode` becomes the cookie value). This is an excellent cookie value because you will always be able to reference the item's implementation directly by casting `lParam` appropriately. The result item structure `RESULTDATAITEM` is similar in content and also has an `lParam` member.

An item's constructor initializes both the scope and result data-item structures. All snap-in item classes must add something similar to the following:

```
CMMCPrimaryRootItem::CMMCPrimaryRootItem()
{
  ZeroMemory(&m_scopeDataItem, sizeof(SCOPEDATAITEM));
  m_scopeDataItem.mask = SDI_STR | SDI_IMAGE | SDI_OPENIMAGE | SDI_PARAM;
```

```
m_scopeDataItem.displayname = MMC_CALLBACK;
m_scopeDataItem.nImage = 0;          // May need modification
m_scopeDataItem.nOpenImage = 0;      // May need modification
m_scopeDataItem.lParam = (LPARAM) this;

ZeroMemory(&m_resultDataItem, sizeof(RESULTDATAITEM));
m_resultDataItem.mask = RDI_STR | RDI_IMAGE | RDI_PARAM;
m_resultDataItem.str = MMC_CALLBACK;
m_resultDataItem.nImage = 0;          // May need modification
m_resultDataItem.lParam = (LPARAM) this;

// This item will contain child items. Result items don't set this!
m_scopeDataItem.cChildren = 0;
m_scopeDataItem.mask |= SDI_CHILDREN;
}
```

All items have a method called `GetScopePaneInfo`. This allows an item to expose a current version of the SCOPEDATAITEM structure. You will need a new updated SCOPE-DATAITEM structure if you want to change an item's icon or display name, for instance. All snap-in item classes must add something similar to the following:

```
HRESULT CMMCPrimaryRootItem::GetScopePaneInfo(SCOPEDATAITEM
  *pScopeDataItem)
{
  if (pScopeDataItem->mask & SDI_STR)
    pScopeDataItem->displayname = m_bstrDisplayName;
  if (pScopeDataItem->mask & SDI_IMAGE)
    pScopeDataItem->nImage = m_scopeDataItem.nImage;
  if (pScopeDataItem->mask & SDI_OPENIMAGE)
    pScopeDataItem->nOpenImage = m_scopeDataItem.nOpenImage;
  if (pScopeDataItem->mask & SDI_PARAM)
    pScopeDataItem->lParam = m_scopeDataItem.lParam;
  if (pScopeDataItem->mask & SDI_STATE)
    pScopeDataItem->nState = m_scopeDataItem.nState;

  // TODO: Add code for SDI_CHILDREN
    return S_OK;
}
```

The `GetResultPaneInfo` method is similar to `GetScopePaneInfo` and is called whenever a current RESULTDATAITEM structure is required. The RESULTDATAITEM structure has one exception. Any items added to the scope pane may end up displayed in the result pane (like folders in Windows Explorer). This is the purpose of the `bScopeItem` member; it is set to true whenever a scope item is displayed in the result pane. All snap-in item classes must add something similar to the following:

```
HRESULT CMMCPrimaryRootItem::GetResultPaneInfo(RESULTDATAITEM
  *pResultDataItem)
{
```

```
  if (pResultDataItem->bScopeItem)
  {
    if (pResultDataItem->mask & RDI_STR)
    pResultDataItem->str =
        GetResultPaneColInfo(pResultDataItem->nCol);
    if (pResultDataItem->mask & RDI_IMAGE)
      pResultDataItem->nImage = m_scopeDataItem.nImage;
    if (pResultDataItem->mask & RDI_PARAM)
      pResultDataItem->lParam = m_scopeDataItem.lParam;


    return S_OK;
  }

  if (pResultDataItem->mask & RDI_STR)
    pResultDataItem->str = GetResultPaneColInfo(pResultDataItem->nCol);
  if (pResultDataItem->mask & RDI_IMAGE)
    pResultDataItem->nImage = m_resultDataItem.nImage;
  if (pResultDataItem->mask & RDI_PARAM)
    pResultDataItem->lParam = m_resultDataItem.lParam;
  if (pResultDataItem->mask & RDI_INDEX)
    pResultDataItem->nIndex = m_resultDataItem.nIndex;


  return S_OK;
}
```

The `GetResultPaneColInfo` method is added by the Visual Studio snap-in wizard and is intended to make it easier to retrieve column information when an item is displayed in the result pane. The `m_bstrDisplayName` member commonly is accessed whenever an item's display name is needed; it is part of the `CSnapInItemImpl` base class. The display name is usually retrieved for result pane items when `GetResultPaneColInfo` is called (the display name is normally a column index of zero). Here is what the method looks like:

```
LPOLESTR CMMCPrimaryRootItem::GetResultPaneColInfo(int nCol)
{
  if (nCol == 0)
    return m_bstrDisplayName;

  // TODO: Return the text for other columns
  return OLESTR("Override GetResultPaneColInfo");
}
```

The `Notify` method is very important. This is where the snap-in item will receive notifications from the console. There are many different notifications (some of which were outlined earlier), and we shall cover these in more detail later in the chapter. The wizard adds the following code that includes a default implementation for the

MMCN_ADD_IMAGES notification. The snap-in responds to the MMCN_ADD_IMAGES notification by supplying the console with the images that the item intends to use. In practice, a single bitmap contains all the icons for the whole snap-in. The add images code is similar to that introduced earlier.

```
HRESULT CMMCPrimaryRootItem::Notify( MMC_NOTIFY_TYPE event, long arg,
  long param, IComponentData* pComponentData, IComponent* pComponent,
  DATA_OBJECT_TYPES type)
{
  HRESULT hr = S_FALSE;

  // Need the correct IConsole interface pointer
  CComPtr<IConsole> spConsole;
  if (pComponentData != NULL)
    spConsole = ((CMMCPrimary*)pComponentData)->m_spConsole;
  else
    spConsole = ((CMMCPrimaryComponent*)pComponent)->m_spConsole;

  switch (event)
  {
  case MMCN_ADD_IMAGES:
    {
      IImageList* pImageList = (IImageList*) arg;

      // Load bitmaps
      HBITMAP hBitmap16 = LoadBitmap(_Module.GetResourceInstance(),
        MAKEINTRESOURCE(IDB_MMCPRIMARY_16));

      HBITMAP hBitmap32 = LoadBitmap(_Module.GetResourceInstance(),
        MAKEINTRESOURCE(IDB_MMCPRIMARY_32));

      // Add images to console
      hr = pImageList->ImageListSetStrip((long*)hBitmap16,
        (long*)hBitmap32, 0, RGB(255, 0, 255));

      break;
    }
  }
  return hr;
}
```

In the add images code, why are there different calls for obtaining the IConsole interface? During snap-in initialization, a call is made to IComponentData::Initialize and shortly after, another call is made to IComponent::Initialize. The IUnknown interface passed into these two different `Initialize` calls will reveal different `IConsole` interface pointers. Each `IConsole` object may have a different set of supported interfaces and some methods may respond differently. Item notification handlers should use the correct `IConsole` interface. Going back to the `CMMCPrimaryRootItem` class declaration, you should have noticed the declaration of some static members. All item classes must declare these members because they are used by ATL to expose the item information through the `IDataObject` interface. Recall that an `IDataObject` represents an item. The next statements initialize these static members. The following sets up the item's GUID. Recall that this must be unique for every *item type* (that is, every class). The `m_NODETYPE` holds a binary version of the GUID and the `m_SZNODETYPE` has the string form.

```
static const GUID CMMCPrimaryRootItemGUID_NODETYPE =
  {0xf5852eee, 0x67e4, 0x4150, {0x9c, 0xdf, 0xae, 0x1e, 0x93, 0x16,
  0xa, 0xf5}};

const GUID* CMMCPrimaryRootItem::m_NODETYPE =
  &CMMCPrimaryRootItemGUID_NODETYPE;

const OLECHAR* CMMCPrimaryRootItem::m_SZNODETYPE =
  OLESTR("F5852EEE-67E4-4150-9CDF-AE1E93160AF5");
```

The following sets up the display name of the item. This applies only to the root item, because all other items use the `m_bstrDisplayName` member.

```
const OLECHAR* CMMCPrimaryRootItem::m_SZDISPLAY_NAME =
  OLESTR("MMC WMI Administration");
```

The following sets up the snap-in's class identifier (CLSID) to which the item belongs.

```
const CLSID* CMMCPrimaryRootItem::m_SNAPIN_CLASSID = &CLSID_MMCPrimary;
```

Figure 9.10 shows what the snap-in looks like so far.

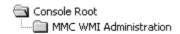

Figure 9.10 Snap-in with root item

■ Adding Your Own Namespace Items

All snap-ins have a root namespace in the scope pane. In Figure 9.10, the MMC WMI Administration item is the snap-in's *root item*. We shall extend the namespace by adding a new item to the scope pane.

Adding items to a namespace involves using the `IConsoleNameSpace2` interface and a `SCOPEDATAITEM` structure. You can get a `SCOPEDATAITEM` structure from the item using its `GetScopeData` method (this is implemented in `CSnapInItemImpl`). Once you have the `SCOPEDATAITEM` structure, you can call `InsertItem` to add the item to the scope pane. When the `InsertItem` method returns, the `ID` member of the `SCOPEDATA-ITEM` structure contains the `scope item` handle. This handle can be used later to manipulate the scope item using other methods on the `IConsoleNameSpace2` interface. To limit long snap-in startup times, you should design your snap-ins so that items are created and added when a scope pane item is expanded. Before we discuss adding a scope item, we want explain a bit more about notifications. All notifications have two parameters: `arg` and `param`. These parameters will have different meanings depending on the type of notification MMC is delivering. This is similar to a Windows message that has `WPARAM` and `LPARAM` parameters. For a `MMCN_EXPAND` notification, the `param` parameter is the `scope item` handle of the item being expanded. You can consider this the parent for new items and should use it as the relative parent. This will correctly position the new scope item in the correct place within the scope pane. Of course you could choose to ignore the `param` parameter and use another `scope item` handle if you wish, although we don't think this is common.

Finally, a call to `InsertItem` will add the item to the namespace. Here are the relevant portions of the `Notify` method implementation:

```
HRESULT CMMCPrimaryRootItem::Notify( MMC_NOTIFY_TYPE event, long arg,
  long param, IComponentData* pComponentData, IComponent* pComponent,
  DATA_OBJECT_TYPES type)
{
HRESULT hr = S_FALSE;

CComPtr<IConsole> spConsole;
... .. ...
.. ..

switch (event)
{
case MMCN_EXPAND:
  {

    // Need namespace interface to insert an item
    CComQIPtr<IConsoleNameSpace2> spNamespace(spConsole);
```

```
// Create item to add
CMMCPrimaryServicesItem* pItem = new CMMCPrimaryServicesItem;

// Get items scope data item structure
SCOPEDATAITEM* pScopeItem = NULL;
hr = pItem->GetScopeData(&pScopeItem);

// Set this items parent
pScopeItem->relativeID = param;

if (SUCCEEDED(hr))
  hr = spNamespace->InsertItem(pScopeItem);

    break;
  }
... ... ..
.. ..
  .
  }


  return hr;
}
```

As you can see in the code fragment, we created a new item class called CMMC-
PrimaryServicesItem. This will be the container for all the Windows services (we
cover it later when we add result pane items). Before adding items to either the scope
or the result pane, you should set up the display name. Do something like this in your
own snap-ins:

```
CMMCPrimaryServicesItem::CMMCPrimaryServicesItem()
{
  ... ... ..
  .. ..
  m_bstrDisplayName = L"Services";
}
```

Figure 9.11 shows what the snap-in looks like so far.

Figure 9.11   Snap-in with Service item

■ Adding Your Own Columns

A scope pane item normally adds the columns that its result pane item counterparts will populate. Adding columns is easy: The scope item responds to the MMCN_SHOW notification and calls `IHeaderCtrl::InsertColumn` to add the columns that are required. The MMCN_SHOW notification indicates that the result pane has the focus, and it is an ideal time to add some columns (if required). The MMCN_SHOW notification's `arg` parameter is true when the item is selected.

The following code fragment inserts three columns.

```
switch (event)
{
case MMCN_SHOW:
  {
    CComQIPtr<IHeaderCtrl> spHeader(spConsole);

    if(arg == TRUE)
      {
        hr = spHeader->InsertColumn(0, L"Name",
          LVCFMT_LEFT, MMCLV_AUTO);

        hr = spHeader->InsertColumn(1, L"Status",
          LVCFMT_LEFT, MMCLV_AUTO);

        hr = spHeader->InsertColumn(2, L"Startup Type",
          LVCFMT_LEFT, MMCLV_AUTO);
      }
    break;
  }
... ... ..
.
}
```

The first parameter in `InsertColumn` specifies the column number. Column numbers do not have to be contiguous, for example, 0, 1, 2, and 3. The following is also valid: 0, 2, 8, and 11. The second parameter is the column title. The third parameter specifies how

Figure 9.12 Snap-in with columns

the column should be displayed (left, right, center), and the fourth parameter specifies the column width. We shall see these columns being populated when we add the result pane items later. Figure 9.12 shows what the snap-in looks like so far.

■ Adding Your Own Result Items

Adding result pane items is usually the job of the scope item (the namespace) when it is selected. When a scope item is selected for the first time, it receives two notifications from the console. First, an *expanded* notification is delivered (it is only sent once) and can be used to create the result item (CSnapInItem) objects. The CSnapInItem objects typically are stored in a list for later retrieval. Second, a *selected* notification is delivered. This is when the snap-in would add the result items in the list to the result pane.

An STL list is probably the easiest way to store the result CSnapInItem objects. Here's the declaration:

```
typedef std::list<CSnapInItem*> TChildItemList;
```

Add a TChildItemList member to the scope item class so that result items can be accessed later. In the class that follows, we add a couple of reusable methods that can be used to populate the TChildItemList member (with PopulateResultItems) and display the items in the result pane (with DisplayResultItems).

```
class CMMCPrimaryServicesItem:
  public CSnapInItemImpl<CMMCPrimaryServicesItem>
{
protected:
  TChildItemList m_listChildItems;

  void PopulateResultItems();
  void DisplayResultItems(IConsole* pConsole);
  ...  ...  ..
  ..
};
```

Do something similar to the next code fragment to create the result items for the namespace:

```
case MMCN_EXPAND:
  {
    PopulateResultItems();
    break;
  }
```

The following code should be familiar to you by now (it is based on discussions from Chapter 7). It connects to WMI and obtains all the `Win32_Service` management objects. As each management object is obtained, a result item is created and is added to the `m_listChildItems` list. Notice that the `IWbemClassObject` interface is passed to the result item constructor. We shall expand on this later. The code that we really are interested in from a snap-in perspective is highlighted in bold font.

```
void CMMCPrimaryServicesItem::PopulateResultItems()
{
  CComPtr<IWbemLocator> spLoc;
  HRESULT hr = spLoc.CoCreateInstance(CLSID_WbemLocator);

  CComBSTR bstrNamespace(_T("\\\\.\\root\\CIMV2"));
  CComPtr<IWbemServices> spServices;

  // Connect to CIM
  hr = spLoc->ConnectServer(bstrNamespace, NULL, NULL, 0,
    NULL, 0, 0, &spServices);

  // Setup security
  hr = CoSetProxyBlanket(spServices, RPC_C_AUTHN_DEFAULT,
    RPC_C_AUTHZ_NONE, NULL, RPC_C_AUTHN_LEVEL_CONNECT,
    RPC_C_IMP_LEVEL_IMPERSONATE, NULL, EOAC_NONE);

  // Get list of objects
  CComPtr<IEnumWbemClassObject> spEnumInst;
  hr = spServices->CreateInstanceEnum(CComBSTR("Win32_Service"),
    WBEM_FLAG_SHALLOW, NULL, &spEnumInst);
  bool bFinished = false;
  while (!bFinished)
  {
    ULONG uNumOfInstances = 0;
    CComPtr<IWbemClassObject> spInstance;
    HRESULT hrNext = spEnumInst->Next(10000, 1, &spInstance,
      &uNumOfInstances);

    if (hrNext == WBEM_S_FALSE)
      bFinished = true;
    else
    {
      // Add child item for result pane
      CMMCPrimaryWinServiceItem* pItem =
        new CMMCPrimaryWinServiceItem(spInstance);

      m_listChildItems.push_back(pItem);
    }
  }
}
```

When the scope item is selected, it will receive an `MMCN_SHOW` notification. The `MMCN_SHOW` notification indicates that the result pane has the focus and that this is an ideal time to display the result items. The `MMCN_SHOW` handler should iterate through the `m_listChildItems` list and add each item to the result pane.

Here is the code to handle the `MMCN_SHOW` notification. The `IConsole` interface is passed to our helper method because it is required to access the result pane through `IResultData`.

```
case MMCN_SHOW:
{
  if(arg == TRUE)
  {

    // Add columns code here!
    ... .. ..
    .. ...


    // Add items in result pane
    DisplayResultItems(spConsole);
  }
  break;
}
```

Result pane items are added using the `IResultData::InsertItem` method, which takes a `RESULTDATAITEM` structure. The `RESULTDATAITEM` structure should be obtained using the item's `CSnapInItem::GetResultData` method. This is similar to the way we got the scope data item structure that was discussed earlier. Here is the code for the helper method:

```
void CMMCPrimaryServicesItem::DisplayResultItems(IConsole* pConsole)
{
  // Get the IResultData interface from the console
  CComQIPtr<IResultData> spResult(pConsole);

  TChildItemList::iterator itrItem = m_listChildItems.begin();
  for (; itrItem != m_listChildItems.end(); itrItem++)
  {
    if (*itrItem)
    {

      // Get the result pane info for the node
      LPRESULTDATAITEM pResultItem = NULL;
      HRESULT hr = (*itrItem)->GetResultData(&pResultItem);
```

```
      if (SUCCEEDED(hr))
        hr = spResult->InsertItem(pResultItem);
    }
  }
}
```

So far, the scope pane services item has completed everything it needs to do. It has created the result items and added them to the result pane. Coding the result items is our next focus. We need to figure out how each result item (a Windows service) should display itself.

Before a Windows service item can be displayed, we need somehow to obtain information about the service. If you recall from the code fragments earlier, the CMMC-PrimaryWinServiceItem class took an IWbemClassObject interface (the service) in its constructor. The simplest way to extract this information is to make a local copy of the Win32_Service properties. A good reason for making a copy as soon as possible is that the IWbemClassObject is not guaranteed to be valid indefinitely. The following code fragment was introduced in Chapter 7. It enumerates through all the Win32_Service properties, allowing us to make a local copy in what we call a *property map*. Let's see what the constructor looks like:

```
CMMCPrimaryWinServiceItem::CMMCPrimaryWinServiceItem(
  IWbemClassObject* pService)
{
  ... ... ..
  ... .. .
  ...

  // Get properties from the service
  HRESULT hr = pService->BeginEnumeration(WBEM_FLAG_NONSYSTEM_ONLY);

  CComBSTR bstrName;
  CComVariant varValue;
  while (pService->Next(0, &bstrName, &varValue, 0, NULL) ==
    WBEM_S_NO_ERROR)
  {
    m_PropertyMap[bstrName.m_str] = varValue;

    // Free memory for next iteration
    bstrName.Empty();
    varValue.Clear();
  }

  pService->EndEnumeration();

  // Set-up the display name
  m_bstrDisplayName = V_BSTR(&m_PropertyMap[L"DisplayName"]);
}
```

Notice how the display name is set up—it uses the `DisplayName` property that originally came from the `Win32_Service` object. It is important to set up `m_bstrDisplayName` because it is used in several places by the ATL snap-in framework.

Here is the `m_PropertyMap` declaration:

```
class CMMCPrimaryWinServiceItem:
  public CSnapInItemImpl<CMMCPrimaryWinServiceItem>
{
protected:
  TWMIPropertyMap m_PropertyMap;
  ... ... ..
  .. ...
  ..
};
```

The `TWMIPropertyMap` type is an STL map keyed on the name of the property. The property value is contained in a `CComVariant`. Here is the `TWMIPropertyMap` declaration:

```
typedef std::basic_string<WCHAR> wstring;
typedef std::map<wstring, CComVariant> TWMIPropertyMap;
```

Next, the service item must populate the columns that the scope item set up. Recall the discussion earlier on `GetResultPaneColInfo`. `GetResultPaneColInfo` is a helper method that returns a string for each of the columns. The column number referenced by `nCol` maps to the number used when `InsertColumn` was called. The following code populates the column values. Notice how the values are obtained from the local property map.

```
LPOLESTR CMMCPrimaryWinServiceItem::GetResultPaneColInfo(int nCol)
{
  if (nCol == 0)
    return m_bstrDisplayName;
  else if (nCol == 1)
  {
    // We only want 'Started' to appear on service items
    if (V_BOOL(&m_PropertyMap[L"Started"]) == VARIANT_FALSE)
      return L"";
    else
      return L"Started";
  }
  else if (nCol == 2)
    return V_BSTR(&m_PropertyMap[L"StartMode"]);
  else
    return OLESTR("Override GetResultPaneColInfo");
}
```

Figure 9.13 shows what the snap-in looks like so far.

Figure 9.13 Snap-in with result pane items

■ Setting Up and Handling Verbs

As briefly mentioned earlier, verbs help in maintaining common activities across all snap-ins. The responsibility of an item is to set up the verbs it supports. In this section, we shall enable the refresh verb; when it is triggered by the user, it will get delivered to the item via a `MMCN_REFRESH` notification. However, not all verbs use notifications as their delivery mechanism. A properties verb, for instance, results in a call to `IExtend-PropertySheet::CreatePropertyPages`. Table 9.5 lists the most common verbs and how they get delivered (other verbs will be covered later).

To manipulate verbs requires the `IConsoleVerb` interface that can be obtained from a call to `IConsole::QueryConsoleVerb`. The best time to set the verbs (using `Set-VerbState`) is during the `MMCN_SELECT` notification. `MMCN_SELECT` is sent when an item's selected state changes. The item is selected if the `arg` parameter is true. The following code fragment enables the refresh verb:

```
case MMCN_SELECT:
{
```

Table 9.5 Common Snap-in Verbs

Verb	Delivery Mechanism
MMC_VERB_REFRESH	Delivered through the `MMCN_REFRESH` notification.
MMC_VERB_RENAME	Delivered through the `MMCN_RENAME` notification.
MMC_VERB_DELETE	Delivered through the `MMCN_DELETE` notification.
MMC_VERB_PROPERTIES	Delivered through `IExtendPropertySheet`. Both `QueryPagesFor` and `Create-PropertyPages` get called. Only primary snap-ins can enable this verb because they own the item. However if extension snap-ins create namespace or result items, then they own it and therefore can also enable the properties verb.
MMC_VERB_PRINT	Delivered through the `MMCN_PRINT` notification.

```
  if (arg) // Item selected
  {
    CComPtr<IConsoleVerb> spVerb;
    hr = spConsole->QueryConsoleVerb(&spVerb);

    // Enable the refresh verb
    hr = spVerb->SetVerbState(MMC_VERB_REFRESH, ENABLED, TRUE);
  }
}
```

Enabling the refresh verb causes the verb to appear on the Item's Context menu and toolbar. When a user triggers the refresh verb, an MMCN_REFRESH notification is delivered to the item. The most basic way to refresh a namespace item (the services item, in this case) is to remove all the result items and re-create the list. This is what the following refresh verb handler does:

```
case MMCN_REFRESH:
{
  DeleteResultItems(spConsole);

  PopulateResultItems();

  DisplayResultItems(spConsole);
}
```

This conveniently brings us to the deletion of items. We have created a helper method DeleteResultItems that removes result items and physically deletes the result pane CSnapInItem objects. Here is what has been added to the services class:

```
class CMMCPrimaryServicesItem:
  public CSnapInItemImpl<CMMCPrimaryServicesItem>
{
protected:
  void DeleteResultItems(IConsole* pConsole);
  .. ...
  ..
};
```

As with inserting, deleting items also requires the IResultData interface. This time we call DeleteItem, passing the item's HRESULTITEM handle. Deleting a scope pane item is similar except that you call IConsoleNameSpace::DeleteItem, passing a HSCOPEITEM handle. Here is the code for the DeleteResultItems helper method:

```
void CMMCPrimaryServicesItem::DeleteResultItems(IConsole* pConsole)
{
  // Get the IResultData interface from the console
  CComQIPtr<IResultData> spResult(pConsole);
```

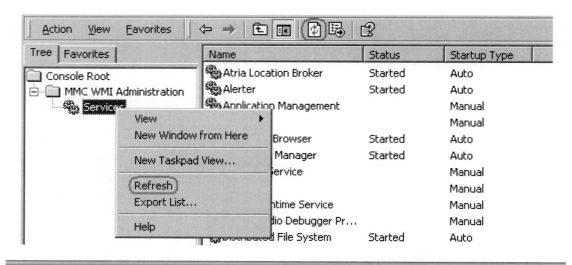

Figure 9.14 Snap-in with refresh verb enabled

```
TChildItemList::iterator itrItem = m_listChildItems.begin();
for (; itrItem != m_listChildItems.end(); itrItem++)
{
  if (*itrItem)
  {

    LPRESULTDATAITEM prdi = NULL;
    HRESULT hr = (*itrItem)->GetResultData(&prdi);

    hr = spResult->DeleteItem(prdi->itemID, 0);

    delete *itrItem;
    *itrItem = 0;
  }
 }
}
```

Figure 9.14 shows what the snap-in looks like now. Notice that the refresh verb is displayed on the Context menu and toolbar.

■ Adding Your Own Menus

The MMC console allows snap-ins to add menu items in only a few places. Limiting the number of places where menu items can be added helps in maintaining a consistent user interface between snap-ins and also aids the snap-in extension mechanism.

The menu in Figure 9.15 is a typical Item Context menu without any verbs enabled. The menu highlights four places where snap-ins can add menu items: TOP, NEW, TASK, and VIEW.

- **NEW**—New operations are performed here. Creating a new, shared directory is an example. Menu items here can be added by both primary and extension snap-ins.
- **TASK**—All other tasks are placed under this submenu. If you want to add any behavior to your scope or result item, this is the right place. For instance, a user in the Windows 2000 Users and Computers snap-in has a menu task Reset Password.... Result pane items that have a only small number of context menu items generally do not use the All Tasks submenu. They instead use the top menu region only. Menu items here can be added by both primary and extension snap-ins.
- **TOP**—It is common to find that all items in the TASK menu also appear in the TOP menu. Extension snap-ins are encouraged not to extend the TOP menu, so a user will have to use the All Tasks submenu to access the extended menu options.
- **VIEW**—Extending this submenu is useful if you want different views or employ a mechanism to filter the data presented in the result pane. Menu items here can be added by both primary and extension snap-ins.

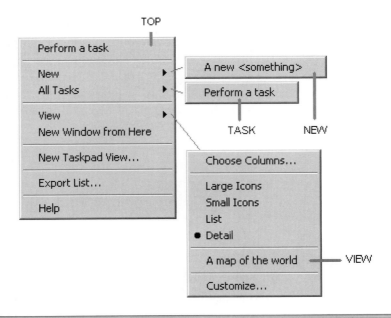

Figure 9.15   Snap-in menu structure

To create the context menu items with ATL is easy: Only one macro identifies a menu resource, SNAPINMENUID. The menu resource in Visual Studio looks similar to Figure 9.16. In this example, all of the four regions have one menu item each. Add the menu items for the regions you want to support in your snap-in.

Adding context menus requires the snap-in to support the IExtendContextMenu interface. The IExtendContextMenu interface effectively gives the snap-in the option to add menu items that can be responded to later by performing the desired operation. The bold font shows the new additions (note that this is only the result pane object):

```
class CMMCPrimaryComponent:
  public CComObjectRootEx<CComSingleThreadModel>,
  public CSnapInObjectRoot<2, CMMCPrimary >,
  public IExtendContextMenuImpl<CMMCPrimaryComponent>,
  public IComponentImpl<CMMCPrimaryComponent>
{
  BEGIN_COM_MAP(CMMCPrimaryComponent)
    COM_INTERFACE_ENTRY(IComponent)
    COM_INTERFACE_ENTRY(IExtendContextMenu)
  END_COM_MAP()
  .. ... .
  ... ..
  .
};
```

After creating the menu resource, the next step is to use the SNAPINMENUID macro in your class. This identifies a menu resource that ATL will translate into snap-in specific calls. This approach for adding menus is excellent. You work with menu resources in your projects and the IExtendContextMenuImpl::AddMenuItems implementation iterates through the menu, making calls to the console-provided interface IContextMenuCallback. Adding this macro makes it possible for you to see the menu items in your snap-in.

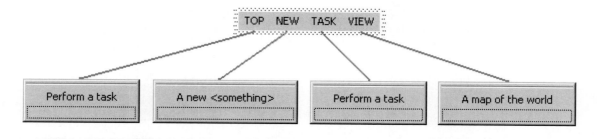

Figure 9.16 Snap-in menu resource structure

Next, we must handle the menu commands when the user activates them. This is the purpose of the `SNAPINCOMMAND_ENTRY` macro. It routes a menu command from `IExtendContextMenu::Command` to a method in the item's class. In the class declaration that follows, we add a couple of helper functions to make it easy to stop and start Windows services using WMI.

```
class CMMCPrimaryWinServiceItem:
  public CSnapInItemImpl<CMMCPrimaryWinServiceItem>
{
public:
  .. ... ..
  ... .
  .

  BEGIN_SNAPINCOMMAND_MAP(CMMCPrimaryWinServiceItem, FALSE)
    SNAPINCOMMAND_ENTRY(ID_TASK_START, OnTaskStartService)
    SNAPINCOMMAND_ENTRY(ID_TASK_STOP, OnTaskStopService)
  END_SNAPINCOMMAND_MAP()

  SNAPINMENUID(IDR_WINSERVICE_MENU)

  void UpdateMenuState(UINT id, LPTSTR pBuf, UINT *flags);
  . ... ..
  ... .
  ..

protected:
  HRESULT OnTaskStartService(bool &bHandled, CSnapInObjectRootBase *pObj);
  HRESULT OnTaskStopService(bool &bHandled, CSnapInObjectRootBase *pObj);

  // Helper methods
  HRESULT WMIConnect(IWbemServices** ppServices);
  HRESULT StartStopService(bool bStart);
};
```

The two menu item handlers for starting and stopping Windows services are straightforward. They use the `StartStopService` helper method to perform the task. As you will see later, toolbar buttons also end up calling these methods. Here are the handlers:

```
HRESULT CMMCPrimaryWinServiceItem::OnTaskStartService(bool &bHandled,
  CSnapInObjectRootBase *pObj)
{
  return StartStopService(true);
}
```

```
HRESULT CMMCPrimaryWinServiceItem::OnTaskStopService(bool &bHandled,
  CSnapInObjectRootBase *pObj)
{
  return StartStopService(false);
}
```

The `StartStopService` helper executes either the `StartService` or `StopService` method on the Windows service, depending on the `bStart` parameter. Calling WMI method calls is discussed in Chapter 7.

To reference and manipulate a management object requires an object path. An *object path* is a WMI term that identifies a management object by specifying the machine, namespace, class, and key properties. Given that the machine and namespace information is provided when connecting to WMI, a relative object path specifies just the class and key properties of the management object and can be accessed easily via the `__RELPATH` property. We use this property to execute a WMI method against the correct Windows service. As you will see later, the `__RELPATH` property also is useful during the `MMCN_PROPERTY_CHANGE` notification. Here is the helper method:

```
HRESULT CMMCPrimaryWinServiceItem::StartStopService(bool bStart)
{
  HRESULT hr = S_OK;

  // Connect to WMI using a helper method that wraps up ConnectServer
  CComPtr<IWbemServices> spServices;
  hr = WMIConnect(&spServices);

  // This is the relative object path of the Windows service
  CComBSTR bstrNTService(V_BSTR(&m_PropertyMap[L"__RELPATH"]));

  // Which WMI method do we want to call?
  CComBSTR bstrMethod;

  if (bStart)
    bstrMethod = "StartService";
  else
    bstrMethod = "StopService";

  // Execute WMI method
  CComPtr<IWbemClassObject> spOutParams;
  hr = spServices->ExecMethod(bstrNTService, bstrMethod, 0, NULL,
    NULL, &spOutParams, NULL);

  CComVariant varReturnValue;
  hr = spOutParams->Get(L"ReturnValue", 0, &varReturnValue, 0, 0);
```

```
    if (V_I4(&varReturnValue) != 0)
    {
      // Windows service method failed. Convert to HRESULT
      hr = HRESULT_FROM_WIN32(V_I4(&varReturnValue));
    }

    // Update property map so the UI can correctly reflect changes
    if (bStart && SUCCEEDED(hr))
      m_PropertyMap[L"Started"] = CComVariant(true);
    else if (!bStart && SUCCEEDED(hr))
      m_PropertyMap[L"Started"] = CComVariant(false);

    // Update the item's column information
    RESULTDATAITEM* prdi = 0;
    hr = GetResultData(&prdi);

    CComQIPtr<IResultData> spResult(m_spCachedConsole);
    hr = spResult->UpdateItem(prdi->itemID);

    return hr;
  }
```

Notice that the item's property map entry, `Started`, is updated to reflect the status of the Windows 2000 service correctly. The `Started` status is used when an item is requested to populate the columns in the result pane. This activity is forced when the `IResultData::UpdateItem` method is called. If you want to change the icon of an item in the result pane, you need to call `IResultData::SetItem`.

You probably have gathered by now that we have only two menu items: Start and Stop. Unfortunately, both menu options are available and the user can execute both of them. This does not make much sense, especially when we already know whether the service is running. To resolve this, we can dim the Stop menu item for a service that has already started. Hidden deep in atlsnap.h is a method called `UpdateMenuState` that can be overridden. This method is called whenever a menu is about to be displayed. It provides an opportunity to change the menu flags and the description. That is why the `UpdateMenuState` method was added to the earlier class declaration. The following code implements the behavior we want:

```
void CMMCPrimaryWinServiceItem::UpdateMenuState(UINT id, LPTSTR pBuf,
  UINT *flags)
{
  if (id == ID_TASK_START)
  {
    // Service already started, grey Start menu item
    if (V_BOOL(&m_PropertyMap[L"Started"]) == VARIANT_TRUE)
      *flags |= MFS_GRAYED;
```

Figure 9.17 Snap-in item with custom menu

```
    }
    else if (id == ID_TASK_STOP)
    {
      // Service already stopped, grey Stop menu item
      if (V_BOOL(&m_PropertyMap[L"Started"]) == VARIANT_FALSE)
        *flags |= MFS_GRAYED;
    }
  }
```

The `id` parameter in the preceding code fragment is the menu identifier used in the menu resource. The `pBuf` parameter is the menu item text that you can change (if you want to). Changing the menu text is useful when you want to toggle the purpose of a menu item. The `flags` parameter constitutes any of the Win32 `MFS_xxxx` flags.

Figure 9.17 shows what the snap-in looks like so far. Notice the dimmed menu item.

■ Adding Your Own Toolbars

Creating toolbars with ATL is similar to creating menus. Just add a macro into the toolbar map in the item's class. The macro identifies a toolbar resource that contains the button bitmaps and IDs. The toolbar resource in Visual Studio looks similar to Figure 9.18.

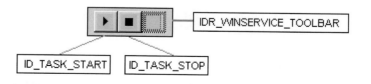

Figure 9.18 Snap-in toolbar resource

Now that we are adding a toolbar for result pane items, it is necessary for the snap-in's result pane object to support the `IExtendControlbar` interface. The `IExtendControlbar` interface gives the snap-in an opportunity to add toolbar items and later to respond to them. The mechanism used to respond to toolbar actions is the same as that used by Context menu items. If toolbars are used for any scope pane items, then you must also extend the supported interfaces on the scope pane object. The bold font shows the new additions:

```
class CMMCPrimaryComponent:
  public CComObjectRootEx<CComSingleThreadModel>,
  public CSnapInObjectRoot<2, CMMCPrimary >,
  public IExtendContextMenuImpl<CMMCPrimaryComponent>,
  public IExtendControlbarImpl<CMMCPrimaryComponent>,
  public IComponentImpl<CMMCPrimaryComponent>
{
  BEGIN_COM_MAP(CMMCPrimaryComponent)
    COM_INTERFACE_ENTRY(IComponent)
    COM_INTERFACE_ENTRY(IExtendContextMenu)
    COM_INTERFACE_ENTRY(IExtendControlbar)
  END_COM_MAP()
  .. ... .
  ... ..
    .
};
```

Unlike Context menus, a snap-in can add several toolbars to an item. All toolbars are specified through the `SNAPINTOOLBARID_MAP` macros. Our snap-in has just one toolbar and is added to the map using the `SNAPINTOOLBARID_ENTRY` macro. Behind the scenes, adding the toolbar is done when `IExtendControlbarImpl::SetControlbar` is called. Handling notifications from the toolbar is processed through `IExtendControlbarImpl::ControlbarNotify`. When a user clicks a button, ATL's `ControlbarNotify` method delegates the notifications to the same handlers used by the Context menus. Here are the new additions to the item:

```
class CMMCPrimaryWinServiceItem:
  public CSnapInItemImpl<CMMCPrimaryWinServiceItem>
{
public:
  .. ... ..
  ... .
    .
  // These were already defined in previous section
  BEGIN_SNAPINCOMMAND_MAP(CMMCPrimaryWinServiceItem, FALSE)
    SNAPINCOMMAND_ENTRY(ID_TASK_START, OnTaskStartService)
```

```
        SNAPINCOMMAND_ENTRY(ID_TASK_STOP, OnTaskStopService)
    END_SNAPINCOMMAND_MAP()

    BEGIN_SNAPINTOOLBARID_MAP(CMMCPrimaryWinServiceItem)
      SNAPINTOOLBARID_ENTRY(IDR_WINSERVICE_TOOLBAR)
    END_SNAPINTOOLBARID_MAP()

    BOOL UpdateToolbarButton(UINT id, BYTE fsState);
    . ... ..
    ... .
    ..
};
```

Unfortunately, we have the same problem with enabling and disabling the toolbar buttons as we did with the menu items. Both the start and the stop toolbar buttons are available, and the user can execute both of them. Like `UpdateMenuState`, toolbars can be controlled by overriding `UpdateToolbarButton`. This method is called whenever a toolbar button is about to be displayed and offers an opportunity to set the button state. The `UpdateToolbarButton` method must return false to disable the toolbar button. The following code implements the behavior we want:

```
BOOL CMMCPrimaryWinServiceItem::UpdateToolbarButton(UINT id, BYTE
  fsState)
{
  if (id == ID_TASK_START)
  {
    // Service already started, grey Start toolbar button
    if (V_BOOL(&m_PropertyMap[L"Started"]) == VARIANT_TRUE)
      return FALSE;
  }
  else if (id == ID_TASK_STOP)
  {
    // Service already stopped, grey Stop toolbar button
    if (V_BOOL(&m_PropertyMap[L"Started"]) == VARIANT_FALSE)
      return FALSE;
  }

  if (fsState == ENABLED)
    return TRUE;
  return FALSE;
}
```

Figure 9.19 shows what the snap-in looks like so far. Notice the dimmed toolbar button.

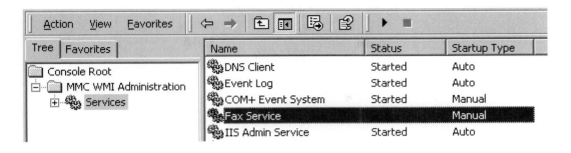

Figure 9.19 Snap-in item with toolbar

■ Adding Your Own Property Pages

Property pages typically are used to display and manipulate properties of an item. For instance, an item representing a shared directory may have properties that specify how many users can access the share. This information could be displayed and changed on the item's property page.

There are two mechanisms for adding your own property pages: (1) Enable the item's properties verb, and (2) provide a customized property sheet that is launched separately without using the properties verb. This section will focus on the former.

The following is a typical property sheet lifecycle:

1. Enable the item's properties verb. This is the most common approach to supplying your own property sheets within an MMC snap-in. First, it's relatively easy to implement, and second, it provides a standard means for extension snap-ins to add their own property pages to an item.

2. When the user activates the properties verb, the console asks your item to add its pages by calling `IExtendPropertySheet::CreatePropertyPages`.

3. When properties on a page change, a property-changed notification is sent to the item. The item performs the appropriate response to commit the change.

Supporting property sheets in the result pane requires the result pane object to support the `IExtendPropertySheet` interface. If you use property sheets for any scope pane items, then you must also extend the supported interfaces on the scope pane object. The bold font shows the additions:

```
class CMMCPrimaryComponent:
  public CComObjectRootEx<CComSingleThreadModel>,
  public CSnapInObjectRoot<2, CMMCPrimary >,
```

```
    public IExtendContextMenuImpl<CMMCPrimaryComponent>,
    public IExtendControlbarImpl<CMMCPrimaryComponent>,
    public IExtendPropertySheetImpl<CMMCPrimaryComponent>,
    public IComponentImpl<CMMCPrimaryComponent>
{
  BEGIN_COM_MAP(CMMCPrimaryComponent)
    COM_INTERFACE_ENTRY(IComponent)
    COM_INTERFACE_ENTRY(IExtendContextMenu)
    COM_INTERFACE_ENTRY(IExtendControlbar)
    COM_INTERFACE_ENTRY(IExtendPropertySheet)
  END_COM_MAP()
  .. ... .
     ... ..
      .
};
```

The next step is to enable the properties verb. When the user triggers the verb, it
will result in the console calling `QueryPagesFor` and `CreatePropertyPages`. You've already seen how to enable verbs; but in this case, we shall make the properties verb the
default action. Double-clicking an item automatically triggers the properties verb. The
following code fragment enables the properties verb:

```
case MMCN_SELECT:
{
  if (arg) // Item selected
  {
    CComPtr<IConsoleVerb> spVerb;
    hr = spConsole->QueryConsoleVerb(&spVerb);

    // Enable the properties verb and make it the default
    hr = spVerb->SetVerbState(MMC_VERB_PROPERTIES, ENABLED, TRUE);
    hr = spVerb->SetDefaultVerb(MMC_VERB_PROPERTIES);
  }
}
```

Enabling the properties verb causes the verb to appear on the Item's Context menu
and toolbar. The Context menu will highlight the properties verb in bold font to indicate that this is the default action. Figure 9.20 shows what a Windows service item's
Context menu looks like.

Before a snap-in item can add any pages (a potentially heavyweight process), the
console first queries if there are any pages to add through `QueryPagesFor`. The `type` parameter specifies the context that the console is using to display the property pages.
Currently, there are four recognized contexts: `CCT_SCOPE`, `CCT_RESULT`, `CCT_SNAPIN_
MANAGER`, and `CCT_UNINITIALIZED`. The `CCT_SCOPE` and `CCT_RESULT` contexts query for
property pages for either the scope or the result panes, respectively. The `CCT_SNAPIN_
MANAGER` context queries for wizard pages to display during snap-in initialization. The

Figure 9.20   Snap-in item with properties verb enabled

CCT_SNAPIN_MANAGER and CCT_UNINITIALIZED contexts currently are not used by verbs. QueryPagesFor should respond with S_OK if pages need to be added and S_FALSE if there are no pages for the supplied context.

The next task is to implement the item's CreatePropertyPages method. This is where the item adds its property pages for the supplied context. The console provides the property sheet and the snap-in provides the property pages by adding them using the IPropertySheetCallback::AddPage method (interface supplied through the lpProvider parameter). The Visual Studio snap-in wizard provides a sample implementation of a property page that uses the CSnapInPropertyPageImpl ATL class. You can use this class as the basis for your own pages.

Here is the Windows service item class with the new additions to add property pages.

```
class CMMCPrimaryWinServiceItem:
  public CSnapInItemImpl<CMMCPrimaryWinServiceItem>
{
  .. ... .. .
  ... ...
  ..

  STDMETHOD(QueryPagesFor)(DATA_OBJECT_TYPES type)
  {
    if (type == CCT_RESULT)
      return S_OK;              // Yes. We support property pages for
                                // result pane items
    return S_FALSE;             // We do not support property pages for
                                // other contexts
  }

  STDMETHOD(CreatePropertyPages)(LPPROPERTYSHEETCALLBACK lpProvider,
    long handle, IUnknown* pUnk, DATA_OBJECT_TYPES type);
```

```
    {
      // We only support the result pane for this item
      if (type == CCT_RESULT)
      {
        // Create the property page. It will get destroyed
        // later...The second parameter to the property page
        // class constructor should be true for only one page as
        // it destroys the notification handle.
        CMMCWinServiceGeneralPage* pPage =
          new CMMCWinServiceGeneralPage(handle, true, _T("General"));

        // Provide access to the item so we can use the property map
        pPage->SetItem(this);

        // Add the property page's HPROPSHEETPAGE handle
        lpProvider->AddPage(pPage->Create());

        // TODO: Continue to add additional pages here...

        return S_OK;
      }
      return E_UNEXPECTED;
    }
};
```

CreatePropertyPages has a few other parameters that are worth examining. When any of the property pages have changed, you should call MMCPropertyChangeNotify. This will fire an MMCN_PROPERTY_CHANGE notification that will find its way back to the item. The item should formulate an appropriate response to this notification, perhaps persisting any changes made in the property sheet. CreatePropertyPages passes the notification handle through handle, which MMCPropertyChangeNotify uses. When the property pages have finished with the handle it should be freed (typically by only one of the property pages) with a call to MMCFreeNotifyHandle. Note that the notification handle is valid only for primary snap-ins. The pUnk parameter provides access to either the IComponent or the IComponentData implementation of the snap-in (depending on where CreatePropertyPages is called). This may or may not prove to be useful in your own snap-ins. The type parameter is the supplied context of the type of pages that should be added to the property sheet or wizard. Figure 9.21 is the property sheet for a Windows service item.

Although you can use the ATL CSnapInPropertyPageImpl class to implement your property pages, if you have your own class there is no problem in using it as long as it can return a HPROPSHEETPAGE handle.

The following code is the property page class declaration that was used in the code fragment earlier. This property page class is based on the sample implementation

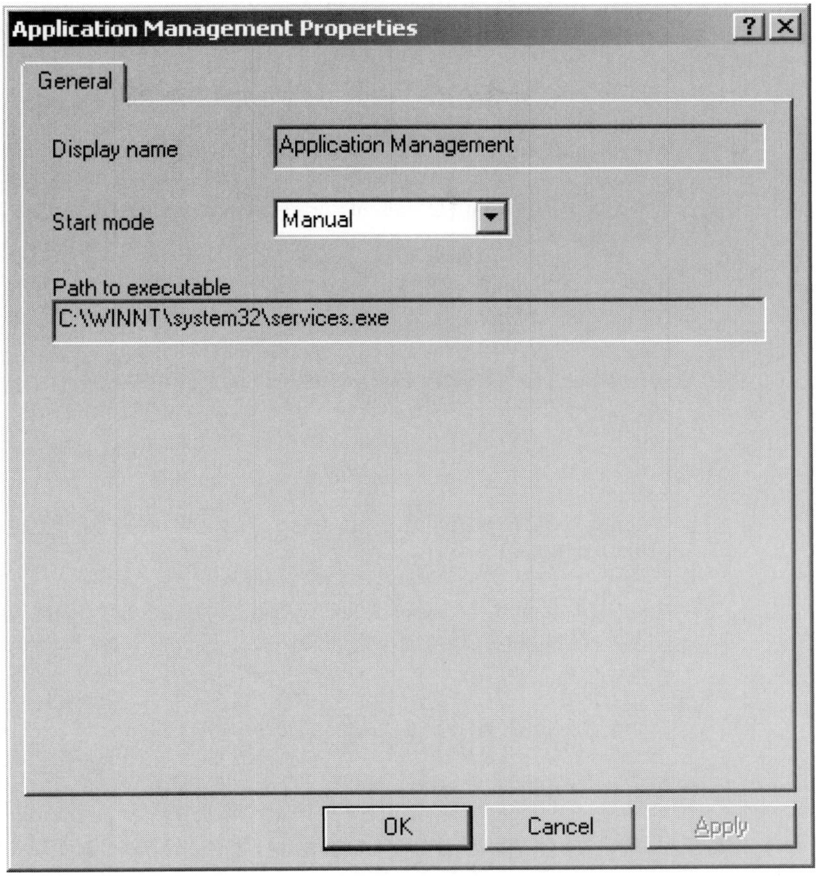

Figure 9.21   Snap-in item's property sheet

provided by the Visual Studio snap-in wizard. We have highlighted points of interest in bold font.

```
class CMMCWinServiceGeneralPage:
  public CSnapInPropertyPageImpl<CMMCWinServiceGeneralPage>
{
public:
  CMMCWinServiceGeneralPage(long lNotifyHandle,
    bool bDeleteHandle = false, TCHAR* pTitle = NULL):
    CSnapInPropertyPageImpl<CMMCWinServiceGeneralPage>(pTitle),
    m_lNotifyHandle(lNotifyHandle), m_bDeleteHandle(bDeleteHandle) { }
```

```
    ~CMMCWinServiceGeneralPage();
    enum { IDD = IDD_WINSERVICEGENERAL_PAGE};

    BEGIN_MSG_MAP(CMMCWinServiceGeneralPage)
      MESSAGE_HANDLER(WM_INITDIALOG, OnInitDialog)
      COMMAND_CODE_HANDLER(BN_CLICKED, OnUpdate)

      CHAIN_MSG_MAP(CSnapInPropertyPageImpl<CMMCWinServiceGeneralPage>)
    END_MSG_MAP()

public:
    HRESULT PropertyChangeNotify();

    void SetItem(CMMCPrimaryWinServiceItem* pItem);

    BOOL OnApply();

protected:
    LRESULT OnInitDialog(UINT uMsg, WPARAM wParam, LPARAM lParam,
      BOOL& bHandled);

    LRESULT OnUpdate(WORD wNotifyCode, WORD wID, HWND hWndCtl,
      BOOL& bHandled);

protected:
    long m_lNotifyHandle;        // The change notification handle
    bool m_bDeleteHandle;        // Should this page delete the notification
                                 // handle?

    CMMCPrimaryWinServiceItem* m_pItem; // The item being manipulated
};
```

The `SetItem` method allows the item to associate itself with the property page and should be called by the item before the property page is added to the console's property sheet. This enables the property page to communicate and manipulate the item. The communication primarily involves accessing the item's property map, which is a copy of the management object's property values. Here is the implementation of the `SetItem` method that simply stores the item's object address for later use.

```
    void SetItem(CMMCPrimaryWinServiceItem* pItem)
{
    m_pItem = pItem;
}
```

The following code is a typical `OnInitDialog` message handler. It sets up all the controls on the page and populates them with values from the item's property map. In the following code fragment, we set up three user interface controls:

```
LRESULT OnInitDialog(UINT uMsg, WPARAM wParam, LPARAM lParam, BOOL&
  bHandled)
{
  USES_CONVERSION;    // using ATLs conversion macros

  TWMIPropertyMap& rProp = m_pItem->GetPropertyMap();

  // Display service display name
  CWindow wndName(GetDlgItem(IDC_WINSERVICE_NAME));
  wndName.SetWindowTextW(V_BSTR(&rProp[L"DisplayName"]));

  // Display service executable path
  CWindow wndExePath(GetDlgItem(IDC_WINSERVICE_PATH));
  wndExePath.SetWindowTextW(V_BSTR(&rProp[L"PathName"]));

  // Set-up the Start Mode combo box
  CWindow wndMode(GetDlgItem(IDC_WINSERVICE_STARTMODE));
  wndMode.SendMessage(CB_ADDSTRING, 0, LPARAM(_T("Automatic")));
  wndMode.SendMessage(CB_ADDSTRING, 0, LPARAM(_T("Manual")));
  wndMode.SendMessage(CB_ADDSTRING, 0, LPARAM(_T("Disabled")));

  // Display the service's Start Mode in the combo box
  wndMode.SendMessage(CB_SELECTSTRING, 0,
    LPARAM(OLE2T(V_BSTR(&rProp[L"StartMode"]))));

  return TRUE;
}
```

The `OnUpdate` method enables the apply button (by calling `SetModified`) whenever a user changes properties on the property page. The start mode combo box is the only editable control on the property page.

Developing snap-in property pages is usually more lightweight as they merely manipulate an item's property map. This reduces the functionality contained within the property page and moves it to the item class. The result is that all the load and save operations are encapsulated in the item. With this strategy in mind, the implementation of `OnApply` sets new values in the item's property map and fires a property-changed notification, as in the following code:

```
BOOL OnApply()
{
  // Get selected start mode text
  CWindow wndMode(GetDlgItem(IDC_WINSERVICE_STARTMODE));
  int nIndex = wndMode.SendMessage(CB_GETCURSEL);

  TCHAR szMode[20];
  wndMode.SendMessage(CB_GETLBTEXT, nIndex, LPARAM(szMode));
```

```
        // Change the item's property
        TWMIPropertyMap& rProp = m_pItem->GetPropertyMap();

        rProp[L"StartMode"] = szMode;

        // Send notification to item
        PropertyChangeNotify();

        return TRUE;
    }
```

A key statement in the above code is the call to `PropertyChangeNotify`. This generates an `MMCN_PROPERTY_CHANGE` notification, where the item will know that it has been changed and that it should perform the necessary operations to save the changes.

The Visual Studio snap-in wizard–generated code provides no support for property-changed notifications, and it is left to the developer to implement them. We shall cover this shortly, but for now note that the item's object address is passed in the `LPARAM` parameter of the `MMCPropertyChangeNotify` call. This will be used later to route the notification to the correct item.

```
        HRESULT PropertyChangeNotify()
        {
          return MMCPropertyChangeNotify(m_lNotifyHandle, long(m_pItem));
        }
```

When all the pages have finished with the notification handle, only one page should free the handle. This is what the wizard-generated code looks like:

```
        ~CMMCWinServiceGeneralPage()
        {
          if (m_bDeleteHandle)
            MMCFreeNotifyHandle(m_lNotifyHandle);
        }
```

The main issue with the `MMCN_PROPERTY_CHANGE` notification is that when `IComponent::Notify` is called, the `lpDataObject` reference is null. As will be discussed later in the chapter, this parameter provides important information that ATL uses to route notifications to the appropriate item. As this is null for property-changed notifications, we have to find another way to identify the object that is sending the notification. This is where the `LPARAM` parameter of the `MMCPropertyChangeNotify` call comes in. First, let's see what the wizard-generated code looks like for `IComponent::Notify`:

```
        STDMETHOD(Notify)(LPDATAOBJECT lpDataObject, MMC_NOTIFY_TYPE event,
          long arg, long param)
        {
```

```
    if (lpDataObject != NULL)
      return IComponentImpl<CMMCPrimaryComponent>::Notify(lpDataObject,
        event, arg, param);

    // TODO: Add code to handle notifications that set lpDataObject == NULL.
    return E_NOTIMPL;
}
```

To implement our new policy, we must obtain the LPARAM parameter passed into the MMCPropertyChangeNotify call. The LPARAM value eventually makes its way through to the param parameter of the MMCN_PROPERTY_CHANGE notification. Because the param value is an item's object address, we can simply cast it to a CSnapInItem pointer. A call to the item's GetDataObject method will obtain an IDataObject representation of the item. The IDataObject can be used now to route the notification as normal back to the item. The following code fragment demonstrates:

```
STDMETHOD(Notify)(LPDATAOBJECT lpDataObject, MMC_NOTIFY_TYPE event,
  long arg, long param)
{
  if (lpDataObject != NULL)
  {
    return IComponentImpl<CMMCPrimaryComponent>::Notify(lpDataObject,
      event, arg, param);
  }
  else if (event == MMCN_PROPERTY_CHANGE)
  {
    // Get item pointer from MMCPropertyChangeNotify
    CSnapInItem* pItem = reinterpret_cast<CSnapInItem*>(param);

    // Get item's IDataObject
    CComPtr<IDataObject> spDataObject;
    pItem->GetDataObject(&spDataObject, CCT_RESULT);

    // Deliver the notification to the correct item
    return IComponentImpl<CMMCPrimaryComponent>::Notify(
      spDataObject, event, arg, param);
  }

  return E_NOTIMPL;
}
```

The above implementation is only for the result pane object. If you plan to support property pages for scope pane items, then similar code is required for the scope pane object.

To handle the MMCN_PROPERTY_CHANGE notification, we have created a helper function called SetServiceStartMode that calls the ChangeStartMode method on the

`Win32_Service` class. We call `SetServiceStartMode` to reflect the service's start option that was selected in the item's property page. This is what the handled notification looks like:

```
case MMCN_PROPERTY_CHANGE:
{
  SetServiceStartMode();
}
break;
```

■ Refocusing an Item's Property Sheet

On occasion, you will find that it is necessary to refocus a property sheet programmatically. Property sheets cannot be programmatically closed by the snap-in. This must be done by the user. All property sheets run in their own thread and can be hidden from view easily by focusing another window. Before a snap-in can refocus an item's property sheet, it needs to compare the open property sheet with the associated item. The same applies when the properties verb is triggered and the property sheet is displayed. If the property sheet becomes hidden, the user should be able to re-trigger the properties verb to display the already open property sheet. Unfortunately, a wizard-generated snap-in has no implementation for comparing items. To resolve this, both the `IComponent` and `IComponentData` interfaces should implement the `CompareObjects` method.

The following code fragment takes a very simple approach. It compares the item's object address to determine if the compare succeeds or fails. It extracts the item's object pointer from the `IDataObject` using the `CSnapInItem::GetDataClass` method. If the two pointer values are the same, then we are looking at the same item.

```
STDMETHOD(CompareObjects)(LPDATAOBJECT lpDataObjectA,
  LPDATAOBJECT lpDataObjectB)
{
  CSnapInItem* pItemA = 0;
  DATA_OBJECT_TYPES typeA;
  CSnapInItem::GetDataClass(lpDataObjectA, &pItemA, &typeA);

  CSnapInItem* pItemB = 0;
  DATA_OBJECT_TYPES typeB;
  CSnapInItem::GetDataClass(lpDataObjectB, &pItemB, &typeB);

  // Is this the same item?
  if (pItemA == pItemB)
    return S_OK;
  else
    return S_FALSE;
}
```

By implementing the `CompareObjects` method, the desired functionality outlined earlier will now work. That is, if an item's property sheet becomes hidden and a user triggers the properties verb, the already open property sheet will be refocused as the topmost window.

To refocus a property sheet programmatically requires the use of the console-provided `IPropertySheetProvider` interface. Let's look at how you can use this interface. The `m_spCachedConsole` and `m_pCachedComponent` members you see below were cached during a new revision of the `Notify` method. The `m_spCachedConsole` is the snap-in's `IConsole` interface and the `m_pCachedComponent` is a pointer to our own `IComponent` implementation.

```
bool CMMCPrimaryWinServiceItem::RefocusPropertySheet()
{
  HRESULT hr = S_FALSE;

  // Get the property sheet provider from the console
  CComQIPtr<IPropertySheetProvider> spPropSheet = m_spCachedConsole;

  // Get an IDataObject of ourselves
  CComPtr<IDataObject> spData;
  hr = GetDataObject(&spData, CCT_RESULT);

  // We get this because we need the HRESULTITEM
  RESULTDATAITEM* prdi = 0;
  hr = GetResultData(&prdi);

  // If the property sheet is found, it is displayed
  hr = spPropSheet->FindPropertySheet(long(prdi->itemID),
    LPCOMPONENT(m_pCachedComponent), spData);

  if (hr == S_OK)
    return true; // Property sheet refocused
  else
    return false; // No property sheet
}
```

The crucial call in this code is `FindPropertySheet`. The first parameter is the property sheet's cookie value. For the properties verb, this is the `HRESULTITEM` item ID. The second parameter is either the `IComponent` or `IComponentData` implementations of the snap-in. The third parameter is the `IDataObject` of the item being refocused. `FindPropertySheet` returns `S_OK` if the item's property page was found and displayed and `S_FALSE` if it was not.

The `GetDataObject` call creates an `IDataObject`, which represents the item being refocused. The `GetResultData` call provides access to the item's `itemID` handle (the cookie value). Make the appropriate code changes if you are planning to refocus a scope pane item. This includes calling `GetScopeData` and using a `HSCOPEITEM` handle.

■ Adding Your Own Help

The Microsoft Management Console provides two possible options for adding help in your snap-in. MMC itself uses the HTML Help system, and the preferred strategy is that you integrate with this. This obviously requires that you create an HTML Help file in which all the topics, including your own, can be accessed via the MMC help index and search tabs. The alternative is to use WinHelp or your own proprietary help system. This is becoming more unpopular as vendors increasingly use the HTML Help system.

Follow these steps to integrate help in your snap-in:

1. Ensure that you have an HTML Help file. Most commercial product development projects have a documentation team that provides the compiled HTML Help files (.chm).

2. Extend your snap-in scope pane object (`IComponentData`) to support the `ISnapinHelp2` interface. When the `ISnapinHelp2` interface is called, your help file will be added to the MMC help file collection. If your help file links to other HTML Help files, then you must also specify these so they, too, can be added to the MMC help file collection.

3. Handle the `MMCN_CONTEXTHELP` notification and call `IDisplayHelp::ShowTopic` specifying the help topic URL. The console provides the `IDisplayHelp` interface.

The `ISnapinHelp2` interface allows the snap-in to add its help files to the MMC help file collection by implementing the `GetHelpTopic` and `GetLinkedTopics` methods. `GetHelpTopic` returns the file path of the snap-in's HTML Help file. The file path is a Unicode string created with `CoTaskMemAlloc`. `GetLinkedTopics` returns a string of all the linked HTML Help files (which are separated by semicolons). The `ISnapinHelp2` interface is queried for early during the snap-in initialization.

This is what our snap-in (scope pane object) looks like now. The new additions are highlighted in bold font:

```
class CMMCPrimary:
  public CComObjectRootEx<CComSingleThreadModel>,
  public CSnapInObjectRoot<1, CMMCPrimary>,
  public IComponentDataImpl<CMMCPrimary, CMMCPrimaryComponent>,
  public ISnapinHelp2,
  public CComCoClass<CMMCPrimary, &CLSID_MMCPrimary>
{
public:
```

```
.  ... ..
... ..
..

STDMETHOD(GetHelpTopic)(LPOLESTR* lpCompiledHelpFile)
{
  CComBSTR bstrHelpFile("SomeHelpFile.chm");

  *lpCompiledHelpFile = static_cast<LPOLESTR>(CoTaskMemAlloc(
    ((bstrHelpFile.Length() +1) * sizeof(OLECHAR))));

  ocscpy(*lpCompiledHelpFile, bstrHelpFile);

  return S_OK;
}

STDMETHOD(GetLinkedTopics)(LPOLESTR* lpCompiledHelpFiles)
{
  return E_NOTIMPL; // No linked help files
}

BEGIN_COM_MAP(CMMCPrimary)
  COM_INTERFACE_ENTRY(IComponentData)
  COM_INTERFACE_ENTRY(ISnapinHelp2)
END_COM_MAP()
... ..
..
};
```

When users want help for a particular item, they display it by selecting the Help menu option on the item's Context menu. The console responds by sending a help notification to the item, but only if the snap-in supports the `ISnapinHelp2` interface.

When the snap-in supports the `ISnapinHelp2` interface, all item context menus include a Help menu option and the console's standard Help Topics menu item on the Help menu. A user triggering a Help menu option results in an `MMCN_CONTEXTHELP` notification being sent to the item. The next step is to handle this notification and instruct the console to display the help topic. The `IDisplayHelp::ShowTopic` method requires an HTML Help file URL that references the desired topic. The format of the URL is:

```
helpfilename::topicfilename
```

The code fragment that follows it uses the following URL:

```
SomeHelpFile.chm::/Topic_one.htm
```

You should do something similar to the following code to handle the `MMCN_CONTEXTHELP` notification:

```
case MMCN_CONTEXTHELP:
{
  CComQIPtr<IDisplayHelp> spHelp(spConsole);

  // Display help
  hr = spHelp->ShowTopic(L"SomeHelpFile.chm::/Topic_one.htm");
}
break;
```

This moves your help strategy toward providing help for every item type.

If you do not have an HTML Help file for your snap-in, then you should not support the `ISnapinHelp2` interface. In this scenario, the console will display the Help on <snap-in name> menu option and when the option is activated, the console will send a `MMCN_SNAPINHELP` notification to the result pane object (`IComponent`). You should handle this notification to display your own non-HTML Help–based help. This is useful if you use another help system. If you plan to support page-level help in your property pages, then you must not use the `IDisplayHelp` interface, but rather the `MMCProperty-Help` API call. From what we have observed, most help for dialogs and property pages has moved toward using the WinHelp API "What's this?" context help.

A display of the help topic in the previous code fragment on a property page would look like this:

```
MMCPropertyHelp(L"SomeHelpFile.chm::/Topic_one.htm");
```

■ Primary (Standalone) Snap-in Registration

Snap-in registration is key to the MMC architecture. As the console is the center point for all administration tools, some kind of registration is necessary so that all the tools can be located and displayed through the snap-in selection dialogs. This registration is made in the registry. All snap-ins make two types of registrations: (1) Because snap-ins are COM components, they must make the appropriate COM runtime registrations, and (2) snap-ins must let MMC know that they are available through MMC specific registrations.

The Visual Studio snap-in wizard generates an ATL registry script that incorporates both types of registration. All COM registrations are similar for all COM components and so we shall not cover this explicitly.

The MMC specific registrations are stored in the `HKEY_LOCAL_MACHINE` portion of the registry under `Software\Microsoft\MMC\Snapins`. All snap-ins register their CLSID (class identifier) under this key. The COM object referenced by the CLSID must support the `IComponentData` interface. Our demonstration snap-in is registered under `...\MMC\Snapins\{E131584D-6EFD-4624-9547-B328834BAC31}`. Let's look at the ATL registry script and continue examining it detail:

```
HKLM
{
  NoRemove Software
  {
    NoRemove Microsoft
    {
      NoRemove MMC
      {
        NoRemove Snapins
        {
          ForceRemove {E131584D-6EFD-4624-9547-B328834BAC31} =
            s 'MMCPrimary'
          {
            val NameString = s 'MMC WMI Administration'
            val About = s '{7BE5E087-CDD5-479D-B64C-FA294EF61390}'
            NodeTypes
            {
              {F5852EEE-67E4-4150-9CDF-AE1E93160AF5}
              {DF2FB296-321D-4f62-9D6E-12895AACA79E}
              {55BC8974-CEDE-4123-91C1-E2A6CDAF7A7D}
            }
            StandAlone
          }
        }
        NoRemove NodeTypes
        {
          ForceRemove {F5852EEE-67E4-4150-9CDF-AE1E93160AF5}
          {
          }
          ForceRemove {DF2FB296-321D-4f62-9D6E-12895AACA79E}
          {
          }
          ForceRemove {55BC8974-CEDE-4123-91C1-E2A6CDAF7A7D}
          {
          }
        }
      }
    }
  }
}
```

The value under the `NameString` key is the name of the snap-in. This name gets displayed in the Add Standalone Snap-in dialog, through the Add/Remove Snap-ins menu item (page 409) and also the About property sheet. Unfortunately, because the snap-in name is stored in the registry, it is difficult to localize, especially when your product provides a dynamic means of supporting different languages.

All standalone snap-ins should add the `StandAlone` key. If it does not exist, then the snap-in will not appear in the Add Standalone Snap-in dialog. Extension-only snap-ins should not create the `StandAlone` key.

The value under the `About` key is the CLSID of the about co-class. The console will `CoCreate` this to display the snap-in's details and icons.

The `...\MMC\Snapins\{E131584D-6EFD-4624-9547-B328834BAC31}\NodeTypes` key (in our demonstration snap-in) are the published item GUIDs. All snap-ins that want to allow extension snap-ins to extend their items must publish the GUIDs of those item types. Recall the following from earlier in the chapter:

```
static const GUID CMMCPrimaryRootItemGUID_NODETYPE =
    {0xf5852eee, 0x67e4, 0x4150, {0x9c, 0xdf, 0xae, 0x1e, 0x93, 0x16,
    0xa, 0xf5}};

const GUID* CMMCPrimaryRootItem::m_NODETYPE =
    &CMMCPrimaryRootItemGUID_NODETYPE;

const OLECHAR* CMMCPrimaryRootItem::m_SZNODETYPE =
    OLESTR("F5852EEE-67E4-4150-9CDF-AE1E93160AF5");
```

Every item has a GUID associated with it. These GUIDs should appear under the `...\NodeTypes` key. If you inspect the preceding snap-in registry script, you will see that the root item's GUID (`F5852EEE-67E4-4150-9CDF-AE1E93160AF5`) is registered. You can also deduce that there are three item types in the demonstration snap-in. Many developers forget to update the registry script when they add new item types to the snap-in.

The `...\MMC\NodeTypes` key has entries for all the items that can be extended. The primary snap-in usually makes empty entries for the item types it publishes. Extension snap-ins will make additional registrations under these keys.

■ More on How ATL Delegates Tasks to an Item

By now, you have seen sufficient code fragments that demonstrate how to manipulate items and how items communicate with the console through `IDataObject`. You have also witnessed that items can create an `IDataObject` representation of themselves using `GetDataObject`. The reverse is also true. You have seen that `GetDataClass` can obtain the items object pointer from an `IDataObject`. This functionality is possible because the `IDataObject` keeps a pointer to the C++ `CSnapInItem`–based class using a custom data format called CCF_GETOBJECTDATA (defined in atlsnap.h). This is the key to how ATL snap-in templates work. Given any IDataObject, the snap-in can gain access to the original C++ CSnapInItem item.

Virtually all the snap-in interface methods have an IDataObject parameter. ATL extracts the CSnapInItem object from the IDataObject using the CCF_GETOBJECTDATA format and then forwards the call or notification to the correct item. The following code fragment demonstrates how ATL does this. The bold font shows where the call is forwarded to the item:

```
STDMETHOD(Notify)(LPDATAOBJECT lpDataObject, MMC_NOTIFY_TYPE event,
  long arg, long param)
{
  HRESULT hr = E_POINTER;

  if (lpDataObject)
  {
    CSnapInItem* pItem = 0; // Will be the original C++ object
    DATA_OBJECT_TYPES type; // either CCT_SCOPE or CCT_RESULT

    // A helper method that uses the CCF_GETOBJECTDATA data format
    // and turns it into a CSnapInItem pointer of the item
    hr = m_pComponentData->GetDataClass(lpDataObject,
      &pItem, &type);

    // Delegate notification to the item that must receive it
    if (SUCCEEDED(hr))
      hr = pItem->Notify(event, arg, param, this, NULL, type);
  }

  return hr;
}
```

Knowing this detail is useful when you want to implement an MMC interface that is not supported by ATL.

■ Renaming Items

If your snap-in needs to be able to rename items either in the scope or result panes, then you must enable the rename verb. The rename verb provides an in-place editing experience and when completed results in an MMCN_RENAME notification being sent to the item. To demonstrate this, we have created a new scope pane node that can be renamed.

The first task is to enable the rename verb. The following code fragment should be familiar to you:

```
case MMCN_SELECT:
{
  if (arg) // Item selected
  {
    CComPtr<IConsoleVerb> spVerb;
    hr = spConsole->QueryConsoleVerb(&spVerb);

    // Enable the rename verb
    hr = spVerb->SetVerbState(MMC_VERB_RENAME, ENABLED, TRUE);
  }
}
```

The rename verb will now appear on the item's Context menu and, when triggered, the item turns into an in-place edit control. The user commits the new name either by selecting another item or by pressing carriage return. When this happens, an MMCN_RENAME notification is sent to the item with the new name contained within the param parameter. It is up to the item whether to accept or reject the new proposed value. Returning S_FALSE indicates that the item rejected the change and S_OK indicates that the item accepted the change. As part of the name change, maintain the item's integrity by updating the internal variables such as m_bstrDisplayName. Call SetItem to literally update the user interface with your new changes. In fact, you can use SetItem to perform any update to the user interface. You can use this technique if you need to change the icon image or (in this case) update the display name. This also includes populating columns with new values. Let's look at the notification handler:

```
case MMCN_RENAME:
{
  // Update with new name
  m_bstrDisplayName = reinterpret_cast<LPOLESTR>(param);

  // We need the scope item structure so SetItem can be called
  SCOPEDATAITEM* psdi = 0;
  hr = GetScopeData(&psdi);

  // Update the user interface for the item
  CComQIPtr<IConsoleNameSpace2> spNamespace(spConsole);
  hr = spNamespace->SetItem(psdi);

  // Set hr to S_FALSE to disallow the rename, otherwise return S_OK.
}
break;
```

Figure 9.22   Renaming snap-in item

The screen shot in Figure 9.22 shows how our snap-in is looking so far. You can see the new item that is being edited.

■ Drag and Drop

Drag-and-drop functionality is prevalent in applications today because it provides an easier-to-use experience. Management applications are no exception. Occasionally you will want to make it easy for users to grab objects and drop them elsewhere in your management environment. Users already have become accustomed to this concept. A user can grab a folder in Windows Explorer and either copy it or move it to another location. Implementing drag-and-drop functionality is not always perceived as an easy thing to do. Microsoft has made drag and drop in MMC snap-ins very straightforward to support. All you need to do is enable verbs and respond to notifications.

There are two types of drag-and-drop operations: (1) Items can be copied and dropped elsewhere only, and (2) items can be copied or moved to another location. The drag-and-drop support is limited in that it has an affinity with the MMC process. This means that items cannot be dropped into another MMC console; they can be dropped only within the same console. Items can be dragged and dropped across result and scope pane boundaries. Let's examine the steps required to *copy* items:

1. The source item must enable `MMC_VERB_COPY`. This displays a toolbar button and Copy is placed on the item's Context menu. Enabling this verb says, "I can be copied."

2. The target item must enable `MMC_VERB_PASTE`. This displays a toolbar button and Paste is placed on the item's Context menu. Enabling this verb says, "I can copy other items."

3. The target item must handle `MMCN_QUERY_PASTE` and `MMCN_PASTE` notifications.

The `MMCN_QUERY_PASTE` notification queries the destination item whether the source item can be pasted. If the target item responds with `S_OK`, it effectively means, "Yes. I can perform the paste operation for the source item." The console will then issue the `MMCN_PASTE` notification to complete the drop operation. Let's examine the steps required to *copy* and/or *move* items:

1. The source item must enable `MMC_VERB_COPY` and `MMC_VERB_CUT`. This displays both the Copy and Cut toolbar buttons and adds them to the item's Context menu. Enabling `MMC_VERB_CUT` says, "I can be removed from this location."

2. The target item must enable `MMC_VERB_PASTE`.

3. The target item must handle `MMCN_QUERY_PASTE` and `MMCN_PASTE`. The `MMCN_PASTE` notification must also return an `IDataObject` of the source item to be removed. Depending on the operation (copy or move), the source data object may or may not get used.

4. If a *move* drag-and-drop operation is being performed, you should remove the source item when the snap-in receives an `MMCN_CUTORMOVE` notification. The source item's `IDataObject` is contained within the notification's **arg** parameter.

Let's consider which drag-and-drop operations we want to support in the demonstration snap-in. Now we have two scope pane items: The first item lists the Windows services on the local machine, and the second could list a small subset of services to monitor. It would be handy to drag a Windows service from the Services list and drop it into the new Group item list (see the small screen shot in Figure 9.22). For example, if users wanted to monitor only the Fax and Telephony services, they could drag and drop them into the Group list. The Group scope item would display only the Fax and Telephony service items.

Let's focus on copying items. Enable the `MMC_VERB_COPY` verb on the source item and then enable the `MMC_VERB_PASTE` verb on the target item. (Previous code samples demonstrate how to enable verbs. See "Setting Up and Handling Verbs," p. 436.) Enabling these verbs will cause the console to send `MMCN_QUERY_PASTE` and `MMCN_PASTE` notifications to the target item. The following code fragment uses helper functions to handle the notifications:

```
case MMCN_QUERY_PASTE:
{
  hr = QueryPaste(reinterpret_cast<LPDATAOBJECT>(arg));
}
break;

case MMCN_PASTE:
{
  hr = PasteObject(reinterpret_cast<LPDATAOBJECT>(arg),
    reinterpret_cast<LPDATAOBJECT*>(param), spConsole);
}
break;
```

For the query paste notification, we decided that we could paste any Windows service item. This means that we can drop any Windows service into the Group item.

The following implementation uses Run-Time Type Information (RTTI) to determine the class type of a pointer, and if the item is a CMMCPrimaryWinServiceItem class, it allows the paste operation to go ahead. In a commercial snap-in, it is likely that you would perform more comprehensive checks to ensure that the item could be pasted. For instance, we could have checked the Current Item list, and if the item already had been added, deny the paste.

```
HRESULT CMMCPrimaryGroupItem::QueryPaste(LPDATAOBJECT lpDataObject)
{
  HRESULT hr = S_OK;

  // Get snap-in item pointer from the IDataObject
  CSnapInItem* pItemQuery = 0;
  DATA_OBJECT_TYPES objtype;
  hr = CSnapInItem::GetDataClass(lpDataObject, &pItemQuery, &objtype);

  // Use RTTI to determine if we can paste objects of this type
  CComBSTR bstrClassName = typeid(*pItemQuery).name();
  if (bstrClassName == _T("class CMMCPrimaryWinServiceItem"))
  {
    hr = S_OK; // Yes. We can paste objects of this type
  }
  else
  {
    hr = S_FALSE; // Not a supported object to paste
  }

  return hr;
}
```

If the query was successful, the console issues an MMCN_PASTE notification that is handled by the following helper method. It assumes that the paste is acceptable, obtains the WMI object's relative path, and uses this information to create a brand-new item. We add the new item to our internal list and then attempt to add it to the result pane. The code highlighted in bold font is used for move operations. We will discuss move operations shortly.

```
HRESULT CMMCPrimaryGroupItem::PasteObject(LPDATAOBJECT lpDataObject,
  LPDATAOBJECT* lpNewDataObject, IConsole* pConsole)
{
  HRESULT hr = S_OK;

  // Get snap-in item pointer
  CSnapInItem* pItemQuery = 0;
  DATA_OBJECT_TYPES objtype;
  CSnapInItem::GetDataClass(lpDataObject, &pItemQuery, &objtype);
```

```
        // Query paste should have already identified that this object of
        // type CMMCPrimaryWinServiceItem* is okay.
        CMMCPrimaryWinServiceItem* pServiceItem =
            reinterpret_cast<CMMCPrimaryWinServiceItem*>(pItemQuery);

        // We need the items property map so we can extract the __RELPATH
        TWMIPropertyMap& rProp = pServiceItem->GetPropertyMap();

        // Connect to WMI to get the object
        CComPtr<IWbemServices> spServices;
        hr = WMIConnect(&spServices);

        // Getting object from WMI
        CComPtr<IWbemClassObject> spInstance;
        hr = spServices->GetObject(V_BSTR(&rProp[L"__RELPATH"]),
          WBEM_FLAG_RETURN_WBEM_COMPLETE, NULL, &spInstance, NULL);

        // Create new item to add to the result pane
        CMMCPrimaryWinServiceItem* pCopyItem =
          new CMMCPrimaryWinServiceItem(spInstance);

        // We want to store this as we need to display the items in the
        // result pane (during MMCN_SELECT)
        m_listChildItems.push_back(pCopyItem);

        // Get the result pane info for the new item
        LPRESULTDATAITEM pResultItem = NULL;
        hr = pCopyItem->GetResultData(&pResultItem);

        // Add the item to the result pane
        if (SUCCEEDED(hr))
        {
            CComQIPtr<IResultData> spResult(pConsole);
            hr = spResult->InsertItem(pResultItem);
        }

        // This paste may be as a result of a cut or move operation. In which
        // case we need to return the item to be deleted.
        *lpNewDataObject = lpDataObject;

        return hr;
    }
```

Let's now focus on moving items from one place to another. Apart from enabling the MMC_VERB_COPY verb, the source item must also enable MMC_VERB_CUT. If the user decides to move the item from one location to another, the `MMCN_CUTORMOVE` notification is sent to the snap-in's `IComponent` or `IComponentData` interface. The purpose of this notification is to remove the source item provided in the `arg` parameter. This ordinarily involves removing the item from the user interface and then physically freeing the memory resources that maintain the item's state. Let's look at how the `MMCN_CUTORMOVE` notification is handled:

```
STDMETHOD(Notify)(LPDATAOBJECT lpDataObject, MMC_NOTIFY_TYPE event,
                  long arg, long param)
{
  if (lpDataObject != NULL)
  {
    return IComponentImpl<CMMCPrimaryComponent>::Notify(
      lpDataObject, event, arg, param);
  }
  else if (event == MMCN_PROPERTY_CHANGE)
  {
      // Handle property change notifications
  }
  else if (event == MMCN_CUTORMOVE)
  {

    // Get the item from the IDataObject
    CSnapInItem* pItemCut = 0;
    DATA_OBJECT_TYPES objtype;
    CSnapInItem::GetDataClass(reinterpret_cast<LPDATAOBJECT>(arg),
      &pItemCut, &objtype);

    // Use RTTI to determine if we can delete this object
    CComBSTR bstrClassName = typeid(*pItemCut).name();
    if (bstrClassName == _T("class CMMCPrimaryWinServiceItem"))
    {
      CutOrMoveWinService(pItemCut);
    }

    return S_OK;
  }
  return E_NOTIMPL;
}
```

The first task in this code sample is to determine the item's class. We decided that we can move only items that are Windows services. If the item is a Windows service (`CMMCPrimaryWinServiceItem`), then we call a helper function `CutOrMoveWinService` to complete the move. Note that the item has been copied already and the only task left is to remove the source item referenced in the `arg` parameter. Let's look at what might be done to physically remove the source item:

```
void CMMCPrimaryComponent::CutOrMoveWinService(CSnapInItem* pItemToCut)
{
  CMMCPrimaryWinServiceItem* pItem =
    reinterpret_cast<CMMCPrimaryWinServiceItem*>(pItemToCut);

  // Get parent item
  CMMCPrimaryServicesItem* pParent =
    reinterpret_cast<CMMCPrimaryServicesItem*>(pItem->GetParentItem());

  // Iterate through all items until we reach the item to cut or move
  TChildItemList& rChildList = pParent->GetChildItemList();

  TChildItemList::iterator itrService = rChildList.begin();
  for (; itrService != rChildList.end(); itrService++)
  {
    // Is this the item we want to cut or move?
    if ((*itrService) == pItemToCut)
    {

      // We need the itemID
      LPRESULTDATAITEM prdi = NULL;
      HRESULT hr = pItemToCut->GetResultData(&prdi);

      // Remove the item from the result pane
      CComQIPtr<IResultData> spResult(m_spConsole);
      hr = spResult->DeleteItem(prdi->itemID, 0);

      // Free memory and remove the object from our internal list
      // of the real object
      delete *itrService;
      rChildList.erase(itrService);

      break;
    }
  }
}
```

In this snap-in's implementation, the result items are stored in the scope item (namespace) using a `TChildItemList` member. To remove the result item involves finding it in the scope item's `TChildItemList` so that the result item's `HRESULTITEM` handle can be obtained. After an attempt is made to remove the result item from display (using its handle), the next step is to free the memory resources allocated to the item, and then to remove it from the `TChildItemList` member.

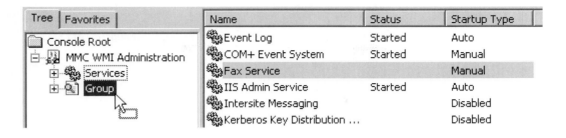

Figure 9.23   Dragging snap-in items from result pane to scope pane item

The screen shot in Figure 9.23 shows the Fax service being dragged and about to be dropped in the Group item.

■ Accessing Web Sites

On occasion, your software requirements may include accessing a Web site. For example, an administration application might need to access a support site, submit problem reports, or run some aspects of your administration environment through a Web server. Creating an item to access a Web site is easy. All that is required is to override the `GetResultViewType` method in the `CSnapInItem`-derived class. The following is a generalized class that can use any Web site URL:

```
class CMMCPrimaryWebSiteItem:
  public CSnapInItemImpl<CMMCPrimaryWebSiteItem>
{
public:
  ... ... ...
  ... . ..
  ..
  CMMCPrimaryWebSiteItem(LPOLESTR lpszURL, LPOLESTR lpszDisplayName)
  {
    .. ... . ..
    ... .
    m_bstrURL = lpszURL;
    m_bstrDisplayName = lpszDisplayName;
  }

  STDMETHOD(GetResultViewType)(LPOLESTR *ppViewType, long
  *pViewOptions)
  {
```

```
      // Allocate memory for URL
      *ppViewType = static_cast<LPOLESTR>(
        CoTaskMemAlloc(sizeof(OLECHAR) * (m_bstrURL. Length() +1)));

      // Copy URL that MMC will use to go to
      wcscpy(*ppViewType, m_bstrURL);

      // Ensure standard list view is not selected
      *pViewOptions = MMC_VIEW_OPTIONS_NOLISTVIEWS;
      return S_OK;
   }

protected:
   CComBSTR m_bstrURL; // The Web Site's URL
};
```

The Web site display name and URL are passed when the scope pane item is created. The item's display name is copied to m_bstrDisplayName and the Web site's URL is copied to m_bstrURL. MMC determines what the result pane view should be by calling GetResultViewType. Here the item can instruct MMC to use an alternate view. The ppViewType out-parameter allows the snap-in to specify a string moniker. The string is allocated by the snap-in and will get freed by MMC when MMC no longer requires the string. The pViewOptions out-parameter specifies one or more result pane view options. To display a Web page requires only one of the options to be set, MMC_VIEW_OPTIONS_NOLISTVIEWS. This instructs MMC not to use the standard list view control. MMC becomes reliant entirely on the ppViewType parameter to determine what view to display.

You must not specify the http:// portion when specifying a Web URL. For instance, http://www.microsoft.com becomes www.microsoft.com. MMC will interpret www.microsoft.com as a Web-based URL. The following code fragment from the CMMCPrimaryRootItem class demonstrates how the scope pane item is created and added as a child of the root item. Notice the format of the URL being passed to the constructor of the CMMCPrimaryWebSiteItem class.

```
case MMCN_EXPAND:
{
  CComQIPtr<IConsoleNameSpace2> spNamespace(spConsole);
  . ... ..
  ... .
    .
  CMMCPrimaryWebSiteItem* pWebSite =
    new CMMCPrimaryWebSiteItem(L"www.microsoft.com",
      L"Microsoft's Web Site");

  InsertScopeItem(spNamespace, pWebSite, param);
}
break;
```

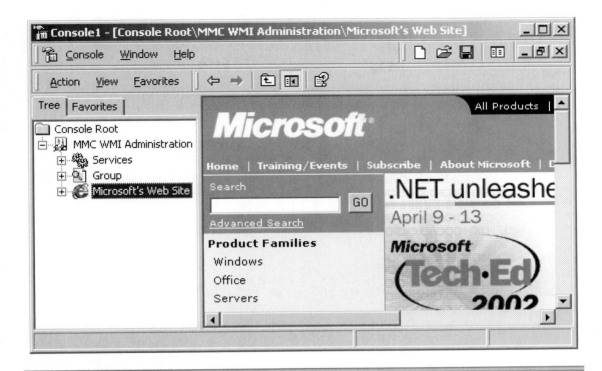

Figure 9.24   Snap-in item displaying a Web page

The screen shot in Figure 9.24 shows the Web site item that displays the Microsoft home page.

■ Displaying Custom Views

To display a custom view other than the standard list view control, you need to develop an ActiveX control. An ActiveX control allows you the freedom to have the user interface that best suits your administration environment. You may have noticed that some of the Windows 2000 snap-ins display custom views in the result pane, such as the disk management tool.

Creating an item to use an ActiveX control is very similar to creating an item to access Web sites (as in the previous section). You must override the `GetResultViewType` method in the `CSnapInItem`-derived class. The following class displays the standard Windows 2000 calendar ActiveX control:

```
class CMMCPrimaryAXControlItem:
   public CSnapInItemImpl<CMMCPrimaryAXControlItem>
```

```
{
public:
  .. ... ...
  ... . ..
  ..
  CMMCPrimaryAXControlItem()
  {
    .. ... . ..
    ... .
    m_bstrDisplayName = L"Calendar Control";
  }

STDMETHOD(GetResultViewType)(LPOLESTR *ppViewType, long *pViewOptions)
{
  // The following GUID is the standard calendar control
  CComBSTR bstrCtrl(L"{8E27C92B-1264-101C-8A2F-040224009C02}");

  // Allocate memory for GUID string
  *ppViewType = static_cast<LPOLESTR>(
    CoTaskMemAlloc(sizeof(OLECHAR) * (bstrCtrl.Length() +1)));

  // Copy CLSID of ActiveX control so that MMC can display the control
  wcscpy(*ppViewType, bstrCtrl);

  // Ensure standard list view is not selected
  *pViewOptions = MMC_VIEW_OPTIONS_NOLISTVIEWS;
  return S_OK;
}
};
```

Like the Web site example in the previous section, MMC calls GetResultViewType to determine the view to display in the result pane. To display a custom view through an ActiveX control, you specify the ActiveX control's class identifier (CLSID) in string form through the ppViewType out-parameter. MMC will evaluate the string and determine that it is a class identifier for a COM component. MMC loads the control and hosts it within the result pane issuing Object Linking and Embedding (OLE) method calls for the control to display its user interface. Developing OLE ActiveX controls is beyond the scope of this book.[3] The screen shot in Figure 9.25 shows the calendar control as the scope item's user interface.

More than likely, the OLE control that is displayed in the result pane will require some sort of initialization. MMC supports this scenario by sending the snap-in item an

3. For more information about developing OLE ActiveX controls, we recommend reading *ATL Internals* by Brent Rector and Chris Sells, ISBN 0-201-69589-8.

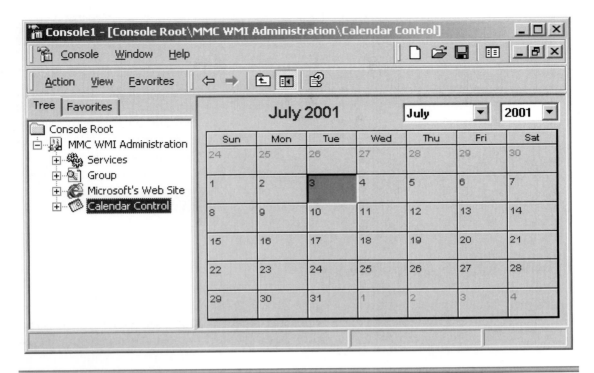

Figure 9.25 Snap-in item hosting an ActiveX control

`MMCN_INITOCX` notification immediately after the control is loaded. This is your opportunity to initialize the control in the item's `Notify` implementation. The following code sample demonstrates how to initialize the calendar control to July 3, 2001:

```
case MMCN_INITOCX:
{
  // Use ATLs IDispatch helper class
  CComDispatchDriver spCalendar = LPUNKNOWN(param);

  // Set calendar control properties
  // date == 3 July 2001
  spCalendar.PutPropertyByName(L"Day", &CComVariant(3));
  spCalendar.PutPropertyByName(L"Month", &CComVariant(7));
  spCalendar.PutPropertyByName(L"Year", &CComVariant(2001));
}
```

Notice that the above code makes use of ATL's `CComDispatchDriver` class. This is a helpful class if you do not want to import or include header files that contain the COM interface definitions. The `IUnknown` interface of the OLE control is passed through the `param` parameter during the `MMCN_INITOCX` notification. It is up to you to perform whatever is necessary to initialize the control.

You can also obtain the OLE control's `IUnknown` interface by calling the `Query-ResultView` on the `IConsole` interface. This allows you to delegate calls from the MMC snap-in to the control. For example, the control may have a refresh operation that you may want to expose to the user via the MMC refresh verb. The refresh action easily can be delegated to the control when the appropriate item receives an `MMCN_REFRESH` notification. The implementation of the notification handler either could use a cached (reference counted) copy of the control's `IUnknown` interface (cached from the `MMCN_INITOCX` notification) or call `QueryResultView` to get the control's `IUnknown` interface from the console. After access to the control is established, the snap-in can call the appropriate refresh method to complete the delegated action.

■ Developing Extension Snap-ins

Extension snap-ins make the Microsoft Management Console environment different from other management user interfaces. Generally, other management environments provide no means of adding new administration tasks. If the management environment did offer an extension mechanism, it was always a proprietary solution. For instance, suppose you were to add some voice mail features for users in an e-mail environment. You could add your application's administration tasks to the Exchange System Administrator in Microsoft Exchange 5.5. Luckily, Microsoft Exchange 5.5 does provide a mechanism to add your own property pages by implementing a DLL that exports a few functions. However, if another e-mail system were used, there would be another API to hook into and you would face the additional possibility that no such extension mechanism even exists. The result is that you end up with a fragmented administration extension mechanism for virtually every kind of administration environment. The extension mechanism provided by MMC is comprehensive, is well thought out, and most importantly, offers a unified API for developing administration applications and extending them. We regard the extension mechanism to be one of the most powerful features of MMC.

To enable the extension mechanism requires that a primary snap-in properly register the item types that can be extended. Typically, as you have little idea of how others might want to extend the management environment, you should register all the item types used within the snap-in.

The extension snap-in can then register to extend one or more of the user interface elements of a particular item type. This includes:

- Extending a scope item's namespace
- Extending an item's Context menu

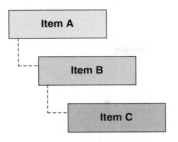

Figure 9.26 Snap-in extension mechanism

- Extending an item's toolbar
- Extending an item's property sheet
- Extending an item's task pad

The extension mechanism is so powerful that an extension snap-in can extend another extension snap-in. Consider the diagram in Figure 9.26.

Suppose that *Item A* was added to the scope pane by a primary standalone snap-in. An extension snap-in can extend *Item A*'s namespace and add its own, *Item B*. The snap-in adding *Item A* is the primary snap-in for *Item B*. The snap-in adding *Item B* has full control over the item and if extended becomes a primary snap-in. *Item B* can be extended by another extension snap-in adding *Item C*. The snap-in adding *Item B* is the primary snap-in for *Item C*.

How does the extension snap-in mechanism work? Every item type has a unique GUID associated with it and should be registered by the primary snap-in. An extension snap-in registers to extend the item type, specifying what type of user interface it is extending (namespace, property sheet, menu, and so forth). When the console invokes the extension snap-in (Figure 9.27), it must bind to the primary snap-in's item: For instance, *Item A* is wrapped by *Item A binding*.

If the primary snap-in's (*Item A*) namespace is extended, then notifications sent to the primary snap-in's `IComponentData::Notify` are also sent to the extension snap-in's

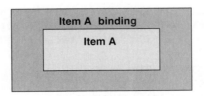

Figure 9.27 Snap-in extension item binding

item binding *(Item A binding)* through its `IComponentData::Notify` as well. The notifications that are delivered to the extension snap-in depend on what is being extended. If only a Context menu is extended, then `MMCN_EXPAND` notifications will not be forwarded to the extension snap-in. The extension snap-in will be queried for the Context menu items it wants to add.

Extension snap-ins cannot alter the behavior of primary snap-ins; they only can add behavior to them. For instance, an extension snap-in cannot enable the properties verb to an item in the primary snap-in.

Developing extension snap-ins does not really differ from the techniques you have already seen in this chapter. For instance, adding scope pane items and adding property pages or a menu item are still the same. The differences are:

- A special item class binds to the primary snap-in's item.
- Extension snap-in's registration is slightly different.

Let's focus on the item class that binds (or wraps) to the primary snap-in's item. We shall make an extension snap-in that adds only a Context menu item to a primary snap-in item. This menu item will be labeled "An example action" and will be added to all Windows service items.

The following is the complete class declaration for the extension snap-in's co-class. It was generated for the most part by the Visual Studio snap-in wizard in which we specified only that we wanted to extend context menus.

```
class CMMCExtension:
  public CComObjectRootEx<CComSingleThreadModel>,
  public CSnapInObjectRoot<1, CMMCExtension>,
  public IComponentDataImpl<CMMCExtension, CMMCExtensionComponent>,
  public IExtendContextMenuImpl<CMMCExtension>,
  public CComCoClass<CMMCExtension, &CLSID_MMCExtension>
{
public:
  CMMCExtension();
  ~CMMCExtension();

  EXTENSION_SNAPIN_DATACLASS(CWinServiceExtItem)

  BEGIN_EXTENSION_SNAPIN_NODEINFO_MAP(CMMCExtension)
    EXTENSION_SNAPIN_NODEINFO_ENTRY(CWinServiceExtItem)
  END_EXTENSION_SNAPIN_NODEINFO_MAP()

  BEGIN_COM_MAP(CMMCExtension)
    COM_INTERFACE_ENTRY(IComponentData)
    COM_INTERFACE_ENTRY(IExtendContextMenu)
  END_COM_MAP()
```

```
DECLARE_REGISTRY_RESOURCEID(IDR_MMCEXTENSION)
DECLARE_NOT_AGGREGATABLE(CMMCExtension)

STDMETHOD(Initialize)(LPUNKNOWN pUnknown);

static void WINAPI ObjectMain(bool bStarting)
{
  if (bStarting)
    CSnapInItem::Init();
}
};
```

As you can see, virtually everything appears the same as a primary snap-in, except for the statements in bold text. These statements enable the extension snap-in to bind to the primary snap-in's item. The `EXTENSION_SNAPIN_DATACLASS` macro effectively creates a member variable that represents a permanent binding to the primary snap-in item. The next step is to make the binding communicate with the primary snap-in. This is the job of the `EXTENSION_SNAPIN_NODEINFO_MAP` macro, which will be discussed in the next section.

An extension snap-in can extend any number of primary snap-in items. If an extension snap-in were to extend two different items (perhaps even in different primary snap-ins), then you would need to create another extension data class and add another entry in the extension item map, like this:

```
EXTENSION_SNAPIN_DATACLASS(CWinServiceExtItem)
EXTENSION_SNAPIN_DATACLASS(CAnotherExtItem)

BEGIN_EXTENSION_SNAPIN_NODEINFO_MAP(CMMCExtension)
  EXTENSION_SNAPIN_NODEINFO_ENTRY(CWinServiceExtItem)
  EXTENSION_SNAPIN_NODEINFO_ENTRY(CAnotherExtItem)
END_EXTENSION_SNAPIN_NODEINFO_MAP()
```

In the following code sample, let's examine the `CWinServiceExtItem` class[4] that binds to the primary snap-in item. This class looks like any other `CSnapInItemImpl` class except that it has one difference: It has `TRUE` in the template parameter list (in bold font). This parameter is used only in extension snap-ins in which an item is binding to a primary snap-in item. In all other cases, this parameter is not specified and defaults to `FALSE`.

```
class CWinServiceExtItem: public CSnapInItemImpl<CWinServiceExtItem, TRUE>
{
public:
```

4. The snap-in wizard–generated code initially used the name `CMMCExtensionExtData`, which we changed to `CWINServiceExtItem`.

```
CWinServiceExtItem();
~CWinServiceExtItem();
.. ... ..
... .
.
BEGIN_SNAPINCOMMAND_MAP(CWinServiceExtItem, FALSE)
  SNAPINCOMMAND_ENTRY(ID_TASK_ANEXAMPLEACTION, OnTaskExampleAction)
END_SNAPINCOMMAND_MAP()

SNAPINMENUID(IDR_MMCEXTENSION_MENU)

protected:
  HRESULT OnTaskExampleAction(bool &bHandled,
    CSnapInObjectRootBase   *pObj)
  {
    MessageBox(NULL, _T("An example action for a Windows Service"),
      _T("Extension snap-in"), MB_OK);

    return S_OK;
  }
  ... ... ..
  .. ...
  ...
};
```

As you can see, we have specified the menu (using the SNAPINMENUID macro) and implemented a handler (OnTaskExampleAction) for the one and only Context menu item that we added to the All Tasks Context menu. We discussed the same type of code earlier in the chapter (p. 441).

Figure 9.28 shows what the snap-in looks like so far. Notice that All Tasks menu is added to include the Extension Snap-ins Context menu item.

When the "An example action" Context menu is triggered by the user, the handler displays the message box in Figure 9.29.

■ Exchanging Information between Primary and Extension Snap-ins

In the previous section, there was no context information to identify the Windows service being managed. When the message box popped up, it was effectively a blind action, with no regard for which Windows service was selected. In most cases, this will not be adequate. The extension snap-in certainly will want some context information to perform the appropriate task. As we mentioned earlier in the chapter, the IDataObject interface provides a perfect solution for exchanging information. The IDataObject interface is the key for primary snap-ins to publish context information and for extension snap-ins to subscribe to it.

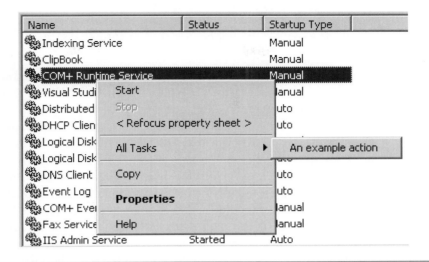

Figure 9.28   Extension snap-in adding a menu item

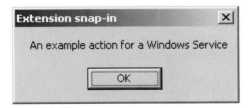

Figure 9.29   Extension snap-in example action

Let's focus on publishing information in a primary snap-in. Given that the extension snap-in is extending Windows service items, the primary snap-in will need to publish some information that an extension snap-in can use effectively. As witnessed earlier, the __RELPATH WMI property contains the relative path of a WMI management object. A more complete and absolute reference would be the __PATH property (a fully qualified path containing machine and namespace information). For our purposes, the WMI relative path is more than enough context information.

Let's publish the relative path in the primary snap-in. But before we dive into the details, let's examine the information already published by ATL and the associated clipboard formats:

- The item's GUID in binary form (CCF_NODETYPE)
- The item's GUID in string form (CCF_SZNODETYPE)

- The item's display name (CCF_DISPLAY_NAME)
- The snap-in's class identifier (CCF_SNAPIN_CLASSID)

The clipboard formats used above are registered when the `CSnapInItem::Init` is called in the snap-ins `ObjectMain` DLL initialization method. What we need to do is extend the published information to include the relative object path of the Windows service. The published formats can be of any type such as a GUID or some other binary structure. We usually publish Unicode strings for easy access, and this is what we shall do to expose the relative object path.

Publishing your own formats involves overriding the `CSnapInItem::FillData` method. The easiest approach in implementing this is to copy the method from atlsnap.h and extend it by publishing additional information. Let's call the new format we shall publish `CCF_WINSERVICE_RELPATH`. If the extension snap-in requests this format, then the primary snap-in must fill the stream (`pStream`) with the appropriate information, in this case, a Unicode string containing the relative object path of the service. Let's look at the code:

```
STDMETHODIMP CMMCPrimaryWinServiceItem::FillData(CLIPFORMAT cf,
                                                 LPSTREAM pStream)
{
  // Copied from atlsnap.h
  ULONG uWritten = 0;

  if (cf == m_CCF_NODETYPE)
    return pStream->Write(GetNodeType(), sizeof(GUID), &uWritten);

  if (cf == m_CCF_SZNODETYPE)
    return pStream->Write(GetSZNodeType(),
      (ocslen((OLECHAR*)GetSZNodeType()) + 1)* sizeof(OLECHAR),
      &uWritten);

  if (cf == m_CCF_DISPLAY_NAME)
    return pStream->Write(GetDisplayName(),
      (ocslen((OLECHAR*)GetDisplayName()) + 1) * sizeof(OLECHAR),
      &uWritten);

  if (cf == m_CCF_SNAPIN_CLASSID)
    return pStream->Write(GetSnapInCLSID(), sizeof(GUID), &uWritten);

  // Publish the snap-ins additional information
  CLIPFORMAT cfWinServerRelPath =
    CLIPFORMAT(::RegisterClipboardFormat(_T("CCF_WINSERVICE_RELPATH")));
```

```
    if (cf == cfWinServerRelPath)
    {
      // Get the relative object path of the service
      BSTR bstrRelPath = V_BSTR(&m_PropertyMap[L"__RELPATH"]);

      // Write it out to the stream for the extension snap-in to read
      return pStream->Write(bstrRelPath,
        (SysStringLen(bstrRelPath) + 1) * sizeof(OLECHAR), &uWritten);
    }


    return DV_E_CLIPFORMAT;
}
```

You've probably gathered by now that only one `IDataObject` format can be requested at a time. If `CCF_WINSERVICE_RELPATH` is requested, we obtain the relative object path from the item's property map and write it to the `IStream`. Note that if `CCF_WIN-SERVICE_RELPATH` is already registered, then `RegisterClipboardFormat` will return the existing clipboard format value.

Let's move on to the extension snap-in. The Visual Studio snap-in wizard included the following:

```
class CWinServiceExtItem: public CSnapInItemImpl<CWinServiceExtItem,
TRUE>
{
public:
  CWinServiceExtItem();
  ~CWinServiceExtItem();
  .. ... ..
  ... .
  .
protected:
  IDataObject* m_pDataObject;

public:
  virtual void InitDataClass(IDataObject* pDataObject,
    CSnapInItem* pDefault)
  {
    m_pDataObject = pDataObject;
    // The default code stores off the pointer to the Dataobject the class
    // is wrapping at the time. Alternatively you could convert the
    // dataobject to the internal format it represents and store that
    // information.
  }
  CSnapInItem* GetExtNodeObject(IDataObject* pDataObject,
    CSnapInItem* pDefault)
```

```
      {
        // Modify to return a different CSnapInItem* pointer.
        return pDefault;
      }
    };
```

The `InitDataClass` method is used only for extension snap-in items that bind to primary snap-in items. Its main purpose is to give the extension snap-in an opportunity to extract (or subscribe to) information provided by the primary snap-in item. The `pDataObject` parameter is the `IDataObject` of the primary snap-in item to which we are binding. The `pDefault` parameter is the permanent item binding set up by the `EXTENSION_SNAPIN_DATACLASS` macro.[5]

The `GetExtNodeObject` method is a way of delegating the extraction of primary snap-in item information through another `CSnapInItem`-based object.[6]

The tasks left are to implement the `InitDataClass` method and to extract the primary snap-in item information using the `pDataObject` parameter. The only context information the extension snap-in cares about is the relative object path of the Windows service.

Let's look at how this might be done:

```
class CWinServiceExtItem: public CSnapInItemImpl<CWinServiceExtItem,
TRUE>
{
public:
  CWinServiceExtItem();
  ~CWinServiceExtItem();
  .. ... ..
  ... .
      .
protected:
  IDataObject* m_pDataObject;
  CComBSTR m_bstrRelPath;

public:
virtual void InitDataClass(IDataObject* pDataObject,
  CSnapInItem* pDefault)
{

  // Cache copy for ourselves
  m_pDataObject = pDataObject;

  // Prepare IDataObject format for the CCF_WINSERVICE_RELPATH
  FORMATETC formatetc = {
```

---

5. We have never found a practical use for the `pDefault` parameter.
6. We have never found a practical use for the `GetExtNodeObject` method.

```
            ::RegisterClipboardFormat(_T("CCF_WINSERVICE_RELPATH")),
        NULL, DVASPECT_CONTENT, -1, TYMED_HGLOBAL};


        // Allocate memory for the data, lets hope that 256 Unicode
        // characters is okay
        STGMEDIUM stgmedium = { TYMED_HGLOBAL, NULL};
        stgmedium.hGlobal = GlobalAlloc(0, 512);


        // Extract the information from the primary snap-in item
        if (SUCCEEDED(pDataObject->GetDataHere(&formatetc, &stgmedium)))
        {
          // Store in local data member for later access
          m_bstrRelPath = static_cast<LPOLESTR>(stgmedium.hGlobal);
        }


        // Free memory
        if (stgmedium.hGlobal)
          GlobalFree(stgmedium.hGlobal);
    }
    ... ... ..
    .. ...
    ...
  };
```

Notice how the format was specified: It requested the `CCF_WINSERVICE_RELPATH` from
the primary snap-in item. However, you must be sure to allocate enough memory to
hold data that you are extracting. After extracting the information, store it in a suitable
place for later retrieval, in this case, `m_bstrRelPath`.

The extension snap-in bound item now has the context information it needs to execute tasks, in this case, the relative path contained within the `m_bstrRelPath` member.

The next step is to use this information in our simple Context menu handler. We
just display the relative path:

```
HRESULT OnTaskExampleAction(bool &bHandled, CSnapInObjectRootBase *pObj)
{
  TCHAR szBuffer[512];
  sprintf(szBuffer, _T("An example action for a Windows Service (%ls)"),
    m_bstrRelPath);

  MessageBox(NULL, szBuffer, _T("Extension snap-in"), MB_OK);

  return S_OK;
}
```

Figure 9.30 shows what the `OnTaskExampleAction` handler displays.

Figure 9.30 Extension snap-in adding a menu item with context information

■ Extension Snap-in Registration

Like primary standalone snap-ins, extension snap-ins make two types of registrations: (1) COM component registration and (2) MMC registration. The Visual Studio snap-in wizard generates an ATL registry script that incorporates both types of registration. All COM registrations are similar for all COM components, so we shall not explicitly cover this.

The MMC specific registrations are stored in the HKEY_LOCAL_MACHINE portion of the registry under Software\Microsoft\MMC. Our demonstration extension snap-in is registered under ...\MMC\Snapins\{08B017E8-47AD-4D1B-A928-94FFD77E9950}, similar to the registration of primary standalone snap-ins. The real difference is in the registrations made under the ...\MMC\NodeTypes key.

Let's look at the ATL registry script and then examine it in detail:

```
HKLM
{
  NoRemove Software
  {
    NoRemove Microsoft
    {
      NoRemove MMC
      {
        NoRemove Snapins
        {
          ForceRemove {08B017E8-47AD-4D1B-A928-94FFD77E9950} =
          s 'WMI Administration Extension'
          {
            val NameString = s 'WMI Administration Extension'
            val About = s '{2FC11162-83EE-47ED-87DA-490D7402230C}'
          }
        }
        NoRemove NodeTypes
        {
          NoRemove {55BC8974-CEDE-4123-91C1-E2A6CDAF7A7D}
```

```
          {
            NoRemove Extensions
            {
              NoRemove ContextMenu
                {
                  val {08B017E8-47AD-4D1B-A928-94FFD77E9950} =
                    s 'WMI Administration Extension'
                }
              }
            }
          }
        }
      }
    }
  }
```

The registrations made under the `...\MMC\NodeTypes` key are the primary snap-in items that we have extended. Recall the previous primary snap-in registry script that made empty registration place holders for the items it published (p. 461). The extension snap-in registry script extends these items with additional registrations.

In the preceding registry script, we add the `Extensions` key, which can contain one or more of the following: `NameSpace`, `ContextMenu`, `ToolBar`, `PropertySheet`, and `Task`. Each of these subkeys specifies the type of extension of the extension snap-in. As you can see from this registry script, the extension snap-in extends only Context menus for the Windows service items. The class identifier (CLSID) value is the extension snap-in's co-class.

■ Making MMC Snap-ins Theme Aware

Unlike previous versions of Windows, Windows XP introduces new user interfaces that are called *visual styles*. A visual style affects how applications display buttons, dialogs, and other common controls. An application that displays buttons, dialogs, and other common controls in the active visual style is said to be *theme aware*. It should be the goal for all applications to become theme aware. The visual impression of a theme-aware application makes it look at home under Windows XP. Users of Windows XP rapidly get accustomed to the hot-spotting of controls as the mouse moves over them, as well as its visual appearance. Users will quickly notice if your application does not fit in with the user interface. Paying close attention to the user interface in MMC snap-ins is important because MMC itself is theme aware. Property pages that it hosts will appear out of place, presenting a mixed style of controls, if the snap-in is not theme aware. Look at the primary MMC snap-in example in Figure 9.31.

Notice first that the page uses the classic solid dialog background color instead of a white-to-grey gradation. If you look closely, you will see a white border around the page.

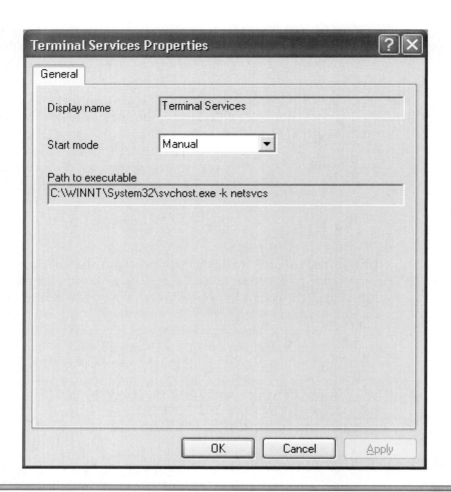

Figure 9.31 MMC snap-in: Not theme aware

Second, the edit controls and combo box use the classic visual style. Although this is not a complex page, it is easy to tell that it does not fit in with the Windows XP visual style. Fortunately, Microsoft makes it reasonably easy to make an application or DLL theme aware. (If your application uses OLE controls, then the task is a bit more involved. Check the Platform SDK for additional information in using the theme-aware APIs.)

The first task in making an MMC snap-in DLL theme aware is to declare it as *isolation* aware. This introduces special code within the Platform SDK header files to use the theme-aware controls, especially property sheets. Include the following statement before any other header files in stdafx.h:

```
#define ISOLATION_AWARE_ENABLED TRUE
```

The code introduced by this declaration will make the DLL automatically use the theme-aware controls if it is running under Windows XP. Note that the DLL is compatible with other versions of Windows with no other operating system specific dependencies being introduced. The `ISOLATION_AWARE_ENABLED` definition becomes active only when the DLL is linked to the new common controls.

In a visual style other than the classic one, all the standard controls have been moved into the common controls DLL, COMCTL32.DLL, so the key in making an application or DLL use the Windows theme-aware controls is to link to the new common controls. This is achieved by making a manifest that is an XML-based file. The manifest is included in the application or DLL's resources and is queried for by the Windows executable loader. The following XML document is stored in a file called `MMCPrimarySnapin.dll.manifest`:

```
<?xml version="1.0" encoding="UTF-8" standalone="yes"?>
<assembly xmlns="urn:schemas-microsoft-com:asm.v1" manifestVersion
="1.0">
<assemblyIdentity
  version="1.0.0.1"
  processorArchitecture="X86"
  name="MMCPrimarySnapin.MMCPrimary.1"
  type="win32"
/>
<description>WMI Service primary snap-in</description>
<dependency>
  <dependentAssembly>
    <assemblyIdentity
      type="win32"
      name="Microsoft.Windows.Common-Controls"
      version="6.0.0.0"
      processorArchitecture="X86"
      publicKeyToken="6595b64144ccf1df"
      language="*"
    />
  </dependentAssembly>
</dependency>
</assembly>
```

The items highlighted in bold font are the replaceable portions of the manifest. You should complete them with your version number, component identifier, and description. Windows XP and the .NET Framework introduce a new concept called an *assembly*. At a very basic level, an assembly is a collection of files. In many cases, it probably is a single DLL. Global assemblies are registered with the operating system and are stored in a secure area of the file system. The result of the example manifest is that all the user-interface controls (standard and common controls) that an application or DLL uses will use the new common controls version 6.0.

The next step is to include the above manifest in the application or DLL. Declare the following resource identifier in the resource.h file:

```
#define MANIFEST_RESOURCE_ID 2
```

This is followed by linking the manifest file into the executable's resources. Include the following DLL's resource file (.rc):

```
MANIFEST_RESOURCE_ID RT_MANIFEST "MMCPrimarySnapin.dll.manifest"
```

When the application or DLL is loaded after compilation, it will use the new common controls library. Because the new common controls library is theme aware, all

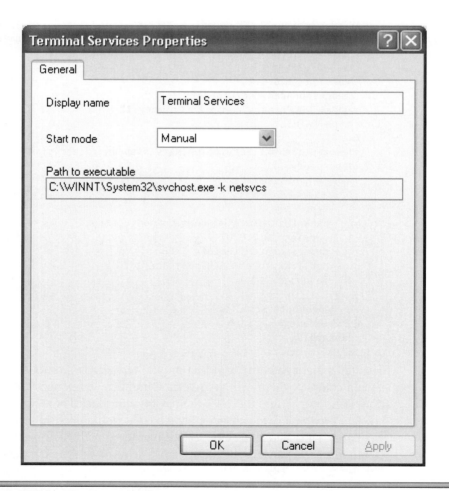

Figure 9.32 MMC snap-in: Theme aware

common controls displayed in your application will also become theme aware. The screen shot in Figure 9.32 shows a theme-aware version of the property page from Figure 9.31.

■ Summary

We began this chapter by noting the importance of a standardized unified administration environment. This environment had to be extensible and support many different types of administration. A quick tour of all the interfaces defined within MMC followed. We distinguished between the interfaces provided by the console and the interfaces the snap-in should implement. The snap-in demonstration first discussed the `IComponentData` and `IComponent`, two of the most important interfaces that a snap-in must implement. After we demonstrated how to add scope and result items, more discussion provided a how-to guide for extending the administration user interface with menus, property pages, and toolbars. In addition, we showed how to incorporate an ActiveX control to customize the result pane view for a scope item and how to access Web sites easily.

We discussed and demonstrated some advanced features like drag and drop and how to programmatically refocus a property sheet. We showed you how ATL delegates calls to the appropriate items and more about the `IDataObject` interface and some of its interactions with other objects, such as in extension snap-ins.

To make the demonstration snap-in relevant to this book, we showed how to express WMI management objects in the user interface, conveniently using the management object's relative path to carry out operations against the correct Windows service.

We discussed and demonstrated extension snap-ins in detail, in which the most important part was how extension snap-ins bind to a primary snap-in. The extension snap-in architecture is rich and allows for the partitioning of snap-in development within a large team.

Ten Fast Facts: Developing MMC Snap-ins

1. The Microsoft Management Console is the center point for all administration tools. It allows administrators to set up frequently accessed administration tools and, because all snap-ins have a similar look and feel, it reduces the total cost of ownership.

2. MMC provides a comprehensive snap-in hosting architecture providing support for standalone and extension snap-ins. Standalone snap-ins can be run on their own and can be extended in a number of ways, allowing administration tool developers to leverage existing administration environments. Extension snap-ins also can be extended by other extension snap-ins.

3. Developing MMC snap-ins is a combination of using a number of MMC-provided COM interfaces and a snap-in providing MMC with implementations of a few COM interfaces that deliver the administration user interface.

4. Standalone snap-ins must support the `IComponentData` and `IComponent` interfaces. Extension snap-ins can support either or both of these interfaces depending on the type of extension.

5. The `IComponentData` interface is the snap-in's primary interface and allows the extension of scope pane items. The `IComponent` interface implements the result pane and allows the extension of result pane items.

6. Snap-ins that want to display context menus, property sheets, and toolbars must support `IExtendContextMenu`, `IExtendPropertySheet`, and `IExtendControlbar` interfaces respectively.

7. MMC has a number of specific verbs such as rename, delete, and properties. Verbs help in maintaining a consistent user interface and a set of common operations across all snap-ins.

8. Primary and extension snap-in items (both scope and result pane items) should publish key information. This opens up the MMC extension architecture for other extension snap-ins to provide new and related user interface extensions to the administration tool set.

9. If you require a customized user interface that differs from the default list view in the result pane, then consider developing a custom OLE control.

10. Develop your snap-ins against the latest Platform SDK so that they can be made theme aware and fit in with Windows XP visual styles.

Chapter 10

Developing WMI Scripts
for Administrators

If you have spent any amount of time managing computer systems in industry, it is probably safe to assume that at some point, through no fault of your own, you have had to deal with a system management crisis. It is said that the Chinese language, developed long before system administration, views crisis as a type of opportunity (although we doubt this means a "crisamatunity," as Homer Simpson once said). The purpose of this chapter is to look at the ways that WMI minimizes these opportunities for administrators and promotes more productive use of your time. Don't be mistaken: network cards still will fail, user accounts will need resetting, and disks will need defragmenting, but with the suite of tools provided by Microsoft, you will be prepared better for at least some eventualities and better able to automate a great many of your day-to-day tasks.

In the past decade alone, the role of system administrators and support staff has increased in complexity with every advance in enterprise infrastructure. Despite these advances it seems that the reactive ethos of system management remains, ensuring that a large percentage of time is spent resolving previously unforeseen catastrophes in an ad hoc manner. For Microsoft and the DMTF, this signalled that it was time for enterprise system management to catch up with the rest of technology. Consequently, Microsoft Windows Management Instrumentation (WMI) was born with a view to providing a more efficient way to manage systems and your time. Microsoft has developed a suite of tools built to gain maximum leverage and enable administrators to embrace proactive as well as reactive management strategy. Using these tools administrators can actually try to anticipate events, such as a server disk running out of space, and have an automated sequence of tasks in place to deal with it.

Until now we have discussed the core technologies and architecture of WMI, but have addressed its use only from the perspective of a developer. To redress any potential imbalance, Chapters 10 and 11 are written specifically with a view to targeting those at the *sharp end* of reducing the total cost of ownership. Whereas past chapters focused upon the role of both the developer and the administrator, we now examine a number of scenarios specific to administrators and the solutions to them offered by WMI.

Let's look at the various tools at your disposal as an administrator and see if we can make your life easier at work and save you some money on shoe leather.

■ Scripting, WMIC, and the CIM Studio

Microsoft provides a variety of tools and technologies for those who wish to manage their systems using WMI. We shall examine three particular approaches:

- The WMI CIM studio (for Windows 98 and above)
- Windows Management Instrumentation Command-line (WMIC) (for Windows XP)
- Visual Basic Scripting for WMI (for Windows 98 and above)

This chapter introduces scripting for beginners and then introduces the WMI Application Programming Interface (API) in the context of a series of examples. Chapter 11 examines how to tackle writing your own scripts for WMI as an adjunct to the material presented here and introduces the Windows XP tool, WMIC. The WMI CIM studio is mentioned in both chapters, however, those unfamiliar with it should refer to Chapter 4 for a detailed introductory tutorial.

■ Administration and the WMI CIM Studio

If you have read Chapter 4, you are already familiar with the function and purpose of the WMI CIM Studio. From an administrator's perspective, the Studio provides an invaluable way of moving through the CIM repository to gain an insight into exactly what data you can retrieve from WMI, as well as a way of managing system settings. Its primary purpose here is to assist us in moving through the wealth of management information available from the CIM repository and in tracking down classes that may be of interest. In fact, being able to script proficiently is only half of the struggle to gain maximum advantage from WMI. The other half comes from understanding the structure of the CIM repository and being able to move through it to locate relevant classes and associations.

■ Administration and the WMIC

WMIC is part of Microsoft Windows XP Professional's new suite of command-line tools and is an effective tool for administrators who wish to effect changes upon small groups of machines or produce reports garnered from WMI's management data. We shall look at how we can use WMIC to automate management tasks and as a command line–driven utility for local and remote system configuration and management in the next chapter.

■ Administration and Scripting

Perhaps the most advanced feature of the WMI management suite of tools for administrators is the client-side scripting mechanism supported by the Windows Scripting Host. Although comparatively simple in relation to the COM interface model for developers discussed in Chapters 7 and 8, scripting is nonetheless a powerful means for retrieving information from WMI and for automating day-to-day tasks and providing proactive solutions to system management. Although we are leveling our discussion at administrators, the examples and techniques discussed here are relevant also to software developers, because scripting and WMIC (to some extent) are excellent ways to test WMI-instrumented products.

■ Guiding Principles

Much that you need to know about administration for WMI can be found on Microsoft's MSDN Web site (http://msdn.microsoft.com) as well as on numerous third party sites. Acres of documentation exist to assist those new to scripting, WMIC, or the WMI CIM Studio to discover even the smallest minutiae of information; so why bother with this chapter?

One of the common problems people find when learning a new technology today is not that they cannot find enough information but more often that they find too much and do not know where to begin, or they do not have the time to extract what they need. To learn WMI using the existing Microsoft documentation (which provides a commendable level of detail), is somewhat akin to attempting to learn the English language by reading a thesaurus: The material is very informative but somewhat overpowering for a beginner. With this in mind, this chapter attempts to:

- Cut a swathe through the documentation so you do not have to!
- Provide examples, suggestions, and best practices that are targeted at providing a manageable level of detail for someone just starting out with scripting and WMI.

After readers are more accomplished, the Microsoft sources available on the Web provide an excellent source of reference and should become an invaluable tool. The purpose of this chapter therefore is not to replace the official documentation, but rather to provide a quick introduction to the relevant issues that builds upon readers' existing knowledge to make them productive as quickly as possible.

■ Prerequisites

To get the most from this chapter, first make sure that you have read Chapters 1 through 4 and are familiar with CIM terminology: classes, instances, schemas, namespaces, and so forth. You should also be familiar with the WMI CIM Studio and have a good general knowledge of the Windows platforms. We assume that as an administrator you have a general knowledge of desktop and server hardware and of basic network topologies and concepts: routers, gateways, and so forth. The chapter does not assume a prior knowledge of scripting, but some basic knowledge of batch files will be helpful to your understanding of the concepts we explain.

■ Chapter Structure

The chapter tackles one of the more challenging tools for administrators to master: the scripting API for WMI. This section assumes not that readers have scripted before but that they have some prior knowledge of batch file language or log on scripts and so feel comfortable with the basics of program execution and program flow of control. The introduction examines simple scripting examples that illustrate basic script structure, variables and constants, and basic input and output. The chapter then introduces the concept of attaching to WMI namespaces and the security considerations and potential pitfalls associated with the different techniques. The bulk of the chapter introduces a series of practical examples for interacting with WMI, including retrieving data, modifying data, deleting data, and creating data, all of which are tasks administrators commonly perform with WMI. As part of this process, we introduce the basic use of the Windows GUI to enable scripts to elicit and provide feedback in a format consistent with the users' experience, as well as accepting input from the command line.

Throughout the chapter, we introduce readers to a series of best practices for writing professional WMI scripts for system administration. We anticipate that practicing these techniques will enable readers to write maintainable, readable, and usable scripts.

■ VBScript Boot Camp

The purpose of this section is to introduce you to the fundamentals of scripting, the Windows Scripting Host (WSH), and the scripting API for WMI in as short a time as possible. To achieve this, we made certain sacrifices with regard to the level of detail and topics covered. We present only the bare essentials. Consequently, some details have been omitted in favor of concentrating on the pragmatic aspects of scripting for WMI. For example, although often the WMI API offers more than one way to achieve a goal, because of limited space we chose the most broadly applicable to the widest number of scenarios. Therefore, we do not claim that our examples represent the definitive approach to tackling a problem in WMI (nor the leanest or most efficient). They do, however, convey a series of best practices with explanations that will enable administrators to write professional-level scripts quickly and simply. We also hope that the examples represent a cross-section of the tasks that system administrators will want to perform with WMI, thus providing a starting point from which to script productively in as short a time as possible. We anticipate that upon completing the examples given here and in Chapter 11, readers should feel confident enough to write their own more complex scripts using the reference material available from Microsoft.[1]

Although it is true that scripting is not as simple as the MSDOS batch file language or log on scripts for network operating systems, over the years it has become an increasingly powerful tool for system administrators. With the introduction of WMI and the scripting API for WMI there has never been a more compelling reason to learn to script. The material covered here will introduce you to scripting for WMI and in doing so will teach you the basics of scripting. Scripting skills are generally applicable to all types of system maintenance, whether governed by WMI or not, and can be broadly applied to the automation of day-to-day repetitive tasks. Despite the initial overhead associated with learning to script for WMI, the investment will ultimately repay you by making your time more productive. The sample scripts provide clear examples of the kind of power you can harness to impress colleagues and employers.

■ JavaScript vs. VBScript

The WSH can interpret both JScript and VBScript as part of its standard installation, and the choice between the two is largely arbitrary in scripting for WMI. We use VBScript in our examples because although we do not require the platform independence of JScript, we do require the interoperability with Component Object Model (COM). VBScript has built in support for collections that commonly are returned by COM objects. VBScript, a subset of the Visual Basic for Applications (VBA) language, is developed and supported by Microsoft, which is actively interested in maintaining and promoting its future use.

Terminology Checkpoint:

Throughout this section we refer to the *syntax* and *semantics* of a language. The syntax of a language governs its grammatical usage and spelling. Unlike humans,

1. Detailed information on scripting and all Microsoft technologies is available on the Microsoft MSDN Web site, http://msdn.microsoft.com.

computers understand only information fed to them in a very precise form. The syntax of the language dictates this form. Semantics refer to the intended meaning of a command (that is, what it does). In the English language, we could say that "I, in the bar, went" is a simple example of a syntax error whereas, "We went into the bar," although syntactically correct is semantically wrong if one person went in to the bar alone. In other words, the conveyed meaning is not the intended meaning. Syntax and semantic errors (sometimes referred to as *logic errors*) are two types of error programmers commonly encounter.

■ Setting Up Your System for Scripting

Regardless of the version of Windows you run, you should download the latest version of Microsoft Windows Scripting Host and Windows Script Debugger (free from the Microsoft Web site). Installing these will ensure that all the file associations and script engines are configured correctly on your system and that you have the latest functionality. It will also allow you to run the examples in this chapter.[2]

> **Note:** Windows XP users should download the Windows 9x/Me/NT4.0 version of Windows Scripting Host.

■ Scripting and Administration

The typical workload of a system administrator covers a wide variety of tasks. In Table 10.1 we provide examples of common administrative tasks that for which WMI scripting is useful. We shall cover each of these aspects in the chapter.

■ What Is the Windows Scripting Host?

The Windows Scripting Host (WSH) is a small binary executable that resides in the ..//Windows/system32 folder. It is shipped with Windows 98, Windows 2000 (Server and Professional), Windows XP, and IIS4.0. Microsoft describes it as a "language independent scripting host for the Windows operating system," which in plain English means that you can use a variety of scripting languages with it if you have installed the necessary ActiveX scripting engine. Because standard WSH supports Microsoft Visual Basic Scripting (VBScript) and JavaScript (JScript), both of which install as part of Internet Explorer 3.0 and later, to run scripts, you need to install WSH on your system.

2. Microsoft Windows Scripting Host (version 5.6 approximately 700k) can be downloaded from: http://www.microsoft.com/msdownload/vbscript/scripting56.asp.

Table 10.1 Matching Common Administrative Tasks to WMI Equivalent

Type of Task	Example	WMI Scripting Programmatic Equivalent
Tracing the source of a fault.	Discovering which disk controller is attached to which disk drive partition.	Association traversal.
Checking the status of a managed object.	Check the processes and services currently running on local/remote machine(s).	Instance retrieval.
	Find user accounts that are locked or disabled.	Instance retrieval using a WQL query.
	Find the status of a specific user account.	
Changing the state of a managed object.	Setting a user account to be locked.	Instance modification.
Creating a new managed object.	Create a new instance of a managed object. For example a new process (i.e., run Notepad. exe), create a new directory, service or share, etc.	Instance creation.
Deleting a managed object.	Removing a print job from a print queue.	Instance deletion.
Effecting changes in state on a managed system.	Rebooting a system or enabling DHCP.	Method invocation.
Responding to changes in the managed environment.	Disk space below 10Mbytes.	Event triggered script.

■ Scripts

A script is merely a plain text file, very similar in some respects to an MSDOS batch file. It contains a series of commands that the WSH passes to the relevant scripting engine for interpretation into actions. WSH determines to which engine to pass the script based upon the file suffix of the script. For scripts written in VBScript, the file suffix is *.vbs* and for scripts written in JScript, the file suffix is *.js*. The association between the suffix and the ActiveX scripting engine is stored in the registry under the following key:

```
HKEY_LOCAL_MACHINE\SOFTWARE\Microsoft\Windows Scripting Host\Script
Extensions
```

Two further file types that are of interest to the WSH are *.wsf* and *.wsh*. Files with these extensions contain references to other script files as part of the script. This programming approach makes it possible to intermix scripts written in different languages and to store functions collectively as libraries. Space limitations prevent our addressing these file types in our introduction to WMI scripting.

■ Scripting vs. Compiled Languages

In scripting, unlike compiled languages such as C++, you do not need to go through building and compilation before you can execute a script. In other words, you do not need to create an executable (.exe file) to run the file. This simplifies the process of coding and debugging but affects the performance of the script in relation to such compiled languages. The performance reduction, however, is nominal because most scripts are relatively small and the tasks administrators require them to perform are relatively simple, compared to a full-blown Windows application.

The benefits of writing scripts for WMI follow in summary:

- They are easy to use after you master the basic syntax.
- They can do everything that MSDOS batch files can do and a lot more.
- They can be written to perform tasks ranging from the retrieval of a log-in name to e-mailing all of the services running on a given machine to you.
- They enable you use the professional-looking Windows GUI to write scripts, which is not possible from MS-DOS.
- They can take action in response to events while they are unattended.[3]

BEST PRACTICE!   Script Signing

Administrators who are concerned about the potential security risks associated with running scripts can take advantage of Microsoft's new scripting security model introduced with Windows Scripting Host 5.6. It provides a series of Crypto API tools that can create and verify digital signatures. Using these tools, it is possible to *sign* a script, and to view and manage certificates, certificate revocation lists (CRLs), and certificate trust lists (CTLs). This means that you can create a script and sign it to ensure that when it executes on a host no one has tampered with it and it comes from authorized source.[4]

---

3. Anyone who questions the potential power of scripting should think back to the outbreak of the I Love You (Love Letter) worm. Written in VBScript and sent as an attachment in an e-mail message, it is an infamous testament to the power of scripting and the Windows Scripting Host. An MSDOS batch file could never have achieved a fraction of this functionality!

4. For more information on the Crypto API tools see: http://msdn.microsoft.com/library/en-us/script56/html/wsconWinTrust.asp.

■ The Windows Scripting Host

Microsoft developed the Windows Scripting Host (WSH) to provide a way to interact with the Windows operating system by executing scripts directly on the Windows desktop or from within the command console. Microsoft also provides a command-line driven equivalent, CSCript.exe, that will allow you to run scripts from the command line. In our discussion we shall use the Windows-based version, WSCript.exe, so that we can interact with the Windows GUI. If you surf the Web, you may already be aware that scripts can be embedded in HTML documents to perform routine tasks such as verifying the fields in a form. WSH enables us to write standalone scripts and execute them directly without embedding them in HTML.

Scripts can be executed in any of the following ways:

- They can be added to HTML documents and activated with Internet Explorer V3.0 or later.
- They can be added to Active Server Pages (.asp) using Internet Information Services (IIS).
- They can be executed as standalone scripts using the Windows Scripting Host.

Because of the types of tasks administrators undertake, we shall concentrate upon writing standalone scripts that are interpreted by the Windows Scripting Host.

■ Your First Script

Rather than attempt to introduce a large amount of theory off the cuff, let's start by typing and running our first script (Figure 10.1). If you are too impatient to type the scripts, you can download them all from our Web site at http://www.wbem.co.uk.

```
'Example        1
'Author:        Craig Tunstall 26/04/2002          } annotation
'Description:   A simple script to display a greeting using a
'               variable and constant value
Option Explicit

Const   MESSAGE = "Welcome"        } variable/constant declaration
DIM strMyInput

strMyInput = " to scripting"
MsgBox ("This is a string literal")                 } program
MsgBox ("This is a constant: " & MESSAGE)             body
MsgBox ("This is a constant and variable: " & MESSAGE & strMyInput)
```

Figure 10.1 First script

To write using VBScript you need a simple text editor like Windows Notepad or Wordpad. If you use Windows Wordpad you should make sure that you save your work as a text document because the extra formatting instructions in the other formats will cause errors in running the script. The other downside of using Wordpad is that error messages typically refer to specific line numbers and Wordpad does not have the facility to display line numbers. This can become confusing if your scripts grow to any great length. To avoid this problem you can use Notepad or a dedicated program editor (of which numerous shareware or freeware examples are available for download from the Web).[5] The Windows script debugger already has a line number facility for identifying errors.

> **Note:** The Microsoft Notepad GoTo… facility on the Edit menu only works with the Word Wrap feature switched off.

> **Hint:** Scripting is not case sensitive, so you can use upper case and lower case indiscriminately and it will mean the same to the WSH.

Now save the file to disk before attempting to run it. To run the script you can double-click the file in Explorer or right-click it and select Open. Assuming that you have typed everything correctly and installed the Windows Scripting Host, your script should generate three separate dialog boxes, one at a time, as shown in Figure 10.2.

Congratulations, you have successfully typed and run your first script! Now let us look at how it works.

You can see from the example that the program starts by listing some comments explaining who wrote the script, when they wrote it, and a simple description of what it does. We refer to this as *annotation* and shall explain its importance shortly. Next we

Figure 10.2 Results of running example1.vbs

5. A particularly good product is the Textpad text editor from Helios, http://www.textpad.com, that is available for trial as shareware.

specify an option for the WSH, Option Explicit. This affects the way the script is parsed before it is interpreted. We shall discuss this in detail shortly. Next we define a single constant value called MESSAGE and assigned it a value, "Welcome," using the equals (=) sign. We also declare a variable called strMyInput using the DIM statement.

We then enter the program body, which is the part of the script that tells WSH what to do with all of the constants and variables defined previously and how to behave. First we assign the string value, "to scripting," to our variable. Next we have a series of calls to MsgBox function (short for Message Box), which displays a simple dialog box with an OK button. Each MsgBox contains some text, the first a string literal, the second a string literal and constant, and the third a string literal, constant, and variable. We shall provide more detailed definitions of all these terms as the chapter progresses. A *string literal* is a fancy way of describing a piece of text enclosed in quotation marks. In the last two calls to MsgBox we used the ampersand (&) symbol to concatenate the data before displaying it to the screen.

Now let's type another example (Figure 10.3) that illustrates GUI-based input and output and the use of variables.

This script initially behaves much the same as the last one until the point at which the variable strMyInput is assigned the value, "to scripting." Then its behavior alters and an input box is placed on the screen using the InputBox function that displays in Figure 10.4.

The input box is displayed *before* the message box when we run the script because it appears in the script before the MsgBox call. Any input is then stored in the variable strMyInput, overwriting its initial value. The last MsgBox call then displays this value to

```
'Example:        2
'Author:         Craig Tunstall 26/04/2002
'Description:    A simple script to get some input using InputBox and
'                then display it using the MsgBox function

Option Explicit

Const MESSAGE = "Welcome"
DIM strMyInput

strMyInput = " to scripting"
strMyInput = InputBox("Please enter some text:")

MsgBox ("This is a string literal")
MsgBox ("This is a constant: " & MESSAGE)
MsgBox ("This is what you entered: " & strMyInput)
```

Figure 10.3 GUI output using script

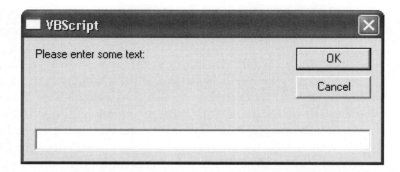

Figure 10.4 The result of calling the `InputBox` function

the screen by referring to the `strMyInput`. This shows us how variables can be overwritten at run-time. Try changing the script as follows and running it to see what happens.

```
strMyInput = InputBox("Please enter some text:")
```

to

```
MESSAGE = InputBox("Please enter some text:")
```

Hint: You will receive an error, and the script will not run.

In reality, the first line that assigns a value to `strMyInput` would be superfluous because the variable is later assigned a value from the results of the input box.

Don't worry at this point if you do not understand every statement in the examples. Their purpose is to introduce you to the basics of variables and constants, input and output, and basic program structure. Having typed these, let's look at some theory behind VBScript and programming in general and introduce some additional principles with which you will need to be familiar before you start scripting.

■ Indentation

Scripts are more highly structured than batch files, and to make them readable and maintainable and to help track down syntax errors, we use indentation. Scripts should always follow a consistent indentation convention to emphasize the flow of the program. If called upon to amend an existing script always adhere to the existing indentation style or modify the indentation style for the entire source.

- Use tabs to indent lines of code where necessary.

- Use vertical spaces (carriage returns) to segment logical sections of the script (for example, program body and variable/constant declaration).

- Use horizontal spaces to separate statements and their outcome.

BEST PRACTICE! Code Indentation

Always indent your code. It will improve readability and maintainability and help you locate syntax errors.

Annotation

It is considered good practice to always annotate a script. Annotation enables programmers to quickly recognize what the program does, who wrote it, and when it was written. Typically programmers annotate the start of the script and any subroutines, complex statements, arguments to routines, and control structures. If you are modifying an existing script, also ensure that you update the comments to reflect any changes. As a general rule scripts should include enough comments that another programmer can interpret your code, but not so many that they overwhelm readers, thus obscuring the code.

To annotate in VBscript, you have two choices: either to use the ' character or to use the REM keyword (short for REMark). Both allow you to put a textual description of what the script does until the end of that line. Remember to use the ' character or REM at the beginning of each new line immediately before your text to avoid syntax errors.

Annotating your code saves somebody else having to read through your work line by line to understand the purpose of the script. Although this type of annotation is not required for your script to run, it is definitely considered good practice and can save a lot of time when you go back to your scripts.

BEST PRACTICE! Code Annotation

Always annotate your scripts with at least the author's name, the date the script was written or modified, and the purpose of the script.

■ Variants, Variables, and Constants

In the previous examples, we declared a constant called MESSAGE. We did so using the const keyword and assigning it a value of "Welcome." The string literal was enclosed in quotation marks to delimit the string so that WSH knows where it starts and ends. Anything enclosed in quotation marks is classified as a string literal. Because MESSAGE is a constant, it cannot be changed while the script is running (that is, it remains *constant* throughout the running of the script). This explains the error message you received earlier if you altered the script to assign MESSAGE, the value taken from the input box. If we wish to create values that can be changed during the running script, we declare variables using the *DIM* statement (note that there are actually three variations of this statement—ReDIM, Public, and Private—but for the purpose of the boot camp we use only DIM). Note also that variable and constant names must be unique within the scope that they are declared.

The purpose of variables and constants in any programming language is to keep track of data components in a convenient and easy to remember way. Without variables and constants, we would find ourselves placing data in areas of memory manually and then having to remember where we placed them and what they were for! In the not-so-distant past when people programmed in assembly language, you literally chose a free spot in memory and placed your data there. Whenever you wanted to retrieve that data, you had to refer explicitly to that memory address using a numeric value. Variables and constants provide us with an automatic way of storing this data in memory.

VBScript has only a single data type, referred to as a Variant. Variants are able to contain different types of data (that is, strings, numbers, objects) depending on how they are used. From the perspective of a programmer this makes life really simple. Also, because Variant is the only data type in VBScript, it is also the data type returned by all functions in VBScript. When we declare variables, they are all of type Variant.

Software engineers classify programming languages as either strongly or loosely typed depending upon how strict the language is with regard to its type declaration and the combining of types. For example, in C++ you must first declare the *type* (that is, if it is a string or a numerical value) of a variable before you can assign it a value. Because VBScript uses Variants, we classify it as loosely typed. You therefore can forego having to assign an explicit type to any variables you use. You can also combine variables and constants regardless of type.

■ Use Meaningful Variable Names

Although it is tempting while hacking away at a piece of script to use any variable or constant name that comes to mind, it is a lot easier to understand the flow of a script, maintain it, and track errors if you use meaningful variable and constant names. For example, variable X13DA may have had some cryptic meaning at its inception but is unlikely to have the same meaning six months later and will probably mean nothing to someone else trying to maintain your script.

Different software companies have different naming conventions for variables, constants, objects, and so forth. Indeed you may decide that you should follow this example and define a naming convention of your own. When doing so, try to capture in the naming scheme the purpose of the variable, constant, or function as well as its type. For example, name your variables and constants in a way that indicates whether they are variables (that is, they can change during the execution of the script), constants (that is, they cannot change during the execution of the script), or functions. In scripting, variable and constant names can be up to 255 characters long, but it is advisable to keep them to between six and twenty characters; otherwise, they become cumbersome.

For example, we shall use the following naming convention:

Numeric variables are prepended with *n*	that is, `nCounter`
String variables are prepended with *str*	that is, `strMyString`
Array variables are prepended with *a*	that is, `aAnArray`
Objects are prepended with *obj*	that is, `objAnObject`
Constants are entirely uppercase	that is, `MYCONST`

BEST PRACTICE! Variable Naming

Always use a consistent naming convention when writing scripts and always use meaningful variable names.

■ VBScript Functions

Microsoft provides over 90 built-in functions with VBScript to assist you in performing a variety of common programming tasks. These functions save you having to write complex code when performing tasks like placing a dialog box on the screen, converting date values, or displaying a picture to the screen. In the examples so far, we have used the `MsgBox` and `InputBox` function to output information.

```
MsgBox ("This is a string literal")
MsgBox ("This is a constant: " & MESSAGE)
MsgBox ("This is what you entered: " & strMyInput)
```

For a detailed explanation of the available functions and their purpose, see http://msdn.microsoft.com/library/en-us/script56/html/vtoriFunctions.asp.

▪ The WSH Object Model

The main motivation for writing any program is to achieve some goal, whether it is displaying a simple text message on the screen or accessing some data from a database. The process of writing our scripts to perform certain types of administrative tasks is simplified by calling upon prewritten methods or properties that are stored in the WSH object model. When you run a script using the WSH, you automatically gain access to the object model that it provides. Each object in the object model potentially contains a number of methods and properties that are all related by function. For example, the WshNetwork Object contains methods that relate to network drives and printers and properties that hold the user name, computer name, and domain name. The WSH object model defines 14 objects, broadly categorized as either helper functions or script execution and troubleshooting functions. You can use the helper functions in your scripts to perform tasks such as mapping network drives or retrieving and modifying environment variables, creating shortcuts, and reading and writing from the system registry. The execution and troubleshooting interfaces allow output to the screen and manipulation of the WSH. We cannot describe each of these in detail here, but shall mention those that we use in our examples. For more information on the WSH object model, see http://msdn.microsoft.com/library/en-us/script56/html/wsori WSHLanguageReference.asp.

▪ Program Statements and Keywords

For our programs to actually perform some actions, we must issue commands to tell the system what we want it to do. To make this happen, we use statements that have associated actions. These statements are predefined by the programming language and learning them is part and parcel of coding in any language. To make things easier to remember, the statement names give some indication of their function and are usually referred to as *keywords*. For example, the *constant* keyword is short for *constant*. Each programming language has its own set of keywords. The only limitation is that you need to remember that you cannot use one of these reserved keywords to name your variables. For example, you cannot name a variable Set because this would lead to confusion: The system would not know whether you were referring to the variable or to the VBScript keyword. With some practice, however, you will find yourself reusing certain statements, making the coding process a lot more fluid. Also, certain patterns will begin to emerge in your programming, thus simplifying and speeding up your scripting time. In our Example 1 and Example 2, `const` and `DIM` are keywords that belong to the VBScript language.

Table 10.2 provides a list of VBScript keywords with brief descriptions. For a more detailed outline of their function and arguments, please refer to the MSDN Web site at http://msdn.microsoft.com/library/en-us/script56/html/vtoriStatements.asp.

Table 10.2 VBScript Keywords

Keyword	Description
`Call`	An optional keyword used to pass control of the script to a sub or function procedure.
`Class`	Used to declare class definitions.
`Const`	Declares a constant value.
`Dim`	Declares one or more variables.
`Do...Loop`	Used to repeat a block of statements until a condition is true or while a condition is true.
`Erase`	Used in conjunction with fixed-sized arrays to clear their contents.
`Execute`	Used to execute one or more statements.
`ExecuteGlobal`	Used to execute one or more statements in the global namespace of the script.
`Exit`	Used to forcibly exit do…loop, for each…next, functions or subroutines.
`For Each...Next`	Iterates through a group of statements for each element in a collection or array.
`For...Next`	Iterates through a block of statements a specified number of times.
`Function`	Declares the name, arguments, and code that form the body of a Function procedure.
`If...Then...Else`	Conditionally executes a block of statements, depending on the value of an expression.
`On Error`	Enables or disables error-handling by the system. Typically used as `On Error Resume Next`, which disables the global Err object.
`Option Explicit`	Used to force explicit declaration of variables in a script with the DIM, ReDIM, Private, and Public statements.
`Private`	Used to declare private variables.
`Property Get`	Used in a class block to specify a name, arguments, and code that return a value.
`Property Let`	Used in a class block to specify a name, arguments, and code that set a value.
`Property Set`	Used in a class block to specify a name, arguments, and code that set a reference to a value.
`Public`	Used to declare public values.
`Randomize`	Generates a random number. Used in conjunction with the `Rnd` function that returns a random number.
`ReDim`	Declares a dynamic array.
`REM`	Short for Remark and used to add comments to a script. Is same as '.
`Select Case`	Executes one of several groups of statements depending on the value of an expression.
`Set`	Used to assign an object reference to a variable or property.
`Sub`	Declares a subroutine within a script. The block of code that forms the subroutine must be terminated by the statement End Sub.

Continued

Table 10.2 *Continued*

Keyword	Description
While...Wend	Repeats a block of statements while a condition is true.
With	Allows reference to be made to an object's functions unqualified. This is useful if repeated calls need to be made to functions on the same object.
Empty	Used to indicate an uninitialized variable value. This is not the same thing as a variable being set to null.
False	Equivalent to 0.
Nothing	Used in conjunction with set to disassociate an object variable from any object.
Null	Used to indicate that a variable contains no valid data.
True	Equivalent to 1.

■ The Option Explicit Statement

In all of our examples, we shall use the Option Explicit statement. This tells the interpreter to check the script more stringently for the declaration of variables using the DIM, Private, Public, and ReDim. This statement must appear before any other statements in the script. But why would we specify something that will make our lives harder? We don't. Without Option Explicit it is possible to introduce errors in your script that can be hard to track down at a later date. Using Option Explicit makes you more aware of the variables that you have declared and their purpose within the script.

> **BEST PRACTICE!** Variable Declaration
>
> Always declare the Option Explicit statement at the start of your scripts.

■ Connecting to a Local or Remote Namespace

Our next example takes the first step toward interacting with WMI using a script. It connects to a namespace in the CIM repository. From reading the previous chapters, you should be aware of the purpose of namespaces in CIM. When connected you are able to retrieve, set, delete, or create management information. If you want to interact with WMI, then you must first connect to a namespace.

In the example in Figure 10.5, we have built upon Example 2 and defined a new variable called objNamespace to hold a namespace object. The script still uses an input box, but we have modified this to request the name of the machine to which you wish to connect. WMI accepts a machine name or an IP address as a parameter. The script introduces the use of the `GetObject` statement to attempt to connect to a WMI namespace on a remote machine using the `WINMGMTS` *moniker* (don't worry; we shall discuss `WINMGMTS` and monikers in more detail shortly). We say *attempt* because the successful completion of the task is due to many factors outside the control of the script, including the availability of the destination machine, network conditions, and our security context. Let's assume, however, that the statement successfully connects to the default namespace on the target machine.

```
Set objNamespace =
Getobject("WINMGMTS:{impersonationlevel=impersonate}\\" &
    strMyInput)
```

If we wanted to specify a target namespace other than the default then we could append it, as follows, to the end of the `WINMGMTS` call.

```
Set objNamespace =
GetObject("WINMGMTS:{impersonationlevel=impersonate}//"&
    "root/anothernamespace"}
```

A *moniker* is an alias for a sequence of calls and settings. Microsoft provided the `WINMGMTS` moniker to simplify the process of attaching to the default CIM namespace

---

```
' Example:        3
' Author:         Craig Tunstall 26/04/2002
' Description:    A simple script to attach to a namespace

Option Explicit

Const MESSAGE = "Connected to "
DIM strMyInput, objNamespace

strMyInput = InputBox("Please enter a machine name:")

Set objNamespace = Getobject("WINMGMTS:{impersonationlevel=impersonate}\\"
& strMyInput)

MsgBox(MESSAGE & strMyInput)
```

Figure 10.5 Scripts That interact with the GUI

Note: Because we haven't discussed error checking yet we shall assume that the `GetObject` call always returns successfully (that is, attaches to a namespace).

with default privileges. In its simplest form the `WINMGMTS` moniker can attach to the default namespace on the local machine as follows:

```
Set objNamespace = GetObject("WINMGMTS:")
```

This is functionally equivalent to the following series of calls which we discuss shortly:

```
DIM objLocator, ojNamespace

Set objLocator = CreateObject("WbemScripting.SWbemLocator")

Set objNamespace = objLocator.ConnectServer(,"root\CIMV2")

objNamespace.Security_.ImpersonationLevel =
wbemImpersonationLevelImpersonate
```

By doing so we accept the following (Figure 10.6) default settings, which are OS configurable. In Windows XP this value can be altered using the `WMIMGMT` snap-in that can be called using Start/Run, wmimgmt.msc.

Default settings for `WINMGMT` are:

- Namespace: \\root\CIMV2_
- Impersonation level: impersonate (WMI core version 1.5 above)
- Authentication level: pktprivacy

As we mentioned earlier, it is also possible to attach to a namespace by using the `SWbemLocator` method, `ConnectServer`. Thus, we can replace our call to `WINMGMTS` as follows:

```
DIM objLocator, ojNamespace

Set objLocator = CreateObject("WbemScripting.SWbemLocator")

Set objNamespace = objLocator.ConnectServer(,"root\CIMV2")

objNamespace.Security_.ImpersonationLevel =
wbemImpersonationLevelImpersonate
```

Although `Connectserver` uses more lines of code, it is possible to specify a username and password when connecting to a namespace, which you are not able to do if you use `WINMGMTS`.

```
ConnectServer(Servername,NameSpace,Username,Password,Locale,Authority,
Securityflags)

service.Security_.ImpersonationLevel = wbemImpersonationLevel
  Impersonate
service.Security_.AuthenticationLevel = wbemAuthenticationLevelIPkt
  Integrity
```

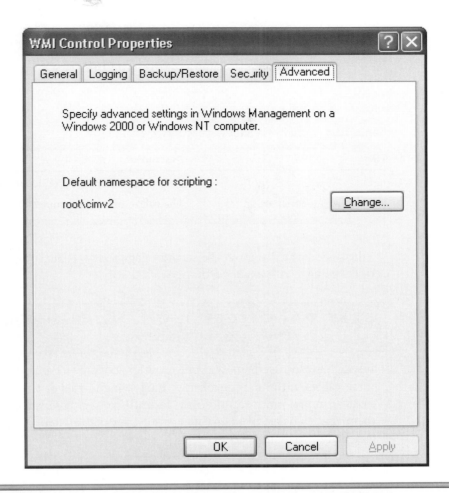

Figure 10.6 The WMI Control Advanced tab can be used to set the default namespace on a machine

Where:

- *Servername* is the name of destination machine—that is, Machinename, 145.123.123.1
- *Namespace* is the destination namespace—that is, \root\CIMV2
- *Username* is the user name—that is, Administrator
- *Password* supplies the password
- *Locale* specifies the LCID. For example, ms_809 for UK English and ms_409 for US English. If not specified, then it simply takes the default for the host machine.

- *Authority* specifies whether an alternative Kerberos or NTLM domain is required for authentication. It should be formed as follows:

  ntlmdomain:domainname or kerberos:domainname\Servername

- *Securityflags:* Only two options are currently available (see Table 10.3).

Table 10.3 Security Flags for ConnectServer

Flag	Description
Null	Wait indefinitely until connection establishes
WbemConnectFlagUseMaxWait	The call returns in 2 minutes or less

It is good practice to set the security flag to `wbemconnectflagUseMaxWait` if your script is going to run unattended.

> **BEST PRACTICE!** Using a password and username to attach to a namespace
>
> If specifying the username and password for accessing a namespace, avoid placing these values in the script explicitly using string literals or constants as this warrants an unnecessary security risk. Instead, specify these values at runtime, use them, and then destroy them (by resetting the variable to null) as soon as you have attached to the namespace.

> **BEST PRACTICE!** Retrieving locale-specific information
>
> You may recall from Chapters 3 and 4 that WMI can contain locale-specific information. If you are connecting to a namespace that stores information from multiple locales or simply from a different locale from your own, you possibly will need to specify the locale of the information you wish to retrieve. This would be especially true if you were attempting to connect to a namespace hosted on a machine based in a foreign country. If you do not specify this value, you run the risk of retrieving your data in the default locale of the target machine. There are two ways of retrieving locale-specific information, depending on whether you are connecting to a namespace: You can use the `WINMGMTS` moniker or `SWbemLocator.ConnectServer`.

Using WINMGMTS, you enclose the locale value in [] square brackets as follows:

```
Set objNamespace =
    GetObject("WINMGMTS:[locale=ms_809]!root\CIMV2:Win32_LogicalDisk")
```

This call retrieves the localized class definition for Win32_LogicalDisk. Alternatively, using SWbemLocator.ConnectServer, you specify it as follows:

```
Set objLocator = CreateObject("WbemScripting.SWbemLocator")
Set objNamespace = objLocator.ConnectServer(, "root\CIMV2",,, "ms_809")
```

Having specified your locale, in both cases you must then use the flag wbemFlag-UseAmendedQualifiers when performing any subsequent calls that read or write to locale-specific information. For example:

```
Set objwbemobject = _
objNamespace.Get("Win32_LogicalDisk", wbemFlagUseAmendedQualifiers)
```

We introduce the Get function later in the chapter.

Top Tip: The underscore _ character in VBScripting allows a statement to carry across to a new line. Always ensure that it is preceded by a single white space. Note that the underscore character cannot be used to break up sting literals so that they carry across to a new line.

■ Security Issues

The issue of security has always been of importance in distributed systems, especially when potentially system-critical management data is at stake. To combat malicious attacks that attempt to abuse WMI Microsoft, employ two Distributed COM (DCOM) mechanisms, *impersonation* and *authentication,* that you can use when connecting to a namespace using WINMGMTS or ConnectServer. The impersonation level dictates if and how you hand over your credentials to a trusted third party. The authentication level dictates if and how you verify that you are who you say you are.

To illustrate this point further imagine that you walk into a Main Street bank and request a transfer of funds. Before proceeding with the transfer the bank clerk must first authenticate that *you* are the owner of the account. To prove you are the owner, you could provide visual confirmation: a bank card, driver's license, or passport. These are forms of authentication.

> **Note of Interest:** It is worth noting that in banking and system security they commonly refer to this as "two-factor" authentication. For example, an ATM requires both your card (a physical factor) and your PIN number (a personal factor).

Next, the clerk may need to swipe your bank card to gain access to your details on the banking system and carry out the transaction. This is a process of impersonation. Ordinarily the clerk could not gain access to your account but with these details is able to carry out the requested task. At the end of the transaction, the clerk returns the card, and you leave the bank.

Setting the level of impersonation and authorization prior to connecting to a namespace is an important aspect of ensuring that your code works and is secure. Using too high a level of impersonation represents an unwarranted security risk, whereas giving too little may not allow the task to be carried out. In other words, it is a balancing act between these two states. Microsoft's default settings are sufficient in most cases for connecting to a namespace although in certain situations you may want to reconsider the impersonation and authentication setting, for example, if you are connecting to one or more remote namespaces, especially if you are connecting across an untrusted network such as the Internet.

The impersonation level (Table 10.4) defines two aspects of your interaction. First, it determines whether or not you show your credentials to the target process. Second, it dictates whether that machine can then use your security context to carry out the request.

There are varying strengths of authentication depending on how vulnerable to attack is the type of connection you are making (see Table 10.5). With each increase in strength is an associated overhead of processing time and bandwidth to carry out the authentication. Although negligible in terms of DSL connections and today's high-end processors, this could become an issue if you are connecting to a server across a low-bandwidth analog 56k line. It is important to understand that authentication works both for you and the machines to which you are trying to connect. For example, if you set the authentication level to None and tried to connect to a namespace hosted on a remote Windows 2000 server, the connection will most probably fail. This is because that machine has no way of authenticating you and consequently will not allow you access to its resources.

It is also possible to identify the authentication authority. At present the two accepted values are:

- ■ `WINMGMTS: {authority=ntlmdomain:domainname}`
- ■ `WINMGMTS: {authority=kerberos:domainname\Servername}`

Finally, it is also possible to specify which privileges to deny or allow on your local machine (see Table 10.6). When communicating across a network to a remote host,

Table 10.4 Security Impersonation Levels

Impersonation Level	Description
Anonymous	Will fail on calls to most remote machines as it hides the credentials of the caller. This would be like trying to withdraw money from your bank without providing valid proof of identity.
Identify	Will also fail on calls to most remote machines as this allows the target to query the credentials of the caller but not adopt those credentials to carry out the request. This would be like allowing the bank clerk to see your credentials but not allowing the clerk to use them when carrying out your request.
Impersonate	This allows the remote machine to both retrieve and use the credentials of the caller. Works in most cases for connections to remote machines. This would be like providing adequate proof of ID and supplying the clerk with your bank card so that your request can be carried out. This is the default setting for WMI version 1.5 and above.
Delegate (Windows 2000 and XP only)	This setting not only allows the remote machine to use your credentials but also any subsequent machines it connects to while carrying out your request. Use with caution as the further your credentials are carried around the network, the more vulnerable they are to attack. Using our banking metaphor, this would be like giving your bank card to the bank clerk who could then potentially pass it around the bank to numerous people in an attempt to get the job done: not advisable unless you are very confident about all of the host machines in your network.

Table 10.5 Security Authentication Levels

Authentication Level	Description
None	No authentication is used. Not recommended!
Connect	Authenticates the credentials of the caller only when the connection is first made to the destination machine.
Call	Authenticates only at the beginning of each call when the destination machine receives a request.
Pkt	Authenticates all data, packet by packet, from the client. This is the default setting for WMI.
PktIntegrity	Authenticates that no data has been modified during transit between the source and destination machine.
PktPrivacy	Authenticates all previous impersonation levels and encrypts the argument value of each remote procedure call.

Table 10.6 Security Privilege Constants*

Privilege Constant	Description
CreateToken	Required to create a primary token.
PrimaryToken	Required to assign the primary token of a process.
LockMemory	Required to lock physical pages in memory.
IncreaseQuota	Required to increase the quota assigned to a process.
MachineAccount	Required to create a machine account.
Tcb	Identifies its holder as part of the trusted computer base. Some trusted, protected subsystems are granted this privilege.
Security	Required to perform a number of security-related functions, such as controlling and viewing audit messages. This privilege identifies its holder as a security operator.
TakeOwnership	Required to take ownership of an object without being granted discretionary access. This privilege allows the owner value to be set only to those values that the holder may legitimately assign as the owner of an object.
LoadDriver	Required to load or unload a device driver.
SystemProfile	Required to gather profiling information for the entire system.
Systemtime	Required to modify the system time.
ProfileSingleProcess	Required to gather profiling information for a single process.
IncreaseBasePriority	Required to increase the base priority of a process.
CreatePagefile	Required to create a paging file.
CreatePermanent	Required to create a permanent object.
Backup	Required to perform backup operations.
Restore	Required to perform restore operations. This privilege enables you to set any valid user or group SID as the owner of an object.
Shutdown	Required to shut down a local system.
Debug	Required to debug a process.
Audit	Required to generate audit-log entries.
SystemEnvironment	Required to modify the nonvolatile RAM of systems that use this type of memory to store configuration information.
ChangeNotify	Required to receive notifications of changes to files or directories. This privilege also causes the system to skip all traversal access checks. It is enabled by default for all users.
RemoteShutdown	Required to shut down a system using a network request.
Undock	Required to remove computer from docking station.
SyncAgent	Required to synchronize directory service data.
EnableDelegation	Required to enable computer and user accounts to be trusted for delegation.

*Taken from Microsoft MSDN documentation

this becomes the responsibility of the COM RPC. You will need to set the privileges if you want to perform certain tasks such as requesting that the machine shut down. However, be careful not to revoke any privileges that may interfere with the actual purpose of your script. This option is not applicable to Windows 98 because of the different security model (or absence thereof):

- `WINMGMTS:{(Security,!RemoteShutDown)}` will stop this machine performing remote requests to shut down.

To deny a certain privilege, use an exclamation sign (!) before it.

Deciding on the Level of Security Required

The settings for the impersonation and authentication levels is largely dictated by the type of task you wish to carry out and how it is instrumented within WMI (that is, a provider or static within the CIM repository). Microsoft suggests that you should check the documentation for the provider you are using, but at present this is problematic. Many of the built-in providers do not explicitly document the implementation/authentication settings needed to carry out specific tasks, in which case you must assume that the default settings are sufficient. In reality the setting depends on a process of trial and error, reading the error messages you get when calls fail, and generally using common sense.

BEST PRACTICE!   Connecting to a namespace

Our example uses the `WINMGMTS` moniker to improve readability but also explicitly defines the level of impersonation as *impersonate*. The reason for this is that versions of WMI earlier than 1.5 were configured to have a default impersonation level of Identify. Unless you specifically set the impersonation level in your calls, there is always a possibility that when connecting to a remote machine the call will fail. Notice also that we have explicitly defined the namespace to connect to, as this setting can equally be modified and cause your scripts to go awry.

```
Set objNamespace =_
    GetObject("WINMGMTS:{impersonationlevel=impersonate}//"&"root/another-namespace"}
```

Data Input

Sometimes when you write a script you want to be able to enter the parameters at runtime rather than specifying them explicitly in the script. This makes the script more flexible. A classic example that would warrant this approach could be specifying the machine name or domain name at runtime so that your script can carry out its function.

As part of the VBScript boot camp introduction we shall look at two possible ways of doing this: one for unattended operation and one for attended. The first unattended way is to feed in the parameters at the command line when initially calling the script. The script can then capture and use these *arguments* using the `WSCript.Arguments` property that is part of the WSH object model mentioned earlier. Type the script in Figure 10.7 and then call it from the Start/Run menu by typing the following:

```
C:\example4.vbs machinename username <return>
```

```
'Example:        4
'Author:         Craig Tunstall 02 May 2002
'Description:    Simple script to accept command line parameters and output
'                them to the screen

DIM objArguments, strMachine, strUsername, strPassword

Set objArguments = WScript.Arguments

' Store these values in meaningful variable names
strMachinename = objArguments(0)
strUsername = objArguments(1)

' notice that the arguments start at 0
MsgBox("The machine name is: " & strMachinename)
MsgBox("The user name is: " & strUsername)
```

Figure 10.7 Input through the command line
Note: If you do not supply the correct number of arguments in this example, then the script will fail.

Each parameter you entered is retrieved by the `Arguments` property and then displayed using the call to `MsgBox`. The numeric value passed to `objArguments(n)` refers to the argument passed to the script starting with zero as the first entry (in our case `machinename`).

The second way of retrieving input is the `InputBox` function that uses the Windows GUI. We have already encountered this function in an earlier example, but here it is again with a few more parameters.

Figure 10.8 displays three separate input boxes and stores the values entered by the user in each of the three separate variables, `strServerName`, `strUsername`, and

```
'Example:       5
'Author:        Craig Tunstall 02 May 2002
'Description:   Simple script using input boxes to retrieve input

DIM strServerName, strUsername, strPassword

strServername = InputBox("Enter server name: ","Server Name Input Box",
  "Default server name")
strUsername = InputBox("Enter user name:", "User name Input Box",
  "Administrator")
strPassword = InputBox("Enter password:", "Password Input Box")
```

Figure 10.8   Input through the GUI

strPassword. The first parameter passed to the input box is the text prompt displayed that tells the user what data is required. The second parameter is the title of the input box. Notice that we have added default values for the server name and username as an optional third parameter to speed up the process of entering the details.

Error Detection

Broadly speaking, two types of errors should concern us when writing scripts. There are those errors that are part of the script, syntax and semantic errors, that we mentioned briefly earlier. These errors can be found during development and testing and are highlighted largely by WSH and judicious use of the script debugger. The second, more insidious kind of error happens as a result of problems outside the scope of the script. For example, a router that the script is trying to connect to may not be responding or a faulty network card prevents communication with the outside world. For this type of problem, our scripts need to have a mechanism in place to catch the error and provide as much information as possible about it.

To deal with these errors we employ a function that is part of the WMI scripting API, SWbemError. This function provides a more detailed account of WMI-related errors than the standard WSH Err routines that we also shall use to catch other types of errors. To use our own error-checking routine we must first turn off the WSH standard error-checking routine. To do so, at the beginning of your script before any other statements enter the following line:

```
On Error Resume Next
```

This literally means "on error resume at the next statement in the script." This stops the error from being caught by WSH (which would normally terminate the script and report the error to you). But why is this useful? Many types of administrative scripts need to run unattended; therefore, it is not particularly useful for them to behave in the default manner because nobody will be there to see the error. Using On Error Resume Next makes it the responsibility of the programmer to detect any errors and take the appropriate action. The error-checking technique we propose introduces the use of subroutines, using the sub statement. A subroutine in VBScript is a simple but effective way of saving time by reusing blocks of code that you may need to use repeatedly within your script. By delimiting a block of code with the Sub and End sub statements, as you can see in the excerpt below, you create a subroutine within your script that you can call repeatedly. Subroutines typically are placed at the end of the script after the main body of code.

```
Sub MySubRoutine
'Enter my block of statements here
' And here.....'
' Then end the subroutine using EndSub
End sub
```

Having declared the MySubRoutine, it is then possible to evoke it using the *call* statement as follows (note that you do not have to use the call statement but we do so in the examples to improve the readability of the script).

```
Call MySubRoutine()
```

Using subroutines, we can also pass parameters as in the example in Figure 10.9.

```
' Example:        6
' Author:         Craig Tunstall 26/04/2002
' Description:    An example of passing a value to a subroutine

Option Explicit

DIM strMyInput

strMyInput = InputBox("Please enter some text: ")
Call DisplayText(strMyInput)

Sub DisplayText(strText)

  MsgBox ("This is what you entered: " & strText)

End sub
```

Figure 10.9 Calling subroutines

Multiple parameters can also be passed using the comma as a delimiter. Notice that the value you type in the input box is held first in variable `strMyInput`, which is then passed to the subroutine `DisplayText`. After inside subroutine, `DisplayText`, the variable assumes a new name, `strText`, which is then displayed as part of the `MsgBox` call.

```
Call CheckWMIError()
Call CheckStdError()
```

For our error checking we define two subroutines: `CheckWMIError` and `CheckStdError`. We call `CheckWMIError` after we perform any task that calls the WMI API to check for an error and we call `CheckStdError` in all other cases when we want to check for more general WSH errors.

In both subroutines in Figure 10.10 we introduce the use of the conditional If…then statement. Using this statement it is possible to execute a block of statements in response to certain conditions being met. In our error-checking subroutines the condition is `Err <> 0`, which checks to see if the global WSH object Err contains an error code. More precisely, if `Err` is not equal to zero an error has occurred in your script. If true the routine then displays an error message box. It converts the value into a string representing the hexadecimal value of the number using the `Hex` function and then proceeds to list the description for the error. If the `CheckWMIError` subroutine has been called, then extended WMI error information is appended to the error message. Finally the subroutine clears the `Err` object back to zero and then stops the execution of the script with the WSH object model method `WScript.quit(0)`. The value enclosed in the parentheses is optional and can be used to indicate under what conditions the script terminated. See Figure 10.11 for an example of the Error dialog boxes in action.

As you can see the code blocks for both subroutines are quite detailed, which is why we place the code in a subroutine and call it as necessary in our examples. Notice how we have indented the block of statements within the If…then statement to help make the script more readable.

If you examine the code within the calls to `MsgBox` you will see references made to `VbCr` and `VbTab`. These are VBScript constants that can be used for formatting text. Table 10.7 provides a complete list of the available formatting constants and their descriptions.

In our error-detection routine, we have also enhanced the appearance of the message box by using an additional flag, `vbExclamation`. To access these features on the `MsgBox` function you must ensure that you declare a variable to which it will return a value. In our case this is `nMsgResult`. Without this the call will fail. We have deliberately changed the appearance of the `MsgBox` so that it highlights that an error has occurred in a way that is consistent with the look and feel of the Windows GUI. You will also notice that the message box plays the exclamation Wav when it is displayed.

```
'Example:          7
'Author:           Craig Tunstall
'Description:       This is an excerpt and will not run on its own. Cut and
'                   past into your own scripts to use.

Sub CheckStdError()

DIM nMsgResult

If Err.number <> 0 then
  nMsgResult = MsgBox ("Error Number: " & VbTAB & "0x" & _
  Hex(Err.Number) & vbCr & "Error Type: " & VbTAB & _
  Err.Description,vbExclamation, "Standard Error Information")
    Err.clear
    WScript.quit
  End if
End sub

Sub CheckWMIError()

  DIM nMsgResult,WMIError

  If Err.number <> 0 then
    Set WMIError = CreateObject("WbemScripting.SWbemLastError")
    nMsgResult = MsgBox ("Error Number: " & VbTAB & "0x" & _
      Hex(Err.Number) & vbCr & "Error Type: " & VbTAB & _
      Err.Description & vbCr & "Operation: " & VbTAB & _
      WMIError.Operation & vbCr & "Parameter Info: " & VbTAB & _
      WMIError.ParameterInfo & vbCr & "Provider Name: " & VbTAB & _
      WMIError.ProviderName & vbCR & "Error Description: " & VbTAB & _
      WMIError.Description, vbExclamation, _
      "WMI Extended Error Information")
    Err.Clear
    WScript.quit
  End if
End sub
```

Figure 10.10 Subroutines to display errors

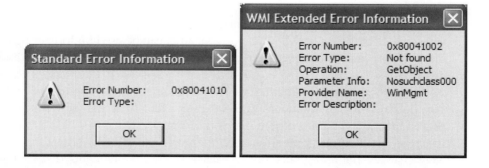

Figure 10.11 The Standard Error and WMI Extended Error Information dialog boxes

Table 10.7 VBScript Constants

Constant	Description
vbTab	Inserts a horizontal tab into output.
VbLf	Inserts a line feed into output.
vbCr	Inserts a carriage return into output.
vbCrLf	Inserts both a carriage return and line feed into output.
vbNewLine	Inserts a platform-specific new line into the output.

Each of the constants in Table 10.8 can be used with the **MsgBox** function to change its appearance to match the message it conveys.

Table 10.8 MsgBox Appearance Constants

Constant	Description
vbInformation	Displays the information message icon in the message box.
vbQuestion	Displays the warning question mark icon in the message box.
vbCritical	Displays the critical message icon in the message box.
vbExclamation	Displays the warning message icon in the message box.

You can also modify the behavior of the message box using the constants in Table 10.9.

Table 10.9 MsgBox Modal Constants

Constant	Description
vbSystemModal	The user must respond to the message box before the application is allowed to continue.
vbApplicationModal	All applications are suspended until the user acknowledges the message box.

For example, if you wanted to create a message box that both displayed the exclamation icon and suspended all currently running applications, you could specify it as follows:

```
DIM nMsgResult
nMsgResult = MsgBox("Look at me!",vbApplicationModal+vbExclamation,
  "Modal Exclamation message box")
```

Both error dialogs in Figure 10.11 use the `VbExclamation` constant to change the appearance of `MsgBox`es.

BEST PRACTICE! User/Script Interaction
If writing an attended script, always provide consistent and accurate feedback to the user at all stages of a script's execution. This includes error notification and notification of the successful completion of a task.

■ Error Logging (NT/2000/XP Only)

If your scripts are going to run unattended, dialog boxes are not the ideal way to keep track of any successes or failures that have occurred in your absence. WSH supports event logging so that you can write to the application event log and view the information later. This can be an invaluable way of tracking whether a script successfully executed or the type of errors it encountered. It also provides the exact date and time that the error occurred.

BEST PRACTICE! Tracking Unattended Script Behavior
Storing information in the application event log is a powerful feature for tracking the behavior of your scripts, but use this feature sparingly. Do not use it as a debugging tool and report only the information vital to tracking the event.

First, create a `WSCript` object for accessing the `LogEvent` function.

```
Set wshshell = CreateObject("WSCript.Shell")
```

Then to generate an event, place a call to this object's `LogEvent` function. This tells the WSH to write directly to the application event log. The `LogEvent` function takes two parameters: The first tells the event log what type of event has taken place and the second is the text it displays in the description field of the event. In the following example, the first parameter is 1, which tells the event log to list this as an error. The string literal is the text that will be placed in the description of the event.

```
Wshshell.LogEvent 1, "My error description"
```

There are a number of different options depending on the type of event you are reporting, as shown in Table 10.10.

Table 10.10 Event Logging Types

Value	Description	Value	Description
0	Success	4	Information
1	Error	8	Audit success
2	Warning	16	Audit failure

The event log error notification subroutine is shown in Figure 10.12. It is very similar to CheckWMIError() but writes its output to the event log instead. Notice that we included the name and path of the script for which the error occurred, using the WScript.ScriptFullName property.

The LogWMIError routine will produce the output in Figure 10.13 within the application event log. Note that it will record the source as WSH.

■ WMI Scripting Data Retrieval

Having successfully attached to a namespace, we now look at one of the most common tasks you will want to perform—the task of retrieving data from WMI. The first thing you will need to do before retrieving any data is find the names of the classes that represent the managed objects in which you are interested. The most common way to find this information is through the WMI CIM Studio and its search facility. This process is covered later in the chapter. For the sake of brevity, let's assume that we have already performed the search and have decided to use the Win32_NetworkLoginProfile class held in the root/CIMV2 namespace. This class contains information about the currently logged-on user accounts.

In this case, because we are attaching locally to WMI, we do not need to specify a machine name. Also, because we do not need to supply a user and a password, we can use the WINMGMTS moniker. As explained as one of our best practices, we can implicitly accept the default value for authentication but must always explicitly define the setting for impersonation as being impersonate.

```
'Example:        8
'Author:         Craig Tunstall 26/04/2002
'Description:    This is an excerpt and will not run on its own. Cut and
'                paste into your own scripts.

Sub LogStdError()
  DIM nMsgResult,WSHshell

  If Err.number <> 0 then
    Set WSHshell= CreateObject("WSCript.Shell")
    WSHshell.LogEvent 1,"Script name: " & vbTAB & WScript.ScriptFullname & _
      vbcr & "Error Number: "& VbTAB & "0x" & Hex(Err.Number) & vbCr & _
      "Error Type: " & VbTAB & Err.Description

    Err.clear
    WScript.quit
  End if
End sub

Sub LogWMIError()
  DIM nMsgResult,WMIError,WSHshell

  If Err.number <> 0 then
    Set WSHshell= CreateObject("WSCript.Shell")
    Set WMIError = CreateObject("WbemScripting.SWbemLastError")
    WSHshell.LogEvent 1, "Script name: " & vbTAB &
      WSCript.ScriptFullname & vbCR & "Error Number: " & VbTAB & "0x" & _
      Hex(Err.Number) & vbCr & "Error Type: " & VbTAB & _
      Err.Description & vbCr & "Operation: " & VbTAB & _
      WMIError.Operation & vbCr & "Parameter Info: " & VbTAB & _
      WMIError.ParameterInfo & vbCr & "Provider Name: " & VbTAB & _
      WMIError.ProviderName & vbCR & "Error Description: " & VbTAB & _
      WMIError.Description

    Err.Clear
    WScript.quit
  End if
End sub
```

Figure 10.12 Subroutines to record errors in the Windows event log

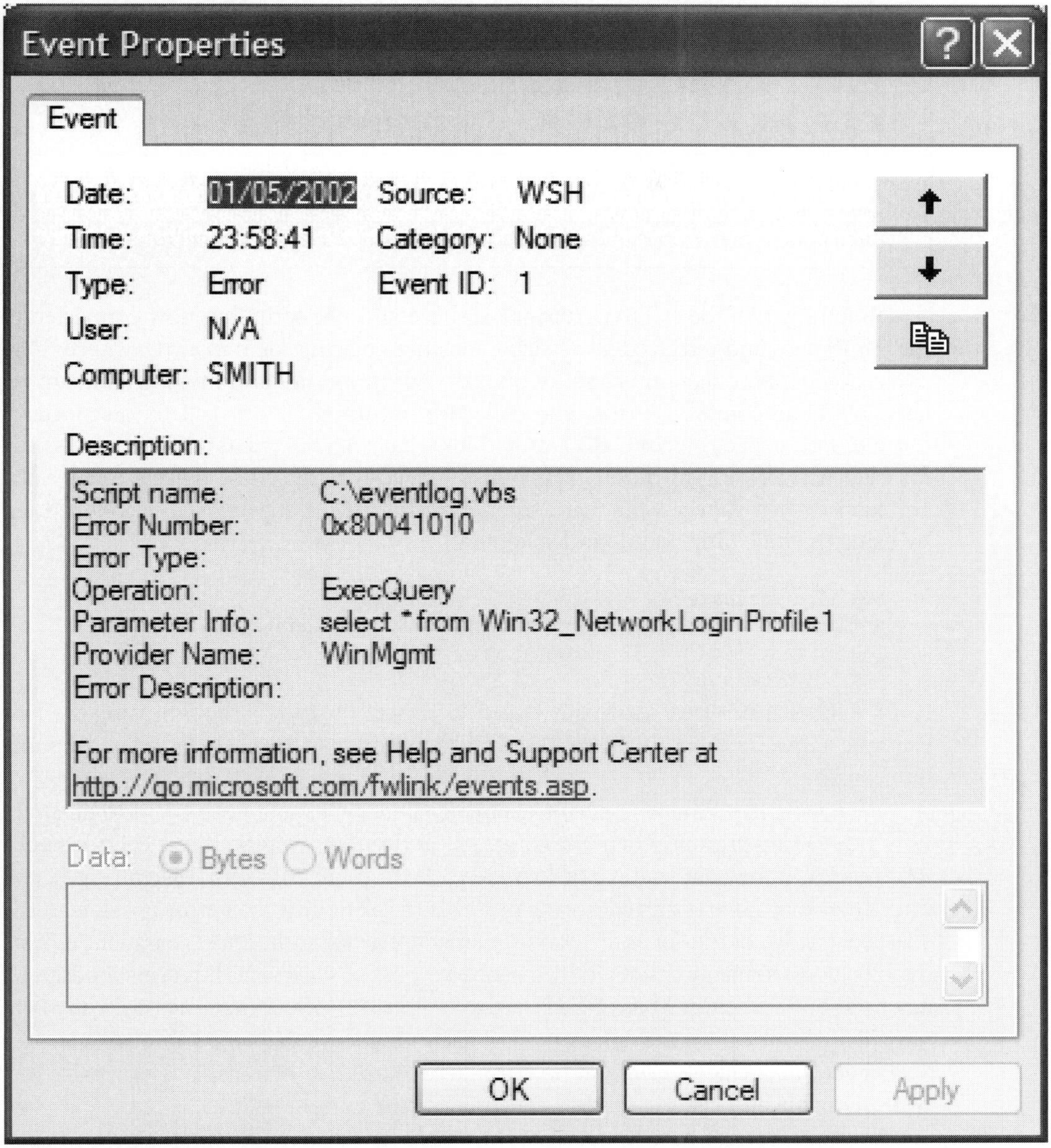

Figure 10.13 Event generated by `LogWMIError`

To retrieve all of the available instances of a class, we use the `InstancesOf` function that belongs to `SWBemServices`, which is part of the WMI API.

BEST PRACTICE! Using `InstancesOf`

```
Set objNamespace = GetObject("winmgmts:{impersonationlevel=
   impersonate}\\")
Set objLoginProfiles = objNamespace.InstancesOf("Win32_NetworkLoginProfile")
```

Assuming that the call to `GetObject` is successful, the script has now connected to the namespace and retrieved all available instances placing them in `objLoginProfiles` as a *collection*. A collection is a set of objects with properties and methods that are related by some common factor. The collection returned by our call to `InstancesOf` (`"Win32_NetworkLoginProfile"`) is stored in `ObjLoginProfiles` as a set of objects, one for each network log-in profile. It is our job to go through these objects one by one and inspect their values. Note that we could further reduce the amount of code written by using the following compound statement.

```
Set objNamespace =
GetObject("winmgmts:{impersonationlevel=impersonate}\\").
   InstancesOf("Win32_NetworkLoginProfile")
```

The choice between the two is largely a personal matter, although using the first example allows reuse of the `WINMGMTS` object to interact with other classes in the same namespace.

We have also included the error-checking subroutines in Figure 10.14 to illustrate how you can incorporate them into a script. Notice that we placed one call to `Check-WMIError()` immediately after our first two calls to the WMI API. This will catch any errors that may have occurred during our calls to WMI. Our next error check is in the statement block of our *for each...next* statement. The for *each...next* statement repeats the block of statements delimited by the *next* part of the statement. It repeats for each element in our collection (that is, each instance of `Win32_` `Win32_NetworkLogin-Profile` returned by our call to `InstancesOf`). For each iteration it calls the subroutine `Check-StdError()` to check for errors. If no error has occurred, it then displays a message box with the name and last log-on date and time for the current user.

You may wonder how we arrive at the names that display the various properties of our management data. For example, the `MsgBox` function refers to `Profile.Name` and `Profile.LastLogon`. These values are made from the element name declared in the *for each...next* statement and the name of the property we want to display, taken directly from the `win32_` class definition. To find out the choice of properties for a class, use the WMI CIM Studio, locate the class, enumerate all the instances, and then look at the instance data.

```vbscript
'Example:        9
'Author:         Craig Tunstall
'Description:    This example retrieves the network login name and date from
'                WMI and displays it using a message box

option explicit
on error resume next

DIM objNamespace, objNetworkLoginProfiles, Profile, nMsgBox

Set objNamespace = GetObject("winmgmts:{impersonationlevel=impersonate}\\")

Set objNetworkLoginProfiles =
  objNamespace.InstancesOf("Win32_NetworkLoginProfile")
Call CheckWMIError()

for each Profile in objNetworkLoginProfiles
  call CheckStdError()
  nMsgBox=MsgBox("Network Login Name: " & vbTAB & Profile.Name & VbCR & _
    "Last logon: " & vbTAB & Profile.LastLogon, vbInformation, _
    "Current User Details")
Next

' **** Beginning of our error checking subroutines ****
Sub CheckStdError()
DIM nMsgResult
  If Err.number <> 0 then
    nMsgResult = MsgBox ("Error Number: " & VbTAB & "0x"' & _
      Hex(Err.Number) & vbCr & "Error Type: " & VbTAB & _
      Err.Description,vbExclamation,"Standard Error Information")

    Err.clear
    WScript.quit
  End if
End sub

Sub CheckWMIError()
  DIM nMsgResult,WMIError

  If Err.number <> 0 then
    Set WMIError = CreateObject("WbemScripting.SWbemLastError")
    nMsgResult = MsgBox ("Error Number: " & VbTAB & "0x" & _
    Hex(Err.Number) & vbCr & "Error Type: " & VbTAB & Err.Description & _
    vbCr & "Operation: " & VbTAB & WMIError.Operation & vbCr & _
    "Parameter Info: " & VbTAB & WMIError.ParameterInfo & vbCr & _
    "Provider Name: " & VbTAB & WMIError.ProviderName & vbCR & _
    "Error Description: " & VbTAB & WMIError.Description, _
    vbExclamation, "WMI Extended Error Information")

    Err.Clear
    WScript.quit
  End if
End sub
```

Figure 10.14 Retrieving the network log-in name and date from WMI

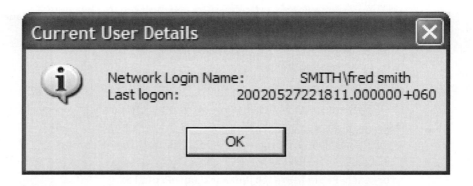

Figure 10.15 Example of a date value without formatting

Having run this script, you will notice a slight problem with the output. Instead of listing the date and time the current user logged on, it displays a string similar to the one in Figure 10.15.

■ Displaying Date and Time Values (XP Only)

To successfully display, parse, or set date and time values retrieved from your calls, the WMI API provides the SWbemDateTime function (Figure 10.16). To use it in your scripts you must first create an object as follows:

```
Set dateTime = CreateObject("WbemScripting.SWbemDateTime")
```

Then take the initial WMI value and convert it using the following:

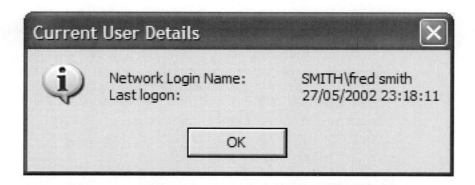

Figure 10.16 Example of date formatting using SWBemDateTime

```
dateTime.Value = object.LastLogon
```

before displaying it using:

```
MsgBox("Date:" & datetime.GetVarDate)
```

Here are the modifications to Example 9 so that it displays the date and time properly:

```
DIM objNamespace, objNetworkLoginProfiles, Profile, nMsgBox,
  objDatetime

Set objNetworkLoginProfiles = objNamespace.ExecQuery("SELECT * FROM
Win32_NetworkLoginProfile WHERE UserType='Normal Account'")
```

which result in the following more user-friendly date and time format:

```
set objDateTime = CreateObject("WbemScripting.SWbemDateTime")

for each Profile in objNetworkLoginProfiles
    call CheckStdError()
    objDateTime.Value = Profile.LastLogon
    nMsgBox=MsgBox("Network Login Name: " & vbTAB & Profile.Name & VbCR &
        "Last logon: " & vbTAB & vbTAB & objDateTime.GetVarDate,
        vbInformation, "Current User Details")
Next
```

> **Note:** We have used `ExecQuery` instead of `InstancesOf` to refine the set of instances returned by the script. If we used `InstancesOf` we would retrieve all available accounts on the target machine including system accounts. For Windows XP users, the script would fail when it attempted to convert the date on the system accounts, which do not store a `lastlogon` value.

■ Retrieving Subsets of Instances

The `InstancesOf` function is a simple way of retrieving all of the instance information for a given class; however, in some cases we may want only to retrieve a specific subset of the data available. For example, many processes can run on a machine at a given time and retrieving all of them is needlessly inefficient. To remedy this, it is possible to refine the exact set of data returned by a call to WMI using the `ExecQuery` function and a WQL statement (Figure 10.17). Please refer to the tutorial in Chapter 4 for constructing WQL queries.

```
' Example:      10
' Author:       Craig Tunstall
' Description:  This example uses a WQL query to retrieve a subset of
'               data from WMI and displays it using a message box.
'               It gets the default printer and displays
'               a selection of details.

option explicit
on error resume next

DIM objNamespace, objPrinterProfiles, Profile, nMsgBox

Set objNamespace = _
  GetObject("winmgmts:{impersonationlevel=impersonate}\\")

Set objPrinterProfiles = _
  objNamespace.ExecQuery _
  ("SELECT * FROM Win32_Printer WHERE Default=true")

if objPrinterProfiles.count = 0 then
  nMsgBox = MsgBox("No default printer available", _
  vbInformation, "Printer dialog")
  WScript.quit
end if

for each Profile in objPrinterProfiles
  nMsgBox=MsgBox("Printer: " & vbTAB & Profile.Name & VbCR & _
  "Shared: " & vbTAB & Profile.Shared & vbcr & "Status: " _
  & vbTAB & Profile.Status,VbInformation,"Default Printer" _
    "Settings")
next
```

Figure 10.17   Uses a WQL query to get the default printer

Note that although there can be only one default printer on a system, we still need to treat whatever is returned from ExecQuery as a collection of potentially more than one object. In Example 11 (Figure 10.18) we enumerate (that is, list) all those services on the host machine that are stopped and whose start mode is manual.

You can also use the ExecQuery command to retrieve a specific instance of a class by specifying its key value in the WQL query string. For example, the excerpt in Figure 10.19 would return only the details of the alerter service.

```
' Example:      11
' Author:       Craig Tunstall
' Description:  This example uses a WQL query to retrieves a subset of
'               data from WMI and displays it using a message box

option explicit
on error resume next
DIM objNamespace, objProcess, Process, nMsgBox

Set objNamespace = _
  GetObject("winmgmts:{impersonationlevel=impersonate")

Set objService = _
  objNamespace.ExecQuery("SELECT * FROM Win32_Service WHERE _
  startmode='Manual' AND started=FALSE")

if objService.count = 0 then
  nMsgBox = MsgBox("No Services match the criteria", vbInformation, _
      "Services dialog")
  WScript.quit
end if

for each Service in objService
  nMsgBox=MsgBox("Service: " & vbTAB & Service.Name & VbCR & _
      "State: " & vbTAB & Service.State & vbcr & "Status: " & _
      vbTAB & Service.Status,VbInformation,
      "Manual Services Stopped Dialog")
next
```

Figure 10.18 Uses a WQL query to list Windows services not started

```
Set objProcess = objNamespace.ExecQuery("SELECT * FROM Win32_Service
WHERE name='alerter'")
```

Figure 10.19 A WQL query to get the *alerter* Windows services

---

BEST PRACTICE! Use the Get Method

When retrieving a specific instance of a class, assuming you know its key value, it is more efficient to use the `SWBemServices.Get` method. This bypasses the need for WMI to parse a WQL query before returning the instance.

```
Set objProcess = objNamespace.Get("Win32_Service.name='alerter'")
nMsgBox=MsgBox("Process:" & vbTAB & objProcess.Name & VbCR & "State:" & vbTAB & _
    objProcess.State & vbcr & "Status:" & vbTAB & _
    objProcess.Status,VbInformation)
```

BEST PRACTICE! Use Semisynchronous Calls to ExecQuery

In some cases when using the `ExecQuery` call, certain types of WQL query can result in large quantities of data being returned to your script. Typically WMI would wait until the query was complete and all the data gathered before returning the data to your script, thus slowing the script's performance. To avoid this potential bottleneck and improve the performance of your script, you can tell WMI to perform the `Exec-Query` call semisynchronously. To do this, set two flags, `wbemFlagReturnImmediately` and `wbemFlagForwardOnly`, as part of the `ExecQuery` call. They tell WMI to return the data as soon as the provider supplies it rather than waiting for the entire collection to be assembled, as is the case with synchronous calls. Notice that we have specified the flag's combined value as `48` (decimal) in the call to `ExecQuery`.

```
Set objPrinter = objNamespace.ExecQuery("SELECT * FROM Win32_Printer
WHERE
    Default=true",, 48)
```

Note: Don't forget the two commas immediately after the query!

■ WMI Data Modification Scripting Example

To modify the data you have retrieved from WMI is very simple, assuming that the provider supports the operation. Unfortunately, WMI currently is not very clear at conveying whether or not a class is updatable. In theory, a class should contain the class qualifiers, `SupportsCreate`, `SupportsDelete`, and `SupportsUpdate`, for this purpose. (`SupportsCreate` indicates that the class will support the creation of instance, `Sup-`

portsDelete that the class supports instance deletion, and SupportsUpdate that the class supports instance modification.) To determine if these qualifiers are present, use the WMI CIM Studio to navigate to the class in question and then check for the qualifiers under the Object Qualifiers menu option. In practice however, the Win32_Schema does not use these qualifiers, which means it is often a case of trial and error to determine what the class will allow you to do. We anticipate, however, that Microsoft will implement these qualifiers in a future release of WMI. An alternative measure is to examine the object class in CIM Studio to see what method it supports and use its method to modify data. To do so, we first retrieve the data from WMI, change its value to our new setting, and then use the SWBemObject Put_ method (Figure 10.20).

```
' Example:        12
' Author:         Craig Tunstall
' Description:    This example uses a WQL query to retrieve all the user
'                 accounts that have been disabled and uses the put_method
'                 to enable them. It also uses the MsgBox vbYesNo flag to
'                 prompt the user whether or not to enable the account

option explicit

on error resume next

DIM objNamespace, objUserAccounts, Useraccount, nMsgResult

Set objNamespace = GetObject("winmgmts:{impersonationlevel=impersonate}\\")

Set objUserAccounts = objNamespace.ExecQuery("SELECT * FROM Win32_UserAccount
  WHERE disabled=TRUE")

if objUserAccounts.count = 0 then
  nMsgResult = MsgBox("All accounts are enabled", vbInformation,
    "Accounts dialog")
  WScript.quit
end if

for each UserAccount in objUserAccounts
  nMsgResult = MsgBox("Enable user account: "& UserAccount.Name & "?", _
    vbSystemModal+ vbYesNo + vbQuestion, "Locked User Account")

  If nMsgResult = vbYES Then
    UserAccount.disabled=FALSE
    UserAccount.Put_
    nMsgResult= MsgBox (UserAccount.Name & " has now been enabled." & _
      vbCr & "Fullname: " & UserAccount.fullname,vbInformation, _
      "User Account Enabled")
  end if
next
```

Figure 10.20   Example script that enables disabled user accounts

We also introduce some additional logic to this example and allow the user to choose whether or not to enable the account. This is achieved by setting the vbYesNo flag on the call to MsgBox so that it prompts the user with the choice of a yes or no button. We have also made the dialog box modal using vbSystemModal and displayed a question mark using the flag vbQuestion (Figure 10.21).

After the user makes a choice, we test the result (stored in nMsgResult) to see if the user clicked the yes button (vbYes). If true, the if statement block then changes the user account from disabled to enabled and uses the Put function to send the information back to WMI. The script then provides visual confirmation with a dialog box that indicates that the job was a success. Table 10.11 lists the constants available for MsgBox to alter its buttons.

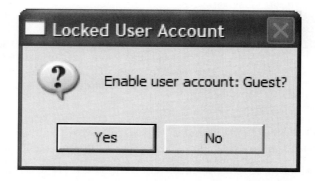

Figure 10.21 A MsgBox with the vbYesNo, vbSystemModal, and vbQuestion flags set

Table 10.11 MsgBox Button Constants

Constant	Description
vbOKOnly	Displays a single OK button. Test for vbOk.
vbOKCancel	Displays OK and cancel buttons. Test for vbOk and vbCancel.
vbAbortRetryIgnore	Displays abort, retry, and ignore buttons. Test for vbAbort, vbRetry, and vbIgnore.
vbYesNoCancel	Displays yes, no, and cancel buttons. Test for vbYes, vbNo, and vbCancel.
vbYesNo	Displays yes and no buttons. Test for vbYes and vbNo.
vbRetryCancel	Displays retry and cancel buttons. Test for vbRetry and vbCancel.

If when experimenting with the `Put` method, you may receive the following error:

Error: Provider is not capable of the attempted operation
Code: 80041024
Source: SWbemObjectEx (win XP) or SWbemObject

This indicates that the provider for that class does not support the `Put` method. Consequently you will not be able to change the data through VBScript.

▣ Data Deletion Scripting Example

Deleting instance data from WMI is a relatively simple task. First you must retrieve the data you want to delete using, for example, `InstancesOf`, `ExecQuery`, or `get`. Next you call the `SWbemServices` delete method on the specific object you wish to delete. A common problem when doing this, however, is that the provider does not support this action. Again, in the absence of documentation or the Supports Delete qualifier, it is a trial-and-error process to determine whether you can carry out this task on the required object. In Figure 10.23, we provide the user with a choice of whether or not to perform the deletion of a printer configuration using the `MsgBox` function.

Figure 10.22 shows a message box eliciting a response from the user before performing actions such as deletion. This is good practice depending on the purpose of the script.

▣ Data Creation Scripting Example

Data creation in WMI uses the `SpawnInstance` method of `SWBemObject`. As you did in the delete method, you must retrieve the object you wish to create and then create a

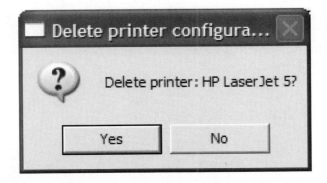

Figure 10.22 Using `MsgBox` to elicit a response from the user

```
' Example:        13
' Author:         Craig Tunstall
' Description:    This example retrieves all the currently installed printers
'                 and then gives the user the option to delete them one
'                 at a time.

option explicit

on error resume next

DIM objNamespace, objPrinter, PrinterInstance, nMsgResult

Set objNamespace = GetObject("winmgmts:{impersonationlevel=impersonate}\\")

Set objPrinter = objNamespace.ExecQuery("SELECT * FROM Win32_Printer")

If objPrinter.count = 0 Then MsgBox("No Printers installed!")

for each PrinterInstance in objPrinter
  nMsgResult = MsgBox("Delete printer: "& PrinterInstance.Name & "?", _
    vbSystemModal+ vbYesNo + vbquestion, "Delete printer configuration")

  If nMsgResult = vbYes Then
    PrinterInstance.Delete_
    nMsgResult= MsgBox (PrinterInstance.Name & " has now been deleted
      from the system." & vbCr, vbInformation,"Printer Deleted")
  end if
next
```

Figure 10.23   Retrieves all the currently installed printers and offers an option to delete

new instance. You do this with a call to the `SpawnInstance` method (see Figure 10.24). If successful, you then can populate the properties of the instance before committing it to WMI with the `Put` method.

Again, many providers do not appear to support this method, and it is a trial-and-error process to determine which ones do and do not in the absence of the Supports Create qualifier.

■ Association Traversal Using VBScript

Associations in CIM are, arguably, one its greatest strengths. It is possible by using an association to determine the exact relationships between managed objects. For exam-

```
' VBScript excerpt for creating an instance of Win32_Printer

DIM objNamespace, objPrinter, ObjNewUser
Set objNamespace = GetObject("winmgmts:{impersonationlevel= _
  impersonate}\\")
Set objPrinter = objNamespace.ExecQuery("SELECT * FROM _
  Win32_Printer.DeviceID="HP Laserjet 5")

ObjNewPrinter=objPrinter.SpawnInstance_()
ObjNewPrinter.DeviceID="New Printer Config"
ObjNewPrinter.Description="This is our new printer config"
' See Win32_Printer for description of other properties
ObjNewPrinter.Put_
```

Figure 10.24 Creating a printer configuration

ple, with associations you can determine which disk is connected to which controller card, which in turn is connected to which motherboard, and so on. The following example demonstrates how to use associations to track down associated managed objects, using the `ExecQuery` method. It passes a WQL query that uses the AssocClass qualifier to specify the association class in which we are interested. The script starts by iterating through each of the available parallel ports on the host machine and then using the association class `Win32_PrinterController` to determine which, if any, printers are attached to that port (Figure 10.25). As with many of the examples given here, the WMI CIM Studio plays a large part in discovering and understanding the relationships between these managed objects. For more information on forming WQL queries for associations, refer to Chapter 4.

■ Executing Methods Using VBScript

To execute a method in VBScript, you first must retrieve the managed object and then call the method directly. You can use the WMI CIM Studio to browse the available methods on a CIM class using the Method tab in the right pane. Always check with WMI CIM Studio to determine whether any parameters are required in the method call. In the example in Figure 10.26, we call the `PrintTestPage` method on the WMI class `Win32_Printer`, which results in a test page being printed.

```
' Example:        14
' Author:         Craig Tunstall
' Description:    This example uses a WQL query to traverse the association
'                 between each parallel port on the host machine and any
'                 printers that may be attached.

option explicit
on error resume next

DIM objNamespace, objPrinter, ParallelPort, nMsgResult,PrinterCollection,
AttachedPrinter

Set objNamespace = GetObject("winmgmts:{impersonationlevel=impersonate}\\")

Set objPrinter = objNamespace.InstancesOF("Win32_ParallelPort")

If objPrinter.count = 0 Then
  MsgBox("No parallel ports available")

for each ParallelPort in objPrinter
  Set PrinterCollection = objNamespace.ExecQuery("ASSOCIATORS OF
    {Win32_ParallelPort.DeviceID='" & ParallelPort.DeviceID & "'}
    WHERE " & "AssocClass=Win32_PrinterController Role=antecedent")

If PrinterCollection.count = 0 Then
  nMsgResult=MsgBox("There are no printers attached", vbInformation,
    ParallelPort.DeviceID)

  for each AttachedPrinter in PrinterCollection
    nMsgResult = MsgBox ("Printer " & AttachedPrinter.DeviceID &
      " is attached to " & ParallelPort.DeviceID,
      vbInformation,ParallelPort.DeviceID)
  next
next
```

Figure 10.25 Find printers attached to a parallel port

■ Summary

Thus concludes our VBScript boot camp introduction to scripting for WMI. During Chapter 10, we covered the basic issues surrounding writing an administrative script for WMI and introduced some of the components you will need to write professional administrative WMI scripts. These include program layout, input and output, error

```
' Example:        15
' Author:         Craig Tunstall
' Description:    This example uses retrieves the default printer and sends
'                 a test page to it by executing the PrintTestPage method

option explicit

DIM objNamespace, objPrinter, nMsgResult,PrinterCollection, DefaultPrinter

Set objNamespace = GetObject("winmgmts:{impersonationlevel=impersonate}\\")

Set objPrinter = objNamespace.ExecQuery("SELECT * FROM Win32_Printer WHERE
  Default=true")

For each DefaultPrinter in ObjPrinter
  DefaultPrinter.PrintTestPage()
  nMsgResult = MsgBox("Test page sent to: " & DefaultPrinter.name,
    vbInformation, "Test Page Dialogue")
Next
```

Figure 10.26   Finds the default printer and prints the test page

checking routines, and a series of best practices to avoid common scripting problems. In Chapter 11, we look at the issues of writing your own script for the first time and study the Windows XP command-line tool, WMIC.

Ten Fast Facts: Summary of VBScript Boot Camp

1. Use meaningful names for all artifacts in your script (for example, objects, variables, constants, and functions).

2. Use subroutines as a useful way to avoid needlessly repeating blocks of commonly used code.

3. Decide upon the required level of impersonation when connecting to a WMI namespace and specify it explicitly in your calls.

4. Use the WINMGMT moniker unless you need to specify a username and password.

5. Always specify the locale when making your calls to avoid queries failing because WMI is trying to access the wrong locale.

6. Always try to catch extended error information from calls to WMI specific functions, because this will help locate the source of the fault.

7. Always annotate your scripts with the author's name, date of creation/modification, purpose of script, or modification to script.

8. Always use Option Explicit and declare your variables using DIM, ReDIM, Public, or Private. This will help you to keep track of your variable use and prevent potential problems that might occur later.

9. Avoid using default values (for example, the default namespace) where possible when connecting to WMI because they can be changed on the client machine and cause your scripts to fail unexpectedly.

10. Don't ever turn error checking off while developing your script but do use it when running your script after it has been debugged. Use error routines, such as the ones presented here, to track your errors and write the output to the screen or event log.

Chapter 11

WMI Scripting and WMIC

Having introduced the basics of scripting for WMI in Chapter 10, we focus in this chapter on the process of writing your own scripts. We examine the thought processes involved as a series of steps and examine practical issues such as how your script will interact with its environment, what type of execution model it will adopt, and how to debug it. In the latter part of the chapter, we introduce the Windows XP command-line driven tool WMIC and give examples of its use in interactive and noninteractive mode.

■ Identifying the Correct Course of Action

Regardless of whether you intend to use WMIC, VBScript, or WMI CIM Studio, there are a number of steps you should take before committing to any particular course of action. The following guide aims to help you through the process of selecting the right tool.

Make a Note of the Problem Description

It is important to note down the problem from the perspective of what you need to do in as much detail as possible, even if it amounts to only a few lines. Although this may seem like overkill for a relatively small task, it is good practice when you're just starting off, and it helps you think about the problem. If you cannot write a clear and concise description of what you are trying to achieve then you will definitely have trouble writing a script (for example) to perform the task!

Here's an example problem description:

Enable DHCP on all the machines on the third floor that are members of the Accounts department. Configure the DHCP server for the third floor to lease out its IP addresses for seven days and to set the default gateway to 127.0.0.1 (Note: For the sake of argument we have used the local loopback address).

Divide the Problem into Its Constituent Parts

Some problems can be broken further into smaller constituent parts and you may find that different tools can address different problems. Breaking the task into subtasks can simplify the process of solving the problem. If there is any order in which the tasks should be performed, make sure that you capture that as well. For example:

Task 1: Modify the settings on the DHCP server so that it leases IP addresses for seven days at a time.

Task 2: Change the default gateway to 127.0.0.1.

Task 3: Configure the machines on the third floor from static IP addresses to DHCP.

Decide Which Hardware or Software Components You Are Going to Manage

One of the most important tasks to perform before using any of the WMI administrative tools (that is, WMI CIM Studio, WMIC, or the scripting API) is first deciding which components you are going to manage and second, finding their equivalent CIM classes. Assuming that you know which components you wish to manage, the next step is to locate their classes. To do this you first must decide which namespace contains the management information that is most relevant for your managed component (see Chapter 4 for a list of namespaces and their purposes).

Selecting a Namespace

For administrators root\CIMV2, root\WMI, and root\Microsoft are the best places to start looking for administrative management information. For example, the root\ WMI namespace contains a vast amount of management information not available elsewhere.

After you have selected the relevant namespace, you must then search for the class that best captures the management information in which you are interested. To help you do this Microsoft provides a good search facility in WMI CIM Studio (which is part of the WMI SDK and can be downloaded from the Microsoft site—see earlier chapters for the URL). To provide a practical example, let's use WMI CIM Studio to tackle Task 3 of our example and determine if any classes in the root\CIMV2 namespace hold DHCP related-information.

First, start WMI CIM Studio and navigate to the root/CIMV2 namespace, which, if you recall from previous chapters, holds the majority of classes for local management information. Now click the search binoculars in the class view and select each of the search options so that class names, property names, and class descriptions are all active. Now type the acronym DHCP and click the Go! button to search for any related classes. Doing this returns a list of class names that have DHCP as part of their class name, class description, or property name.

Notice that all three search options have been selected in Figure 11.1.

In this case, our search returns only two classes: `Win32_BaseService` and `Win32_NetworkAdapterConfiguration`. Now inspect each class and its description, using the help icon to get their details. Based on the descriptions it appears that the required class is `Win32_NetworkAdapterConfiguration`. Now that we have found the relevant class, we will inspect its methods and properties. In the case of the class `Win32_NetworkAdapterConfiguration` there are two things of interest: a method called

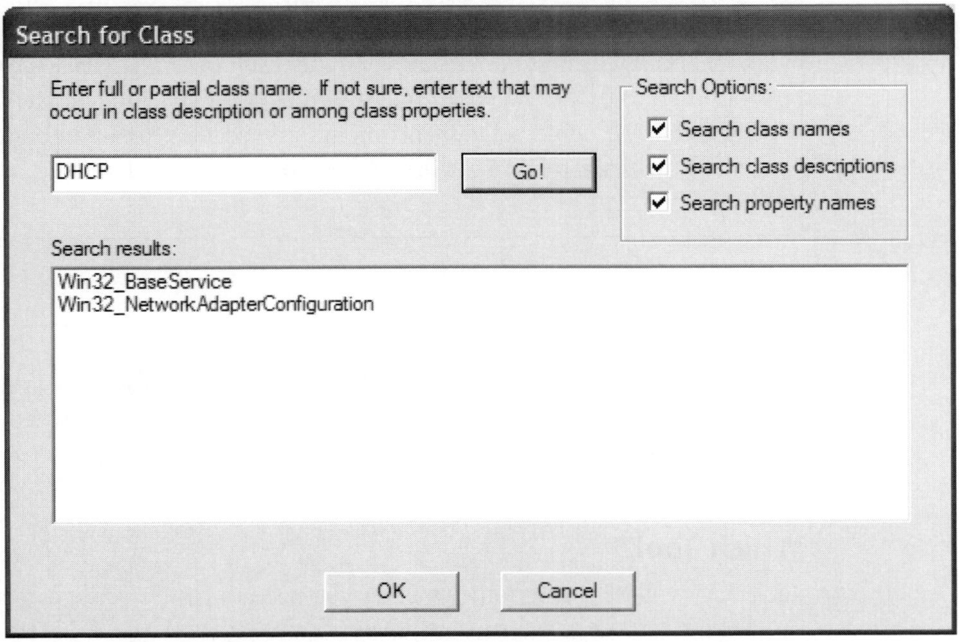

Figure 11.1 The Search dialog of the WMI CIM Studio

EnableDHCP() and a property called DHCPEnabled. The following description comes from the class information in WMI CIM Studio.

The description for method EnableDHCP( ): "The EnableDHCP method enables the Dynamic Host Configuration Protocol (DHCP) for service with this network adapter. DHCP allows IP addresses to be dynamically allocated. The method returns an integer value that can be interpreted as follows:

0—Successful completion, no reboot required

1—Successful completion, reboot required, and so forth

The description for property DHCPEnabled: "The DHCPEnabled property indicates whether the dynamic host configuration protocol (DHCP) server automatically assigns an IP address to the computer system when establishing a network connection. Values: TRUE or FALSE. If TRUE, DHCP is enabled."

BEST PRACTICE! Properties vs. Methods

Whenever presented with the choice of using a method or a property that appears to perform the same function, it is advisable to use the method. If you use a method, your script can elicit more feedback about the outcome of the call and take action accordingly. For example, if the result of a call to EnableDHCP() were 1 as opposed to 0, then we would need to reboot the machine before DHCP would be enabled. We could achieve this programmatically if required by retrieving the primary instance of class Win32_OperatingSystem and calling its shutdown method.

Hint: When you have found the classes you are looking for, also check the associations because these can be a really useful way of tracing a fault to its conclusion and finding classes that can provide additional information on your managed object.

Which Tool?

Table 11.1 will help determine whether you need to write a script to perform the task or whether you use a tool such as WMIC, Scripting, or WMI CIM Studio.

In the context of our running example, we decide the following, for example:

Table 11.1 Administration Tools

Tool	Strengths
Scripting	Tasks that are performed at regular intervals or in response to an event.
	Tasks that have many steps.
	Tasks that require a GUI for input or output.
	Tasks that use many managed objects.
WMIC	Tasks that do not have too many steps.
	Tasks that are performed regularly (noninteractive mode) or once only (interactive mode).
	Situations that cannot use or don't require a GUI (for example, telnetting into a machine).
	Tasks that require management data in a formatted output.
WMI CIM Studio	Tasks that involve a single namespace at a time.
	Tasks that do not have a vast amount of steps or repetition.
	Situations that require a user-friendly interface and search facility (for example, browsing the CIM repository).

Task 1 performed once only, therefore WMIC or WMI CIM Studio.

Task 2 performed once only, therefore WMIC or WMI CIM Studio.

Task 3 performed n times (where n is the number of machines on the third floor) is a candidate for scripting.

If you are performing a task only once and do not anticipate performing it again on a regular basis, then you would be best advised to use either WMI CIM Studio or WMIC to do the job. In our example, Tasks 1 and 2 could be carried out this way. If the task requires some degree of repetition and/or has many steps, that is, you need to carry it out weekly or need to repeat it on multiple machines, then consider scripting. Scripting also is ideal for situations in which you need to get user feedback to complete a task using a GUI. The user, in this instance, could be another administrator. WMIC, although capable of behaving in a scripted manner, is more suitable for smaller tasks that do not require a GUI.

The following steps apply only to scripting.

Decide Whether Your Script Should Run Locally or Remotely on the Target Machines

How the script will connect to the namespace largely will dictate the security issues that need to be addressed. If you are connecting remotely (that is, across a network), you need to determine if a username and password are explicitly required and what level of authentication and impersonation are needed. If you are connecting locally, then your script automatically assumes your current credentials and you cannot specify a username and password. The only setting you can change is the impersonation level. Changes to the authentication level other than `pktprivacy` will fail.

Always try to use the `WINMGMTS` moniker where possible to assist readability and cut down the complexity of the script, but remember that if a username and password are required then you must use the `SWBemLocator.connectserver` method instead (see Chapter 10 for more details).

In our fictitious example, we are going to run the script locally and attach across the network remotely to the target namespace of each of the machines in the Accounts department. We shall assume that we have administrator-level privileges for all of the machines in the department, and that we do not need to use a unique password and username explicitly for each machine.

Decide Whether Your Script Will Run Unattended or Attended

Whether your script executes attended or unattended dictates the type of input and output techniques you will use. Check Table 11.2 for the available choices for the material presented here.

Although by no means a definitive list, it provides a discussion point for your own script.

Determine the Variables and Constants

Now to determine the variables and constants you may need in your script. A simple technique (also used in Chapter 5, Schema Design) is to examine your problem de-

Table 11.2 Attended and Unattended Inputs and Outputs

Style	Input	Output
Attended	Messageboxes	Messageboxes
	Inputboxes	Event log
	Command line arguments	
Unattended	Command line arguments	Event log

scription and select the nouns as candidate variables and constants. For example in our problem defined earlier, we specified our basic requirements as being

> "Enable DHCP on all the machines on the third floor that are members of the Accounts department. Configure the DHCP server for the third floor to lease out its IP addresses for seven days and to set the default gateway to 127.0.0.1."

We then broke these requirements into three separate tasks, of which Task 3 was suitable for scripting.

> "Enable DHCP on all the machines on the third floor that are members of the Accounts department."

From this simple description, we produce the following constants and variables.

Candidate Constants
Members of the Accounts department all belong to the Accounts domain. We could therefore declare this as a constant using the following statement:

```
Const ACCOUNTS = "accounts"
```

Candidate Variables
We need the following variables:

A variable to hold the namespace object

A variable to hold the result from the `EnableDHCP()` method

A variable to hold the name of the target machine, and so forth

> **Note:** When you start writing your script you often will find yourself adding or deleting variables and constants as you go along. Don't worry, this is a normal part of the development process, which is why we define them as *candidate* variables and constants; they are used only as a guide to start the scripting process.

Determine the Sequence of Steps in the Task

Here we break the task into its individual steps. For example, "Enable DHCP on all the machines on the third floor that are members of the Accounts Department," can be broken into the following steps:

1. Gather the names of all machines in the Accounts department. For example, this could be done by retrieving the names of those machines that are members of the Accounts group.

2. For each machine in the domain perform the following:

   a. Attach to target namespace of root\CIMV2

   b. Retrieve the instance of `Win32_NetworkAdapterConfiguration` where Index=1 (Note that Index=1 retrieves the primary NIC for that machine)

   c. Call the method `EnableDHCP` on the `NetworkAdapterConfiguration` object and check result

   d. If value is 1 then initiate reboot on machine

   e. Go to next machine (2a)

Using the examples given in Chapter 10, we can now begin to see how we may implement each one of these steps. This, then, can be our guide when we start writing the script.

■ Script Deployment and Execution

A variety of options is available to you for delivering your scripts. These options assume that you are operating in a networked environment.

Local Execution and Storage

The most straightforward approach is to execute your scripts locally from the machine on which they are installed (Figure 11.2). If you do this and use the default security settings, then the script only will be able to perform options available to the currently logged-on user because it assumes their security context. This can be advantageous if

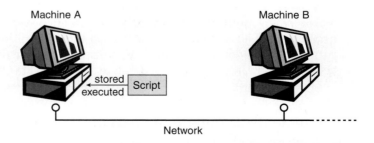

Figure 11.2 The script is stored and runs locally

you do not need the script to perform any tasks requiring administrator-level privileges. The disadvantage of this approach is that the script is not updated centrally, and if you make changes to one script then you will need to update all installations of the script.

Local Execution from a Shared Resource

Very similar in essence to the previous option, here the script is stored on a shared drive to which all users have access. This removes the problem of keeping the script up to date (Figure 11.3). The disadvantage of this approach is that the script then presents a single point of failure, and if security precautions are not taken and the script is damaged, corrupted, or interfered with, then its impact will be more widespread.

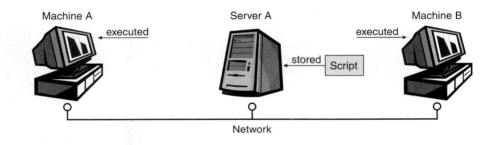

Figure 11.3 The script is stored centrally on a shared drive and runs locally

Remote Connection across a Network

Write the script so that it attaches remotely across the network to the client machine, using a NetBIOS name or TCP/IP address (Figure 11.4). This approach is secure because the script relies on your security privileges to access the destination machine's resources.

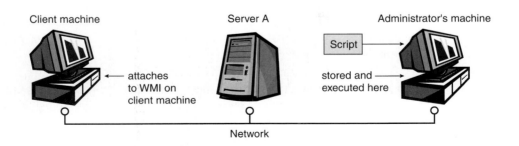

Figure 11.4 The script is stored locally and attaches across the network to the remote namespace

Remote Invocation of a Script (Available Only with Windows Script v5.6)

Use remote invocation of the script using WSH's remote scripting feature, which is new to Windows Script v5.6. This feature transfers the script across the network to the client machine using DCOM, where it then is executed as a local process using your security context (Figure 11.5). For this option to work you must have privileges to execute the WSH on the remote machine and also the latest version of WSH installed (version 5.6).

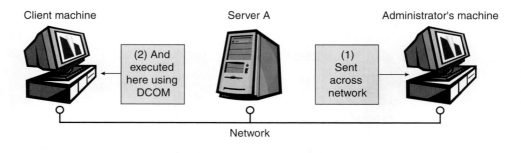

Figure 11.5 The script is stored locally, copied across the network, and executed as a process in the remote machine

WSH uses an object called WSHRemote to start the remote script (Figure 11.6). First you must create an object of WSHController and then invoke its CreateScript function, passing to it the name of the script you wish to use and the destination UNC machine name. You can then start the script on the destination machine by calling the Execute method. You can confirm the status of the script by checking the WSHRemote status property where a value of 0 indicates that the job has been created but is not yet running, 1 means that the script is running remotely, and 2 means the job has completed. If the script ceases to respond or complete its task after a predetermined amount of time you can call upon the terminate method.

The example in Figure 11.6 takes a machine name and script name from the command line and executes the script on the remote machine. It then waits until the script is complete by testing its status before displaying a Confirmation dialog box.[1]

1. For more detailed information, please refer to the documentation for Windows Scripting Host 5.6, available as a help file at Microsoft's MSDN Web site.

```
'Example:        16
'Author:         Craig Tunstall 02 May 2002
'Description:    This is an example of remote scripting. The script takes
'                two command line parameters, the name of the machine to
'                run the script on and the name of the script

Option Explicit

DIM objArguments, strMachinename, strScriptname

Set objArguments = WScript.Arguments

'store the arguments in meaningful variable names

if objArguments.count <> 2 then
  MsgBox("Usage: <scriptname> machinename scriptname")
  WScript.quit
end if

strMachinename = objArguments(0)
strScriptname = objArguments(1)

Dim objRemoteScript,objController

Set objController = WScript.CreateObject("WSHController")
Set objRemoteScript = objController.CreateScript(strMachinename,strScriptname)
objRemoteScript.Execute

Do Until objRemoteScript.Status = 2
  WScript.Sleep 50
Loop

MsgBox("Script:" & strScriptname & " completed running on " & strMachinename)
```

Figure 11.6   Running a script on a remote machine

Script Execution Methods

Having written your script, you then will want to decide how to trigger its execution. This typically falls into one of two categories: *attended* or *unattended execution*. Attended execution is self explanatory and depends upon someone being present to initiate the script and then provide feedback where necessary. There are numerous options for unattended execution.

Executing Scripts at Start Up

By associating the script as part of the user's log-on profile (Windows XP/NT/2000 only) it is possible to trigger the script's execution whenever the user logs on. In this instance the script assumes the user's credentials while executing and is performed when the user first logs on (and unless you explicitly write the script otherwise, it will be performed every time the user logs on). On a Windows 9x/Me/Win XP/NT4.0/2000 installation it is also possible to place the script in the startup folder, which will ensure that the script gets executed every time the machine starts. Note that in all cases the target machine must have the Windows scripting host installed. Although neither approach is particularly eloquent, both are simple to configure.

Execute the Script Using the Windows Scheduler

Users of Windows 98 and earlier can schedule a script to run using the Windows task scheduler, which is included as standard and found under the Accessories/System Tools folder. With this utility you can specify the name of your script using the browse facility and then schedule it to run every day, week, month, once, at startup, or whenever you log on.

The Windows task scheduler (Figure 11.7) can be used to trigger your script only once or at regular intervals.

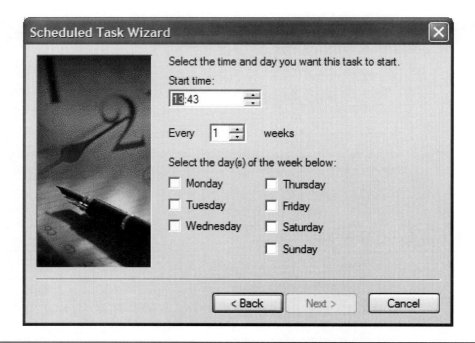

Figure 11.7 The Windows task scheduler

Event-driven Script Execution (Windows XP Only)

Here the script is triggered in response to an intrinsic event in the system and must be defined using a WQL query. There are several limitations to this approach. First, there must be a class present in the CIM repository that represents the event you want to monitor. If not, you will have to write an event provider and define new classes to expose the event. Second, the script runs under LocalSystem credentials, which restricts its access to network shares and environment variables because it is not able to access the data for a particular user's account.

For more information see the `ActiveEventConsumer` class in the `\root\subscription` namespace.

▇ Sending E-mail

In some situations, normally when you want to maintain a time-sensitive record of an event in your system, it is useful to be able to use e-mail in conjunction with WMI. That way, the information arrives at your inbox where you can view it at your discretion. Users of Windows XP have this facility supported with the `SMTPEventConsumer` class held in the `root\subscription` namespace. This class consists of a number of properties that, among other things, allow the user to configure to whom the e-mail is sent, the subject line, the message itself, and the name of the SMTP server. By creating an instance of an event filter and binding it with an instance of `SMTPEventConsumer`, it is possible to configure WMI to notify you by e-mail of events such as a disk running low on free space.

For users of Windows versions earlier than XP, there is no integrated WMI e-mail facility that can be triggered in response to events. Although we cannot recreate this facility entirely in VBScript, we can develop a subroutine that sends e-mails using an `Outlook` object and then pass this routine our management information. Although not triggered in response to an event, the script could be scheduled to run at regular intervals using the Windows task scheduler, as we discussed earlier. The following VB-Script in Figure 11.8 retrieves the list of services on the host machine that are set to start up automatically (that is, startup='auto') but currently are in the stopped state. After the script has connected to the `CIMV2` namespace and retrieved this information with a call to `Execquery`, it then calls the `PostEmail` subroutine. `PostEmail` takes three parameters: the subject line, the destination address, and the message body. For it to work on your machine, you must be running a MAPI compliant e-mail package such as Microsoft Outlook. MAPI is an acronym for Mail Application Programming Interface: It was defined by Microsoft and became a de facto standard for interfacing with e-mail applications.

The variable `strRecipient` (in Figure 11.8) stores the e-mail address of the person to whom the message will be sent. The `strsubject` variable simply contains the text

Figure 11.8 Sends an e-mail of all Windows services

```
'Example:        17
'Author:         Craig Tunstall 02 May 2002
'Description:    Catalogues all of the services currently running on the
'                host machine and sends an email to the address specified
'                in strEmailAddr. In order for this to work you must have
'                Microsoft Outlook installed on your system
'                N. B. Does not work on Windows XP

option explicit
on error resume next

DIM objNamespace, objService, Service, nMsgBox,
strMsgBody,strRecipient,strSubject

' define the items for the e-mail
strRecipient = "insertyouname@mailprovider.com"
strSubject = "Services currently running on machine: "

Set objNamespace = GetObject("winmgmts:{impersonationlevel=impersonate}\\")

Set objService = objNamespace.ExecQuery("SELECT * FROM Win32_Service WHERE
startmode='Auto' AND state='Stopped'")

If objService.count = 0 then
  MsgBox("No matches")
  WScript.quit
end if

for each Service in objService
  strMsgBody = strMsgBody & "Service: " & Service.Name & vbTAB &
  vbTAB & vbTAB & "State: " & Service.State & vbTAB & vbTAB &
  "Status: " & Service.Status & vbCr
next

call PostEmail(strMsgBody,strRecipient,strSubject)

' The PostEmail subroutine takes three parameters, the contents of the
' email, the strEmailAddr address and strSubjectline line

Sub PostEmail(strEmailcontents, strEmailAddr,strSubjectline)
  ' This constant is used in the call to the outlook object to create
  ' a blank email message
  Const BLANKEMAIL = 0

  Dim objOutl, objMAPI, objMailItem, ServiceSet, Service, SystemSet, System
```

```
' Create Outlook object reference
Set objOutl = WScript.CreateObject("Outlook.Application")

' obtain an object reference to "Mapi" name space
Set objMAPI = objOutl.GetNameSpace("MAPI")

' create a new mail item object
Set objMailItem = objOutl.CreateItem(BLANKEMAIL)

' set the mail object properties
objMailItem.Recipients.Add strEmailAddr

Set objSystemSet = GetObject("winmgmts:").
  InstancesOf ("Win32_ComputerSystem")

for each System in objSystemSet
  objMailItem.Subject = strSubjectline & System.Name
next

objMailItem.Body = strEmailcontents

' We are now ready to connect to our MAPI compliant email client
' i.e. outlook

objMAPI.Logon "profile", "password"
objMailItem.Send
objMAPI.Logoff
nMsgBox=MsgBox("E-mail created for " & strEmailAddr, vbInformation,
  "Email dialogue")
end sub
```

that you want to display in the subject heading of your e-mail message. The strMsg-Body variable contains the message that will be the main body of your e-mail.

```
' Create Outlook object reference
Set objOutl = WScript.CreateObject("Outlook.Application")
```

This statement assigns our object variable, objOutl, to an Outlook application object. Outlook is the name of our automation server and Application is the name of the type of the object. From this point on, if we need to call any of the functions in Microsoft Outlook, we do so using the variable objOutl followed by a period and then the name of the property or method that we need to call.

Remember that we cannot use whitespaces or extended characters (such as the exclamation point) in our variable names, so we normally use something short and to the point to help us remember it. Objects are an abstraction mechanism that provide a storage place for complex data types. In this case we have created an object of type "`Outlook.Application`".

```
Set objMAPI = objOutl.GetNameSpace("MAPI")
```

Here we obtain a namespace object of type `MAPI` by making a call to `GetNameSpace` using our recently created `objOutl` object. This currently is the only supported type for Microsoft Outlook, Visual Basic, and VBScript. This object is assigned to our object variable `objNameSpace`. We shall call the methods on this object later on in our program.

```
Set objMailItem = objOutl.CreateItem(BLANKEMAIL)
```

At this stage in the program we use our Outlook object (`objOutl`) to create a new e-mail message item. The constant `BLANKEMAIL` is passed to `CreateItem` to instruct it to create a new blank e-mail message. We then can fill this item in with the fields for the subject header and message body.

```
objMailItem.Recipients.Add strEmailAddr
```

This section of the program calls the add recipient function from our `ObjMailItem` object variable. Also included in the call is the variable `strEmailAddr` that we passed in by our call to `PostEmail`. In short, this function adds the contents of the variable recipient to the newly created message as a recipient address. Now our e-mail message has a destination address. If we wanted to send this message to multiple recipients we could repeatedly call `objMailItem.Recipients.Add` with each of the different recipient names.

```
Set objSystemSet = GetObject("winmgmts:").InstancesOf
("Win32_ComputerSystem")
for each System in objSystemSet
    objMailItem.Subject = subject & System.Name 'subject
next
```

Next we retrieve all available instances of `Win32_ComputerSystem` and assign these to our object variable `SystemSet`. We then append the e-mail subject line with the name of the machine from which this information has come, using the name property of `Win32_Computersystem`.

```
objMailItem.Body = strEmailcontents
objMAPI. Logon "profile", "password"
objMailItem.Send
objMAPI. Logoff
nMsgBox=MsgBox("E-mail created for " & strEmailAddr, vbInformation,
    "Email dialogue")
```

The final section of the script logs on to the MAPI provider using the permissions granted to the current user's profile and then invokes the **send** method on `objMailItem`.

After doing this, the script again logs out of the mail system. Next we display a dialog box confirmation message that the system has created an e-mail message. It includes the name of the e-mail recipient.

Type the code exactly as shown in the example, and let's run the program to see what it does. Once it is executed, you should be presented with a dialog box notifying you that the message has been created and placed in your outbox. If you now check your e-mail outbox, you should have a message pending that lists the current automatic services that are stopped.

■ Setting Up Your System for Debugging and Testing

Having typed the examples, let's now look at the issue of debugging. *Debugging* is the term programmers commonly use to describe the process of removing syntax or semantic errors (also known as *logic errors* or "bugs") from programs. Typically, this involves reading through the program repeatedly to trace a spelling mistake or grammatical error to its source and is a process all programmers go through when developing software, no matter how experienced they are. Unfortunately, you normally will not be aware of the bugs in your scripts until you attempt to run a script and it fails. Depending upon the type of fault that caused the failure, the WSH ordinarily will point you toward the source of the error by referring to a specific line in your script. The only exceptions to this rule are semantic errors that occur when the program doesn't behave quite as you wanted or expected. For these types of error you need to step through the script, line by line, examining the script's behavior at each stage to understand where things start to go wrong. Fortunately Microsoft provides us with a free tool, the Microsoft Windows Script Debugger, to help track down syntactical and semantic errors.

Microsoft Windows Script Debugger (approx. 600k)

To debug scripts you need the Windows Script debugger. This is available from the following URL:

http://msdn.microsoft.com/downloads/sample.asp?url=/MSDN-FILES/027/
001/731/msdncompositedoc.xml

Having installed the debugger, let's configure your system to simplify the process of debugging and testing your scripts.

Note: Before typing the following registry code, make sure that you have sufficient privileges to modify the system registry.

Navigate to the Start/Run menu, type the text in Figure 11.9, and click the OK button.

Figure 11.9 Use Notepad to create a new file called scriptdebug.reg

> **Warning:** Changing values in the Windows registry, if not carried out correctly, can have dire consequences that can affect your machine's performance and/or configuration. All changes effected via a .reg file are immediate and there is no undo facility (although is it possible to roll back to an earlier version of your registry—this is potentially a time-consuming task). Type and run the following code exactly as printed (or download from our Web site). Click yes to create a new file and in your new instance of Windows Notepad type the text in Figure 11.10 and save to an easily locatable directory.

```
REGEDIT4

[HKEY_CLASSES_ROOT\VBSFile\Shell\Debug]
@="&Debug on Error"

[HKEY_CLASSES_ROOT\VBSFile\Shell\Debug\Command]
@="WScript.exe \"%1\" //D"

[HKEY_CLASSES_ROOT\VBSFile\Shell\ForcedDebug]
@="&Forced Debug"

[HKEY_CLASSES_ROOT\VBSFile\Shell\ForcedDebug\Command]
@="WScript.exe \"%1\" //X"
```

Figure 11.10 Registry changes to enable script debugging

Now locate `scriptdebug.reg` with the file explorer, double-click it, and click yes to allow it to update the registry. Files appended with the .reg are associated with the Windows registry and double-clicking them adds their contents. The new registry settings capitalize upon two of the options available for the Windows Scripting Host and the keys within the registry that allow you to add new features to the right-click menu for specific file types. We have added these options to simplify the process of debugging your scripts. For more Windows Scripting options go to the Start/Run menu option and type:

```
Wscript.exe /?
```

Having updated the registry, you should have two new options whenever you right-click a .vbs (Visual Basic script) file (Figure 11.11).

Figure 11.11   The two new settings available on the Context menu for .vbs files

The first new option, Debug on Error, executes your script and ensures that if it encounters an error while attempting to run, the debugger is called. The second new option, Forced Debug, starts your script within the debugger regardless of whether any errors have been encountered. This can be useful if you wish to observe the step-by-step execution of your script, for example, to track down logical errors.

▪ Debugging Your Scripts

Having updated the registry, you should now have two new options added to the right mouse context menu for Visual Basic script files (suffix .vbs). To reiterate, these options were:

- Debug on Error: This option calls the debugger only if your program encounters an error while executing.
- Forced Debug: This option launches your script within the debugger and allows you to step through your program line by line.

To illustrate the use of these debug options, let's take a look at one of our sample scripts with the debugger in Forced Debug mode.

First, locate `example2.vbs` using the file explorer and right-click it to bring up the Context menu. Select Forced Debug from the list to initiate the debugger (as in Figure 11.12).

The initial screen displays your script with the first program statement highlighted. At this point the debugger has frozen the script and is waiting for your command before proceeding. Notice that the Window screen is read-only: Subsequently you cannot modify your script within the debugger unless you save it under a different name using the File/Save As option. Now open the View menu and select the Command Window option from the drop-down menu. This produces another stand-alone window that enables you to type commands and interact with the debugger and your script. This can be used, for example, to inspect or set the value of variables in your script or even to enter actual VBScript statements to see the outcome. For example, you can issue VBScript statements, such as `MsgBox`, to it. The only limitation of the command window is that you can enter only one line at a time: It is possible, however, to enter multiple commands using the colon as a separator.

Return focus to the main window by left-clicking it. You can use the cursor keys or the mouse to position the cursor anywhere throughout your script. Select the last `MsgBox` statement from our script and press F9 to highlight this as a breakpoint. You should now see a red circle appear next to the line you selected (as in Figure 11.13).

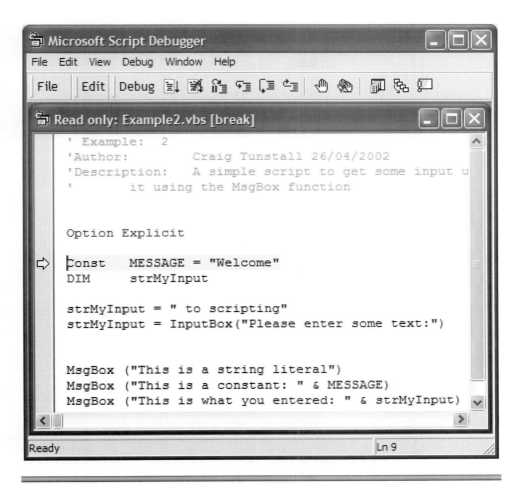

Figure 11.12 The Windows Script debugger main screen

Breakpoints are a really useful way of stopping the program's execution at specified locations, for example, to inspect the value of variables. Let's step through our script one
line at a time until the first breakpoint and use the command window to inspect the
value of the variable strMyInput before it is displayed to the screen using the message
box function.

Use the F5 key to run the script: Enter some text in the input box and click OK. If
you wanted to step through the script one line at a time, you alternatively could use
the F8 key. Now, in the command window, type the text in Figure 11.14 and press the
return key.

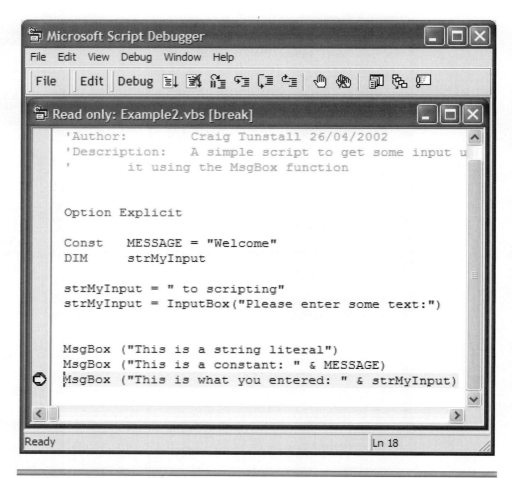

Figure 11.13 Setting breakpoints in the debugger using F9

Figure 11.14 The command window can retrieve the value of variables

You should be presented with the text that you just typed to the text input box. Now, from the command window, let's change the value of this text again: Type the text in Figure 11.15 and press the return key.

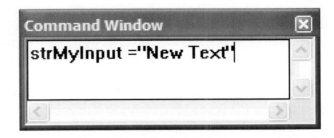

Figure 11.15　The command window also can be used to set the value of variables

Now press F5 again to continue execution of the program, and you will see that the output has been changed to your new value.

The debugger can be an invaluable tool for tracking down logic errors in your scripts. If the outcome of a script is not as expected, by judicious use of breakpoints and using the command window for variable inspection, you can gain insight into what exactly is happening behind the scenes when your script runs.

■ Windows Management Instrumentation Command-line (WMIC)

Administrators of Windows XP have an additional tool in their system management armory, the WMI Command-line or WMIC. As the name suggests, this is a command-line driven tool that can access local or remote CIM repositories and retrieve, modify, add, or delete data in them. With WMIC, Microsoft introduces a new term to system management, *Alias*. An Alias is a simplified term that refers to a more complex query that retrieves and formats information from the CIM repository. Microsoft's rationale for Aliases is that the traditional paths and class names for data in the CIM repository are syntactically unfriendly and fairly long for the command line (especially when you consider the 1024 char buffer limit). Aliases alleviate this and help to simplify performing system administrative tasks. Another interesting feature of Aliases is that WMIC will allow you to define your own, thus enabling you to tailor the management of your system.

WMIC operates in one of two modes: interactive and noninteractive. In noninteractive mode you can call WMIC from batch files or from the command prompt. In interactive mode you are presented with a special command prompt.

WMIC also contains a number of options that allow you to control the format of the output it generates. For example, you can transfer information between heterogeneous systems in XML or display your output on the local intranet using HTML-compatible data to allow easy dissemination of information.

As well as the built-in help feature in WMIC, an extensive overview of the command settings and syntax is available in the Windows XP Help and Support Center, which you can activate from the Start menu. After you have activated it, type `WMIC` and click the search button to retrieve a list of the available information. Consequently, this section of the chapter does not provide an exhaustive definition of the syntax of WMIC. It is an introductory tutorial that illustrates the use of the syntax and highlights some of its more useful features that you might use in day-to-day administrative tasks.

Note that WMIC will install and run only if you are an administrator member of the administrators' group. This is regardless of the permissions granted using `wmimgmt.msc` at the namespace level.

▪ Using WMIC

As mentioned, WMIC can operate in one of two modes: interactive or noninteractive. Interactive mode starts WMIC and provides you with a special command prompt to issue your WMIC-specific commands. Noninteractive mode starts WMIC, performs the requested actions, and then returns to the calling function, be it the command line or a script (in this sense, it can be a batch file, VBScript, or Jscript). This is useful if you wish to automate certain commands, perhaps by adding WMIC commands to existing batch files. Let's look at WMIC in interactive mode.

▪ Interactive Mode

To activate WMIC in interactive mode, move to the command prompt from the Windows Start menu, type `WMIC`, and press the return key. This triggers the execution of the file `wmic.exe` that is held in the `%SystemRoot%\wbem` folder. WMIC installs on demand, so there will be some initial gargling as Windows XP installs the executable and compiles a number of MOF files into the CIM repository the first time you run it. To be precise, it compiles the files `Cli.mof`, `Cliegaliases.mof`, and `Cliegaliases.mfl` into the `root/Cli` namespace of the CIM repository. `Cli.mof` contains the class descriptions for the Aliases, whereas `Cliegaliases` contains the actual instances. Aliases, as we shall discover, are a useful tool for simplifying day-to-day tasks and provide a way for the administrator to govern the presentation of management information.

Each time you execute WMIC after its initial installation, it compiles only `Cliega-liases.mof` and `Cliegaliases.mfl` into the repository to update the instances of Microsoft's Aliases. `Cliegaliases.mof` and `Cliegaliases.mfl` also can be found in the `%SystemRoot%\wbem` folder on your machine. We shall look at `Cliegaliases.mof` and `Cliegaliases.mfl` later. Let's practice using WMIC in interactive mode: Open a session of the command prompt and type `WMIC`, then press the key.

You can tell that you now are operating WMIC in interactive mode because the command prompt has changed to `wmic.root\cli>` and is waiting for your input. The command prompt keeps track of the *role* setting. A role in WMIC is really a namespace in the CIM repository that holds the information for your Aliases (by default this is `root\cli`, which you can see by looking at the command prompt in Figure 11.16). Microsoft introduced the notion of an Alias with WMIC to simplify the management of your environment. Aliases replace syntactically complex strings of classes, instances, and WQL queries with simplified keywords. The great thing about this approach is that you can create and tailor your own Aliases. Microsoft provides a series of default Aliases that you can browse by issuing the `/?` command (Figure 11.17) from the WMIC prompt: This command also lets you view a list of commands and global switches.

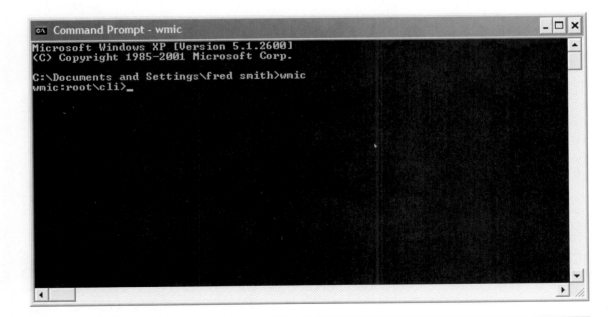

Figure 11.16   The WMIC command prompt

Figure 11.17 offers quite a few new terms to learn, but WMIC has an interactive help facility to assist you. Also, remember that WMIC is not case sensitive. Simply type the name of the command about which you would like to know more, followed by /?.

The global switches listed initially are the configuration settings for your current instance of WMIC. For example, these global switches define the machines to which you will connect, your username or password, and so forth. Most of these can keep their default settings. However, if you want to connect to multiple machines across the network or configure output styles, then understanding these configuration switches is essential.

Next all of the available Aliases are listed with brief descriptions of their purposes. As you will see, Microsoft provides more than 70 predefined Aliases for commonly carried-out tasks—quite a lot to read on the screen at one time. We shall configure WMIC to write all of the available commands and Aliases to a text file for reference.

Finally, beneath the Aliases is a series of commands, CLASS, PATH, CONTEXT, and QUIT/EXIT. In addition to these commands are numerous additional verbs such as ASSOC, GET, and SET that allow you to construct precise statements about the information you would like to retrieve or change in the CIM repository. We shall take a closer look at these later in the chapter.

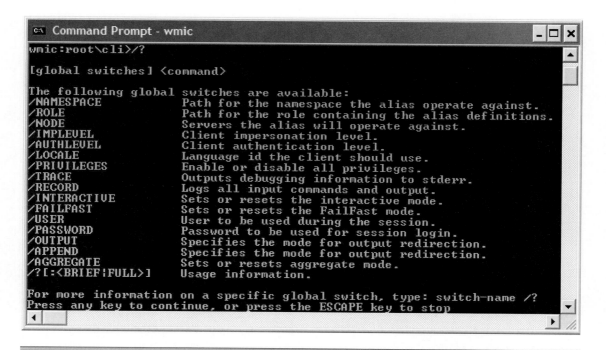

Figure 11.17 The /? sequence retrieves all available switches, Aliases, and commands

Configure WMIC to write all output to `commands.txt`, a file on the C drive:

```
Wmic:root\cli>/output:c:\commands.txt
```

Now issue the command to send a full listing of all the available commands to the file:

```
Wmic:root\cli>/?:full
```

Now return the output value to its default setting:

```
Wmic:root\cli>/output:STDOUT
```

The `/?:full` command sends a comprehensive listing of the available functions to `commands.txt`. The final command tells WMIC to redirect output back to the standard output stream, STDOUT, which by default is the command prompt screen. STDOUT, STDIN, and STDERR are common programming terms. STDIN and STDOUT refer to the input or output streams respectively and STDERR is the stream to which all errors are sent. STDIN is by default in the keyboard and STDOUT and STDERR are in the command prompt screen. If you now move to the root of the C:\ drive and open the file `commands.txt`, you will find a detailed description of the global switches, commands, and Aliases.

■ Configuring WMIC

Next, we shall inspect the configuration of WMIC (Figure 11.18) using the `context` command. From the WMIC command prompt type:

```
Wmic:root\Cli>context
```

As you can see from Figure 11.18, WMIC is attached to the `root\CIMV2` namespace: It gathers its Aliases from the default role `root\cli`. It is also connected to node SMITH (p. 590), which in this instance is the local machine, although we could also specify multiple nodes here to enable us to manage more than one machine. WMIC is configured by default to use impersonation level access that uses the account credentials of the current user for actions carried out locally. If you are attaching to namespaces on remote machines, then you may want to increase the security level to delegate (available on Windows 2000 machines and later) to enable your credentials to be used during calls to other computers. The only caveat is that this may represent an unnecessary security risk and so should be used sparingly. The authentication level is set to its default value of Pkt (packet), which ensures that all outbound data is authenticated to ensure it does, in fact, originate from the intended client. This certifies that you are not receiving erroneous data from a malicious third party. Note that all

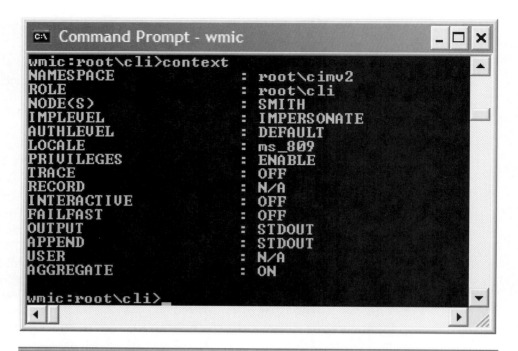

Figure 11.18 WMIC configuration

local connections to WMI on your machine use the highest possible authentication level of PktPrivacy, which authenticates all previous impersonation levels and encrypts the argument value of each remote procedure call. Any attempt to set this value to any other setting on your local machine will result in any subsequent calls to an Alias, a PATH, or a CLASS failing to retrieve any data.

The locale setting dictates any language-specific settings for the namespace you are accessing. This may at first appear to be a fairly trivial switch; however, make sure that this setting matches the locale of the namespace on the machine that you are accessing; otherwise, you will encounter error messages such as 0x8004100e, Invalid Namespace when trying to use Aliases.[2]

Hint: Take the last three digits of your hex locale ID and append them with ms_ to set WMIC's locale switch. For example US English hex value is 0x409 = ms_409, UK English hex value 0x809 = ms_809.

---

2. For a table of languages and LCIDs (LoCale IDentifiers), see http://msdn.microsoft.com/library/en-us/script56/html/vsmscl_CID.asp.

> **Top Tip:** If you experience problems while using WMIC, the first place to look for clues is the `%SystemRoot%\wbem/logs/wmic.log` file. Another good place to search for information is the Windows Help and Support Center. Type the error code that WMIC gives you, which normally starts with 0x800xxxxx, and use the search facility to check for Microsoft Knowledge Base information.

The PRIVILEGES switch is enabled by default and allows or revokes your privileges during operations in WMIC. The TRACE switch is set to OFF by default but when set to ON writes all debug information to the screen (referred to as STDERR, for *Standard Error*). Enabling the trace facility is very helpful when you are trying to resolve and detect problems. The RECORD switch is also OFF by default but when set to ON takes a filename to which it writes all of your commands and their output in XML format. The INTERACTIVE switch is, by default, OFF and dictates whether or not WMIC must confirm its actions with you. In reality, this means that WMIC will not prompt you for confirmation before deleting a class or instance from the namespace. This setting is useful if you intend to make unattended calls to WMIC, for example, from batch files. The FAILFAST switch is also useful because it enables commands to fail after a predetermined amount of time rather than waiting indefinitely for a response when your machine is running scripts unattended. Setting FAILFAST to ON would enable the script to move to the next command after a predetermined amount of time rather than hanging indefinitely if a remote machine were not responding to your requests setting.

In summary, the switches are as follows:

/NAMESPACE: Defines the namespace against which all your PATH and CLASS commands will be carried out. Aliases do not rely on this setting because they contain their own reference to a namespace as part of the connection property. (Remember that WMIC is not case sensitive.) By default in WMIC, the /namespace switch is set to `root\cimv2`. Note that all namespace paths are relative unless you start them with a double backslash (\\). If you wish to change the namespace value to something that does not reside beneath the current namespace use, for example:

```
Wmic:Cli>/namespace:\\root\someothernamespace
```

/ROLE: Defines the namespace that contains your Alias configuration data. By default this is the namespace `\\root\Cli` but this can be changed if you wish to define your own namespace to hold your own Aliases (remember that you can store your own user-defined Aliases in `\\root\Cli`). For example:

```
Wmic:Cli>/role:\\root\myownroles
```

`Wmic:root\cli>/role:\\.`—this sets the role to no namespace

> **Top Tip: Wigwams.** When forming namespace paths in WMIC the syntax can be confusing and it can be easy to mix up the order of the forward slash with the backward slash. One simple way of remembering the order is to think of a wigwam /\ with the two slashes in opposing directions. Remember the wigwam— forward slash followed by one or more backward slashes.
>
> For example: `/namespace:\mynamespace` or `/role:\mynamespace`

/NODEs: Defines which machines WMIC will access on your network. This feature is actually pretty powerful because it enables you to carry out tasks simultaneously on multiple machines. The only caveat is that you cannot mix administration of local and remote machines in the same session. This is because WMIC will not allow you to supply a username and/or password when attaching to local namespaces and takes your current credentials instead, for example:

```
Wmic:Cli>/node:machine1,machine2,machine3
```

/IMPLEVEL: Is short for impersonation level. Please refer to the earlier section on security for scripting to get a complete list of options. For example:

```
Wmic:Cli>/implevel:impersonate
```

/AUTHLEVEL: Is short for authentication level. This switch defines the level of authentication used with each of your actions. Again, please refer to the earlier section on security for scripting to get a complete list of options.

```
Wmic:Cli>/authlevel:Pkt
```

/LOCALE: Defines the language settings for your interactions. For example, if the machine to which you are attaching is based in the United States and you are based in the United Kingdom, you still will need to change locale (despite the obvious similarities in languages) from ms_809 UK English to ms_409 US English. Failing to do so would result in WMIC failing when it tries to retrieve locale-specific information, for example:

```
Wmic:Cli>/locale:ms_409
```

/PRIVILEGES: Enables or disables privileges during your interaction with WMIC, for example:

```
Wmic:Cli>/privileges:enable
```

/TRACE: Can be set to on or off and dictates whether WMIC explicitly provides output for every task it undertakes. In most cases you will want this set to off, which is the default. For example:

```
Wmic:Cli>/trace:off
```

/RECORD: Places all output (including the commands you type) to a user specified file, for example:

```
Wmic:Cli>/record:output.txt
```

/INTERACTIVE: Dictates whether or not delete commands are confirmed or not. This is useful if you are running WMIC unattended from a batch file. By default this value is off. For example:

```
Wmic:Cli>/interactive:off
```

/FAILFAST: Dictates whether WMIC times out after two minutes of trying to complete a command before continuing. For example:

```
Wmic:Cli>/failfast:disable
```

/OUPUT: Dictates whether the output from your commands goes to the standard output stream (STDOUT), the Windows clipboard where it can then be pasted into most Windows applications, or to a file (specified by a filename).

```
Wmic:Cli>/output:disable
```

/APPEND: Is the same as OUTPUT but appends the data to any existing output rather than overwriting it. This is useful if you wish to keep a progressive log of changes to your managed environment over time.

```
Wmic:Cli>/append:disable
```

/USER: Allows you to provide a specific username when logging on to WMI. This value can be reset using, for example:

```
wmic:root\cli>/user: " " " "
```

/PASSWORD: Allows you to provide a password for the username. This is also called automatically when you define a username, for example:

```
Wmic:Cli>/password:disable
```

/AGGREGATE: Can be set to either on or off and allows you to aggregate the results of multiple queries, for example:

```
Wmic:Cli>/aggregate:on
```

▪ Interacting with WMIC

The three main commands in WMIC that you can use to get management information from WMI are the Aliases, CLASS, and PATH commands. If you are familiar with the CIM repository, then the CLASS and PATH commands should feel quite natural to you. The CLASS command retrieves class information about managed objects whereas the PATH command retrieves the actual data associated with the class (the instance information). As an administrator, you probably will be most interested in the latter.

Both commands accept schema class names and paths to the CIM repository as part of their syntax. If you are not comfortable with this, then you may feel slightly more at home using Aliases. Despite syntactic differences, you more or less can do the same thing with both types of commands although Aliases have the slight edge of allowing you to format the output generated from them.

From the command prompt type the following:

```
Wmic:Cli>path Win32_NetworkAdapter
```

which is semantically identical to the following built-in Microsoft Alias:

```
Wmic:Cli>nic
```

Both commands retrieve information about the network cards installed on the current machine.

Now type at the command prompt:

```
Wmic:Cli>class Win32_NetworkAdapter
```

This retrieves all of the class schema information for the class `Win32_Network-Adapter`. There is no semantic equivalent for Aliases.

You can find additional information on the use of each Alias, command, or global switch from the WMIC prompt by typing its name followed by `/?:full`. The full switch ensures that all available information, including its description, is returned. If you want less information, use the `brief` switch. For example, let's look at the help information for the Alias baseboard:

```
Wmic:root\cli>baseboard /?:full
```

This should present results similar to the screenshot in Figure 11.19.

At the top of the screen you can see a brief description of the function of the Alias, which in this case tells us that it returns information about the motherboard on our system. Next is a description of the syntax for using the Alias written in BNF (Backus Naur Form).

> **Note:** BNF is named after its inventors, John Backus and Peter Naur. BNF is a way of defining the syntax of formal languages. In BNF a vertical line (|) indicates alternatives and square brackets ([]) indicate optional parts. The vertical line character is represented by 'vline' and spaces are represented by the word 'space'. Words enclosed in "<" and ">" are called nonterminals because they can be further broken into constituent parts, whereas symbols and characters like "A", "+", or "—" that cannot be broken are called terminals.[3]

---

3. Microsoft provides a comprehensive breakdown of the WMIC langauge using BNF that is available from the Windows XP Help and Support Center or the Microsoft Web site (http://www7.software.ibm.com/vad.nsf/Data/Document4639).

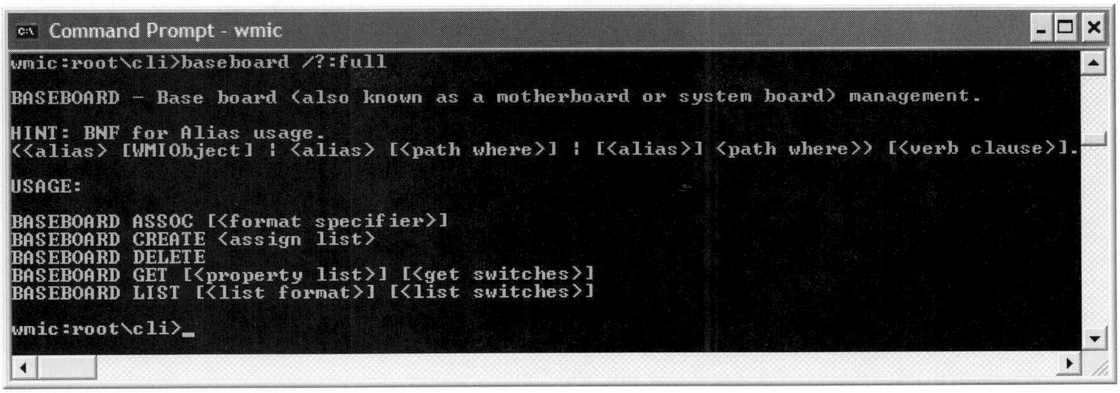

```
Command Prompt - wmic                                        _ □ ✕

wmic:root\cli>baseboard /?:full

BASEBOARD - Base board (also known as a motherboard or system board) management.

HINT: BNF for Alias usage.
((alias) [WMIObject] | (alias) [(path where)] | [(alias)] (path where)) [(verb clause)].

USAGE:

BASEBOARD ASSOC [(format specifier)]
BASEBOARD CREATE (assign list)
BASEBOARD DELETE
BASEBOARD GET [(property list)] [(get switches)]
BASEBOARD LIST [(list format)] [(list switches)]

wmic:root\cli>_
```

Figure 11.19 Usage information on an Alias

■ The WHERE Clause

WHERE enables you to refine your query for information and is useful in situations in which you want to receive a specific subset of information. For example, if we retrieved a comprehensive list of all of the services on our system, we could use the following Alias or path statement without a WHERE clause.

```
Wmic:Cli>Path win32_service
```

or

```
Wmic:Cli>Service
```

Let's imagine that we wanted only to get information about a specific service, called alerter. We could refine our statement so that it retrieved only this specific instance of the class in which a given property met certain criteria. For example, using the WHERE clause:

```
Wmic:Cli>Path win32_service where name="alerter"
```

or

```
Wmic:Cli>service where name="alerter"
```

which would retrieve the instance information for only the alerter service. It also is possible to use a variety of conditions (Table 11.3) with a WHERE clause (+,=,<,>=,!=). For

Table 11.3 Comparison Operators

Symbol	Description	Symbol	Description
>	Is greater than	=	Is equal to
>=	Is greater than or equal to	!=	Is not equal to
<	Is less than		

example, if we wished to list all those services that are currently not set to auto for the startmode then we could use the following:

```
Wmic:Cli>service where startmode!="auto"
```

Remember always to enclose strings in double quotes. Numerical values do not need to be treated this way.

■ Verbs

Verbs allow us to refine our list even further. For example, to retrieve only the displayname and description for each of the services that match our criteria, we could use the get verb:

```
Wmic:Cli>service where startmode!="auto" get displayname,description
```

or

```
Wmic:Cli>Path Win32_Service where startmode!="auto" get displayname,
   description
```

To retrieve the list of available verbs, end the statement with /? as follows:

```
Wmic:Cli>service where startmode!="auto" /?
```

All cases will be a subset of the verbs listed in Table 11.4.

To obtain a detailed explanation of their parameters, switches, and use simply type them as follows:

```
aliasname verb /?:full
e.g. nic assoc /?:full
```

Table 11.4 List of WMIC Verbs

Verb	Description	Example
Assoc	Returns all associated instances. This is a useful way of determining which components are associated to each other.	nic assoc
Create	Creates a new instance and creates property values for it. Note that the provider must support this switch in order for it to work.	nic create index=11
Delete	Deletes the current instance or instances. Can also delete a class. Use with caution!	nic delete index=1 OR nic delete Will attempt to delete all instances of the class!!!
Get	Can be used to retrieve specific properties	nic where deviceID< 3 get name,status,deviceid
List	Alters the display of data. Can be used to specify what information is displayed. **Note: This verb is available ONLY when using Aliases!**	nic list brief|full|instance|system|status
Set	Changes the values of a given property. Multiple properties can be changed by separating each with a comma.	Service where name="alerter" set Description="My new description"
Call	Calls a function that belongs to a class	Service where name="alerter" call pauseservice This causes the alerter service to pause. You could achieve the same effect by calling the pauseservice verb defined as part of the alias. Service where name="alerter" pauseservice

■ Adverbs

Adverbs allow us to refine our query even further. They are additions to the verbs given above. To retrieve a list of adverbs, enter the name of the verb (in conjunction with an Alias name or path) and use /?:full. At the time of writing only the list verb has any adverbs.

■ Looping WMIC Commands

The list and get verbs have two special switches that allow you to repeatedly loop a query as many times as you desire (within reason). For example, type the following:

```
service where name="alerter" get status, name /every:2 /repeat:5
```

This will result in the status of the alerter service being displayed five times, once every two seconds, unless a key is pressed. We also can do this with the list verb as follows:

```
service where name="alerter" list brief /every:2 /repeat:5
```

This shows that the list and get verbs are really very similar. List, in reality, is a set of canned output formats that describe using the adverbs brief, full, instance, status, and system, whereas get allows you to define exactly which properties are retrieved.

■ Types of Output

Microsoft provides an additional number of eXtensible Stylesheet Language Transform (XSL) files to assist in the formatting of WMIC's data (which is all in XML format). Type the following:

```
Wmic:root\cli>/output:d:\nic.htm
Wmic:root\cli>nic get /format:hform.xsl
```

These two commands tell WMIC first to write all output to a file called `nic.htm` on the d drive, and second to retrieve data on the available network cards and format it into an HTML-compatible table using `hform.xsl`. XSL Transform files act as stylesheets with a series of template rules that convert the XML data generated by WMIC into a variety of formats. This is another powerful feature of WMIC that will allow administrators to tailor the output of WMIC into custom formats.[4,5]

The XSL files in Table 11.5 are installed with WMIC by default.

■ Aliases

In Figure 11.20, the Connection object defines the parameters required when connecting to WMI, for example, a username, password, or authentication method. The description property provides a description of the Alias. The Formats array contains a list of properties to be shown for this Alias. Microsoft documents this as a list of lists indexed by the format name (for example, FULL, BRIEF, INSTANCE, or a user-defined qualifier). The FriendlyName string provides the name for the Alias. The name must

4. For a detailed description of both XML and XSL, visit the World Wide Web Consortium Web site at http://www.3w.org/.

5. If you are interested in creating your own SXL files, IBM provides a free XSL stylesheet editor (approximately 5Mb) that can be downloaded from http://www7.software.ibm.com/vad.nsf/Data/Document4639.

Table 11.5   Supplied XSL Files for Outputting WMIC Results

Name	Description
wmiclimofformat.xsl	Converts XML data to MOF format. If Aliases or other WMI objects are defined in XML format, this XSL can be used to convert them to MOFs so that they can be MOFCOMPed. - /FORMAT:MOF format.
wmiclitableformat.xsl	—/ALL or /FORMAT:TABLE
wmiclitableformatnosys.xsl	Same as wmiclitableformat.xsl except that it does not have the ability to display WMI "system" properties (properties for the WMI path of instances, etc.).
wmiclivalueformat.xsl	/VALUE format—one line per value.
mof.xsl	Converts XML data to MOF format. If Aliases or other WMI objects are defined in XML format, this XSL can be used to convert them to MOFs so that they can be MOFCOMPed.
xml.xsl	To output XML data in XML format. All WMIC data is extracted in XML format, so this format will give you data the way that WMIC sees it. This can be useful for creating your own XSL files. Outputting data in XML format is also useful if you want to provide the data to systems that accept XML data.
hform.xsl	HTML output—the data is displayed in a vertical table (one row per property or instance name). The table can be very long.
htable.xsl	HTML output—the data is displayed in a horizontal table (one row per instance). The table can be very wide.
texttable.xsl	The same as wmiclitableformatnosys.xsl.
texttablewsys	The same as wmiclitableformat.xsl.
textvaluelist	Similar to wmiclivalueformat.xsl except that property names are not included on each line and the format is more compact.

be unique in the context of the namespace in which the Alias is defined. As mentioned earlier with respect to scripting, Alias names cannot match keywords, thus, you cannot name your Alias CLASS, QUERY, PATH, or RESTORE because they appear in the same location in the syntax. Next, the PWhere property defines a From/where clause (that is, a WQL query without the Select clause). The query string may contain substitution parameters (tokens preceded by a # mark) indicating where values may be substituted into the query string. The parameter values are taken from the tokens immediately after the Alias if the token cannot be resolved to a switch or verb—this allows, for example, a command such as "nic 1" where the PWhere value for the nic Alias is "WHERE DeviceID=#" and the target is "Select * from Win32_NetworkAdapter."

```
class MSFT_CliAlias
{
  MSFT_CliConnection Connection;
  String Description;
  MSFT_CliFormat Formats[];
  STRING FriendlyName;
  STRING PWhere;
  MSFT_CliQualifier Qualifiers[];
  STRING Target;
  MSFT_CliVerb Verbs[];
};
```

Figure 11.20 The basic structure of an Alias in MOF format stored in the `root\cli` namespace by default

The value of 1 is taken by PWHERE and replaces the #, giving "WHERE DeviceID=1." Then this is appended to the target, forming "Select * from Win32_NetworkAdapter WHERE DeviceID=1." Next the qualifiers applicable to this Alias are held in an array. The Target string defines the object to be operated on through the Alias. The string may be a simple class name or a WQL query. If the `Target` property is empty, only verbs based on command-line utilities may be used by the Alias. The Verbs array is the list of verbs supported by the Alias.

You can also view Aliases and make modifications using the CIM Studio. Let's take a quick detour and have a look under the hood of Aliases to further understand the concept. Start WMI CIM Studio and navigate to the `root\cli` namespace. From here you should be presented with the set of classes (as in the screenshot in Figure 11.21).

The right hand pane in Figure 11.21 is an enumeration of the `MSFT_CliAlias` instances.

The classes held in the `root\cli` namespace are defined specifically for WMIC. These are all part of the MSFT schema of classes that are designed to facilitate, among other things, policy extensions, remote events, and WMIC-specific functions. Select `MSFT_CliAlias` and click the enumerate button in the top right. In the right hand pane we have enumerated all instances of class `MSFT_CliAlias` as this is the class of most interest to us with respect to Aliases. If you enumerate this class, you will be presented with all of the currently available Aliases. The friendly name is the name you can use in WMIC, and, as you can see, many of them are self-describing, with names like Printer, Registry, or OS. Scroll down the right pane until you see the friendly name of NIC (short for Network Interface Card). Highlight this row and go to the object using either a double-click or right mouse click. You should be presented with the information (in Figure 11.22) in the right pane.

The `Connection` property holds an object of type `MSFT_CliConnection`. The value of this object holds details of the target namespace to which your Aliases will connect.

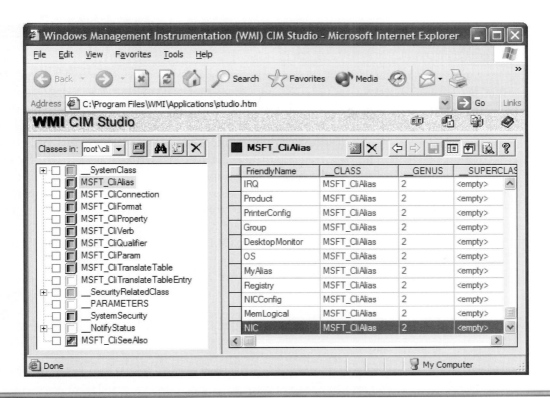

Figure 11.21 The MSFT_CliAlias class in the root\Cli namespace

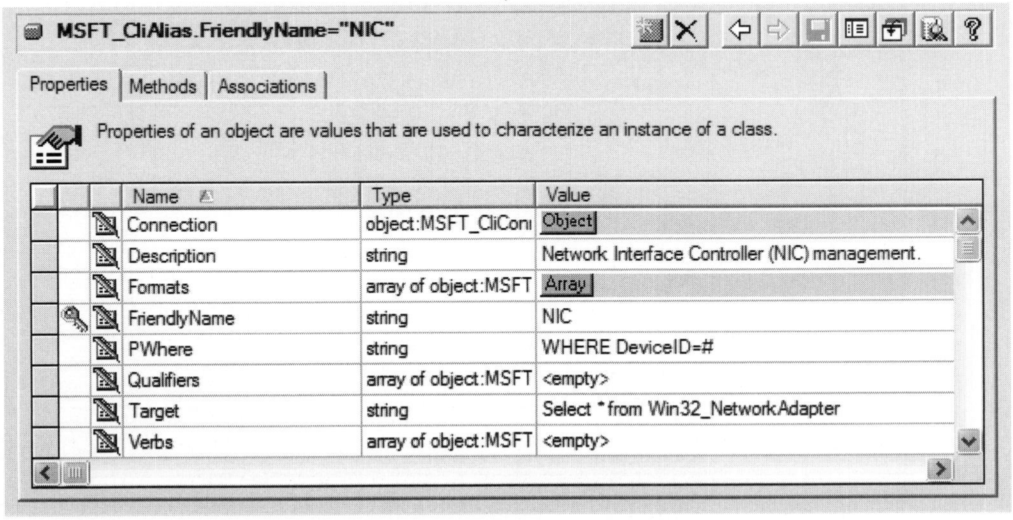

Figure 11.22 The NIC Alias, up close and personal

In most cases, you will retrieve your information from the CIMV2 namespace because it holds much of the system-specific information relevant to you as an administrator. Click the object button in the Value column to explore this in more detail: Note that the value of the Namespace property in this case is root\CIMV2. This object allows you to attach to CIM repositories located on remote machines by specifying the server name, username, and password. Unfortunately, these properties seem to have little effect upon the behavior of the Aliases, which instead access the machine specified in the global switches /node and /user. We also warn against setting these properties here because they hold the password value undisguised by the traditional star characters, which leaves the machine open to snooping and subsequent abuse.

Clicking the Connection value brings up the Embedded Object dialog (Figure 11.23) for class MSFT_CliConnection.

The next property is the description for the Alias and details its purpose. After that is the Format property, which contains an array of objects that dictate how the output is formatted for the Alias. This is of particular interest to us if we wish to customize the fields shown in the output from an Alias and the way in which they are displayed (Figure 11.24).

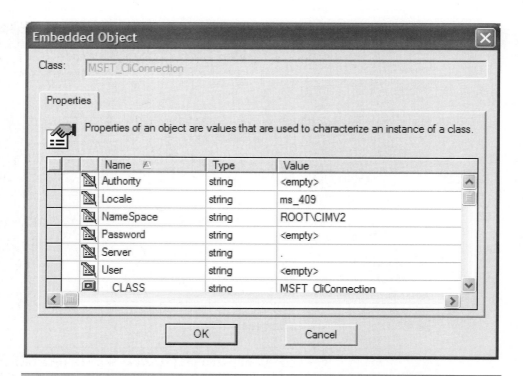

Figure 11.23 The Embedded Object dialog for class MSFT_CliConnection

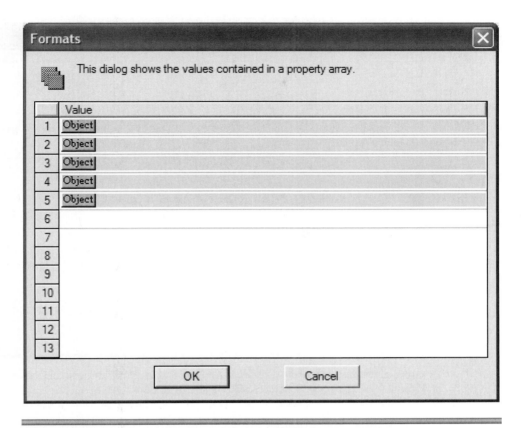

Figure 11.24   An array of objects associated with the Formats property

Figure 11.24 is an array of objects associated with the Formats property. Each one of these represents a different style of layout, for example, BRIEF|FULL|INSTANCE| SYSTEM|STATUS, that can be called from WMIC. If you click the topmost object number (1), you will be presented with a dialog box (Figure 11.25) that displays the properties of the STATUS format option. This is defined for table format (the only other option is LIST), which makes the output very wide because it lists the properties of the class in columns from left to right across the screen. The Properties array contains the list of the properties that are displayed by the format.

Each object defines the layout of the data and the properties that are displayed.

As mentioned earlier, the FriendlyName property is a key property that must be unique for the instance and also is the name you use in WMIC. PWhere is used to retrieve specific instances of the CIM class defined in the property Target. The hash character (#) indicates that a numeric value is assigned by users when they call the Alias. To accept a string value from the command line, enclose the hash symbol in single quotes, '#'. The Qualifiers property holds an array of the qualifiers applicable to the Alias.

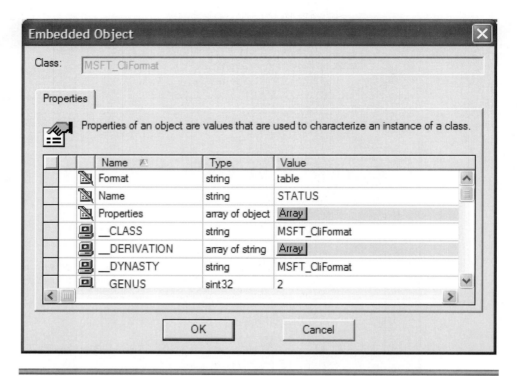

Figure 11.25 Properties of the STATUS format option

The `Target` property can contain either a class name or, more commonly, a WQL clause. The `Verb` property details the verbs that can be used in conjunction with the Alias. In this example, there are no verbs that can validly be used in conjunction with the Alias. To see the Alias in action, let's activate it in WMIC. First, move from the Start menu to the command prompt option and type `wmic` at the prompt. Now type the name of the Alias, `nic` (remember, WMIC is not case sensitive). You should be presented with something similar to the image in Figure 11.26.

As you can see, you have retrieved a comprehensive list of all of the network interface cards, both logical and physical, available on your machine. To save this output, you could simply pipe all of the information to an output file by specifying its name in the `/output` global switch as follows:

```
Wmic:root\cli>/output:d:\nic.txt
```

Or to cut and paste the information into a Windows GUI–based application we could specify:

```
Wmic:root\cli>/output:clipboard
```

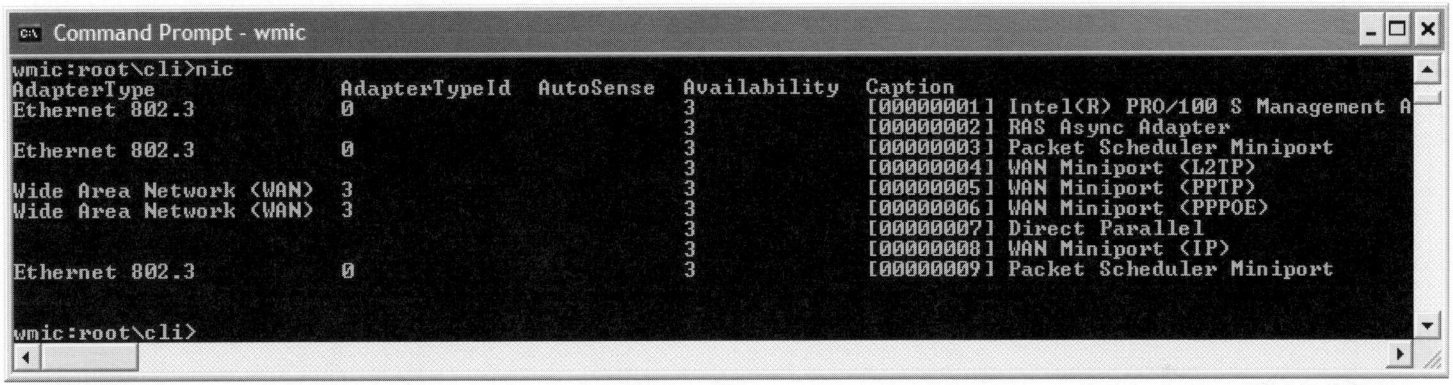

```
cx   Command Prompt - wmic

wmic:root\cli>nic
AdapterType                AdapterTypeId  AutoSense  Availability  Caption
Ethernet 802.3             0                         3             [00000001] Intel(R) PRO/100 S Management A
                                                     3             [00000002] RAS Async Adapter
Ethernet 802.3             0                         3             [00000003] Packet Scheduler Miniport
                                                     3             [00000004] WAN Miniport (L2TP)
Wide Area Network (WAN)    3                         3             [00000005] WAN Miniport (PPTP)
Wide Area Network (WAN)    3                         3             [00000006] WAN Miniport (PPPOE)
                                                     3             [00000007] Direct Parallel
                                                     3             [00000008] WAN Miniport (IP)
Ethernet 802.3             0                         3             [00000009] Packet Scheduler Miniport

wmic:root\cli>
```

Figure 11.26   The NIC Alias in action

587

To send our output to the screen later, we could use the following command:

```
Wmic:root\cli>/output:STDOUT
```

STDOUT is the default screen on most operating systems.

■ Creating or Modifying Aliases Using the CIM Studio

One of the most powerful features of WMIC is that you can tailor it to suit your own needs by customizing certain aspects of it. This includes potentially customizing or modifying Aliases to simplify the syntax of day-to-day tasks and also creating your own canned output formats to determine which properties are shown and how they are displayed. The only caveat is that you must determine before creating your own Alias whether Microsoft already has implemented it for you. Microsoft includes more than 70 built-in Aliases as part of WMIC: They can be viewed either typing /? in WMIC or by inspecting the MSFT_CliAlias class in the root\Cli namespace using the WMI CIM Studio.

We will examine three ways of creating your own Alias: one using the MOF language, one from the command line of WMIC using the create command, and one using the WMI CIM Studio.

Considerations

1. Decide which components you wish to manage and locate their classes in the CIM repository using the WMI CIM Studio. Typically, the best place to start looking is the root\CIMV2 namespace. After you are in the namespace, use the help button to retrieve descriptions of candidate classes and their properties to help you decide whether this class contains the information you need.

2. Decide from which machines (nodes) on the network you are going to retrieve this information. Do any of the machines use Kerberos authority or NTLM? You must specify this in the Alias.

3. Identify the locale of each machine you will be accessing. Make a note, because you will need to specify this in the Alias.

4. Determine whether you will need a username and password to access these machines. Are they the same for all the machines? Remember, you cannot define specific username/password pairs for specific nodes: All nodes in a WMIC session require the same username and password.

Creating a Simple Alias from the WMIC Command Line

It is also possible to create an Alias from the command line using Alias. Start WMIC in interactive or noninteractive mode and type the following:

```
Alias create friendlyname="MyAlias", PWhere="WHERE AdapterType='#'",
    target="SELECT * FROM Win32_NetworkAdapter" < >
```

If successful, WMIC will return "instance creation successful." This will result in a new Alias called MyAlias being created and stored locally in the CIM repository. MyAlias returns a list of the currently installed network adapters with the option to filter the results by frame type. Notice that we have enclosed the hash in single quotes, because it is a string value. To test it from the interactive command prompt, making sure to enclose the string value in double quotes, type:

```
wmic:root\Cli>MyAlias "Ethernet 802.3" <return>
```

Using WMIC in Noninteractive Mode

In noninteractive mode it is possible to use WMIC to access WMI on the local machine or across the network to a remote machine from within a batch file. Here we shall take a brief look at the pros and cons of doing so.

To call WMIC in noninteractive mode, you must append all commands, Aliases, and switches after the call to WMIC, each separated by a space. For example, to retrieve the context of WMIC from the command line, you would type the following and then press the return key:

```
C:\ WMIC CONTEXT
```

If you irreparably damage the existing Alias instances or classes while experimenting with the CIM studio, you can recompile them into the CIM repository by typing:

For classes: `c:\mofcomp cli.mof`

For instances: `c:\mofcomp Cliegaliases.mof`

`c:\mofcomp Cliegaliases.mfl`

This will restore the classes and instances to their initial states, but will not delete any existing instances you may have created.

You must take certain precautions when running your batch files unattended and accessing WMIC. For example, make sure that you have set the namespace, role, and node global switches before making any calls. Also ensure that FAILFAST and INTERACTIVE are OFF before proceeding. You will probably want to write the output to a file for later viewing.

Aliases are recommended for use with WMIC in noninteractive mode because they improve readability and sparingly use the 1024-character limitation of the command line. Fully qualified paths potentially could eat up vast numbers of characters.

Suppose that we wish to publish a table of the currently installed software on a machine when the user first boots up. This table would allow administrators to keep track of potential irregularities, such as the installation of unlicensed software or software that is not work-related. To set this up, we could append the `autoexec.bat` file to call WMIC as follows:

```
WMIC /FAILFAST:off /LOCALE:ms_409/INTERACTIVE:off/OUTPUT:c:\table.htm
    Product get name,vendor /format:hform.xsl
```

> **Note:** Always specify switches before Aliases, otherwise they have no effect. Aliases and switches must be separated by spaces.

This call will result in the name and vendor of all the software products installed on the host machine being written to the file `table.htm` in tabular HTML format, using the format defined in `hform.xsl` (Figure 11.27).

WMIC commands can be configured to format the output in a variety of predesigned styles. These formats are also customizable because WMIC works with XSL documents. Using the output switch ensures that everything in the file `table.htm` is

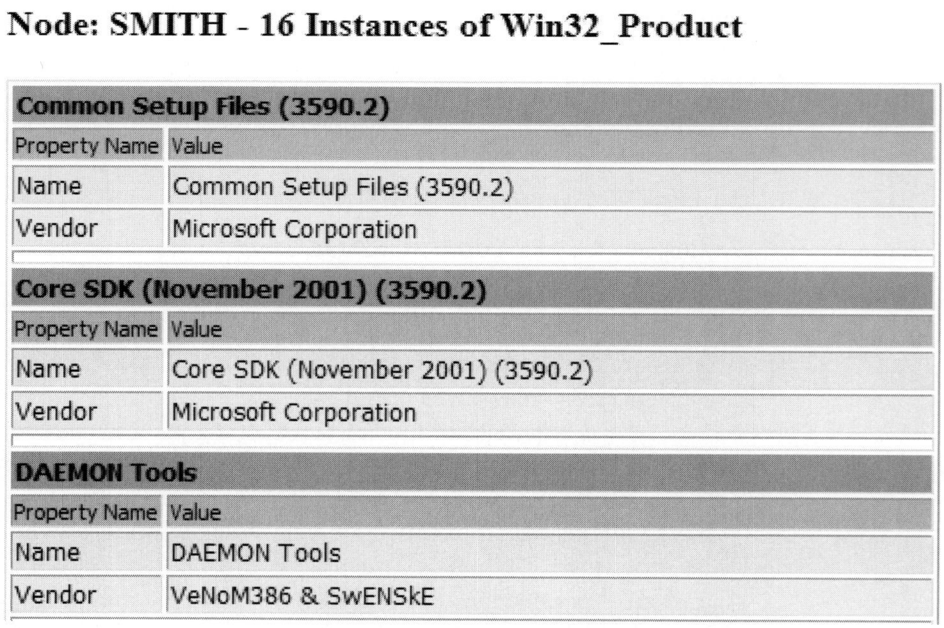

Node: SMITH - 16 Instances of Win32_Product

Common Setup Files (3590.2)	
Property Name	Value
Name	Common Setup Files (3590.2)
Vendor	Microsoft Corporation

Core SDK (November 2001) (3590.2)	
Property Name	Value
Name	Core SDK (November 2001) (3590.2)
Vendor	Microsoft Corporation

DAEMON Tools	
Property Name	Value
Name	DAEMON Tools
Vendor	VeNoM386 & SwENSkE

Figure 11.27 WMIC can format the output in a variety of predesigned styles

overwritten each time it runs. If, however, you wanted to keep track of the changes over the weeks, you would use the /append switch instead, as follows:

```
WMIC /FAILFAST:off /LOCALE:ms_409 /INTERACTIVE:off /APPEND:table.htm
    Product list format brief /format:hform.xsl
```

WMIC does not accept multiple queries on a single command line. For example, the following would fail.

```
WMIC /LOCALE:ms_409 nic: /LOCALE Product list format brief /
format:hform.xsl
```

> **BEST PRACTICE!**   Usernames and Passwords
>
> Never declare passwords and usernames using the /password and username switches when using WMIC in noninteractive mode from a batch file. This represents an unwarranted security risk.

■ Summary

By learning to use WMI Scripting and WMIC, administrators are able to plan and implement a proactive management strategy, as well as to automate complex day-to-day tasks. The WMI architecture is Microsoft's most extensive management architecture to date: The tools examined in this chapter and in Chapter 10 provide relatively simple, but powerful, ways to benefit from it.

WMIC is an essential tool for carrying out single queries on one or more machines. This is perfect for administrative tasks with a relatively small number of steps. WMIC is also extremely simple to use, ensuring that administrators can begin to obtain results from it in a relatively short time. WMIC has powerful formatting abilities that are easily extensible by designing custom XSL formats of your own. The Alias feature makes WMIC particularly easy to use without any prior knowledge of the structure of the CIM. In interactive mode, WMIC allows users to issue commands one at a time and query WMI on local or remote machines. In noninteractive mode, existing batch files can be updated so that they can also harness the power of WMIC.

WMI Scripting is a step beyond the previous capabilities of the MS-DOS batch file language and of the scripting capabilities of the WSH object model alone. In providing the WMI API, Microsoft has provided administrators with a unique opportunity to develop simple management tools of their own within reasonable time. After the initial overhead of learning to script, the rapid development time of scripts compared with the complexity of the tasks they can undertake via WMI offer a real step forward in the enterprise system management arena.

Ten Fast Facts: WMIC Tips

1. WMIC can be used to access local or remote CIM repositories and retrieve, modify, add, or delete data in them.

2. WMIC introduces a new term to system management, *Alias*. An Alias is a simplified term that refers to a more complex query that retrieves and formats information from the CIM repository.

3. WMIC can operate in one of two modes, interactive and noninteractive. Interactive mode starts WMIC and provides you with a special command prompt to issue your WMIC-specific commands. Noninteractive mode starts WMIC, performs the requested actions, and then returns to the calling function.

4. WMIC is configured by default to use impersonation level access that uses the account credentials of the current user for actions carried out locally.

5. The three main commands in WMIC that you can use to get management information from WMI are the Aliases, CLASS, and PATH commands. The CLASS command retrieves class information about managed objects whereas the PATH command and Aliases retrieve the actual data associated with the class (the instance information).

6. WMIC provides help on each of its commands. Append with /? to retrieve help for a specific command (or verb associated with a command).

7. The WHERE clause enables you to refine your WMIC queries to allow you to receive a specific subset of information.

8. Verbs in WMIC allow the user to refine the set of data returned by a query. Adverbs are additions to verbs that refine the query even further.

9. Output from WMIC can be modified using XSL documents. Microsoft provides a number of XSL documents but users can also define their own to tailor the output to suit the needs of their organization.

10. It is possible to create your own Aliases to simplify the administration of your target environment. This can be done using the WMI CIM Studio or by writing and compiling a MOF file.

Chapter 12

Developing WMI Providers

One of the most powerful features of Windows Management Instrumentation (WMI) is that it allows developers to expose their own management objects through a provider. WMI offers a lot of infrastructure that makes writing providers reasonably straightforward. Let's look at the big picture of current approaches used by developers to expose their management interfaces.

If you're a developer of a client-side project, then it's likely that you don't have any facility to manage and monitor the software. Managing and monitoring client applications is sometimes viewed as more of a problem than managing and monitoring server-side applications. Microsoft has already led the way by making Microsoft Office and Internet Explorer expose management objects. Microsoft Office exposes more than 100 classes (in the `root\MSAPPS10` namespace) and Internet Explorer exposes around ten classes (in the `root\CIMV2\Applications\MicrosoftIE` namespace). This allows administrators to remotely monitor and manage large numbers of client machines in the network.

If you're a developer of a server-side project, then you almost definitely have some management requirement. Traditionally, server-side development projects have implemented their own infrastructure for local and remote administration. This may have been a combination of custom DCOM interfaces, writing values directly into the registry, or using some other mechanism (such as a file), all of which are completely proprietary and require special knowledge to manage the environment. Writing your own DCOM administration interfaces may seem like an easy route at first but after writing a WMI provider, you will soon realize that WMI offers a lot of the plumbing that you might otherwise have to implement. Here are a few reasons why writing a WMI provider can benefit you:

- Uses an industry standard class-based schema. The benefit here is that the classes can be very precise in their definition. This allows others to understand and use your classes easily. A class-based schema allows you to encapsulate objects logically in the management environment.

- Allows access to management objects either through the scripting interface or through a programming language such as C++ and C#.

- Provides an infrastructure for executing WQL queries. If a provider doesn't support query optimization, WMI can still perform the query by enumerating all the management objects for a class. In short, you get free query support.

- Allows simpler deployment. Developing DCOM solutions requires a proxy-stub DLL to be installed on each client machine. Accessing WMI management objects requires no additional installation on client machines if they're running Windows 2000/XP or Windows ME.

- Provides an infrastructure to publish events when something interesting happens. Clients can capture these events across the network by making an event subscription.

- Optimizes the marshalling of high-performance data across the network. When accessing high-performance objects on another machine, WMI on the remote machine caches the objects and transmits only minimal data sets over the network.

- Provides a logical and unified administration model.

Let's focus on the last point in the list. Some development projects store their administration information in several places. These could include the Active Directory, an XML file, a database, the Internet, the registry, or some other storage medium. The storage medium is sometimes referred to as the *local cache*. Let's consider the following WMI class:

```
class Sample_MyUser
{
  [key] string Name;                 // Stored in a database
  boolean OnLine;                    // Retrieved from the Internet
  boolean UserAlreadyLoggedOn;       // Obtained at runtime
  string PhoneNumber;                // Retrieved from the Active Directory
  Sample_Preferences Options;        // Stored in an XML file
  boolean EnableUser;                // Stored in Registry
};
```

This class clearly demonstrates how we logically can encapsulate a user in code in which the data for each of the properties has originated from a different data source.

From a client programming perspective, the client never needs to use any other APIs to access the properties exposed by the class. The client's only programming requirement is to use the WMI `IWbemServices` interface. In a traditional programming environment, this encapsulation is lost: The client needs to write code to access all the different data sources separately. Encapsulation is not the only feature that is lost; scripting support and querying are lost, too. The solution is to write a provider that accesses all the data from the different data sources and then deploy the provider on the machine that is exposing the management objects. Any client can then connect to the machine to access the data. At a general level, providers fall into two categories: *push providers* and *pull providers*. Figure 12.1 illustrates.

Pull providers pull instance or property data from the local cache and pass it to WMI. Hence, a pull provider implements its own data retrieval. Typically, a pull provider accesses data that is dynamic and/or changes frequently. There are six different types of pull providers:

- **Class.** A class provider can generate class definitions dynamically. For instance, the WMI Performance Counter provider generates WMI classes based on the counter definitions. We do not explicitly discuss class providers in this chapter.

- **Instance.** An instance provider exposes the management objects that are available for one or more classes. An instance provider can support instance enumeration, retrieval, creation, modification, and deletion of management object data. An instance provider needs to store and provide access to its own data.

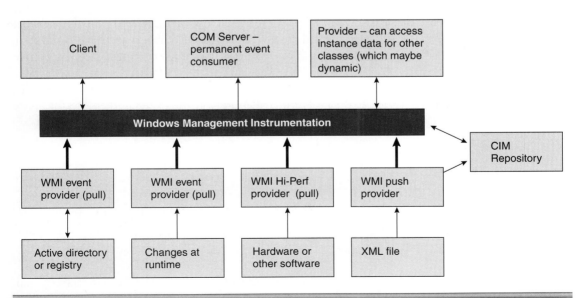

Figure 12.1   WMI client/provider architecture

The WMI Event Log provider is an example of an instance provider. Instance provider development probably is the most common type.

■ **Method.** A method provider implements one or more methods in one or more classes. This type of provider generally is coupled with instance providers.

■ **Event.** An event provider can publish both intrinsic and extrinsic events. This type of provider generally is coupled with instance providers.

■ **Property.** A property provider implements dynamic property access for one or more classes. Properties are accessed using either a class, instance, or property context.

■ **Hi-Perf.** A high-performance provider allows very fast and efficient access to constantly changing data. This is how Win32 performance counters are exposed.

Push providers push, that is, write, instance data into the CIM repository. The CIM repository is managed by WMI, which means that the data storage, data access, and event notification are provided by WMI.

In addition to these types of providers is a permanent event consumer provider. An event consumer is an application that requests events from WMI. There are two types of event consumers: temporary event consumers and permanent event consumers. Chapter 7 covers temporary event consumers in detail. Permanent event consumers offer on-demand event delivery and are more like a client than a provider. The main advantage of a permanent event consumer is that it does not have to be running when the event occurs.

The rest of this chapter assumes that you are familiar with C++ programming, COM (Component Object Model), and ATL (Active Template Library). It also assumes that you have read Chapter 7 and are aware that management objects can be created, updated, deleted, enumerated, and queried, and that properties on objects can be manipulated, methods can be executed, and you can subscribe to receive WMI events. This chapter is a detailed discussion on how to write providers to expose your own management objects. By the end of this chapter, you should be knowledgeable about virtually every key aspect of writing a WMI provider.[1]

■ Where to Start

Developing a WMI provider requires that some schema be in place first. If you're developing an instance provider, then you need to have designed your class schema and

---

1. During this chapter, we use the terms "management object," "managed object," "object," and "instance" interchangeably.

added it to the CIM repository. The schema includes some qualifiers to specify how the class, property, or method is implemented.

We shall cover most of the different types of providers in this chapter. As we discuss each type of provider, we shall include information on the schema being implemented and the provider registration.

■ Developing an Instance Provider

An instance provider exposes instances for one or more classes. You develop an instance provider when a class's instance data originates from a data source other than the CIM repository. As already mentioned, this data or local cache can originate from a variety of sources. This may include a hardware device, a database, a file, the registry, and so forth.

The first step is to design the class schema for the management objects. We shall implement a fruit basket. This is a simple schema with three classes that includes an association class. Most real-world objects will have an association: This provider implementation demonstrates how you can integrate such a class. Figure 12.2 describes a rough outline of the class schema that we shall implement.

As you develop your schema, you will realize that you need to understand all the interactions between your classes. We call this "The rules of the management environment." Here are the rules for the management environment we have defined:

There can be zero, one, or more fruit baskets. A fruit basket can contain one or more items of fruit. Many items of fruit can exist but only as long as they are in a basket. An item of fruit can reside only in one basket. After an item of fruit is assigned to a basket, it cannot be changed. An item of fruit cannot be deleted specifically. When a basket is deleted, so are all of the items of fruit contained within it.

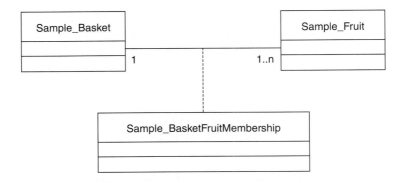

Figure 12.2 WMI instance provider class schema

Let's have a look at the class definitions that will be implemented. Here's the first class:

```
[
  dynamic: ToInstance,
  provider("FruitBasketProv"): ToInstance,
  SupportsUpdate,
  SupportsDelete
]
class Sample_Basket
{
  [key] string Name;
  uint8 Capacity;
};
```

This is a simple class with two properties. The first property is the name of the basket. No two baskets can have the same name because `Name` is a key property. The purpose of key properties is that they uniquely specify how an object is referenced which determines what appears in the `__Path` property. Hence, if a class doesn't have a key property, then any objects of that class cannot be referenced, which has the side effect that objects cannot be created. The `Capacity` property merely specifies how many items of fruit the basket can contain.

The next step is to mark the class as implemented by an instance provider. This requires the `dynamic` qualifier, which indicates that the class's instances are created dynamically. The `provider` qualifier informs WMI who will provide the instances. This qualifier specifies the name of a registered WMI provider. The `ToInstance` flavor specifies that the qualifier be propagated to instances.

Before diving into the details of writing a provider, you should assess the capabilities that a provider requires. An instance provider can create, update, enumerate, delete, get an object, and support query optimization. Not all of our classes support all of these features: It is common for different classes to support different combinations of supported provider functions. Incorporate this design activity during your schema design. WMI classes that support the standard mechanism for creating, updating, and deleting management objects should have the `SupportsCreate`, `SupportsUpdate`, and `SupportsDelete` qualifiers respectively. The `Sample_Basket` class supports the following provider functions:

- Update basket instance data (note that the class is qualified as supporting this feature by specifying the `SupportsUpdate` qualifier).
- Get a basket instance.
- Delete a basket instance (note that the class is qualified as supporting this feature by specifying the `SupportsDelete` qualifier).
- Enumerate all basket instances.

Let's move to the `Sample_Fruit` class:

```
[
  dynamic: ToInstance,
  provider("FruitBasketProv"): ToInstance,
  SupportsUpdate
]
class Sample_Fruit
{
  [key] string Name;
  uint16 Weight;

  [implemented, static, constructor]
  boolean AddFruitToBasket([in] string FruitName,
    [in] string BasketName);
};
```

This is another simple class that has only two properties. The `Name` property uniquely identifies an item of fruit and the `Weight` property stores how heavy the fruit item is. The class also has a method called `AddFruitToBasket`. In our schema, this is the only way to create a basket that does not already exist, and it is also the only way to add an item of fruit and associate it with a specific basket. Apply the `constructor` qualifier to methods that create instances (which `AddFruitToBasket` does). WMI does not use the `constructor` qualifier, which is for information purposes only. The `implemented` qualifier indicates that the method has an implementation that is supplied by a method provider. The `static` qualifier effectively means the method can be called without reference to any instances of the class. This is the same concept as in object-oriented programming. We shall discuss the details of the `AddFruitToBasket` method later when method providers are covered.

The `Sample_Fruit` class will support the following provider functions:

- Update fruit instance data (note the class is qualified as supporting this feature by specifying the `SupportsUpdate` qualifier).
- Get a fruit instance.
- Enumerate all fruit instances.
- Execute a method.

The `Sample_BasketFruitMembership` class links the fruit to the basket. This is called an *association*. Associations describe the relationship between instances of two classes. The properties of an association class include object references to the two instances.

```
[
  association,
  dynamic: ToInstance,
```

```
      provider("FruitBasketProv"): ToInstance
    ]
    class Sample_BasketFruitMembership
    {
      [key] Sample_Basket ref Basket;
      [key] Sample_Fruit ref Fruit;
    };
```

The `Basket` reference identifies the basket in the relationship and the `Fruit` reference identifies the item of fruit in the relationship. Apart from the object reference properties, the `association` qualifier is what makes this an association class.

The `Sample_BasketFruitMembership` class supports the following provider functions:

- Get an instance of the relationship between the basket and an item of fruit.
- Enumerate all relationship instances.

Now that we have defined our schema and determined the provider capabilities we need, let's discuss the COM interfaces that need to be implemented.

An instance provider is a COM component (in or out of process server) that supports two interfaces: `IWbemProviderInit` and `IWbemServices` (see Figure 12.3). All providers implement the `IWbemProviderInit` interface, and WMI uses it to initialize the provider. The `IWbemServices` interface is implemented for class, instance, and method providers. An instance provider usually implements the `CreateInstanceEnumAsync` and `GetObject-Async` methods. Optionally (depending on the requirements of the schema), the provider may implement `DeleteInstanceAsync`, `PutInstanceAsync`, and `ExecQueryAsync`.

■ Provider Registration

Apart from the COM registration requirements, a WMI provider also must register itself with WMI. This is achieved by creating instances of provider-related classes within the CIM repository. Without the WMI registration process, it would be impossible for class, instance, and property providers to be referenced by classes and properties.

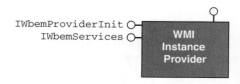

Figure 12.3 WMI instance provider component

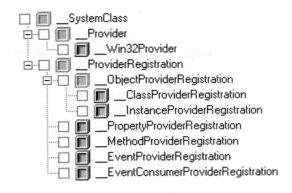

Figure 12.4 WMI provider registration class hierarchy

Provider registration is a two-step process. The first step includes the initialization and security requirements of the provider,. The second step is to register what kind of provider it is, for example, whether it is an instance or method provider.

The first step requires a __Win32Provider instance to register the provider. The second step requires an instance of a class derived from __ProviderRegistration to specify the type of the provider referenced by the __Win32Provider instance. Figure 12.4 shows the class hierarchy of the classes used in provider registrations.

Let's take a quick tour of the base class, __Provider, before we focus on the __Win32Provider registration.

```
[abstract]
class __Provider: __SystemClass
{
  [key] string Name;
};
```

The Name property uniquely identifies the provider registration. The name used by the Name property can be referenced by other classes and instances when specifying a provider. A class or instance can specify a provider by using the provider qualifier, which usually is accompanied by a dynamic qualifier. The __Win32Provider class looks like this:

```
class __Win32Provider: __Provider
{
  [not_null] string CLSID;
  string ClientLoadableCLSID;
  string DefaultMachineName;
  datetime UnloadTimeout;
```

```
        boolean InitializeAsAdminFirst;
        sint32 ImpersonationLevel = 0;
        sint32 InitializationReentrancy = 0;
        boolean PerUserInitialization = FALSE;
        boolean PerLocaleInitialization = FALSE;
        boolean Pure = TRUE;


    };
```

The CLSID property must be supplied because it identifies the COM component that WMI must load (by calling CoCreateInstance). The COM component must implement the IWbemProviderInit interface. The ClientLoadableCLSID property is used by high-performance providers to load the provider in-process if the client and provider reside on the same machine.

The DefaultMachineName property specifies the computer on which to launch the provider. If the provider runs on the local computer, then this should have a null value.

The UnloadTimeout property specifies how long WMI allows the provider to remain idle before it is unloaded. According to the documentation, providers typically request that WMI wait no longer than 5 minutes. However, the current version of WMI ignores this property. WMI unloads the provider based on the timeout value specified by the ClearAfter property in a class derived from __CacheControl in the root namespace. Microsoft recommended that providers set UnloadTimeout property because it will be used in future versions of WMI.

The InitializeAsAdminFirst property specifies whether the provider requires that it be initialized using an administration-level security context under WMI. The ImpersonationLevel property specifies whether the provider requires the security context of the caller to access system-level objects. The PerUserInitialization property specifies whether the provider is initialized once for each and every user (caller) making service requests against the provider. We discuss these three properties in more detail later in the chapter.

The PerLocaleInitialization property specifies that the provider be initialized each time a user connects to the namespace using a different locale.

The InitializationReentrancy property specifies how WMI should control the initialization of the provider. This property can be one of the following:

0: All provider initialization must be serialized.

1: All provider initializations in the same namespace must be serialized.

2: No provider initialization serialization is required.

The Pure property specifies whether the provider is a pure or nonpure provider. Most providers are pure providers because they exist to service requests from clients, such as an instance provider. A nonpure provider transitions to the role of a client after it has finished servicing client requests. For instance, a push provider would be a nonpure provider. After a push provider has updated the CIM repository with data during its initialization, it no longer has any responsibilities, other than waiting to be unloaded or to transition to the role of a client. It is important for WMI to distinguish between pure and nonpure providers so that it can determine when it is safe to shut down. WMI must wait for all operations involving nonpure providers to finish before it can safely shut down.

Here's a typical provider registration:

```
instance of __Win32Provider
{
  Name = "FruitBasketProv";
  CLSID = "{9BE34D0B-B648-471C-9608-1E6FAE67A7F7}";
  ClientLoadableCLSID = NULL;
  DefaultMachineName = NULL;
  ImpersonationLevel = 1;
  InitializationReentrancy = 0;
  InitializeAsAdminFirst = FALSE;
  PerLocaleInitialization = FALSE;
  PerUserInitialization = TRUE;
  Pure = TRUE;
  UnloadTimeout = NULL;
};
```

Notice that the schema described in the previous section used the `provider` qualifier to specify the `FruitBasketProv` provider to service requests. The `FruitBasketProv` instance is the first step in provider registration.

A MOF registration file typically will contain instances that complete the second step of the provider registration. These instances are derived from `__ProviderRegistration` (as can be seen from the class hierarchy displayed earlier). Let's have a quick look at this base class:

```
[abstract]
class __ProviderRegistration: __SystemClass
{
  __Provider ref provider;
};
```

The `__Win32Provider` registration is referenced by all instances derived from `__ProviderRegistration` through the `provider` property.

As we cover each type of provider, we shall provide more details on how the provider should be registered.

■ Provider Initialization

Shortly after it loads a provider, WMI initializes the provider through its `IWbemProviderInit` interface. The `IWbemProviderInit` interface has only one method, `Initialize`. Depending on the provider's registration, `Initialize` can be called with different values. For instance, a provider may have been registered with per-user or per-locale initialization. We shall discuss this later.

Provider initialization is your opportunity to initialize state or devices correctly so that the provider can function properly. Let's look at the `IWbemProviderInit` interface.

```
interface IWbemProviderInit
{
HRESULT Initialize(
  LPWSTR wszUser,                      // User name
  LONG lFlags,                         // Must be zero, reserved
  LPWSTR wszNamespace,                 // Namespace loading the provider
  LPWSTR wszLocale,                    // Initialization locale
  IWbemServices* pNamespace,           // The providers local IWbemServices
  IWbemContext* pCtx,                  // Context for making WMI calls
  IWbemProviderInitSink* pInitSink);   // Report initialization status
};
```

The `wszUser` parameter is the name of the user accessing the provider. This parameter is passed only if the provider registration requested per-user initialization. This can be useful if you want to alter your provider capabilities on a per-user basis (like making properties read-only, for example).

The `wszNamespace` parameter is the name of the namespace that loads the provider. It is possible for a provider to service requests for more than one namespace. However, it is common for a provider implementation to service requests within a single namespace. Use this parameter if your provider targets more than one namespace and each namespace has different initialization requirements.

The `wszLocale` parameter is the locale for which the provider is being initialized. This parameter is passed only if the provider registration requested per-locale initialization. This can be useful if your provider has different initialization requirements for each supported locale. The format of this parameter starts with "`MS_`" and the Win32 LCID locale identifier (in hex) is appended. US English is "`MS_409`" and German is "`MS_407`."

Often a provider needs to be able to make service requests back into WMI. This is typical when spawning an instance of a class or getting a method's in/out parameter definitions. The `pNamespace` parameter is the provider's own local `IWbemServices` interface that is capable of servicing any requests made by the provider.

It is possible that during provider initialization, the provider may want to execute WMI requests in another namespace, even a namespace on another machine. Your first act, in this instance, may be to perform something similar to the following:

```
CComPtr<IWbemLocator> spLoc;
hr = spLoc.CoCreateInstance(CLSID_WbemLocator);

CComBSTR bstrNamespace("\\\\SomeMachine\\root\\SomeNamespace");

CComPtr<IWbemServices> spServices;
hr = spLoc->ConnectServer(bstrNamespace, NULL, NULL, 0,
  NULL, 0, 0, &spServices);
```

Doing this during provider initialization may result in an access denied error. To avoid this, you should use the `CLSID_WbemAdministrativeLocator` service instead of the standard `CLSID_WbemLocator` service. Create your locator service like this:

```
CComPtr<IWbemLocator> spLoc;
hr = spLoc.CoCreateInstance(CLSID_WbemAdministrativeLocator);
```

This technique applies only to providers that are in-process COM servers. Out-of-process COM servers should use the standard `CLSID_WbemLocator` service.

The `pCtx` parameter is the context used by WMI when making calls to the `IWbemServices` interface through the `pNamespace` parameter. Neglecting to pass the `pCtx` parameter can cause WMI to start an infinite loop.

The `pInitSink` parameter reports initialization status back to WMI. The `IWbemProviderInitSink` interface has just one method, `SetStatus`. A provider must call `SetStatus`, passing either `WBEM_S_INITIALIZED` or `WBEM_E_FAILED`. `WBEM_S_INITIALIZED` indicates that the provider is fully initialized and is ready to accept requests. `WBEM_E_FAILED` indicates that the provider failed to initialize and is not functional.

We've already determined that an instance provider will need to implement the `IWbemProviderInit` and `IWbemServices` interfaces. So let's look at a minimal ATL implementation.

```
class CInstance:
  public CComObjectRoot,
  public CComCoClass<CInstance,&CLSID_Instance>,
  public IWbemProviderInit,
  public IWbemServicesImpl<CInstance>
{
public:
  CInstance() {}
```

```
BEGIN_COM_MAP(CInstance)
  COM_INTERFACE_ENTRY(IWbemProviderInit)
  COM_INTERFACE_ENTRY(IWbemServices)
END_COM_MAP()

DECLARE_REGISTRY_RESOURCEID(IDR_Instance)
protected:
  CComPtr<IWbemServices> m_spLocalServices;

public:
  STDMETHOD(Initialize)(LPWSTR wszUser, LONG lFlags,
    LPWSTR wszNamespace, LPWSTR wszLocale,
    IWbemServices *pNamespace, IWbemContext *pCtx,
    IWbemProviderInitSink *pInitSink);
};
```

The `IWbemServicesImpl` C++ template class in this declaration is an `IWbemServices` implementation that returns `WBEM_E_NOT_SUPPORTED` for all the interface methods. Some of these interface methods will be overridden as new provider functionality is implemented.

The fruit basket provider has no special initialization requirements, but a provider must perform a minimal set of tasks. A provider should keep a reference on the `IWbem-Services` interface passed through `pNamespace`. The reference is held by `m_spLocal-Services`. As you'll see later in the chapter, the `m_spLocalServices` member will become very useful when we start exposing management objects. A provider must also call `IWbemProviderInitSink::SetStatus` to report the provider initialization status to WMI. WMI uses this information to determine if the provider is capable of servicing requests. `SetStatus` always returns `WBEM_S_NO_ERROR`.

Let's look at the implementation for `IWbemProviderInit::Initialize`:

```
STDMETHODIMP CInstance::Initialize(LPWSTR wszUser, LONG lFlags,
  LPWSTR wszNamespace, LPWSTR wszLocale, IWbemServices *pNamespace,
  IWbemContext *pCtx, IWbemProviderInitSink *pInitSink)
{
  ObjectLock lock(this);

  // Cache a copy of the local namespace
  m_spLocalServices = pNamespace;

  HRESULT hrStatus = WBEM_S_INITIALIZED;

  try
  {
    //
    // TODO: Add your initialization code here
    //
```

```
  }
  catch(...)
  {
    hrStatus = WBEM_E_FAILED;
  }

  // Let WMI know your initialized
  pInitSink->SetStatus(hrStatus, 0);

  return WBEM_S_NO_ERROR;
}
```

For more complex providers, the initialization requirements may be more involved than in this simple example. Just to be thread-safe, we use ATL's `ObjectLock` to synchronize access to all methods implemented in a provider.

■ Enumerating Objects

All instance providers should be capable of enumerating the objects they expose. Implementing this functionality is usually the best place to start, because you can immediately start testing your provider with the CIM Studio (shipped with the Platform SDK). To enumerate your managed objects requires that you iterate through your local cache, create instances of your objects, and pass them onto WMI. The fruit basket provider will use the registry for its local cache of data. The registry needs to store many baskets, each containing many items of fruit. Figure 12.5 shows the registry structure we shall use.

From Figure 12.5, you can determine that there are two baskets (*MyBasket1* and *MyBasket2*), with *Basket1* containing two items of fruit, *Apple1* and *Apple2*. Likewise,

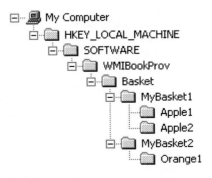

Figure 12.5 Fruit basket registry structure

MyBasket2 has only one item of fruit, *Orange1*. Each basket will store the basket's capacity in a DWORD value, *Capacity,* and each item of fruit will have a DWORD value, *Weight.* To expose all the baskets in our provider involves enumerating all the baskets under the Basket key. We store the data under the HKEY_LOCAL_MACHINE registry key because the provider will be loaded by WMI, which is run under the local system account.

To expose the enumeration through a provider requires the implementation of CreateInstanceEnumAsync. The IWbemServices interface contains many methods, including synchronous and asynchronous versions. Providers only implement the asynchronous versions, the ones ending with ...Async.

Let's look at the CreateInstanceEnumAsync method:

```
interface IWbemServices
{
HRESULT CreateInstanceEnumAsync(
  const BSTR strClass,            // Class to enumerate
  LONG lFlags,                    // Optional flags
  IWbemContext* pCtx,             // Context for making WMI calls
  IWbemObjectSink* pResponseHandler);  // Returned managed objects
};
```

An instance provider can service many different classes in one or more namespaces; the class that is to be enumerated is passed by WMI to the provider through the strClass parameter. A provider must use this parameter and create only instances that pertain to the referenced class (that is, exposing management objects for a specific class). Names of abstract classes are never passed through the strClass parameter.

The lFlags parameter contains the flags that a client passes to WMI: WMI passes the flags to the provider. WBEM_FLAG_SEND_STATUS is the only flag that you're likely to use. This flag requests that the provider send progress information about the call so that WMI can pass the information to the client. The provider exposes its management objects and progress status information through the pResponseHandler parameter (which is an IWbemObjectSink interface). Let's see what the IWbemObjectSink interface looks like:

```
interface IWbemObjectSink
{
HRESULT Indicate(
  LONG lObjectCount,              // Number of objects passed
  IWbemClassObject **ppObjArray);  // Array of objects

HRESULT SetStatus(
  LONG lFlags,                    // Call status
  HRESULT hResult,                // Call result or progress
  BSTR strParam,                  // For PutInstanceAsync only
  IWbemClassObject *pObjParam);   // For complex error/status
};
```

The provider calls the `Indicate` method to pass one or more instances that satisfy a request. If there are three objects that satisfy a request, then the provider will call the `Indicate` method three times.

The `SetStatus` method allows the provider to notify WMI with call status information; this includes call completion and call progress information. The `SetStatus` method's `lFlags` parameter can be either `WBEM_STATUS_COMPLETE` or `WBEM_STATUS_PROGRESS`. When the provider has completed the service request, it must call `SetStatus`, passing the `WBEM_STATUS_COMPLETE` flag. The `hResult` parameter must contain the outcome of the completed operation. If a client passes `WBEM_FLAG_SEND_STATUS` to an `IWbemServices` interface method (such as `CreateInstanceEnumAsync`), then the provider should make calls to `SetStatus` regularly so that the client continually can be informed with the service request. Some providers don't handle the `WBEM_FLAG_SEND_STATUS` flag, so it effectively becomes ignored. If you choose to implement this feature, then your provider should call `SetStatus`, passing `WBEM_STATUS_PROGRESS` in the `lFlags` parameter, and the `hResult` parameter, should contain both the progress and total information. The progress value is contained in `LOWORD(hResult)`, which is usually represented as a percentage. The total value is contained in `HIWORD(hResult)` and usually represents the total number of instances. However, depending on how you want to present the information to the client, you can choose how to encode your status information in the `hResult` parameter. The `strParam` parameter allows the provider to return an object path of a newly created instance. A provider should complete this parameter in implementations of `PutInstanceAsync` that create objects.

The `pObjParam` parameter allows the provider to return very rich information about an error or the status of an operation. This is useful especially where the error and/or status cannot simply be encapsulated in an HRESULT. When writing your own providers, keep this in mind if you want richer information provided to the client. The `pObjParam` parameter works like any other `IWbemClassObject` instance. Properties on the instance can be inspected for the desired information.

Let's look at the new additions in the provider implementation:

```
class CInstance:
  public CComObjectRoot,
  public CComCoClass<CInstance,&CLSID_Instance>,
  public IWbemProviderInit,
  public IWbemServicesImpl<CInstance>
{
  . . . . .
  . . .
  . .
public:              // IWbemServices
  STDMETHOD(CreateInstanceEnumAsync)(const BSTR Class, long lFlags,
    IWbemContext *pCtx, IWbemObjectSink *pResponseHandler);
```

```
protected:            // Enum implementation for each class
  HRESULT EnumBasket(IWbemObjectSink *pResponse, IWbemContext *pCtx);

  HRESULT EnumFruit(IWbemObjectSink *pResponse, IWbemContext *pCtx);

  HRESULT EnumFruitBasket(IWbemObjectSink *pResponse,
    IWbemContext *pCtx);

protected:            // Helpers
  HRESULT CreateInstance(LPOLESTR lpszClassName,
    IWbemClassObject** ppObject, IWbemContext *pCtx);
  .......
  ....
  .
};
```

In the provider's implementation of `CreateInstanceEnumAsync`, you should check to ensure that the provider supports the enumeration of the requested class: if it does, it should route the service request to another method. That's why you see `EnumBasket`, `EnumFruit`, and `EnumFruitBasket` in the previous declaration. To make the code sample readable, we created a helper method (`CreateInstance`) that we use to create the instances of our management objects.

First, let's look at `CreateInstanceEnumAsync`:

```
STDMETHODIMP CInstance::CreateInstanceEnumAsync(const BSTR Class,
long lFlags, IWbemContext *pCtx,
IWbemObjectSink *pResponseHandler)
{
  ObjectLock lock(this);
  HRESULT hr = WBEM_S_NO_ERROR;

  try
  {
    // Handle service request based on class name
    if (CompareClass(Class, L"Sample_Basket"))
      hr = EnumBasket(pResponseHandler, pCtx);
    else if (CompareClass(Class, L"Sample_Fruit"))
      hr = EnumFruit(pResponseHandler, pCtx);
    else if (CompareClass(Class, L"Sample_BasketFruitMembership"))
      hr = EnumFruitBasket(pResponseHandler, pCtx);
    else
      hr = WBEM_E_INVALID_CLASS; // Provider does not support the class

    // Tell WMI that the service request is complete
    pResponseHandler->SetStatus(WBEM_STATUS_COMPLETE,
      hr, NULL, NULL);
```

```
      }
      catch(...)
      {
        hr = WBEM_E_PROVIDER_FAILURE;

        pResponseHandler->SetStatus(WBEM_STATUS_COMPLETE,
          hr, NULL, NULL);
      }

      return hr;
    }
```

The `CompareClass` function you see in this code sample is a simple wrapper for the Win32 API function, `CompareString`. If the class name referenced by `Class` is not supported, then the provider should return `WBEM_E_INVALID_CLASS`. An enumeration request needs access to the `IWbemObjectSink` interface so that the provider can pass one or more instances of a class to WMI and possibly supply call progress information. The `IWbemContext` interface is also required so that new instances can be spawned using the correct `IWbemServices` context.

The following code sample is the implementation for providing all of the instances of the `Sample_Basket` class. The code for `EnumFruit` and `EnumFruitBasket` is not included here. The lines of code in bold font are the main steps for exposing your own management objects. First, the management object is created in memory and the values of its properties are obtained and then set by calling `Put`. Finally, the management object is passed to WMI by calling `Indicate`.

```
    HRESULT CInstance::EnumBasket(IWbemObjectSink *pResponse,
      IWbemContext *pCtx)
    {
      USES_CONVERSION;
      HRESULT hr = WBEM_S_NO_ERROR;

      // Open the basket key to enumerate the baskets
      CRegKey regBasketEnum;
      LONG lReg = regBasketEnum.Open(HKEY_LOCAL_MACHINE,
        _T("Software\\WMIBookProv\\Basket"), KEY_ENUMERATE_SUB_KEYS);

      if (lReg == ERROR_SUCCESS)
      {
        DWORD dwRegIndex = 0;
        LONG lRegBasket = 0;

        do
        {
          // Get the basket name for each iteration
          WCHAR szBasketName[128];
```

```
    lRegBasket = RegEnumKeyW(regBasketEnum, dwRegIndex++,
      szBasketName, 128);

    if (lRegBasket == ERROR_SUCCESS)
    {
      // Create managed object
      CComPtr<IWbemClassObject> spObject;
      hr = CreateInstance(L"Sample_Basket", &spObject, pCtx);

      // Set Name property of the managed object
      CComVariant varName(szBasketName);
      hr = spObject->Put(L"Name", 0, &varName, 0);
      CComBSTR
      bstrBasketPath(L"Software\\WMIBookProv\\Basket\\");
      bstrBasketPath += szBasketName;

      // Open appropriate registry keys to get Capacity property
      CRegKey regBasket;
      lReg = regBasket.Open(HKEY_LOCAL_MACHINE,
        OLE2T(bstrBasketPath), KEY_QUERY_VALUE);

      if (lReg == ERROR_SUCCESS)
      {
        // Get Capacity value from registry
        DWORD dwCapacity = 0;
        lReg = regBasket.QueryValue(dwCapacity, _T("Capacity"));

        if (lReg == ERROR_SUCCESS)
        {
          // Set Capacity property for the managed object
          CComVariant varCapacity((int)dwCapacity);
          varCapacity.ChangeType(VT_UI1);

          hr = spObject->Put(L"Capacity", 0, &varCapacity, 0);
        }
      }

      // Pass managed object to WMI
      hr = pResponse->Indicate(1, &spObject.p);
    }
  }
  while (lRegBasket == ERROR_SUCCESS);
}

return hr;
}
```

The `CreateInstance` helper method wraps up the creation of instances. First, we obtain the management class and second, we create the management object by calling `SpawnInstance`. The new spawned management object requires its properties to be set before it is passed to WMI. Notice that `m_spLocalServices` that was cached earlier is now used.

```
HRESULT CInstance::CreateInstance(LPOLESTR lpszClassName,
  IWbemClassObject** ppObject, IWbemContext *pCtx)
{
  HRESULT hr = WBEM_S_NO_ERROR;

  if (m_spLocalServices)
  {
    // Get class definition
    CComPtr<IWbemClassObject> spClass;
    hr = m_spLocalServices->GetObject(CComBSTR(lpszClassName), 0,
      pCtx, &spClass, NULL);

    // Create instance of class
    hr = spClass->SpawnInstance(0, ppObject);
  }

  return hr;
}
```

■ Getting an Object

All providers should be able to obtain a specific object from your management environment. When a client makes a specific request for a management object, it creates an object path that uniquely identifies the management object. An object path contains the class and one or more key property/value pairs to identify the object. It can also optionally include the machine and namespace details. Here is an example that uniquely identifies a user account:

```
Win32_UserAccount.Domain="GWCOLE",Name="Administrator"
```

A string such as the one above gets passed to the provider's `GetObjectAsync` method. For a more detailed explanation of object paths, please refer to Chapter 7.

Let's look at the `GetObjectAsync` method:

```
interface IWbemServices
{
HRESULT GetObjectAsync(
  const BSTR strObjectPath,                 // Requested object
```

```
    LONG lFlags,                              // Optional flags
    IWbemContext* pCtx,                       // Context for making WMI calls
    IWbemObjectSink* pResponseHandler );      // Returned managed object
};
```

When a client makes a request for a specific management object using an object path, WMI passes the object path to the provider through the strObjectPath parameter. The provider verifies that the object exists, then creates and populates the properties of the object. Finally, the provider returns an IWbemClassObject object back to WMI through the sink provided by WMI (pResponseHandler). WMI in turn passes the object back to the client.

The lFlags parameter contains the flags that a client passes to WMI. If you expect your get operation to be lengthy, then you should consider implementing progress information when the lFlags parameter specifies WBEM_FLAG_SEND_STATUS. Most providers implementations of GetObjectAsync don't respond to WBEM_FLAG_SEND_STATUS because a get operation is usually fast.

Let's look at the new additions in the provider implementation:

```
class CInstance:
  public CComObjectRoot,
  public CComCoClass<CInstance,&CLSID_Instance>,
  public IWbemProviderInit,
  public IWbemServicesImpl<CInstance>
{
  .....
  ...
  ..
public:              // IWbemServices
  STDMETHOD(GetObjectAsync)(const BSTR ObjectPath, long lFlags,
    IWbemContext *pCtx, IWbemObjectSink *pResponseHandler);

protected:           // GetObject implementation for each class
  HRESULT GetBasket(IWbemObjectSink *pResponse, IWbemContext *pCtx,
    ParsedObjectPath* pObjectPath);

  HRESULT GetFruit(IWbemObjectSink *pResponse, IWbemContext *pCtx,
    ParsedObjectPath* pObjectPath);

  HRESULT GetFruitBasket(IWbemObjectSink *pResponse, IWbemContext *pCtx,
    ParsedObjectPath* pObjectPath);

protected:           // Helpers
  VARIANT GetObjectPathKey(LPCWSTR lpszPropName,
    ParsedObjectPath* pObjectPath);
  .......
  ....
  .
};
```

As with the `CreateInstanceEnumAsync` implementation, `GetObjectAsync` also checks to ensure that the provider supports the requested class. If the class is supported, the request is routed to a method that is capable of obtaining the object. This is the purpose of the `GetBasket`, `GetFruit`, and `GetFruitBasket` methods in the preceding class declaration. To decode the object path passed by WMI, we have created a helper method called `GetObjectPathKey`. Fortunately, Microsoft has provided a WMI object path parser in the Platform SDK. The parser is implemented through a set of header and .cpp files. The `CObjectPathParser` class is used to decode and encode an object path. The `ParsedObjectPath` class represents an object path in which the machine, namespace, class, and key properties can be inspected individually. You'll see the `CObjectPathParser` and `ParsedObjectPath` classes used throughout this chapter.

Let's have a look at `GetObjectAsync`:

```
STDMETHODIMP CInstance::GetObjectAsync(const BSTR ObjectPath, long lFlags,
  IWbemContext *pCtx, IWbemObjectSink *pResponseHandler)
{
  USES_CONVERSION;
  ObjectLock lock(this);
  HRESULT hr = WBEM_S_NO_ERROR;

  try
  {

    CObjectPathParser objPath;
    ParsedObjectPath* pParsedPath;

    // Parse object path for the desired object
    objPath.Parse(ObjectPath, &pParsedPath);

    // Handle service request based on class name
    if (CompareClass(pParsedPath->m_pClass, L"Sample_Basket"))
      hr = GetBasket(pResponseHandler, pCtx, pParsedPath);
    else if (CompareClass(pParsedPath->m_pClass, L"Sample_Fruit"))
      hr = GetFruit(pResponseHandler, pCtx, pParsedPath);
    else if (CompareClass(pParsedPath->m_pClass,
        L"Sample_BasketFruitMembership"))
      hr = GetFruitBasket(pResponseHandler, pCtx, pParsedPath);
    else
      hr = WBEM_E_INVALID_CLASS; // Provider does not support the class

    // Tell WMI that the service request is complete
    pResponseHandler->SetStatus(WBEM_STATUS_COMPLETE,
      hr, NULL, NULL);
  }
  catch(...)
  {
    hr = WBEM_E_PROVIDER_FAILURE;
```

```
    pResponseHandler->SetStatus(WBEM_STATUS_COMPLETE,
        hr, NULL, NULL);
}


    return hr;
}
```

The general technique applied here is to parse the object path and use the `Parsed-ObjectPath` class so that individual key properties can be obtained. Like `Create-InstanceEnumAsync`, we need access to the `IWbemObjectSink` interface so that the provider can create a single object instance (if it exists).

The following code sample is the implementation for obtaining a management object for the `Sample_Basket` class. The code for `GetFruit` and `GetFruitBasket` is not included here. The code in bold font includes the key steps for exposing a management object, which is first created in memory, followed by setting the object's property values. Finally, the provider calls `Indicate` to pass the management object to WMI.

```
HRESULT CInstance::GetBasket(IWbemObjectSink *pResponse,
    IWbemContext *pCtx, ParsedObjectPath* pObjectPath)
{
    USES_CONVERSION;
    HRESULT hr = WBEM_S_NO_ERROR;
    CComPtr<IWbemClassObject> spObject;


    // Get the name of the requested basket from the object path
    CComVariant varBasketName(GetObjectPathKey(L"Name", pObjectPath));


    CComBSTR bstrBasketPath(L"Software\\WMIBookProv\\Basket\\");
    bstrBasketPath += V_BSTR(&varBasketName);


    // Check if basket exists?
    CRegKey regBasket;
    LONG lReg = regBasket.Open(HKEY_LOCAL_MACHINE, OLE2T(bstrBasketPath),
        KEY_QUERY_VALUE);


    if (lReg == ERROR_SUCCESS)
    {
        // Basket exists, create an instance and return it to WMI
        hr = CreateInstance(L"Sample_Basket", &spObject, pCtx);


        // Populating the properties of the Sample_Basket class
        hr = spObject->Put(L"Name", 0, &varBasketName, 0);


        DWORD dwCapacity = 0;
        lReg = regBasket.QueryValue(dwCapacity, _T("Capacity"));
```

```
        if (lReg == ERROR_SUCCESS)
        {
          CComVariant varCapacity((int)dwCapacity);
          varCapacity.ChangeType(VT_UI1);

          hr = spObject->Put(L"Capacity", 0, &varCapacity, 0);
        }
      }

      // Pass the requested object to WMI
      if (spObject)
        hr = pResponse->Indicate(1, &spObject.p);
      return hr;
    }
```

The `GetObjectPathKey` helper method makes it easy to get a key property value from a parsed object path. The `lpszPropName` parameter specifies a key property and, if it exists, returns it as a VARIANT. The key properties are contained within an array in the `ParsedObjectPath` object (passed as `pObjectPath`).

```
    VARIANT CInstance::GetObjectPathKey(LPCWSTR lpszPropName,
      ParsedObjectPath* pObjectPath)
    {
      CComBSTR bstrPropName(lpszPropName);

      // Object paths can specify multiple properties
      for (int nKeyIndex = 0;
        nKeyIndex < int(pObjectPath->m_dwNumKeys);
        nKeyIndex++)
      {
        // Is this the property we're after?
        if (bstrPropName == pObjectPath->m_paKeys[nKeyIndex]->m_pName)
          return pObjectPath->m_paKeys[nKeyIndex]->m_vValue;
      }

      return CComVariant(); // Property not found
    }
```

■ Deleting an Object

The previous two sections covered the functionality that is needed to make a read-only instance provider. If your management requirement extends to creating, updating, or deleting management objects, then you need to implement `PutInstanceAsync` and `DeleteInstanceAsync`, respectively. You may find that in your schema design some management objects should not be deleted directly. For instance, if you're designing a schema related to hardware devices, then it is not possible to create or delete such objects.

Deleting a management object is straightforward. WMI passes an object path that the provider should verify to ensure that it references a real instance and then, literally, remove the management object.

Let's look at the `DeleteInstanceAsync` method:

```
interface IWbemServices
{
HRESULT DeleteInstanceAsync(
  const BSTR strObjectPath,              // Object to delete!
  LONG lFlags,                           // Optional flags
  IWbemContext* pCtx,                    // Context for making WMI calls
  IWbemObjectSink* pResponseHandler);    // Progress status
};
```

When a client wishes to remove a management object from the management environment, it must specify an object path. The object path is passed through the `strObject-Path` parameter: It is the provider's responsibility to verify that the object reference is valid.

As in the `GetObjectAsync` discussion, if you expect your delete operation to be lengthy, then you should consider implementing progress information when `WBEM_FLAG_SEND_STATUS` is specified through the `lFlags` parameter.

Let's look at the new additions in the provider implementation:

```
class CInstance :
  public CComObjectRoot,
  public CComCoClass<CInstance,&CLSID_Instance>,
  public IWbemProviderInit,
  public IWbemServicesImpl<CInstance>
{
  .....
  ...
  ..
public:                 // IWbemServices
  STDMETHOD(DeleteInstanceAsync)(const BSTR ObjectPath, long lFlags,
    IWbemContext *pCtx, IWbemObjectSink *pResponseHandler);

protected:              // GetObject implementation for each class
  HRESULT DeleteBasket(IWbemObjectSink *pResponse, IWbemContext *pCtx,
    ParsedObjectPath* pObjectPath);
  .......
  ....
  .
};
```

After the `DeleteInstanceAsync` method has checked that it supports the requested class, it should handle the request by removing the object from the local cache. The fruit basket schema requires only that the `Sample_Basket` class support the deletion of objects (that is, baskets). The provider has just one delete method, `DeleteBasket`.

Let's have a look at `DeleteInstanceAsync`:

```
STDMETHODIMP CInstance::DeleteInstanceAsync(const BSTR ObjectPath,
  long lFlags, IWbemContext *pCtx, IWbemObjectSink *pResponseHandler)
{
  USES_CONVERSION;
  ObjectLock lock(this);
  HRESULT hr = WBEM_S_NO_ERROR;

  try
  {
    CObjectPathParser objPath;
    ParsedObjectPath* pParsedPath;

    // Parse object path for the desired object
    objPath.Parse(ObjectPath, &pParsedPath);

    // Handle service request based on class name
    if (CompareClass(pParsedPath->m_pClass, L"Sample_Basket"))
      hr = DeleteBasket(pResponseHandler, pCtx, pParsedPath);
    else if (CompareClass(pParsedPath->m_pClass, L"Sample_Fruit"))
      hr = WBEM_E_NOT_SUPPORTED; // Delete operation not supported
    else if (CompareClass(pParsedPath->m_pClass,
        L"Sample_BasketFruitMembership"))
      hr = WBEM_E_NOT_SUPPORTED; // Delete operation not supported
    else
      hr = WBEM_E_INVALID_CLASS; // Provider does not support the class

    // Tell WMI that the service request is complete
    pResponseHandler->SetStatus(WBEM_STATUS_COMPLETE,
      hr, NULL, NULL);
  }
  catch(...)
  {
    hr = WBEM_E_PROVIDER_FAILURE;

    pResponseHandler->SetStatus(WBEM_STATUS_COMPLETE,
      hr, NULL, NULL);
  }

  return hr;
}
```

You should have noticed that a specific error code, WBEM_E_NOT_SUPPORTED, was returned for the classes that do not support the deletion of objects. You may find that your providers support a specific class, but not for your specific operation. In cases like this, in which the provider capabilities vary between classes, you should return an appropriate error code.

The following code sample is the implementation for deleting a management object for the Sample_Basket class. It begins by verifying the object path, then deletes all the baskets and the contained items of fruit using ATL's CRegKey class.

```
HRESULT CInstance::DeleteBasket(IWbemObjectSink *pResponse,
 IWbemContext *pCtx, ParsedObjectPath* pObjectPath)
{
  USES_CONVERSION;
  HRESULT hr = WBEM_S_NO_ERROR;

  CComBSTR bstrBasketPath(L"Software\\WMIBookProv\\Basket");

  // Check basket exists?
  CRegKey regBasket;
  LONG lReg = regBasket.Open(HKEY_LOCAL_MACHINE, OLE2T(bstrBasketPath),
    KEY_WRITE);

  if (lReg == ERROR_SUCCESS)
  {
    CComVariant varBasketName(GetObjectPathKey(L"Name", pObjectPath));

    // Delete basket from registry
    lReg = regBasket.RecurseDeleteKey(OLE2T(V_BSTR(&varBasketName)));
  }

  if (lReg != ERROR_SUCCESS)
    hr = WBEM_E_PROVIDER_FAILURE;

  return hr;
}
```

■ Creating or Updating an Object

If any of the classes implemented by a provider support the creation or the updating of management objects, then you need to implement the PutInstanceAsync method. None of the classes in the fruit basket schema support the creation of objects through PutInstanceAsync. However, there is a requirement to update the properties of both the Sample_Basket and Sample_Fruit classes.

Let's look at the `PutInstanceAsync` method:

```
interface IWbemServices
{
HRESULT PutInstanceAsync(
  IWbemClassObject* pInst,            // Object to create or update!
  LONG lFlags,                        // Optional flags
  IWbemContext* pCtx,                 // Context for making WMI calls
  IWbemObjectSink* pResponseHandler); // Progress status
};
```

When a client wants to create or update a management object, it creates an in-memory version of the object and populates its properties. It then passes the management object to WMI, which in turn passes it to the provider through the `pInst` parameter. It is the provider's responsibility to retrieve the property values from the `IWbemClassObject` interface and persist them to the local cache.

The `lFlags` parameter specifies what kind of operation `PutInstanceAsync` should perform. If the client passes `WBEM_FLAG_CREATE_ONLY`, then the provider must allow only the creation of objects. If the object already exists, then the provider should return an appropriate error, such as `WBEM_E_ALREADY_EXISTS`. If not, the provider should create the object in its local cache. If the client passes `WBEM_FLAG_UPDATE_ONLY`, then the provider must allow updates to be performed only against an already existing object. Updating, similar to creating objects, should return an appropriate error, such as `WBEM_E_NOT_FOUND`, if the object doesn't exist. If the object does exist, the provider should update (persist) the object's properties in its local cache. If the client passes `WBEM_FLAG_CREATE_OR_UPDATE`, then the provider should do what is necessary to persist the object to the local cache. A provider must handle all of these three flags. If you expect your creation or updating operation to be lengthy, then you should consider implementing progress information when `WBEM_FLAG_SEND_STATUS` is specified.

Let's look at the new additions in the provider implementation:

```
class CInstance :
  public CComObjectRoot,
  public CComCoClass<CInstance,&CLSID_Instance>,
  public IWbemProviderInit,
  public IWbemServicesImpl<CInstance>
{
  .....
  ...
  ..
public:                 // IWbemServices
  STDMETHOD(PutInstanceAsync)(IWbemClassObject *pInst, long lFlags,
    IWbemContext *pCtx, IWbemObjectSink *pResponseHandler);
```

```
protected:                // PutInstance implementation for the basket class
  HRESULT PutBasket(IWbemObjectSink *pResponse, IWbemContext *pCtx,
    IWbemClassObject* pInst, long lFlags);

  HRESULT PutFruit(IWbemObjectSink *pResponse, IWbemContext *pCtx,
    IWbemClassObject* pInst, long lFlags);

protected:                // Helpers for PutBasket
  bool FindBasket(LPCTSTR lpszBasketName);

  HRESULT UpdateBasket(IWbemClassObject* pInst);
  .......
  ....
  .
};
```

After the `PutInstanceAsync` method has verified that it supports the requested class, it should handle the request by creating or updating the object in the local cache. The `PutBasket` and `PutFruit` methods update instances of `Sample_Basket` and `Sample_Fruit`, respectively.

`PutInstanceAsync` is the only method that does not pass an object path. Instead, it passes an `IWbemClassObject` created by the client. Inspect the `__CLASS` system property to determine the object's class.

Let's look at `PutInstanceAsync`:

```
STDMETHODIMP CInstance::PutInstanceAsync(IWbemClassObject *pInst,
  long lFlags, IWbemContext *pCtx, IWbemObjectSink *pResponseHandler)
{
  USES_CONVERSION;
  ObjectLock lock(this);
  HRESULT hr = WBEM_S_NO_ERROR;

  try
  {
    // What class is this instance?
    CComVariant varClass;
    hr = pInst->Get(L"__CLASS", 0, &varClass, 0, 0);

    // Handle service request based on class name
    if (CompareClass(varClass.bstrVal, L"Sample_Basket"))
      hr = PutBasket(pResponseHandler, pCtx, pInst, lFlags);
    else if (CompareClass(varClass.bstrVal, L"Sample_Fruit"))
      hr = PutFruit(pResponseHandler, pCtx, pInst, lFlags);
    else if (CompareClass(varClass.bstrVal,
      L"Sample_BasketFruitMembership"))
      hr = WBEM_E_NOT_SUPPORTED; // Update or create not supported
```

```
        else
          hr = WBEM_E_INVALID_CLASS; // Provider does not support the class

        // Tell WMI that the service request is complete
        pResponseHandler->SetStatus(WBEM_STATUS_COMPLETE,
          hr, NULL, NULL);
      }
      catch(...)
      {
        hr = WBEM_E_PROVIDER_FAILURE;

        pResponseHandler->SetStatus(WBEM_STATUS_COMPLETE,
          hr, NULL, NULL);
      }

      return hr;
    }
```

When handling a particular class, you must implement appropriate actions for
WBEM_FLAG_CREATE_OR_UPDATE, WBEM_FLAG_UPDATE_ONLY, and WBEM_FLAG_CREATE_ONLY.
The following should demonstrate the sort of logic required.

```
HRESULT CInstance::PutBasket(IWbemObjectSink *pResponse,
IWbemContext  *pCtx, IWbemClassObject* pInst, long lFlags)
{
  USES_CONVERSION;
  HRESULT hr = WBEM_S_NO_ERROR;

  // The name of the basket, we need this to determine whether or not the
  // object exists
  CComVariant varName;
  hr = pInst->Get(L"Name", 0, &varName, NULL, NULL);

  if (lFlags == WBEM_FLAG_CREATE_OR_UPDATE)
  {
    bool bFound = FindBasket(OLE2T(V_BSTR(&varName)));

    if (bFound)
      hr = UpdateBasket(pInst);
    else
      hr = WBEM_E_NOT_SUPPORTED;
  }
  else if (lFlags & WBEM_FLAG_UPDATE_ONLY)
  {
    bool bFound = FindBasket(OLE2T(V_BSTR(&varName)));
```

```
      if (bFound)
        hr = UpdateBasket(pInst);
      else
        hr = WBEM_E_NOT_FOUND;
    }
    else if (lFlags & WBEM_FLAG_CREATE_ONLY)
      hr = WBEM_E_NOT_SUPPORTED;
    else
      hr = WBEM_E_INVALID_PARAMETER;


    return hr;
}
```

The `FindBasket` method helps the provider determine what actions it should take when updating basket objects. If the basket doesn't exist, then it cannot be updated (as in the preceding example). The `FindBasket` helper method attempts to open the basket's registry key to determine whether or not it exists. If the basket exists, then true is returned, otherwise false.

```
bool CInstance::FindBasket(LPCTSTR lpszBasketName)
{
  USES_CONVERSION;

  CComBSTR bstrBasketPath(L"Software\\WMIBookProv\\Basket\\");
  bstrBasketPath += lpszBasketName;

  CRegKey regBasket;
  LONG lReg = regBasket.Open(HKEY_LOCAL_MACHINE, OLE2T(bstrBasketPath),
    KEY_QUERY_VALUE);

  if (lReg == ERROR_SUCCESS)
    return true;
  else
    return false;
}
```

The `UpdateBasket` helper method helps the provider persist basket properties to the local cache. It retrieves all the properties from the object (in bold font in the code sample that follows) and writes the properties to the registry. If this fails, an appropriate error is returned to WMI and, ultimately, to the client.

```
HRESULT CInstance::UpdateBasket(IWbemClassObject* pInst)
{
  USES_CONVERSION;
  HRESULT hr = WBEM_S_NO_ERROR;
```

```
          // Get the Name of the basket
          CComVariant varName;
          hr = pInst->Get(L"Name", 0, &varName, NULL, NULL);

          CComBSTR bstrBasketPath(L"Software\\WMIBookProv\\Basket\\");
          bstrBasketPath += V_BSTR(&varName);

          // Open the basket's registry key
          CRegKey regBasket;
          LONG lReg = regBasket.Open(HKEY_LOCAL_MACHINE, OLE2T(bstrBasketPath),
            KEY_WRITE);

          // Get the Capacity property from the basket
          CComVariant varCapacity;
          hr = pInst->Get(L"Capacity", 0, &varCapacity, NULL, NULL);

          // Write the object's properties to the local cache
          lReg = regBasket.SetValue(DWORD(V_UI1(&varCapacity)), _T("Capacity"));

          if (lReg != ERROR_SUCCESS)
            hr = WBEM_E_PROVIDER_FAILURE;

          return hr;
      }
```

■ Querying for Your Objects

One of the great benefits of writing a provider is that WMI automatically provides the infrastructure to support WQL queries. When a client issues a query that involves one of your classes, WMI first checks if query optimization is supported through the provider registration. If the provider does not support query optimization, WMI then processes the query by evaluating all the objects returned by `CreateInstanceEnumAsync`, if the provider implements this. The result is that by supporting `CreateInstanceEnum-Async`, you get free query support.

Query optimization usually involves retrieving only the properties that have been requested by the client. For example, if the client makes the following query:

```
SELECT * FROM Win32_UserAccount WHERE Domain="DOMAIN_A"
```

`SELECT *` requests that all properties of a `Win32_UserAccount` object must be populated. This can be considered lazy if the client intends to use just two or three properties from the object. Recall that some properties can originate from a variety of sources that include the Internet, a hardware device, or another server (using RPC). All of these data sources have the potential to be very expensive both in processor cycles and in time. Clients can optimize queries by specifically stating the properties they intend to use. Let's revise the previous query:

`SELECT FullName, SID` `FROM Win32_UserAccount WHERE Domain="DOMAIN_A"`

`SELECT FullName, SID` now specifies that the client is interested in only two properties: `FullName` and `SID`. If your provider does not support query optimization, then when a client issues a query, WMI will call your provider's implementation of `Create-InstanceEnumAsync`, which retrieves all of the properties in all of the objects. WMI will process and evaluate each object. If the object satisfies the query, WMI will pass the object to the client with only the `FullName` and `SID` properties populated. However, if the provider does support query optimization, then the provider should obtain only the `FullName` and `SID` properties and create an object with the two properties populated. When WMI receives the object, it verifies that the object does, in fact, satisfy the query and finally passes it on to the client. If the `WHERE` clause includes properties, then you should also include them in the properties that you populate.

Retrieving just the requested properties is one level of optimization. Another level of optimization is in the management objects that get passed to WMI. This involves the processing of the `WHERE` clause. In the above query, `WHERE Domain="DOMAIN_A"` specifies a property `Domain` that has a value `DOMAIN_A`. This kind of query allows the provider to exclude all other objects that are not in `DOMAIN_A`. This ultimately means that a subset of objects is passed to WMI. If the client passes a complex query with several WQL operators, it is unlikely that the provider will evaluate each object against such a query because (1) the provider would need access to a good query processor, and (2) the development effort to implement query support would be too great. The good news is that WMI provides an infrastructure in which the provider passes a rough subset of objects that WMI uses to do the complex evaluation. That is, WMI processes the set to ensure that each object satisfies the query and then delivers the final set of management objects to the client. Figure 12.6 demonstrates what happens.

The fruit basket provider does not implement any query optimization support. If it were to offer this facility, the provider would need to implement the `ExecQueryAsync` method. Let's look at this method:

```
interface IWbemServices
{
HRESULT ExecQueryAsync(
  const BSTR strQueryLanguage,        // The query language to use
  const BSTR strQuery,                // The actual query
  long lFlags,                        // Optional flags
  IWbemContext* pCtx,                 // Context for making WMI calls
  IWbemObjectSink* pResponseHandler); // Returned objects
};
```

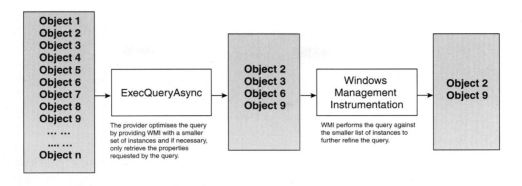

Figure 12.6   Query processing from provider to client

The `strQueryLanguage` parameter specifies the type of query to perform. The current implementation of WMI supports only WQL.

The `strQuery` parameter is the query that WMI or the client wishes the provider to perform. If a client issues an `ASSOCIATORS` query, WMI may break up the query and issue several standard WQL queries under the cover. The provider passes back the objects that roughly satisfy the query through the `pResponseHandler` parameter (using the `Indicate` method).

Queries can sometimes take a significant amount of time, so you may want to consider implementing progress information when `WBEM_FLAG_SEND_STATUS` is specified in the `lFlags` parameter.

■ Instance Provider Registration

Earlier in the chapter, we covered the first step of the provider registration. The second step completes the registration process by specifying the type of provider and its particular capabilities.

For an instance provider, an instance of the `__InstanceProviderRegistration` class must be made within the CIM repository. This class details the capabilities of an instance provider and derives from the abstract class, `__ObjectProviderRegistration`. Let's tour this base class:

```
[abstract]
class __ObjectProviderRegistration: __ProviderRegistration
{
  boolean SupportsPut = FALSE;
  boolean SupportsGet = FALSE;
  boolean SupportsDelete = FALSE;
  boolean SupportsEnumeration = FALSE;
```

```
[
  ValueMap{    "WQL:UnarySelect", "WQL:References",
               "WQL:Associators", "WQL:V1ProviderDefined"}
] string QuerySupportLevels[];


[
  Values{"Pull", "Push", "PushVerify"}
] sint32 InteractionType = 0;
};
```

The SupportsPut property specifies whether the instance provider supports data modification, which includes creating and updating objects. If the provider supports either of these functions, then the provider must implement the IWbemServices::PutInstance-Async method. If not, WMI makes no attempt to call the provider and immediately returns WBEM_E_PROVIDER_NOT_CAPABLE (the same reaction for the rest of the nonsupported provider features). A provider may or may not want to include this facility, depending on whether the schema includes instances that can be created or updated.

The SupportsGet property is similar to SupportsPut but pertains to the retrieval of an instance from the provider. If the provider supports this function, then the provider must implement the IWbemServices::GetObjectAsync method. It is generally considered good practice that all providers support the retrieval of objects.

The SupportsDelete property is similar, but pertains to the deletion of instances. If it is supported by the provider, then the provider must implement the IWbemServices::DeleteInstanceAsync method. A provider may or may not want to implement this facility depending on whether the schema includes instances that can be deleted.

The SupportsEnumeration property is similar but pertains to the enumeration of instances exposed by the provider. If it is supported by the provider, then the provider must implement the IWbemServices::CreateInstanceEnumAsync method. It is generally considered good practice (in our opinion, an absolute must) that all providers support the retrieval of all management objects exposed by the provider.

The QuerySupportLevels property specifies the level of query optimization that the provider supports. In general, if a provider supports query processing, it includes the "WQL:UnarySelect" string in the QuerySupportLevels array. If the provider supports one or more of the other features (such as "WQL:V1ProviderDefined"), then it can include the capability in the array as well. The "WQL:V1ProviderDefined" capability allows the provider to extend the WQL vocabulary to include other clauses, such as ORDER BY. Include the "WQL:References" or "WQL:Associators" capabilities if your provider can process either REFERENCES OF or ASSOCIATORS OF statements. If the provider cannot process these types of WQL statements, WMI will formulate standard WQL queries and issue them against the provider (assuming it supports "WQL:UnarySelect").

If the query passed to the provider is too complex, the provider can let WMI handle the query by returning WBEM_E_TOO_COMPLEX.

The InteractionType property specifies what kind of instance provider it is. Generally, instance providers are pull providers, which means that the value of this property is almost always zero. This property has more meaning if you are developing a push provider. Push providers normally are registered as class providers and the `InteractionType` property must be set to 1. The `__ObjectProviderRegistration` base class is used for both class and instance provider registrations.

The `__ObjectProviderRegistration` class under Windows XP adds two more properties: `SupportsBatching` and `SupportsTransactions`. These are currently documented as "not used." The `__InstanceProviderRegistration` class defines the already defined `Provider` property as the class's key property.

```
class __InstanceProviderRegistration: __ObjectProviderRegistration
{
  [key] __Provider ref Provider;
};
```

Here is a typical registration for an instance provider. Notice that it supports nearly all the instance provider capabilities except query optimization.

```
instance of __InstanceProviderRegistration
{
  Provider = "__Win32Provider.Name=\"FruitBasketProv\"";
  SupportsGet = TRUE;
  SupportsPut = TRUE;
  SupportsDelete = TRUE;
  SupportsEnumeration = TRUE;
};
```

■ Developing a Method Provider

Method providers implement behavior for management classes and management objects. When you design your schema, you should consider what actions need to be or could be performed. For instance, if you had a management object that represented a telephony device, one of the actions that you might want to perform is to dial a telephone number. This is an example of adding behavior to the class or object.

You develop a method provider when one or more classes in your schema defines a method. The `Sample_Fruit` class in our schema defines a method called `AddFruit-ToBasket`. This method adds an item of fruit to a basket. If the basket doesn't exist, then the basket is created before the item of fruit is assigned to the basket. Chapter 7 outlines other considerations for method design.

Here is the `Sample_Fruit` class declaration as we defined it earlier:

```
[
  dynamic: ToInstance,
  provider("FruitBasketProv"): ToInstance,
  SupportsUpdate
]
```

```
class Sample_Fruit
{
  [key] string Name;
  uint16 Weight;

  [implemented, static, constructor]
  boolean AddFruitToBasket([in] string FruitName, [in] string BasketName);
};
```

The `AddFruitToBasket` method takes two input parameters. The `BasketName` parameter specifies the *basket* to which an item of *fruit* should be assigned. The item of fruit is specified by the `FruitName` parameter. Methods can take a combination of input and output parameters that can be of any WMI data type. This includes instances of other classes that get passed as objects.

A method provider is a COM component (in-process or out-of-process server) that supports two interfaces: `IWbemProviderInit` and `IWbemServices` (see Figure 12.7). The `IWbemServices` interface has many methods, of which only the `ExecMethodAsync` requires an implementation.

■ Executing Methods

All method providers implement the `ExecMethodAsync` method. Depending on the input and output parameter complexity, method providers can be reasonably straightforward to implement. The simplest implementation is a static method that takes no input or output parameters. More complex methods are those that use a combination of input and output parameters of varying types, including objects.

Let's look at the `ExecMethodAsync` method:

```
interface IWbemServices
{
  HRESULT ExecMethodAsync(
  const BSTR strObjectPath,      // Class or object path
  const BSTR strMethodName,      // Method being called
  LONG lFlags,                   // Optional flags
```

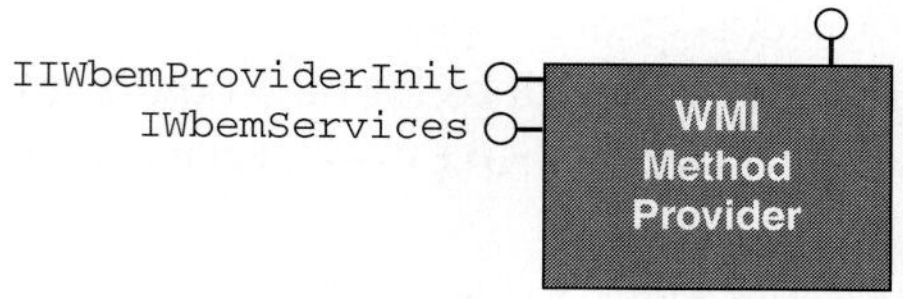

Figure 12.7 WMI method provider component

```
    IWbemContext* pCtx,              // Context for making WMI calls
    IWbemClassObject* pInParams,     // Method input parameters
    IWbemObjectSink* pResponseHandler);  // Method output parameters
};
```

The `strObjectPath` parameter is an object path that specifies either a class reference or an object path. To explain the differences, let's examine the following declaration:

```
class Sample_Class
{
  [key] string Name;
  [static, implemented] void foo();
};
```

If a method provider implemented the previous `foo` method, it should expect the `strObjectPath` parameter to contain a relative class reference, such as `Sample_Class`. The method provider should check this parameter to determine if it supports the referenced class. If the static method declaration changed to something such as:

```
class Sample_Class
{
  [key] string Name;
  [implemented] void foo();
};
```

then a method provider implementing `foo` should expect the `strObjectPath` parameter to contain a relative object reference, such as `Sample_Class.Name="SomeValue"`. This uniquely identifies an object against which the method should be performed. The method provider should check that the object exists before performing the operation.

The `strMethodName` parameter is the name of the method, such as `"foo"`. A method provider can implement one or more methods in one or more classes.

Again, if you expect your method operation to be lengthy, then you should consider implementing progress information when `WBEM_FLAG_SEND_STATUS` is specified through the `lFlags` parameter.

Here is a typical code fragment of what a client does to pass the in-parameters to a WMI method.

```
// Get the class definition so we can get access to the method in-parameters
CComPtr<IWbemClassObject> spClass;
hr = spServices->GetObject(L"Sample_Class", 0, NULL, &spClass, NULL);

// Get the methods in-parameters
CComPtr<IWbemClassObject> spInParamsDefinition;
hr = spClass->GetMethod(L"foo", 0, & spInParamsDefinition, NULL);
```

```
// Spawn an instance of the in-parameters for client to populate
CComPtr<IWbemClassObject> spInParams;
hr = spInParamsDefinition ->SpawnInstance(0, &spInParams);

// Setup required for the method in-parameters
CComVariant varInParam(int(12345));
hr = spInParams->Put(L"MyParamName", 0, & varInParam, 0);

// Execute method
CComPtr<IWbemClassObject> spOutParams;
hr = spServices->ExecMethod(bstrClass, bstrMethod, 0, NULL,
  spInParams, &spOutParams, NULL);
```

When a client spawns an instance of the in-parameters, it populates all the properties with real values. Each property in the in-parameter instance represents an in-parameter in the method's argument list. WMI passes the `spInParams` instance straight to the method provider through the `pInParams` parameter. The provider must extract the property values for it to perform the desired operation.

If the method being executed has any out-parameters (including the return value), then the provider performs similar operations as in the preceding code fragment. The provider creates an instance of the out-parameters and populates each property that maps to the method's output parameter. The return value for a method exists in a property called `ReturnValue`, hence, none of your method out-parameters can use this name. The provider passes the out-parameters to WMI using the `IWbemObjectSink::Indicate` method (`pResponseHandler`).

Let's look at the implementation for the method provider. We omit the `IWbemProviderInit` implementation because it is the same as the one for the instance provider.

```
class CInstance:
  public CComObjectRoot,
  public CComCoClass<CInstance,&CLSID_Instance>,
  public IWbemProviderInit,
  public IWbemServicesImpl<CInstance>
{
  .....
  ...
  ..
public:                // IWbemProviderInit
  STDMETHOD(Initialize)(LPWSTR wszUser, LONG lFlags,
    LPWSTR wszNamespace, LPWSTR wszLocale,
    IWbemServices *pNamespace, IWbemContext *pCtx,
    IWbemProviderInitSink *pInitSink);

public:                // IWbemServices
  STDMETHOD(ExecMethodAsync)(const BSTR strObjectPath,
    const BSTR strMethodName, long lFlags, IWbemContext *pCtx,
    IWbemClassObject *pInParams, IWbemObjectSink *pResponseHandler);
```

```
protected:              // method implementation
  HRESULT Method_AddFruitToBasket(IWbemClassObject *pInParams,
    IWbemObjectSink *pResponse, IWbemContext *pCtx,
    ParsedObjectPath* pObjectPath);
  .......
  ....
  .
};
```

The method provider is required to implement only one WMI method, `AddFruit-ToBasket`. This is implemented by `Method_AddFruitToBasket`. Let's see how `ExecMethodAsync` processes its parameters and executes the WMI method call:

```
STDMETHODIMP CInstance::ExecMethodAsync(const BSTR strObjectPath,
  const BSTR strMethodName, long lFlags, IWbemContext *pCtx,
  IWbemClassObject *pInParams, IWbemObjectSink *pResponseHandler)
{
  USES_CONVERSION;
  ObjectLock lock(this);
  HRESULT hr = WBEM_S_NO_ERROR;

  try
  {
    CObjectPathParser objPath;
    ParsedObjectPath* pParsedPath;

    // We want this so we can determine the class name
    objPath.Parse(strObjectPath, &pParsedPath);

    // We don't support Sample_Basket and Sample_FruitBasketMembership
    // classes.
    if (CompareClass(pParsedPath->m_pClass, L"Sample_Fruit") &&
      CComBSTR(strMethodName) == L"AddFruitToBasket")
    {
      // This calls the method's implementation
      Method_AddFruitToBasket(pInParams, pResponseHandler, pCtx,
        pParsedPath);
    }
    else if (CompareClass(pParsedPath->m_pClass, L"Sample_Basket"))
      hr = WBEM_E_NOT_SUPPORTED;
    else if (CompareClass(pParsedPath->m_pClass,
        L"Sample_FruitBasketMembership"))
      hr = WBEM_E_NOT_SUPPORTED;
    else
      hr = WBEM_E_INVALID_CLASS;

    // Tell WMI that the service request is complete
    pResponseHandler->SetStatus(WBEM_STATUS_COMPLETE,
      hr, NULL, NULL);
```

```
    }
    catch(...)
    {
      hr = WBEM_E_PROVIDER_FAILURE;

      pResponseHandler->SetStatus(WBEM_STATUS_COMPLETE,
        hr, NULL, NULL);
    }

    return hr;
}
```

After it is determined that the provider supports the class and method, the method's implementation is executed by calling a function (Method_AddFruitTo-Basket) that implements the WMI method. The next code fragment should contain nothing new. It uses two helper methods, GetEnumFruitMap and FindFruitInMap, which help identify whether an item of fruit already exists. The Method_AddFruitTo-Basket first retrieves the in-parameters and then checks them to ensure that it has valid values to execute the operation. After the method has attempted to perform its operation, it creates and populates the method's out-parameters and passes them back to WMI. In our particular case, the only out-parameter is the method's return value, which is called ReturnValue. This sequence of actions will be similar for every method implementation. The bold font in the following code shows where the method's in-parameters are obtained and where the out-parameters are set and returned to WMI.

```
HRESULT CInstance::Method_AddFruitToBasket(IWbemClassObject *pInParams,
  IWbemObjectSink *pResponse, IWbemContext *pCtx,
  ParsedObjectPath* pObjectPath)
{
  USES_CONVERSION;
  HRESULT hr = WBEM_S_NO_ERROR;
  bool bRetVal = false;

  // Get the method's BasketName in-parameter
  CComVariant varBasket;
  HRESULT hrBasket = pInParams->Get(L"BasketName", 0, &varBasket, 0, 0);

  // Get the method's FruitName in-parameter
  CComVariant varFruit;
  HRESULT hrFruit = pInParams->Get(L"FruitName", 0, &varFruit, 0, 0);

  // Ensure that we have both parameters to perform method function
  if (SUCCEEDED(hrBasket) && V_VT(&varBasket) != VT_NULL &&
    SUCCEEDED(hrFruit) && V_VT(&varFruit) != VT_NULL)
  {
```

```
      // Helper function to create a map of all the basket and fruit items
      TBasketFruitMap mapFruit;
      GetEnumFruitMap(mapFruit);


      if (FindFruitInMap(OLE2T(V_BSTR(&varFruit)), mapFruit))
      {
        // We can't add the fruit item it is already added to a basket
        hr = WBEM_E_ALREADY_EXISTS;
      }
      else
      {
        // Fruit name not used. Can create and assign the item of fruit.
        tstring szBasketPath(_T("Software\\WMIBookProv\\Basket\\"));
        szBasketPath += OLE2T(V_BSTR(&varBasket));


        // Create the basket if it doesn't already exist
        CRegKey regBasket;
        LONG lReg = regBasket.Create(HKEY_LOCAL_MACHINE,
          szBasketPath.c_str(), NULL, REG_OPTION_NON_VOLATILE,
          KEY_WRITE);


        if (lReg == ERROR_SUCCESS)
        {
          tstring szFruitPath(szBasketPath);
          szFruitPath += _T("\\");
          szFruitPath += OLE2T(V_BSTR(&varFruit));


          // Create and assign item of fruit
          CRegKey regFruit;
          LONG lReg = regFruit.Create(HKEY_LOCAL_MACHINE,
            szFruitPath.c_str(), NULL, REG_OPTION_NON_VOLATILE,
            KEY_WRITE);


          if (lReg == ERROR_SUCCESS)
            bRetVal = true; // Used in WMI methods return value
        }
      }
    }


  // Setup the out-parameters
  CComPtr<IWbemClassObject> spClass;
  hr = m_spLocalServices->GetObject(CLASS_FRUIT, 0, pCtx, &spClass, NULL);


  // Get out-parameter definition
  CComPtr<IWbemClassObject> spOutClass;
  hr = spClass->GetMethod(L"AddFruitToBasket", 0, NULL, &spOutClass);
```

```
// Spawn out parameter instance to pass to WMI
CComPtr<IWbemClassObject> spOutParams;
hr = spOutClass->SpawnInstance(0, &spOutParams);

// Set method's return value
CComVariant varReturn(bRetVal);
hr = spOutParams->Put(L"ReturnValue", 0, &varReturn, 0);
// Pass out-parameters to WMI
hr = pResponse->Indicate(1, &spOutParams.p);

return hr;
}
```

■ Method Provider Registration

Earlier in the chapter, we covered the first step of the provider registration. The second step completes the method provider registration.

Method provider registration is much simpler than for all the other providers. There are no additional capabilities except to redefine the `Provider` property to be the class's key property.

```
class __MethodProviderRegistration: __ProviderRegistration
{
  [key] __Provider ref Provider;
};
```

Here is a typical method provider registration:

```
instance of __MethodProviderRegistration
{
  Provider = "__Win32Provider.Name=\"FruitBasketProv\"";
};
```

■ Developing an Event Provider

Delivering events is one of WMI's most useful features. It enables management objects to indicate when something interesting has happened, either as an intrinsic or extrinsic event. The example schema used thus far throughout this chapter has some scope for delivering events. Our instance provider exposes management objects that can be created by calling the `AddFruitToBasket` method by specifying a basket name that does not already exist. When a management application creates a new basket, an event provider can deliver (publish) this interesting event to WMI. All management applications that subscribe for a new basket notification will receive an event indicating that a basket has been created. Intrinsic events usually provide management applications with enough detail about an object so that there is no need to make a separate call to `GetObject`.

To review from Chapter 7, there are three types of events: intrinsic, extrinsic, and timer.

1. Intrinsic events: These occur in response to changes to namespaces, classes, and instances. Changes to instances are the most useful event notifications.

2. Extrinsic events: These are custom-defined events. These types of events allow great flexibility in managed applications to deliver specialized events. They can be separate from activity on other management objects. The `Win32_Power-ManagementEvent` class is a good example.

3. Timer events: These are events that are delivered by WMI using preconfigured information. There are no provider mechanisms for timer events because WMI effectively becomes the provider.

If a provider creates, modifies, or deletes instances, as in our case, then it should publish the intrinsic events `__InstanceCreationEvent`, `__InstanceModification-Event`, and `__InstanceDeletionEvent`. To keep our sample event provider implementation simple, we shall only publish an `__InstanceCreationEvent`. This event will be published to WMI after the `AddFruitToBasket` method has successfully created a new basket.

Like all the other providers you've seen, an event provider is also a COM component (an in-process or out-of-process server). It must support the `IWbemProviderInit` and `IWbemEventProvider` interfaces (see Figure 12.8). WMI initializes the provider through the `IWbemProviderInit` interface, and the `IWbemEventProvider` interface requires an implementation for its one and only method, `ProvideEvents`.

To test the provider's event notification capability, go to Appendix A for a short tutorial on using the WMI SDK event tools. If you are using Microsoft Visual Studio .NET, then Appendix B covers a short tutorial on using the WMI server explorer, which includes support for making event subscriptions.

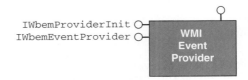

Figure 12.8 WMI event provider component

■ Firing Events

Before writing an event provider, let's consider the type of mechanisms available to publish events. The preferred approach is to develop an event provider. This is preferred because the provider implementation can be decoupled from the other providers and also is a single source for the events. Another benefit is that other users and developers of management applications can use a tool such as CIM Studio to view the event registrations. They can enumerate the instances of the __EventProviderRegistration class and inspect the EventQueryList property.

The second approach is to use the QueryObjectSink method on the IWbemServices interface. This allows a client or management application such as a Windows 2000/XP service to publish events directly to WMI without developing a provider. Typically, this is used for extrinsic events, but it also works for intrinsic events.

All event providers must implement the IWbemEventProvider interface:

```
interface IWbemEventProvider
{
HRESULT ProvideEvents(
  IWbemObjectSink* pSink,       // To deliver events to WMI
  long lFlags);                 // Reserved, must be zero
};
```

The ProvideEvents method is called by WMI only once, when the first client application makes a subscription for an event published by the provider. The ProvideEvents method typically creates its own thread, which is used to publish the events.

When an event provider is ready to publish an event, it should pass the event to WMI using the pSink parameter (IWbemObjectSink). Publishing the event is completed when Indicate is called.

Let's look at the implementation for the event provider. We omit the IWbemProviderInit implementation because it is the same as the one for the instance provider.

```
class CEvent:
  public CComObjectRoot,
  public CComCoClass<CEvent,&CLSID_Event>,
  public IWbemProviderInit,
  public IWbemEventProvider
{
public:
  CEvent() {}

  BEGIN_COM_MAP(CEvent)
    COM_INTERFACE_ENTRY(IWbemProviderInit)
    COM_INTERFACE_ENTRY(IWbemEventProvider)
  END_COM_MAP()
```

```
DECLARE_REGISTRY_RESOURCEID(IDR_CEvent)
.....
...
..

// IWbemProviderInit
public:
  STDMETHOD(Initialize)(LPWSTR wszUser, LONG lFlags,
    LPWSTR wszNamespace, LPWSTR wszLocale,
    IWbemServices *pNamespace, IWbemContext *pCtx,
    IWbemProviderInitSink *pInitSink);

// IWbemEventProvider
public:
  STDMETHOD(ProvideEvents)(IWbemObjectSink *pSink, long lFlags);

// Helpers for event provider
protected:
  static void ThreadProvideEvents(void *param);

  static void GetBasketList(tstringlist& slBaskets);

  static void FireEventNewBaskets(tstringlist& listOrigBaskets,
    IWbemServices* pServices, IWbemObjectSink* pEventSink);

  static HRESULT EventCreateInstance(LPOLESTR lpszClassName,
    IWbemClassObject** ppObject, IWbemServices *pServices);
};
```

The `EventCreateInstance` helper method is similar to the `CreateInstance` helper method we discussed earlier. This makes it convenient to create a new instance (event) of a specified class. The `EventCreateInstance` will be used to create the event and also to create a basket instance for the event's `TargetInstance` property.

The `ProvideEvents` implementation will create a thread that will monitor changes to the basket local cache. When a new basket change is detected, the thread will fire the event to WMI. The only information needed by the thread is the provider's local `IWbemServices` interface and the `IWbemObjectSink` interface. The `IWbemServices` interface will create the instances required for the event and the event's `TargetInstance` property. The `IWbemObjectSink` interface will publish the events. To pass both of these into the thread requires a small structure:

```
typedef struct tagTEventProvThread
{
  CComPtr<IWbemServices> m_spLocalServices;
  CComPtr<IWbemObjectSink> spEventSink;

} TEventProvThread;
```

The following simple implementation of `ProvideEvents` requires only the newly defined structure to be completed and passed to the thread via the thread creation API:

```
STDMETHODIMP CEvent::ProvideEvents(IWbemObjectSink *pSink, long lFlags)
{
  TEventProvThread* pThreadParams = new TEventProvThread;

  pThreadParams->m_spLocalServices = m_spLocalServices;
  pThreadParams->spEventSink = pSink;

  HANDLE hThread = HANDLE(_beginthread(ThreadProvideEvents, 0,
    pThreadParams));

  return WBEM_S_NO_ERROR;
}
```

The first task for the thread is to extract the thread parameters and monitor changes to the registry (because this is the provider's local cache). As soon as some activity happens, the provider determines whether a new basket was added and fires an event. The following thread never exits. In your own provider implementation, you probably will want to change this to be more robust according to good programming techniques.

```
void CEvent::ThreadProvideEvents(void *param)
{
  CoInitializeEx(NULL, COINIT_MULTITHREADED);

  // Extract thread parameters
  TEventProvThread* pThreadParams =
    reinterpret_cast<TEventProvThread*>(param);

  // Open registry key to monitor
  CRegKey regBaskets;
  LONG lReg = regBaskets.Open(HKEY_LOCAL_MACHINE,
    _T("Software\\WMIBookProv\\Basket"), KEY_READ);

  while (true)
  {
    // Retrieve the list of baskets so we can later determine if a
    // new basket had been added.
    tstringlist listBasket;
    GetBasketList(listBasket);

    // Wait for a notification from the registry
    LONG lResult = RegNotifyChangeKeyValue(regBaskets.m_hKey, TRUE,
      REG_NOTIFY_CHANGE_NAME, NULL, FALSE);
```

```
      if (lResult == ERROR_SUCCESS)
      {
        // Activity happened in the registry, if a new basket was
        // added, fire an event
        FireEventNewBaskets(listBasket, pThreadParams->m_spLocalServices,
          pThreadParams->spEventSink);
      }
    }
    CoUninitialize();
  }
```

The `RegNotifyChangeKeyValue` returns only when there is activity for the specified
key. The only activity that will be monitored is specified by `REG_NOTIFY_CHANGE_NAME`,
which monitors whether a subkey is added or deleted.

To determine whether any changes have occurred, a list of all the baskets is obtained before waiting for notifications from the registry. When a registry notification is
received, the new basket list is compared with the original basket list. If there is a new
basket entry, we shall create the event and fire it. Here is the implementation of `Get-
BasketList` that retrieves all the baskets that currently exist:

```
void CEvent::GetBasketList(tstringlist& slBaskets)
{
  CRegKey regBasketEnum;
  LONG lReg = regBasketEnum.Open(HKEY_LOCAL_MACHINE,
    _T("Software\\WMIBookProv\\Basket"), KEY_ENUMERATE_SUB_KEYS);

  DWORD dwRegIndex = 0;
  LONG lRegBasket = 0;

  do
  {
    WCHAR szBasketName[128];
    lRegBasket = RegEnumKeyW(regBasketEnum, dwRegIndex++,
      szBasketName, 128);

    if (lRegBasket == ERROR_SUCCESS)
      slBaskets.push_back(W2T(szBasketName));
  }
  while (lRegBasket == ERROR_SUCCESS);
}
```

The `FireEventNewBaskets` function does all the work. It determines if there is a new
basket and, if there is, begins to create and populate the event and then publishes it to
WMI. The bulk of this function should be familiar to you by now: It uses the ATL registry class and STL lists.

Before diving into the code, let's quickly review what an __InstanceCreation-
Event looks like.

```
class __InstanceCreationEvent: __InstanceOperationEvent
{
};
```

An instance creation event derives from __InstanceOperationEvent, which looks
like this:

```
class __InstanceOperationEvent: __Event
{
  object TargetInstance;
};
```

The TargetInstance property represents a copy of the new instance that we just now
created. In our case, this is an instance of the Sample_Basket class. The portions of the
following code in bold font are the main duties of an event provider: (1) to create an
in-memory version of the newly created management object, which will be used to
populate the event's TargetInstance property; (2) create the event and populate its
properties, specifically, the TargetInstance property; and (3) fire the event to WMI.

```
void CEvent::FireEventNewBaskets(tstringlist& listOrigBaskets,
  IWbemServices* pServices, IWbemObjectSink* pEventSink)
{
  HRESULT hr = WBEM_S_NO_ERROR;

  // Get new list of baskets
  tstringlist listCurBaskets;
  GetBasketList(listCurBaskets);

  // Compare original list of baskets against the new list
  tstringlist::iterator itrCurBasket = listCurBaskets.begin();
  for (; itrCurBasket != listCurBaskets.end(); itrCurBasket++)
  {
    bool bFound = false;

    tstringlist::iterator itrBasket = listOrigBaskets.begin();
    for ( ; itrBasket != listOrigBaskets.end(); itrBasket++)
    {
      // Is this is a new basket
      if ((*itrBasket) == (*itrCurBasket))
        bFound = true;
    }

    if (!bFound) // We have a new basket
    {
      // Prepare registry path to get new basket information
```

```
CComBSTR bstrBasketPath(L"Software\\WMIBookProv\\Basket\\");
bstrBasketPath += (*itrCurBasket).c_str();

CRegKey regBasket;
LONG lReg = regBasket.Open(HKEY_LOCAL_MACHINE,
  OLE2T(bstrBasketPath), KEY_QUERY_VALUE);

CComPtr<IWbemClassObject> spTargetInst;

if (lReg == ERROR_SUCCESS)
{
  // Create an instance for the TargetInstance property of
  // the event
  hr = EventCreateInstance(L"Sample_Basket", &spTargetInst,
    pServices);

  // Populate the newly created basket's properties
  CComVariant varBasketName((*itrCurBasket).c_str());
  hr = spTargetInst->Put(L"Name", 0, &varBasketName, 0);

  DWORD dwCapacity = 0;
  lReg = regBasket.QueryValue(dwCapacity, _T("Capacity"));

  if (lReg == ERROR_SUCCESS)
  {
    CComVariant varCapacity((int)dwCapacity);
    varCapacity.ChangeType(VT_UI1);

    hr = spTargetInst->Put(L"Capacity", 0, &varCapacity, 0);
  }
}

// We have a completed TargetInstance, so now create the event
CComPtr<IWbemClassObject> spEvent;
hr = EventCreateInstance(L"__InstanceCreationEvent",
  &spEvent, pServices);

if (spEvent)
{
  // Populate the TargetInstance property of the event
  CComVariant varTargetInst(spTargetInst);
  hr = spEvent->Put(CComBSTR("TargetInstance"), 0,
    &varTargetInst, 0);
  // Fire the event to WMI!
  hr = pEventSink->Indicate(1, &spEvent.p);
}
      }
    }
  }
}
```

We have told you about the two interfaces that you must implement for an event provider. There are two additional interfaces that you might want to consider: `IWbem-EventProviderQuerySink` and `IWbemEventProviderSecurity`.

The `IWbemEventProviderQuerySink` interface is implemented by providers that want to know what event queries the provider currently is servicing. Providers can use this information to optimize performance of the event provider. Here is the interface:

```
interface IWbemEventProviderQuerySink
{
HRESULT NewQuery(
  unsigned long dwId,             // WMI provided ID for query
  WBEM_WSTR wszQueryLanguage,     // Query language of wszQuery
  WBEM_WSTR wszQuery);            // Event query

  HRESULT CancelQuery(
    unsigned long dwId);          // WMI provided ID for query
};
```

The `dwId` parameter is a WMI-generated ID that providers can use to track event queries. When WMI calls `NewQuery`, the provider can track the query until `CancelQuery` is called.

The `wszQueryLanguage` parameter specifies the type of event query subscription. The current implementation of WMI supports only WQL. The `wszQuery` parameter specifies the event query for the events for which a client wants to receive notifications.

The `IWbemEventProviderSecurity` interface is implemented by event providers who want to restrict access to their events. When a client or management application subscribes for event notification, if this interface is implemented, WMI will check with the provider to determine if it is all right to continue the event subscription. Here is the interface:

```
interface IWbemEventProviderSecurity
{
HRESULT AccessCheck(
  WBEM_CWSTR wszQueryLanguage,    // Usually 'WQL'
  WBEM_CWSTR wszQuery,            // Event query request
  long lSidLength,                // Length of the security descriptor
  const BYTE* pSid);              // The security descriptor
};
```

The `wszQuery` parameter is the requested event query by the client or management application. If a provider offers different security access levels based on the query, then the provider should also check the security descriptor in the `lSidLength` and `pSid` parameters. In most cases, the provider may care to inspect only the security descriptor. If the event provider wishes to deny access for an event subscription, it should return `WBEM_E_ACCESS_DENIED`.

So far we've covered the preferred approach of publishing your own events. The second approach is based on publishing an event without writing a provider. This is typically used where an administration application might want to notify a Windows 2000/XP service of some interesting event and vice versa. An example might be to fire an event when a Windows service encounters an unhandled exception.

In the previous event provider sample code, WMI passed an event sink (`IWbem-ObjectSink`) to the provider, which the provider later used to deliver events. The second technique of firing events is somewhat similar. A call to `QueryObjectSink` on the `IWbemServices` interface supplies an `IWbemObjectSink` event interface. The use of the `IWbemObjectSink` interface is the same as an event provider, that is, you call `Indicate` to publish an event to WMI. The following client-side sample code demonstrates this (using hard-coded values for a new instance of a basket):

```
// Access WMI
CComPtr<IWbemLocator> spLoc;
hr = spLoc.CoCreateInstance(CLSID_WbemLocator);

CComBSTR bstrNamespace(_T("\\\\.\\root\\WMIBook"));
CComPtr<IWbemServices> spServices;

// Connect to WMI to get access to the namespace via IWbemServices
hr = spLoc->ConnectServer(bstrNamespace, NULL, NULL, 0,
  NULL, 0, 0, &spServices);

// Create a target instance so we can populate the
// TargetInstance property of the event
CComPtr<IWbemClassObject> spTargetInstClass;
hr = spServices->GetObject(CComBSTR("Sample_Basket"), 0,
  NULL, &spTargetInstClass, NULL);

CComPtr<IWbemClassObject> spTargetInst;
hr = spTargetInstClass->SpawnInstance(0, &spTargetInst);

// Populate the basket's properties
CComVariant varBasketName("MyBasket");
hr = spTargetInst->Put(L"Name", 0, &varBasketName, 0);

CComVariant varCapacity(int(4));
varCapacity.ChangeType(VT_UI1);
hr = spTargetInst->Put(L"Capacity", 0, &varCapacity, 0);

// Create the event
CComPtr<IWbemClassObject> spEventClass;
hr = spServices->GetObject(CComBSTR("__InstanceCreationEvent"), 0,
  NULL, &spEventClass, NULL);
```

```
CComPtr<IWbemClassObject> spEvent;
hr = spEventClass->SpawnInstance(0, &spEvent);

// Populate the event's properties
CComVariant varTargetInst(spTargetInst);
hr = spEvent->Put(CComBSTR("TargetInstance"), 0, &varTargetInst, 0);

// Ask WMI for an event sink so we can publish events
CComPtr<IWbemObjectSink> spEventSink;
hr = spServices->QueryObjectSink(0, &spEventSink);

// Publish the __InstanceCreationEvent
hr = spEventSink->Indicate(1, &spEvent.p);
```

■ Event Provider Registration

Earlier in the chapter, we covered the first step of the provider registration. The second step completes the event provider registration.

The only additional requirement for event provider registration is specifying the WQL event queries that the provider is capable of servicing. This is done through the `EventQueryList` property.

```
class __EventProviderRegistration: __ProviderRegistration
{
  [key] __Provider ref Provider;
  string EventQueryList[];
};
```

A provider must add all the WQL event queries that it can support to the `Event-QueryList` array. This registration also proves useful to the users of your classes or events to identify the event notifications that are available from your provider. Here is a typical event provider registration:

```
instance of __EventProviderRegistration
{
  Provider = "__Win32Provider.Name=\"FruitBasketEventProv\"";
  EventQueryList =
  {
    "SELECT * FROM __InstanceCreationEvent WHERE TargetInstance
      ISA \"Sample_Basket\""
  };
};
```

This registration says that the event provider supports only event notifications for newly created baskets.

Developing an Event Consumer Provider

In the previous section, you saw how you can publish events to WMI, and in Chapter 7, you saw how client (or services) applications could subscribe for event notification as a temporary event consumer. This means that if the Windows 2000/XP service or client application is not running, then the event will not be delivered or handled. WMI offers a permanent event consumer as another solution for a more robust event delivery. The permanent event consumer is developed as a WMI provider and is referred to as an *event consumer provider*. This robust event delivery system is a powerful mechanism for handling events even when the application is not running. Here is a scenario in which this robust event delivery system might be used:

> You decide that you would like to build automatic software update distribution in your software. You could achieve this by setting up a timer instruction that will fire an event once a month. By subscribing to the event, you could handle the notification by developing a permanent event consumer provider. The provider could check a Web site and automatically patch the updated files. This process runs independent of the software being distributed. You may identify other scenarios in which a more robust event delivery system may allow you to creatively solve problems. WMI delivers event subscriptions to permanent event consumer providers by loading the provider and passing the event notification to it.

Like all the other providers you've seen, an event consumer provider is also a COM component (an in-process or out-of-process server). It must support the `IWbemProviderInit` and `IWbemEventConsumerProvider` interfaces. WMI initializes the provider through the `IWbemProviderInit` interface. The `IWbemEventConsumerProvider` interface requires an implementation for the one and only method, `FindConsumer`.

Handling Event Notifications

Permanent event subscription is very different from temporary event subscription. It is based on a configuration held within the CIM repository. The event consumer provider

Figure 12.9 WMI event consumer provider component

receives notifications through a logical consumer. A logical consumer contains configuration information that the provider can use to determine how it should deal with the event. Logical consumers are related directly to the provider through the class type of the logical consumer (in the provider registration). This means that an event consumer provider must define its own class for its logical consumers. The class must be derived from `__EventConsumer`, and it must define a key property so that instances of the logical consumers can be created. You can set up several logical consumers that you can later tie to different event queries (filters). Event filters define the event subscriptions for logical consumers by creating instances of the `__EventFilter` class. However, to tie an event filter to an event consumer requires that an association be created with the `__FilterToConsumerBinding` class. Figure 12.10 is the hierarchy of the classes used by permanent event consumers. Note that the `Sample_WMIBookEventConsumer` class is defined for our sample provider.

Let's look at creating a logical consumer class for our provider. First, let's examine the base class, `__EventConsumer`, because our new class must derive from it to add our own configuration details for each consumer.

```
[abstract]
class __EventConsumer: __IndicationRelated
{
  string MachineName;
  [units("bytes")] uint32 MaximumQueueSize;
  [read] uint8 CreatorSID[];
};
```

The `MachineName` property defines the name of the computer to which WMI must send all events. The `MaximumQueueSize` property defines the limit for the maximum number of bytes of the queued events. Finally, the `CreatorSID` property is a security identifier that uniquely identifies the user who created the permanent event consumer. Notice the lack of key properties: It is left to the derived class to define the key properties required to properly reference a logical consumer. Here is a new event consumer class that represents the consumer configuration of the new provider that we are about to develop:

```
class Sample_WMIBookEventConsumer: __EventConsumer
{
  [key] string Name;
  boolean EnableBeep;
};
```

We shall identify our consumers by name, hence the key property called `Name`. In the provider implementation you will see, when our provider receives an event, it will make a beep sound, hence the configuration property, `EnableBeep`. Creating a class doesn't automatically enroll a permanent event consumer provider to consume events. To create a logical consumer, we must create an instance of our new class that will be

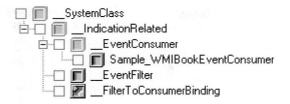

Figure 12.10 WMI event consumer provider classes

stored in the CIM repository. The following code will create a logical consumer called
MyEventConsumer.

```
instance of Sample_WMIBookEventConsumer
{
  EnableBeep = TRUE;
  Name = "MyEventConsumer";
};
```

This completes the consumer registration. Next, event filters must be created for the
required event subscriptions. This is a simple task of creating instances of the __Event-
Filter class. In the following filter, we will subscribe for the events that are generated by
our new provider. We call this query filter MyEventConsumerFilter.

```
instance of __EventFilter
{
  Name = "MyEventConsumerFilter";
  QueryLanguage = "WQL";
  Query = "SELECT * FROM __InstanceCreationEvent WHERE TargetInstance
    ISA \"Sample_Basket\"";
};
```

We now need to tie the logical consumer to the event filter. No event notifications
will get delivered to the event consumer provider without this step. It is important that
you completely specify a fully qualified object path that also includes the machine name.

```
instance of __FilterToConsumerBinding
{
  Consumer = "\\\\GCOLE\\ROOT\\WMIBook:
    Sample_WMIBookEventConsumer.Name=\"MyEventConsumer\"";

  Filter = "\\\\GCOLE\\ROOT\\WMIBook:
    __EventFilter.Name=\"MyEventConsumerFilter\"";
};
```

In the preceding example, when an event matches the event subscription in MyEvent-
ConsumerFilter, WMI will deliver the event to the logical consumer, MyEventConsumer
(loading the logical consumer if required).

Let's summarize. We created a class that defines the properties that specify what a logical consumer should do upon receipt of an event. We created a logical consumer that specified whether it should make a beep sound upon receipt of an event. Next, we defined an event filter for the event notifications we want to receive. Finally, we tied the logical consumer to the event filter, which completes the event subscription for the permanent event consumer. The benefit of separating the event filters, logical consumers, and bindings is that an event filter can be used for many logical consumers and a logical consumer can subscribe to many event filters.

Let's move on to developing the provider. Apart from initialization, all event consumer providers must implement the `IWbemEventConsumerProvider` interface:

```
interface IWbemEventConsumerProvider
{
HRESULT FindConsumer(
  IWbemClassObject *pLogicalConsumer,        // The logical consumer
  IWbemUnboundObjectSink **ppConsumer);      // The consumer sink
};
```

The `FindConsumer` method is called by WMI whenever it needs to deliver an event to a particular logical consumer. The `pLogicalConsumer` parameter is the same instance referenced by the `Consumer` property in the `__FilterToConsumerBinding` association. After the provider has found or created an appropriate event sink, the provider returns it through the `ppConsumer` output parameter. WMI will use the sink to deliver the events to the provider. Here's the returned event sink interface:

```
interface IWbemUnboundObjectSink
{
HRESULT IndicateToConsumer(
  IWbemClassObject *pLogicalConsumer,        // The logical consumer
  long lNumObjects,                          // Number of events
  IWbemClassObject **apObjects);             // Array of events
};
```

Like the `FindConsumer` method, the `pLogicalConsumer` parameter is the WMI representation of the logical consumer. The provider can inspect properties of the `pLogicalConsumer` instance to determine what actions it must take to process the event. In our example provider, `pLogicalConsumer` is the `Sample_WMIBookEventConsumer.Name="MyEventConsumer"` instance that we created earlier. The `lNumObjects` parameter specifies how many events are being passed in the `apObjects` parameter.

Let's look at the implementation for the event consumer provider. We omit the `IWbemProviderInit` implementation because it is the same as the one for the instance provider.

```
class CEventConsumer :
  public CComObjectRoot,
  public CComCoClass<CEventConsumer, &CLSID_EventConsumer>,
```

```
    public IWbemProviderInit,
    public IWbemEventConsumerProvider
{
public:
  CEventConsumer() {}

  BEGIN_COM_MAP(CEventConsumer)
    COM_INTERFACE_ENTRY(IWbemProviderInit)
    COM_INTERFACE_ENTRY(IWbemEventConsumerProvider)
  END_COM_MAP()

  DECLARE_REGISTRY_RESOURCEID(IDR_EventConsumer)

// IWbemProviderInit
public:
  STDMETHOD(Initialize)(LPWSTR wszUser, LONG lFlags,
    LPWSTR wszNamespace, LPWSTR wszLocale,
    IWbemServices *pNamespace, IWbemContext *pCtx,
    IWbemProviderInitSink *pInitSink);

// IWbemEventConsumerProvider
public:
  STDMETHOD(FindConsumer)(IWbemClassObject* pLogicalConsumer,
    IWbemUnboundObjectSink** ppConsumer);

};
```

The FindConsumer method's responsibility is to find and, if necessary, create an event sink for a particular consumer. Let's see how this might be done:

```
STDMETHODIMP CEventConsumer::FindConsumer(
  IWbemClassObject* pLogicalConsumer,
  IWbemUnboundObjectSink** ppConsumer)
{
  ObjectLock lock(this);
  HRESULT hr = WBEM_E_NOT_FOUND;

  *ppConsumer = 0; // Init out-param

  // Get the class of the event consumer
  CComVariant varClass;
  hr = pLogicalConsumer->Get(CComBSTR("__CLASS"), 0, &varClass, 0, 0);

  // Check that we can support this event consumer
  if (_wcsicmp(V_BSTR(&varClass), L"Sample_WMIBookEventConsumer") == 0)
  {
    // Create permanent event consumer
    CComObject<CEventConsumerSink>* pEventSink = 0;
    hr = CComObject<CEventConsumerSink>::CreateInstance(&pEventSink);
```

```
  // Query for the out-going interface
  hr = pEventSink->QueryInterface(IID_IWbemUnboundObjectSink,
    (LPVOID*)ppConsumer);
}
else
  hr = WBEM_E_NOT_FOUND;

return hr;
}
```

The first task is to check that the provider supports its accompanying logical consumer class, `Sample_WMIBookEventConsumer`. Because this is a particularly simple implementation, the provider creates an event sink that WMI will eventually release. In a more complex provider, you may want to check other properties to determine what kind of sink you want to pass back to WMI.

If WMI does not have an active sink to which to deliver the event, it loads the provider (by calling `CoCreateInstance`) and initializes it through the `IWbemProviderInit` interface. WMI then calls the `FindConsumer` method to gain access to the sink. WMI holds on to the sink for a short while before it releases it.

Let's have a look at the `CEventConsumerSink` class implementation in more detail. This is where the real processing of the events takes place.

```
class CEventConsumerSink:
  public CComObjectRootEx<CComSingleThreadModel>,
  public IWbemUnboundObjectSink
{
public:
  CEventConsumerSink() {}

  BEGIN_COM_MAP(CEventConsumerSink)
    COM_INTERFACE_ENTRY(IWbemUnboundObjectSink)
  END_COM_MAP()

// IWbemUnboundObjectSink
public:
  STDMETHOD(IndicateToConsumer)(IWbemClassObject* pLogicalConsumer,
    long lNumObjects, IWbemClassObject** apObjects);
};
```

The only method that the provider needs to implement is `IndicateToConsumer`. WMI calls this method to deliver the events to the provider through the `apObjects` parameter. This is where the provider should perform its processing of the event. In the following implementation, all the provider does is make a beep sound if configured to do so:

```
STDMETHODIMP CEventConsumerSink::IndicateToConsumer(
  IWbemClassObject* pLogicalConsumer, long lNumObjects,
  IWbemClassObject** apObjects)
```

```
{
  ObjectLock lock(this);
  HRESULT hr = WBEM_S_NO_ERROR;

  // Get the class of the event consumer
  CComVariant varClass;
  hr = pLogicalConsumer->Get(CComBSTR("__CLASS"), 0, &varClass, 0, 0);

  // Check that we can support this event consumer
  if (_wcsicmp(V_BSTR(&varClass), L"Sample_WMIBookEventConsumer") == 0)
  {
    // Get event consumer properties
    CComVariant varBeep;
    hr = pLogicalConsumer->Get(CComBSTR("EnableBeep"), 0, &varBeep, 0, 0);

    // WMI can que events and send them all together in one call
    for (int nIndex = 0; nIndex < lNumObjects; nIndex++)
    {
      // This is a simple event handler, just retrieves the class.
      CComVariant varEventType;
      hr = apObjects[nIndex]->Get(CComBSTR(_T("TargetInstance")), 0,
        &varEventType, 0, 0);

      // Get event object
      CComQIPtr<IWbemClassObject> spEvent = V_UNKNOWN(&varEventType);

      // Get the class of the event (you may want to do this so
      // that you can determine what to do with this event. This
      // implementation does nothing with this information.)
      CComVariant varEventTypeClass;
      hr = spEvent->Get(CComBSTR(_T("__CLASS")), 0,
        &varEventTypeClass, 0, 0);

      // Make a beep sound if the consumer is configured as such
      if (V_BOOL(&varBeep))
        Beep(1500, 250);

      // Received event of type < V_BSTR(&varEventTypeClass) >
    }
  }
  else
    hr = WBEM_E_NOT_FOUND;

  return hr;
}
```

Be prepared to handle more than one event because WMI can queue events and send them all at once. This is typically the case when the provider cannot process the event notifications as fast as they are being delivered. This is a very simple provider that only makes a beep sound. In a commercial provider you will have to process more serious events. Did you notice that the provider checked to make sure that it could process the event by looking at the logical consumer that subscribed for the event? In addition, you also would check the class of the event to ensure that you can process it.

▪ Permanent Event Consumer Provider Registration

Earlier in the chapter, we covered the first step of the provider registration. The second step completes the event consumer provider registration.

As already discussed, all permanent event consumer registrations are held within the CIM repository. The general approach is to create your event subscriptions using the `__EventFilter` class and create your own logical consumers using your own class derived from `__EventConsumer`, which is in our case `Sample_WMIBookEventConsumer`. The logical consumer and event subscriptions are then bound together with an association class, `__FilterToConsumerBinding`.

The second step of the event consumer provider registration requires an instance of the `__EventConsumerProviderRegistration` class. The registration contains a provider reference and the event consumer classes supported by the provider. WMI uses the `ConsumerClassNames` property to link an event consumer to a specific provider.

```
class __EventConsumerProviderRegistration: __ProviderRegistration
{
  [key] __Provider ref Provider;
  [key] string ConsumerClassNames[];
};
```

Here is a typical event consumer provider registration. Notice that our logical consumer class (`Sample_WMIBookEventConsumer`) is registered against our provider in the `ConsumerClassNames` property. Whenever WMI needs to deliver an event to the `Sample_WMIBookEventConsumer` consumer, WMI can determine which provider to load and delivers the event to it.

```
instance of __EventConsumerProviderRegistration
{
  Provider = "__Win32Provider.Name=\"FruitBasketPermEventProv\"";
  ConsumerClassNames = { "Sample_WMIBookEventConsumer"};
};
```

▪ Developing a Property Provider

A property provider retrieves and modifies property values for instances that are stored in the CIM repository. If your schema is based on storing instances in the CIM repository, then you may have a requirement for a property provider. If one or more properties in an instance rely on dynamic information, then your first act usually is to develop an instance provider (requiring you to implement your own local cache for the instance data). In this situation, a property provider can dynamically provide the property for an instance.

We shall implement a very simple schema for our sample property provider. The class will contain two properties: a key property and a property that will be provided by a property provider. Let's have a look at the class:

```
class Sample_Chapter
{
  [key] sint32 ChapterNumber;
  boolean FileReadOnly;
};
```

The class is supposed to represent a chapter that is stored as a document on a disk drive. The `ChapterNumber` property represents the number of the chapter and the `FileReadOnly` property represents whether the document file is read-only or not. The `FileReadOnly` property will be provided by the property provider.

Let's create an instance of the `Sample_Chapter` class in the CIM repository:

```
[
  DynProps,
  InstanceContext("E:")
]
instance of Sample_Chapter
{
  ChapterNumber = 12;

  [
    PropertyContext("\\My Documents\\WMIProvChapter.doc"),
    Dynamic,
    Provider("WMIPropertyProv")
  ]
  FileReadOnly;
};
```

Note the use of the `DynProps` qualifier: It indicates that an instance contains values provided by a dynamic property provider. When an instance uses the `DynProps` qualifier, it means that one or more properties have both the `Dynamic` and `Provider` qualifiers. The `Dynamic` qualifier specifies that the property be supplied dynamically by the provider specified in the `Provider` qualifier. Whenever a property provided value is `Dynamic`, the property must also specify the `PropertyContext` qualifier. Property providers can make use of three different context qualifiers: `ClassContext`, `Instance-Context`, and `PropertyContext`. The context qualifiers: can provide additional context information about a class, instance, and property. For a property provider to achieve anything useful requires a property context.

- The `ClassContext` qualifier is applied to a class in which the context information is the same for every instance.
- The `InstanceContext` qualifier is applied to an instance in which the context information applies to every property.
- The `PropertyContext` qualifier is applied to a property in which there is very specific context information that only applies to a single property.

In the sample instance above, the `InstanceContext` qualifier specified the disk drive on which the chapter resided. Although not a particularly good example of an instance context, it demonstrates the use of an instance context within a provider. The `PropertyContext` qualifier specified a relative file path to the chapter's document file. This is a reasonably good example of the property context because the `FileReadOnly` property pertains to the actual document, `"\My Documents\WMIProvChapter.doc"`.

All three context qualifiers can contain any string that will mean something to the property provider. In the above example, we just happened to use file system–based strings.

Like all the other providers you've seen, a property provider is a COM component (in process or out-of-process server). It must support the `IWbemProviderInit` and `IWbemPropertyProvider` interfaces (see Figure 12.11). WMI initializes the provider through the `IWbemProviderInit` interface, and the `IWbemPropertyProvider` interface requires an implementation to get and set properties.

■ Exposing Dynamic Properties

The sample property provider implementation will expose `FileReadOnly` only as a dynamic property. In addition, the provider will support only the retrieval of the property. Setting the property will not be possible in this implementation. However, it could be achieved easily by using the appropriate Win32 APIs.

Figure 12.11 WMI property provider component

Let's look at the implementation for the property provider. We omit the `IWbemProviderInit` implementation because it is the same as the one for the instance provider.

```
class CProperty:
  public CComObjectRoot,
  public CComCoClass<CProperty, &CLSID_Property>,
  public IWbemProviderInit,
  public IWbemPropertyProvider
{
public:
  CProperty() {}

  BEGIN_COM_MAP(CProperty)
    COM_INTERFACE_ENTRY(IWbemProviderInit)
    COM_INTERFACE_ENTRY(IWbemPropertyProvider)
  END_COM_MAP()

  DECLARE_REGISTRY_RESOURCEID(IDR_Property)

// IWbemProviderInit
public:
  STDMETHOD(Initialize)(LPWSTR wszUser, LONG lFlags,
    LPWSTR wszNamespace, LPWSTR wszLocale,
    IWbemServices *pNamespace, IWbemContext *pCtx,
    IWbemProviderInitSink *pInitSink);

// IWbemPropertyProvider
public:
  STDMETHOD(GetProperty)(long lFlags, const BSTR strLocale,
    const BSTR strClassMapping, const BSTR strInstMapping,
    const BSTR strPropMapping, VARIANT* pvValue);

  STDMETHOD(PutProperty)(long lFlags, const BSTR strLocale,
    const BSTR strClassMapping, const BSTR strInstMapping,
    const BSTR strPropMapping, const VARIANT* pvValue)
  {
    return WBEM_E_NOT_SUPPORTED;
  }
};
```

Because the provider will not allow the setting of the `FileReadOnly` property, the `PutProperty` method is not implemented and returns an appropriate HRESULT to WMI. Let's take a closer look at the `GetProperty` method:

```
interface IWbemPropertyProvider
{
HRESULT GetProperty(
  long lFlags,                    // Must be zero
```

```
        const BSTR strLocale,          // Locale
        const BSTR strClassMapping,    // Class context
        const BSTR strInstMapping,     // Instance context
        const BSTR strPropMapping,     // Property context
        VARIANT *pvValue);             // The returned property value
    };
```

The `strLocale` parameter is a user-specified locale that is obtained during the initial connection to WMI. This can be used in cases where the returned property value is localized. If the property is not localized, the provider implementation can ignore the locale parameter.

The `strClassMapping`, `strInstMapping`, and `strPropMapping` parameters correspond to `ClassContext`, `InstanceContext`, and `PropertyContext` respectively. However, you can expect the `strPropMapping` parameter to be present because any property supplied by a property provider also declares the property context. All of the context strings passed through to the provider are completely user-defined by the schema designer.

The `pvValue` output parameter is the value of the property that will be returned to the caller. The value of the property is based on the supplied contexts and locale. Notice that no parameters specify the class or property names. Carefully consider how you divide and reference your property provider implementations and how you encode the context strings.

Let's have a look at how you might develop the `GetProperty` method:

```
STDMETHODIMP CProperty::GetProperty(long lFlags, const BSTR strLocale,
  const BSTR strClassMapping, const BSTR strInstMapping,
  const BSTR strPropMapping, VARIANT* pvValue)
{
  ObjectLock lock(this);
  HRESULT hr = WBEM_S_NO_ERROR;

  // Create a full file path based on the instance and property contexts
  CComBSTR bstrFile(strInstMapping);
  bstrFile += strPropMapping;

  // Quick attempt to make sure there is a filepath
  if (bstrFile.Length() > 0)
  {

    // Determine if file is read only
    V_VT(pvValue) = VT_BOOL;
    V_BOOL(pvValue) =
      (GetFileAttributesW(bstrFile) & FILE_ATTRIBUTE_READONLY) ?
      VARIANT_TRUE : VARIANT_FALSE;
  }
```

```
      else
        hr = WBEM_E_NOT_FOUND; // No instance or property contexts

      return hr;
    }
```

The code sample demonstrates how you can use the context strings to formulate a fully qualified file path. The file path is then passed to the `GetFileAttributes` API to determine whether or not the file is read-only. The code in bold font is the value that will be returned to the caller.

■ Property Provider Registration

Earlier in the chapter we covered the first step of the provider registration. The second step completes the property provider registration. Registering property providers requires you to specify the capabilities of the two most basic operations you can do with a property: property retrieval and property modification.

The `SupportsPut` property specifies whether the property provider supports property modification. If the provider supports this function, then the provider must implement the `IWbemPropertyProvider::PutProperty` method. If not, WMI makes no attempt to call the provider and will immediately return `WBEM_E_PROVIDER_NOT_CAPABLE`. The `SupportsGet` property has the same reaction.

The `SupportsGet` property specifies whether the property provider supports property retrieval. If the provider supports this function, then the provider must implement the `IWbemPropertyProvider::GetProperty` method. Here is the `__PropertyProviderRegistration` class definition:

```
class __PropertyProviderRegistration : __ProviderRegistration
{
  [key] __Provider ref Provider;
  boolean SupportsPut = FALSE;
  boolean SupportsGet = FALSE;
};
```

Here is a typical property provider registration. Notice that the registration supports only property retrieval.

```
instance of __PropertyProviderRegistration
{
  Provider = "__Win32Provider.Name=\"MyPropertyProv\"";
  SupportsGet = TRUE;
  SupportsPut = FALSE;
};
```

■ Developing a Push Provider

A push provider allows you to create instances and update properties that reside within the CIM repository. This is useful for data that is not dynamic and solves the problem of having to create and manage your own local cache. This includes the data storage, data access, and event notification that are provided by WMI. Push providers are the simplest to develop because the only interface you need to implement is `IWbem-ProviderInit` (see Figure 12.12).

In practice, developing push providers is not very common. However, you may find that in your solution developing a push provider is a perfect match.

Let's implement a very simple solution for our sample push provider. All it will do is create an instance of a specific class and update one of its properties. Here is the class definition:

```
class Sample_SomeClass
{
  [key] string Name;
  uint32 NumberOfUpdates;
};
```

The `Name` property is an arbitrary name that will be a key property and therefore uniquely identify an instance.

The `NumberOfUpdates` property will be incremented by one every time the provider is initialized.

■ Pushing Data to the CIM Repository

A push provider should perform the following sequence of tasks:

1. Identify whether there are any objects that you need to create. If there are, then you must create the objects in the CIM repository.

2. Identify whether there are any objects that you need to remove. If there are, remove them from the CIM repository.

Figure 12.12 WMI push provider component

3. Update the properties of your instances that now exist. This may involve obtaining the property values from some other data source.

A push provider's class declaration looks like this:

```
class CPushInstance:
  public CComObjectRoot,
  public CComCoClass<CPushInstance,&CLSID_PushInstance>,
  public IWbemProviderInit
{
public:
  CPushInstance() {}

  BEGIN_COM_MAP(CPushInstance)
    COM_INTERFACE_ENTRY(IWbemProviderInit)
  END_COM_MAP()

  DECLARE_REGISTRY_RESOURCEID(IDR_PushInstance)

// IWbemProviderInit
public:
  STDMETHOD(Initialize)(LPWSTR wszUser, LONG lFlags,
    LPWSTR wszNamespace, LPWSTR wszLocale,
    IWbemServices *pNamespace, IWbemContext *pCtx,
    IWbemProviderInitSink *pInitSink);
};
```

Our push provider will ensure that a specific instance of the `Sample_SomeClass` class exists and that its object path can be referenced by `Sample_SomeClass.Name=` `"MyClass"`. If the object already exists, the provider will retrieve the `NumberOfUpdates` property and add one to it. The updated property is then written back to the CIM repository. Let's take a look at the implementation:

```
STDMETHODIMP CPushInstance::Initialize(LPWSTR wszUser, LONG lFlags,
  LPWSTR wszNamespace, LPWSTR wszLocale, IWbemServices *pNamespace,
  IWbemContext *pCtx, IWbemProviderInitSink *pInitSink)
{
  ObjectLock lock(this);
  HRESULT hrStatus = WBEM_S_INITIALIZED;

  try
  {
    CComBSTR bstrPath;
    bstrPath = (_T("Sample_SomeClass.Name=\"MyClass\""));

    // Check if the object we want to update exists?
    CComPtr<IWbemClassObject> spInstance;
```

```
HRESULT hr = pNamespace->GetObject(bstrPath,
  WBEM_FLAG_RETURN_WBEM_COMPLETE, NULL,
  &spInstance, NULL);


if (SUCCEEDED(hr))
{
  // Get a property from the object that we want to update
  CComVariant varUpdate;
  hr = spInstance->Get(CComBSTR(_T("NumberOfUpdates")), 0,
    &varUpdate, 0, 0);


  // In this simple implementation, we're just incrementing
  // the property by one.
  V_I4(&varUpdate) += 1;


  // Write new property
  hr = spInstance->Put(CComBSTR("NumberOfUpdates"), 0,
    &varUpdate, 0);
}
else
{
  // Our object does not exist, lets create one. First, we need to
  // get the class definition so we can spawn an instance of it.
  CComPtr<IWbemClassObject> spClass;
  hr = pNamespace->GetObject(CComBSTR("Sample_SomeClass"),
    WBEM_FLAG_RETURN_WBEM_COMPLETE, NULL, &spClass, NULL);


  // Make new object
  hr = spClass->SpawnInstance(0, &spInstance);


  // Set some properties on the object
  CComVariant varInstName(_T("MyClass"));
  hr = spInstance->Put(CComBSTR("Name"), 0, &varInstName, 0);
  CComVariant varInstUpdate(int(1));
  hr = spInstance->Put(CComBSTR("NumberOfUpdates"), 0,
    &varInstUpdate, 0);
}


  // Commit to create instance in CIM repository
  hr = pNamespace->PutInstance(spInstance,
    WBEM_FLAG_CREATE_OR_UPDATE | WBEM_FLAG_OWNER_UPDATE,
    NULL, NULL);
}
catch(...)
{
  hrStatus = WBEM_E_FAILED;
}
```

```
        // Let WMI know we've finished
        pInitSink->SetStatus(hrStatus, 0);

        return hrStatus;
    }
```

■ Push Provider Registration

Earlier in the chapter we covered the first step of the provider registration. The second step completes the push provider registration.

Registering a push provider is disguised as a class provider. It is not an instance provider because instances are not exposed dynamically. A push provider requires that the classes it supports be previously defined. The class definitions do not need to have any special qualifiers to take advantage of a push provider.

Registration for a push provider requires an instance of the `__ClassProvider-Registration` class. The `InteractionType` property is set to 1 to indicate that this is a push provider. The `InteractionType` property was covered earlier in the chapter (in the section on instance provider registration).

```
instance of __ClassProviderRegistration
{
  Provider = "__Win32Provider.Name=\"MyPushProv\"";
  InteractionType = 1;
};
```

Note that when making the `__Win32Provider` registration, you must ensure that the `Pure` property is set to false because a push provider does not need to hang around to service any other requests.

■ Security Considerations

Depending on the requirements of the provider, you may need to provide secure access to your objects. This means that the provider can restrict access to operations and information. Here are three reasons that you might want secure access:

1. Your provider uses system-level objects such as a file or the registry. The correct security context might be required to service the request. For instance, altering a registry value may require users of a particular security group and therefore requires the provider to impersonate the user (who may be on another machine) executing the operation.

2. You may want the provider to impersonate a user so that all security operations can be audited (if enabled by the administrator).

3. You may decide to perform your own security, in which case the provider could inspect the security descriptor to determine if access is allowed.

Fortunately, Microsoft has made it very easy for providers to impersonate the client's security context. It requires a two-step process. The first step is to impersonate the client making the request. This involves making the appropriate security calls in the provider. The second step is to correctly register the provider so that WMI can ensure that the security context will be correctly impersonated.

Let's take a closer look at how the client security context manages to get to the provider. When WMI passes the client an `IWbemServices` interface, the client (using the COM run time) creates a proxy that is used to communicate with the WMI service. The proxy resides in its own thread in the client process and therefore has its own security context. The COM run time ensures that the security context used by the proxy ends up at the stub (see Figure 12.13). It is the client's responsibility to ensure that the proxy's security context is set up correctly using `CoSetProxyBlanket`.

For a provider to impersonate a client request requires `CoImpersonateClient` and `CoRevertToSelf`. Because the WMI architecture is built on COM, these APIs are provided as part of the COM run time. The implementation of virtually all the methods in the `IWbemServices` interface should call `CoImpersonateClient` whenever the client's security context is required for an operation. When the provider is finished with the security context (perhaps after accessing system-level objects, such as the registry), it should call `CoRevertToSelf` to switch back to the provider's security context.

Let's see how a provider typically impersonates a client's security context:

```
STDMETHOD(GetObjectAsync)(const BSTR ObjectPath, long lFlags,
  IWbemContext *pCtx, IWbemObjectSink *pResponseHandler)
{
  HRESULT hr = WBEM_S_NO_ERROR;
```

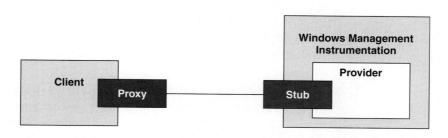

Figure 12.13 Remote access boundaries between clients and providers

```
// This impersonates the client's security context. Any calls made
// after this will be in the client's security context and therefore
// can be audited.
CoImpersonateClient();

try
{
  //
  // TODO: Add your code here. May set hr to WBEM_E_ACCESS_DENIED.
  //
}
catch(...)
{
  hr = WBEM_E_FAILED;
}

// Go back to the providers security context.
CoRevertToSelf();

return hr;
}
```

If the provider requires switching the client security context back and forth within the implementation, it can do so simply by making multiple impersonate/revert-to-self calls:

```
CoImpersonateClient();
// Do operation in client security context
CoRevertToSelf();
// Do operation in provider security context
CoImpersonateClient();
// Do operation in client security context
CoRevertToSelf();
```

For more information, review the section on security in Chapter 7.

The second step for enabling provider security is the provider's registration. Earlier in the chapter we covered provider registration in detail. Recall that __Win32-Provider registration includes the security and initialization requirements of a provider. This is what the __Win32Provider class looks like:

```
class __Win32Provider: __Provider
{
  [not_null] string CLSID;
  string ClientLoadableCLSID;
  string DefaultMachineName;
  datetime UnloadTimeout;
```

```
    boolean InitializeAsAdminFirst;
    sint32 ImpersonationLevel = 0;
    sint32 InitializationReentrancy = 0;
    boolean PerUserInitialization = FALSE;
    boolean PerLocaleInitialization = FALSE;
    boolean Pure = TRUE;
};
```

The `ImpersonationLevel` property must be set to 1 and the `PerUserInitialization` property must be set to TRUE. The `ImpersonationLevel` specifies that when the provider calls `CoImpersonateClient` and `CoRevertToSelf`, the provider will impersonate the client correctly. The `PerUserInitialization` specifies that whenever a user accesses the objects exposed by a provider, the provider is initialized and given the opportunity to perform any specific security initialization.

If the provider needs to use the administration-level thread security token during initialization, then the registration must also set the `InitializeAsAdminFirst` property to TRUE. Although a call to `CoImpersonateClient` will not fail, the provider will use WMI's security context instead of the client's. This is useful when you want the provider to have privileged access to system-level objects during initialization.

■ Summary

This chapter has introduced you to the most popular kinds of WMI providers that can be written to expose some aspect of your management environment. You learned how you can easily expose management objects through an instance provider. This type of provider has to manage how and where it stores its data (the local cache). However, if you don't want to use the registry or a file to store the data, you may choose to store the data in the CIM repository in a subnamespace (perhaps called `data`). You should design the capabilities of the provider along with the schema.

Next, you saw how you can provide behavior for your classes and objects by implementing a method provider. Review Chapter 7 for guidelines on method design. You learned that as well as passing standard WMI types like `sint32`, you can also pass objects as in and out parameters.

You learned how you can develop an event provider to expose events in your management environment. This is a very powerful feature, so think of creative ways that you can incorporate this type of information in your management schema. The sample provider exposed an intrinsic event that is always linked to classes, instances, or namespaces. You can publish events that have no relation to classes, instances, or namespaces, such as the power management event classes, for example. Consider the possibilities of the types of events you could publish for your own system.

You were introduced to one of the most powerful WMI features, robust event delivery through permanent event consumer providers. This allows you to create an in or out of process COM server that will be activated by WMI to deliver an event. This can be completely separate from the main application and provides interesting opportunities to solve interesting problems in an elegant way.

Next, you saw how you could easily provide properties dynamically for instances held in the CIM repository. Property providers offer an easy way out for providing dynamic properties without having to write a full blown instance provider. However, you'll need to carefully choose what contexts you need to use and how they are encoded.

Although push providers are not very popular, you saw how you could develop one to expose your management objects within the CIM repository. There isn't much scope for controlling what happens to the instances you create, delete, or update. However, the nature of a push provider usually means that the instances that need to be pushed reside on some other data source.

Finally, you learned how you can easily impersonate client security contexts. This is useful when a provider makes calls to APIs that require access rights to system-level objects such as a file or the registry.

Ten Fast Facts: Developing WMI Providers

1. Expose your management environment through WMI! This will help you unify your administration interfaces for your hardware and software. You can use WMI to access your management objects in a user interface administration tool (such as MMC), and it may also help system administrators make scripts for routine administration tasks.

2. Think about your schema design first, before developing a WMI provider. Review Chapter 5 and Chapter 6 to learn more about schema design.

3. Be aware of the types of WMI providers that can be developed and their merits. In particular, instance, method, and event providers are the most common.

4. All WMI providers must support the `IWbemProviderInit` interface. Instance and method providers must support the `IWbemServices` interface. Event providers must support the `IWbemEventProvider` interface.

5. Keep your mind open when looking for a solution that requires a robust event delivery system. Permanent event consumer providers may be the solution.

6. When developing your WMI providers, consider making them local COM servers. This will allow you overall control of the process from which the information is exposed; for instance, you will be able to specify the security context in which the provider is launched.

7. At a minimum, it is best practice for instance WMI providers to support `Create-InstanceEnumAsync` and `GetObjectAsync`. This will enable users and management applications to determine what management objects are available and to gain access to a specific management object.

8. Consider the security requirements for your WMI provider. Note that WMI's security model is based on DCOM security. Separate from DCOM security is namespace security, controlled via an access control list (ACL).

9. When examining your management environment, consider what external events exist outside the scope of your management objects. Review Chapter 7 for a detailed discussion of the differences between intrinsic and extrinsic events.

10. On the Web site that accompanies this book is an ATL-like WMI provider framework that will make your provider development easier.

Chapter 13

High-Performance Instrumentation

The computing world has long required the instrumentation of applications with detailed trace information and techniques to monitor system usage. The most basic trace instrumentation that many development organizations employ is a debug logging facility. Debug logging is usually achieved by writing text statements into a text file that may include the time, a thread identifier, and the subsystem or component writing the trace statement. This basic form of instrumentation has aided many organizations to resolve problems by inspecting the log file to determine the program flow at the time a problem occurred. The log file has other benefits apart from identifying where a particular problem occurred. A developer can use the log file for performance profiling by inspecting the tick count (time) and identify portions of code that take too long to complete. A developer can identify multithreaded problems by seeing the sequence of calls made between threads and components. Even if a problem cannot be easily reproducible, a developer can ascertain from the log file where additional instrumentation should be added and make the section of code more robust.

Every line or statement written to a debug log file can be viewed as an event, hence the name of a new instrumentation technology introduced in Windows 2000, *event tracing*. Event tracing allows applications to fire and capture events extremely fast. An event tracing session can be monitored in real time or be written to a binary log file that is managed by the operating system. Every event is a binary structure that has some predefined fields, such as a time stamp, the type of event, and its version. Most events are extended with customized fields or structures to supply additional information about the activity. To achieve the same outcome as a debug log file, an event-tracing event would contain a single custom string field that would verbosely describe the event. The Windows 2000/XP kernel exposes many event traces that include activity with processes, threads, file and disk activity, TCP/IP, loading images such as DLLs and executables, registry access, and hard and soft page faults. There are also event traces for the various security subsystems used by Windows. Windows XP extends the existing kernel events with new versions to provide even more detail about what is happening in the kernel.

Problems in applications that output text statements or events to a debug log file are much more difficult to properly evaluate and resolve because the information provided in the file is only at an application level. Suppose a server-side mail-oriented application builds on top of MAPI (Messaging API). MAPI itself builds on top of the operating system, which uses the remote procedure call layer (RPC), which, in turn, causes the TCP/IP network layer to be exercised (and not forgetting the security authentication that goes on behind the scenes). The e-mail server, in turn, uses the message store, the Active Directory, and so the list goes on. When a customer has a problem in which a MAPI call is taking a significant amount of time, where do you start? The text debug log file will not be able to give you all the detail that is required to identify and resolve difficult problems. For instance, it may turn out that the MAPI call is taking too long because of an isolated network problem. It is unlikely you'll be able to identify this problem when looking at a flat text file. This is because you don't know what is going on with the components on which you are building. If all the components on which you are building expose useful event traces, then it is possible to get a three-dimensional view of the problem.

Event tracing doesn't stop there! A single event in an event trace can have a parent event. This opens up the possibility to have child events that detail a larger event. Suppose an application has to perform a complex calculation. It could fire a start calculation event followed by child events that detail the calculation's progress, which might finally end in a stop calculation event. So, not only can you drill down through all the components to the operating system, but you may also be able to drill through all the child events and their child events. This cannot easily be achieved with a flat text file.

Since the release of Windows NT 3.1, all applications have been able to read and write high-performance counters. High-performance counters offer a very fast solution for monitoring system utilization. This form of instrumentation is different from event tracing because the information communicated is based on a single value for a single counter at that moment. Performance counters are arranged into objects that can contain one or more counters and each counter in turn may have one or more instances. For example, a particular Process object has some counters like Thread Count for which there are several Instances (that is, currently running applications). This is one example of the instrumentation provided by the operating system. In fact, Windows includes many performance counters; other examples include Memory, IP, Processor, and System. To make such an instrumentation technique useful, a monitoring application continually must retrieve the counter values in a loop that allows an ongoing graph or log to be updated. For example, the performance monitor supplied with Windows is a graphical application that can display graphs for one or more performance counters. A developer who wishes to identify whether an application leaks memory over a long period can set up the performance monitor to monitor the Private Bytes counter from the Process object. If the graph goes up, then the application is leaking memory. If the graph is stable, then the application is well behaved. This is one example that demonstrates how tremendously useful software instrumentation is. It is also an example of how noninstrumented applications can benefit from the instrumentation provided through the Windows operating system. Many server-side applications now instrument or expose high-performance counters to help administrators in planning for system capacity. Writing code to access performance counters is not user-friendly and requires the use of the registry APIs. To overcome the difficulties of accessing the performance counters, Microsoft developed the Performance Data Helper (PDH) library. This makes it significantly easier to write code to monitor performance counters.

The main difference between event tracing and performance counters is that it is hard to track individual resources with performance counters. Performance counters offer a way to view system utilization, such as memory usage. Performance counters cannot be used easily for debug logging, for tracking resources or operations such as a disk drive, or for monitoring registry access.

This chapter aims to bring you up to speed with event-tracing technology. Although specifically aimed at Windows XP, many of the event-tracing APIs are available in Windows 2000.

■ Overview of Event Tracing

Event tracing is a subsystem that is deeply integrated in the Windows operating system and is considered part of the Windows Management Instrumentation tool set (see Figure 13.1). Event tracing is super fast and provides new scope for resolving problems and monitoring and tracking resources. The most fundamental aspect of event tracing is an *event*. An event can be best described as an activity of interest. For example, the Windows operating system's TCP/IP stack is instrumented with event traces that describe activities such as connect, send, receive, and disconnect. Each event typically includes additional information about the activity: In the case of the TCP/IP stack, more information is provided about the connection and details of what was sent or received. The subsystem that implements event tracing is referred to as the *event tracer* and is implemented in the Windows kernel.

Events are fired (published) by an event-tracing provider, also known as an event-tracing logger. Any application that you develop can be an event-tracing provider and it can be engaged in one or more event-tracing sessions. The event tracer temporarily holds the events fired by a provider in nonpaged system memory buffers. The event tracer manages the buffers and if necessary, it also manages the dumping of them to an event trace log file on disk. An event-tracing session can be associated only with a single event-tracing provider. Hence, if you want event traces from several subsystems or components, then an event-tracing session must be created to record the events from each provider.

The structure of an event is usually published as a class in the WMI repository and is sometimes referred to as an *event trace*. Hence you'll often see the terms *class* and *event trace* used interchangeably. There are no limits to how many different event traces a provider can instrument. The kernel, for example, publishes nine different event traces. Each event trace fired by a provider is further defined by its *event type*. For instance, the kernel event trace for the TCP/IP stack has event types connect, send, receive, and disconnect. The interpretation of an event depends on its event type. For instance, the TCP/IP details for a connect event are different from the details exposed for a read or write event. Although there are some system-defined event types, an event-tracing provider is free to define its own.

Event-tracing sessions cannot be started, stopped, or queried without an event-tracing controller. An event-tracing controller is an application under Windows XP that can initiate up to a maximum of 32 event-tracing sessions of which 29 are available for applications. Under Windows 2000, the global logger and the kernel logger have reserved sessions. Windows XP reserves a third session for internal use.

Event traces cannot be processed or inspected without an event-tracing consumer. A consumer is an application that can either process the event traces in real time or open an already existing event trace log file from disk. Depending on the volume of event traces being fired, a real-time consumer must process the events super fast to not lose events from the nonpaged memory buffers. If the event tracer fills all the available buffers, it starts dropping events. When postprocessing event trace log files, a consumer can specify and process several log files at once. Hence, if you have event traces from several subsystems or components, you can get the event tracer to process them and provide you with a chronological event stream.

A single application can be both an event-tracing controller and an event-tracing consumer.

■ Controlling Event Traces

Controlling event traces is critically important because it allows event-tracing sessions to be started and stopped. This ultimately provides a log file either for later analysis or to monitor the events in real time. Conveniently, the operating system can manage the dumping of events to a log file. The log file is stored in binary format and can be con-

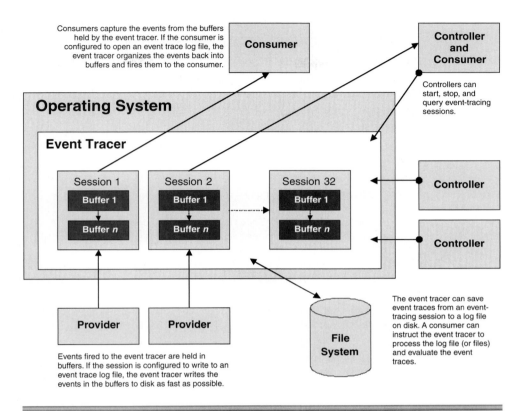

Consumers capture the events from the buffers held by the event tracer. If the consumer is configured to open an event trace log file, the event tracer organizes the events back into buffers and fires them to the consumer.

Consumer

Controller and Consumer

Controllers can start, stop, and query event-tracing sessions.

Operating System

Event Tracer

Session 1	Session 2	Session 32
Buffer 1	**Buffer 1**	**Buffer 1**
Buffer _n_	**Buffer _n_**	**Buffer _n_**

Controller

Controller

Provider

Provider

Events fired to the event tracer are held in buffers. If the session is configured to write to an event trace log file, the event tracer writes the events in the buffers to disk as fast as possible.

File System

The event tracer can save event traces from an event-tracing session to a log file on disk. A consumer can instruct the event tracer to process the log file (or files) and evaluate the event traces.

Figure 13.1   Event-tracing architecture

figured to log the events circularly, sequentially, or incrementally. Monitoring the events live is convenient as well because not only can the events be monitored in real time, you also might have other requirements based on retrieving the events as soon as they are available. For instance, you may have a requirement to process the events in real time so that they can be stored in an alternative format or transmitted over the network to a shared logging or tracing server. Obviously, this distributed approach would degrade network performance if thousands of events were to occur every few seconds. The Windows XP kernel can generate 10,000 events in just a few seconds. If you're considering a distributed tracing approach, carefully evaluate what you send over the network.

Starting a Kernel Event-Tracing Session

Starting an event-tracing session requires two essential pieces of information. First, you must specify the event-tracing provider that will generate the required events, and second, you must specify where the events must be delivered (either a log file or delivery in real time). Calling `StartTrace`, if successful, will start the event-tracing session using the session's configuration supplied through an `EVENT_TRACE_PROPERTIES` structure. When a session is in progress, calling `ControlTrace` will allow the session's configuration and statistics at that moment to be obtained. We will discuss more on this later in the chapter.

Let's start with the first call that must be made to initiate an event-tracing session, `StartTrace`. The following code starts the NT Kernel Logger session (starting other event-tracing providers will be covered later):

```
void StartEventTracing()
{
  // Setup the Event Tracing session properties.
  // The MakeTraceProperties is a private helper function.
  PEVENT_TRACE_PROPERTIES pTraceProps =
    MakeTraceProperties(_T("NT Kernel Logger"),
      _T("C:\\MyEventTrace.etl"));

  // This tell the Event Tracer to log to a file sequentially
  pTraceProps->LogFileMode |= EVENT_TRACE_FILE_MODE_SEQUENTIAL;

  // Requesting TCP/IP and registry events from the NT Kernel Logger
  pTraceProps->EnableFlags |= EVENT_TRACE_FLAG_NETWORK_TCPIP |
    EVENT_TRACE_FLAG_REGISTRY;

  // Start the session.
  TRACEHANDLE hTraceSession = 0;
  ULONG ulError = StartTrace(&hTraceSession, _T("NT Kernel Logger"),
    pTraceProps);

  LocalFree(pTraceProps);
}
```

The step prior to calling `StartTrace` is to set up the session's configuration through an `EVENT_TRACE_PROPERTIES` structure. This is a variable length structure that requires that enough memory be allocated to hold both the structure and the two strings that are tagged at the end of the structure, one string for the name of the session and the other to specify the log file path. After creating and performing the minimum initialization for the `EVENT_TRACE_PROPERTIES` structure, the event trace log file that should be written to is set. The `EVENT_TRACE_FILE_MODE_SEQUENTIAL` flag instructs the session to write the events to the log file sequentially. Because the maximum log file size has not been set, this means that the log file will continue to grow indefinitely. Because we're setting up a session to monitor the NT Kernel Logger, the next step is to specify the kernel events that are required. In this case, we request events from access to the registry and the TCP/IP stack. Finally, the event-tracing session is started by calling `StartTrace`.

Let's look at `StartTrace` in more detail. Here is the function's declaration:

```
ULONG StartTrace(PTRACEHANDLE TraceHandle, LPCTSTR InstanceName,
  PEVENT_TRACE_PROPERTIES Properties);
```

If `StartTrace` is successful in starting the desired event-tracing session, it returns a `TRACEHANDLE` through the `TraceHandle` parameter. It is sometimes useful to keep the returned `TRACEHANDLE` because you can gather statistics about the session, update the session's operating configuration, and stop the session. However, as you'll see later, there are other techniques to reacquire the session handle if you don't have it. The `TRACEHANDLE` is considered closed when the session is stopped.

To uniquely identify a session, a session name must be provided through the `InstanceName` parameter. Other applications may have started their own sessions, and they probably would be unhappy if your application changed their operating configurations or stopped their sessions altogether. This is why a unique session name must be supplied that has the added benefit that an application's session can be easily identified when enumerating all the active event-tracing sessions. (This is covered later in the chapter.) However, that said, NT Kernel Logger is a special case and its session name must be "NT Kernel Logger" (this is one of the operating system's reserved sessions).[1]

The session's configuration is passed through the `Properties` parameter. When `StartTrace` returns, it updates the members of the `EVENT_TRACE_PROPERTIES` structure to provide some initial statistics and the final outcome of the session's configuration (some configuration details might not have been specified and some sensible defaults are automatically assigned).

Setting Up a Session's Configuration

Let's cover the `EVENT_TRACE_PROPERTIES` structure in more detail. As already mentioned, this is a variable-length structure that stores the session's configuration and run-time statistics. Figure 13.2 shows a rough layout highlighting that the variable length members `LoggerNameOffset` and `LogFileNameOffset` point to offsets from the start of the structure.

The following privately defined macro calculates the offset described above which will be used in the `MakeTraceProperties` helper function.

```
#ifndef ByteOffset
  #define ByteOffset(X, Offset) \
    reinterpret_cast<LPTSTR>(Offset ? (DWORD(X) + DWORD(Offset)) : NULL)
#endif
```

1. This is defined by the `KERNEL_LOGGER_NAME` macro in `evntrace.h`.

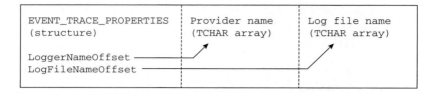

Figure 13.2 EVENT_TRACE_PROPERTIES structure

We have arbitrarily decided that it is unlikely the log file path will be longer than 1024 characters. The session name must not be larger than 1024 characters. Here are the definitions we will use:

```
#define SESSION_NAME_STRLEN      1024
#define LOGFILE_NAME_STRLEN      1024
```

The helper function MakeTraceProperties is used by all code samples in this chapter to create and complete the minimum initialization of an EVENT_TRACE_PROPERTIES structure. Let's look:

```
PEVENT_TRACE_PROPERTIES MakeTraceProperties(
  LPCTSTR lpszProvider = _T(""), LPCTSTR lpszLogFile = _T(""))
{
  PEVENT_TRACE_PROPERTIES pTraceProps = 0;

  // Calculate how big we need our structure
  ULONG ulSizeNeeded = sizeof(EVENT_TRACE_PROPERTIES) +
    (SESSION_NAME_STRLEN * sizeof(TCHAR)) +
    (LOGFILE_NAME_STRLEN * sizeof(TCHAR));

  // Allocate memory for structure
  pTraceProps = reinterpret_cast<PEVENT_TRACE_PROPERTIES>(
    LocalAlloc(LPTR, ulSizeNeeded));

  RtlZeroMemory(pTraceProps, ulSizeNeeded);

  // Fill standard members
  pTraceProps->Wnode.BufferSize = ulSizeNeeded;
  pTraceProps->Wnode.Flags = WNODE_FLAG_TRACED_GUID;

  // Correctly specify the offsets for the variable length strings
  pTraceProps->LoggerNameOffset = sizeof(EVENT_TRACE_PROPERTIES);
```

```
pTraceProps->LogFileNameOffset =
  pTraceProps->LoggerNameOffset +
  (SESSION_NAME_STRLEN * sizeof(TCHAR));

// Copy Provider and Log file path
LPTSTR lpszLoggerName =
  ByteOffset(pTraceProps, pTraceProps->LoggerNameOffset);

LPTSTR lpszLogFileName =
  ByteOffset(pTraceProps, pTraceProps->LogFileNameOffset);

_tcsncpy(lpszLoggerName, lpszProvider, SESSION_NAME_STRLEN -1);
_tcsncpy(lpszLogFileName, lpszLogFile, LOGFILE_NAME_STRLEN -1);

return pTraceProps;
}
```

It should be obvious that the first few statements calculate the memory requirements, including enough room for the two strings tagged at the end of the structure. The size of the structure is recorded in the `Wnode.BufferSize` member. It is essential that the `Wnode.Flags` member contain the `WNODE_FLAG_TRACED_GUID` that indicates that the structure contains event-tracing information. The next step is to specify the string offsets correctly and copy the session name and log file path to the appropriate positions within the structure. The `LoggerNameOffset` member is set up only for "NT Kernel Logger" sessions because it is a special case, as you will see later. The `LoggerNameOffset` member should always be allocated enough memory because when the session's configuration and statistics are queried for, using `ControlTrace`, the `LoggerNameOffset` member will contain the session name.

To understand more about the statistics and configurations that are available for an event-tracing session, let's discuss the members of the `EVENT_TRACE_PROPERTIES` structure.

```
typedef struct _EVENT_TRACE_PROPERTIES {
  WNODE_HEADER Wnode;
//
// data provided by caller
  ULONG BufferSize;              // buffer size for logging (kbytes)
  ULONG MinimumBuffers;          // minimum to preallocate
  ULONG MaximumBuffers;          // maximum buffers allowed
  ULONG MaximumFileSize;         // maximum logfile size (in MBytes)
  ULONG LogFileMode;             // sequential, circular
  ULONG FlushTimer;              // buffer flush timer, in seconds
  ULONG EnableFlags;             // trace enable flags
  LONG AgeLimit;                 // age decay time, in minutes
```

```
    // data returned to caller
      ULONG NumberOfBuffers;            // no of buffers in use
      ULONG FreeBuffers;                // no of buffers free
      ULONG EventsLost;                 // event records lost
      ULONG BuffersWritten;             // no of buffers written to file
      ULONG LogBuffersLost;             // no of logfile write failures
      ULONG RealTimeBuffersLost;        // no of rt delivery failures
      HANDLE LoggerThreadId;            // thread id of Logger
      ULONG LogFileNameOffset;          // Offset to LogFileName
      ULONG LoggerNameOffset;           // Offset to LoggerName
    } EVENT_TRACE_PROPERTIES, *PEVENT_TRACE_PROPERTIES;
```

The `Wnode` member contains specific information about the `EVENT_TRACE_PROPERTIES` structure (for instance, its size).

All events delivered to an event-tracing session are held in nonpaged system memory buffers until they either are written to disk or are delivered to a real-time monitor. A minimum of four buffers is required, although this depends on the expected throughput of events. If a high throughput of events is expected, a combination of the minimum preallocated buffers, the maximum number of buffers, and the buffer size should be increased to prevent events from being lost. The number of preallocated buffers can be specified through the `MinimumBuffers` member. If a value less than four buffers is specified, Windows XP automatically ups it to the minimum requirements. The maximum number of allocated buffers can be specified through the `Maximum-Buffers` member. If the operating system finds that all the available allocated buffers are full, it automatically will allocate more buffers, up to the specified `MaximumBuffers`, to hold the undelivered events. If the maximum number of allocated buffers has been reached, events will be lost. If the `MaximumBuffers` member is zero, Windows XP will automatically calculate a minimum maximum default based on the buffer size and how much memory the machine has. The size of each buffer can be specified through the `BufferSize` member. The default buffer size for the NT Kernel Logger is 4KB; for other providers, it is 8KB. However, the buffer size can be set from 1KB to 1024KB. Both the `MinimumBuffers` and `MaximumBuffers` can be increased significantly, but this will depend on the size of the buffer (`BufferSize`) and how much memory the machine has.

To determine what really is happening with the session's buffer configuration, the `EVENT_TRACE_PROPERTIES` structure has `NumberOfBuffers`, `FreeBuffers`, and `Events-Lost` read-only members. The `NumberOfBuffers` member says how many buffers currently are allocated. This usually is less than configured `MaximumBuffers` but, if `NumberOfBuffers` reaches the same size as `MaximumBuffers`, then the minimum `Maxi-mumBuffers` might need reconsideration. To further determine if this is the case, check the `FreeBuffers`. This is the number of allocated buffers not currently in use that are ready for use in the session's buffer pool. If the `FreeBuffers` is near zero and `NumberOf-Buffers` is near `MaximumBuffers`, then the session's configuration needs reconsideration because there is danger of losing events. The most definite indicator that the buffer configuration is not large enough for the throughput of events is that `EventsLost` is anything greater than zero. If necessary, a session's buffer configuration can be updated while the session is still in progress. As with most software systems, there are periods when data throughput is high and when it is low. Event tracing behaves similarly, which is why the session buffer pool can be flexibly configured. When thousands of events can get delivered in just a few seconds, there is more need to make the buffer pool large enough so that no events are lost. When the event throughput returns to a low state, the unused allocated buffers are no longer required. The operating system automatically frees the unused buffers based on the `AgeLimit`. This is specified in minutes and if none (zero) is supplied, Windows XP defaults it to 15 minutes.

The `BuffersWritten` member tells how many buffers have been written to disk or have been delivered to a real-time monitor. Combined with the buffer size and the average size of an event, this can be a good indicator of how many events have been generated, saved, and processed. If problems occur in writing events to the log file, then the `LogBuffersLost` member will contain the number of buffers that were lost. Likewise, the `RealTimeBuffersLost` tells the number of buffers that could not be delivered in real time.

When configuring an event-tracing session to write to a log file, how often the buffers are scheduled to be flushed to disk can be specified through the `FlushTimer` member. This is specified in seconds. If zero, each buffer will be flushed when it becomes full. Setting the `FlushTimer` to one second may cause each buffer (even if not full) to be flushed to disk more frequently (every second) depending on the throughput of events.

Event-tracing sessions can be easily configured for managing the storage or delivery of events. Table 13.1 describes the flags that can be used when setting up the `LogFileMode` member.

Using the `EnableFlags` member is applicable only when using the NT Kernel Logger. Because of the very high throughput of events generated by the NT Kernel Logger, the `EnableFlags` member allows the precise specification of the kernel activities in which the session is interested. Table 13.2 describes the possible flags that can be combined.

When setting up the `EVENT_TRACE_PROPERTIES` structure to pass into a call to `StartTrace`, there are two ways in which you can specify the event-tracing provider. The first, which works only for the NT Kernel Logger, is to complete the string pointed to by `LoggerNameOffset` with `"NT Kernel Logger."` This combined with the `EnableFlags` set will automatically start a kernel session. The second approach involves specifying the globally unique identifier (GUID) of the event-tracing provider. All providers are uniquely identified by a GUID, which is sometimes referred to as the provider's control GUID. Specifying the provider's control GUID is necessary to start a session using any other event-tracing provider. Completing the `Wnode.Guid` member specifies

Table 13.1 LogFileMode Flags

LogFileMode **Flags**	**Comment**
EVENT_TRACE_FILE_MODE_APPEND (Windows XP only)	Append new events to an existing sequential log file. Do not use with EVENT_TRACE_REAL_TIME_MODE or EVENT_TRACE_FILE_MODE_CIRCULAR.
EVENT_TRACE_FILE_MODE_CIRCULAR	Write events to a log file. When the file reaches the maximum size, the oldest events are replaced with newer events. Do not use with EVENT_TRACE_REAL_TIME_MODE or EVENT_TRACE_FILE_MODE_SEQUENTIAL.
EVENT_TRACE_FILE_MODE_NEWFILE (Windows XP only)	Automatically switches to a new log file when the file reaches the maximum size. The specified file name must be a formatted string (i.e., it must contain a %d). Each time a new file is created, a counter is incremented and its value is used. The formatted string is used as the file name. Do not use with EVENT_TRACE_FILE_MODE_CIRCULAR.
EVENT_TRACE_FILE_MODE_PREALLOCATE (Windows XP only)	When a session is created with StartTrace, the log file is extended to the MaximumFileSize. The file occupies the entire space during logging, for both circular and sequential log files. When the session is stopped, the log file is reduced to the size needed. This flag is useful if there is concern about running out of disk space during the session.
EVENT_TRACE_FILE_MODE_SEQUENTIAL	Write events to a log file sequentially. Stop when the file reaches the maximum size. Do not use with EVENT_TRACE_FILE_MODE_CIRCULAR.
EVENT_TRACE_REAL_TIME_MODE	Deliver the events to consumers in real time. Do not use with EVENT_TRACE_FILE_MODE_CIRCULAR or EVENT_TRACE_FILE_MODE_SEQUENTIAL.

Table 13.1 *Continued*

LogFileMode **Flags**	**Comment**
EVENT_TRACE_RELOG_MODE (Windows XP only)	Logs the event without including EVENT_TRACE_HEADER. The logger was started to relog one or more existing log files to a new log file. Therefore, the variable portion of the relogged event already has a header from the old log file.
EVENT_TRACE_USE_GLOBAL_SEQUENCE (Windows XP only)	Use sequence numbers that are unique across event-tracing sessions. See TraceMessage for usage details.
EVENT_TRACE_USE_LOCAL_SEQUENCE (Windows XP only)	Use sequence numbers that are unique only for an individual event-tracing session. See TraceMessage for usage details.
EVENT_TRACE_USE_PAGED_MEMORY (Windows XP only)	Use paged memory. This setting is recommended so that events do not use up the nonpaged system memory.
EVENT_TRACE_PRIVATE_LOGGER_MODE	A private event-tracing session is a user-mode event-tracing session that runs in the same process as its event trace provider. This will be discussed in more detail later in the chapter.

Table 13.2 EnableFlags Flags

EnableFlags **Flags**	**Comment**
EVENT_TRACE_FLAG_DISK_FILE_IO	File I/O events.
EVENT_TRACE_FLAG_DISK_IO	Physical disk I/O events.
EVENT_TRACE_FLAG_IMAGE_LOAD	Image load events.
EVENT_TRACE_FLAG_MEMORY_HARD_FAULTS	Hard page fault events.
EVENT_TRACE_FLAG_MEMORY_PAGE_FAULTS	All page fault events.
EVENT_TRACE_FLAG_NETWORK_TCPIP	TCP/UDP events.
EVENT_TRACE_FLAG_PROCESS	Process events.
EVENT_TRACE_FLAG_THREAD	Thread events.
EVENT_TRACE_FLAG_REGISTRY	Registry access events.
EVENT_TRACE_FLAG_DBGPRINT	DbgPrint(ex) calls.

the provider's control GUID and also makes the string pointed to by `LoggerNameOff-set` redundant. The kernel provider can be specified using either of these two approaches. If using the latter approach to start a kernel session, ensure that the `Wnode.Guid` member contains `SystemTraceControlGuid`.[2] If the session is configured to store the event trace in a log file, the string pointed to by `LogFileNameOffset` specifies the file path. This, obviously, is not required when monitoring events in real time.

The `LoggerThreadId` member contains the thread identifier of the event-tracing session.

The header for the `EVENT_TRACE_PROPERTIES` structure (accessed through `Wnode`) uses a `WNODE_HEADER` structure. Let's have a look:

```
typedef struct _WNODE_HEADER
{
  ULONG BufferSize;       // Size of buffer inclusive of this ULONG
  ULONG ProviderId;       // Provider Id of driver returning this buffer
  union
  {
    ULONG64 HistoricalContext;    // Logger use
    struct
    {
      ULONG Version;              // Reserved
      ULONG Linkage;              // Linkage field reserved for WMI
    };
  };

  union
  {
    ULONG CountLost;              // Reserved
    HANDLE KernelHandle;          // Kernel handle for data block
    LARGE_INTEGER TimeStamp;      // Timestamp as returned in units of
                                  // 100ns since 1/1/1601
  };
  GUID Guid;              // Guid for data block returned with results
  ULONG ClientContext;
  ULONG Flags;
} WNODE_HEADER, *PWNODE_HEADER;
```

The size of the entire `EVENT_TRACE_PROPERTIES` structure (including the two variable length strings) is recorded in the `BufferSize` member. This must be set up soon after the `EVENT_TRACE_PROPERTIES` structure has been created.

If access to the session's `TRACEHANDLE` is not available, you can query for it using `ControlTrace`. The `StopEventTracing` code sample later in the chapter will explain

---

2. `SystemTraceControlGuid` is defined in `evntrace.h`.

more about this, but for now, we just want to highlight that the `HistoricalContext` member can contain the `TRACEHANDLE` of a session when it is queried.

The `Guid` member, as described earlier, contains the event-tracing provider's control GUID. The `TimeStamp` member is not used by the `EVENT_TRACE_PROPERTIES` structure. The `Flags` member must be set to `WNODE_FLAG_TRACED_GUID`, which says that this structure contains event-tracing information.

Querying the Session's Configuration and Statistics

If you care deeply about the state of a session while it is in progress, you can use `ControlTrace` to query its statistics. This is useful in determining whether any events are lost or simply to see how many buffers have been written. Combined with other configurations, this can give an indication of event throughput. Let's look at a code sample that outputs all of the available configurations and statistics for an NT Kernel Logger session:

```
void QueryEventTracing()
{
  // Setup the Event Tracing session properties
  PEVENT_TRACE_PROPERTIES pTraceProps = MakeTraceProperties();

  // We can also perform a query without a session handle
  ULONG ulError = ControlTrace(NULL, _T("NT Kernel Logger"),
    pTraceProps,
    EVENT_TRACE_CONTROL_QUERY);

  _tprintf(_T("\nQuerying 'NT Kernel Logger'\n\n"));

  _tprintf(_T("\t*Read-only properties\n"));
  _tprintf(_T("\t\tEvents lost %d\n"), pTraceProps->EventsLost);
  _tprintf(_T("\t\tFree buffers %d\n"), pTraceProps->FreeBuffers);
  _tprintf(_T("\t\tLog buffers lost %d\n"), pTraceProps->LogBuffersLost);
  _tprintf(_T("\t\tLogger thread ID %d\n"), pTraceProps->LoggerThreadId);
  _tprintf(_T("\t\tNumber of buffers %d\n"), pTraceProps-
    >NumberOfBuffers);
  _tprintf(_T("\t\tBuffers written %d\n"), pTraceProps->BuffersWritten);
  _tprintf(_T("\t\tProvider ID %d\n"), pTraceProps->Wnode.ProviderId);
  _tprintf(_T("\t\tReal-time buffers lost %d\n"),
    pTraceProps->RealTimeBuffersLost);
  _tprintf(_T("\t\tTrace flags %d\n"), pTraceProps->Wnode.Flags);
  _tprintf(_T("\t\tTrace session handle %d\n"),
    pTraceProps->Wnode.HistoricalContext);

  // Read/write properties
  _tprintf(_T("\n\t*Read/Write properties\n"));
  _tprintf(_T("\t\tAge limit (minutes) %d\n"), pTraceProps->AgeLimit);
```

```
_tprintf(_T("\t\tBuffer size (KB) %d\n"), pTraceProps->BufferSize);
_tprintf(_T("\t\tFlush timer (seconds) %d\n"), pTraceProps-
  >FlushTimer);
_tprintf(_T("\t\tLogger name %s\n"), ByteOffset(pTraceProps,
  pTraceProps->LoggerNameOffset));
_tprintf(_T("\t\tLog file path %s\n"), ByteOffset(pTraceProps,
  pTraceProps->LogFileNameOffset));
_tprintf(_T("\t\tMaximum buffers %d\n"), pTraceProps->MaximumBuffers);
_tprintf(_T("\t\tMaximum log file size (MB) %d\n"),
  pTraceProps->MaximumFileSize);
_tprintf(_T("\t\tMinimum buffers %d\n"), pTraceProps->MinimumBuffers);
_tprintf(_T("\t\tProvider GUID %ls\n"),
  CComBSTR(pTraceProps->Wnode.Guid));
_tprintf(_T("\t\tTrace log mode %d\n\n"), pTraceProps->LogFileMode);


LocalFree(pTraceProps);
}
```

Once again, the first task is to create an EVENT_TRACE_PROPERTIES structure with
MakeTraceProperties. The next call to ControlTrace queries the NT Kernel Logger
session for its configuration and statistics. The rest of the code sample merely prints
the details of each member of the structure. Here is the output:

```
Querying 'NT Kernel Logger'

  *Read-only properties
   Events lost 1680
   Free buffers 24
   Log buffers lost 0
   Logger thread ID 2364
   Number of buffers 27
   Buffers written 112
   Provider ID 0
   Real-time buffers lost 0
   Trace flags 0
   Trace session handle 65535

  *Read/Write properties
   Age limit (minutes) 15
   Buffer size (KB) 4
   Flush timer (seconds) 0
   Logger name NT Kernel Logger
   Log file path C:\MyEventTrace.etl
   Maximum buffers 26
   Maximum log file size (MB) 0
   Minimum buffers 4
   Provider GUID {9E814AAD-3204-11D2-9A82-006008A86939}
   Trace log mode 513
```

The QueryEventTracing function used ControlTrace in a way that did not require a TRACEHANDLE. To discuss this further, let's look at the ControlTrace declaration:

```
ULONG ControlTrace(TRACEHANDLE TraceHandle, LPCWSTR InstanceName,
    PEVENT_TRACE_PROPERTIES Properties, ULONG ControlCode);
```

If a TRACEHANDLE is available, it should be used to perform one of the actions specified by the ControlCode parameter. If the TRACEHANDLE is passed through the TraceHandle parameter, the InstanceName parameter should be set to NULL. TraceHandle and InstanceName should not be used at the same time. If a TRACEHANDLE is not available, then the session name must be specified through the InstanceName parameter: This should be the same session name that was supplied in the call to StartTrace. Note that using the session's name will cause ControlTrace to acquire TRACEHANDLE internally, which will add a very small performance loss. Given that most of the time this is a reasonably rare operation, it won't make a lot of difference because these functions are highly efficient and super fast.

Regardless of the operation specified in ControlCode, the Properties parameter will always return the most recent configuration and statistics for the session. The ControlCode can be only one of the actions in Table 13.3.

To update or change a session's configuration, you should perform a query, make the appropriate alteration, and then update the session.

Calling ControlTrace using the EVENT_TRACE_CONTROL_QUERY action[3] will query the current statistics for a specific session. To update a session's operating parameters, call ControlTrace using the EVENT_TRACE_CONTROL_UPDATE action. Finally, to programmatically force the event tracer to flush the currently active buffer, use the EVENT_TRACE_CONTROL_FLUSH action to call ControlTrace.

Stopping the Session

When you decide that the session no longer needs to be active, you should stop it. The most common among a number of reasons for stopping a session is that the application

Table 13.3 ControlCode Flags

ControlCode **Flags**	**Comment**
EVENT_TRACE_CONTROL_QUERY	Retrieves only session configuration and statistics.
EVENT_TRACE_CONTROL_STOP	Stops the session.
EVENT_TRACE_CONTROL_UPDATE	Updates the session's configuration.
EVENT_TRACE_CONTROL_FLUSH	Flushes the session's active buffers. For Windows XP only.

---

3. Note that QueryTrace, UpdateTrace, and FlushTrace have been superseded by ControlTrace.

no longer requires a debug trace or that the real-time monitor application has been closed. The next code sample demonstrates how to stop a session, as well as how the TRACEHANDLE for a specific session can be reacquired. Let's have a look:

```
void StopEventTracing()
{
  // Setup the Event Tracing session properties
  PEVENT_TRACE_PROPERTIES pTraceProps = MakeTraceProperties();

  // We can get the session handle by performing a query
  ULONG ulError = ControlTrace(NULL, _T("NT Kernel Logger"),
    pTraceProps,
    EVENT_TRACE_CONTROL_QUERY);

  // Get the session handle
  TRACEHANDLE hTraceSession =
    TRACEHANDLE(pTraceProps->Wnode.HistoricalContext);

  // Stop the session.
  ulError = ControlTrace(hTraceSession, NULL, pTraceProps,
    EVENT_TRACE_CONTROL_STOP);

  LocalFree(pTraceProps);
}
```

After the EVENT_TRACE_PROPERTIES structure has been created and initialized, the next step demonstrates how to reacquire the TRACEHANDLE. First, query for the session's configuration using ControlTrace and extract the TRACEHANDLE from it through the Wnode.HistoricalContext member. The next call to ControlTrace uses the newly acquired TRACEHANDLE and stops the session by using the EVENT_TRACE_CONTROL_STOP action. StopTrace can also be used to stop a session; however, it has been superseded by ControlTrace.

Starting Event-Tracing Sessions

All of the code samples so far have demonstrated how to start, query, update, and stop the kernel event-tracing session. Starting a kernel session is a special case and starting a session for other providers is slightly different. First, other providers cannot be referenced by a name in the way the NT Kernel Logger can. A GUID must be specified to reference the provider that must be started. In the following code sample, we shall start a session to report events for the Domain Name Service: Its provider's control GUID is 1540ff4c-3fd7-4bba-9938-1d1bf31573a7. Second, the provider has to be enabled for it to start tracing events. Let's have a look:

```
void StartEventTracingProvider()
{
```

```
// Guid for DNS provider {1540ff4c-3fd7-4bba-9938-1d1bf31573a7}
GUID DNS_EVENTTRACER =
{ 0x1540ff4c, 0x3fd7, 0x4bba, { 0x99, 0x38, 0x1d, 0x1b, 0xf3, 0x15,
  0x73, 0xa7 } };


// Setup the Event Tracing session properties
PEVENT_TRACE_PROPERTIES pTraceProps =
  MakeTraceProperties(_T(""), _T("C:\\MyEventTraceProvider.etl"));


// Setup session to start the following event tracing provider
pTraceProps->Wnode.Guid = DNS_EVENTTRACER;


// This tells the Event Tracer to log to a file sequentially
pTraceProps->LogFileMode |= EVENT_TRACE_FILE_MODE_SEQUENTIAL;


// Start the session.
TRACEHANDLE hTraceSession = 0;
ULONG ulError = StartTrace(&hTraceSession, _T("My DNS Session"),
  pTraceProps);


// Normal providers must be enabled to get events
ulError = EnableTrace(TRUE, 0, 0, &DNS_EVENTTRACER, hTraceSession);


LocalFree(pTraceProps);
}
```

In the code sample, we have marked the differences between starting the NT Kernel Logger and other providers in bold font. First, we declare the provider's control GUID (DNS_EVENTTRACER). Next, we specify the control GUID in the Wnode.Guid member of the EVENT_TRACE_PROPERTIES structure. Finally, we start the provider emitting the required events using EnableTrace. Let's have a look at EnableTrace in more detail.

```
ULONG EnableTrace(ULONG Enable, ULONG EnableFlag, ULONG EnableLevel,
  LPCGUID ControlGuid, TRACEHANDLE TraceHandle);
```

As we shall discuss later, EnableTrace ends up calling the provider's control function, which is registered when the provider initializes and registers its GUID with the operating system's event tracer. This ultimately means that the provider defines the interpretation Enable, EnableFlag, and EnableLevel parameters. All providers should interpret Enable as either TRUE (to start emitting events) or FALSE (to stop emitting events). The EnableFlag parameter can specify the type of events the provider should produce. This can be a similarly defined set of bit-mask flags such as those used to enable the various event traces from the kernel. However, many providers may not publish their enabled flags, so good providers should always treat a value of zero as meaning all traces. The EnableLevel parameter is the detail level of the events produced by the provider. A provider can define its detail level from 0 to 255, and the interpretation of this value is user defined.

The ControlGuid parameter specifies the provider's control GUID and the session handle is passed through the TraceHandle parameter.

Querying for Active Event-Tracing Sessions

From time to time, it is useful to determine the event-tracing sessions that currently are running on a machine. A maximum of 32 sessions is allowed, of which 3 are reserved by the operating system, leaving 29 sessions available. To query for all active sessions requires a call to QueryAllTraces. Let's have a look:

```
void QueryAllEventTraces()
{
  // Max 32 Event Tracing sessions
  PEVENT_TRACE_PROPERTIES parProps[MAX_TRACESESSIONS];

  for (int nIndex = 0; nIndex < MAX_TRACESESSIONS; nIndex++)
  {
    // Setup the Event Tracing session properties
    parProps[nIndex] = MakeTraceProperties(_T(""), _T(""));
  }

  ULONG ulNumOfTraceSessions = 0;
  ULONG ulRetVal = QueryAllTraces(parProps, MAX_TRACESESSIONS,
    &ulNumOfTraceSessions);

  _tprintf(_T("\nCurrently active sessions\n\n"));

  for (nIndex = 0; nIndex < ulNumOfTraceSessions; nIndex++)
  {
    // Display basic details
    _tprintf(_T("\t%s - %s\n"),
      ByteOffset(parProps[nIndex], parProps[nIndex]->LoggerNameOffset),
      ByteOffset(parProps[nIndex], parProps[nIndex]->LogFileNameOffset));
  }

  // Free memory
  for (nIndex = 0; nIndex < MAX_TRACESESSIONS; nIndex++)
    LocalFree(parProps[nIndex]);
}
```

The first task we perform in the code sample is to create an array of 32 EVENT_ TRACE_PROPERTIES structures. This is large enough to retrieve all the configuration and statistics for all the sessions. The call to QueryAllTraces returns the number of sessions that are active: These are listed and output to the console. The only detail we display is the name of the session and the log file path. Here is an example output:

```
Currently active sessions

   NT Kernel Logger - C:\MyEventTrace.etl
```

The `QueryAllTraces` function is quite simple:

```
ULONG QueryAllTraces(PEVENT_TRACE_PROPERTIES *PropertyArray,
  ULONG PropertyArrayCount, PULONG LoggerCount);
```

The `PropertyArray` parameter is an array of pointers to `EVENT_TRACE_PROPERTIES` structures that will hold the configuration and statistics of each active session. The `PropertyArrayCount` is the number of elements allocated in `PropertyArray`. Finally, the number of active session details in the properties array is returned by `LoggerCount`.

Querying for Registered Event-Tracing Providers

When starting a session for an event-tracing provider, it is important to ensure that the provider currently is running before starting the session. Unfortunately, `StartTrac` and `EnableTrace` do not report an error if the provider is not running currently. This gives the impression that the session is running happily when, in reality, it is not. However, sessions that have been started without the provider being loaded are valid, because when the provider loads and registers itself with the event tracer, the event tracer will attempt automatically to enable the provider so that it will generate the required event traces. When a provider loads, it calls `RegisterTraceGuids` to register with the operating system's event tracer. When a provider closes or exits, it calls `UnregisterTraceGuids` to remove its control GUID from the event tracer's internal active GUID list. If you want to identify whether the provider you're starting is currently registered, you can call `EnumerateTraceGuids` (available only under Windows XP and later). Let's have a look:

```
void QueryRegisteredTraceGuids()
{
  // Array for 128 registered GUIDs, although this can be higher
  PTRACE_GUID_PROPERTIES parProps[MAX_TRACEGUIDS];

  for (int nIndex = 0; nIndex < MAX_TRACEGUIDS; nIndex++)
  {
    // Setup the registered GUID properties
    parProps[nIndex] = reinterpret_cast<PTRACE_GUID_PROPERTIES>(
      LocalAlloc(LPTR, sizeof(TRACE_GUID_PROPERTIES)));
```

```
        ZeroMemory(parProps[nIndex], sizeof(TRACE_GUID_PROPERTIES));
}


// Get list of registered GUIDs
ULONG ulGuidCount = 0;
ULONG ulError = EnumerateTraceGuids(parProps, MAX_TRACEGUIDS,
  &ulGuidCount);
_tprintf(_T("\n%d Currently registered GUIDs\n\n"), ulGuidCount);
_tprintf(_T("\t<       GUID       > \tGuid Type\n"));
_tprintf(_T("\t\tIsEnabled \tEnableFlags \tEnableLevel \tLoggerID\n"));
_tprintf(_T("\n\t---------------\n\n"));

for (nIndex = 0; nIndex < ulGuidCount; nIndex++)
{
  // Display details
  _tprintf(_T("\t%ls \t%s \n\t\t%s \t\t%d \t\t%d \t\t%d\n\n"),
    CComBSTR(parProps[nIndex]->Guid),
    parProps[nIndex]->GuidType == 0 ? _T("Provider") : _T("Event"),
    parProps[nIndex]->IsEnable == 1 ? _T("True") : _T("False"),
    parProps[nIndex]->EnableFlags, parProps[nIndex]->EnableLevel,
    parProps[nIndex]->LoggerId);
}


// Free memory
for (nIndex = 0; nIndex < MAX_TRACEGUIDS; nIndex++)
  LocalFree(parProps[nIndex]);
}
```

Details of each registered provider or event class are supplied through a TRACE_GUID_PROPERTIES structure. The EnumerateTraceGuids function requires an array of TRACE_GUID_PROPERTIES pointers large enough to retrieve all the registration information. This becomes the first task in the code sample we just now examined. We made up a theoretical maximum of 128 registered elements (identified through MAX_TRACEGUIDS). However, this can be higher when more software uses the event-tracing system. After EnumerateTraceGuids is called, the details of each registration are output to the console.

Let's examine the TRACE_GUID_PROPERTIES structure in detail:

```
typedef struct _TRACE_GUID_PROPERTIES {
  GUID      Guid;
  ULONG     GuidType;
  ULONG     LoggerId;
  ULONG     EnableLevel;
  ULONG     EnableFlags;
  BOOLEAN   IsEnable;
} TRACE_GUID_PROPERTIES, *PTRACE_GUID_PROPERTIES;
```

The `Guid` member contains the event-tracing GUID registration referenced by `GuidType`. Currently, the event-tracing system supports two types of GUID registrations: providers and events. If the `GuidType` member contains 0, then the registration details (`LoggerId`, `EnableLevel`, `EnableFlags`, and `IsEnable`) are for a provider. If `GuidType` contains 1, it identifies an event class registration. Unfortunately, the current event-tracing implementation in Windows XP does not provide the event class registrations.

The `LoggerId` member contains the thread identifier of the event-tracing session. The current state of each provider is supplied through `EnableLevel`, `EnableFlags`, and `IsEnable` members. The `LoggerId` member is valid only if `IsEnable` is TRUE.

Executing the `QueryRegisteredTraceGuids` function produces the following output:

```
22 Currently registered GUIDs

    <                 GUID              >   Guid Type
         IsEnabled         EnableFlags       EnableLevel      LoggerID


    ----------------------------------------------------------------

    {8D316658-850B-4A3E-B79D-0F300A80EF5B}    Provider
         True              0                 0                3

    {196E57D9-49C0-4B3B-AC3A-A8A93ADA1938}    Provider
         False             0                 0                0
    . ... .. .
    ... ...
    .. .

    {1B1D4FF4-F27B-4C99-8BD7-DA8F1A74051A}    Provider
         True              0                 0                2

    {F33959B4-DBEC-11D2-895B-00C04F79AB69}    Provider
         False             0                 0                0
    .. .. ... .
    ... . ...
    ... .

    {58DB8E03-0537-45CB-B29B-597F6CBEBBFD}    Provider
         False             0                 0                0
```

Although we have shortened the above output, it does show that two providers are involved in event-tracing sessions and that the rest of the registrations are not enabled for any event-tracing sessions.

Calling the `EnumerateTraceGuids` function is quite simple:

```
ULONG EnumerateTraceGuids(PTRACE_GUID_PROPERTIES *GuidPropertiesArray,
    ULONG PropertyArrayCount, PULONG GuidCount);
```

The `GuidPropertiesArray` parameter is an array of pointers to `TRACE_GUID_PROPERTIES` structures that will hold the provider and event registration details. The `Property-ArrayCount` is the number of elements allocated in `GuidPropertiesArray`. Finally, the number of registered provider and event GUIDs is returned by `GuidCount`. If the supplied array is too small, `EnumerateTraceGuids` will return `ERROR_MORE_DATA` and a larger array should be allocated. Note that the registration details for the kernel provider are not listed in the `GuidPropertiesArray` out-parameter. This is because the kernel provider is a special case with a reserved session, named "NT Kernel Logger".

Out of the 22 event-tracing providers in Windows XP, details for only eight providers have been published (check Table 13.4).

Starting Private Event-Tracing Sessions

So far we've discussed starting kernel and normal sessions. The differences between these types of sessions are quite small. The only real difference is that normal sessions require the provider's control GUID and an additional call to `EnableTrace` to start generating events. There is another way to initiate a normal session: a private session. Before we delve into this, let's reevaluate `StartTrace`.

Whether for a kernel or a normal session, `StartTrace` sets up a thread that manages and dumps the session's buffers either to a log file or to a real-time monitoring application. The `LoggerThreadId` member of the `EVENT_TRACE_PROPERTIES` structure contains the thread identifier that `StartTrace` sets up. Figure 13.3 shows this.

Table 13.4 Published Event-Tracing Providers

Event-tracing Provider GUID	Comment
{9e814aad-3204-11d2-9a82-006008a86939}	NT Kernel Logger
{1540FF4C-3FD7-4BBA-9938-1D1BF31573A7}	Domain Name Service (DNS)
{94A984EF-F525-4BF1-BE3C-EF374056A592}	Windows Print Spooler
{F33959B4-DBEC-11D2-895B-00C04F79AB69}	Active Directory—Net Log-on
{CC85922F-DB41-11D2-9244-006008269001}	Local Security Authority
{C92CF544-91B3-4DC0-8E11-C580339A0BF8}	NTLM Security Protocol
{BBA3ADD2-C229-4CDB-AE2B-57EB6966B0C4}	Active Directory—Kerberos
{DAB01D4D-2D48-477D-B1C3-DAAD0CE6F06B}	Advanced Configuration and Power Interface (ACPI)

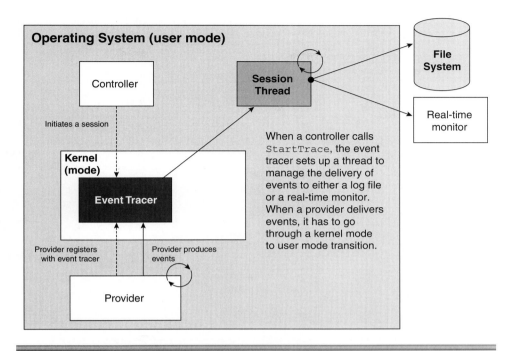

Figure 13.3 Starting a kernel or normal session

The advantage of this solution is that a provider publishes the events only once but several sessions can be receiving the events in their buffers. Not only can the events be logged to a file, but another session also can be monitoring the same event trace actively at the same time. The disadvantages include that only a maximum of 32 sessions can be active at one time and that the sessions have to pass through a kernel mode to a user-mode transition. The transition occurs when the user-mode provider delivers the event to the kernel, which is then delivered to the user-mode session thread. To overcome these disadvantages, an event-tracing controller can initiate a *private session*.

A private event-tracing session is a user-mode session that runs in the same process as its event trace provider. Private event-tracing sessions are less expensive because they avoid kernel mode to user mode transitions. However, they come with other limitations. A private session can record events only for the threads of the process in which it is running. There can be only one private session per process, and it cannot be used with any real-time delivery. Further, events generated by a private session do not include execution times in the event detail. If you can live with these limitations, then it is possible to have more than 32 actively executing sessions. The diagram in Figure 13.4 shows a private session.

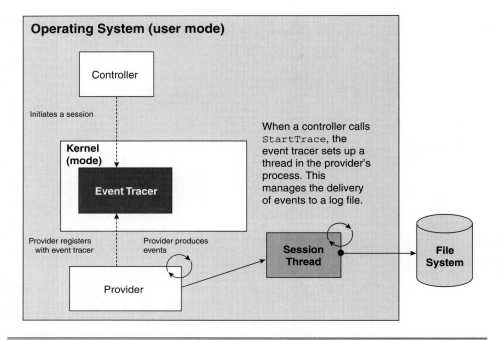

Figure 13.4 Starting a private session

The difference in starting a private event-tracing session is that you specify the EVENT_TRACE_PRIVATE_LOGGER_MODE flag and ensure that it is accompanied with one of the file logging options. The following code demonstrates:

```
// Setup the Event Tracing session properties
PEVENT_TRACE_PROPERTIES pTraceProps =
  MakeTraceProperties(_T(""), _T("C:\\MyPrivateEventTrace.etl"));

pTraceProps->Wnode.Guid = DNS_EVENTTRACER;

// This tells the Event Tracer to setup a private session and output
// logging to a file (sequentially)
pTraceProps->LogFileMode |= EVENT_TRACE_PRIVATE_LOGGER_MODE |
  EVENT_TRACE_FILE_MODE_SEQUENTIAL;

// Start the private session.
TRACEHANDLE hTraceSession = 0;
ULONG ulError = StartTrace(&hTraceSession, _T("My Private DNS Session"),
  pTraceProps);

ulError = EnableTrace(TRUE, 0, 0, &DNS_EVENTTRACER, hTraceSession);
```

When the private session's log file is created, the process's identifier is appended to the supplied file path. The file path in the code sample, when created, will look something like `C:\\MyPrivateEventTrace.etl_3788`.

Another perceived disadvantage is that `QueryAllTraces` cannot be used to find which private event-tracing sessions are currently active. However, calling `Enumerate-TraceGuids` will identify whether the provider currently is in a session.

■ Developing an Event-Tracing Provider

Before we cover analyzing event trace log files, it is important to know how the information is exposed from the provider. This will help you more easily to understand how to interpret the events.

When developing your own applications or components, seriously consider exposing event traces. Integrating the event-tracing technology into your applications is not hard. Some useful C++ templates accompany this book. As each application and component is instrumented with events traces, debugging problems will take you to new levels of analysis. You don't have to instrument all of your applications at once, but as each new component is developed, integrate the event-tracing technology even if you have to coexist with other debugging mechanisms that might already be employed for your project. Over time, you'll be able to better analyze problems with other subsystems for which you have no control, such as the kernel and the Windows XP security subsystems.

The first step in making an application or component an event-tracing provider is to define the events (schema) that you want to trace. To discuss how to instrument an application, we shall develop a very simple lift simulator. The lift will travel between floors 0 to 9 and once in a while will complain about having some fault. Three event classes are involved to instrument this problem domain briefly:

1. An event to describe when the lift is going up
2. An event to describe when the lift is going down
3. An event to expose the nature of the fault

The screen shot in Figure 13.5 shows the lift simulator provider in action.[4] You can easily see that when the lift starts to go down, it is marked with a *start* event. Also, its event details provide more detail of where the lift is and where it is going. After the lift has started to travel (that is, when it is in progress), *checkpoint* events mark when it

---

4. The screen shot is taken from an application that Gwyn Cole developed to analyze event traces and control event-tracing sessions. It can be found on the Web site that accompanies this book.

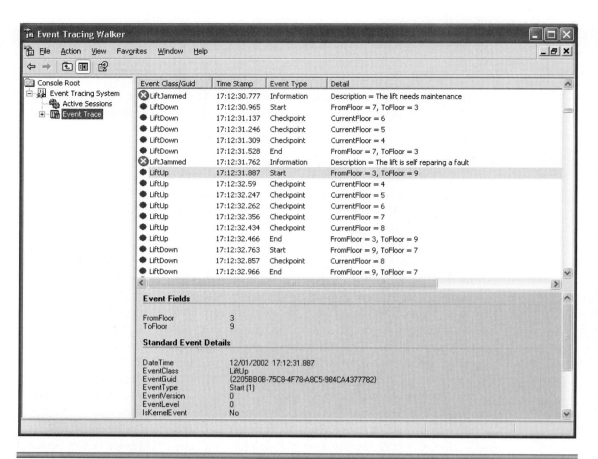

Figure 13.5 Lift Simulator event trace

passes each floor. Notice that the event is still classified as a LiftDown event class; however, its event details are different from the start event. This is because the interpretation of the event details is not only dependent on the event class but also on the version of the event and the event type. The flexibility of an event type allows much more freedom to add new tracing to an already existing event class because all that is required is to define a new event type and its associated details structure. If the details of an existing event type change, you should update the event version for the whole event class. Finally, when the lift stops, it is marked with a *stop* event. The start and stop events use identical detail structures even though they use different event types. The *start, stop,* and *checkpoint* are standard event types; a few others also are defined in `evntrace.h`. We shall discuss the standard event types later in the chapter.

Defining the Event Class Schema

All events use a standard structure called EVENT_TRACE_HEADER that describes common details for every event. However, for most applications, an event without user-defined detail doesn't provide any real benefit. Fortunately, each event can have its own customized data tagged on at the end of the EVENT_TRACE_HEADER structure. Defining your own schema thus simply becomes a task to define some structures. Let's start with the structure that describes the detail for *start* and *stop* event types.

```
typedef struct tagLIFTSIM_UP_DOWN
{
  LONG lFromFloor;
  LONG lToFloor;
} *PLIFTSIM_UP_DOWN, LIFTSIM_UP_DOWN;
```

It is as simple as that! All that is left is to tag the LIFTSIM_UP_DOWN structure to the end of the EVENT_TRACE_HEADER structure, like this:

```
typedef struct tagEVENT_LIFTSIM_UP_DOWN
{
  EVENT_TRACE_HEADER Header;
  LIFTSIM_UP_DOWN Data;
} *PEVENT_LIFTSIM_UP_DOWN, EVENT_LIFTSIM_UP_DOWN;
```

We've now defined an event that can be used in our event-tracing provider. However, this is only for two of the three event types in our event class schema: start and stop. The reason that the LIFTSIM_UP_DOWN structure is defined separately is to make it easier to reuse and cast the event details when performing analysis in an event-tracing consumer (covered later). The checkpoint event type has a different structure. Here is its definition:

```
typedef struct tagLIFTSIM_MOVINGFLOOR
{
  LONG lCurrentFloor;
} *PLIFTSIM_MOVINGFLOOR, LIFTSIM_MOVINGFLOOR;
```

```
typedef struct tagEVENT_LIFTSIM_MOVINGFLOOR
{
  EVENT_TRACE_HEADER Header;
  LIFTSIM_MOVINGFLOOR Data;
} *PEVENT_LIFTSIM_MOVINGFLOOR, EVENT_LIFTSIM_MOVINGFLOOR;
```

Before we can use these structures, we shall need to register the application as an event-tracing provider, which requires both the registration of the provider and its supported event classes. All event-tracing providers have a control GUID because this is how the operating system's event tracer communicates with the provider. Here is this application's control GUID. Note that you would generate a new GUID for your application or component.

```
// {8D316659-850B-4a3e-B79D-0F300A80EF5B}
static const GUID PROVGUID_LIFTSIM =
{0x8d316659, 0x850b, 0x4a3e, {0xb7, 0x9d, 0xf, 0x30, 0xa, 0x80, 0xef,
0x5b}};
```

Next, the GUIDs to uniquely identify events also must be defined. Every event class that you wish to define must have its own GUID. Here are the GUID declarations for the `LiftUp`, `LiftDown`, and `LiftJammed` classes:

```
// {2205BB0B-75C8-4f78-A8C5-984CA4377782}
static const GUID LIFTSIM_UP =
{0x2205bb0b, 0x75c8, 0x4f78, {0xa8, 0xc5, 0x98, 0x4c, 0xa4, 0x37, 0x77,
0x82}};
```

```
// {2205BB0C-75C8-4f78-A8C5-984CA4377782}
static const GUID LIFTSIM_DOWN =
{0x2205bb0c, 0x75c8, 0x4f78, {0xa8, 0xc5, 0x98, 0x4c, 0xa4, 0x37, 0x77,
0x82}};
```

```
// {2205BB0D-75C8-4f78-A8C5-984CA4377782}
static const GUID LIFTSIM_JAMMED =
{0x2205bb0d, 0x75c8, 0x4f78, {0xa8, 0xc5, 0x98, 0x4c, 0xa4, 0x37, 0x77,
0x82}};
```

Registering an Application as an Event-Tracing Provider

Because the lift simulator is a simple application, its implementation is an excellent example for visualizing what is required to register and emit events. Here is the `main` function, which registers itself as an event-tracing provider and goes on to wait for the instruction to generate its events:

```
extern "C" int _tmain()
{
  // Initialise global variables
  g_hProvider = 0;
  g_dwEnableLevel = 0;
  g_dwEnableFlags = 0;
  g_bTracerActive = false;

  g_lCurrentFloor = 0;
```

```
        // Include event class registration GUIDs
        TRACE_GUID_REGISTRATION tgrEventClasses[3];
        ZeroMemory(tgrEventClasses, sizeof(tgrEventClasses));

        // The three event classes this provider supports
        tgrEventClasses[0].Guid = &LIFTSIM_UP;
        tgrEventClasses[1].Guid = &LIFTSIM_DOWN;
        tgrEventClasses[2].Guid = &LIFTSIM_JAMMED;

        // Register this application as an event-tracing provider
        TRACEHANDLE hRegProvider = 0;
        ULONG ulReg = RegisterTraceGuids(ControlCallback, NULL,
          (LPCGUID)&PROVGUID_LIFTSIM, 3, tgrEventClasses,
          NULL, NULL, &hRegProvider);

        while ( <some condition > )
        {
          if (g_bTracerActive)
          {
            // Emit the lift simulated events
            ProvideEvents();
          }
        }

        // We're finished, remove this as an event-tracing provider from the
        // OS event tracer's internal registered provider list
        ulReg = UnregisterTraceGuids(hRegProvider);

        return 0;
    }
```

The `main` function starts off by initializing some global variables. The global variables will be set by the provider's control call-back function, `ControlCallback`. The `g_hProvider` variable stores the provider's `TRACEHANDLE`. Access to the provider's `TRACEHANDLE` is required if the application wants to produce events. The `g_dwEnableLevel` and `g_dwEnableFlags` variables allow other code in the application to determine what events it should produce. The `g_bTracerActive` variable determines whether or not the application starts generating events. The `g_lCurrentFloor` variable keeps track of the current floor that the simulator is on.

As briefly mentioned, the provider registration also must include the event classes for which it will be generating events. This is specified through an array of `TRACE_GUID_REGISTRATION` structures. Each element in the array represents a single event class. This, together with the applications path and the control call-back function, must be supplied to `RegisterTraceGuids`. After the call to `RegisterTraceGuids`, the application awaits the instruction to start producing events from an event-tracing controller (that is, through `StartTrace` and `EnableTrace`). When the application closes, it must call `UnregisterTraceGuids` to inform the operating system's event tracer that it is going away and will no longer be a registered provider.

Let's take a closer look at the `TRACE_GUID_REGISTRATION` structure:

```
typedef struct _TRACE_GUID_REGISTRATION {
    LPCGUID Guid;        // Guid of data block being registered or updated.
    HANDLE RegHandle;   // Guid Registration Handle is returned.
} TRACE_GUID_REGISTRATION, *PTRACE_GUID_REGISTRATION;
```

Before passing the structure to `RegisterTraceGuids`, the `Guid` member must be set. All event classes are referenced by a GUID; thus, no other details about the class are required. When `RegisterTraceGuids` returns, it populates the `RegHandle` member with a handle that can be used for calls to `CreateTraceInstanceId` and `TraceEventInstance`. These event-tracing calls are for producing hierarchical events (covered later).

Without calling `RegisterTraceGuids`, an application cannot become an event-tracing provider, so let's look at this function in more detail:

```
ULONG RegisterTraceGuids(WMIDPREQUEST RequestAddress, PVOID
RequestContext,
    LPCGUID ControlGuid, ULONG GuidCount,
    PTRACE_GUID_REGISTRATION TraceGuidReg, LPCSTR MofImagePath,
    LPCSTR MofResourceName, PTRACEHANDLE RegistrationHandle);
```

For the operating system's event tracer to communicate with the provider, the provider must supply a call-back function through `RequestAddress`. This primarily will be called from the event tracer but usually will be triggered as a result of an event-tracing controller calling `EnableTrace`. The `RequestContext` parameter is a user-defined value that will get passed to the `RequestAddress` function. In a C++ application, this parameter could be the address of a C++ object or some other user-defined cookie value.

The provider's GUID is passed through the `ControlGuid` parameter and the number of event class registrations referenced by `GuidCount` is passed in the `TraceGuidReg` array. The definition of event classes is usually documented in the WMI repository under the `EventTrace` class in the `root\WMI` namespace. If the provider wants to document or publish the structure of its event classes, then the `MofImagePath` parameter should contain the path of the executable or DLL that contains a Windows resource of the compiled binary MOF file. The actual reference to the resource is supplied by `MofResourceName`. Both `MofImagePath` and `MofResourceName` can be NULL if the provider wants keep the structure of the event classes private.

Upon a successful provider registration, `RegisterTraceGuids` will return a `TRACEHANDLE` referenced by `RegistrationHandle` that will be used later when the provider unregisters itself. The `RegistrationHandle` is valid only in a call to `Unregister-TraceGuids`. The `UnregisterTraceGuids` function is very straightforward:

```
ULONG UnregisterTraceGuids(TRACEHANDLE RegistrationHandle);
```

Developing the Provider's Control Call-Back Function

Apart from registering the application as an event-tracing provider, the next most important development task is to code the provider's control call-back function. As already mentioned, this is the primary communication between the operating system's event tracer and the provider. Let's have a look at the implementation for the lift simulator:

```
ULONG __stdcall ControlCallback(WMIDPREQUESTCODE RequestCode,
  PVOID Context, ULONG *reserved, PVOID Buffer)
{
  ULONG ulStatus = ERROR_SUCCESS;

  switch (RequestCode)
  {
    case WMI_ENABLE_EVENTS:
    {
      g_hProvider = GetTraceLoggerHandle(Buffer);
      g_dwEnableLevel = GetTraceEnableLevel(g_hProvider);
      g_dwEnableFlags = GetTraceEnableFlags(g_hProvider);
      g_bTracerActive = true;

      break;
    }
    case WMI_DISABLE_EVENTS:
    {
      g_hProvider = 0;
      g_dwEnableLevel = 0;
      g_dwEnableFlags = 0;
      g_bTracerActive = false;

      break;
    }
    default:
    {
      ulStatus = ERROR_INVALID_PARAMETER;
    }
  }
  return ulStatus;
}
```

As you can see, it is simple. The event tracer calls this function and the `Request-Code` is either `WMI_ENABLE_EVENTS`, to inform the provider that it should start emitting events, or `WMI_DISABLE_EVENTS`, to tell it to stop emitting events. However, it is ultimately up to the provider to interpret what is meant by being enabled and disabled.

For the application to determine which tracing flags and which tracing-level values were passed to `EnableTrace`, the control call-back function must call `GetTraceLoggerHandle` to retrieve a valid `TRACEHANDLE`. Retrieval of the `TRACEHANDLE` also is necessary if the provider wants to produce events in calls to `TraceEvent` (to be discussed in more detail). The event-tracing flags can be obtained with a call to `GetTraceEnableFlags` and the tracing level with a call to `GetTraceEnableLevel`. The `Buffer` parameter is exclusively for use by the `GetTraceLoggerHandle` call.

The `Context` parameter is a user-defined cookie value that previously was supplied in a call to `RegisterTraceGuids`.

Producing an Event Trace

Finally, we shall generate some events. Generating events is very simple. All that is required is to create and initialize the appropriate event structure (defined earlier) and pass it to `TraceEvent`. The `TraceEvent` function passes the event to the kernel's event tracer, which ultimately delivers it to the session's active buffer. Before a provider calls `TraceEvent`, it should recognize whether the provider has been enabled to generate events.

Before integrating `TraceEvent` into your application, you should have a clear understanding of the sequence of events and their event types that need to be generated. The diagram in Figure 13.6 describes the schema that will be instrumented.

The diagram attempts to highlight that an event class can have many versions and that each version has a set of supported event types. However, for the lift simulator, there is only one version, version zero. Whenever the lift goes up, it will start with an `EVENT_TRACE_TYPE_START` event followed by several (if necessary) checkpoint events of type `EVENT_TRACE_TYPE_CHECKPOINT`. Finally, when the lift stops at the desired floor, the entire `LiftUp` operation will end with an `EVENT_TRACE_TYPE_END` event. Although specific event types could have been defined, it would not make reasonable sense to define them because the standard event types describe the `LiftUp` operation perfectly. The structures described in the diagram's event types are not exactly the same as those defined for the provider; however, the binary memory representation is the same and makes for easier visualization of the event structure. Let's look at a portion of the lift simulator code to see how it produces some of the events. The following portion is from the *up operation*:

```
LONG lStartFloor = g_lCurrentFloor;
LONG lEndFloor = rand() % 10;
```

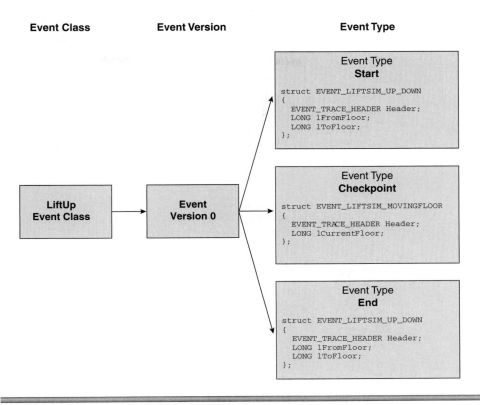

Figure 13.6   Event-trace schema for Lift Simulator

```
// Make sure the final destination floor is greater than the floor we are
// currently on.
while (lEndFloor <= lStartFloor)
  lEndFloor = rand() % 10;


// Move floors
for (LONG lFloor = lStartFloor; lFloor <= lEndFloor; lFloor++)
{
  if (lFloor == lStartFloor || lFloor == lEndFloor)
  {


    // We are at either the starting floor or the ending floor
    EVENT_LIFTSIM_UP_DOWN Event = {0};
    Event.Header.Size = sizeof(EVENT_LIFTSIM_UP_DOWN);
    Event.Header.Guid = LIFTSIM_UP;
    Event.Header.Flags = WNODE_FLAG_TRACED_GUID;
```

```
    if (lFloor == lStartFloor)
      Event.Header.Class.Type = EVENT_TRACE_TYPE_START;
    else
      Event.Header.Class.Type = EVENT_TRACE_TYPE_END;

    Event.Data.lFromFloor = lStartFloor;
    Event.Data.lToFloor = lEndFloor;
    // Generate the event
    ulError = TraceEvent(g_hProvider, (PEVENT_TRACE_HEADER)&Event);
  }
  else
  {

    // We are moving between floors
    EVENT_LIFTSIM_MOVINGFLOOR Event = {0};
    Event.Header.Size = sizeof(EVENT_LIFTSIM_MOVINGFLOOR);
    Event.Header.Guid = LIFTSIM_UP;
    Event.Header.Flags = WNODE_FLAG_TRACED_GUID;

    Event.Header.Class.Type = EVENT_TRACE_TYPE_CHECKPOINT;
    Event.Data.lCurrentFloor = lFloor;

    // Generate the event
    ulError = TraceEvent(g_hProvider, (PEVENT_TRACE_HEADER)&Event);
  }

  // Takes time to move between floors
  Sleep(rand() % 250);
}

// New floor
g_lCurrentFloor = lEndFloor;
```

Pay special attention to the items in bold font. Notice that although we are using two different event structures for the LiftUp operation (EVENT_LIFTSIM_UP_DOWN and EVENT_LIFTSIM_MOVINGFLOOR), the Event.Header.Guid member contains the LiftUp operation's GUID that defines the events as being from the same event class. The Event.Header.Class.Type member contains the event type information. This, combined with the event class and the version, allows a consumer to properly interpret the data structure attached to the event during analysis. Finally, the event is generated from a call to TraceEvent. Notice, however, that it must have access to the provider's TRACE-HANDLE (obtained during the control call-back function).

Let's move on to examine the EVENT_TRACE_HEADER structure. This structure is used for all event generation via TraceEvent. It also represents all the detail that is common to all generated events.

```
typedef struct _EVENT_TRACE_HEADER {  // overlays WNODE_HEADER
  USHORT          Size;               // Size of entire record
  union {
    USHORT        FieldTypeFlags;     // Indicates valid fields
    struct {
      UCHAR       HeaderType;         // Header type-internal use only
      UCHAR       MarkerFlags;        // Marker-internal use only
    };
  };
  union {
    ULONG         Version;
    struct {
      UCHAR       Type;               // event type
      UCHAR       Level;              // trace instrumentation level
      USHORT      Version;            // version of trace record
    } Class;
  };
  ULONG           ThreadId;           // Thread Id
  ULONG           ProcessId;          // Process Id
  LARGE_INTEGER   TimeStamp;          // time when event happens
  union {
    GUID          Guid;               // Guid that identifies event
    ULONGLONG     GuidPtr;            // use with WNODE_FLAG_USE_GUID_PTR
  };
  union {
    struct {
      ULONG       ClientContext;      // Reserved
      ULONG       Flags;              // Flags for header
    };
    struct {
      ULONG       KernelTime;         // Kernel Mode CPU ticks
      ULONG       UserTime;           // User mode CPU ticks
    };
    ULONG64       ProcessorTime;      // Processor Clock
  };
} EVENT_TRACE_HEADER, *PEVENT_TRACE_HEADER;
```

The structure starts off by wanting the Size, which includes the EVENT_TRACE_HEADER structure and all the space required by all the event's custom fields.

The most important information for clearly stating the class, version, and type of the event starts with completing the Guid member. This contains the event class's GUID. If you want to avoid a GUID assignment, then a pointer to a GUID can be referenced instead. To do this requires setting up GuidPtr and updating the Flags member with WNODE_FLAG_USE_GUID_PTR. We prefer the GUID assignment to the Guid member because it is less difficult to identify the class during analysis. The version of the event can be updated through the Class.Version member and the level of the event can be assigned to Class.Level. To complete the event identification requires an event type, which is assigned to `Class.Type`. As already mentioned, a provider can define its own event types: These must be greater than 0x09. Table 13.5 describes the standard event types.

The kernel defines a number of its own event types: Examine the `evntrace.h` for more detail.

Some of the fields are not for public use and are used by the event tracer internally. However, the `FieldTypeFlags` member provides additional information about which members of the structure are valid (Table 13.6). Note that `TraceEvent` and the event tracer will update specific members of the structure, `TimeStamp`, for example. Be aware that any flags set in `FieldTypeFlags` may be altered.

Table 13.5 Standard Event Types

`Class.Type` **Flags**	**Comment**
EVENT_TRACE_TYPE_INFO	Informational event. This is the default event type.
EVENT_TRACE_TYPE_START	Start event. Use to trace the initial state of a multistep event.
EVENT_TRACE_TYPE_END	End event. Use to trace the final state of a multistep event.
EVENT_TRACE_TYPE_DC_START	Collection start event. This is used by the NT Kernel Logger to state which threads and processes have been set up for event-tracing data collection. In other applications, this could be used to state which resources/devices/operations are set up for generating event traces.
EVENT_TRACE_TYPE_DC_END	Collection end event Check EVENT_TRACE_TYPE_DC_START for more details.
EVENT_TRACE_TYPE_EXTENSION	Extension event. Use for an event that is a continuation of a previous event. For example, use the extension event type when an event trace records more data than can fit in a session buffer.
EVENT_TRACE_TYPE_REPLY	Reply event. Use when an application that requests resources can receive multiple responses. For example, if a client application requests a URL, and the Web server reply is to send several files, each file received can be marked as a reply event.
EVENT_TRACE_TYPE_DEQUEUE	Dequeue event. Use when an activity is queued before it begins. Use EVENT_TRACE_TYPE_START to mark the time when a work item is queued. Use the dequeue event type to mark the time when work on the item actually begins. Use EVENT_TRACE_TYPE_END to mark the time when work on the item completes.
EVENT_TRACE_TYPE_CHECKPOINT	Checkpoint event. Use this for an event that is not at the start or end of an activity.

Table 13.6 FieldTypeFlags Flags

FieldTypeFlags **Values**	**Comment**
EVENT_TRACE_USE_NOCPUTIME	The KernelTime, UserTime, and ProcessorTime members are not used.
EVENT_TRACE_USE_PROCTIME	The ProcessorTime member is valid.

The ThreadId and ProcessId members contain the thread and process identifiers that generated the event. The TimeStamp member is the exact time the event was generated. The ThreadId, ProcessId, and TimeStamp members are completed by TraceEvent.

The Flags member contains information about the event structure. It is important that this member be initialized with WNODE_FLAG_TRACED_GUID. This flag, effectively, says that this structure contains event-tracing information. In addition, the Flags member can contain a combination of bit-mask values shown in Table 13.7.

The KernelTime member contains the elapsed execution time for kernel mode in-structions and the UserTime member contains the elapsed execution time in user

Table 13.7 Flags Bit-Mask Values

Flags **Values**	**Comment**
WNODE_FLAG_USE_GUID_PTR	Use this to indicate that the event class is referenced by a pointer to the GUID. If this is the case, the GuidPtr member must contain a valid pointer to a GUID.
WNODE_FLAG_USE_MOF_PTR	The event data appended to this structure is stored in an array of MOF_FIELD structures.
	Note that this is not commonly used. Specifying the event's custom data like this has a limitation of only 16 MOF_FIELD structures. The structure looks like this:

	``
	typedef struct _MOF_FIELD {
	  ULONG64 DataPtr; // Pointer to data
	  ULONG Length; // Length of MOF field
	  ULONG DataType; // Type of data
	} MOF_FIELD, *PMOF_FIELD;
	``

	The DataType member has no documented values. However, it seems sensible to use the WMI CIMTYPE enumeration values.

mode. A private event-tracing session uses the `ProcessorTime` member and does not use the `KernelTime` and `UserTime` members.

The `TraceEvent` function is quite simple:

```
ULONG TraceEvent(TRACEHANDLE TraceHandle, PEVENT_TRACE_HEADER EventTrace);
```

The provider's `TRACEHANDLE` that was obtained in the control call-back function must be passed in `TraceHandle`. The event structure containing any custom fields must be passed into `EventTrace`.

Kernel-mode device drivers can also generate events and, interestingly, they register themselves with the operating system's event tracer using `IoWMIRegistration-Control` and generate events with `IoWMIWriteEvent`.

Producing a Hierarchical Event Trace

Event tracing also includes the ability to group events hierarchically. Generating events with `TraceEvent` produces a stream of events that have no association with other events. However, as you saw earlier in the chapter, we used the event-type field to help in distinguishing a flat series of events to either track an operation or to monitor a resource. Additionally, a cookie or a handle that can specifically reference a particular operation or object could also be included with the event's custom fields. This can help as well in associating a large number of events to a specific operation or resource. Event tracing with `TraceEvent` is the most common approach because it makes analyzing several event-tracing log files in which the event time order will interleave events from different sources easier. That said, grouping events in a way that makes it easier to associate one event from another can't be ignored.

One such example is in the lift simulator described earlier. It has three classes of events: `LiftUp`, `LiftDown`, and `LiftJammed`. Both `LiftUp` and `LiftDown` attempt to group events by monitoring the lift's progress with *start* and *end* events. If the lift travels more than one floor, several checkpoint events in between the *start* and *end* events help in tracking the progress of the operation. The *checkpoint* and *end* events in reality are associated with the *start* of the lift's movement. The `LiftJammed` event can't be associated with any other event, so this would remain as a normal traced event. The diagram in Figure 13.7 shows how the lift simulator might look if it used hierarchical events as opposed to a flat series of events. An event trace can contain a mix of both types of events.

All events generated by `TraceEvent` simply are called *events*. In generating hierarchical events, each event is called an *event instance* so that all child event instances can be associated with the correct parent event instance.

Let's review some of the event-tracing provider registration. All the event classes that a provider wishes to expose must be registered with `RegisterTraceGuids`. This takes an array of `TRACE_GUID_REGISTRATION` structures that register the GUIDs of the event classes stored in the `Guid` member. If `RegisterTraceGuids` is successful, it returns

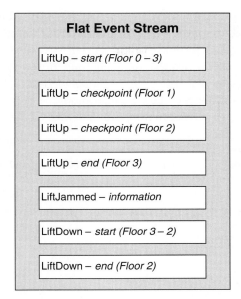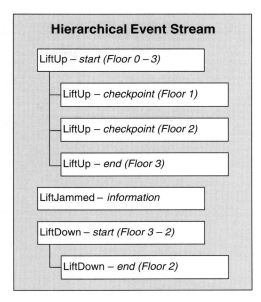

Figure 13.7   Flat versus hierarchical event trace

a handle for each class in the `RegHandle` member of the `TRACE_GUID_REGISTRATION` structures. Without access to the `RegHandle`, it is impossible to generate hierarchical event traces. Here is the registration code:

```
TRACE_GUID_REGISTRATION tgrEventClasses[3];
tgrEventClasses[0].Guid = &LIFTSIM_UP;
tgrEventClasses[1].Guid = &LIFTSIM_DOWN;
tgrEventClasses[2].Guid = &LIFTSIM_JAMMED;

TRACEHANDLE hRegProvider = 0;
ULONG ulReg = RegisterTraceGuids((WMIDPREQUEST)ControlCallback, NULL,
  (LPCGUID)&PROVGUID_LIFTSIM, 3, tgrEventClasses,
  (LPCTSTR)szModulePath, NULL, &hRegProvider);
```

Similar, but not quite the same, are the provider's event structures. For `Trace-Event`, the event structures begins with `EVENT_TRACE_HEADER`. For hierarchical event tracing, the event structure must begin with `EVENT_INSTANCE_HEADER` and also is followed by optional custom fields. Here is an example:

```
typedef struct tagEVENTINST_LIFTSIM_UP_DOWN
{
  EVENT_INSTANCE_HEADER Header;
  LIFTSIM_UP_DOWN Data;
} *PEVENTINST_LIFTSIM_UP_DOWN, EVENTINST_LIFTSIM_UP_DOWN;
```

As you've already seen, generating flat events is straightforward: You need only complete the event structure and pass it to `TraceEvent`. Generating hierarchical events requires an instance identifier to be created before the event structure can be completed. The instance identifier makes it possible uniquely to identify a specific operation. When analyzing hierarchical event traces, the instance identifier allows you to associate child and parent event instances correctly. Create a unique instance identifier for an event instance by calling `CreateTraceInstanceId`, like this:

```
EVENT_INSTANCE_INFO UpEvtInst = {0};
 ulError = CreateTraceInstanceId(tgrEventClasses[0].RegHandle,
 &UpEvtInst);
```

It is important to note from this example that the first parameter uses the event class registration handle returned by `RegisterTraceGuids`. Here is the prototype of the `CreateTraceInstanceId` function:

```
ULONG CreateTraceInstanceId(HANDLE RegHandle,
  PEVENT_INSTANCE_INFO   pInstInfo);
```

The `RegHandle` parameter contains the event class handle provided by the `Register-TraceGuids`. Internally, `CreateTraceInstanceId` uses the event class's `RegHandle` to verify and locate that the event class registration exists and to obtain its GUID. Unlike a standard event, an event instance's event class GUID cannot be specified in the `EVENT_INSTANCE_HEADER` structure. The instance identifier is returned by the `pInstInfo` parameter. Let's look at the `EVENT_INSTANCE_INFO` structure:

```
typedef struct EVENT_INSTANCE_INFO {
  HANDLE      RegHandle;
  ULONG       InstanceId;
} EVENT_INSTANCE_INFO, *PEVENT_INSTANCE_INFO;
```

The `RegHandle` parameter contains the event class's registration handle, which is the same as the one supplied in the first parameter to `CreateTraceInstanceId`. The unique event instance identifier is placed in the `InstanceId` member.

Let's look at a code sample that generates an instance event.

```
EVENTINST_LIFTSIM_UP_DOWN Event = {0};
Event.Header.Size = sizeof(EVENTINST_LIFTSIM_UP_DOWN);
Event.Header.Flags = WNODE_FLAG_TRACED_GUID;

// The event instance's event type
Event.Header.Class.Type = EVENT_TRACE_TYPE_START;
```

```
// Custom event data
Event.Data.lFromFloor = lStartFloor;
Event.Data.lToFloor = lEndFloor;

// Generates an instance event
ulError = TraceEventInstance(g_hProvider,
  (PEVENT_INSTANCE_HEADER)&Event, &UpEvtInst, NULL);
```

This code should look quite familiar by now. The event structure is set up and is passed to `TraceEventInstance` to generate the event. Notice that the third parameter uses the event instance information (`EVENT_INSTANCE_INFO`) structure that was initialized by `CreateTraceInstanceId`. Let's examine `TraceEventInstance` prototype:

```
ULONG TraceEventInstance(TRACEHANDLE TraceHandle,
  PEVENT_INSTANCE_HEADER EventTrace, PEVENT_INSTANCE_INFO pInstInfo,
  PEVENT_INSTANCE_INFO pParentInstInfo);
```

Like `TraceEvent`, the `TraceHandle` parameter is the provider's `TRACEHANDLE`. The event that the provider wishes to generate is passed to the `EventTrace` parameter. The event's instance details, created by `CreateTraceInstanceId`, must be passed to `pInstInfo`. If the event instance has a parent, be sure to pass the parent's instance details to `pParentInstInfo`. Before examining the `EVENT_INSTANCE_HEADER` structure, let's look at a complete code sample that produces a child instance event:

```
// Create instance for child event
EVENT_INSTANCE_INFO MovingEvtInst = {0};
ulError = CreateTraceInstanceId(tgrEventClasses[0].RegHandle,
  &MovingEvtInst);

// Setup child event
EVENTINST_LIFTSIM_MOVINGFLOOR Event = {0};
Event.Header.Size = sizeof(EVENT_LIFTSIM_MOVINGFLOOR);
Event.Header.Flags = WNODE_FLAG_TRACED_GUID;

Event.Header.Class.Type = EVENT_TRACE_TYPE_CHECKPOINT;

// Event custom data
Event.Data.lCurrentFloor = lFloor;

// Generate child instance event. Both the event instance and parent
// event instance details are passed into TraceEventInstance.
ulError = TraceEventInstance(g_hProvider,
  (PEVENT_INSTANCE_HEADER)&Event, &MovingEvtInst, &UpEvtInst);
```

Although the `EVENT_INSTANCE_HEADER` structure is similar to the `EVENT_TRACE_` `HEADER`, it is different in the following ways.

1. It does not have a `Guid` member because the GUID is obtained from the event class registration.

2. It has a `RegHandle` member that holds the event class registration handle and the `InstanceId` member uniquely identifies the event.

3. It has both `ParentRegHandle` and `ParentInstanceId` members to record the parent instance's event class registration handle and instance identifier.

For additional information about the other members, check the `EVENT_TRACE_` `HEADER` structure discussed earlier. Here is the `EVENT_INSTANCE_HEADER` structure:

```
typedef struct _EVENT_INSTANCE_HEADER {
  USHORT          Size;
  union {
    USHORT        FieldTypeFlags;      // Indicates valid fields
    struct {
      UCHAR       HeaderType;          // Header type - internal use only
      UCHAR       MarkerFlags;         // Marker - internal use only
    };
  };
  union {
    ULONG         Version;
    struct {
      UCHAR       Type;
      UCHAR       Level;
      USHORT      Version;
    } Class;
  };
  ULONG           ThreadId;
  ULONG           ProcessId;
  LARGE_INTEGER   TimeStamp;
  ULONGLONG       RegHandle;
  ULONG           InstanceId;
  ULONG           ParentInstanceId;
  union {
    struct {
      ULONG       ClientContext;       // Reserved
      ULONG       Flags;               // Flags for header
    };
    struct {
      ULONG       KernelTime;          // Kernel Mode CPU ticks
      ULONG       UserTime;            // User mode CPU ticks
    };
    ULONG64       ProcessorTime;       // Processor Clock
```

```
};
ULONGLONG       ParentRegHandle;
} EVENT_INSTANCE_HEADER, *PEVENT_INSTANCE_HEADER;
```

Unfortunately, there is a big problem with hierarchical event tracing in the released version of Windows XP. It is badly broken! The event class GUIDs are `GUID_NULL`, which means that it is impossible to identify to which class the events belong. We hope that eventually a Windows XP service pack will fix this problem. Under Windows 2000, hierarchical event tracing works just fine.

■ Analyzing Event-Trace Log Files

Analyzing events from an event-trace log file or a real-time session is the most important aspect of the event-tracing technology. It allows the possibility of analyzing event traces from an application and its components through to the subsystems upon which the application builds, right down to the kernel and including kernel mode device drivers. For the first time, software truly can track operations and resources through every subsystem. This provides a complete perspective for resolving problems. Here are a few examples:

When an application opens and reads a file, an event-tracing session will be able to confirm the disk I/O activity involved as well as to determine whether the file was read from the in-memory file cache.

If an application performs badly on a particular machine, it will be possible to identify if a lot of paging occurs at specific times of poor performance. If this is the case, perhaps the machine requires more memory.

If an application is having problems communicating with a particular server within the enterprise, a consumer will be able to filter network activity to that server.

Processing an Event-Trace Log File

You should know by now that an event-tracing session can log only to a single log file. To monitor all the subsystems that an application builds upon requires several sessions to record the activity in several log files. Analyzing several log files can be an ugly business. One of the real benefits of the event-tracing consumer APIs is that they can consume several log files and produce a time-ordered stream of events. Suppose there is a situation in which you have a distributed application on several servers. Tracking operations and resources between two or more systems is traditionally difficult, and in most cases, analyzing problems for such applications is poor, usually because marrying activities between several (possibly text-based) log files is not easy and is awkward.

Let's look at some code that analyzes an event trace:

```
const LPCTSTR ET_FILE = _T("C:\\LiftSim.etl");

EVENT_TRACE_LOGFILE log = {0};

// Allocate memory for log file name
log.LogFileName = reinterpret_cast<LPTSTR>(LocalAlloc(LPTR,
  (_tcslen(ET_FILE) +1) * sizeof(TCHAR)));

// Copy log file name to EVENT_TRACE_LOGFILE structure
_tcscpy(log.LogFileName, ET_FILE);

// Setup event callback. This will be called for every event.
log.EventCallback = GenericEventCallback;

// Setup buffer callback. This will be called at the end of every buffer.
log.BufferCallback = GenericBufferCallback;

// Setup as many log files that you want processed
TRACEHANDLE hTraceLog[1];
hTraceLog[0] = OpenTrace(&log);

// Process all the log files. This is a synchronous call
ULONG ulError = ProcessTrace(hTraceLog, 1, NULL, NULL);

// Clean up
ulError = CloseTrace(hTraceLog[0]);
```

This code sample sets up and analyzes the log file (`C:\LiftSim.etl`) until all its events have been processed. The first task is to create and initialize an `EVENT_TRACE_LOGFILE` structure. This contains information about which log file to open and the call-back functions that will process the events within the file as they are processed. Opening the log file simply requires a call to `OpenTrace` and passing the `EVENT_TRACE_LOGFILE` structure to it. On returning, `OpenTrace` provides a `TRACEHANDLE` that is used for processing the file with `ProcessTrace`. The `ProcessTrace` function executes synchronously, which means that you may want to consider calling it on another thread. When `ProcessTrace` is executing, it delivers a time-ordered stream of events to the call-back specified by `EventCallback`, and as each buffer is processed, a notification is delivered to the call-back specified by `BufferCallback`. After the log file has been dealt with, `CloseTrace` is called to clean up. Multiple log files can be specified through `ProcessTrace` because it takes an array (`hTraceLog`) of opened log file handles. More on these APIs is covered later.

The Event Call-Back Function

The event call-back function is critical to gaining access to the events. The call-back function is provided by a consumer and when `ProcessTrace` is called, it calls the call-back for every event in the log file. If there is a requirement to process thousands of events as quickly as possible, you should aim to make the call-back as efficient as possible. The following is a very simple event call-back that outputs only the event class's GUID and the version number:

```
void WINAPI ASimpleEventCallback(PEVENT_TRACE pEvent)
{
  // Display event class GUID and the version of the event
  _tprintf(_T("EventGuid = %ls, EventVersion = %d\n"),
    CComBSTR(pEvent->Header.Guid), pEvent->Header.Class.Version);
}
```

The event is passed in `pEvent`, which is a pointer to an `EVENT_TRACE` structure. Let's look at this in more detail:

```
typedef struct _EVENT_TRACE {
  EVENT_TRACE_HEADER    Header;            // Event trace header
  ULONG                 InstanceId;        // Instance Id of this event
  ULONG                 ParentInstanceId;  // Parent Instance Id.
  GUID                  ParentGuid;        // Parent Guid;
  PVOID                 MofData;           // Pointer to Variable Data
  ULONG                 MofLength;         // Variable Datablock Length
  ULONG                 ClientContext;     // Reserved
} EVENT_TRACE, *PEVENT_TRACE;
```

The `Header` member uses an `EVENT_TRACE_HEADER` structure that was discussed earlier. This contains general information that is common to every event in an event trace.

The `InstanceId`, `ParentInstanceId`, and `ParentGuid` members are used by hierarchical event tracing. All hierarchical events are referenced by *instance* values as well as by the event class, version, and type details. The `InstanceId` specifically references a transaction. The `ParentInstanceId` references who the event's parent transaction is. A `ParentInstanceId` of zero indicates that the instance supplied by `InstanceId` is an event at the root of the hierarchical tree. The instance's GUID can be obtained from the `Header.Guid` member, and if the `ParentInstanceId` is greater than zero, the `Parent-Guid` member contains the parent's event class GUID.

An event's custom data that the provider tagged on at the end of the `EVENT_TRACE_HEADER` structure can be obtained during analysis through the `MofData member`; its length is supplied by `MofLength`. Why the events in the provider were structured like this should now make sense.

```
typedef struct tagLIFTSIM_MOVINGFLOOR
{
  LONG lCurrentFloor;
```

```
} *PLIFTSIM_MOVINGFLOOR, LIFTSIM_MOVINGFLOOR;
typedef struct tagEVENT_LIFTSIM_MOVINGFLOOR
{
  EVENT_TRACE_HEADER Header;
  LIFTSIM_MOVINGFLOOR Data;
} *PEVENT_LIFTSIM_MOVINGFLOOR, EVENT_LIFTSIM_MOVINGFLOOR;
```

We can easily reuse and cast the `MofData` member to the desired `LIFTSIM_MOVING-FLOOR` structure. Designing your events like this makes it a little easier to ensure that the events generated by the provider can be interpreted correctly by a consumer.[5] Assuming that the event class, version, and type have been identified correctly, here is how to gain access to the customized event data:

```
PLIFTSIM_MOVINGFLOOR pData =
  reinterpret_cast<PLIFTSIM_MOVINGFLOOR>(pEvent->MofData);
```

When a provider makes its events public, it usually publishes the event structures using WMI. The `EventTrace` base class in the `root\WMI` namespace contains inherited classes that describe the following:

1. The existence of the provider and the GUID with which it can be referenced
2. The event classes of the events that the provider can generate and their GUIDs
3. The supported event types of the event class and the properties of the class document (how to interpret the event)

It is up to the consumer to generate a structure based on the information obtained from WMI. This is how you would make structures to interpret events from the kernel, for instance. Figure 13.8 shows the print spooler's documented class hierarchy.

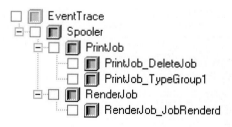

Figure 13.8　Print spooler's event-trace schema

---

5. If the provider and consumer use a shared header file describing the custom event data.

The first event in all event-tracing log files supplies details about the session that created the log file. In fact, this is done for every log file that is processed. Figure 13.9 shows the order in which events and buffers will occur. The left event stream shows what happens when a single log file is processed. The right event stream shows what happens when two or more log files are processed. The only difference is that for every log file processed, the event call-back function will receive an `EventTraceGuid`[6] event with the session details that recorded the log file. The session details can be extracted via the event's custom data. Simply cast the event's `MofData` member to a pointer of a `TRACE_LOGFILE_HEADER` structure.

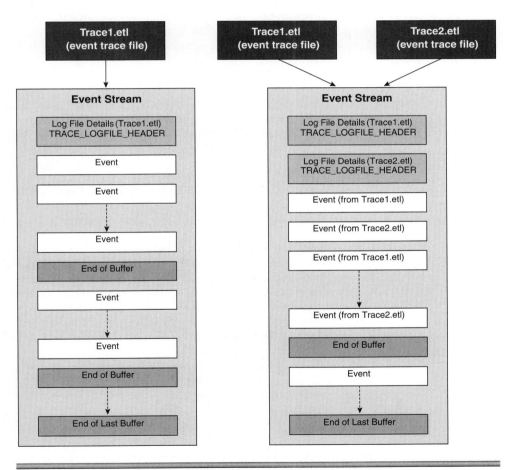

Figure 13.9 Processing single versus multiple event-tracing log files

6. `EventTraceGuid` is defined in `evntrace.h`.

Let's have a look at the event call-back function used by the earlier code sample. The items in bold font highlight the places in the code that event-class and event-type[7] checks are performed to properly determine how the event's `MofData` member should be interpreted, if at all. Because event analysis is important, we have included the whole function. Its purpose is to output all the details of an event and, if the event is from the lift simulator, extract and interpret its custom data. The lift simulator is discussed in detail in the provider section of the chapter.

```
void WINAPI GenericEventCallback(PEVENT_TRACE pEvent)
{
  // Details from the TRACE_LOGFILE_HEADER structure that help to interpret
  // event information
  static ULONG ulTimerResolution = 1;
  static bool bPrivateSession = false;

  try
  {
    // For each log file processed, you get an event that describes
    // the contents of the log file or real-time monitor.
    if(IsEqualGUID((pEvent->Header.Guid), EventTraceGuid) &&
      pEvent->Header.Class.Type == EVENT_TRACE_TYPE_INFO)
    {
      PTRACE_LOGFILE_HEADER tlhSession =
        Reinterpret_cast<PTRACE_LOGFILE_HEADER>(pEvent->MofData);

      if (tlhSession)
      {
      // We can find easily find out whether this is a log from
      // a private session. We will use this for determining what
      // aspects about the kernel, user and processor time
      // members can be displayed. Private session can only use
      // the ProcessorTime member.
      bPrivateSession =
        tlhSession->LogFileMode & EVENT_TRACE_PRIVATE_LOGGER_MODE;

      // The resolution of the timer used in the log file.
      if (tlhSession->TimerResolution > 0)
        ulTimerResolution = tlhSession->TimerResolution / 10000;
      }
    }

  // Display event class and event version
  _tprintf(_T("\nEventGuid = %ls, EventVersion = %d\n"),
    CComBSTR(pEvent->Header.Guid), pEvent->Header.Class.Version);
```

7. As this is a simple consumer for this book, we have omitted code to check the version of the events.

```c
      // Display event type and event level
      _tprintf(_T("\tEventType = %s, EventLevel = %d\n"),
        GetEventTypeAsString(pEvent->Header.Class.Type),
        pEvent->Header.Class.Level);


      // Display event time stamp
      TCHAR szDateTime[80];
      GetTimeStampAsString(pEvent->Header.TimeStamp, szDateTime,
        sizeof(szDateTime) / sizeof(TCHAR));


      _tprintf(_T("\tTimeStamp = %s\n"), szDateTime);


      // Display supported timings
      _tprintf(_T("\tCPUTimeSupported = %s, ProcessorTimeSupported = %s\n"),
        pEvent->Header.FieldTypeFlags & EVENT_TRACE_USE_NOCPUTIME ?
          _T("No") : _T("Yes"),
        pEvent->Header.FieldTypeFlags & EVENT_TRACE_USE_PROCTIME ?
          _T("Yes") : _T("No"));


      if (!bPrivateSession ||
      !(pEvent->Header.FieldTypeFlags & EVENT_TRACE_USE_NOCPUTIME))
      {
        // Display all timings
        _tprintf(_T("\tKernelTime = %d (%d ms), UserTime = %d (%d ms), ")\
          _T("ProcessorTime = %d (%d ms)\n"),
          pEvent->Header.KernelTime,
          pEvent->Header.KernelTime * ulTimerResolution,
          pEvent->Header.UserTime,
          pEvent->Header.UserTime * ulTimerResolution,
          pEvent->Header.ProcessorTime,
          pEvent->Header.ProcessorTime * ulTimerResolution);
      }
      else if (pEvent->Header.FieldTypeFlags & EVENT_TRACE_USE_PROCTIME ||
        bPrivateSession)
      {

        // Display Processor timing only. Note that private session
        // only support the processor time.
        _tprintf(_T("\tProcessorTime = %d (%d ms)\n"),
          pEvent->Header.ProcessorTime,
          pEvent->Header.ProcessorTime * ulTimerResolution);
      }


      // Decoding custom event fields/details. To retrieve a pointer to
      // the data, cast the MofData member to the desired type.

      if (IsEqualGUID(pEvent->Header.Guid, LIFTSIM_UP) ||
        IsEqualGUID(pEvent->Header.Guid, LIFTSIM_DOWN))
```

```
    {
      if (pEvent->Header.Class.Type == EVENT_TRACE_TYPE_START ||
        pEvent->Header.Class.Type == EVENT_TRACE_TYPE_END)
      {
        // LiftUp and LiftDown start and stop events use the same
        // data structure
        PLIFTSIM_UP_DOWN pData = (PLIFTSIM_UP_DOWN)pEvent->MofData;

        _tprintf(_T("\tFromFloor = %d, ToFloor = %d\n"),
          pData->lFromFloor, pData->lToFloor);
      }
      else if (pEvent->Header.Class.Type == EVENT_TRACE_TYPE_CHECKPOINT)
      {
        // LiftUp and LiftDown checkpoint events use a different
        // data structure
        PLIFTSIM_MOVINGFLOOR pData =
          (PLIFTSIM_MOVINGFLOOR)pEvent->MofData;

        _tprintf(_T("\tCurrentFloor = %d\n"), pData->lCurrentFloor);
      }
      else
        _tprintf(_T("\t<Unknown event type>\n"));
    }
    else if (IsEqualGUID(pEvent->Header.Guid, LIFTSIM_JAMMED))
    {
      if (pEvent->Header.Class.Type == EVENT_TRACE_TYPE_INFO)
      {
        // LiftJammed information events use a different
        // data structure
        PLIFTSIM_JAMMED_INFO pData =
          (PLIFTSIM_JAMMED_INFO)pEvent->MofData;

        _tprintf(_T("\tFault Description = %ls\n"),
          pData->szDescription);
      }
      else
        _tprintf(_T("\t<Unknown event type>\n"));
    }
  }
  catch (...)
  {
    // Do something meaningful
  }
}
```

For simplicity, the above code won't be able to properly interpret event timings when processing several event-tracing log files. In your own solutions, consider using an alternative method to store the information provided by the static members, `ulTimer-Resolution` and `bPrivateSession`. The previous function is called `GenericEvent-Callback` because it will be called for every event processed by `ProcessTrace`. Later, we discuss how events can be filtered by their class. Hence there can be several event-handling functions.

The following is a portion of the output produced by the preceding sample code. The items in bold font highlight the event class and its type as well as the custom data that is extracted from the `MofData` member. The {2205BB0C-75C8-4F78-A8C5-984CA4377782} GUID identifies the event as the "lift going down" (`LiftDown`) and last event {2205BB0D-75C8-4F78-A8C5-984CA4377782} is identified as the "lift requiring attention" (`LiftJammed`).[8]

```
EventGuid = {2205BB0C-75C8-4F78-A8C5-984CA4377782}, EventVersion = 0
  EventType = Start, EventLevel = 0
  TimeStamp = 12/01/2002 17:18:58.074
  CPUTimeSupported = Yes, ProcessorTimeSupported = No
  KernelTime = 3 (0 ms), UserTime = 0 (0 ms), ProcessorTime = 3 (0 ms)
  FromFloor = 2, ToFloor = 0


EventGuid = {2205BB0C-75C8-4F78-A8C5-984CA4377782}, EventVersion = 0
  EventType = Checkpoint, EventLevel = 0
  TimeStamp = 12/01/2002 17:18:58.215
  CPUTimeSupported = Yes, ProcessorTimeSupported = No
  KernelTime = 3 (0 ms), UserTime = 0 (0 ms), ProcessorTime = 3 (0 ms)
  CurrentFloor = 1


EventGuid = {2205BB0C-75C8-4F78-A8C5-984CA4377782}, EventVersion = 0
  EventType = End, EventLevel = 0
  TimeStamp = 12/01/2002 17:18:58.340
  CPUTimeSupported = Yes, ProcessorTimeSupported = No
  KernelTime = 3 (0 ms), UserTime = 0 (0 ms), ProcessorTime = 3 (0 ms)
  FromFloor = 2, ToFloor = 0


EventGuid = {2205BB0D-75C8-4F78-A8C5-984CA4377782}, EventVersion = 0
  EventType = Information, EventLevel = 0
  TimeStamp = 12/01/2002 17:18:58.418
  CPUTimeSupported = Yes, ProcessorTimeSupported = No
  KernelTime = 3 (0 ms), UserTime = 0 (0 ms), ProcessorTime = 3 (0 ms)
  Fault Description = The lift needs maintenance
```

8. Check the provider section for more details about the events produced by the lift simulation provider.

The Buffer Call-Back Function

All event traces are organized in a sequence of buffers, each of which contains many trace events. Each event is essentially a variable-length record and only so many events can be stored in a buffer that is at least 1KB in size (default is 8KB). The size of each event without any custom data tagged on it is around 30–40 bytes. Also note that a buffer can contain a small number of events. This is the case when the buffer has been flushed prematurely to disk before it was full. This could be a result of the session being stopped while the buffer was half full, or Windows deciding to flush the buffer to disk (perhaps triggered by the session's FlushTimer), or an event-tracing controller making a call to ControlTrace using the EVENT_TRACE_CONTROL_FLUSH action. The buffer call-back function is called at the end of every buffer processed by ProcessTrace.

The following buffer call-back function is very simple because all it does is keep a record, which is output to the console, of how many buffers have been processed so far.

```
ULONG WINAPI GenericBufferCallback(PEVENT_TRACE_LOGFILE pLog)
{
  static ULONG ulBufferNum = 0;

  ulBufferNum++;

  // Would normally inspect details of the EVENT_TRACE_LOGFILE structure
  printf("\nEnd of Buffer %d\n\n", ulBufferNum);

  // Return TRUE to continue processing next buffer or FALSE to stop
  return TRUE;
}
```

Given that ProcessTrace is a synchronous function, it does not return until all the buffers have been processed. This sometimes is not desirable for some consumer applications. Fortunately, ProcessTrace can be interrupted by the buffer call-back returning FALSE, which prevents the processing of further buffers.

The EVENT_TRACE_LOGFILE structure will be discussed in more detail.

The Consumer Event-Tracing APIs

As you've already seen from the earlier code samples, an event consumer uses Open-Trace, ProcessTrace, and CloseTrace API calls. However, two more API calls assist in filtering events by their class: SetTraceCallback and RemoveTraceCallback. These will be discussed later.

Every event-tracing log file and real-time monitoring session needs to be opened with OpenTrace. This will provide a special TRACEHANDLE that ProcessTrace can use. So let's have a look at the prototype of this function:

```
TRACEHANDLE OpenTrace(PEVENT_TRACE_LOGFILE Logfile);
```

Before `OpenTrace` can be called, an `EVENT_TRACE_LOGFILE` structure needs to be initialized and set up. This structure contains information about the event-trace log file or real-time monitoring session. Let's discuss the various members:

```
struct EVENT_TRACE_LOGFILE {
  LPTSTR                    LogFileName;     // Logfile Name
  LPTSTR                    LoggerName;      // LoggerName
  LONGLONG                  CurrentTime;     // timestamp of last event
  ULONG                     BuffersRead;     // buffers read to date
  ULONG                     LogFileMode;     // LogFile Mode.

  EVENT_TRACE               CurrentEvent;    // Current Event from this stream
  TRACE_LOGFILE_HEADER LogfileHeader;        // logfile header structure
  PEVENT_TRACE_BUFFER_CALLBACK               // callback before each buffer
                       BufferCallback; // is read
  //
  // following variables are filled for BufferCallback.
  //
  ULONG                     BufferSize;
  ULONG                     Filled;
  ULONG                     EventsLost;
  //
  // following needs to be propagated to each buffer
  //
  PEVENT_CALLBACK           EventCallback;   // callback for every event
  ULONG                     IsKernelTrace;   // TRUE for kernel logfile
  PVOID                     Context;         // reserved for internal use
};
```

When setting up the structure to read an event-trace log file, ensure that the `LogFileName` member is completed: It should contain the path of the log file. Monitoring real-time sessions requires that the `LoggerName` member contain the session name. Monitoring real-time sessions will be discussed later.

To process all the events from the log file, the `EventCallback` member must contain a pointer to a call-back function that `ProcessTrace` can call for each and every event. To receive notifications upon the completion of every buffer, the `BufferCallback` member should contain a pointer to a buffer call-back function. Although the `EventCallback` (more important) and `BufferCallback` members can be NULL, it is uncommon. One possible reason for having both members NULL is to open the log file and retrieve details about it.

The `EVENT_TRACE_LOGFILE` structure is used by both `OpenTrace` and the buffer call-back function. When used in a buffer call-back, the time stamp of the last event in the buffer is recorded in the `CurrentTime` member. `OpenTrace` makes no use of the `CurrentTime`. According to the documentation, the `BuffersRead` member is supposed to report the number of buffers processed to date while reading a log file. However, this is zero upon the completion of every buffer. The session's logging options that were used to create the log file or real-time monitoring session can be retrieved from the `Log-FileMode` member. For instance, if `OpenTrace` opens a log file that was configured to record the events sequentially on disk, `LogFileMode` would contain `EVENT_TRACE_FILE_MODE_SEQUENTIAL`. During the processing of an event trace, `CurrentEvent` provides access to the last event in the buffer. According to the documentation, the `BufferSize` member is supposed to contain the size of each buffer in bytes, but we have found it to be zero. It can be found in `LogfileHeader.BufferSize`. The `Filled` member contains the number of bytes in the buffer that have valid data. The number of events that were lost and not stored in the buffer can be determined by looking at `EventsLost`.

Analyzing kernel event-trace log files or monitoring a kernel real-time session, `OpenTrace` will always set the `IsKernelTrace` member to TRUE; for normal event traces it is FALSE.

The `TRACE_LOGFILE_HEADER` structure contains more information about the log file. Specifically, it contains information about how to interpret event timings and the operating system on which the log file was created. This structure is used by `EVENT_TRACE_LOGFILE` and is also the `EventTraceGuid` event's custom data. Let's have a look:

```
typedef struct _TRACE_LOGFILE_HEADER {
  ULONG          BufferSize;              // Logger buffer size in Kbytes
  union {
    ULONG          Version;               // Logger version
    struct {
      UCHAR        MajorVersion;
      UCHAR        MinorVersion;
      UCHAR        SubVersion;
      UCHAR        SubMinorVersion;
    } VersionDetail;
  };
  ULONG          ProviderVersion;     // defaults to NT version
  ULONG          NumberOfProcessors;  // Number of Processors
  LARGE_INTEGER  EndTime;             // Time when logger stops
  ULONG          TimerResolution;     // assumes timer is constant!!!
  ULONG          MaximumFileSize;     // Maximum in Mbytes
  ULONG          LogFileMode;         // specify logfile mode
  ULONG          BuffersWritten;      // used to file start of Circular File
  union {
    GUID LogInstanceGuid;             // For RealTime Buffer Delivery
    struct {
      ULONG        StartBuffers;      // Count of buffers written at start.
      ULONG        PointerSize;       // Size of pointer type in bits
      ULONG        EventsLost;        // Events losts during log session
      ULONG        CpuSpeedInMHz;     // Cpu Speed in MHz
    };
  };
  LPWSTR         LoggerName;
  LPWSTR         LogFileName;
```

```
    TIME_ZONE_INFORMATION TimeZone;
    LARGE_INTEGER  BootTime;
    LARGE_INTEGER  PerfFreq;              // Reserved
    LARGE_INTEGER  StartTime;             // Reserved
    ULONG          ReservedFlags;         // Reserved
    ULONG          BuffersLost;
} TRACE_LOGFILE_HEADER, *PTRACE_LOGFILE_HEADER;
```

We won't cover every member in this structure because most of them are pretty obvious. Let's examine a few of them that you might want to use.

The `ProviderVersion` and `VersionDetail` members contain the operating system's build and version numbers, respectively. The start time of the session can be determined by `StartTime`, and the time the session was stopped can be found in `EndTime`. The `PerfFreq` member provides the frequency of the high-resolution performance counter that the log file or real-time session used when it was created. This is usually the speed of the machine in hertz. The `TimerResolution` member provides timing information that allows the correct interpretation of the kernel, user, and processor timings within the log file's events. `TimerResolution` contains the resolution of the hardware timer, in units of 100 nanoseconds.

Processing events from event-trace log files or real-time sessions is represented by an array of (`OpenTrace` provided) `TRACEHANDLE`s. The `ProcessTrace` function is straightforward:

```
ULONG ProcessTrace(PTRACEHANDLE HandleArray, ULONG HandleCount,
   LPFILETIME StartTime, LPFILETIME EndTime);
```

The array of `TRACEHANDLE`s is supplied through `HandleArray` and the number of elements within the array is passed in the `HandleCount` parameter. The `StartTime` and `EndTime` parameters allow the restriction of events by delivering only the events of interest during the period starting with `StartTime` and ending with `EndTime`. If both of these are NULL, no time restriction is applied.

Finally, when `ProcessTrace` has finished, all the `TRACEHANDLE`s in the `HandleArray` should be closed with `CloseTrace`. Note that `CloseTrace` closes only handles created by `OpenTrace`.

```
ULONG CloseTrace(TRACEHANDLE TraceHandle);
```

■ Monitoring Real-Time Event-Tracing Sessions

To monitor events in real time requires the set up of a real-time session and a real-time consumer to receive the events. The consumer will receive the events only as each buffer becomes full or is flushed. Coding up a controller to start a real-time session is virtually the same as you have seen in earlier sections of this chapter. The only notable difference is that no log filename is specified in the string pointed to by `LogFileName-Offset` because a real-time session has no filename. Also, the `LogFileMode` contains the `EVENT_TRACE_REAL_TIME_MODE` flag, which is what really specifies the session's events to be delivered in real time. Finally, the name of the real-time session is passed into `StartTrace`. The following sample code starts a real-time session for event traces from the lift simulator:

```
// Setup the Event Tracing session properties
PEVENT_TRACE_PROPERTIES pTraceProps = MakeTraceProperties();


pTraceProps->Wnode.Guid = PROVGUID_LIFTSIM;


// This tells the Event Tracer to setup a real-time session
pTraceProps->LogFileMode = EVENT_TRACE_REAL_TIME_MODE;


// Start the session.
TRACEHANDLE hTraceSession = 0;
ULONG ulError = StartTrace(&hTraceSession,
  _T("LiftSim real-time session"), pTraceProps);


ulError = EnableTrace(TRUE, 0, 0, &PROVGUID_LIFTSIM, hTraceSession);


LocalFree(pTraceProps);
```

After the real-time session is started, another application or thread can process events in real time (remember that `ProcessTrace` is a synchronous function call). To monitor a specific real-time session requires the `EVENT_TRACE_LOGFILE` structure to specify the real-time session name correctly in `LoggerName` and set `LogFileMode` to include `EVENT_TRACE_REAL_TIME_MODE`. The following code sample receives real-time events from the real-time session started earlier.

```
const LPCTSTR ET_RT_SESSION = _T("LiftSim real-time session");


EVENT_TRACE_LOGFILE log = {0};


// Allocate memory for session name
log.LoggerName = reinterpret_cast<LPTSTR>(LocalAlloc(LPTR,
  (_tcslen(ET_RT_SESSION) +1) * sizeof(TCHAR)));


// Copy session name to EVENT_TRACE_LOGFILE structure
_tcscpy(log.LoggerName, ET_RT_SESSION);
```

```
// Setup event callback. This will be called for every event.
log.EventCallback = GenericEventCallback;

// We want to monitor a real-time session
log.LogFileMode = EVENT_TRACE_REAL_TIME_MODE;

// Setup as many log files that you want processed
TRACEHANDLE hTraceLog[1];
hTraceLog[0] = OpenTrace(&log);

// Process all the log files. This is a synchronous call
ULONG ulError = ProcessTrace(hTraceLog, 1, NULL, NULL);

// Clean up
ulError = CloseTrace(hTraceLog[0]);
```

As you can see, starting and monitoring events in real time is similar to the techniques identified earlier in the chapter. Remember that you will get to see the events only when the buffer becomes full or is flushed. This means that for sessions with large buffers and/or providers that don't produce many events, you won't get access to the events for a measurable amount of time. To overcome this limitation, you can either set up the session's `FlushTimer` automatically to flush the buffers more regularly or programmatically call `ControlTrace` to flush the buffers manually. If you expect a variable throughput of events from a particular provider, perhaps another controller can adjust the buffer size automatically and flush the timer to suit the frequency of events.

■ Providing and Analyzing Lightweight Events

Event-tracing providers can use what is considered a lightweight approach for generating events, as opposed to calling `TraceEvent` normally. The lightweight function `TraceMessage` generates informational events that include the event's data supplied through a variable argument list. The advantage of `TraceMessage` is that it is not only considered lightweight but is also simpler to call from within a provider. The fact that it produces only informational events clearly states its intended use. The Windows Software Trace Preprocessor (WPP) uses `TraceMessage` to generate events from within an application. The WPP is a set of macros: When inserted into an application's source code, it is preprocessed before the compiler does the compilation. One of the objectives of `TraceMessage` and WPP is to be as easy as using `printf` style logging in an application. One of the suggested uses of `TraceMessage` is to provide additional information in checked/debug builds. We highly encourage you not to consider `TraceMessage` as an alternative for all of an application's event tracing, because when an event-trace log file or real-time session is processed, it is much harder to analyze than a trace with `TraceEvent` generated events.

The lift simulator provider generates events detailing the lift's actions and its progress. The following code provides more information about what the lift is about to do before it starts the chosen operation:

```
// One of the variable arguments will be a string
WCHAR szActionMsg[32];
ZeroMemory(szActionMsg, sizeof(szActionMsg));


wcscpy(szActionMsg, L"The next action is ");


// Generate event
ULONG ulError = TraceMessage(g_hProvider,
  TRACE_MESSAGE_SEQUENCE | TRACE_MESSAGE_GUID | TRACE_MESSAGE_TIMESTAMP
  | TRACE_MESSAGE_SYSTEMINFO, &MYINFOEVENT, 502,
  szActionMsg, sizeof(szActionMsg), nAction, sizeof(nAction), NULL, 0);
```

One of the variable parameters is a string. The string is declared to be of a fixed length so that it is easier to interpret the event during analysis. The call to `TraceMessage` uses most of the flag parameters that can be passed to it. As each flag is used, the structure of the resulting event's data will be affected. The second variable argument is the action about to be performed. When this is coupled with the first variable argument, the resulting trace message would read something like this (in a `printf` style output), "The next action is 2." Finally, the variable argument list is terminated with NULL values.

Let's discuss `TraceMessage` in more detail:

```
ULONG __cdecl TraceMessage(TRACEHANDLE LoggerHandle,
  ULONG MessageFlags, LPGUID MessageGuid, USHORT MessageNumber, ...);
```

Like `TraceEvent`, the `LoggerHandle` parameter is the `TRACEHANDLE` that was obtained in the provider's control call-back function.

All events generated by `TraceMessage` contain almost no information in the `EVENT_TRACE` structure when processed by a consumer. The event's custom data is used to store both the variable arguments and extra data specified by the `MessageFlags` parameter. The only members of the `EVENT_TRACE` structure used by `TraceMessage` include:

1. `Class.Version`, which contains the flags passed in `MessageFlags`. Note that the flags specified alter the outcome of the custom data.

2. The lower `DWORD` of `Version` contains the number of each occurrence of the message/event that is supplied in the `MessageNumber` parameter. The value and meaning of the `MessageNumber` parameter are user-defined.

3. Both the `MofData` and `MofLength` members are used to provide access to the data specified for inclusion by `MessageFlags` and the variable argument list.

The `MessageGuid` parameter can specify either the class (GUID) of the message or a `DWORD` component identifier that is user-defined.

The variable argument list contains the message's information in pairs of `PVOID` and `ULONG` parameters. The `PVOID` argument specifies data and the `ULONG` argument specifies the length of the data (in bytes) referenced by `PVOID`. The argument list must be terminated with a NULL and 0.

Table 13.8 contains the flags that can be passed into the `MessageFlags` parameter. Note that these are in the correct evaluation order when analyzing an event generated by `TraceMessage`.

The `TraceMessage` function is available only under Windows XP and later.

Analyzing Lightweight Events

Analyzing events generated by `TraceMessage` always reveals an event class containing `GUID_NULL`. This effectively means the event has no class. This is one of the reasons why it is more difficult to analyze event traces with these types of events.

Table 13.8 `MessageFlags` Flags

`MessageFlags` **Flags**	**Comment**
`TRACE_MESSAGE_SEQUENCE`	Include a sequence number in the message.
	Note that sequence numbers will be generated only if the session supplies either `EVENT_TRACE_USE_LOCAL_SEQUENCE` or `EVENT_TRACE_USE_GLOBAL_SEQUENCE`.
`TRACE_MESSAGE_GUID`	The message type and that the `MessageGuid` parameter contains a GUID.
`TRACE_MESSAGE_COMPONENTID`	The component to which the message pertains. The `MessageGuid` parameter contains a `DWORD`.
`TRACE_MESSAGE_TIMESTAMP`	Includes the time that the message was generated.
`TRACE_MESSAGE_PERFORMANCE_TIMESTAMP`	Time stamp is the performance counter (not the system clock).
	This flag is valid only if `TRACE_MESSAGE_TIMESTAMP` is also specified.
`TRACE_MESSAGE_SYSTEMINFO`	Includes the thread identifier (TID) and process identifier (PID) in which the message was generated.

As already mentioned, an event trace processed with `ProcessTrace` can be supplied with an event call-back function to analyze the events within the log file or real-time session. However, it is important to note that all events are delivered to the call back. To separate or filter events by their event class is possible with the use of `Set-TraceCallback`. This sets the event call-back function for a specific event class and is irrespective of any particular `ProcessTrace` session within the process. When `ProcessTrace` encounters an event that has a registered event call-back for an event class, it calls that call-back function. This is in addition to the generic call-back function specified for the `ProcessTrace` session that still gets called. This technique of specifically filtering events of a specific class will become useful when analyzing event traces that contain events generated by `TraceMessage`.

Let's call `SetTraceCallback` to filter what is probably a `TraceMessage` event:

```
ulError = SetTraceCallback(&GUID_NULL, TraceMessageEventCallback);
```

The code says that for this process, whenever `ProcessTrace` encounters an event that has a class GUID of `GUID_NULL`, call the `TraceMessageEventCallback` function. It probably is wise to filter `TraceMessage` events for processing by another call-back function because they can be very intricate to implement. Structures pointed to by the `MofData` member will vary, depending on the flags and variable arguments that were passed to `TraceMessage`. The following example structure will decode the preceding `Trace-Message` event:

```
typedef struct tagLiftSimMsgTypeOVerBitmask43
{
  // TraceMessage members
  DWORD SeqNumber;
  GUID guid;
  FILETIME ft;
  DWORD TID;
  DWORD PID;

  // Variable arguments for MYINFOEVENT class
  WCHAR szMsg[32];
  ULONG nAction;
} LiftSimMsgTypeOVerBitmask43;
```

The `SeqNumber` member is included in the structure because the `TraceMessage` call that generated the event specified the `TRACE_MESSAGE_SEQUENCE` flag. The `guid` member is included because of the `TRACE_MESSAGE_GUID` flag. If the `TraceMessage` had specified `TRACE_MESSAGE_COMPONENTID` flag, then the `guid` member would be replaced with a `DWORD` for the component identifier. You get the picture: It becomes very intricate. Instead of making structures for every combination of flags passed to `TraceMessage`, it is probably better to walk the memory pointed to by `MofData` before processing the variable arguments. If no flags are specified in a call to `TraceMessage`, then the resulting data structure contains only the variable arguments. Hence, it is important to evaluate the flags correctly in the proper order. The diagram in Figure 13.10 shows the correct order of declaration of the resulting structure.

Whenever `SetTraceCallback` sets up a filter and it no longer is required, `RemoveTraceCallback` should be called to remove the call-back registration from the process, like this:

```
ulError = RemoveTraceCallback(&GUID_NULL);
```

▪ Summary

This chapter has introduced you to the benefits of event tracing and provided a complete and thorough discussion about the event-tracing APIs: Every API and structure has been covered. You've seen how to turn your existing applications into event-tracing providers by simply making a couple of API calls. In addition, you've been given everything you need to know to develop your own controllers and consumers. We have used these same techniques to develop a general purpose event-tracing analyzer, which is available on the Web site that accompanies this book.

Start integrating event traces in your own applications so that in time you'll be in a better position to investigate problems at customer sites. Using the event-tracing

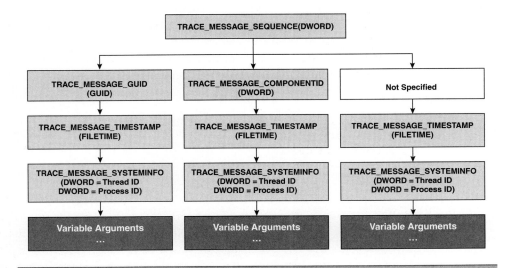

Figure 13.10 Interpreting `TraceMessage` events

technology opens up the possibility of obtaining event traces from subsystems apart from your own. This is a real benefit, especially in multiteam projects for large systems. Event tracing paves the way for unified debug, resource, operation, and capacity planning activities that have not been previously possible, especially when the kernel, device drivers, and security activity are included.

The event-tracing APIs are super fast, so any time-sensitive operation should not be affected by using them. In fact, on multiprocessor systems, each processor is allocated a separate active buffer to eliminate contention.

One other interesting area is event-tracing security. This is an ACL stored in the registry: If an ACL exists for the provider, the operating system's event tracer will apply the configured security credentials. Hence, it is possible to receive an access-denied error from the event-tracing APIs. Check the Platform SDK for more information on event-tracing security.

A limitation of the event-tracing system is that events delivered to a consumer may not appear in the exact time order that the events were delivered to the event tracer. This is true only if there are multiple events within the same millisecond. The lightweight function `TraceMessage` does offer the facility to sequence the events, but unfortunately, there is no equivalent for `TraceEvent`.

Event tracing is one of three high-performance instrumentation techniques available in Windows. There are also performance counters that make it easy to monitor system utilization. If you want to expose counters for your own application, you can check out some of the new features in ATL 7.0 in this area. If you want to gain access to performance counters from a client point of view, you can visit the Performance Data Helper (PDH) library.

An alternative to exposing performance counters is to develop a high-performance WMI provider. This makes it easy to expose WMI objects that can be accessed through the normal WMI APIs, as well as being optimized for very high performance both within an application and for transmissions over a network. The last few sections of Chapter 7 discuss how to query high-performance data as a client.

Ten Fast Facts: High-Performance Instrumentation

1. The main difference between event tracing and performance counters is that it is hard to track individual resources with performance counters. Performance counters offer a way to view system utilization, such as memory usage. Performance counters cannot be used easily for debug logging, for tracking resources or operations such as a disk drive, or for monitoring registry access.

2. Event-tracing controllers start and stop event-tracing sessions. An application that produces an event trace is known as an event-tracing provider. Event-tracing consumers analyze event-tracing log files and monitor the events in real time.

3. Event-tracing controllers can start sessions using the `StartTrace` API and later stop using `ControlTrace` passing the `EVENT_TRACE_CONTROL_STOP` flag.

4. Event-tracing providers can produce both events and event instances. Event instances are used for hierarchical event-tracing.

5. An event-tracing provider must implement a call-back function prototyped by `WMIDPREQUEST` and register it using `RegisterTraceGuids`. When the provider shuts down, it must unregister itself using `UnregisterTraceGuids`.

6. Event-tracing providers produce events using `TraceEvent`, and for hierarchical events they must use `CreateTraceInstanceId` and `TraceEventInstance`.

7. A list of registered event-tracing providers can be obtained using `Enumerate-TraceGuids`.

8. A list of active event-tracing sessions can be obtained using `QueryAllTraces`.

9. Analyzing event traces involves using consumer APIs `OpenTrace`, `ProcessTrace`, and `CloseTrace`. One of the real benefits of the event-tracing consumer APIs is that they can consume several log files and produce a time-ordered stream of events.

10. Event-tracing providers that want to produce informational events can do so using `TraceMessage`.

Appendix  A

WMI Event SDK Tools

Chapters 7, 8, and 12 covered subscribing and publishing WMI events. The aim of this appendix is to show how you can refine or test your event queries for an administrative script or an application development project. The WMI SDK comes with a number of tools that include CIM Studio, WMI Event Registration, WMI Event Viewer, and WMI Object Browser. CIM Studio is covered in Chapter 4. In this appendix, we shall focus on the WMI Event Registration and WMI Event Viewer tools.

Chapter 7 covered the three different types of events—intrinsic, extrinsic, and timer instructions—in detail. The WMI event tools allow you to set up event consumers to receive any WMI event. The main benefit of the event tools is that they allow visualization and inspection of virtually every aspect of an event. This is an invaluable resource for a developer. From an event consumer's point of view, they provide a toolset to refine and test event queries. From an event provider's perspective, they facilitate testing, which helps to ensure that the provider is working properly.

Let's start a tutorial that sets up and monitors a couple of event queries. We shall use the examples from Chapters 7 and 8. The first event query will monitor when the CD-ROM drive changes and has media, such as a music CD, loaded. The second event query will monitor events from an interval timer instruction.

From the Start menu, run the WMI Event Viewer tool. This tool has two functions. First, it allows you to view events from previously set-up consumers. Second, it allows you to load the WMI Event Registration tool to set up the event queries and consumers. Figure A.1 shows what you'll see.

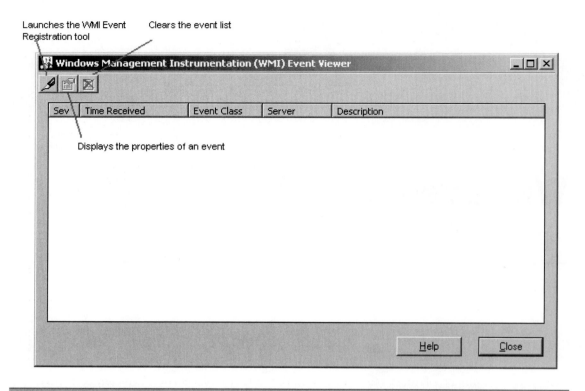

Figure A.1 WMI Event Viewer

Let's start by setting up an event query. To do so, launch the WMI Event Registration facility by pressing the first button on the top left of the toolbar. The WMI Event Registration tool enables the set up of event queries (also called filters), timer instructions, and event consumers. After these are set up, the WMI Event Viewer will instantiate the event consumers to receive the events. Figure A.2 shows what the WMI Event Registration tool looks like.

The left pane lists the selected configuration, which can be Consumers, Filters, or Timers. The right pane lists either event queries (filters) or consumers, depending on the configuration that is selected in the left pane. The configuration in the left pane displays currently set-up items or the creation of new items, such as timers, queries, and consumers. The right pane allows consumers and event queries to be associated with each other. More on this later.

Let's start by making a new event query. Select Filters and right-click the __EventFilter item, as in Figure A.3.

Select the New Instance menu item. This displays a property sheet that allows the event query configuration to be entered. First, you'll need to supply a name that

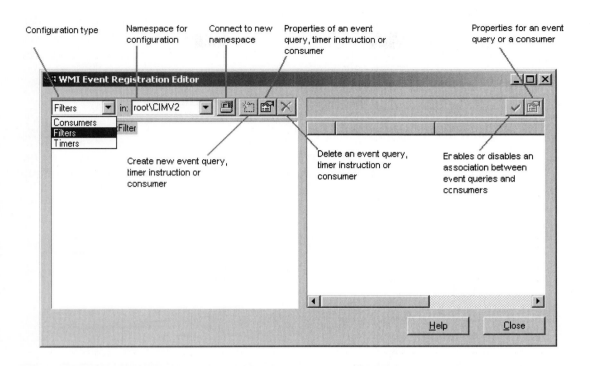

Figure A.2 WMI Event Registration

Figure A.3 Creating a new event query

uniquely identifies the event query. Supplying a good name will make it easy to identify the query when it is associated with an event consumer. Second, enter the event query for the events that you want to receive. Enter the following query that was covered in detail in Chapters 7 and 8:

```
SELECT * FROM __InstanceModificationEvent WITHIN 5
  WHERE TargetInstance ISA "Win32_CDROMDrive" AND
  TargetInstance.MediaLoaded = true
```

Briefly, the query requests events when the CD-ROM drive has changed and media has been loaded. Last, enter the type of the event query. The only currently supported type is WQL. Figure A.4 shows how this information is entered.

	Name △	Type	Value
▦ CreatorSID	array of uint8	Array
🔑 ▦ Name	string	CDROMWithMediaLoaded
▦ Query	string	SELECT * FROM __InstanceModifica
▦ QueryLanguage	string	WQL
🖳 __CLASS	string	__EventFilter

Figure A.4 Entering configuration for new event query

The next step is to create an event consumer with which the newly configured event query can be associated. This is an important step because only consumers can make event subscriptions to WMI. The WMI Event Registration facility makes it easy to set up a consumer and associate it with one or more event queries. Select the Consumers configuration in the left pane and right-click the EventViewerConsumer item as in Figure A.5.

Figure A.5 Creating new event consumer

Select the New Instance menu item. This displays a property sheet that allows the event consumer configuration to be entered (Figure A.6). First, you'll need to supply a name that uniquely identifies the event consumer. As with setting up an event query, supplying a good name will make it easier to identify the consumer when it is associated with an event query. Second, enter a description. This will be displayed in the WMI Event Viewer when the consumer receives an event. Entering a description is useful to distinguish events received by this consumer when multiple consumers are receiving events (Figure A.12). Last, enter the severity of the events subscribed to by this consumer. A value of zero will display an error icon in the WMI Event Viewer when an event arrives. The `Severity` property can be used to visualize the importance of an event. As you can see from Figure A.12, there is a warning icon for the events being subscribed to from the CD-ROM Media Loaded consumer and an informational icon for the events received by the Timer Event consumer. Set the `Severity` property to zero for an error icon, one for a warning icon, or two for an information icon.

			Name △	Type	Value
			CreatorSID	array of uint8	Array
			Description	string	Win32_CDROMDrive has changed a
			MachineName	string	\<empty\>
			MaximumQueueSize	uint32	\<empty\>
			Name	string	CDROM Media Loaded
			Severity	uint8	1
			_CLASS	string	EventViewerConsumer

Figure A.6 Entering configuration for new event consumer

Finally, the new consumer needs to be associated with the CD-ROM Media Loaded event query. The right pane lists all the available event queries with which the consumer can be associated. As only one query has been set up, only one query is listed. To associate the query to the consumer, press the green check toolbar button and a green check will appear next to the query, as in Figure A.7.

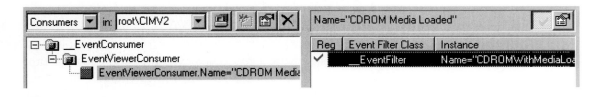

Figure A.7 Associating an event query to an event consumer

Closing the WMI Event Registration tool returns you to the WMI Event Viewer. The Event Viewer automatically updates itself when registrations are created or deleted. In the example in Figure A.8, we opened the CD-ROM and closed it with a music CD placed on the tray. This action caused the CD-ROM management object to change, and the event query was ultimately satisfied because the MediaLoaded event property became true. Notice that there is a warning icon because the consumer's configuration had the `Severity` property set to one.

Sev	Time Received	Event Class	Server	Description
⚠	3/28/2002 9:30:40 AM	__InstanceModificationEvent	BART	Win32_CDROMDrive has changed an

Figure A.8 WMI Event Viewer displaying newly received event

Let's continue and create an interval timer instruction and an event query to subscribe for the timer event. In addition, we shall create another consumer to receive the new timer events. Reopen the WMI Event Registration facility with the WMI Event Viewer. Select the Timers configuration in the left pane and right-click the __IntervalTimerInstruction item, as in Figure A.9.

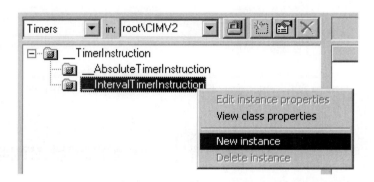

Figure A.9 Creating new time instruction

Select the New Instance menu item. This displays a property sheet that allows the timer instruction configuration to be entered (Figure A.10). First, you'll need to supply a timer identifier (that is, its name) to reference the timer instruction uniquely. As noted already, make a point of supplying a good name. Second, set the interval time between events in milliseconds. In the example in Figure A.10, WMI will fire a timer event every two seconds.

		Name △	Type	Value
	⊞	IntervalBetweenEver	uint32	2000
	🔧	SkipIfPassed	boolean	false
🔑	🔧	TimerId	string	TwoSecondTimer
	🖥	__CLASS	string	__IntervalTimerInstruction

Figure A.10   Entering configuration for new interval timer instruction

The next step is to create an event query that will capture the timer events fired by the new timer instruction. You'll need to go through steps similar to those that were used to create the CD-ROM event query, except that the query you enter in the screen in Figure A.4 will subscribe for the new timer events. Here's the timer event query:

```
SELECT * FROM __TimerEvent WHERE TimerId = "TwoSecondQuery"
```

Although the above event query could be associated with the CD-ROM Media Loaded consumer, we prefer to create another consumer to receive the timer events, because it demonstrates setting multiple consumers, and the event queries associated with the consumer can have a different class of severity. The events received by the CD-ROM Media Loaded consumer display a warning icon and those received by the Two Second Timer consumer display an information icon. Figure A.11 shows the timer query being associated with the Two Second Timer consumer.

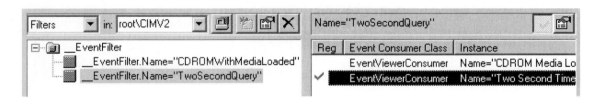

Figure A.11   Associating a timer event query to an event consumer

When you return to the WMI Event Viewer screen, you'll see multiple events being received by multiple consumers, as in Figure A.12. This is how you'll be able to visualize your event queries and monitor various types of events across the network. Using the WMI event SDK tools can provide a very simple means for a system administrator to monitor activity from servers with a network.

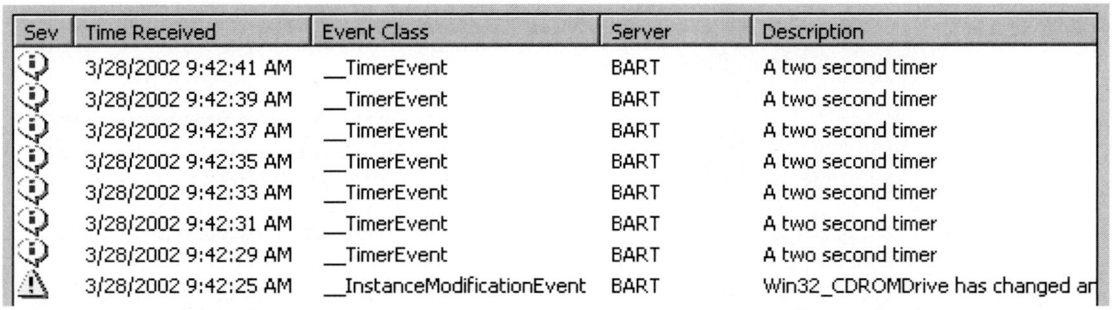
Sev
Time Received
Event Class
Server
Description
3/28/2002 9:42:41 AM __TimerEvent BART A two second timer
3/28/2002 9:42:39 AM __TimerEvent BART A two second timer
3/28/2002 9:42:37 AM __TimerEvent BART A two second timer
3/28/2002 9:42:35 AM __TimerEvent BART A two second timer
3/28/2002 9:42:33 AM __TimerEvent BART A two second timer
3/28/2002 9:42:31 AM __TimerEvent BART A two second timer
3/28/2002 9:42:29 AM __TimerEvent BART A two second timer
3/28/2002 9:42:25 AM __InstanceModificationEvent BART Win32_CDROMDrive has changed ar

Figure A.12 WMI Event Viewer displaying events from multiple consumers

To examine the detail of an event, either double-click an event or press the properties toolbar button. Figure A.13 shows the event detail of the CD-ROM drive `_InstanceModificationEvent` in Figure A.12. The `_InstanceModificationEvent` event is covered in detail in Chapter 7. However, note that both the `PreviousInstance` and `TargetInstance` properties are embedded objects. The WMI Event Viewer allows embedded objects to be displayed in detail by pressing the object button.

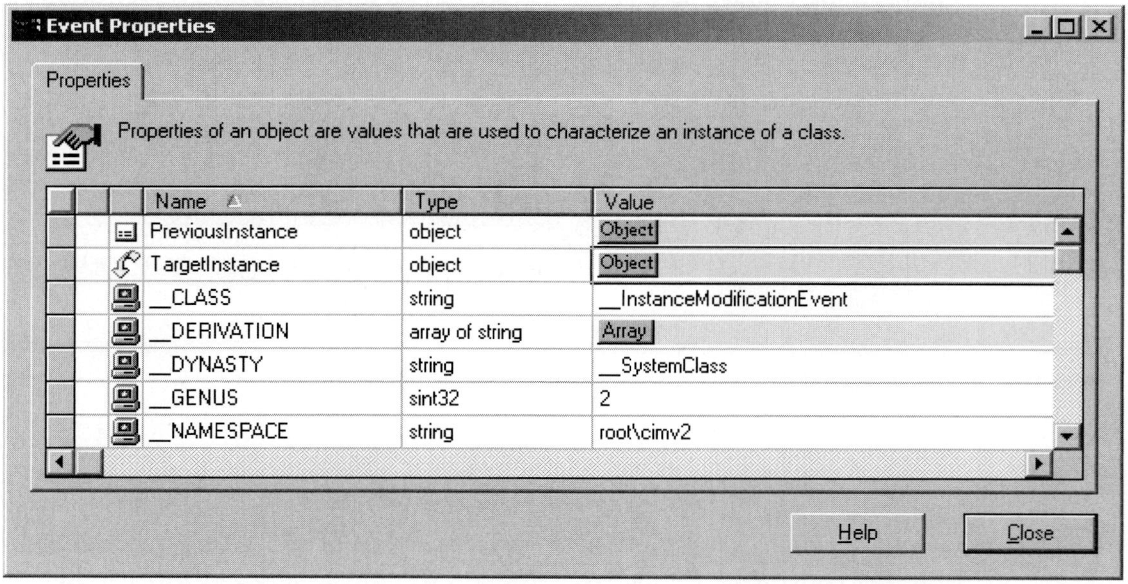
Event Properties
Properties
Properties of an object are values that are used to characterize an instance of a class.
Name
Type
Value
PreviousInstance object Object
TargetInstance object Object
__CLASS string __InstanceModificationEvent
__DERIVATION array of string Array
__DYNASTY string __SystemClass
__GENUS sint32 2
__NAMESPACE string root\cimv2
Help
Close

Figure A.13 Viewing an event in the WMI Event Viewer

Pressing the object button (next to the `TargetInstance` property) displays the recently changed CD-ROM management object: See the screen shot in Figure A.14. All the properties of the `Win32_CDROMDrive` object can be inspected and you'll also notice that the `MediaLoaded` property is *true,* which is a requirement of the event query.

The WMI event SDK tools are very useful: You'll find yourself using them continuously during your software development projects or administrative tasks. The more you use WMI events, the more you'll realize just how useful they are.

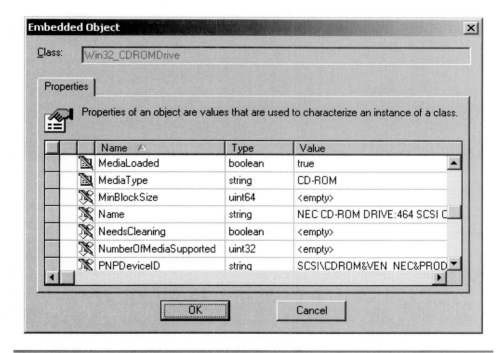

Figure A.14   Viewing `TargetInstance` property

Appendix B

WMI Server Explorer

Microsoft has developed the WMI Server Explorer extension for Visual Studio.NET, a new tool for interacting with WMI in the integrated development environment. The Server Explorer is a useful aid that allows you to manipulate and manage various components of a machine. By default, there are facilities in the server explorer to access the Windows event log, services, performance counters, message queues, and SQL Server database connections. To add the WMI Server Explorer extension, you must download and install it from the Microsoft Web site. Go to http://www.microsoft.com/downloads/ and perform a keyword search for "Management (WMI) Extensions for VS.NET" to link to the WMI Server Explorer download page.

In some ways, the WMI Server Explorer extension is similar to the WMI Object Browser, which is a tool that ships with the WMI SDK. The WMI Server Explorer uses association classes to link related management objects together. Before delving into a tutorial, let's see what the server explorer looks like (Figure B.1).

The items listed under "Management Classes" are the WMI classes included in the server explorer by default. "Management Events" allows you to subscribe for WMI event notifications. More on this later.

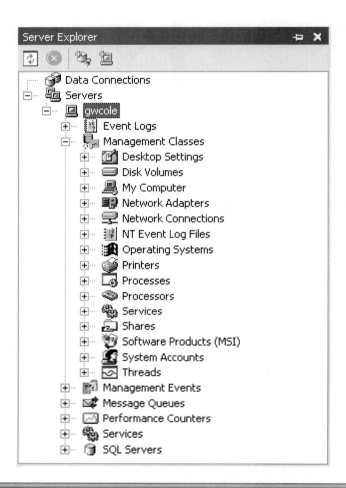

Figure B.1 The Visual Studio .NET Server Explorer

■ Manipulating Management Objects in the Server Explorer

Let's go through a short tutorial in using the WMI Server Explorer. The WMI Server Explorer allows you to add management classes from any WMI namespace into the view you see in Figure B.1. The WMI Server Explorer displays the class's management objects and any association classes relating management objects to one another. Let's start by adding the Fruit Basket management classes that we discussed in Chapter 12. There are two main classes, `Sample_Basket` and `Sample_Fruit`, and an association class, `Sample_BasketFruitMembership`, to link which fruit belongs in which basket.

To add a management class to the WMI Server Explorer view, right-click on Management Classes and select the Add Classes...menu option. Figure B.2 shows the Add Classes dialog that allows you to select the namespace and the classes within them that you would like to add to the WMI Server Explorer view. Figure B.2 shows the `Sample_Basket` and `Sample_Fruit` classes being added.

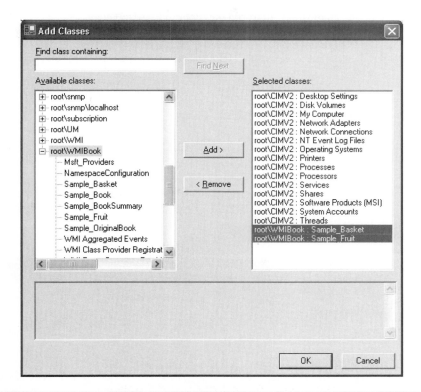

Figure B.2 Add Classes dialog

After pressing the OK button you'll see the selected classes get added to the view. Figure B.3 shows a simplified view of what the newly added items will look like.

Figure B.3 The newly added management classes

Notice that the full class names are displayed. If you want your classes to have a different display name, "Fruit Basket" instead of "Sample_Basket," you must add the DisplayName qualifier to the management class, as in the following MOF declaration.

```
[
  dynamic: ToInstance,
  provider("FruitBasketProv"): ToInstance,
  SupportsUpdate,
  SupportsDelete,
  DisplayName("Fruit Basket"): ToInstance ToSubClass
]
class Sample_Basket
{
  [key] string Name;
  uint8 Capacity;
};
```

To highlight the similarities between the WMI Object Browser and the WMI Server Explorer, the screen shot in Figure B.4 shows how the WMI Object Browser displays the fruit basket called "The Basket." Notice that "The Basket" management object is associ-

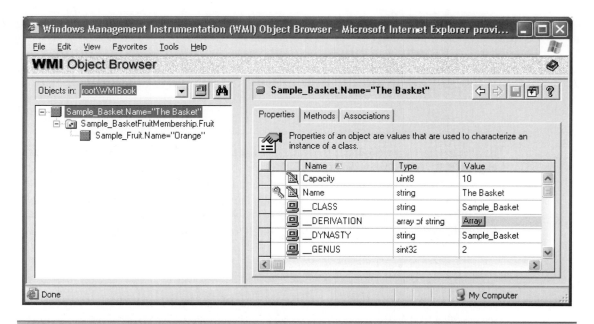

Figure B.4 The WMI Object Browser showing the fruit basket objects

ated with only one item of fruit, "Orange." If the basket had multiple items of fruit, these would also be listed. The right pane shows the basket's properties and a tab for invoking any methods, as well as a tab for showing the object relationships diagrammatically.

Let's see how the same fruit basket is displayed in the WMI Server Explorer. Figure B.5 shows a portion of the view. Notice that we added the `DisplayName` qualifiers to the `Sample_Basket` and `Sample_Fruit` classes. The "Fruit Basket" class has one basket called "The Basket." Through the association class, the basket contains one item of fruit, "Orange." As you can see, this is very similar to the view you see in the WMI Object Browser.

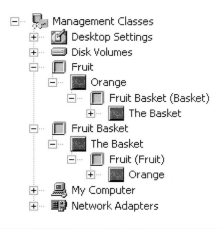

Figure B.5 The WMI Server Explorer showing the fruit basket objects

The properties of a management object also can be displayed. To do this, right-click the "The Basket" management object and select the Properties menu option. You will see a Properties window similar to the one in Figure B.6.

Management class and object methods can also be invoked with the WMI Server Explorer. The methods appear on the item's menu. For example, right-click the Fruit management class and you'll see the menu option AddFruitToBasket…(as in Figure B.7).

Select the AddFruitToBasket menu option and you will see the dialog in Figure B.8. To invoke the method, complete the method parameters and press the invoke button. To add an item of fruit called "Apple" to a basket called "The Cool Basket," complete the `FruitName` and `BasketName` method parameters respectively. After a method has been invoked, the Results list shows the methods `ReturnValue` and any other output parameters.

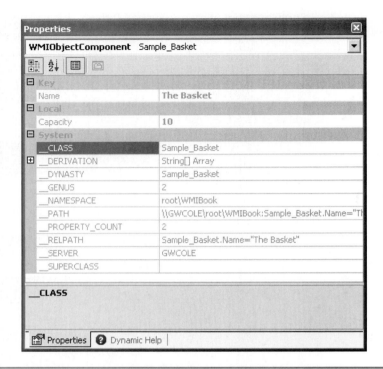

Figure B.6 The WMI Server Explorer properties window

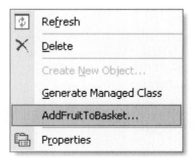

Figure B.7 The *Fruit* class menu

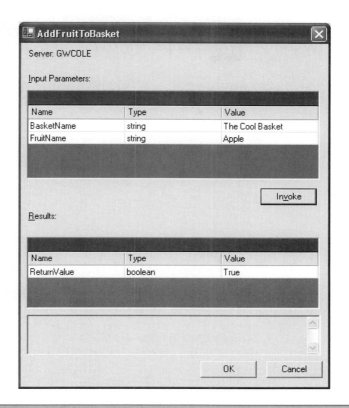

Figure B.8 The AddFruitToBasket method dialog

Also notice that the menu in Figure B.7 has a menu option titled Generate Managed Class. In a .NET C# development project, this will create a C# class that wraps up access to the management class in question. This is very handy if you want easy access to WMI objects within your development projects. The following is a much cut-down extract of the class generated.

```
public class Fruit: System.ComponentModel.Component {

  // Private property to hold the name of WMI class which created
    this class.
  private static string CreatedClassName = "Sample_Fruit";

  ... ... ..
  .. ...
  ...
  .
```

```csharp
// Gains access to the WMI Sample_Fruit.Name property
[Browsable(true)]
[DesignerSerializationVisibility(DesignerSerializationVisibility.
  Hidden)]
public string Name {
  get {
    return ((string)(curObj["Name"]));
  }
}

... ... ..
... ...
...
..


// Gains access to the WMI Sample_Fruit.Weight property
[Browsable(true)]
[DesignerSerializationVisibility(DesignerSerializationVisibility.
  Hidden)]
[TypeConverter(typeof(WMIValueTypeConverter))]
public System.UInt16 Weight {
  get {
    if ((curObj["Weight"] == null)) {
      return System.Convert.ToUInt16(0);
    }
    return ((System.UInt16)(curObj["Weight"]));
  }
}

... ... ..
.. ... .
.. ..
...


// Gains access to the WMI Sample_Fruit enumeration and WQL queries
public static FruitCollection GetInstances(string condition) {
  return GetInstances(null, condition, null);
}

..........
........
.....
..


// A wrapper for the WMI Sample_Fruit class method, AddFruitToBasket.
 public static bool AddFruitToBasket(string BasketName, string
FruitName) {
 bool IsMethodStatic = true;
```

```
if ((IsMethodStatic == true)) {
  System.Management.ManagementBaseObject inParams = null;
  System.Management.ManagementClass classObj =
    new System.Management.ManagementClass(null,
      "Sample_Fruit", null);
  inParams = classObj.GetMethodParameters("AddFruitToBasket");
  inParams["BasketName"] = BasketName;
  inParams["FruitName"] = FruitName;
  System.Management.ManagementBaseObject outParams =
    classObj.InvokeMethod("AddFruitToBasket", inParams, null);
  return System.Convert.ToBoolean(outParams.
    Properties["ReturnValue"].Value);
}
else {
  return System.Convert.ToBoolean(0);
}
}


 . . . . . . . . . .
  . . . . . . . .
   . . . . .
    . .
}
```

■ Subscribing for Event Notification in the Server Explorer

Chapters 7, 8, and 12 covered subscribing and publishing WMI events. To be able to refine and test your event queries within the integrated development environment is a real benefit. You may do this for an administrative script or for an application development project. The WMI Event Registration and WMI Event Viewer, discussed in Appendix A, are among the number of tools in the WMI SDK. Because the WMI Server Explorer is a separate downloadable extension, it is not part of the WMI SDK.

Chapter 7 covered the three different types of events—intrinsic, extrinsic, and timer instructions—in detail. The WMI Server Explorer allows you to set up temporary event consumers to receive any WMI event. From an event consumer point of view, the WMI Server Explorer provides a means to refine and test event queries. From an event provider perspective, the WMI Server Explorer facilitates testing, which helps to ensure that the provider is working properly.

So let's continue the tutorial and set up and monitor an event query. We will use an example from Chapters 7 and 8. The event query will monitor when the CD-ROM drive changes and has media loaded, such as a music CD.

To add a management event query to the WMI Server Explorer view, right-click the Management Events and select the Add Event Query...menu option. Figure B.9 shows the Build Management Event Query dialog that allows you to set up the event query.

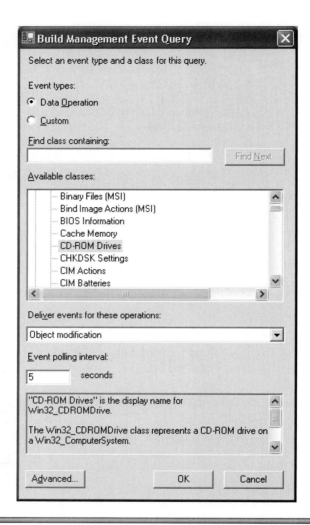

Figure B.9 The Build Management Event Query dialog

The dialog's user interface allows you develop a query without having to know all the class names, event query syntax, and other details to create an event query. The query that we would like to set up will be equivalent to the following, which was covered in detail in Chapters 7 and 8:

```
SELECT * FROM __InstanceModificationEvent WITHIN 5
  WHERE TargetInstance ISA "Win32_CDROMDrive" AND
  TargetInstance.MediaLoaded = true
```

Briefly, the query requests events when the CD-ROM drive has changed and media has been loaded. When first entering the dialog in Figure B.9, you are presented with a list of all the WMI namespaces in the list titled "Available classes." Figure B.10 shows what the list looks like before it was expanded in Figure B.9. Expand the `root\CIMV2` namespace and scroll down until you find the CD-ROM Drives item (as in Figure B.9). Selecting this will ensure that the resulting query will include the `Win32_CDROMDrive` management class.

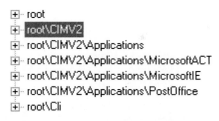

Figure B.10   The available classes list

Next, change the Deliver events for these operations selection to Object modification. Selecting Object Modification will ensure that the resulting query will include the `__InstanceModificationEvent` intrinsic event class.

Next, ensure that the Event polling interval is set to 5. This will ensure that the resulting query will include the `WITHIN 5` clause.

To make the event query more specific, you will need to press the advanced button. Figure B.11 shows the Advanced Query Options dialog.

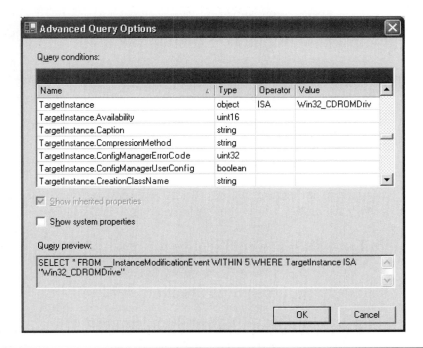

Figure B.11   The Advanced Query Options dialog

The lower portion of the dialog shows the WQL event query so far. The next task is to add the `MediaLoaded = true` condition to the event query. This involves finding the `MediaLoaded` property in the target instance class, `Win32_CDROMDrive`. Entering the desired operator and the desired value will cause the event query to be updated, as in Figure B.12.

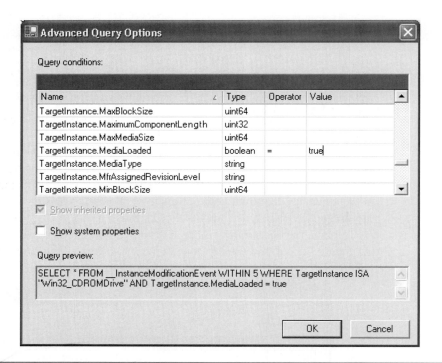

Figure B.12 Specifying the `MediaLoaded=true` condition

Press OK again on the Build Management Event Query dialog. After the WMI Server Explorer registers the event query subscription, you'll see the event query item appear as in Figure B.13.

Figure B.13 The CD-ROM event query subscription

Finally, when an event occurs, it will appear in the output window in Visual Studio.NET, as in Figure B.14. Note that the output of the event is on a single line.

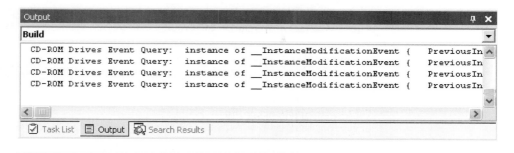

Figure B.14 The Visual Studio .NET output window

Expanding the text from one of the events provides every detail of the event. The following is the last event in Figure B.14 expanded. The items in bold demonstrate that the `MediaLoaded` property did indeed change to be in a loaded state.

```
CD-ROM Drives Event Query: instance of __InstanceModificationEvent
{
  PreviousInstance = instance of Win32_CDROMDrive
  {
    Availability = 3;
    Capabilities = {3, 7};
    Caption = "HITACHI DVD-ROM GD-5000";
    ConfigManagerErrorCode = 0;
    ConfigManagerUserConfig = FALSE;
    CreationClassName = "Win32_CDROMDrive";
    Description = "CD-ROM Drive";
    DeviceID = "IDE\\CDROMHITACHI_DVD-ROM_GD-
5000_0212_\\5&35C6CA11&0&0.0.0";
    Drive = "D:";
    Id = "D:";
    Manufacturer = "(Standard CD-ROM drives)";
    MediaLoaded = FALSE;
    MediaType = "CD-ROM";
    Name = "HITACHI DVD-ROM GD-5000";
    PNPDeviceID = "IDE\\CDROMHITACHI_DVD-ROM_GD-
5000_0212_\\5&35C6CA11&0&0.0.0";
    SCSIBus = 0;
    SCSILogicalUnit = 0;
    SCSIPort = 1;
    SCSITargetId = 0;
```

```
      Status = "OK";
      SystemCreationClassName = "Win32_ComputerSystem";
      SystemName = "GWCOLE";
    };

    TargetInstance = instance of Win32_CDROMDrive
    {
      Availability = 3;
      Capabilities = {3, 7};
      Caption = "HITACHI DVD-ROM GD-5000";
      ConfigManagerErrorCode = 0;
      ConfigManagerUserConfig = FALSE;
      CreationClassName = "Win32_CDROMDrive";
      Description = "CD-ROM Drive";
      DeviceID = "IDE\\CDROMHITACHI_DVD-ROM_GD-
      5000_0212_\\5&35C6CA11&0&0.0.0";
      Drive = "D:";
      DriveIntegrity = TRUE;
      FileSystemFlagsEx = 524293;
      Id = "D:";
      Manufacturer = "(Standard CD-ROM drives)";
      MaximumComponentLength = 110;
      MediaLoaded = TRUE;
      MediaType = "CD-ROM";
      Name = "HITACHI DVD-ROM GD-5000";
      PNPDeviceID = "IDE\\CDROMHITACHI_DVD-ROM_GD-
      5000_0212_\\5&35C6CA11&0&0.0.0";
      SCSIBus = 0;
      SCSILogicalUnit = 0;
      SCSIPort = 1;
      SCSITargetId = 0;
      Size = "644122624";
      Status = "OK";
      SystemCreationClassName = "Win32_ComputerSystem";
      SystemName = "GWCOLE";
      TransferRate = 3264;
      VolumeName = "MP3";
      VolumeSerialNumber = "9ED67994";
    };
  };
```

Glossary

Alias

An Alias is an abstraction introduced as part of the Windows XP command line tool WMIC. It provides simplified keywords, or Aliases, in place of more complex queries that retrieve and format information from the CIM repository. Using an Alias makes it easier to specify a complex query from the command line.

Association

An association is a special management class that illustrates the relationships that exist between management objects.

CIM (Common Information Model)

The common information model defines a model that represents the manageable elements of the enterprise. It is a core concept of the WBEM initiative and was defined by the DMTF. The CIM describes the management environment through namespaces, classes, objects, properties, standard data types, and methods.

CIM repository

The CIM repository is the store that holds enterprise management information. It uses the Common Information Model as a template for structuring the data held in the repository, and it is implementation specific.

Class provider

A class provider can generate class definitions dynamically. For instance, the WMI Performance Counter provider generates WMI classes based on the counter definitions.

Class schema
See *Management schema.*

CMIP (Common Management Information Protocol)
Common Management Information Protocol is part of the Open Standards Interconnect (OSI) body of standards that defines operations and notification services described in the standard called Common Management Information Services (CMIS).

CMIS (Common Management Information Services)
The Common Management Information Services framework defines a set of messages, their structure, and their content for use with network management. It is similar in concept to SNMP but provides more functionality.

COM/DCOM (Distributed Component Object Model)
The Component Object Model (COM) is a Microsoft-defined component software architecture that allows applications and systems to be built from components supplied by different software vendors. The Distributed Component Object Model (DCOM) extends COM by enabling a communication mechanism among objects on different computers. (Source: MSDN)

Data query
Data queries specify which management objects are requested from the management environment. For example, "SELECT * FROM Win32_LogicalDisk".

DMI (Desktop Management Interface)
The Desktop Management Interface (DMI) is a specification defined and managed by the DMTF. It came into existence in 1994 and was the realization of the DMTF's goal to simplify desktop management. It represents the DMTF's first initiative to reduce the complexity of desktop management for vendors and administrators.

DMTF (Distributed Management Task Force)
The DMTF consortium was founded in May of 1992 by a cooperative of eight companies: Digital Equipment Corporation, Hewlett-Packard, IBM, Intel, Microsoft, Novell, SunSoft, and SynOptics. The DMTF now comprises over 200 commercial technology industry providers whose aim is to work together to develop standards for the maintenance, support, and development of management standards for personal computer products.

Event consumer
An event consumer is an application that requests events from WMI. There are two types of event consumers: temporary event consumers and permanent event consumers.

Event provider

An event provider can publish both intrinsic and extrinsic events. This type of provider is generally coupled with instance providers.

Event query

An event query specifies exactly the events to which an event consumer would like to subscribe. For example, "`SELECT * FROM __InstanceModificationEvent WITHIN 30 WHERE TargetInstance ISA "Win32_CDROMDrive"`".

Event tracing

Event tracing is a subsystem that is deeply integrated in the Windows operating system and is considered part of the Windows Management Instrumentation tool set. Event tracing is super fast and provides new scope for resolving problems and monitoring and tracking resources. The most fundamental aspect of event tracing is an *event*.

Event-tracing session

An event-tracing session manages the events delivered to the operating system's event tracer and either stores them to a file or delivers them to an event-tracing real-time monitor.

Event-tracing provider

An event-tracing provider publishes events to one or more event-tracing sessions. There are several providers within the operating system to expose activity in the Windows kernel, security subsystems, and numerous other subsystems. Any application can expose events to the operating system's event tracer.

Event-tracing analysis

This is the process of analyzing event traces either by reading one or more event tracing log files or by monitoring and analyzing the events in a real-time monitor.

Extrinsic event

Extrinsic events are custom-defined events. These are useful for applications to publish events that do not fit in with namespaces, classes, and instances.

Flavors

Qualifiers are characterized by how they are transmitted from parent to child class or from class to instance. Flavors determine the rules by which a qualifier transmits its information.

High-Performance provider

A high-performance (Hi-Perf) provider allows very fast and efficient access to constantly changing data.

HTTP (Hypertext Transfer Protocol)
The transport protocol defined by the W3C that enables the transmission of HTML (Hypertext Markup Language) pages across the Web. HTTP is one of the underlying protocols capable of transmitting XML-managed information.

IETF (Internet Engineering Task Force)
The Internet Engineering Task Force is a standards body that oversees the evolution of the Internet architecture and the smooth operation of the Internet. It has been responsible for defining hundreds of standards for the protocols that proliferate the Internet.

Instance
The term *instance* is interchangeable with *management object* and *managed object*. See *Management object*.

Intrinsic event
Intrinsic events occur in response to changes to namespaces, classes, and instances.

Instance provider
An instance provider exposes the instances that are available for one or more classes. An instance provider can support instance enumeration, retrieval, creation, modification, and deletion of instance data. An instance provider needs to store and provide access to its own data, the local cache.

Key property
A key property or compound key properties define how a management object will be referenced.

Local cache
The *local cache* is a term used in developing WMI providers. It represents the data that dynamic providers use when exposing management objects, properties, and methods. Examples include the Active Directory, an XML file, a database, the Internet, the registry, or some other storage medium.

Managed object
The term *managed object* is interchangeable with *management object* and *instance*. See *Management object*.

Management application
A management application is a program (such as an MMC snap-in) or Web interface that can interact with the management environment to gather, inspect, and manipulate a system's functionality or configuration.

Management class
A management class is the schema to which all management objects (or instances) will conform.

Management namespace
Namespaces are used in WMI to differentiate among the groups of classes and instances that represent particular management environments.

Management object
A management object is an instance of a management class and represents an object whose properties can be inspected to evaluate the state of the managed item. For instance, a shared directory on a personal computer can be represented as a managed item by exposing the name of the share together with its path and a multitude of other properties.

Management schema
A management schema is a set of classes that instrument a particular management environment. For instance, the Win32 schema instruments the various Windows-specific aspects of the operating system. A management schema is also referred to as the *class* schema.

Management scope
A term used by the WMI classes in the .NET Framework to help manage connections to the WMI operating system services.

Method provider
A method provider implements one or more methods in one or more classes. This type of provider is generally coupled with instance providers.

MMC (Microsoft Management Console)
The Microsoft Management Console is Microsoft's answer to providing a consistent user interface in which system administrators can find all their management tools.

MOF (Managed Object Format)
The Managed Object Format is used to define the structure and contents of the CIM schema. A MOF text file describes the classes (and instances) of one or more management objects. The information held in a MOF file can then be imported into the CIM repository.

.NET Framework
The .NET Framework is a new platform that has many new technological features that make it useful for writing, deploying, and running software. A top-level view of the .NET

Framework is that it can be seen as an execution platform that is not tied to a specific processor architecture. The WMI management environment is exposed through the .NET Framework through the System.Management library.

Object path

An object path is a string that can specifically reference either a class or object instance. An object path can either be considered a *fully qualified path* or a *relative path*. Relative object paths omit the machine and namespace names.

Object property

See *Property*.

Object reference

See *Object path*.

Permanent event consumer

Permanent event consumers offer a robust event delivery system and are implemented as loadable (on-demand) components. When an event is delivered to a permanent event consumer, WMI loads the appropriate component (if it has not already been loaded from a previous event delivery) and then passes the event to it.

Property

Property is the term used in WMI to describe the characteristics of a management class or object.

Property provider

A property provider implements dynamic property access for one or more classes. Properties are accessed using a class, an instance, or a property context.

Push provider

A push provider allows you to create instances and update properties that reside within the CIM repository. This is useful for data that is not dynamic and solves the problem of having to create and manage your own local cache. This includes the data storage, data access, and event notification, all of which are provided by WMI.

Qualifiers

Qualifiers are the mechanism by which characteristics can be assigned to any of the elements within a schema. This includes methods, method parameters, properties, classes, and associations.

Role

A role in WMIC is a namespace that defines and contains alias configuration data. By default this is the namespace \\root\Cli. This can be changed by system administrators who wish to define their own namespaces for their own aliases.

Schema
See *Management schema.*

Schema query
Schema queries are used to request class information and/or schema associations.

Script
A script is a plain text file and is similar in some respects to an MSDOS batch file. It contains a series of commands that the Windows Scripting Host (WSH) passes to the relevant scripting engine for interpretation into specific actions. System administrators can write scripts to execute routine administrative tasks within the management environment.

SNMP (Simple Network Management Protocol)
The simple network management protocol is an open network management protocol designed to monitor and control network components such as servers, gateways, and routers. SNMP is an Internet standard defined by the IETF and is part of the TCP/IP suite of protocols.

Timer event
Timer events are a specialized kind of intrinsic event. They are events that are generated and delivered by WMI using preconfigured timer instructions.

Timer instruction
A timer instruction informs WMI when to generate a timer event. There are two types of timer instructions: absolute and interval timer instructions. Absolute timer instructions generate and deliver an event at a specific time. Interval timer instructions are continuously generated and delivered when each interval occurs.

Temporary event consumer
Temporary event consumers are applications (clients or Windows services) that subscribe to WMI for event notification. The event notification is temporary because if the application is not running, the event cannot be delivered.

UML (Unified Modelling Language)
The Unified Modelling Language is used in schema design as a way of creating a visual template of schemas, with the aim of simplifying the overall development process.

WBEM (Web-Based Enterprise Management)
WBEM is an initiative that ties together existing standards with new technologies such as the CIM.

WMI (Windows Management Instrumentation)
The Windows Management Instrumentation is a complete management infrastructure for the Windows operating systems. It integrates WBEM's concept of a common information model for management information into the Windows management framework.

WMIC

Administrators of Windows XP have an additional tool in their systems management armory called the *WMI Command line* or WMIC. As the name suggests, this is a command-line driven tool that can access local or remote CIM repositories and retrieve, modify, add, and delete objects in the management environment.

WMI CIM Studio

A tool supplied by the WMI SDK that allows developers and system administrators to navigate, inspect, manipulate, and search the CIM repository.

WMI Provider

A software component that is loaded by WMI to service a management request. There are several types of providers that can be developed to expose a systems management environment.

WSH (Windows Scripting Host)

The Microsoft Windows Scripting Host (WSH) is a language-independent scripting host for Windows Script compatible scripting engines. It brings simple, powerful, and flexible scripting to the Windows platform, allowing you to run scripts from both the Windows desktop and the command prompt. (Source: MSDN)

W3C (World Wide Web Consortium)

The W3C was founded in 1994 with the objective of developing common protocols for the World Wide Web. The development of these common protocols enables interoperability in an environment that spans the globe, the Internet.

WQL (WMI Query Language)

The WMI Query Language is based on SQL (Structured Query Language) with new keywords to support specific WMI features. This includes data, schema, and event queries.

XML (Extended Markup Language)

XML is a subset of the Standard Generalized Mark-up Language (SGML) and is targeted at data representation. XML has been adopted by the DMTF as a means of representing the information stored in CIM across heterogeneous networks.

ZAW (Zero Administration for Windows)

Microsoft launched the Zero Administration for Windows (ZAW) initiative to show its commitment to the problems and costs associated with complex administrative environments. The aim of the ZAW initiative was to reduce the Total Cost of Ownership (TCO) of running and maintaining a Windows desktop personal computer in the enterprise. It encompassed a variety of technologies including Windows policy-based management and more important, WMI.

Bibliography

Booch, Grady. (1993). *Object-Oriented Analysis and Design with Applications* (2nd Ed.). Menlo Park, CA: Addison-Wesley. [ISBN: 0-805-35340-2]

Booch, Grady, Rumbaugh, James, and Jacobson, Ivar. (1998). *The Unified Modeling Language User Guide.* Reading, Mass: Addison-Wesley. [ISBN: 0-201-57168-4]

Brown, Keith. (2000). *Programming Windows Security.* Boston, MA: Addison-Wesley. [ISBN 0-201-60442-6]

http://msdn.microsoft.com: Microsoft Developer Network (MSDN)

http://www.dmtf.org: Distributed Management Task Force (DMTF)

http://www.ietf.org: Internet Engineering Task Force (IETF)

http://www.microsoft.com: Microsoft website

http://www.rational.com/uml/: Rational Software

http://www.textpad.com: Helios

http://www.w3.org: The World Wide Web Consortium

Kent, William. (1983). "A simple guide to five normal forms in relational database theory." *Communications of the ACM,* 26:2, 120–125.

Priestly, Mark. (2000). *Practical Object-Oriented Design with UML* (2nd Ed). Europe: McGraw-Hill Education. [ISBN: 0-077-09599-5]

Rector, Brent, and Sells, Chris. (1999). *ATL Internals.* Reading, Mass.: Addison-Wesley. [ISBN 0-201-69589-8]

Thompson, J. P. (1989). *Data with Semantics: Data Models and Data Management.* New York: Van Nostrand Reinhold. [ISBN: 0-442-31838-3]

Index

Also from Addison-Wesley

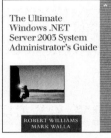

The Ultimate Windows .NET Server 2003 System Administrator's Guide

ROBERT WILLIAMS
MARK WALLA

0-201-79106-4

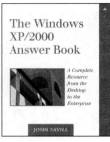

The Windows XP/2000 Answer Book

A Complete Resource from the Desktop to the Enterprise

JOHN SAVILL

0-321-11357-8

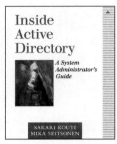

Inside Active Directory

A System Administrator's Guide

SAKARI KOUTI
MIKA SEITSONEN

0-201-61621-1

Managing Enterprise Active Directory Services

ROBBIE ALLEN
RICHARD PUCKETT

0-672-32125-4

Inside Citrix® Metaframe XP™

A System Administrator's Guide to Citrix MetaFrame XP/1.8™ and Windows® Terminal Services

TED HARWOOD

0-7357-1192-5

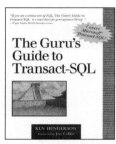

The Guru's Guide to Transact-SQL

KEN HENDERSON

0-201-61576-2

The Guru's Guide to SQL Server™ Stored Procedures, XML, and HTML

KEN HENDERSON

0-201-70046-8

The Administrator's Guide to SharePoint Portal Server 2001

BILL ENGLISH

0-201-77574-3

Register
Your Book

at www.awprofessional.com/register

You may be eligible to receive:

- Advance notice of forthcoming editions of the book
- Related book recommendations
- Chapter excerpts and supplements of forthcoming titles
- Information about special contests and promotions throughout the year
- Notices and reminders about author appearances, tradeshows, and online chats with special guests

Contact us

If you are interested in writing a book or reviewing manuscripts prior to publication, please write to us at:

Editorial Department
Addison-Wesley Professional
75 Arlington Street, Suite 300
Boston, MA 02116 USA
Email: AWPro@aw.com

Visit us on the Web: http://www.awprofessional.com